UN<i>DEFINED</i>

A Spiritual Quest
to Uncover the
Truth and Power
Lying Within

W. E. R. KEYES

Copyright © 2019 W.E.R. Keyes.

All rights reserved. No part of this book may be reproduced, stored, or transmitted by any means—whether auditory, graphic, mechanical, or electronic—without written permission of the author, except in the case of brief excerpts used in critical articles and reviews. Unauthorized reproduction of any part of this work is illegal and is punishable by law.

This book is a work of non-fiction. Unless otherwise noted, the author and the publisher make no explicit guarantees as to the accuracy of the information contained in this book and in some cases, names of people and places have been altered to protect their privacy.

ISBN: 978-1-6847-1116-1 (sc)
ISBN: 978-1-6847-1118-5 (hc)
ISBN: 978-1-6847-1117-8 (e)

Library of Congress Control Number: 2019915287

Because of the dynamic nature of the Internet, any web addresses or links contained in this book may have changed since publication and may no longer be valid. The views expressed in this work are solely those of the author and do not necessarily reflect the views of the publisher, and the publisher hereby disclaims any responsibility for them.

Any people depicted in stock imagery provided by Getty Images are models, and such images are being used for illustrative purposes only. Certain stock imagery © Getty Images.

Lulu Publishing Services rev. date: 10/25/2019

To
All Beings
Nakina
Ashley
My parents & daughter
And
The love that brought me home

CONTENTS

1	The Cellar	1
2	A Dream – The Beginning of the End	14
3	The Dive – The Only Way Forward is Back	24
4	The Game – Winning is Losing	52
5	The Rabbit Hole – The Only Way Out is Through	84
6	The Heart's Silent Song	119
7	The Gilded Carriage	166
8	Let it Go	227
9	Mirrors of Love	256
10	Mirrors of Fear	299
11	The Calling	335
12	The Cave	413
13	Coming Home	503

Un*Defined*

A journey from knowing
To un-knowing
Feeling the truth of something; in something
Far greater than myself
In the midst of worldly chaos
Lies my Being
A silent, endless symphony of oneness
Formless, nameless; without possessions or place
Forever expanding
Reaching for the highest within me
With instinctive harmony
Lifting my soul.

Understanding
Confined by definition
Fearful, desperate, grasping self
Trusting others
Not my Self
Seeking life's miracles
In mindless quandary
Loss the only reward
False measure in mistaken treasure
No honor in empty courage
Beyond the soul light, shining in my eyes.

Invisible tears
Watched by unseeing eyes
Silent screams, echoing through ears gone deaf
Endless heartache
Blood-less, sword-less battles
Tortured mind, wracked body
Spewing precious life essence in meaningless directions
Every step away from my truth
Feeling small, dark, leaden

Silently drowning
A living death.
Searching; searching
Forever seeking
Life's bounty
And love's sweet promise
Until spent, broken
Scorched
Lifeless
In this enticing physical reality
Frivolous nothings, empty shadows
With naught to give
Naught to feed my soul
All empty illusions.

A moment of Grace
A new vision
Hope
Release what falsely binds
Disguised attachments all
Born of fears, fed by desires
Release old, and new ambitions
Deny ego
Forever trapped in its mirrored prison
And rise, rise, rise to the silent whisper of the calling
Soul-knowing the only map
An open heart, the Divine messenger
Through the unseen
Unspoken
Unknown
From something to nothing
From nothing to oneness
All black nothingness
Only I am
Light.

No space, no time
Only my soul's truth
Seeing all that has gone before
All that is yet, to come
No beginning, no ending
No winning, no losing
No longer enslaved by ego battles
All oneness
Joy, pain
Light, dark
Life, death
Self and Universe
All blissful, peaceful
Silence.

But, no
Don't reason or hold onto
Endless nothingness
For she is
Life
Infinite
Abundant
All-knowing, eternity
With every breath
She bestows life and brings death
I feel her in the boughs of my Being
Bathed in ever-lasting, Divine love
And with every breath's soulful embrace and kiss farewell
Timeless, ageless, life
I become in this moment
And forever
Nothing and everything
I am
Un*defined*.

CHAPTER 1

THE CELLAR

She woke up with a start, and whimpered softly as she took in the darkness around her. The cellar was cold, and damp. She glanced towards the small entrance that was somewhere to her right but, she couldn't see anything. She shivered, and desperately tried to stop sobbing. Something warned her that the heavy silence wouldn't take kindly to being disturbed, and that made her even more afraid. Why was it so quiet? Where was everyone? Did they forget about her? She had no idea how long she'd been sitting there. Did anyone notice she was gone? Perhaps it was best if her absence went undetected. She wouldn't be able to explain what she was doing in the cellar, so late at night. She'd never been out alone in the dark before. But, that wasn't the cause of her anxiety. She swallowed hard. She didn't want anyone to find her secret hideout! She shifted nervously, and almost toppled over. Her thin, crossed legs felt stiff, and numb. She had to get back into the house before anyone came looking for her. A surge of fear knotted the insides of her stomach with that thought. She shifted again, and winced from the pain as her skin grazed against rough earth. She slowly got onto her hands, and knees to avoid hitting the wooden ceiling just above her head. She tried crawling towards the exit but, her legs felt like blocks of ice. She fell flat on her face. As she moved her arms into position to lift herself, her fingers brushed against something. She knew instantly, what it was. She froze. Everything was deadly quiet and yet, she distinctly heard the sound of thunder rumbling somewhere in the distance. She welcomed the distraction, and tilted her head to listen out for the raindrops. She loved the rain. But, there was nothing. And yet, the sound of thunder grew louder with every breath that she took. She closed her eyes tightly, hoping to shut out the sound. But, that didn't help. It never occurred to her that it was the sound of her own blood throbbing against her temples. She was trembling; barely breathing as fear slowly engulfed her. She stroked the soft, furry bundle, and was oblivious to the tears rolling down her cheeks. It still felt warm against her fingers. Through her daze, she heard herself whisper to her little friend: "Eve…ry…thing's…. OK. It's go….going…. to be…. fine. You'll see."

However, that small measure of self-directed comfort was not enough to keep reality at bay. As the memories flooded her mind she slumped onto the gravel, and grabbed her head between her hands. She heard herself screaming: "STOP. Pleeeeasssseee…..pleeeaaaaseeeee…. stop." But, it was no use. She remembered crying - for a very long time. And then, lying down on the cold earth, because she felt so tired. She must have fallen asleep. But now, she was wide awake. And it was all coming back to her. Her whole body cringed from the onslaught of the memory, and she scampered directionless across the ground trying to find some way out. She wanted to get as far away as possible, from her thoughts. But, she was forced to stop when she hurtled headfirst into one of the dark corners. The painful thud on her head did little to stop her as she pushed and fought against the walls to put some distance between herself, and the still, furry bundle. Her little, white kitten wasn't moving! Earlier on, she'd forced herself to believe that he was sleeping but, that was a long time ago. He was still not moving! She was petrified. She didn't know what was wrong with him. What if he never woke up!? What if she never got to play with him again? He was her only friend in the whole, wide world. She was overcome by grief. She just leaned against the wall, and sobbed her heart out.

She smiled through her tears as she recalled the first time that she saw him. It was only a few days ago. She couldn't believe her eyes. A tiny, white kitten! All alone in the open, dry fields alongside their house! He stuck out like a flag in the sand-colored, grass. Why was he all alone? Where was his mother? She looked around, scanning the fields and trees but, there was no mother-cat in sight. So she decided to take him back home with her. She picked him up, and snuggled him close to the curve of her neck. She could barely hear the soft, broken cries as he welcomed the warmth, and burrowed even closer. When she approached the doorway at the side of the house, she quickly covered him with her shirt. She glanced around nervously to make sure that no one was around, and then hurriedly crept into her room. She frantically searched for a hiding place, and chose the first one that came to mind. She lifted the warm blanket at the foot of her bed, and gently placed him under it. At dinner that night she was unusually, still. Her fidgety-energy was directed at a far more threatening thought that wouldn't leave her alone. What if they found him!? There would be hell to pay! But, she pushed the thought aside. Trouble didn't bother her – it was her middle name! The thought of losing her new-found friend, however, was something too difficult to contemplate. She wouldn't let that happen! She would have to find a better hiding place. And quickly! That night, to everyone's surprise, she was the first to excuse herself. She headed straight to her bedroom. She was overjoyed when she lifted the blanket, and found the kitten in the exact spot where she'd left him. She picked him up gently, and smothered him with kisses. What was she going to call him?

    She hopped into bed and placed the kitten close to her chest, before pulling the covers over her head. She didn't have to worry about her parents coming into their room at night. They always went straight to bed after dinner. She'd never questioned that but, sometimes she wondered why everyone at home seldom spoke or laughed. Neither did anyone read bedtime stories to her! She'd never heard of them, until she overheard some of the children at school talking about storybooks, and fairy tales. She was intrigued, and couldn't wait to get her hands on one. But, as hard as she tried she just couldn't find one. She remembered spending many an afternoon trying to imagine what the many strange creatures looked like. She knew who her favorite character was long before she even read about him. Peter Pan! She wanted to fly - just like he did! She had to meet him! And there was no doubt in her mind that someday she would. The world was full of magical things – like the stars! She'd often hung around the school corridors during breaks to chat to the other kids about his adventures but, they usually avoided her. They were only interested in her joining them whenever they played hide-and-seek. But, she soon tired of that silly game - she always ended up being the seeker! And she never understood why they kept choosing her for that part! No matter how hard she tried, she could never find them! And when they did make an appearance – all of them suddenly, appearing out of nowhere – they teased her rotten. Then one day, she accidentally discovered them all hiding in the same place. She was so confused. After all, the rules of the game were pretty clear! Everyone had to choose a different hiding place! To make matters worse, they teased her so loudly that all the other kids turned to look at her. That made her so angry! More so, because she didn't understand why they were making fun of her! She always did whatever they told her! Her anger was quickly forgotten in her willful attempts to make the earth open up, and swallow her whole. But, it never did. She just had to stand on the playground, and be laughed at.

    That night she lay in her bed, and couldn't stop smiling. None of it mattered, anymore. Not the fairy tales, the horrid teasing or the stupid games. There was only one thought that held center stage in her mind. She'd found a brand-new friend; one who didn't hide from her or call her names. And no one was going to take him away from her! Ever! She smiled at that thought, and waited for her sister to fall asleep before lifting her little friend out from under the covers. She wanted to play with him – for a little while longer. He was so good - he didn't make a sound. If he stayed that quiet, no one would ever find him. And she could keep him - always! She'd never before, felt so happy about anything. Except, when she was looking at the starry lights, far away in the night sky. She never had to search for them - they were always in the same place. She never understood why she felt comforted by that. And she loved the way that they always twinkled. She was convinced that they were speaking to each other, and often wished she could hear them. But, they were too far away. Sometimes she would stare at them, until tears came to her eyes. She'd discovered that her trick made them look larger and somehow, that made them appear closer. Close enough for her to reach out, and "touch" them. Then she would shut her eyes tightly – to keep the image of the stars floating around in her mind. She loved the giddy feeling as she pretended to swim with the stars inside her head, until they faded away. Then she would open her eyes, and there they were - back in the sky! It was pure magic! She reveled playing with them – in the wonderful spell that they weaved all around her. At other times, she was happy just gazing at them. She never felt alone, whenever she was with them. One day, she would figure out a way to get closer to them. And someday, Peter Pan was going to help make her dream come true! But, tonight was very special. She'd found a new playmate. And he was right there, next to her – not up in the sky! Suddenly, she knew just what she was going to call him. Kitty! She smiled gleefully, and wriggled her toes.

As she drifted off into a deep sleep, for once free of the many thoughts that plagued her before morning, she didn't know that the kitten was already very ill. It had been abandoned by its mother a few days ago. She believed that he slept so soundly beside her, because he liked her. Furthermore, he made no attempt to run away or hide from her. He wanted to be her friend! In her little world she'd never heard the word "rejection" even though, she'd experienced it many times. Then again, she'd never heard the word "love." All she knew that night was a strange, warm feeling right down to her bones as she lay next to Kitty. So much so, that she forgot all about riling her sister with her usual aimless chatter. There were so many things that she wanted to know about the world but, that could wait. Besides, that would only bring on another shouting match. And that always upset her. She didn't want anything spoiling her special time with Kitty. Besides, the shouting would scare Kitty. She wouldn't allow that! Grown-ups were strange creatures! No one wanted to talk to her about anything. She might be six years old but, she had so many questions. One day, she would find all the answers. For now, she would play with Kitty. And one day soon, she would fly amongst her stars!

The next morning, she was up before her sister could come to her side of the bed, and yank the covers off. There was a little bounce in her step, and a little smile on her face as she hurried through her morning routine. For once, she wouldn't have to worry about the "meanies" at school. That was her first thought when she woke up. As she made up her bed, she couldn't help thinking about her first few days at school. She was so excited, especially when she saw other children her own age. She quickly made a few friends, and they had lots of fun during playtime. But, all that changed one afternoon. Her face fell, as she relived the worst day of her life. For some reason, she was feeling very lost that day. And without being aware of it, she started sucking her thumb in class. She hid the act from view, by holding one hand over her mouth. She was staring so intently out the window that she missed her teacher looking in her direction. She was startled out of her slumber-like, state when she heard a shout. She looked around the class to see what the fuss was all about. But, it was only when her teacher approached her desk that it hit her - she was at the center of it! By that time, the entire class was pointing at her, and laughing. "Take that thumb out of your mouth! How many times do I have to tell you?" She was so taken aback, that she just continued staring at her teacher - with her thumb still in her mouth. Then her finger was yanked out of her mouth, and she was instructed to stand in the "naughty corner" for the rest of the day. But, that wasn't the worst of it. As much as she tried to stop herself, she burst into tears in front of the whole class! And it didn't end there. To her horror, the teasing and finger-pointing went on for weeks after that. All she wanted was to forget the whole thing. But, she couldn't – they wouldn't let her! Sometimes things got so bad during playtime that she had to take her lunch back to class, and hide out in one of the toilet cubicles. But, hunger was far easier to live with than being the brunt of laughter, and terrible name calling. Perhaps she would have felt better if she could have understood why sucking her thumb was so bad. Or why no one wanted to play with her, after that. Eventually, like with so many other things that happened during those years, she just overlooked them, and turned the other cheek.

And then, she found Kitty! Her bestest friend! That morning she felt on top of the world. She couldn't stop humming. There was only one thing that bothered her - finding him a safe hiding place. She glanced at her cupboard. It was the best bet. No one went near it, because it was in such a mess. He would be safe there, until she returned home. She carefully placed Kitty in a box, and then grabbed her lunch, and dashed outside to the waiting car. She got into the back seat but, had a tough time settling down – much to the annoyance of her sister. Generally, she was forced to be quiet all the way to school. That morning, however, she couldn't contain her excitement. She spoke, incessantly – about nothing in particular. She continued jabbering, despite the fact that she was talking to her sister's back – she preferred staring out the car window. But, she didn't mind. She was trying to keep herself from thinking about Kitty. She was already missing him terribly. She silently promised herself that she would make up for lost time later that afternoon. And for the first time - in such a long time - she didn't have to worry about the sick feeling in her stomach as they approached the school. When her father stopped outside the school gate, she didn't wait for her sister but, ran on ahead, skipping as she did. They seldom saw each other during the day. Sometimes she saw her sister with her friends during playtime but, she was never invited to join them. In the afternoons, she had to wait at the nearby bus shelter for "big school" to finish and then, tag behind her sister and her friends on the long walk home. Whenever she got too close, she was always given the "look." That made her slowdown immediately – to increase the distance between them. To pass the time, she used to conjure up all sorts of stories in her head. That made the walk a lot more fun. And less lonely. She often wished that she could make the time go faster, and that one day she would wake up, and be a grown up. She hated being the "little sister." Besides the hand-me-downs, no one ever took notice of her. Her sister was always ahead of her – in everything. And she was everyone's favorite! Was something wrong with her? What did she have to do, to be liked by everyone? She sighed sadly. As usual, there were no answers but, each experience compounded the seeds of shame, and rejection imprinted somewhere in her mind.

 The walk home that afternoon was the longest she'd ever known. When they approached the house she raced on ahead. She dashed into their bedroom, and quickly changed into her play clothes. As she pulled a T-shirt over her head, she glanced at herself in the dresser mirror. She grinned, and stuck her tongue at the image that greeted her – a gangly, funny-looking girl with big brown eyes, and large rabbit-teeth sticking out from under her top lip. She gave a soft, whooping sound as she jumped, and made a side heel-tap – a move that she'd perfected playing hopscotch. She'd never felt so excited. Sometimes she played with the other children in the small neighborhood. Mostly she hung out by herself, and wandered around the empty fields looking for hidden 'treasure.' She was happiest there, and filled her hours looking for all sorts of things in the "wild" bush. The others didn't like the "creepy-crawlies" but, she was fascinated by them. And she loved the wide, open spaces. There was nothing between her, and the rest of the world - just earth and the never-ending, blue sky. She'd been warned many times to stay out of the fields. It was dangerous. And frightening things happened to little girls who ventured far from home on their own. So she preferred going by herself – just in case, anyone ratted on her. Not because she was afraid - she just felt safer out there, than she did back home. Besides nothing exciting ever happened indoors. She didn't have any toys or books. But, none of that mattered when she was meandering around in the fields. It was the only place where she could forget about everything, and just enjoy the sun on her skin; the sound of the wind whispering in her hair. Each afternoon was an adventure, and every step took her closer to discovering something magical. She was hit by a thought. Kitty! She must stop day-dreaming! She turned to the cupboard to retrieve her little pet. She moved a few boxes aside, until she located the one that she'd hidden him in. She lifted the lid slowly, and peeked inside. He was still, sound asleep. She smiled. He was just like her - he loved his sleep. Actually, she loved daydreaming under the blankets too but, she didn't have to dream anymore. She had something that she'd always wished for - a best friend! She picked up the kitten, and placed him carefully in the front pouch of her jumper. She sneaked into the kitchen to get her afternoon snack, and made a face when she saw what it was. Bread, and potatoes. She made a face but, grabbed it anyway, and bolted outside. Kitty must be hungry. She would feed him.

That afternoon she sat by herself at the back of the house, and waited patiently for Kitty to wake up. She smiled, as she reminisced over her many adventures in the fields. Finding the baby mice was her very first. She'd almost stepped on them, because they were as brown as the grass but, she managed to stop just in time, with one foot stuck mid-air. She was amazed when she bent down to take a closer look. She'd never before, seen baby mice. They looked a bit scary without hair, and their ears looked way too big for their small heads! And there were so many! Far too many for her to count, back then. She removed her shoes, and placed them inside before walking slowly back to the house – there were pieces of broken glass in the thick grass. But, the pain wasn't the reason for her cautiousness - she'd been cut many times before. She was afraid her wounds would alert the others to her little escapades. And that would spoil all her fun! Back home, she crept into her room, and hid them in a box under her bed. She fed them odd scraps of food – whatever she could lay her hands on at dinner time. The one thing that she didn't count on was how fast they grew. Before long, they were too big to fit in the box. But, she dare not let them out. There was no way that she would be able to catch them all! As difficult as it was to let them go, she decided to take them back to the fields. But, with each passing day she found herself making one excuse after another. One afternoon, they were squeaking really loudly when her sister was in the room. And then, her little secret was out! After that, she didn't know what became of her little friends. She winced, as she remembered the punishment for her little misdemeanor. She frowned. What was so wrong about keeping them? They were so little. And they were all alone out there! Anything could happen to them! She had to keep them safe. That conviction provided some much needed motivation whenever she wanted to overcome her apprehension, and bring her little friends back to the house.

Like the spiders she'd found one rainy afternoon, in the cellar. There they were, just hanging in the corner of the wall on tiny, silver threads! She was amazed. She couldn't understand how such big creatures could move about on wisps of cotton. She sat watching them for hours; tap-tapping on the shiny threads with the tiniest feet that she'd ever seen. She couldn't figure out where their mouths were. So she waited, hoping to catch them in the act of eating something. But, they didn't. She was getting hungry, and guessed that it must be getting close to dinner time. She decided that they must be hungry too, so she carefully removed them, and placed them in an old cardboard box that she found nearby. She fed them breadcrumbs for a few days, and was so glad that they made no noise. Still, it wasn't long before they were discovered. And then, all hell broke loose! There were people running around in all directions, trying to avoid the slowest of creatures! Sure, they had lots of legs but, for all the time that she had them, they had gone nowhere! And they never hurt her! She didn't know why everyone was so scared. She couldn't help giggling, as she bolted outside to find someplace to hide. And when she heard her name being called several times, she remained glued to her hiding place. She knew exactly what awaited her, if she got caught.

But, she couldn't hide forever. She tried putting on a brave face when the time came for her punishment but, that didn't stop the pain. However, it did make her more determined to ignore the little creatures in the fields. Except, for the little snake that she spotted one day on the branch of the guava tree. She watched it crawling around the branches for a long time, as her mind see-sawed about taking him home with her. First, she had to think of a suitable hiding place - one that she hadn't used before. It took a while, before she thought of the perfect place. Her underwear drawer! It was her responsibility to pack away her laundry when she got home – or so, she'd thought. When she opened the drawer a few days later, the snake was nowhere to be seen. She frantically searched her room for it. And then, hurriedly left the house when she couldn't find it. She only returned much later, when she was certain that her father was home. From the fiery looks she received at the dinner table, there was no mistake that her little, wiry friend had been found, and dealt with. She kept her head down, and ate very quickly. She excused herself before anyone else, and went straight to bed. She was glad for the warm safety of the covers when she finally, pulled them over her head. That night, she made herself a promise that she would never again, bring her little friends back to the house. It wasn't safe for them. And for her. And she was having frightening dreams at night. But, she never mentioned them to anyone. What for? She would only get punished all over again, for her "wild" behavior! She didn't know who she was more afraid of – her dreams or people. She decided that it had to be people. Even though she looked, and sometimes behaved like them, she could never understand them - no matter, how hard she tried! In stark contrast, she felt so much closer to the little creatures she found outside. She didn't even look like them! And they never hurt her. Not once!

Her reverie was broken when she felt Kitty's slight movement against her stomach. She lifted him out of her pocket, and tried feeding him but, his mouth remained tightly shut. Then she placed him on the ground and tried playing with him but, he just flopped onto his side, and went straight back to sleep. She decided that he must be very tired. It was best to let him rest. She heard her cousins' voices in the garden. They were talking about climbing the guava tree - one of her favorite pastimes. At first, she hesitated. She didn't want to leave her little friend. Then she remembered the one place that she'd never thought of before. The cellar! No one would look for him there! Everyone hated it, and stayed as far away as possible. She wished that she'd thought about it sooner. She could have kept all her friends down there! And it was dark and quiet – Kitty could rest, until she went back to fetch him later. She picked the frail little thing up, and headed for the nearest cellar entrance. She crawled in, and made straight for her hideaway in the far corner. She placed him gently into the small cradle that she made out of sand. She caressed him, and whispered a promise to be back as soon as she could. And then, she scrambled outside to join the others.

The guava tree was its best at that time of year. It was laden with fruit and the leaves were thick, and full. It was great fun pretending to be a monkey as she weaved her way through the branches, climbing as high as she could to pick the juiciest fruit. The others called her "crazy" and laughed when she made weird sounds, and scratched her armpits. She'd never seen a real, live monkey before but, her father told her that such creatures lived in the forest far, far away. He'd described them and said that they survived on leaves, and fruit. They could also swing from tree to tree, and sometimes slept on the branches at night without falling off! Unbelievable! But, she never doubted anything her father said. Perhaps someday she would get to see a real, live one. Perhaps she would get one for a friend. Until then, she was happy to play "pretend." Much sooner than expected, she heard the usual shout from her mother to wash up for dinner. With a sigh, she climbed down from the tree, and went to get Kitty from the cellar. She knew she was dragging her heels but, there was enough time. There was only one bathroom, and she knew that her sister would get there first. She always did. She was the "good" one. Her mother always said so.

She crawled into the cellar and beetled on hands, and feet towards her hideout. She was forced to look down in that position but, she could still move with surprising speed in the dark. She knew her way around the cellar almost as well, as she knew her way around the fields. And no-one knew about the doorway that led to her secret hideaway. She didn't either, until she'd discovered it one day, quite by accident. It had something to do with the way that the light faded at the far end. It looked as though the wall ended there - just where the light disappeared. But, there was another little entrance at that blind spot. One day, while playing in the cellar she leaned against the 'wall,' and much to her surprise she'd fallen through the darkened doorway! At first, she wanted to share her discovery with her cousins but, then decided against it. She needed some place to hide out at times and, that was the perfect spot. And since no one liked the "smelly" cellar, her secret remained quite safe. She smiled when she spotted Kitty. She slowed down, so as not to disturb him. He looked like he was still, fast asleep. She could see him quite clearly, in the light filtering through the air vents in the wall. She stopped a moment to take in the sight that greeted her, and her heart went out to the little creature lying in the dark. He looked so small, and helpless. She tickled him gently behind one ear, expecting him to look up at her with his beautiful, green eyes. But, he didn't move. She tried again – this time on his slightly exposed belly. Still, he didn't move. She curled both her hands around him, and picked him up. As she did, his little head slumped, and dangled strangely over the side of her hands. She felt something stop inside of her, and she went very, very cold. She didn't quite know when it happened but, she started crying. She wasn't even aware of it, until she felt her hands go moist from the wet fur. They just sat there - for the longest time. She didn't know for how long. She stroked him gently, and continued calling to him softly, wishing for him to wake up. He never stirred. She tried praying. For once, deciding that her fierce grandmother had to be right about something. She was always praying, and nobody could ever be still around her! Except, she didn't know who she was supposed to be praying to. And she felt silly talking to this God-person who was always in hiding. But, she was desperate. She would do anything to get Kitty to wake up. She just couldn't understand why he was so still. And why he wouldn't play with her. She lifted him close to her cheek, and rubbed her face softly against his little body. The tears continued to fall down her cheeks.

From a distance, she heard loud noises on the wooden floors above her. It sounded like people were running around inside the house. She heard them calling something out several times. Somewhere in her mind, it registered that they were calling out to someone. It never occurred to her that they might be looking for her. Then she heard someone call out her name close by. It sounded as though, they were already inside the cellar! She saw a flashlight flicker, a few times. They were coming for them! She shrunk further back into the corner, and clutched the kitten to her chest. She didn't want to go back out there! Not ever, again! Not until, Kitty woke up. If they found them, they would take Kitty away from her! In the grips of the fear that consumed her, she'd completely forgotten that no one knew about her little hide-away. She forced her body into a tiny ball in the corner, and closed her eyes tightly, hoping to shut out the loud sounds around her. She succeeded somewhat but, failed to stop the sick feeling

Undefined

in her belly. Something terrible had happened. She just knew it! But, she couldn't name it. Neither did she want to think about it. She must have fallen asleep. For when she woke up, it was deadly quiet. And so cold. She started sobbing, again. How was she going to go back to that school? Who was she going to play with? But, she knew she would find some way to deal with all of that - the way that she'd always done. There was another pain though, somewhere deep inside her that felt so much worse than anything she'd experienced before. She refused to think about it but, it found a way to echo through her heart. Where did Kitty go? Why did he leave her? She missed him so. She wanted him back. She wished that she knew a song. She was convinced that the silence would stop thundering in her ears, if she could just sing something out loud. She'd learnt a few songs in the school choir but, they were all happy tunes. And she didn't feel very happy. She knew a prayer that they sometimes sang together at home but, she didn't feel like praying, either. It crossed her mind that whatever happened to her friend might be bigger than anything she was familiar with. She recalled something strange that her grandmother had once said: "Only God took people away, forever." She'd never understood who this invisible God was or why It would want to take Kitty away from her. Neither did she understand the meaning of "forever." What was it? Was it a place? Could she go there, and bring him back? It must be very far away, if he couldn't hear her calling him. That's it! Kitty must have gone away to "forever!" Maybe he got tired of waiting for her while she was playing with the other kids, and had fallen into a deep sleep. He must have slipped away in his dreams to go visit a friend there, and gotten lost. She'd also gotten lost when wandering around weird places in her dreams. He was bound to find his way back to her, sometime soon. She would wait for him. She started moaning softly and rocked herself gently backwards, and forwards. The moaning formed its own sad tune. It was a haunting sound, full of longing for something precious that had been found and lost - far too quickly. All that was left in its wake was an aching emptiness. And a ravenous doubt that such a wondrous thing had ever existed, in the first place.

CHAPTER 2

A DREAM – THE BEGINNING OF THE END

She didn't know for how long she was in the cellar. She wished she'd paid more attention whenever her teacher had spoken about the "time" but, she always mixed up the "big" and "little" hands, and said it backwards. Her classmates thought it was funny but, it was no laughing matter to her. She was always in trouble, because of it! And she'd spent many an afternoon on the guava tree pondering her bad luck. Her slow pace in the mornings irritated everyone and they often pointed to the "ticker" on their wrists, and shouted: "Time is going! Hurry up!" And she was usually sent to detention for getting back late to class. She didn't own a watch but, she heard the bell. And she was warned often enough but, just couldn't stop herself from dragging her heels after break. Besides, where could it go? The hands just went round and round in a box, all day long!? Why was everyone desperately trying to catch it? As far as she could tell from the never-ending, frenzy every day no one had ever succeeded. Would she be able to catch it, someday? She doubted it. It wasn't about running fast - she could most certainly do that. Where was the fun in trying to catch something that was already trapped? Did it even exist? She shook her head. Trying to catch time was like trying to catch a feather - the second she reached for it, it floated away! At least she could see, and touch the feather – if she caught it! She sighed. She would probably have to strap a "ticker" to her wrist when she was older. Somehow that thought didn't appeal to her. She suspected that it would make her do strange things – like everyone else around her.

The cold cellar brought her back to her shivering body. She almost dropped Kitty as she placed him on her lap. She stroked him again, and started telling him a story. That should coax him into waking up! But, he remained very still. He was now a lot colder, and quite stiff. She blew warm air onto her hands, and rubbed his body. There, that was sure to warm him up! Without being aware of it, she started moaning again. And that made her feel sleepy. She rested her head against the corner of the wall, telling herself that it would only be for a little while, until Kitty got back from "forever." Then everything would be fine again, and she could go back into the house. She smiled, and thought about her warm bed as she slowly drifted off to sleep. When she woke up, she was lying on her side in the dirt. She felt blissfully warm, and for a moment she thought she was in her bed. But, there was a strong smell of leaves, and damp earth coming from something on top of her. She hesitated, before lifting her head to take a peek. It looked like some sort of blanket but, not one that she'd ever seen before. Whatever it was she was glad for its warmth. She snuggled down into its tickling earthiness, and wriggled her toes happily. Just as she was about to doze off again, she remembered. Kitty! She sat bolt upright. The cellar was now pitch black, and she was very frightened. Where was she? Where was Kitty? From the smell, she gathered that she was still in the cellar. The familiarity was somewhat comforting but, it did little to alleviate her confusion. She recalled that she was waiting for Kitty to return. Did he come back while she was sleeping? Her hands reached for him on her lap but, he wasn't there! She searched the ground using her hands but, he was nowhere to be found! All sorts of thoughts bombarded her little mind as she tried to figure out what had happened to him. To counter her fear, she made herself believe that Kitty was playing hide-and-seek. He was bound to return soon, and tell her all about his game. She had to be brave. And stick with her plan to wait for him. He would be very afraid if he got back, and discovered that she'd left him all alone in the dark cellar! She smiled and once again, pulled the blanket over herself to keep warm. As her eyes drooped, she wondered where the blanket had come from. She'd never seen anything like it! And how did it end up on top of her? Her eyes opened wide as she recalled the scary stories that she'd heard about things roaming about at night. She was very familiar with the creatures that she found during her day-time jaunts but, the creatures of the night suddenly, loomed large and threatening in the dark. She yanked the blanket over her head and the tears started, all over again. She desperately wanted to go back into the house but, she couldn't leave without Kitty.

She heard a soft tinkling sound. She forced herself to open her eyes under the blanket, and strained her ears to listen to the weird sound. But, she was still very drowsy and was about to nod off again, when she spotted a strange glow through the gaps between the leaves. It was coming from the far corner. It looked.... like…...like….a shiny mist wafting through the air. She dropped the blanket, and rubbed the sleep from her eyes. Something was sitting there! Quietly, watching her! It looked like a person but, she wasn't certain. She'd never seen anything like it before! And it was glowing! Its colors changed! And it moved constantly – like a wave! But, it stayed in exactly, the same spot! Now and again, she thought that she recognized a facial expression - of sorts. But, before she could attach an image to it, the "face" changed! She couldn't take her eyes off it. She closed her eyes, and shook her head several times to make sure that she wasn't dreaming. But, when she looked again, there it was - still waving about, and glowing! It slowly dawned on her that the shiny-thing was busy with something. It took a while, before she figured it out. It was playing marbles! She was so surprised that she forgot all about her fear, and confusion. She continued to watch wide-eyed as it dug a hole in the ground, and placed the largest marble – the "Queenie" - inside. And then the shiny-thing floundered around in its waves trying to hit it! But, how? It had no arms! How was it planning to strike, if it couldn't take proper aim? She continued watching in amazement. This was her favorite game! It was the one thing that she was good at! She couldn't suppress her annoyance as the glowing mass continuously failed to hit its mark. It was such an easy shot! The Queenie was less than an arms-length away. Anyone could hit that!

While she contemplated how to approach the weird looking creature, a memory of her first game of marbles flashed through her mind. One afternoon, she'd spotted a group of boys at the far end of the school grounds. They were huddled over something. She was curious. So she approached slowly, and watched them for a while. They were playing a game! One that she'd never seen before! They looked at her, and then promptly, turned away. That made her feel uncomfortable but, she decided

Undefined

to stay, and continue watching. In a short space of time, she managed to figure out what they were doing with the little glass balls, and asked if she could join them. They laughed at her, and said: "Girls can't play marbles." She scoffed. She played cricket! And soccer! But, she remained quiet. Eventually, she was forced to leave. It was getting late, and she still had a long walk ahead of her. But, she returned the following afternoon. Much to her amazement, she was invited to join them. She listened intently as one of them explained what she had to do, and then took the handful of marbles that were handed to her. Her first few attempts were pathetic – she just couldn't get the hang of it. That did little for her credibility with the boys. And they became more impatient with her, with every passing day. But, she refused to give up. It took a few days before she felt confident enough, to hold her own amongst them. And then, she started beating them. She expected them to be upset. Instead, they stopped teasing her, and became more interested in her technique. As the days passed, she really started to enjoy their company. And she was feeling good again, about going to school. Before long, she'd mastered her technique, and was winning most of the games. She soon became "one of the guys." And earned a brand new nickname – one that she was very happy with, compared to all the horrible names that were usually thrown at her. "Queenie." It made her smile every time she heard it. She grew to love the game so much, that she played it almost every afternoon. And now, this glowy-thing was messing it up! She couldn't watch its blundering efforts for a moment longer. Without giving it another thought, she lifted the leafy-blanket, and moved closer.

"You're doing it all wrong" she scolded. "Try bending lower. And keep your elbow close to your side."

She watched as the glowing mass tried to follow her advice. And then it "toppled" over in a heap. It bounced about on the floor a few times; looking like puffs of light-waves. She couldn't help smiling. It reminded her of sand-devils, whirling about in the dust. She liked this glowy-thing. *Whatever it was!*

"Here, let me show you" she offered.

She bent down on her knees, and positioned herself carefully with her elbows close to her sides. She held a marble in her right hand and then slowly extended, and drew her wrist back towards her body a few times – to focus her aim. But, there was more to a successful hit - the way she placed her fingers, and the flick of the wrist. She glanced at the glowy-thing with raised eyebrows - to emphasize what she was about to do. It was still watching her. She curved three of her fingers so that the tips formed a circle alongside the marble that was being held between her forefinger, and thumb. That was her "winning hand" – it held the marble firmly in place while keeping her wrist rock-steady. She shifted slightly, to make sure that she was in the correct position. And then, she flicked the marble from her wrist – not her fingers - in one swift, un-blinking movement. There was a resounding crack. Bull's-eye! She hit the Queenie with such force that it bounced out of the hole, and rolled to the far side of the cellar. She shrieked with delight, and bounded up - throwing her arms up into the air. And hit the top of her head on the cellar ceiling. She cried out in pain, and sank to the floor in a heap. There were no tears as she rubbed her head - just a huge grin on her face. She looked at the glowing, ball of waves with a self-satisfied smirk.

"There! That's how it's done" she said.

"Great shot" the glowy-thing said. "Are you ok?"

She grinned. "Yup. All good. Would you like to play some more?"

"Sure" the bouncing, glowing mass replied.

They played for some time but, the glowy-thing didn't improve at the game. In no time at all, she'd won all the marbles, and they lay in a stacked heap by her side. She took a peek to check how it was coping with losing. She was a bad loser – it always made her feel terrible! But, she didn't detect any sign of disgruntlement, and relaxed. She was certain, however, that it was sad. She could relate to that - she'd often felt like that. She thought about giving it a hug. Maybe that would cheer it up. She hesitated. How was she supposed to do that? She still couldn't make out a face or body! Neither was there a front or back! But, the more time she spent with it, the more convinced she was that it was some kind of person. She still couldn't bring herself to look at it directly but, she decided that she definitely liked being in its presence. For some reason, she felt certain that she could trust it. She didn't feel so on edge around it - like she did at home or at school. And it wasn't afraid of the dark cellar. That impressed her. So she decided to continue playing with it. At least, until Kitty got back. She realized that she'd stopped crying, and the recent events that had gripped her in such turmoil were somewhat, forgotten. Even the strange creature in her secret hideout didn't bother her so much. The aching pain in her heart, however, refused to go away even though she tried her best to ignore it. She still didn't know how to deal with that but, playing marbles – even with something that she'd never seen before – felt so good.

'You don't say much, do you?" she said, hesitantly. She wasn't used to talking to people she knew – let alone, something that she'd only just met.

"I don't have many friends. I talk sometimes but, people seldom listen to me. So I prefer to remain quiet." She was certain that its bright glow dimmed as it spoke.

"That's just like me!" she exclaimed. "I don't have any friends. No one says much at home. But, my teacher always has lots to say! I don't listen to her. I don't like her! She caught me sucking my thumb once and now, everybody knows! They never stop teasing me at school. And….. and….they call me horrible names! No one wants to play with me, anymore! Her words came gushing out before she could stop herself. She sank back against the wall feeling very awkward. She'd never spoken so much, to anyone before.

"I'm sorry. That doesn't sound like much fun." And then, the glowy-thing smiled at her. It looked like a big shiny, teddy bear.

She couldn't help but, smile back.

"But, you found a special friend recently?" the glowing mass asked, softly.

"Errr….mmhmm mmhmm" she muttered, slowly nodding her head. "I found Kitty. In the field outside. I brought him back to the house but, I made sure not to tell any…….." her voice trailed off. "How did you know!? I told no one!"

"I was with you when you found him. And I was with you when you brought him here, earlier this afternoon" it said.

"But, I didn't see you. I've never seen you before. Do you stay close by?" she asked, trying hard to keep the fear out of her voice. She knew everyone in the neighborhood, and she'd never seen this thing before!

"Yes. I stay very close by." The glowy-thing seemed to be shining and dancing, all at once.

She was so excited. All her confusion disappeared.

"Then, you must come play. I know all kinds of games. So you don't have to feel sad about losing at marbles. We can play other games – like catch and hop-scotch, and hide-and-seek. But, if you shine so brightly I'm going to find you in a flash! We can be best friends from now on" she said with heartfelt sincerity. She looked at the glowy-thing with great anticipation; a sad, faraway, longing in her eyes.

"Yes, I'd like that very much. I've been looking for a friend for such a long time" it said.

She clapped her hands with glee.

"Me too. We can be besties. Just like Kitty, and me."

"But, what are you doing out here, so late at night? You should be in bed." The glowy-thing spoke softly.

She felt more than saw its glow reach out, and touch her gently. *No! She must be imagining things! It wasn't a person!* Something just didn't feel right. She felt weird. What …. was…. wrong?

She stopped twirling the marbles in the palm of her hand, and looked directly at the glowing-thing for the first time. She was about to say something. Then stopped. Something told her to look behind her. She swung around. There he was! She could see him clearly in the dim light! She must have been dreaming – that's why she didn't see him before! He was still not moving! What was wrong with him!? Her tears started falling, all over again. She didn't bother wiping them away. Neither did she care that Glow could see her crying. She wasn't certain why that name came to mind. It just did. And then, there was an outburst of words that were barely audible.

"Is he gone to 'forever'?" she whispered. "I didn't mean to hurt him….I would never. Never! He's my…. best…bestest friend. My….only…. friend. I tried feeding him but,….but, he wouldn't eat. I don't know what happened….don't know…. what I did. I don't know why he left……" and her voice trailed off in sobs. "He left me here, all alone. He's gone. I don't want to go back…. to the house….. don't want to go…to… to school! Don't want to go, anywhere…without…. him!" She cried, hysterically.

And then she was struck by a frightening thought. Even if she did go back to the house where was she going to hide when she needed to run away!? Glow now knew her secret hideaway! What if he told everyone? They would know where to find her! And she'd shown him her best marble trick! Why did she do that?

"You didn't kill Kitty, Little One. His mother left him a few days ago. I know you tried to feed him but, he was still very little. He needed milk. You didn't kill him" Glow said, gently.

"I….I…. didn't….. kill him" she repeated faintly.

And then, she was overcome with relief. She didn't know what she would have done if she was the one responsible for Kitty's death. But, then she was hit by the full realization of Glow's words. Kitty was dead!

"He's really….. de….de…..dead? Gone away to …..to…..'forever'? I won't be able to play with him, ever again? He didn't go away, because…. because…..he didn't…..like…. me? I thought….I thought….. he…..he… was….sleeping." She whispered as she looked at Kitty's lifeless, little body. A part of her was still hoping that he would wake up.

"No, Little One. He's dead. But, you didn't kill him. He starved to death - the poor little thing. You found him too late. I'm so sorry. I know how much he meant to you. He died, because he didn't have any milk for some time. He liked you - so very much. If he could, he would have stayed with you much, much longer. For many years….. just to play with you. He liked you, even more than you liked him, because he was very heart-broken when his mother left him."

Glow spoke with so much tenderness that it touched something deep inside her, and brought tears to her eyes. She desperately tried to stop. But, her tears seemed to have a will, all of their own.

"Hush. Hush now, Little One. Shhhhhhhh……shhhhhhhh. It's going to be all right. You are going to be all right" Glow said, gently.

No one had ever spoken to her like that before. So softly. So gently. She was used to being shouted at - all the time. Glow's words sounded different, and had a strange effect on her. It made her feel lost, and hopeful at the same time. She also felt such a closeness to it which confused her, because it wasn't anyone or anything that she was familiar with. And yet, for the first time she didn't feel the need to do anything, other than cry. She usually hid from everyone if she felt like crying – at home or at school. But, with Glow she felt safe enough to feel, and show her feelings. It felt strange being so open about it.

"But, who will be my friend now?" she asked. "Who am I going to play with?"

At that thought, she was struck by such a deep sense of loneliness that she almost choked. She was so happy just a little while ago. She was looking forward to getting home from school - just to be with Kitty. And now Kitty was gone....forever! What was she going to do?

"Don't worry, Little One. Please don't cry. You're not alone. Soon you'll have many new friends. Just stay where you are - with yourself. Everything is going to be OK. You'll see......."

She smiled, sadly. There was a twist at the corners of her little mouth that she wasn't aware of. Glow didn't know where she lived or where she went to school. She hated going there – hated being at home but, she had no choice. She wished she could fly away. Far, far away...and be with the stars.

".....and soon, you'll meet many new, and wonderful people" said Glow.

She wondered what Glow was talking about. The words sounded foreign to her. *They made no sense at all! No one had ever spoken to her of such things! Glow spoke as though it knew who she was, and what was going to happen in the future. How could it know that? No one knew such things!* Her grandmother told her a long time ago, that only God knew what was going to happen in that place called the "future." It had something to do with that other thing called "timing." She didn't understand any of it. More so, because that was very different to what her teacher once said: "Books contained the answers to everything." She tried to recall if she'd read anything about Kitty's strange behavior or who Glow might be. But, she'd only recently started school, and her vocabulary was very limited. Perhaps someday, she will find a book that could answer all her questions. *Maybe someday, she will run into this God-person that Grandma always spoke about. But, when will that be? How long did she have to wait? What was she supposed to do in the meantime?*

"For now, you must focus on yourself – on your thoughts, and your feelings. At times, things will get very scary but, I want you to try and remember that things are not as they appear. And I want you to know that there is so much love around you – from everyone, and everything. You're surrounded by love from the entire Universe.

Always remember that. Believe in nothing else – just that love; with all your heart. Everyone is love, and light. So are you. And someday soon, you'll become all that you believe." Glow spoke with what looked like a smile, and its light seemed to be all around her – embracing her in its warmth.

Glow was shining so brightly that it hurt her eyes. She squinted as she stared at it. She even stopped crying. Only the wet streaks on her dust-covered, cheeks remained.

"And look at you…." Glow continued, softly. Gently. "You're young. Beautiful. With your whole life still ahead of you. You have so much to look forward to. A whole life still to create. So much love and joy still to experience; to share. So much that you have to learn about life; about your Self. And you have a beautiful, little daughter. You still have a whole life-time to share with each other. There is so much that you still have to teach her; that she has to teach you. You love her with all your heart. And she loves you – even though, she's still too little to tell you that herself. She's a little part of you - the best part of you. She's a miracle - just like you. I can't promise that things will be easy while you're here. Or that things will make much sense – now or ever. However, I can promise that one day soon, you'll know who you truly are. Now, and for some time to come you're going to feel confused. You're going to remember things you thought were long forgotten, and feel emotions that you've never acknowledged before. But mainly, you're going to feel very alone, and scared. You'll feel abandoned - by everyone. And very lost. You're going to feel heavy, and very, very dark. To help you make your way towards the light within you, you must try to remember only one thing – you are love. You don't believe that. And you don't know what that feels like right now but, you will. As you progress on your quest, you'll feel that love unfolding within you – as you uncover more of your true Self. Try not to get distracted by your mind. Focus on the love emerging within you – it's all you need to face your truth."

CHAPTER 3

THE DIVE – THE ONLY WAY FORWARD IS BACK

    She couldn't breathe. She wanted to run......never stop. Anywhere! As long as she could get away from there. She had to do something.…... anything! But, as hard as she tried she couldn't move. She realized that she was engulfed in Glow's warm, cocoon of light. She didn't know when or how that happened. She couldn't think straight. And she was trembling so violently that she bit her tongue several times. But, she continued to fight against Glow's tight embrace. She didn't know what she was trying to escape from but, despite her pushing, and shoving Glow refused to let her go. Her face was contorted; her mouth open and dry. She was screaming but, there was no sound coming from her lips. Eventually, exhausted from all the exertion, she slumped into Glow's "arms." She felt a warm sensation slowly seeping throughout her body. She relaxed a bit. As she did, something like an electric current swept through her, from head to toe. She gasped. *What was that!?* She'd never felt anything like it before! She was overcome by fear. Still, she tried picking through her confusing thoughts, until she became aware of an unfamiliar feeling. Despite everything going on inside her body she felt strangely, lighter. She'd never felt like that - at any stage of her life! It distracted her from the mayhem in her mind, and made her aware of the avalanche of emotion rising within her.

    The last thing she remembered was playing marbles. Now she was floating about in Glow's "arms"! Weightless. Silent. Still. As she turned her attention to that warm feeling within, she became aware of how soft she felt. And somewhat, exposed. Or was that what it felt like to be more open? How would she know? That was something else she'd never felt before! And then she noticed that beyond Glow's halo there was nothing but, black space! Fear registered on some level. However, with her newfound detachment she realized that she could observe, and acknowledge the fear without becoming tangled in it. An unfamiliar "feeling" told her that she was safe where she was. She found herself preoccupied with her new level of emotional detachment – it was very unsettling. Usually, she was sucked into her emotions – into a kind of vortex. She'd always regarded her emotions to be an inseparable part of her. It dawned on her that with this unexpected mental shift towards greater detachment, her head wasn't spinning so much. She could now process some of her thoughts. *What just happened in the cellar? Where was Kitty? Where was she!? This place didn't look like the cellar at all! She was floating in black space! Where was everyone!? Where was she!? Who was Glow?* She felt utterly bewildered. Despite that, she unconsciously nodded her head in acceptance of all the weirdness around her. She couldn't help reveling in being a part of something that could only be described as mystical. The maverick in her – a part of her that she'd kept carefully hidden over the years – had often wished for something extraordinary to happen in her life. *Well, it looked like she'd certainly gotten her wish! And it was a lot more than she'd bargained for!* She just couldn't recall if she'd ever defined "extraordinary." Or specified who she wanted to bargain with, for that matter! *Perhaps somewhere therein, lay the loophole. And the answer to all this madness!* Someone once told her that life was a "mystery," and that in order to experience it fully one had to be open to everything that it offered – the good, and the bad. Despite her fear, and confusion she felt strangely at home in this black, empty world! Perhaps this was the "mystery." *Maybe this was some kind of adventure. One that she wouldn't have embarked on willingly – there was never enough time for one! So she had to be dragged into it.* She sighed. *It was all making perfect sense. Finally!*

That she was using well-traversed logic to negotiate her way around the "mystery" wasn't factored into her thinking. She didn't know that she was cursorily processing what was going on using her existing mind-maps. She'd always worked hard to ensure that her life progressed without any major mishap. She liked things to go smoothly. And according to a plan. She also knew that she hated order, and structure. But, she was all about delivery. So she compromised herself – all the time. And in the process, she'd messed up many times when circumnavigating her plans to achieve a faster turnaround time. *The black-white cocoon that she found herself in must be some interim dream space that she'd created in her mind to help her get back on track with her life. And Glow must be a figment of her imagination - the answer to her call for help to fix whatever needed fixing.* She sighed happily. *It was all really, quite simple. Why was she confused? This entire situation would soon be "done and dusted" – like every other challenge that had come her way! There was no need to be all OCD about it! She had her own back – like always.* She gave herself an imaginary "pat on the back." *She would get back to her way of doing things. It was just a matter of time. She knew what she was doing. What had Glow called it again? A quest? Hogwash! She would get herself out of this maze. Nothing got the better of her!* She continued floating around in Glow's warm cocoon, happily caught up in her little mind-game.

So much so, that she was unprepared for what happened next. The questions came at her out of nowhere, and tore her away from her reverie. *She was an adult!? Not a child!? And she had a child of her own!? Where was she? When was she born? What did her child look like? What was she doing in the cellar earlier on? How could she still be a child, with Kitty by her side if she was an adult? What was this space?* She glanced around. Everything remained black, and empty - for as far as she could see. *Where was Glow? It was holding her a second ago! What kind of stupid dream was this?* And yet, despite what was going on in her head she couldn't deny that the whole experience felt more real compared to anything that she'd encountered before. She could recall snippets of her adrenaline-packed life but, the full impact of each experience felt somewhat diluted. It made her realize that her life had whizzed by in a blur of activity. And now, for whatever reason some of those life experiences were slowly wafting through her mind's eye – one snapshot at a time. As much as she wanted to ignore it, the snail's pace of each shot grabbed, and held her attention. It wasn't the actual events that were the focal point but, the emotions associated with each one. It made her realize that she'd seldom given her feelings much thought. At the time, she wasn't even aware that she had any! Somehow this weird space was now highlighting each emotion with such gravity that it made each event come back to life. And things looked very different, somehow. She was taken aback. All this, because of her feelings!? Why did she avoid her feelings before?

She recalled pushing her emotions aside on many occasions. That approach had no doubt, helped her to build the life that she wanted but, she now felt the express need to challenge her usual behavior. Something about her life; something about herself felt completely, out-of-synch. She recalled that she'd often made changes to her life. She'd always tried to make it better in some way. *Now that life – her entire physical world - had mysteriously fallen apart! She was in the middle of nowhere; with no one around - except Glow! What now?* She shifted uncomfortably, as the play of emotions continued invading her senses. *What was the reason for this emotional overload? What was she missing in all this chaos?* Perhaps it had nothing to do with the chaos outside of her. Maybe something was going on with her! *How was she supposed to find that out!? How was she supposed to fix herself!? How could this have happened, when she was the one living inside her own skin!?* She was certain that she'd given a lot of thought to her decisions. She sighed, hopelessly. *If her mind was responsible for getting her into this mess then perhaps, the one thing that she'd ignored for so long – her emotions - could get her out of it. There! She had a plan!*

That change in perspective was a revelation in itself. However, it was no match for a mind hardened by habitual logic. It resumed its self-inflicted, position of control before she could explore her new line of thought. *Who was Glow? What was she doing playing games in the cellar if she was an adult? And where on earth was she now!? There was no ground beneath her! She was floating about in space!* She wasn't aware that returning to familiar mind-territory was the instinctive antidote for the impending panic attack. She was too busy trying to recall what home looked like but, no images came to mind. Neither could she recall what her daughter looked like! She was devastated. More so, because she couldn't fathom why she still looked, and felt like a six-year old if she was an adult! She looked around frantically, hoping to see someone. *Where was everyone!? What was she doing there? Why was she all alone? Why did she feel so strange? Was she in some other world?* She shook her head. *She couldn't exist in two different worlds, at the same time! That was impossible!* She felt herself grow cold as another petrifying thought struck her. *Was she dead?* Her breath stuck in her throat as she tried to hold back her tears. She swung herself around a few times, looking for the one thing that she felt certain of. *Where was Glow?*

She felt dizzy, and nauseous. There was nothing to stand on, and although the space around her was of the darkest shade of black that she'd ever seen, it was somehow emphasizing her thoughts, and emotions. She felt consumed by it all and completely, overwhelmed. Her mind, and body were being torn apart in polar opposite directions and yet, she was becoming more aware of something deep within her – a deep calmness. *How strange!* For the first time, she realized that if she focused on remaining detached she could access a different level of awareness – one that made it possible for her to watch her reactionary thoughts. In that instant, she became aware of herself as the "observer" of her strange experience. She was fascinated. She'd heard of that term but, it never made any sense to her. She had a startling revelation. She could watch herself go through this experience without getting all caught up in it! So that's what it felt like to be an observer! But, if she could observe herself by remaining detached from her thoughts, and emotions then what made her mind think the way that it did? Why did she feel the way that she did? What was the origin of those thoughts, and emotions? *Wasn't she, her thoughts and emotions? What purpose did being the observer serve, if she already had a mind?* If her thoughts were reflective of everything that had already transpired in her physical world, then what was she capable of as the observer, instead of the doer? Was the observer in her also capable of seeing, and feeling? Or were her thoughts, and emotions only part of her physical body? If the observer in her didn't react in any way, then what did it do? She shook her head, trying to rid herself of her confusion. She felt as though she was embodying two different people, at the same time! *What was happening to her?*

"That's the way you're feeling, right now. All you need to do is acknowledge that. Nothing more."

Who said that? Where did it come from? She looked into the blackness, and there was Glow. Right beside her!

"Glow!" she exclaimed. "You're still here. You didn't leave me."

"Of course" said Glow. "Why would I leave? Where would I go?" It was giving her that faceless, smile again. And it didn't question the name that she'd given it. She smiled back, and leaned across to give

Undefined

the creature a hug. Her hands passed straight through Glow, and she ended up falling right into it. Only to find herself in exactly, the same spot when she sat up again - with Glow sitting beside her. It was looking at her with a huge grin on its face. She looked at Glow quizzically. Nothing had changed - it still looked like a fuzzy, multi-colored halo. And yet, everything suddenly felt weirder than ever. If she was overwhelmed by the disappearance of her physical world, then this creature by her side made her intensely aware of just how bizarre her experience was. But, she was so happy to see Glow that she decided not to ask too many questions. *She didn't want to be too much trouble. Not now – when she was making another friend.* Besides, something was happening to her in that black space. She suspected that whatever it was Glow was somehow, intricately involved. She wanted to get to the bottom of this situation – even though she could make no sense of it.

"Where are we?" she asked, forcing herself to sound nonchalant.

"We're here – where we've always been. But, you're still in the cellar, Little One" Glow replied cryptically.

"Little One!? Where was 'here?'" How could she still be in the cellar, and sitting with Glow in space!? They couldn't be in two different places, at the same time! That was impossible!

"You won't allow anything to be possible, other than what you can conjure up with your mind. Despite what you believe, you've never left the cellar – irrespective of where you went in your physical world. In your mind, we're in two different places. But, in this space it's all one - we're all one. And we're always together - even when we're apart. This" – and Glow's light spread into the blackness, as far as her eyes could see – "might appear to be very different but, it's your real world. It's your only, true world. The only one that really matters, anyway. It only looks different, because there are no walls here – anywhere around, or between us. That's the way it has always been. The way of life that you're familiar with, is only a very small aspect of life. And yet, it has made you become far too enmeshed with the perceptions generated by your mind. Perceptions that have made you reinforce the walls that you built to protect yourself - from others, and yourself. The little world that you created was comfortable, and predictable. But, that only supported your illusion of control over your life. It fed your ego. But, if you took the time to stand back from what was going on in your head, you would have seen a very different picture. One very similar to what you're seeing now – absolute, nothingness. There is nothing separating us. The nothingness, is all there Is."

She was listening intently. But, the harder she tried to understand the more confused she became. Her mind was riddled with questions but, she remained silent. She didn't know what to say or do; where to begin - she felt totally, out of her depth. Feeling that uncertain of herself was new. *She'd always known what to do! She was knowledgeable about the world. She was capable of finding the answers that she needed.* Something within her, didn't quite agree. Why was she doubtful? What was so different about this quest? But, she had to agree with Glow. Anything her mind could conjure up would be commonplace in the face of what she was experiencing in this blackness. Somewhere in the back of her mind, she was also questioning whether she could trust her logical mind. But, she would never allow herself to admit that. Something told her that whatever she was going through was more profound than anything she'd encountered before. And for some unbeknown reason, she felt like doing nothing other than, observing her experience. Besides, skepticism was only distracting her. And she felt strongly that it would undermine this quest – whatever it was about! *Why was she being so considerate of something unknown!?* But, she decided to consciously adopt what some part of her had already opted to do – albeit, without permission from her mind. She would observe the silent unfolding of something that was beyond her current level of understanding. Trying to keep track of it all might be difficult but, she couldn't deny that she was becoming more enthralled by the minute! She was slowly becoming more captivated by her quest. And more open to it. She was very aware that her mind was screaming for her to bolt but, something deep within her was gently whispering for her to stay. And the power of that whisper was far greater than her extreme discomfort. Previously she would have known exactly, which one to follow but, now she wasn't so sure. *Nothing was so obvious, anymore. Besides, where would she go? In the blackness she couldn't tell one direction from another! For someone who had always defined her own direction in life that was petrifying!* She wanted nothing more than to get out of there, as fast as she could but, something about that silent space made her stay exactly, where she was.

"What am I doing here? This makes no sense at all!" she exclaimed.

"Has anything in your life made any sense?" Glow asked.

She'd always thought that it did. Until now. "Now that I think about it – no!" *Nothing had ever felt right about her life! Perhaps once......or twice. A long time ago.....*

"When was that?" Glow asked eagerly.

She was certain that she'd not voiced her thoughts. *How did Glow know what she was thinking?*

"When I found Kitty" she said sadly.

"Only then?" asked Glow.

"And when my baby was born" she said softly.

Why was she unable to remember anything about her own child? She couldn't recall the child's birth or visualize her face! What was her name? Surely, she should be able to remember that? As she muddled over her thoughts, it dawned on her that there was something similar about both experiences. *What was it?*

"Ah! Only those two occasions? Nothing felt right, at any other time in your life?" Glow sounded surprised, and knowing at the same time.

"No" she said. With a far-off look in her eyes as she reflected on just how strange her words sounded in the blackness.

"Are you certain?" asked Glow.

"Those were the only two experiences that felt good. And so completely, right." And then it struck her. "But, neither one of them was planned." She spoke quietly - caught up in the emotion of her response that was part memory, and part knowing from some place deep within her. A place that she'd never encountered before. *Where was all this information coming from?*

She realized that her life had been pretty uneventful, even though she'd lived it with the good intention of making a difference in her world. Everything was done at a frenetic pace - time was not negotiable. And everything had to be planned right down to the last detail. She'd always factored in as many variables as she could - to ensure that she covered every possible angle to achieve the desired outcome. Now, with her newly acquired "birds-eye" view of the events in her life, she saw something that she'd never seen before. Her life had passed by without her being aware of it! Finding Kitty, and having her baby were the only two experiences that stood out in her mind! In her entire life! And neither one of them had been planned! Glow burst into tiny sparkles. *What was it doing now?* It took her some time to figure out that the spontaneous burst of sparkles was a form of laughter. She was livid. *What was so funny that it warranted a fireworks display?* But, her indignation was short-lived. It was replaced by wonder as she watched the sparkles slowly filter back together again, and re-form Glow. *What the....!? That was impossible!* Again Glow lit up the blackness with a burst of sparkles - just to prove that it could disintegrate, and re-assemble at whim. This time she suspected that the laughter was directed at the stupid look on her face.

"So there were only two events that you didn't plan, and those are the only ones that you remember? And you're now what..... twenty-five? Yes? And for the most part of your life you've been doing what? Living it in a frenzied daze? You went to school and university. Got married. Worked. That was all planned? And yet, you have no recollection of any of it?" Glow sounded playfully, sarcastic.

Did she really do all of that? She couldn't remember any of it! She was appalled. *Twenty-five years! All gone in a flash!? What did she do with all that time?* She looked at herself again – all she could see was the small, frail body of a child. *How could she still be a child, and be twenty-five years old!?* But, the dissonance was too great. Her mind returned to the driver's seat.

"If that's the way things happened, then I must have done whatever I needed to do. I don't remember any of it. No. Life must have just happened, I guess." *What was she saying? It wasn't like her to be so open about her private life. Why was she confiding in a complete stranger... a......a.....thing? Where was all this information coming from? Again she'd answered using part mind, and part.....what? She didn't know.* She was shaking with anxiety.

"Admirable" said Glow. Shooting sparkles everywhere.

"What's so funny? Who are you? What are you doing here? Why don't you just leave me alone?" she shouted sullenly.

"You can stop this at any time, you know. Just open your eyes" Glow said

"My eyes are open!" she retorted.

Glow's halo bounced around – as though it cracked up laughing again. And it looked like it was sticking out its tongue at her! She was very annoyed. The warm feeling she felt earlier had completely, disappeared and she was feeling cold, and frightened. "If you know all the answers, then just tell me! Let's be done with this madness! Then I can go home!" she shouted.

"You are home" said Glow knowingly.

This was home!? She shook her head hard. *Maybe she was still sleeping? This was the weirdest dream that she'd ever had!*

"And if I told you the answers would you believe me?" Glow challenged.

"Probably not. I don't take kindly to weirdo's telling me what to do in space" she snapped.

"Honest. I like that" said Glow. "We can definitely work with that."

No! She couldn't be asleep! There was no way that all of this was a dream! She must be losing her mind!

"So the things that you planned, you don't remember. And the experiences that you 'stumbled' across left a far greater impression on you? Why?" Glow's voice was gentle, and coaxing at the same time.

What did Glow want with her? That was it! It wanted something! She just couldn't figure out what she had that would be of interest to…..a……a….. glow-worm!

"They just did. Everything went by in such a blur. There was never enough time" she snapped.

She was irritated, and tired. And losing interest with all this heavy stuff. She couldn't see where it was going. If indeed, it was going anywhere! She felt as though she was going around in circles! And she hated that! Something within her, nudged forth an insight. She'd driven herself to achieve her goals, because that gave her a sense of control, and direction. That kind of behavior also led her to assume that she was making progress. And that was the philosophy by which she'd lived. Now, however, she wondered whether her constant restlessness had been pointing her in a different direction. Perhaps she should have questioned that philosophy, instead of religiously adhering to it. Were there other aspects about herself that needed to be questioned? She sighed. *She didn't have time for all this! What was the purpose of asking these questions now? What could she possibly achieve by interrogating herself? The past was behind her - a long time ago!*

"You shouldn't have to force yourself to remember anything, Little One. All moments in your life – good and bad – register on some level, and play an integral part in creating your physical reality. As you reflect on the learning of each experience, you start to build a foundation. Just how strong that foundation is, depends on its building blocks - the values that sustain the highest vision of your soul. Integrity, belief, trust, faith and love. A life where you exist on the outer rim of your consciousness – from the outside in – isn't much of a foundation. Life's meaning extends way beyond everything that you think you 'have to do.' There is so much more to life than merely existing in your physical world. There is an entire ocean of magical experiences just waiting to be discovered. But, it sounds as though you were just dipping your toe in the infinite, ocean of life. How can you experience the wonder of life's creations, if you're not open to it? You've yet to find your magic carpet, and live your best life" said Glow, enticingly.

"I want it all over and done with" she shouted. "As quickly as possible! I found Kitty; had my daughter. That's it. As for the rest of it, it must have happened just like you said. That's all I need to know. There's no need to rehash everything or find a 'magic carpet.' There's no such thing! My life is not a fairy-tale! Let's just get on with this…this….. whatever! Ok!"

She felt as though she was going to explode from anger. Usually, she was quite composed - something that she'd always prided herself on. And now, she found herself in a situation that wasn't only testing it but, was also pushing her to the outer limits on every level. *It was beyond exasperating! Patience was never one of her virtues!* For the first time, she deliberately turned her attention towards what was riling her. *Why was she feeling so….. so……furious? Was it her unfamiliar surroundings? The awkward questions that she'd never bothered with? Was it the uncertainty?* She had a startling revelation. She might have encountered many challenges in her life but, she'd never acknowledged the existence of uncertainty! As much as she loved the thrill of adventure, she had to know where things started, and where they would end. She had a plan – for everything! This "adventure" didn't fit that mold. She didn't have the faintest clue what was going on! She formulated a conclusion. *This was a complete waste of her time. It had to end. If she had a child, and a job somewhere out there, then she had responsibilities that needed to be taken care of. And if she was already twenty-five, then she certainly didn't have time to waste on idle fantasies!* And yet, she couldn't deny that Glow's words had awakened something in her - a level of awareness that she wasn't familiar with. An awareness that made her question things about herself; things that she'd never thought about before. Usually, she had no problem ignoring the things that she didn't want to deal with. Now, however, as much as she attempted to suppress her newfound awareness, and the knowing being unearthed from the hidden recesses within herself, she found it impossible to cross over the invisible threshold that separated this person with heightened awareness, from the one who had "lived" in such blissful ignorance.

"Exactly where would you like to go, Little One? You can't be anywhere else, other than where you are right now. And where you need to go, can only be accessed from here. But first, you have to figure out what's holding you back from this present moment. Ironically, all that outward motion in your physical world is the reason you're feeling so stuck. Whatever needs to happen will happen quite naturally – once you release yourself from that illusion, and embrace this moment" said Glow.

She had the distinct impression that Glow was whirling around, trying to catch its tail.

Except, there was no tail! *Was Glow teasing her? Her outer reality was an illusion!? Feeling stuck was an Illusion!? What nonsense!*

"You said there was nothing holding me here. That I can 'open' my eyes at any time, and leave. But, I've done that already! What am I still doing here!? Why is this happening to me?" She paused as something else struck her. "Did I do something wrong? Did I bring this on myself?" She was struggling to keep the rising hysteria out of her voice.

She'd never before been this close to anyone. Not for this length of time, anyway. She realized that she'd seldom allowed people to get close to her. She was mulling over that when she got a familiar metallic taste in her mouth. She groaned. *Now what!?*

"Am I upsetting you, Little One? Or is this the closest that you've ever been to your Self?"

Her breathing was shallow, and very fast. She was battling to get enough air. *She had to get out of there….fast!* She reached for the common ammunition in her armory – skepticism, and denial.

"Is this a joke? What do you want? This doesn't happen in real life! This doesn't happen in my life! I don't want this! I never asked for this! Stop it now!" she hit back ferociously.

"Are you sure you don't 'want' this? That you didn't 'ask' for this? Do you even know what you want? Or what is 'real?' And if you only set out to obtain what you wanted out of life using your mind, what about the life that your soul desires?" asked Glow.

She hit a resounding blank. Her inability to come up with any answers left her feeling very inadequate. And insecure. Without being conscious of it, she again grasped at a common safety net – her past. *Whatever lay behind her was far better than all this craziness! She wanted it back! If this charade was about facing Kitty's death, and taking responsibility for her other karmic antics then she must have learnt enough by now to fix everything that she'd gotten wrong! It was her choice to go back or stay. Everything would be just fine – as soon as she got back to the way life used to be. She could do anything - once she set her mind to it! She'd faced her fair share of challenges before - she could get herself through whatever else lay in store for her, in her physical world. This entire quest-thing was ridiculous! It was probably just some escapist mind-trap that she'd wandered into. It was now time that she got herself out of it! Enough was enough!* She was shaking with determination. It convinced her of the power of her will. She sighed. It was familiar territory. And it felt good. She didn't like the feeling of being groundless. And she hated the constant see-sawing between her thoughts, and emotions. She was the type of person who set a specific direction, and then stuck to her plans, until she reached her goal. *All this talking was stupid! And exhausting!* She'd never spent this much time on herself - ever!

"Oh you've always had lots to say, Little One. But, none of it really came from a place of truth. We'll get to that in a little while, though. First, tell me why you only remember those two events in your life."

Glow spoke encouragingly; each word uttered slowly. Deliberately.

She hated that soft tone. It made her insides all shaky. And it made her say things that she didn't want to. Things that she didn't even think she remembered…..she caught herself mid-thought. Why couldn't she remember!? This was her life! *Things were coming back to her but, at a snail's pace! Why was it so difficult to remember her past? She wasn't suffering from amnesia!* Was she avoiding something? *She could say anything she wanted about her life!? There was nothing wrong with her! She was fine! It was all good!* She sighed, as she once again encountered the impenetrable fog in her brain. *Why was her head so out of it? She was always, so sharp!* She grasped the next readily available thought. *Glow knew more about her life than it was letting on. How could it possibly know her? She'd never met this thing before! Why was she divulging so much about herself, in the first place? She never spoke about her private life. She never allowed anyone to get this close to her! What was happening to her?*

It dawned on her that there was something about Glow's presence that encouraged her to speak without any fear of being judged. Was that the reason she was opening up to Glow? She didn't feel judged or threatened? Was that the reason for her defensive behavior in the past? She realized, it was the first time that she'd acknowledged the existence of such behavior. Why did she feel the need to defend herself, in the first place? Against whom? Glow was being quite neutral in their discussions. Why was she picking up such a strong undercurrent of judgement? There was no one else around! Was she judging herself? Why would she do that? And if she was, then she wasn't even aware of treating herself so badly! Glow's voice carried a distinct tone of authority but, she didn't feel any pressure to answer. Talking to Glow was like talking with herself! She frowned. There was something interesting about this quest – despite all the weirdness! She was gaining a number of crucial insights into her past behavior. She surmised that she'd never taken very kindly to authority before. She'd seldom, if ever "towed the line." Certainly not, if it was expected or demanded of her! Her compliant behavior in this black space was in stark contrast to her rebellious nature in her physical world. She was baffled. She might not be able to recall everything about her past but, this quest was pushing a number of unfamiliar "buttons!" And she was revealing herself to something that she couldn't identify! And in no way feeling obligated to do so!

There was something else about the nature of her interactions with Glow. Its absence contrasted so sharply with what she'd encountered in her physical world that it made her starkly aware of it. *What was it?* And then, it hit her. Glow was not reacting - she was! Her confusion was slowly replaced by some clarity. The norm in her physical world was usually an exchange of words between egos - not a conversation between human Beings! She was struck by another revelation. That included herself! During those years, she'd been living in the shadow of her own ego! She could now clearly see that, because of her new-found ability to be the observer. She was shattered by that insight. And now that she was conscious of it, she understood why she felt so totally different in Glow's presence. Glow either didn't have an ego or could somehow, control it. She was impressed. *Was it possible to do that?* Could she do that? Was she becoming more aware of her ego as her quest progressed? She was definitely, becoming more aware of her walls! And in the presence of greater awareness those walls were somehow dissolving! *What was happening to her? She had to have defenses! She needed her ego! How was she supposed to survive in the world without them? She had to capitalize on situations if she was going to support herself. No one else would!* She sighed, as she was hit by another insight. Life in the physical world had groomed her well – for the physical world! But, not for this quest in black space! She groaned. She felt more stuck than ever! And then, she was struck by an astounding revelation. She would have to unlearn her old behavioral patterns, and learn new ones if she was to make any kind of progress on this quest! Her old behavior wouldn't get her very far - not with Glow. Besides being able to read her thoughts, it could somehow see straight through her manipulating mind-tactics! Somehow, she needed to steer away from her mind, and move closer to her feelings. She would have to feel her way through this quest! *How on earth was she going to do that!?* She felt daunted. And intrigued, at the same time. And she was keenly aware of a deep respect - for Glow; for herself. And for the black space around her. There was something special – almost magical - about it. Before she could stop herself she answered Glow's question from that unknown place, deep within her.

> "I felt happy" she said quietly. "I was so happy when I found Kitty. And when I had my baby. Everything just faded away - nothing else existed. Each moment spent with them filled every part of me. I only wanted to be with them – always. Nothing more. My world felt completely, full; enchanted. I've never felt like that again."

With that admission she suddenly, felt tired…..so very tired. Something

Undefined

else that she never dared admit to herself. She believed it weakened her edge. She sighed deeply, as she relaxed into that feeling for the first time. And felt something loosen its tight grip on her chest. She felt lighter. Happier. What was it about her past that burdened her so? It struck her that the joy she felt with Kitty, and her baby was like a secret, treasure box that she'd selfishly clutched to her heart - too afraid to share it. She couldn't risk losing it. It was a rare thing - feeling - in her life. She couldn't remember anyone in her family expressing any joy. Or love, for that matter. She shook her head to stop the stream of memories now flowing unbidden, through her mind. *Where was all this information coming from? Why couldn't she stop it?* She was now able to recall certain incidents in her life but, as familiar as they were, they somehow appeared very different to her. Or was she able to see more of her truth in this black space? Courtesy of this uncanny sense of knowing - stemming from an unknown source.

"And the rest of the time? You were unhappy?" asked Glow gently.

"I don't really know what happiness is. But, if you compare everything else to what I felt for Kitty and my baby, then yes, I was…..unhappy." She answered slowly. Totally disbelieving of the story unfolding right before her eyes. Was that her life!?

She was still caught in the depth of emotion cascading through her when she realized something profound. Kitty and her child were very close to her but, there was something far closer - her own heart! And her own life! And she was just beginning to understand just how little she knew about either one! Now that she'd spoken of her unhappiness, she realized that it no longer had such a hold on her. She felt so much, better. Stronger, somehow. And a bit more open to allow the unfolding of another insight. What had caused her to be so completely, out of touch with herself!? She'd always believed that she was happy. She'd always tried to see things in a positive light. And yet, there she was openly admitting for the first time, that she was unhappy! How did that split arise between what she believed, and her physical reality? What was this all knowing, part of her that was bringing things to light? *Why now? It was destroying her world! How could it know her truth – in spite of what she felt inclined to believe in her mind?* She was silent for a long time, as she absorbed what she'd just learnt about herself - aware of nothing other than, her breathing. She'd never before been so acutely aware of every breath. She felt so calm. *And she was floating in black space!* She waved her hands vigorously around in an attempt to shatter any mirage of the blackness if it existed but, her actions failed to have any effect on her surroundings. She slumped over her knees, feeling utterly defeated. Her nerves felt stretched to the limit - like she was going to burst out of herself! *Why couldn't she make any progress on this quest?* That questions had a familiar ring to it. She realized that there were so many occasions in the past, when she'd tortured herself about her progress. *Did she do enough to achieve her goals? Even if she didn't, she couldn't – wouldn't – let things fall apart! She had to hold her life together! She had to stick to her plan!* This quest, however, was providing her with a whole new perspective on control. More importantly, on what was out of her control. The only thing she felt critically important in that moment was to focus on her breath – it helped her to stay close to the stillness. She was extremely unsettled by the things she was saying. More so, because she didn't know where it was all coming from. She was speaking partly from what was in her mind and partly, from some unknown place within her - a place that held far more knowing than her mind! And she was speaking about stuff that she didn't even know existed! And it was flowing out of her like a torrent!

"Why don't you share it with me, Little One? Tell me what your happiness felt like" said Glow gently.

She glanced swiftly at Glow. *Why was it being so insistent? What did happiness have to do with anything?* Again she looked around for some kind of distraction, and caught herself in the act. She couldn't suppress the knowing that this was her usual avoidance tactic. She frowned. She never realized that she was capable of hiding things from herself! She tried to think of something to say - to throw Glow off its line of questioning but, her mind went suddenly blank. Instead, she became mesmerized by Glow's halo. It was like a radar targeting some hidden part of her to reveal unknown truths! Her mind was registering her responses but, was battling to make any sense of it. She didn't know that the content was beyond the existing neural pathways in her brain; that her truth was coming from her soul. But, she felt the truth in her words, and realized that honesty was the invisible thread binding them together in the black space. Glow was looking at her intently. Patiently. She held Glow's gaze, unwaveringly. She felt warmed by the kindness that she saw in its light-filled gaze. It made her feel soft, and warm and yet, she didn't feel weak. She felt a kind of strength that she'd never felt before. She turned her attention to Glow's question.

What did happiness feel like? At first, there were no answers. She had to search for it somewhere past the resistance she felt with her whole body. She closed her eyes, and reached invisible hands to search within its hidden depths. She moved them around slowly; feeling her way in the darkness. And then, she touched something. It felt like a "box." She hesitated. Her treasure! *For how long had it been there? Should she open it? What was inside?* For a while, she simply sat with her hands around the edges of the "box." But, she felt drawn to it - felt an urge to be close to whatever lay within. She opened the "lid" very carefully. And felt her heart quiver when she "saw" what was inside. Her earliest, most cherished memories of Kitty, and her baby were laid out within – untouched! She sighed deeply, and smiled. They were not lost, after all! They were still with her! Exactly, as she remembered them! Her heart burst into song, streaming forth a joy that she believed to be long lost. She'd found her "treasure" again! And with it, she found the words to express what she'd never spoken of.

"They filled the emptiness within me. They warmed my hungry soul for days…..months. Years." She spoke softly, her gaze fixed on the beauty that she saw within. "I never felt alone. I wanted nothing; needed nothing. They helped me go on – for one more day."

For some reason, her mind wandered across to the cold winter nights spent in front of the old fireplace in her father's Victorian house. As a child, she'd often sat at his feet while he read the daily newspaper. They seldom spoke but, she looked forward to spending that time with him. She was transfixed by that memory – she stared into the black nothingness. She shook her head as she struggled to swallow the rising lump in her throat. *Where did that memory come from? She never thought about her childhood!* She only realized much later, that that specific memory had distracted her from closing her "Pandora's box."

The shining halo caught her eye, once more. She smiled at Glow, and continued.

"But, I didn't share those moments with anyone. Not that I didn't want to – I tried a few times but, no one was interested. And even if they were, happiness felt out of place in that house. Everyone lived together - their lives centered on each other. But, there was a constant undercurrent of something or other. Expectations? Duty? Love? Fear, perhaps? And there was an all-pervading sense of a silent, inner battle – they felt impelled to maintain the appearance of a united family but, they also hated feeling that way. And yet, no one expressed how they really felt! It took that expression - a 'love-hate' relationship - to a whole new level! As I grew older, I also started behaving that way. It felt quite natural to not share my thoughts or feelings. I wasn't aware of my behavior - I only knew that I preferred keeping to myself. I didn't realize that simply being in the same environment would compound certain patterns of behavior. And that those behaviors would separate me from myself – from everything that was so dear to my own heart. Furthermore, I would never have counted on some part of me remaining committed to my truth – not after those years!

She paused, and took in a deep breath. "Now you know. That was my happiness, and my sadness. I could never quite tell them apart" she said. Her voice faded away into a whisper.

Again she felt that warm, tingly sensation in every fiber of her body. She took a deep breath, and hugged the feeling tightly to her chest. It reminded her of Kitty - his soft fur against her cheek. And her child's sweet breath when she held her little head close to the base of her neck, rocking her to sleep. She couldn't help smiling. She'd never felt like that for ages! And for so long, she feared that she would never feel like that again. But now, she felt as though something had awakened within her - she felt close to them again. She felt a flicker of light somewhere deep within her – like a spark of renewed hope. She frowned. *She must have imagined it.*

"No, Little One" said Glow. "You felt it. Don't deny what you're feeling."

"How do you know……..." and she stopped. She looked at Glow with a quizzical expression on her face.

Somehow with all the intrigue surrounding her quest, it didn't feel important to understand how Glow could read her thoughts. If anything, Glow's uncanny ability fitted in quite well with all the craziness! *She was after-all, hanging out in black space; talking to a big, bulbous Glow-worm! What could be crazier than that!?*

"Thank you for expressing your thoughts, and feelings to me" said Glow softly. "For trusting me enough - to share them with me. I feel honored. Those two experiences must be very special to you. They remained imprinted on your heart, all this time."

"Yes" she said. Somewhat taken aback by how easy it was to share her innermost thoughts, and feelings with Glow. She felt really good. She'd never been with anyone who felt "honored" by such a simple gesture.

"Not 'simple' Little One. Heartfelt. What about love?" Glow asked.

Love? What was that? Her feelings for Kitty and her child were probably, the closest that she'd ever gotten to that thing called "love." She recalled that whenever she was with them time felt as though, it was at a standstill! She couldn't see beyond those two moments – only Kitty, and her baby existed. And herself. There was an overwhelming sense of mixed emotions from tenderness to fear; and everything else in-between. Whenever she'd been close to them, her whole life felt like it was held in a single breath. She'd never felt so alive. And so afraid - of losing everything that she was holding in her arms. She was hit by a revelation. Why wasn't she aware of those emotions back then!? She was feeling everything right now. And there was nothing to feeling, her feelings! She made a startling discovery about the past, and present in the presence of love. The power of feeling something with all of her heart could never be lost!

"That sounds like love to me" said Glow.

She was exhausted and yet, something within her refused to give up. Each time she felt that she was ready to cave, she miraculously found the strength to lift herself up, and continue with her quest. She still had no idea what she was doing or what was happening to her. The only thing she knew for certain, was that her perspective on life was changing with every moment that she spent in the nothingness. As fast as she arrived at a modicum of understanding by pinning her focus onto some conclusion, something within shifted, and she found herself lost in another mirage of thought. It felt as though, whatever was the source of her inner knowing was overriding every attempt by her mind to regain a sense of control! She knew she was grappling for some sort of closure. But, she also had a strong sense that she was merely grasping at straws. She bit her bottom lip as she was forced to make a shocking admission. She didn't know what she was doing! She'd never experienced anything like this before! She was overcome by anxiety. Nothing felt certain, anymore! She was used to things staying the same for as long as she wanted. Now she only had access to this awareness that was prompting her to not "pin" anything down. Instead, she needed to remain in the observer's seat. And not pay any heed to her rambling thoughts, and emotions. No matter how overwhelmed she was. *What was all this about? What was she looking for?* How could she feel more herself in the nothingness than she'd ever felt before!? How could she feel present in such a space!? She was hit by another revelation. The person she thought herself to be in the past, wasn't the same as the "presence" she now sensed awakening within herself. *What was that feeling?* Why did she never feel it in her physical world? Why was she so aware of it in the nothingness?

"Until now" she said, "I never knew the meaning of all that I've shared with you. I didn't even know that stuff was there! The fact that I'm even capable of feeling joy again, is nothing short of a miracle! I've heard the word 'love' spoken many times. I've even used it, occasionally. But, now that I recall what love actually feels like, I realize that those times don't do it any justice. As a child, I never heard it - anywhere. I only learnt of its existence as a teenager - when I went to the movies. I grew up thinking that that was love. But, now I know it's the furthest thing from the kind of love that I'm capable of feeling. Perhaps my limited view was fitting for the world that I thought I knew. All pink and fluffy – like candy floss. Sweet. Nice to look at. But, with nothing of substance to connect with."

"But, your parents must have told you that they loved you" Glow said.
"No. Not in so many words. But, I'm sure they did" she said, sadly.
"What about other family members? Friends?" Glow asked.
"My immediate family circle was small; insular. And tense all the time. There was definitely, no love lost there. There was the usual bunch – the extended family; a few friends, and neighbors." She was thinking hard as she spoke. Her own words sounded totally foreign to her ears.
"So where did you go to for love? For warmth?" Glow asked.

"Didn't think I needed any. I received food, a bed; a roof over my head. School shoes, once a year" she said. Her head bowed under the weight of something she couldn't quite fathom.

"How did that make you feel? How did you survive without love?" Glow asked, looking at her intently.

She'd never stopped to consider her feelings. It was such an indulgence in a world filled with pragmatic, realism. As for love – can you miss something that you've never known? How did she survive? Did she survive at all or did she merely subject herself to a living death with each passing day? Was that why her life felt so empty? So devoid of any joy? Lifeless? And without meaning? And yet, Glow had mentioned a whole string of events that must be the "story" of her life. And yet, she had no memory of it! Was she even present!? Did she go through her life fully cognizant of what she was doing or was the doer merely a shadow of herself? Was the doer fully or partly under the influence of her ego? And if her life so far was reflective of her ego-self, then who was her real Self? What was that Self really capable of doing? *If she was undergoing some sort of transformation on this quest, what would happen to her mind, and ego? Who was she becoming? Could she survive in her world without all the behavioral tricks that she was familiar with?* If her conditioning was responsible for the way her life turned out, then how did she still get to this place of inner "knowing" – a place beyond the familiar boundaries of her mind? What or who else knew her truth - what she should be devoting her life to, instead of sacrificing it to fulfill her ego's fickle whims? *What was the source of her true reality, if not her mind? If she somehow managed to overcome her conditioning, what then? Would everything about her life change!* She was petrified. *What would happen to her? Where would she end up? How could she live her life without some kind of "rulebook" – even if it was written by her conditioning!?* She couldn't live out the rest of her life in black nothingness! All alone! Who was going to help her?

"Whoa, slow down, Little One" Glow said. "You're going to implode!"

"These questions are driving me insane! I need some answers. Now!" she demanded. "You've turned my whole world on its head!" she said accusingly.

"Was that me or you?" Glow asked softly. Erupting in a blaze of sparkles that looked like it was doing cartwheels.

"This isn't funny!" she shouted.

"It is." And Glow continued flip-flopping in the nothingness, leaving little blobs of light to mark its path in the nothingness.

"Then please tell me……..!" she challenged, sarcastically.

"For someone who planned everything, you certainly got yourself in a fix, Little One. Perhaps your life would have been more to your liking if you didn't make any plans at all. That's funny – don't you think? Maybe your constant planning only led you down the proverbial 'garden path' – it helped you avoid what you needed to confront about yourself. You were constantly moving all right but, you went around in circles, and ended up right back where you started. You're wrong about not knowing what to do on this quest. You didn't know what you were doing back then! And now, with your old life fast disappearing, you're also losing touch with your 'plan.' Neither can you come up with a new one, for what you would like to do next. And there is no escape from this nothingness. That leaves you in an even bigger quandary."

She was so livid, she burst into tears. *Her life might not be much but, it was the only one that she had! And she'd beaten herself up about doing her best!* She straightened her back. *Enough of this ridiculous charade! She wasn't going to hang around, and have some freak of nature tell her what was right or wrong! She was in the driver's seat of her own life – no one else! She decided on the direction of her life! And what she wanted to do with it! She controlled……* and then the irony of her thoughts hit home. *If she was the one in control of her life, then she was responsible for this chaos!* She'd planned, and controlled her life into a standstill! And her benchmark for progress was doing the "right" thing – in the "right" order! At the right time! She'd cultivated her knowledge, and will to be her best allies. She excluded everything from her line of sight – other than what she'd set her mind on doing. Armed with that mind-set, she'd firmly believed that she would attain the success she desired! She believed that it was the "formula" to make the progress she wanted to achieve her life's plans. *What an idiot!* She also started to laugh. Slowly at first, and then uproariously. She couldn't remember laughing at herself – ever!

"And I guess, you're about to tell me where, and how it all went wrong?" she asked between bursts of laughter. She spoke before Glow did.

"I'm going to" she said, half-distractedly. *What was she saying?*

But, her focus was already on the deep, stillness within that was now "speaking" with deafening clarity. If she'd spent all her time in a distracted frenzy chasing one goal after another, and it was all crumbling around her, then what could she achieve by focusing her energy on her uncovering more of her truth? *But, what was she looking for? What was the goal that she needed to attain in this nothingness? There had to be one! There had to be a plan! Nothing was going to happen by magic! Only she could make it happen!* Then she was struck by the strangest revelation. Perhaps this quest had nothing to do with goals or plans. That was her old way of thinking. And she'd never found any meaning doing things that way. She sighed. She was relieved when some questions surfaced above all the confusion. Something told her that they would lead to further insight. *Why was she born? Why was she still alive?*

Glow looked at her intently. She thought she saw some sparkles but, she wasn't sure.

"You're learning fast, Little One" said Glow warmly.

"But, there's more work to be done. Right?" And her questioning gaze shifted to the vast, nothingness.

"Pretty much" said Glow. "But, the answers you need won't be found out there, Little One. You need to look a lot closer to home. You already have all the information that you need."

She looked at Glow, and frowned. *She did? Where? Where did she start?*

"Look within yourself. Start with what you've been avoiding all this time - your past" said Glow.

She felt a mixture of shock and fear as those words grabbed her chest, and squeezed out all the breath in her lungs in one single, merciless grip. *Within herself? What nonsense! What did her past have to do with anything!? What could she possibly remember after all this time? Why couldn't she live her life the way that she'd always done? There was nothing more to be gained by hashing up a meaningless past!* Suddenly, she became aware of the rambling thoughts in her head. And before she knew what she was doing, she reached for the silence within. She felt instantly calmer, and gladly submitted to the peace that she found there. And left the storm to continue raging in her mind. She sighed. What would she do without her stillness? She couldn't deny that she was still feeling stuck. She felt as though she was up against an immovable mountain! This black, nothingness was actually, very fitting! And far from making no sense, it might just be the most sensible thing that she'd ever done! *Although, she had no idea how she'd ended up there! But, she needed to continue if she wanted to live her best life. Where did she begin? Which option would best suit the kind of life that she wanted? What was best for her? Where would her new life take her? Would she get everything that she wanted? What if she failed? What if she ended up being disappointed? She had to think carefully! She had to get it right this time!* She glanced around, hoping to find some indication of the direction she should take. But, there was nothing. *There were no signposts! She didn't know where she was or where she was going!* The only way forward was for her to go back. *That was the last thing she wanted to do!* She burst into tears.

And then, the adventurer in her kicked in. *Well - why not? There was nowhere else for her to go; nothing for her to do. And there was no way out – other than going back! What did she have to lose?* If she continued doing what she'd always done – no matter how much effort she put in – she would end up exactly, where she'd been at the beginning of this saga. And that was exactly, nowhere! Moving forward, wasn't about making "progress" in the usual way. On the contrary, it seemed to be more about releasing whatever was holding her back from her truth. And to figure that out, she needed to go back to her past! She sighed. *She never looked back!* Then again, she'd never thought that her past could have such an impact on her behavior! Or turn her reality into a farce! Was she too hasty in turning a blind eye towards things that she didn't understand? Could the past help her get to know herself better? Could she figure out why she was moving around in circles, despite her best intentions? Could she unravel the knots that she was tied up in? And understand why she'd made certain decisions in her life? Could that knowledge guide her towards her truth? How did she become someone other than her true Self!? Who was this true Self!?

She believed that she'd progressed over the years by doing what she thought was best. But, could she call that "progress" if she'd encountered one dead-end, after another? And made decisions that were not in her best interests? Those dead-ends must have had more significance than she realized. She might have achieved some level of success but, there was something that she'd obviously missed. *What?* She wracked her brains but, only ended up feeling more baffled. All she knew for certain was that she no longer wanted just the proverbial "success" in her life. Whatever she believed in doing with her life, it was far from fulfilling. She now knew that much! She wanted to live a life of depth. And meaning. She wanted to feel, fully alive. She had no understanding what that meant - she couldn't put words to it. *And if she couldn't define it, then she couldn't figure out what it entailed to achieve such a life. But, nothing stopped her from hanging out in the nothingness, until she learnt more. Was that what she was doing there? Figuring herself out? Figuring out her life? How long was that going to take?* How ironic that whatever she'd used to peg some kind of definition to her life was now meaningless! And all that she still had to learn – all that was unknown - held her captivated by its mystery. Why did she allow herself to become deluded by all the forced motion in her life? Why did she believe that it would lead her to the success she desired? Did the rapid attainment of her goals make her complacent? Did her so-called, success fool her into thinking that she didn't need to question what she was doing? Why did she do the things that she'd done? Were any of those goals defined by her Self or did her ego blindside her into adopting them from the world at large, based on all the norms that she'd become indoctrinated by over the years? Was that the reason she'd always felt so separated from her life? Her mind had obviously processed the various events in her life. But, if she used the insights that she'd gained in the nothingness as a reference point, then she doubted that she was fully conscious during those years! She'd survived all those years with little or no conscious awareness of what she was doing or why! She was now beginning to understand that deep feeling of dissatisfaction, and frustration that had plagued her throughout her life. And she was now twenty-five years old, with a child of her own! The life that she'd planned for herself now looked more like an excuse for one. *And to the best of her knowledge, she'd lived it by all the rules!*

She felt the familiar stirrings of an old anger. Although this time, it wasn't directed at anybody else. It was directed at herself! She inhaled sharply. *She didn't like this image of herself - someone who was blind to her own mistakes in judgement!* And some pretty obvious ones at that! That pointed to someone who wasn't very knowledgeable. And she'd worked so painstakingly hard to acquire hers! She'd certainly survived all those years but, she had no recollection of how all that effort could have resulted in her reaching a complete, dead-end! This isolated black, nothingness! All this time, she'd been living something of a make-shift life. And thinking that she was making a success of it! She'd been deluding herself! That explained her fragmented, illusory reality! Something within her stirred ferociously at that thought. She no longer wanted just to survive. Or thrive. That was just ramping up a reality based on her existing patterns of behavior! Life was much more than that. She wanted to feel alive with all of her Being. She wanted to be enamored by it; spend every moment in celebration of this wondrous phenomenon called "life." She wanted to live - not just exist. To revel in its realness - not sugarcoat her experiences with illusions about her life or herself. Yes – that was the polar opposite to her old way of doing things. It sounded extreme. Unfamiliar. Irrational. And she would have to open herself to her unknown soul – to allow her truth to unfold. Without having the faintest idea of what that entailed! But, there was no other way if she wanted to live the life that her soul desired. And from her current vantage point that was far more preferable to being trapped by a shadow of a life, that wasn't based on her truth! A shadow that was invisible; dark and scary. And had its roots deep in her unconscious mind. But, it had made itself known repeatedly through her unfulfilling relationships; mind-numbing work; limiting thought patterns and beliefs. And through decisions that not only disempowered her but, also reinforced treating herself without love or kindness. As real as those experiences were, they were only illusions - none of them reflected her true Self. The knowledge that she prided herself on had helped to expand her physical life in various ways but, it had also ensured that she remained a prisoner of her past; leaving her no room to expand into her soul – to be her true Self. No wonder her life was so meaningless! She'd intellectually conceptualized one based on a host of conditioned criteria, including "good" and "bad"; "right" and "wrong." And the biggest illusion of all – defining specific phases to experience the fullness of life!

And yet, in the nothingness she didn't feel happy about any of it! And those so-called "good" decisions had resulted in her illusory reality! She realized that she no longer held any fixed views on what was good or bad; right or wrong. There was no such thing as the "right time!" Nothing felt right, about anything that she'd done! She just felt highly confused, and very frightened. She might not have had many hopes for her life - other than to make it a success. *But, she certainly didn't like feeling like such a failure about it!* And now, even her view of success looked different. She no longer wanted just the material rewards that came with living a lie in her physical world. She wanted the freedom to express her truth - to honor her true Self. To feel inspired. To treat herself with love, and kindness. To feel happy about all aspects of her life, and her Self - including the "wrong" and "bad." She wanted to honor her Self by living life according to the highest values inscribed in her soul. She no longer wanted to live her life according to the "good" expectations of others or herself. Expectations – like compromise - led her away from her truth. The only form of good that now made sense to her was being one with her true Self. She was hit by a revelation. She might not know what her truth was but, she knew what it felt like to be one with her Self! She recalled feeling that way on rare occasions - whenever she looked at the sky. She'd marveled at the sheer wonder of it, and the many creations beneath it. She was part of all that wonder – if only, a very small part. So why didn't she feel that wonder in her life? Was she being stupid? Idealistic? Naïve? But, she was now convinced that there was something more to her Self, and to life. What else could life possibly be about, if not the Universe bequeathing her that same mystical capability of bringing wonder into her physical reality with the soul she was born with? *Where did that thought come from!?* And yet, after doing it "by the book" for so many years, she felt far from connected to the essence of life. Instead, she felt constantly restless; hopeless, and anxious. Empty. Uninspired. Worthless. Most of the time she felt like such a fraud, and a failure. She felt betrayed. She just couldn't figure out by whom. She stared into the nothingness for a long time, hoping to gain some insight. And then, she had a shocking revelation. No one had betrayed her! She'd betrayed herself! By making ignorant choices out of fear, and not love; by settling for the familiar, rather than embracing the magical, unknown path of her soul. She'd betrayed her Self by compromising the highest values inscribed in her soul. Most of all, she'd betrayed her Self by assuming that the by-product of the person she'd become in her physical world was her true Self! She'd sold out to a life of illusion and mediocrity, instead of owning her truth, and living fully alive!

CHAPTER 4

THE GAME – WINNING IS LOSING

They sat in silence. Glow didn't seem to be in a hurry to go anywhere. Despite her constant urge to escape, she felt rooted to the same spot by some unknown force beyond her control. She was very aware of the emotional turmoil within but, she felt powerless to stop it. And her impatience wasn't helping the situation. She felt like she was being transported backwards, and then forwards through the invisible "pages" of her life. Only to find that when some invisible pause-button was pushed she remained exactly, on the same page! *What was she doing there if her efforts were not getting her anywhere!* She'd always strived to translate her plans into action, as fast as possible. The paradox caught her attention, and she realized that her sense of accomplishment was based on achieving definitive results. *There was nothing wrong with that!* And yet, that approach no longer resonated with her in the nothingness. As uncomfortable as it was, she sat with that feeling. *Why were things not working out in this space as she expected? She wanted to move! To get back to her life! There was nothing wrong with going after what she wanted in life. She'd always done that! There was no other way to achieve success in this world!* She sighed heavily. *When was this nightmare going to end?* She was desperate to do something; to see some tangible outcome. She even found herself wishing for some kind of sign! That was very out of character but, she needed some kind of reassurance. And it would validate that she was on the right track. *She would be ecstatic - if something just moved in the nothingness! Being detached from her emotions wasn't much fun. How was she supposed to make herself feel good about this quest!?*

She felt her underlying restlessness stir again, and her mind found the foothold that it was waiting for. Suddenly, she was bored with everything. *Nothing was happening! If all she achieved in this weird space was more patience, and gratitude then she most certainly, would have made some progress!* On another level, however, the gravity of her situation was far from lost. She was still trying to process whatever she could - as fast as possible. *There had to be some thread of understanding to help her unravel this mystery!* She hated unfinished business or leaving any loose ends. She might have achieved some level of detachment but, she was very aware that there was no scale by which she could keep track of her extreme emotions. *And they were always around, even when she felt detached from them!* For someone who had ignored her feelings all her life, this was an overkill! Whether she liked it or not, she was now being exposed to every nuance of feeling. Her entire body was on high alert, even though she could detect no apparent threat. She would have bolted a long time ago - if only she knew where she was or in what direction to go! She couldn't help thinking that she was being punished by the nothingness. *What on earth did she do to bring this on!?*

But, it wasn't just the mind/body paradox that intrigued her – that was already discounted on some level, by the acceptance of her higher Self. It was the stillness within that she felt drawn to. In that inner space, she felt perfectly calm. And she realized that she was becoming more aware of it, even when she wasn't thinking about it. *What was happening to her? This thing was slowly consuming all of her!* But, in a strange way it was also making the nothingness feel a lot more familiar. She couldn't detect any external factor compelling her to remain there. She'd never felt more "in" her body. And together. And yet, she was fully aware of this still, inner sanctum being somewhat distinct from her physical self, even though it felt very much a part of the silence within, and all around her. *What was she saying!? She was contradicting herself!* But, when she closed her eyes, and followed her breath into the silent, stillness in her physical body she felt it merge seamlessly, with the vast nothingness around her. And when she breathed in, she felt as though she was taking all of the nothingness into her body. *What was this stillness? How could it feel so soundless; so empty? And yet, be so full with an aliveness, and presence that she'd never known before? Was this her soul?* As soon as that thought emerged, she became aware of a flowing sensation. It emanated from that inner stillness – it rose, and filled all of her. And then, it cascaded into the nothingness outside of her. It then circled, and flowed from the nothingness back into her again. She felt energized. Uplifted. Her entire body felt like it was vibrating to some finely tuned, silent melody.

Far from being alienating, the sheer power of that unknown force was drawing her deeper into herself. She felt like she was becoming one with it. The source of it eluded her – it seemed to be coming from everywhere, and nowhere – at the same time! Was this what it felt like to just "be?" She felt her amazement growing. Even if she could, did she really want to end this quest? *If she could fully enter this mystery, she might just have the most amazing adventure of her life! Did she even have such control over something that she didn't understand?* And if she claimed that the major constraint to making a decision about her situation was a lack of knowledge about location or her next course of action, then why was her newfound discernment proffering a degree of insight that refuted that? It was also becoming very apparent that her usual mind games were inadequate to help manage her situation in the nothingness. They were geared towards a way of life, which for all intents and purposes, no longer existed. A way of life that she'd defined using a host of labels. Whatever was happening to her now was far too incomprehensible to be grasped by a mind stymied by old patterns, and illusions. Let alone be categorized or defined!

She was detecting something else – not quite a thought or a feeling. *Where was it coming from? Within or outside of her?* She couldn't pin-point it. It was some kind of "message." She was being "asked" to respect the process. There were no threats or demands. And there was no need for any outward show of commitment – words were not necessary. She was so enthralled that she silently acquiesced. For now, all she knew for certain was that she "heard" something. She felt strangely incapable of making herself do or say anything, contrary to what was being "asked" of her. And yet, her acceptance of that silent voice made her feel more empowered than she'd ever felt before. It was the hardest thing that she'd ever done – agreeing to something she had absolutely no knowledge of or control over.

It was as though her entire repertoire of mind tools, and techniques - everything that she placed such reliance on – were being stripped from her conscious grasp. Including her ability to define everything within the context of goals or time. She was unable to access any of it in this black space, where time didn't seem to exist. If Glow knew what was going on it was not giving anything away. It just sat patiently beside her; without any goal or time constraint in sight. She wondered why she didn't feel afraid. If anything, she felt more safe than ever before. She smiled at the irony. *She was hanging about in black space; doing absolutely nothing! And she felt safe!* In her lightness – almost complete, weightlessness - she felt a strength that she'd never felt before. She was hit by another paradox. True strength felt different. It wasn't at all like the heavy, constant driving that she'd subjected herself to before. If she remained focused on the stillness, and observed what was unfolding around her – in slow motion – whatever she was "doing" felt weightless, effortlessness. As unconscious, as every breath that she took.

Those insights sparked a whole new train of thought. Why did she push herself so hard in the past? Her efforts now looked extreme compared to the lower-than-expected results. What was driving that kind of behavior? A desire for success? Or her insecurities? Again, she was confronted by the irony. She'd always strived to remain strong in the face of demanding odds in both life, and career. Something that she accepted without question, for she believed her career guaranteed the success she wanted. It also catered to two other priorities – her independence, and need for security. And yet, from her vantage point in the nothingness, she now saw how trapped she'd been. Was she really independent, if all she felt was constant anxiety over losing her possessions? What kind of reality did that type of "strength" manifest if her "success" was built on fear, and insecurity? How could she miss something so glaringly obvious, when she'd driven herself to distraction to ensure that nothing escaped her, in her efforts to secure the future she wanted!?

"Glad you're starting to enjoy the process" said Glow.

She smiled at Glow. She did feel lighter but, she couldn't deny her bewilderment. She could now recall a few more memories but, her usual knee-jerk reactions were held in abeyance - as though she wasn't quite done with those experiences. Her perspective was also much broader – it encompassed both a "then," and "now" scenario. As opposed to fixating on powering forward to get to that "future" she was so hell-bent on reaching! And her new level of discernment was granting her a special kind of lens - to see those life experiences in a different light. For the first time she realized that she was looking at them more objectively. And not indulging her proclivity to paint everything using the same brush – either good or bad; right or wrong. Even more surprising was the noticeable absence of opinions, and conclusions stemming from that kind of linear-thinking. She frowned. *Life was so much simpler back then! This nothingness was complicating everything!* That rankled. *She didn't want to conduct a review of her life? Whatever for?* She'd always prided herself on her perspective. Now her perspective about everything was changing in the nothingness - expanding way beyond her familiar boundaries! *She could tell it was happening from all the strange thoughts! And yet, she had no control over it! To make matters worse, the entire process was totally foreign to her! Why was she doing all this thinking - about herself! Why was she going through this hell? She needed to get back to working!* Very slowly, confusion gave way to clarity. In some weird way, this quest was giving her a "bird's-eye" view of her past. It felt as though she was seeing herself for the first time! She was struck by a revelation. She now had the ability to choose whether to accept her past as she remembered, or use her discernment as a "license" to gain a new perspective. That meant not dwelling on any single event, if she intended to do justice to this quest! She had to remain in her awareness; continuously step back and out of herself - something that she was not used to! But, it intrigued her.

However, greater confusion followed hot on the heels of that new perspective. She couldn't understand what had possessed her to make some of her past choices! Suddenly, the past didn't look like the proverbial "walk in the park" anymore. She felt as though she was caught in a time-warp, spinning around one huge paradox. Her "tried and trusted" formula had failed to achieve the success that she'd hoped for! She was nothing more than a puppet dancing to a whole host of tunes! And she had no idea who was pulling the strings or playing the music! She also realized that she no longer felt any real sense of accomplishment over her achievements. *And she'd labored over her career! Why didn't she feel fulfilled? Did viewing her goals as a means to an end have something to do with that?* She shook her head adamantly. *No! She couldn't be wrong! That was how things worked. The whole world worked like that! Things had always worked that way! Life was a transaction - everything was given some arbitrary price tag! And an expiry date! Life as she knew it was all about winning – at any cost! And speed was the ultimate benchmark for success. Things had to get done before everything ran out on the planet! She would be dead long before they discovered some new planet like earth, to live on!* Perhaps it was fear of death that was the overriding cause of her frenzied behavior. *What else could it be?* Whatever the reason, nothing in the world was considered sacred, anymore. Including life itself. She exhaled deeply – she wasn't aware that she was holding her breath. Was that how she'd lived her life? When, and how did she get onto that track? No wonder she felt so empty! And full of despair! When did her mind become the master of her life? *But, if she couldn't use her mind how else was she supposed to live? What kind of life would that be?* She was flabbergasted by those strange thoughts.

As if from a million miles away she heard Glow laughing. The sound of it brought her back to the nothingness with a jerk.

"Come now. Pay attention, Little One. Stay focused on your stillness. There's still a lot of work to be done."

She sighed through her exhaustion. Everything seemed to have more than one meaning. Nothing was as she'd previously thought. And nothing was so obvious, anymore. She was getting all muddled up over her beliefs about life, and herself. She couldn't understand her thinking, let alone the decisions that she'd made! Her previous reality appeared to be one huge mirage floating about in some lost world. *Her life wasn't an illusion? She'd spent years building it! And she couldn't just give up her life's work! What else could she do? Was there some other reality that she wasn't aware of?* She had a weird thought. Was there more than one reality?

Glow laughed. "There are as many realities as your soul wishes to create - once you complete this quest. For now pay attention, Little One. This is important. Otherwise, you'll be stuck in the darkness for much longer than you wish to be."

The significance of what Glow said was lost on her. She was still grappling with her old reality. And everything that she'd lost. So much so, the blessings that came with the nothingness continued to elude her. Although, whenever she did manage to lift herself above the discomfort arising from the extreme uncertainty, she felt more of its mysticism. And magic - like something straight out of a fairy tale. Perhaps the magic and mystery had always been there. She must have lost sight of it, somehow. Did she become so brainwashed by mundanity, and mediocrity that she'd succumbed to an illusion? Did she sell her soul for a mirage? Everything that her mind had given structure to previously, seemed to have evaporated in smoke. There wasn't even anything concrete to look at and yet, she had a distinct image of a smoldering trail of ashes as evidence that something had existed. Something told her that the "door" to her past was closed. That she needed to look forward. *But, she couldn't see any way forward! And neither could she get back to her old life!* Her mind was still foggy but, she was certain of one thing. *There was no visible path unfolding in the nothingness! There was nothing to reassure her that a "new door" would open, and reveal her new life!* Ironically, the one "door" that she'd always used – the one labelled "Escape" – was still wide open somewhere, in her psyche. But, she felt no inclination to use it. She did, however, feel inexplicably bound by some unknown force to stay exactly, where she was. Rational or otherwise she couldn't bring herself to extricate herself from some unwritten commitment. She sighed in frustration. S*he had to fix this mayhem!*

"You can't 'fix' this, Little One. It is, what it is. You're finding it difficult to accept, because you have some preconceived notion of what your life should be. But, your life is perfect - the way it has always been. The way it is now. It's not going to remain like this but, you first have to accept where you are. You can help yourself by scrapping your old notions of the life you wanted. You're only being unkind to yourself by persisting with those outdated patterns of thinking. You'll know that if you allow yourself to expand into your awareness – you'll be able to see your resistance. Just embrace the person that you used to be – the truth will to continue to unfold within you. Don't deny what you're feeling. Try to accept every aspect of the person that you were - as it reveals itself to you. It will lead you to your truth – to the person that you are. Both are a part of your true Self. In the process of becoming all that you are, you can't deny or shut out any aspect of you. Cut yourself some slack, and just be with yourself as you uncover your past. When you surrender to this process exactly, as it is - without any resistance – then you'll see what has been holding you back for so long. Only then will you be able to heal it. Try not to worry about what will replace all that you release. Your true reality lies in your soul. It will unfold quite naturally, without any need to force it" said Glow, reassuringly.

She glanced at Glow with a forlorn look in her eyes. It was watching her patiently, and there was a hint of indulgence shining in its wave-like eyes. Her face softened as she remembered that look. Only one person looked at her like that. She smiled as her thoughts turned to her father. He never spoken of his love for her but, she was beginning to understand that what she saw in his eyes was the truest form of love she'd ever known. It might be only a "look" but, she felt it in every cell of her body. It was pure adoration. For the first time she realized just how much she missed that look in his eyes. She could do no wrong in his eyes. And even if she did, it was forgotten in a flash - the moment that his eyes rested on her. His presence in her life somehow, gave her the permission to do anything. To become anyone that she wanted. Was that the reason she'd strived so hard to be a success? To please him? Without much bidding, she recalled memories that she thought were long forgotten. His warm voice caressed her as she reminisced about his stories of the ocean. She'd never seen the "big, blue water." And she'd hung onto every word as he told her how vast it was. And described the many wonderful creatures that lived in it. She could never imagine anything so huge but, when he mentioned the grainy sand, she saw herself running wildly across the beach trying to catch the wind. She stumbled and fell, and her body hit the ground with a gentle thud. She landed face-first, in the soft sand. She rolled over spluttering, and puffing to remove the sand from her face. Then she opened her eyes, and imagined seeing the bluest sky. There were so many birds! She couldn't count them! She waved her arms about in the sand, pretending that she was flying with them, and weaving in and out amongst the white, puffy clouds. She closed her eyes, and dug her feet into the sand, wriggling her toes. She giggled as the grains of sand tickled her. She wanted to stay lost in that memory, forever. But, Glow was right - there was something important for her to do. She just didn't know what it was. She reluctantly brought herself back to the nothingness.

"What was the most prominent feeling during your life?" asked Glow.

"I didn't feel anything. I just worked" she said quietly.

She'd never given her feelings much thought. Whatever spare time she had was spent reading. It was her favorite thing to do. Most of her notions about life were gained through the lives of the various characters that she'd encountered in those books. *And that was way better than spending time with people!* For the first time, she caught herself in the act of thinking that. Why did she feel that way? It dawned on her that without being aware of it she'd often picked up on the emotions of people around her, without differentiating her own feelings from theirs. She was very confused. Was it case of not being able to feel anything or was she overwhelmed by everything that she could feel? She sighed. Whatever it was, she was just never comfortable with her feelings. And whenever her emotions threatened to overwhelm her – which was most of the time - she quickly distracted herself by doing something or other. She stopped. *It wasn't a distraction! Work was her priority! There was no time to waste, if she intended to get to the top of her chosen field. And whenever she could tear herself away from work, there was more than enough to do around the house.*

"That must have taken a lot of drive, Little One. What was fueling it?" asked Glow, sounding very nonchalant, and whirling around so fast that it looked like a solid, white ball of light. But, she'd spent enough time with Glow to know that its questions were significant. She had the strangest thought. Was Glow throwing her invisible, bread-crumbs!?

Again, she was at a loss for a response. She was never aware of needing any kind of "fuel!" But, her behavior was looking more, and more odd – with every moment that she spent in the nothingness. And the growing feeling of being alienated from the self that she remembered was getting worse. What was driving her? Was it financial gain? She'd come from humble beginnings, and was determined to make her life better. But, as hard as she tried to convince herself of her reasoning, it didn't resonate with her. *This awareness thing was a bomber! She couldn't get away from it!* Besides she knew herself well enough to know that she'd always wanted more of everything – not only, money. She enjoyed the choices that money gave her but, she'd never been one to compromise her standards purely for financial reward. It slowly dawned on her that she'd been looking for something. And she believed that she could find it through her career. She wanted a lot out of life - quality, depth; meaning. Everything, actually. And she was prepared to go all out to get what she wanted. Except, for one small detail. She'd never defined "everything." And waiting patiently for it to materialize wasn't her scene! She preferred to make things happen! Did she waste her time doing the wrong things? Was she looking for meaning in all the wrong places? How could she strive so hard for depth and meaning in her life and yet, be totally oblivious about what she was really looking for? As amazed as she was with her latest tendency towards self-recrimination, she realized that it was helping her to understand her behavior. *When, and how did that happen?*

"When you started taking that head of yours a lot less seriously, Little One" wagging a shiny finger at her. "You'll find that as you clear stuff from your past it will be easier for you to cut out the unnecessary noise. You'll create the space to hear your inner voice" said Glow.

There! Glow did it again! It had read her thoughts! But, she was onto something now – she could feel that familiar eagerness running through her. She would get back to interrogating Glow later. Understanding herself was far more important, right now. What was it about this nothingness that helped her cut straight through the BS? She was used to justifying her decisions. So much so, that those decisions formed the basis of her truth. Now those "truths" were somehow losing their appeal. What was the fuel that sustained her during those years? She thought she had boundless, physical energy. She'd whizzed through her days, doing everything that came her way. Then why did she encounter one dead-end after another in her life, despite her dedicated efforts? Was there a relationship between how empty she felt, and whatever she forced herself to do? Why did she have to force herself, in the first place? As frustrating as this quest was she realized that there could be no progress - on any level – until she got to the bottom of her behavior.

"Well….." Glow prompted. Still weaving, and whizzing around in multi-colored circles of light.

"I don't know. There was always too much to do…..there was never enough time……"

She paused, waiting for her mind to kick into gear - to provide more information. But, it was still strangely, removed. She sighed, hopelessly. She doubted that she could solve anything with her mind in a heavy, fog. *This whole thing was a waste of time!* Glow, however, was hell-bent on pushing ahead.

"Were there any emotions that were stronger than others?" asked Glow.

"Nope. All I can remember are the frequent arguments throughout my childhood. Family relationships were always strained. And there wasn't much of a social network in our small community - people kept to themselves. It was a relief to leave all that controversy behind me by moving to a new city. But, I didn't escape for very long. My new environment soon took on the same undertones. A veritable melting pot of conflict when it came to sex; gender; race; culture; politics. Nothing different to any other time in history, I guess" she said, forlornly.

"And that is the saddest part of all this – that so little has changed, since the dawn of time. History shouldn't repeat itself. There is no merit in that. And don't bury your feelings under superficial generalizations or discount them, because of ignorance. They're far more important than you realize. So there was a lot of conflict…..and….?" Glow persisted.

"Yes. Sometimes loud. More often than not, a silent war. People around me, either exploded with anger or avoided each other – as if that would make the incident simply dissolve! As a child I witnessed a lot but, I never really understood it. I also knew that any questions would be ignored, so I pretended to not see anything. No one spoke of the things that were uppermost on their minds. As an adult, I took refuge from all the drama going on in my life by focusing on my career. It gave me with something more constructive to do with my time, even though it wasn't without its fair share of conflict. However, I managed to escape all that with my travels. That brought a whole different layer, and texture to my life. I didn't bother much with anything after that" she said, trying to sound convincing.

"Are you certain? Things have a way of getting under the skin" said Glow.

"There was no time to entertain frivolity! I was busy all day - every day" she said.

"What did you think of all the conflict?" Glow asked.

"That there are a lot of angry people in the world" she blurted out.

"Perhaps. Did you think your experiences were reflecting what was going on inside you? That you were angry about something or someone? Yourself, perhaps?" Glow queried, softly.

"So I'm to blame?" she snapped, looking at Glow with fierce, unflinching eyes.

"There's more to it than that, Little One. You need to listen more carefully. You'll save a lot of energy. There's so much left unsaid, in the unspoken. It makes all the difference between reacting with your ego, and responding from your inner, stillness. More often than not, you'll find that a response isn't even necessary. You just have to stay present, and listen – hold space for the other person to share their thoughts, and feelings. If both parties do this, a conclusion will be reached that best serves all concerned. That will not only save a lot of time and energy but, it will also prevent egos from re-cycling the same old patterns of behavior." Glow spoke with quiet conviction. Not at all fazed by her look. Glow continued.

"People often serve as mirrors in life - reflecting back your thoughts, and feelings. You do the same for others. It might not be obvious at the time for any number of reasons. But mainly, because you're unaware, and distracted by your ego's constant need to prove itself right. You might also be out of touch with your feelings, until your awareness kicks in, and you can pick up on the patterns being reflected to you. Some emotions might have been suppressed for such a long time, that you believe they are forgotten. But then, you meet someone or some event transpires in your life and suddenly, you're sucked right back into the emotional minefield that you firmly believed was behind you. You tend to act in ways that are difficult to understand, and your behavior triggers the very feelings that you're trying to avoid – like guilt, shame, and fear. In your case, your stubbornness to face certain matters when they arose only compounded your painful experiences. You preferred to ignore your emotions by distracting yourself with your busy-ness. But, far from creating your best life you were caught in cycles of repeating history."

"However, in your attempt to resolve some of the more obvious challenges, you did make a few changes that improved your external circumstances. But, you never got to the core of your problem. As a result, you never changed what you most needed to change - yourself. If you continue ignoring the gentle prodding of your awareness, you'll go through the rest of your lifetime without fully understanding your role in creating your past experiences. You'll remain 'stuck' in a self-perpetuating cycle of pain, rejection, and a whole host of other negative feelings. However, you can set yourself on an entirely different path by focusing your energies on understanding your old behavioral patterns. Avoiding it will only keep your past, and the pain alive. It's possible to suppress certain experiences in your mind but, your mind is not the only container of your past – your whole physical body is. Nothing is ever forgotten. To release that, you need to unpack some of the conflict in your life. What emotion stands out for you when you look at the past? Your anger, perhaps?"

Anger? Pain? Rejection? Avoidance? Suppression? Distraction? Resistance? They all struck a nerve! Some past experiences that had elicited such emotions flashed through her mind. She felt a tingly warmth – something like an electric current – surge through her body. Even if she wanted to ignore her past, she could no longer deny the feelings that were now being unearthed from some hidden reservoir within her. *What was happening to her? Why now? Where were those memories coming from?* She felt heavy; so very exhausted. *Why did she feel so burdened by her past? What was she so angry about?*

"You can now name it. Good" said Glow. "Maybe we can now try going a bit deeper. Who are you so angry with?"

"No one! Myself, I guess." But, her words were met with no response from the silent, sanctum within. It made her aware of an important distinction. There might be some degree of truth to her response but, it wasn't the whole truth.

It slowly dawned on her that she was caught in a vicious cycle. She was constantly angry. At her parents. Her circumstances; at everything, and everyone. Including herself, for landing up in one painful experience after another. She'd done things "by the book," and yet, her life had moved further, and further away from her. It had never felt like her own! Even more surprising was that some part of her had always known that. Sadly, she'd never acknowledged that all-knowing part of her. Neither did she acknowledge the part of her that felt so misplaced by all the mayhem in her life. Then there was the whole gender thing. That just added a whole different layer to her frustration. She shook her head, and snorted. *Life would have been so much easier as a man!* She felt something react violently within her at that thought. *What was that about?* As for the color of her skin – she'd never understood why that made her so different compared to everyone else. She remembered asking questions as a child when she noticed them only accessing places marked "For Blacks." She wanted to see where the others were going – those places marked "For Whites." But, everyone acted as though they saw nothing. And no answers were given. It was only as an adult that she'd come to understand the rampant racism in her country. By that time, the signs were eradicated but, many "doors" remained closed. Many still are. Including the "doors" leading to many hearts, and minds. She'd often wondered what her life would have been like without the many exclusionary restrictions that dictated not only her access to physical locations but, also the opportunities that were made available to her. Things might have changed somewhat, since her childhood but, she couldn't help feeling bitter about missing out on some of those opportunities. Now the nothingness made her aware of other considerations with some serious implications. Were the forced political barriers that continued to stymy socio-economic reform only physical in nature? Or did those experiences become imbedded in her psyche to such an extent that they limited her thinking, and made her see "barriers" in life where there were none!? ? Did she identify with being "Black" or did she see herself as a soul with the Divine right to fulfill her purpose?

She sighed. She was overwhelmed by all the information flooding her senses. But, none of it was as bad as the bit that rose to the surface on the muddied lake of her mind. Something she hated so much, that she'd never dared think about it. Until now. She'd lived her life trying to fit in with that kind of world! She believed that it was a sign of acceptance. And acceptance was important if she desired success. Furthermore, acceptance meant belonging – to what and whom, she had no idea. All she knew was that if she abided with some secret, silent code then life would go along as she expected. To her, that was "normal." If for whatever reason she stepped outside those invisible lines then, she would have to face the consequences. Some of it she could live with - by adapting as best she could. Others however, were unbearable and she was eventually, forced to remove herself from those situations. She was grateful that those consequences no longer entailed being burnt at the stake or some other kind of death sentence - as had been the case for generations before her! Now however, she realized that those "lines" were nothing more than changing goalposts throughout the course of history, depending on who or what she was dealing with! She was horrified. Those "goalposts" were nothing but, an illusion! Each soul was different. There were no "goalposts" to fulfilling a soul purpose! And she'd continuously limited hers to fit in with a mirage! She was also very much aware that there were various, more subtle forms of enforcement against women in many cultures across the world, including her own. Her generation was supposedly, living in more "civilized" times but, forcing recognition of gender parity didn't necessarily, change age-old, perceptions! Or signal respect, and acceptance! She frowned. Civilized or not, the social and cultural norms that imposed such restrictions now looked like a repetitive scene from some grandiose puppet show. And she was given those roles that merely perpetuated an age-old illusion that she'd been conditioned to believe in. She wasn't worthy – not only of her rightful place in the world but, of the life that was hers to live, as her soul desired! She had a startling revelation. Even if she did fit in with those so-called "norms," and was fully accepted by others, she wouldn't be able to live with herself! That unknown part of her that she was slowly becoming more aware of wouldn't respect or accept a false sense of self!

Strong on the heels of that revelation came an anger that she wasn't even aware existed. *Why did she believe that she was someone other than her true Self? How did she come to deny her truth? That pointed to living her life according to a host of expectations that she wasn't even aware of! She couldn't be expected – or expect herself - to be anybody, other than her true Self in this world?* At the same time she realized that false expectations made the world stage, nothing more than a charade! And she'd no doubt, compromised, and limited her Self by accepting such a trade-off – knowingly or not! But, it also compromised, and limited those who expected her to be less than her true Self. It placed a "glass ceiling" on human evolution by limiting soul growth. It kept the scales of the human experience low and precariously off-balance, because of outdated man-made laws, and systems. She sighed. It was such a waste of a soul to have contributed to a way of life that only repeated itself - lifetime, after lifetime! She wished life had an "undo" button - one that would allow her to wipe out what she no longer liked about her life. But, even if that was possible, she would not be able to wipe out what she didn't like about herself! She would just come back to fulfill her soul's truth. Nothing could destroy that! She slowly blew out the air in her lungs. She didn't realize that she was holding onto her breath.

She was relieved that she no longer felt guilty about her rebellious nature towards some of the restrictions that had been placed on her. But, her little antics were in no way capable of changing structures that had kept such belief systems alive, since time immemorial. Then again, those systems and structures weren't in her control. It took a few moments for her to digest that astounding admission. *She'd always believed that everything was in her control!* She would never have thought herself capable of making such a distinction! Or such an admission, for that matter. For some reason, however, she felt lighter. And more empowered. She realized that if she still intended to make something of her life then, she needed to shift her focus away from that world "stage," and devote her energy to what was within her control. She sighed. *And what exactly, was that?* She looked at the nothingness but, there were no answers. *What was she supposed to do now? She didn't know!* The very cornerstone of the beliefs that she'd used to curate an identity in her external world was slowly disintegrating. Somehow she had to find a way to live her truth in the world, without succumbing to the belief that the old, familiar systems provided the only reality that she could have. She was chewing hard on her bottom lip. *That sounded extreme! How was she supposed to make that happen?* But, somehow she had to. She couldn't play the role of "pretend" anymore! Life didn't require her to play a game - it required her to be real. And to have the courage to face the consequences of owning her truth. There would obviously, be certain things that she would have to comply with in the world but, that didn't include comprising the soul purpose that only she had the right to fulfill. She didn't know what angered her more – that things didn't have to be the way they were or the blatant perpetuation of a system that only served a few. Why was all that so-called, power used to uphold an age-old, system that didn't serve everyone? It could be harnessed so much more effectively, to create a better world for all life forms, including human beings! And save the planet! She shook her head sadly. But, she needed to focus - right here; right now. She needed to devote her time, and energy to understanding her own behavior.

"That must have been some kind of anger, Little One. It kept you going like a Trojan for years. But, you're discovering that it's easier to distract yourself with thoughts of the outside world, rather than focusing on what's going on within you. And none of it tells me much about you. I now know that you used your anger to drive yourself towards your goals. I also know of your strong sense of justice, and your desire to make the world a better place. Those traits do reveal aspects of your innate nature, and also give you an inkling of your soul purpose. But, nothing you've said tells me much about you. You're not your accomplishments in your physical world – no matter how important you consider them to be. You're not the sum total of your behaviors; decisions or beliefs that you've been conditioned to adopt. You're not the product of the systems, and structures in your world. You're not your successes or your failures. You're not, your qualifications or career. You're not your parent's daughter. You're not just a wife or a mother. You're not your social circle; your title or status; your culture or religion. You're not 'Black,' 'White' or any other color, or label that has its roots in discrimination. You're a woman but, that's just your physiological makeup. Far more important than your sex or gender are the feminine, and masculine energies that are part of your innate nature. Both are essential for inner harmony, and the expression of your true Self. Your various roles might have helped you to function in your world but, none of them define who you truly are. Everything that you've done before, is only a small fraction of your Being. That is far more than any role; more than anything you could ever choose to do or become in your physical world."

She was more confused than ever.

"You're talking about my entire life! Those roles made me who I am! Gave me a life!" she retorted. She was outraged. *Her whole life was collapsing around her!*

"No, Little One" said Glow firmly. "None of your accomplishments, titles or roles define who you truly are. You're not defined by your outside world. You carry within you, your real world. And whatever you've done so far, isn't everything that you're capable of as an awakened soul – one with all of your Being. That chasm between your external reality and what you feel exists, because the Universe doesn't respond to what you do. It responds to the way you feel, when you're doing what your soul desires. And you can't feel that way without being true to your Self.

"I don't understand. I've tried everything I know. I used every approach; every avenue that was open to me" she said, sullenly.

"Yes, you did" said Glow with a warm, smile "But, you only worked within the limitations of your conditioning. Limitations that not only restricted what you did but, also influenced your relationships with others by forming the basis of the non-relationship with yourself. That conditioning also led you to define yourself using the labels that abound in your world. But, who are you, without your conditioning? And those labels? Who are you beyond your race, culture or religion? Beyond your sex or gender? Who are you without your accomplishments? Or relationships? Without your titles, and possessions? Who are you without your past 'story'? Who are you when you're doing nothing? What did your soul come here to do? Who are you as a Being? You might have tried various options to change your life using your mind but, you certainly haven't tried the most important avenue – the Universal channel available to your Being. The conditioning that confines your mind, and body might have sufficed for the life you had before but, it's standing in the way of your truth now. And neither your physical body nor any system operating in your world are powerful enough, to hold you back from your soul purpose. You're feeling 'stuck,' because you're denying your truth. Your soul only desires one thing - to express its own reality in your lifetime. To do so, you need to break the barriers that are holding you back - break free from anyone, and anything that no longer serves your soul's purpose. That is your highest path. If you don't, you'll remain a victim of your circumstances, and nothing more than a caretaker of a false reality - one that was never yours to begin with."

She was completely, taken aback. *A "victim!" A "caretaker!" She was none of those things! She was her own person! She'd always done her best. She'd always set her sights on winning!*

"Then why do you feel like such a failure, Little One? Why are you feeling so depleted? And lost? Why are you in nothingness?" Glow challenged, gently.

"Well……life…. is….is…..a…..a game!" she stuttered. "Losing is a part of it – just like winning! But, I've worked bloody hard to make mine a success. I've messed up but, I'll bounce back. I always do. I'm just having a bad round now. What 'system' are you talking about? Nothing - no one controls me! I make my own rules! This time is no different" she said, feigning confidence. She regretted it, as soon as the words were out of her mouth. *Why didn't anything resonate with her anymore!?*

"That false bravado might have worked for you before Little One, but it won't help you now – not in this space. In fact, nothing that you used to drive your ego's agenda will work here. You're still pretending - trying to make yourself feel better about sticking to your conditioned status quo. But, you can't make yourself feel better about any of this. You need to see yourself as part of your past – not separate to it. And feel everything that comes up within you – without doctoring it to make yourself feel better about it. To see your Self – all of you as you truly are. That means accepting the good, and the bad. That's being real – about you. Acceptance is the first major lesson in being present with your Self. This quest has been in the making for a long time but, you ignored all the signs, and insisted on holding your fragmented life together. You and your past reality are one, and the same. And the faster you learn to surrender to all that unfolds during this quest, the easier it will be for you to let go of your old reality. All of your physical self has to be aligned, and integrated with your truth – before you can be one with your soul's desire to create your one, true reality. The status quo in your physical world is in the process of crumbling, anyway. That might be hard to believe right now - with things still appearing to be intact. But, it's only a matter of time before that illusion falls to the ground. The changes have already started within - on an energetic level. The effect on dense matter will follow. The outer world is only a reflection of the inner world."

What was Glow talking about? She felt as though she was being slammed by a bulldozer – over, and over again! *She couldn't deny that Glow's words were resonating deeply with her but, she didn't understand any of it!! And it was taking forever! She wanted to get on with her life!*

"There's no rush, Little One. Besides you can't go any faster - your soul has set the pace for this quest" said Glow, encouragingly. "You can only feel you way through it – one feeling at a time. Don't worry about understanding. That will come - when you least expect it. Let's go back to what made you so angry."

She frowned. *Was she just maneuvered back to the one question that she was avoiding?* She sighed. *She might as well get on with it!*

"I didn't know it was anger. I seldom knew what I was feeling. But, no matter what I did one thing was evident - I never felt like I belonged in this world. I did try but, the harder I tried the more pain, and rejection I encountered. I ran myself ragged trying to keep up with the demands on my time. The more I did, the more was demanded of me. I couldn't keep up but, I refused to admit that. Besides I was so used to the pace of my life by then, that even when things did slacken off a bit, I took on more. The word 'no' didn't feature in my dictionary. Nothing was too much of an imposition on my time, and energy. I just continued to give. But, I was just running around in circles! I didn't even know that!"

"Why didn't you stop doing the things that made you unhappy? You could have broken out of that vicious cycle by focusing on the things that made you happy. Do you even know what brings you joy?" Glow asked.

"I tried everything! Why don't you believe me?" she asked.

"Do you, believe in you?" asked Glow.

She raised her eyebrows. "I did my best to deal with every possible scenario up front. There was no time to go back, and fix anything. It had to be done right - the first time round. There was no time for analysis – not with the mountain of work that needed my attention. Everyone wanted something." She paused to take a deep breath, and then shot back: "Why do I have to change? What's wrong with me?" Her voice was raised. She was livid. *Joy was overrated! She had to earn a living!*

"I'm not criticizing you, Little One. You can put down those swords" said Glow, gently. Every word sounded like a caress.

The sound of Glow's voice calmed her down, immediately. Something within her responded to the kindness, and softness reaching out to her. She felt as though she was being held in a warm embrace. She was equally struck by Glow's insight into her suppressed emotions. There was nothing comfortable or nice about their time together. She felt challenged mentally, physically, and emotionally to an extent that she'd never experienced before. And yet, the depth and honesty of their conversation kept her fully engaged. Glow continued, without losing a sparkle.

"If you were continuously experiencing conflict - if that was the general pattern in your life – then your relationships were reflecting something that already exists within you. Your sensitive nature made you vulnerable to the emotions of those around you. And besides being confusing, that would have compounded the intensity of your experiences. Unfortunately, before you could become aware of your behavior, your thoughts morphed those experiences in a number of ways. To make matters worse, your reactionary behavior would have provoked a host of repercussions, both from others and yourself. You tried making sense of it but, all that 'noise' in your head made life far more complicated than it needed to be. A revolving door of emotions that keeps spitting you out to face the same reality is pointing you towards something within yourself. And that's what you're doing here – getting to the core of your behavior. Your truth lies behind all that 'noise.'

Glow was observing her closely. Perhaps waiting for some kind of reaction. There was none. She could relate to everything being said. Glow continued.

"Your attention was always focused on the outside world, rather than on your inner self. And that made you susceptible to being constantly distracted by non-essentials. You also wasted a lot of energy dealing with the fallout from your behavior. You basked in self-righteous anger, instead of getting to the underlying cause of it. You're now facing the repercussions of those behavioral patterns in the nothingness – it was the only way for your soul to get your full attention. You can continue ignoring it but, the harder you try the greater will be your soul's pull-back to bring you face-to-face, with the lies you keep telling yourself. And, until you face your truth you'll remain stuck repeating the same patterns during your lifetime. And no matter which way you insist on looking at it, that's not winning. As challenging as your experiences were, your distracted state merely kept you from doing the real work – on yourself. You could no doubt, justify your behavior, and the barriers you erected on the grounds of self-protection. But, you're also blocking yourself from experiencing the life desired by your soul."

"To your credit, you did try disguising those 'walls' by being nice. That people-pleasing behavior might have fooled others but, you can never fool your Self. Not for long, anyway. And without getting to the root-cause of your anger, you'll only extend yourself further, and further in your efforts to please others. There's nothing wrong with that – if you can remember to give without self-sacrifice. Furthermore, if your actions were geared towards meeting the expectations of others then you realize by now, that not only did you set yourself up for disappointment but, your actions were seldom reciprocated. If anything, more was demanded of you to help you become aware of your unconscious behavior. Those experiences were painful in themselves, and you blamed others for treating you badly – which they sometimes did. But, you were also suppressing your own needs and over-functioning, because of your conditioning. But, that wasn't the only sword you turned on yourself. When you found yourself utterly spent from giving so much of yourself, you sub-consciously rejected people before they rejected you – subjecting yourself to more pain, and suffering. A vicious cycle that only continued to deplete you, until you had nothing more to give."

"It's equivalent to playing a game of chess. Except, once your soul awakens, life ceases to be a game. It becomes real. And only the real you can participate in creating your true reality. If you insist on viewing it as a game, then only one set of rules apply – the laws of the Universe. The key difference is that those laws apply equally to everyone, and you don't have the luxury of chopping and changing them to suit your own agenda. Far from being restrictive, they offer you a blank canvas – for your soul to create the highest vision for your life. There is no way you can lose - all the pieces required to play your best game are already carried within your soul. It just knows what to do – you don't even have to think about it. And the key to entering that state of knowing, is your healed Self – it opens you to your highest potential. The 'chess-board' in this case is the blank canvas that you're born with. But, during the course of your life you became hooked onto the game plans of others. You adopted their 'winning' strategies believing that you can achieve the same success they did. And things look so much easier when you're looking at them through your mind's eye – your ego is constantly working in the background to devise a quick win to outdo your opponents. But, it makes you lose sight of your own game. And your truth. By the time you realize that you haven't quite achieved the success you expected, it's too late - your ego won't accept that it's capable of making any mistakes. So you continue transposing different strategies onto your 'chess-board,' convinced that your 'winning hand' is only one more move away. But, that only keeps you wrapped up in the illusion. You can never win using someone else's soul plan. Each one is unique."

"But, all this time you've been denying your own soul plan. That's the reason you feel like such a loser. If you focus all your energy on following your soul path – your true blueprint - you'll be unstoppable. That's the only 'game' that you're here to play. And even when you think you're losing, you'll be winning. You can never lose when you own your truth, and walk your soul path. It's your winning hand. And no one can play your soul's game – not the way you were born to. All you need to do to become master of it, is to observe – your Self. Remain centered in your stillness. Stay present. Stick with it at all costs. There's nothing about your true Self that needs to be fixed - you just have to remove everything that's standing in its way. And don't worry about fitting in – you're not meant to. No person can do justice to the soul path of another."

It all made…..perfect…. sense. Her experience in most of her relationships - if not all – was exactly, that! She'd never fitted in – no matter how hard she tried. She realized that even as a child, she'd been exposed to a lot of anger. The unspoken, pent-up anger amongst the people in her inner circle was deafening. She didn't understand it then but, she realized that she must have interpreted their silence as a form of exclusion, even if it was unintentional. She'd always felt left out! And when her continuous efforts to be heard were silenced, she not only felt rejected, she felt angry. Without being aware of it, she'd succumbed to the same behavior, and used those "swords" on others whenever those painful memories were triggered. Her behavior had no doubt, contributed to much of her pain being self-imposed but, relatively speaking that was easier to live with, compared to the ongoing rejection from others. To protect herself, she learnt to stay on the periphery of peoples' lives by blending in to the point of being practically, invisible. Or so, she thought. She didn't know that life would always find a way to draw her out. Neither did she realize that she was only looking at one side of that "coin" by failing to factor karma into that equation. The other side of those swords were pointing in her direction! It kept her pain alive by attracting the same experiences – day after day. Month after month. Year after year.

As a result of that pain she was in "fight-flight" mode, all her life! She had to be in control of every situation; of every relationship. It gave her the assurance she needed - knowing that she could protect herself from being hurt. She was struck by another revelation. She'd focused all her efforts on trying to fit in, and she was consumed by frustration whenever her efforts were thwarted. At least, that was the way she'd perceived it. What she didn't realize at the time was that her "failures" were pointing her towards something within herself that she was completely, unaware of. Her outer experiences were not the source of the pain – she was! It was inside of her! And it kept her constantly on edge - alienating her from her Self! Her attempts to compensate for her perceived shortcomings might have gained her some acceptance but, it did very little to ease the discomfort of feeling separated from herself. Trying that hard to be accepted by others, only made the "ground" she stood on, that much shakier. Until eventually, it gave way beneath her, and she'd caved. Not because the Universe had it in for her but, because her world was merely mirroring her false sense of self. A self that she'd rejected, because she didn't know who she truly was! With that admission, she felt something bubbling up inside of her. *What was that?*

"So I was angry, because of being rejected? Right? Meanwhile, I was the one rejecting myself?" she exclaimed excitedly. *It was staring her in the face! How could she have missed it?*

"Not so fast, Little One......." Glow said, softly "......rejection can be a useful guide to understanding one's behavior but, it can also be symptomatic of blind spots in one's character. Your emotional barriers might be invisible but, they're like layers of armor that you used to defend yourself. Anger is only one such layer. And with everything that you perceived the world to be throwing at you, you've built a veritable fortress over time! That kind of behavior might have served as a form of protection in the past but, it also blinded you to your truth. Such extreme denial is also a form of self-sabotage – it prevents you from expressing yourself fully. You're only capable of expressing yourself through the lens of your negative conditioning. Much of it is still blocking you from engaging fully with life - from receiving the gifts that life has to offer you. Your soul didn't arrive on this earth, empty handed. But, you're far from open to the experiences designed by your soul to help you realize your highest potential. If you can continue observing your past in the neutrality of your stillness, you will transcend your negative experiences, and heal yourself. You'll be able to align with your soul, and still uncover the life that you deserve. You can't change anything in your external world – it's only showing you what you need to change within yourself."

"Before you can see what that is, you need to remove everything shielding you from your truth. You need to look more closely at the rejection that you experienced. You were either, intentionally provoking it, because you expected it from the familiar pattern of your experiences or you are unconsciously attracting it, to bring you closer to a wound within. You could also be caught up in the interplay between those two patterns. That inner conflict, even though very painful – helps you deflect what you don't want to deal with. But, until you heal yourself, it will continue to disrupt your life. Sometimes a good gauge for the extent of your inner pain, is the pain that you experience in your outer world. And you experienced a lot of it. However, before you can get to the core of it, you first have to remove the layers of illusion that have prevented you from acknowledging its existence. Time isn't a factor in this process – being honest with yourself is. If you fail to acknowledge the 'seed' that has given rise to your behavior, you'll continue with the patterns that hold you captive in a self-made prison. And you'll repeat the negative patterns that are imprinted on your mind, irrespective of the number of achievements that you notch up in your physical world."

"Those negative patterns have run rampant in your life for years - as you've no doubt discovered. It helped you define your goals, and achieve them. It fed your drive for success, and boosted your ego. But, you fell into a dangerous trap. With your goals not being aligned to your soul purpose, your drive was bound to run out. Like it did before. And each time that it did, you were left 'high and dry'– with your ego still on its pedestal, and your soul far from fulfilled. You used your will to spur you on for brief periods of time but, your ego is no match for your truth, because it will never be all that you are – an eternal, infinite Being. It will always end up playing a game of 'catch up' with your soul's truth. While it does, make no mistake that it will distract you from your true purpose. You can't just blaze a path to get what you want out of life. Then again, you can - if you insist on being deluded by your ego. That is your choice. However, if your ego is your only ally in achieving your goals, and you have to deny your truth to do so, then you'll be sacrificing your full potential. All you'll experience are intermittent bouts of success during your lifetime. With one qualifying distinction – you'll feel constantly at odds with that success. You'll continue searching for some form of fulfillment outside yourself, and hit one wall after another. And without reverence for your truth, inner peace will continue to elude you. This quest might be challenging but, it's nothing compared to the emptiness you'll feel with each passing day of your life, if you continue to deny your truth. This quest is no fool's errand. You won't be led astray – not if your intention is to surrender to the highest values within your soul."

"To transcend your negative experiences you have to first, heal the pain caused by old patterns of behavior. You can't embrace the new while you're still hanging onto everything that no longer serves you. So far your lack of self-awareness helped you exploit various quick-fixes to try, and resolve shortcomings in your character. And you've now run out of those options that entailed seeking answers outside of yourself. There is only one avenue still open to you - to look within for the answers that you seek. It will help you to identify the triggers to your past behaviors by revealing the barriers that you've built around yourself. You'll be able to heal each one by bringing it into the light of your consciousness. The removal of each barrier will serve to open your heart a little more, each time – allowing you to shine your soul's light on the next obstacle that has kept you from your Self. And so you'll proceed with your quest, one conscious, light-filled step at a time - opening your heart with every step to reveal more of your true Self. Each time you uncover a layer, whatever form it takes – good or bad - embrace it with love, and compassion. All of it, is you."

"This is your quest - to uncover your truth, and learn to love your Self. It won't be easy. It's not meant to be. Depending on the extent of your conditioning, finding your truth can be a tumultuous journey. But, it's beyond the ephemeral, physical achievements that you've placed so much emphasis on in your physical world. And the reward is unsurpassed – you'll become one with your Self; one with your soul. One with this, Divine Universe. Only by destroying all the illusions of yourself, will you be able to see the path that your soul desires. In the process, you get to uncover your true reality - one that helps to make the world the place it should be. There is no external map – each person's path is different. Your only 'map' lies within, and your feelings will be your guide to 'reading' it - to help you find your way. Stay true to your deepest feelings – without becoming attached to them. And you'll stay true to your path. I know that feelings are of little significance in your physical world. It's your mental prowess that is highly rewarded. And that's important. But, if your life was to be lived through intellect alone, then all your questions would have been answered by now. And yet, those very answers remain elusive. After centuries on this earth, life still remains a mystery. And yet, the questions aren't un-solvable – the answers are available to anyone who opens themselves to being fully present with their truth. But, the answers aren't 'out there.' They lie within you."

"Your inner world – your consciousness - continues to expand. As does this Universe. Owning your truth every step of the way – no matter, where this quest may lead you - is your consciousness expanding. And your participation in that process is your contribution to the evolution of human consciousness, as a whole. Without your truth being realized, and the individual truths of all of humanity, the evolution of human consciousness will remain incomplete. Consciousness – the only true path for all of humanity – will stagnate. Realities will be limited to conditioning. There is some awareness of this in the physical world but, at this time the scale of that awareness is too small to bring about the changes that you all desire for this planet. The only thing standing in the way of that ultimate, true reality of oneness is the egos' view that human Beings are separate from each other. And that, is reinforced by the belief that the existing, limited reality of this physical world is the only reality on offer. That's an illusion. If you can each heal the wound of separation within you, you can uncover the true reality that lies within each soul. And collectively, you can change the state of this planet."

"Whatever you see around you, is a reflection of the extent of that illusion. If history is repeating itself, then human consciousness hasn't moved past the point that each of you has become trapped by it, within your physical bodies. And the state of that collective energy will continue to be reflected to the people in this world, until it's healed. As within, so without. Similarly, if there is repetition of certain experiences in your life, then you haven't evolved past that point in time when that energy became locked into your consciousness. The brain has always been regarded as the 'seat' of your consciousness but, it extends further than that. Your consciousness is housed in your cellular memory – it extends throughout your physical body. You now have an opportunity to heal those painful patterns, and heal the core wound that caused the separation within you. You can still achieve many goals in your physical life but, let them be in harmony with the true desires of your soul. Without this, you'll always be fighting a war with your truth, and losing. You can afford to lose all the battles that you've fought so far but, you can't afford to lose this war with your truth. There will be no recovery from it – you'll be forever lost in the illusion of a false reality. There is no war fiercer than this one. And no other, will demand more of you. This quest to uncover your truth is your soul's highest gift. And you can pass it forward to all of humanity when you've completed it. However, don't expect loud fanfare or any accolades. There is no worldly reward for a soul walking its true path, towards greater consciousness. The reward is the path itself."

"Use your intellect in your physical world – whenever you need to. But, also stay open to the unknown. Your mental abilities extend only as far, as your ego will allow. Both have helped you to identify opportunities in your world or what you perceived as such. But, they have also defined your limits. By mastering your ego, you can harness your mind to serve your soul's highest vision for your life. It's the only real, opportunity worth pursuing. All other opportunities are illusions. But, deny or fight your inner voice, and you'll subdue the one thing that makes you human – your feelings. Thereby denying your own evolution, and that of all of humanity. If you refuse to heed the lessons that your soul strives to teach you, your body will let you know in no uncertain terms, until you heed the silent call of your soul. Your inner voice will be heard – at any cost to your physical existence. The extent of your physical discomfort, the illness of body, mind or both; any ongoing pain, and suffering in your physical life, is only an indication of the extent to which you're denying your inner voice. Listen to it. You owe your soul that much."

She was totally, blown away. *Who was Glow to be speaking of things that she'd never even heard or thought about before? She needed to listen to her inner voice? What was she supposed to be listening for? What did her inner voice even sound like? How did she distinguish it from her other thoughts? How would she know if it was accurate? How could she trust it? Where did she even begin? Surely, her existing knowledge was more accurate. What did this inner voice know that was superior to her mind, anyway?* She was still caught in this tantalizing new tangent of thought, when Glow's next question took her completely, off guard.

"What made you so angry?" Glow asked.

Undefined

"I don't know!" she snapped, slowly realizing that her pre-occupation with her reveries had left her exposed. But, it was too late to shut herself off from what was threatening to break her wide open.

"Who made you angry? Glow persisted.

"Everyone! I told you!" she retorted.

"Then you must have a very short fuse, Little One!" Glow sniggered, breaking up into small light bulbs, and shooting off in multiple directions.

"I don't! And stop calling me 'Little One!'" she shouted.

"Why does that make you so angry?" Glow continued, in a gentle tone. Refusing to be intimidated by her outburst.

"I'm not…..ANGRY!" she shouted.

"You certainly look angry. And you sound angry" Glow said.

"Stop saying that! I'M NOT ANGRY!" she shouted hysterically.

By now, she was beyond livid. And drained by all the emotional mayhem. She wanted out. She wanted to go back. *But, back to what? More of the same? More stagnation? As far as she could tell from her current experience, everything was a total disaster back there. Wherever "back there" was!* And this? She looked around at the nothingness, for the hundredth time. She still couldn't see anything, familiar. Just black space – all around her. *What was this place? Where was she? Where was she going with all these questions?* She'd never felt so lost in her entire life!! She couldn't even think of a way back to her previous life – it was forever lost in some invisible mist. *There was no way out of this! She didn't even know where she was.* She could feel her anxiety, and anger building. To her horror, she burst into tears. She brushed the tears aside quickly. *That was the last thing she wanted to do! What good would it do?* But, the tears continued to roll down her cheeks.

"I'm sorry, Little One. But, it was necessary to get behind that façade you've had up for so long." Glow spoke kindly. "Now perhaps you can tell me why you're so angry that you're crying."

She stuttered through the tears….

"I feel lost…..and …..and….stuck! I can't move. I can't do, anything……can't think. It makes me scared….have to think. If I stop….can't get away…..will get….. get caught. I…..I….feel….feel trapped." She was now crying, hysterically. Slowly she managed to gain some composure. She straightened up, and looked at Glow. "But,

I'm not supposed to feel like that now. I'm an adult. I'm not supposed to break down! I'm strong. I've always been strong. I have to be. I'm not ….small…..and…..and ….weak. That's not me!"

And even as she spoke, the word "rejection" floated across her mind's eye. As her head took over to grasp that startling revelation, even her tears hesitated, and stopped. So that was the part of her that she'd been suppressing! She considered herself to be strong - not some sniffling, lost, little weakling! But, she did feel little, and lost…and weak. The mere acknowledgement of her feelings made her recoil violently. *She was none that! She was strong!* She shook her head, and centered herself in her stillness. Finally, she understood the tug-of-war raging within her each time that she'd donned the mask of being the "strong" person she insisted on emulating. That image of herself changed nothing; it covered up nothing, because a part of her still felt weak, and abandoned. She'd failed to accept her Self by suppressing her innermost feelings! She'd been abandoning herself! She'd also used her anger as a prop to reinforce her facade. Each time anyone triggered that raw spot, she'd unleashed it. And that also explained why she'd kept anyone she considered weak, at a distance – she didn't want to be reminded of what she was refusing to acknowledge about herself! Her refusal to give-in or even admit that she'd had enough of any situation was her ego's defense mechanism to cover up her weaknesses. She saw all too clearly that taking on more than she could handle to please others, and then exploding with resentment in her private moments from the sheer load wasn't the answer, either. Invariably, the person who ended up with the raw end of the deal was herself! It hit her for the first time, just how easily she'd fallen prey to her old patterns, and the ongoing manipulation by her ego. How could she have been so naïve? So unaware of her own behavior? There must have been multiple occasions when she'd given no conscious thought to what she was doing, and her ego must have had carte blanche dictating its own agenda! She sighed, morosely. She'd fallen into the trap of living up to expectations associated with a false image of herself. She'd been trying to prove that she was somebody, other than herself! She'd let herself down so badly. She recalled Glow's words: "Her true Self will have its say." And what a revelation that was! She crumbled under the weight of it. She tried to lift herself up again but, she couldn't find the strength. She sunk even further beneath hunched shoulders, and buried her face in her hands. She was glad that there was no one around. She doubted if she could have faced them. She couldn't even face herself.

"You've done well, Little One. I'm sorry that was so hard on you. But, it was necessary for you to acknowledge a part of you that you've been refusing to acknowledge for so long. You can't fully own who you truly are, if you suppress voicing those parts of you that you don't like or consider weak. You can't refuse to accept yourself. You're not invisible to your Self. Rest now. We'll continue when you wake up" Glow said, gently.

As Glow spoke, she felt herself engulfed in a soft, warm cloud. She tried to fight it - too afraid to close her eyes. *What if she went to sleep, and never woke up!?* But, she was too overcome by exhaustion to dwell on that thought. As her eyelids drooped, she realized that Glow had once again, disappeared from sight. But, she felt too weak to do anything. She couldn't feel her body. She felt as though she was slowly dissolving into the night sky - floating off into the stars. *What were the stars doing there!?* Just before she slipped into a blissful sleep, she became aware of something so immense; so magical. A sense of endless, intangible oneness. It was indescribably, beautiful. She wanted to reach out, and touch it but, it continued to billow out in waves all around her; gently carrying her with it. She felt a strange sensation of something releasing its hold on her – something, that had been there for a long time. And at the same time, there was a blossoming of a vast, silent, emptiness all around her.... or was it inside of her? She couldn't tell the difference. She felt herself slowly, surrender to the great expanse of oneness between herself, and everything around her – that was only nothingness. She didn't realize it then but, she'd just experienced her first glimpse of eternity.

CHAPTER 5

THE RABBIT HOLE – THE ONLY WAY OUT IS THROUGH

She slept for a long time. Occasionally, she felt a star-burst of energy in her chest; followed by electrical pulses that radiated slowly, throughout her body. Despite everything going on, she felt peaceful. That was so starkly different from the way she usually felt that she couldn't help but, be aware of it. There was something else. *What was that strange feeling? She wasn't doing a thing!* It slowly came to her. She didn't want to do anything! She was happy to remain in the stillness, and watch the riotous emotions within her. Despite that, nothing about her past felt relevant anymore. She realized that she was no longer sleeping. Her eyes were wide open; staring into the nothingness. But, her focus was inward - on her stillness. And how different her past looked in the nothingness. She could now recall various life events in more depth – if only those that she'd already shared with Glow. *Was there something significant about those experiences? Did they hold the key to making headway on her quest?* They now looked nothing more than colored dots, scattered across the nothingness. She was convinced that she had to connect them to see some kind of image but, she didn't know where to begin. Neither could she envision what kind of image she wanted. Her mind didn't seem interested in building scenarios anymore. And she'd lost all sense of time. Even that didn't bother her. Why did she feel as though time had lost its hold on her? Did time exist in the nothingness? Did it even matter? All she was aware of was the extreme dichotomy between meaning and emotion as she contemplated her past, and a lost future. She felt as though she was suspended over a chasm looking forlornly, from one to the other. For some reason, she felt that the only important thing in that moment was to remain present with herself. *She dare not reach for either her past or future to gain some kind of foothold to appease her mind — she would lose her balance, and go hurtling into the unknown depths below!*

She was also aware that her ability to focus on the present moment had magnified in the nothingness. She was becoming more engrossed with its spaciousness. *Did the spaciousness within a single moment ever end? Where were its boundaries?* She was used to burying herself in whatever she was doing. But, it was becoming more evident that she'd never been fully present. Besides everything going on in her head, she was constantly distracted by her hyper-alertness of the outside world. She couldn't help feeling grateful for the level of detachment that she'd attained in the nothingness. She couldn't imagine anything worse than being caught again, in the entangled mass of thought, and emotion of her past experiences. Now she could freely sift through each one, and witness aspects of her Self that she didn't know existed. And some that she thought she'd lost along the way. By holding them in that silent, stillness within, she was making them conscious. She didn't understand what she was doing. She was just going on how she felt - lighter with each attempt. Was she somehow integrating those long, forgotten parts of herself? Was that what Glow meant when it spoke of "the light of her consciousness?" Was she becoming whole again? She was still battling her confusion but, she was also very curious. How could she do something that she had no knowledge or understanding of? What was the basis for her actions in the nothingness? She still didn't know where she was or what her quest in the nothingness was about. But, she was unable to shake a deep, inner knowing that this time with herself was somehow critical. It could just be the most significant time of her life! She couldn't deny her frustration at not being able to place a finger on what was happening to her! But, she no longer felt the usual inclination to decide an outcome by resorting to snap judgements. It was an ability that she'd associated with her intuition. She realized that in her haste to get things done in the past, she'd missed an important distinction. Her behavior wasn't prompted only by a need to find the best solution to a challenge. More often than not, it stemmed from the overriding inclination to be the first one to do so. And her compulsive need to be right. She realized that she might have gotten her way but, she didn't solve anything. Not anything that counted, anyway.

Did her old behavior blind her to other avenues of thought? Did that blinkered approach block her from embracing more worthwhile opportunities? Opportunities that supported her overall wellbeing as opposed to just satisfying her ego? She sighed. *All this information was overwhelming!* She was still grappling with the rapid disintegration of her physical life. *She'd dedicated so much effort to planning, and building it! And it was all gone! She couldn't deal with this, anymore! She was done!* And yet, something within her refused to give in. She realized that her old perspective, and those intellectual distinctions now looked superfluous in the nothingness. Without her mind to reinforce her past actions she was thrown into the throes of a huge sense of loss. It clutched at her heart, and sent her reeling. *Was there anything in her past that she could hang onto? Her whole life was dissolving right before her eyes! Everything, and everyone was gone! Her job; status. Her marriage. Her home. Her possessions. How could she sit there, and be so calm? Why wasn't she fighting for the life that was hers - like she'd always done? Why wasn't she trying to hold onto whatever she could, and rebuild her life? She remembered that much about herself - she was a fighter! She'd always been one. Not this passive nobody that stood watching her entire life fall apart! And now, her identity was being stripped from her! Why was she so still? So calm? Why wasn't she doing something to get out of this mayhem!?*

All that greeted her was the silence - within, and around her. And a sense of joy that was totally out of place with her circumstances. *How could she feel happy at a time like this!? She must be in shock!* She realized that her mind had once again, taken over. If she wanted to be the observer, then she needed to remain centered in her stillness. She was fascinated by the paradox. And her expanded capacity to experience so much, at the same time. *That's not the way she remembered herself!* And yet, she couldn't help being in awe with her increasing level of awareness. It didn't matter what was going on in her mind - it was doggedly chipping away her skepticism. And it all felt as though it was happening in some place - out of time! Did she fall into a moment of time – where there was no time!? So much of what she'd experienced before was swirling around her in a kind of fragmented, cinemascope. *And she was just sitting there watching it!* But, it did make her see that she ignored anything that didn't fit her intended course of action. And the moment that something was completed, she relegated it to the "Done and Dusted" shelf that held the most prominent space in her mind. Now she felt the strange inclination to exercise more patience with herself as her past unfolded. She felt as though she was hanging onto the very edge of the known, and unknown - at the same time! She'd never felt so alive.

"Helloooooo there……. Little One. I missed you. So glad you're back. Did you have a good rest?" Glow was gushing with shiny, sparkles that were flying everywhere.

She wished Glow would go away. She no longer felt like playing games with …..with…..this thing! Was she starting to enjoy this time with herself?

"As I said Little One, you can stop this quest at any time. It's your choice" said Glow.

There! Glow had read her thoughts again!

"How do you know what I'm thinking? Those are my private thoughts!" she said, indignantly.

"Nothing is private here" said Glow. "You see all of me; I see all of you. I feel all of you, and you feel all of me. We're one, and the same - we can't hide from each other. Besides, there is nowhere to hide – anywhere in the Universe."

She scoffed. *What nonsense!* Despite her knee-jerk reaction, she realized that she was still battling to understand Glow's words. *This quest wasn't as simple as she thought.* The words sounded familiar but, when strung together their meaning was far from obvious. And she didn't like that. She liked getting straight to the point. Being concise; it made things so much easier. And that gave her the ability to follow through with swift action. But, as annoyed as she was with this new, open-ended perspective she couldn't help feeling curious. Why was her thinking so linear? And her behavior so polarized? Why was everything in her life far from simple? If she was that capable, then how did she end up being stuck in the nothingness? She sighed in exasperation. *Her curiosity had always gotten the better of her! She was getting, nowhere! What was going on with her mind? Why was she thinking such bizarre thoughts!? Where were these revelations, and insights coming from?* She'd hoped that by now, she would have the answers she was desperately searching for.

"Can you tell me where I am? Why am I here?" she asked in a cajoling tone.

"You know the answer to that, Little One. This is your quest." Glow responded kindly.

"Don't try fobbing me off with that psycho-babble! I'm not stupid! What am I doing here!?" she demanded. She was determined to get to the bottom of this madness.

"Calm down, Little One. There is no 'bottom' in this space. At least, not the kind that you're familiar with. Just accept that you're safe. It won't help fighting what you're going through or getting agitated over it. You'll cover more ground by remaining centered in your stillness. Before entering your quest, you hit another dead-end in your life. You tried various ways to make a break through – to take it forward again. But, you only ran into more "walls." Eventually, you caved. And a whole, new avenue opened up for you. And….lo, and behold…. here you are!" Glow ended with another swirling, flourish; sprinkling sparkles, everywhere.

That did nothing to ease her frustration. *She? "Cave!?" Never! What new "avenue?" Glow knew something. She was certain of it! She didn't like all this cryptic nonsense! Not when her life was falling apart!* She would get to the truth - whatever it was!

"What 'avenue' are you talking about?" she demanded.

"That tone won't work with me" said Glow with a shiny, wagging finger. "Try something gentler. You'll find it somewhere within you. I know you – far too well." And she could have sworn that Glow winked at her!

Damn! She so hoped that she could intimidate it into revealing something. She forgot that Glow could read her thoughts. She was the one feeling intimidated now. And very exposed.

She was struck by an odd realization. Being intimidated didn't feel very good! She recalled using that approach quite a few times, to get her way. Was that how other people felt when she behaved like that? She was horrified. Why did she resort to such unkind, insensitive behavior? Immediately, some part of her decided that she would stop behaving that way. There was something disconcerting about using peoples' fears, and weaknesses against them. And it didn't matter how good her intentions were, or how justified the outcome. Why was she so unaware of her behavior before? More importantly, why did that kind of behavior come so naturally to her? Without any conscious motivation, it struck her that the same principle applied if her reactions were fueled by anger, hatred or any other kind of negative emotion, for that matter. Furthermore, if her intentions didn't serve the highest interest of both parties, then her goal wasn't worth pursuing – whatever it was! Any form of "success" based on someone else's pain or loss was no success at all! Real success could only be achieved by holding herself, and others in a space of compassionate, inclusiveness. She might be her own person but, she wasn't separate from those around her. She was alarmed. *Where did those thoughts come from?*

"Very insightful, Little One" said Glow, encouragingly. "You can only meet others as far as you've met yourself - in the relationship that you have with yourself. That will determine how you treat others – you can only treat them in the same way that you treat yourself. When you're able to accept your weaknesses, and acknowledge all of yourself with compassion, then you'll be able to acknowledge, and accept others for all that they are. You'll discover that everyone is not so different after all. Everyone is carrying their fair share of burdens in life, irrespective of what labels they're given in this physical world – from the richest to poorest; youngest to oldest; normal to abnormal; able to disabled. No one person is better off than the next. It only appears that way to your ego because it is focused on the physical. Beyond the labels are souls of unlimited potential to reach unimaginable heights of Being. It's only when you feel broken and separated from yourself that you'll feel separated from everyone. Because you're separated from your true essence, and your unlimited potential. And the chaos that feeling generates within you, is the chaos you'll project onto your external world" said Glow. All the while swirling and twirling, until it became one big tornado and then, exploded into an avalanche of tiny sparkles. Why did she feel that explosion?

"But, coming back to your question. The trauma caused by the events in your life made you turn away from everything that you were familiar with; life as you knew it. And something made you turn inward towards your silent, stillness. You might not have been aware of your actions at the time but, it served was the catalyst for your quest."

Still? Silent? She? She'd never been still or silent in her entire life! Turn inward? What nonsense! There was no such thing! Why would she turn away from a life that she was intent on making a success? She wouldn't do that to herself! She might have messed up a few times but, she wouldn't deliberately destroy her life! And she had no intention of wasting whatever remained of it on some truth quest! Everything was relative! Her "truth" was taking from the world what applied to her, and using it to make something of herself. As far as she could tell, she didn't do things in half measure. She must have been "living the dream." Why would she turn away from all that? None of this made any sense! She had a career, and a family to see to. She didn't have time for this nonsense! This quest must be some kind of glitch! Everything would return to normal – soon. She still had her whole life ahead of her. And if she ever got back to it, she would make certain to live every second of it - be kinder; more compassionate towards herself, and others. What on earth did she need stillness and silence for? She wanted her life back! In the midst of her rambling, it struck her that there was so much about herself that she didn't understand. Why did she approach life the way that she did? Why did she view her world in a certain way? Was it her conditioning? She recalled that she'd often sought answers but, none of them had alleviated her constant restlessness. Her insecurities and anxiety had accumulated over time, until it became easy to submit to a statement that had the power to frustrate, and dumb her out at the same time. "This is the way things have always been done.' No further explanations were deemed necessary. As a result, all worthwhile forms of innovation were excluded by the invisible wall erected by those words. Was that acceptable on a planet constantly caught in the throes of survival? She shook her head to stop those peculiar thoughts. But, she'd still succeeded in building a life within those invisible "walls." It was hard at times…..

"Just hard?" asked Glow

…..Ok. It was downright, infuriating! She didn't understand why everything had to follow the same old, patterns – with the world being in the state that it was! She'd tried complying with various systems, and processes in her life but, sooner or later she'd given up in sheer frustration. Being held to ransom by that kind of thwarted thinking was soul-destroying! Nonetheless, she'd continued giving the established authorities the benefit of the doubt. *They must know what they were doing – they were at it for much longer than she was!* She realized that over the years that belief had become cemented in her thinking. And without knowing any better, it had become the foundation of her past reality. But, her self-compromising approach boomeranged with disastrous consequences for her life. Despite her best efforts, the next "mountain" was always harder, and higher than the previous one. And she just never got to the top of it! One thing, however, remained consistent throughout - nothing that she did, felt right. Still she persisted with the "known." Hard work had never phased her, and more often than not, it was sheer grit that made her reach the end of the goal-line. That trait of hers was never in short supply – she was grateful for that. For she was determined to get the life that she wanted. Her philosophy on living a successful life was simple. Things either happened the way she wanted, or she made them happen in that way. The same principle applied to time – everything had to happen in the allotted time. It not, then she changed her goal, and pursued something else to bring her the success she wanted. She wanted what she wanted, and was prepared to drive herself beyond her physical, and mental limits to achieve it. There were no surprises in her life. *She hated surprises!*

Her time and energy were devoted to study, and striving for the higher echelons in her career. There were many constraints – money, race, culture. Sex, and gender. Politics. But, as limiting as those restrictions were, she remained resolute about taking her place in the "race" to get ahead in life. *And she still had every intention of winning it!* She thought little of the many sacrifices she was called upon to make that affected both family, and herself. They were necessary – they prepared her to win any battle. And each one was a stepping stone that made her more capable to take on the next. She'd seldom entertained thoughts on why things couldn't be done. Instead, her focus was on accomplishing them. She worked herself into a standstill each day, and then crashed for three or four hours of sleep. The words "stop" or "slowdown" didn't feature in her vocabulary. Neither did "no" or "can't." She could do anything that she set her mind to. That was her "edge." She didn't even "blink" at the constant highs, and lows - it was all necessary in the name of her "plan." It struck her that at some point, attaining her goals had ceased to be the primary motivator. Instead, she'd pursued anything, and everything just to feel the surge of adrenaline in her veins! She had a frightening revelation. That's what had made her feel alive!

She'd heard of meditation, and other relaxation techniques but, there was no time for any of that. In her defense, there was too much to do. She was acquainted with spirituality but, she didn't bother delving into it. She assumed that it was the same as religion. And there was no time for that, either. As a child, she'd experienced her fair share of religious practices, and she decided that she would get back to adhering to it, at some point later in life. First, she had to make something of herself. Until she achieved that, she had to stay in the "game" to give herself a fighting chance against the competition - rat race or not! And if she wanted to win, then she had to work harder than everyone else. And by obeying that unwritten decree, she felt as though she'd somehow secured her place in the human, rat race. Success had nothing to do with passion or happiness; it was about the speed of getting things done. And that required her to constantly pit her skills, and wits against her competitors. In her "book" that was the purpose of life – getting ahead of the pack, and staying there. It was the only way, to get the life that she wanted. That was her spiritual practice. She'd never bothered with meaning. As those thoughts flashed across her mind, she felt herself being catapulted onto a familiar platform – the one on which she'd played out her adrenaline-packed, drama-filled life.

"Did you achieve your success?" Glow interrupted.
"I probably would have, if I wasn't here - in the middle of nowhere!" she snapped.
"Tsk, tsk, tsk……temper…..temper…..temper. Not good for you, Little One" said Glow.

Despite her annoyance, she felt comforted by the familiarity between them. She realized that she was now able to "read" Glow's faceless expressions. That was more than she could say about her interactions with most people. And no matter how much time she spent with others, she'd never felt this level of comfort. Conversations were always difficult; people said one thing, and usually, meant something different. Suddenly, she understood why she'd left so many engagements feeling deflated. Glow was speaking candidly – something, that she wasn't very used to. But, what did that say about her? Was she honest with herself? And she couldn't detect any kind of judgment – something else that she was very sensitive to, since she'd felt judged her entire life! She realized this was the first time that she was having such an honest conversation. And it was being held with something that she'd never met before or able to identify! And yet, her time with Glow felt natural; right, somehow. Furthermore, she felt at ease expressing herself just the way she felt. There was no fear of saying the wrong thing. If there was a sense of the dramatic, it wasn't anything contrived - it stemmed from the nature of the quest itself. She realized in that moment, just how many of her past interactions were shrouded in defensiveness, through fear of judgement. *Was fear the underlying cause of her other psychological hang-ups?* She hit a blank. She wondered whether she would have noticed the sharp contrast between different aspects of her persona, if she'd been occupied with the usual spate of activities in her physical world. Somehow, she doubted it. But, as enlightening as her quest was, she was more disturbed by the revelations coming to her out of nowhere. *As opposed to giving her more clarity, they kept her in a constant state of angst! Was anything about her past real?* Was there anything real about herself? The longer she spent in the nothingness, the more she realized that she wasn't the person that she thought herself to be! And there she was talking to a glowing mirage that was more real than anything that she'd met before! *Maybe Glow was nothing more than a figment of her imagination. She must be still dreaming!*

"No, Little One. You might have been dreaming before but, this is no dream. Now about that success you wanted to achieve. From where I'm sitting, it looks like you were trying to run away from something."

Run away!? Her intention was to live her life fully - not run from it! She shook her head in disgust. But, there was one glaring question that rose above everything else floating around in her head. If her intentions were true, then why did she not manifest the life that she wanted!? Why did her much, sought-after success never materialize? More importantly, why did she never feel successful? She felt like such a failure! She'd changed jobs repeatedly, always hunting for the one career-move that would bring her success, and happiness. Instead, each position was as stifling, and unfulfilling as the next. She'd followed that "pot of gold" to different cities. Only to hit one dead-end, after another! *And now, everything that she'd set out to achieve had fallen apart!* She smirked at the irony. *So much for hard work, and good intentions!* She prided herself on making her own choices. In her mind, "choice" and "success" were synonymous with freedom, and living the independent life that she wanted. She guarded that right with jealous zeal and yet, she'd always felt completely, removed from the life she was living. She'd always felt as though something was missing. She felt its absence constantly, and only became more disillusioned when all her efforts to locate it in her world resulted in one failure, after another. That led to the cop-out decision to just get on with whatever she could, until she figured her life out. But, she'd never figured anything out! Each day found her on the same treadmill getting more impatient, and anxious about missing out on some opportunity or other. The nagging doubt of whether or not she would find what she was looking for, left her feeling constantly insecure, and inadequate. Work was the perfect antidote. As unfulfilling as it was it was easier to deal with, compared to the constant anxiety of not finding what she was looking for. Another realization, slowly dawned on her. By constantly choosing to do something – anything to fill that nagging desperation within her – she'd been grasping at straws! She shook her head sadly. *So much wasted time. And she wasn't any closer to figuring herself out! What was she looking for?*

She buried her head in her hands, and sighed heavily. There were no answers to be found in the nothingness. She could only detect her emotions. She felt as though the life that she'd built – based on the known, and familiar - was in a stand-off with everything unknown about her Self. In the nothingness, however, she could stand back and scrutinize that life, and the person responsible for it. *Perhaps she would be able to see what was missing.* After all, parts of her stripped identity were now laid out in the nothingness like an array of dominoes. She found herself thinking that at any moment, the one domino that she was searching for would miraculously appear, and help her solve the mystery of her quest. But, there was little hope of that. Something told her that "piece" would topple the very identity that she was so attached to. She drew in a sharp breath. She didn't know what she was more afraid of - that a part of her already knew her false identity was going to topple or that she would be the one responsible for bringing it down. She gnawed at her lower lip. Why was she so conflicted? Was she trying to hold aspects of herself together that didn't belong to her true Self? She felt her discomfort escalate. Was she living a lie? Was that why she felt like such a fraud? What was lying beneath the carefully, curated identity that she'd built for herself?

"A good question" Glow quipped.

She glared at Glow. But, it wasn't looking at her. Glow was busy lifting layers of itself, differentiated by various colors of its halo, and peering under them – as though looking for something. She shook her head, and stifled a giggle. This was one time she would have to ignore the distraction – as pleasant as it was. She didn't understand what was happening to her mind but, she was beginning to "get it." She'd always kept very much to herself but, that was a coping mechanism to save time, and energy. Was there another reason for her aloofness? Was she hiding from something or someone? Occasionally, she'd manipulated situations to work in her favor but, that behavior was justified on the grounds of survival. She was more than familiar with her rebellious streak, and she was no angel. Especially, if anyone or anything stood between her, and what she wanted. More so, if any kind of injustice was the basis of an obstacle. It dawned on her that there was a place for that attitude in her career, and when fighting injustice but, using it as a "quick fix" in her life had led her down the proverbial garden-path! That much was evident in this space! Was that the reason her efforts were continuously thwarted - she'd taken shortcuts by suppressing her truth? She'd never thought her truth was important to success or progress. Only to find herself stuck on a merry-go-round of repeating experiences! Sometimes her decisions were deliberate but, more often than not, she realized that she'd unconsciously opted for a particular course of action. She now found that kind of behavior extremely disturbing. Why would she choose to go through life as an automaton? Why did she compromise her awareness in the name of progress? Was she avoiding things about herself, and lying to herself in the process? She hit another blank. Before she could dwell on it she was hit by another revelation. She'd continuously tested her boundaries both mentally, and physically. And although she enjoyed challenging herself, she got bored very easily. At some point, she stopped reaching for the next "challenge" if it meant getting caught in yet, another hype. Was that the "dead-end" that Glow had referred to? Why would she stop, and change her behavior without knowing what she was doing? Did this unknown Self know something that her mind didn't? Was it trying to steer her in some other direction? *But, there were only a limited number of possibilities that were open to her in this physical world! She had to stay on top of things – she couldn't miss out on her one, big opportunity!* Something within, however, refuted those sentiments.

She looked out into the nothingness. Why were there so many boundaries in the physical dimension when the nothingness was making her question their very existence? There would probably always be some boundary or other that she would have to contend with but, in the nothingness she realized something startling. Those physical boundaries didn't only define what she was allowed to do. They went a lot deeper, and limited her perspective on what she regarded as an "opportunity." That contrasted sharply with the absence of any such limitations in the nothingness around her. She didn't feel the need to contain her thinking or test herself, in any way – everything was possible. She didn't sense anything holding her back. Why was her thinking so limited in her physical world? Why was she unable to exercise her awareness to this level before? What was blocking her? What else was hidden from her? If she was responsible for this quest, then she must be in the process of uncovering what was hidden from her. How was it possible to hide something from herself!? Did she develop her defense mechanisms to such an extent that she was able to hide aspects of herself beyond her conscious mind? Or was she becoming aware of what was buried in her subconscious mind? Why did she feel the need to protect herself all the time? She'd obviously not succeeded – pain was the norm in her life!

"Ahhhhh…….we're back at the pain-bit. Good" said Glow.

"I'm going around in circles!" she cried in exasperation.

"It might look like that but, you're making progress, Little One. Each time you uncover a layer of suppressed emotion, you're going a little bit deeper, and revealing more of your true Self" said Glow patiently

"So part of me was angry, because I was hurting? And in addition to hurting myself, I was hurting others? That's the reason for all the pain in my life? I was only getting back what I was putting out into the Universe?" she asked softly. She was having a tough time grasping how her feelings affected those around her, and vice versa – especially, when she'd made a point of keeping hers well hidden. Could anything be hidden from herself – from anyone in this Universe, or was she merely deluding herself? She buried her face in her hands. *All this emo-stuff was so confusing! The impact on her behavior – on her life – even more so!* "Yes, and no" said Glow.

Glow's simple answers jarred her senses but, they resonated deeply with her. She was so used to people speaking volumes, and not saying anything that she appreciated the sincerity - and substance - in those monosyllables. Glow's words had the strange effect of bringing things to the forefront of her mind. And that helped her focus on what was most important. Various incidents flashed through her mind helping her to witness her past actions and gain further insight into the impact of her behavior on others, and herself. Some were intentional, and others were triggered by encounters with "difficult" people. As hard as she tried to understand the nature of those triggers on her reactive behavior, she just couldn't seem to pinpoint the reason. In each instance, however, she'd lashed out in anger causing pain to others, and herself. What was at the root of all that anger? Were the triggers pointing to something within herself that she needed to heal? By doing that could she change her behavior – even towards those whom she didn't like? She knew she could find justifiable reasons for her past behavior but, her new-found awareness now made the desire to be right superfluous. Besides, if her world was a reflection of herself, then she must have been projecting her own anger onto those around her. With that insight came a great sense of shame. She couldn't bear to think of herself as the kind of person who had caused pain to others. And to herself – that pain had merely ricocheted back to her! People deserved better. She deserved better.

"What can I do to stop this vicious cycle?" she asked, her voice full of remorse. "What do I do to stop these triggers, and change my behavior?" *Why was she asking Glow? Was she beginning to trust this weird creature?*

"Yes, you're starting to trust, Little One. A little but, every step in the right direction is a huge leap forward for your consciousness. The bigger question, however, is why you don't trust yourself. Now that you're becoming aware of your triggers, you'll check yourself before responding. That will change your behavior, and how you experience your reality going forward. But, that doesn't take away the past pain that you're holding onto in your physical body. You need to heal it through conscious acknowledgment, and forgiveness" said Glow.

"How do I do that? I can't go back - it's been a long time. I've lost track of those people. She grimaced. She was so embarrassed that she couldn't bring herself to face anyone, let alone speak to them. She wouldn't know what to say. *This entire situation was ridiculous!* "I do trust myself" she grumbled, under her breath.

"You don't have to meet anyone in person, although that would be ideal if you could. Each of us has a higher Self that transcends our physical bodies. All you need to do is recall the incident and acknowledge the pain to them, and to yourself. By holding the deed in a space of love and light, sincerely apologize to them through your higher Self, and they will 'hear' you. All thought is energy. All of life is energy. Verbal communication is not always the most effective means of achieving mutual understanding and respect. People might be physically present but, if they're not mindful in the physical space that they share with others. As a result they talk past each other, and achieve little or no understanding" said Glow.

"What will happen if I meet one of them after this? She was totally baffled.

"They could react in any number of ways. Alternatively, they might have forgotten all about the incident. We're all growing, and constantly changing during our lifetimes. But, the reaction of others is not important. Your own sense of guilt has kept the incident very much alive within you. All that negativity causes blockages within you, and prevents you from emitting your own unique, energetic soul-frequency. And that prevents you from realizing your full potential" explained Glow.

Was that the reason for her heavy, lackluster life? She might not have intentionally set out to harm anyone but, neither could she claim to be oblivious of the fact that some of her actions did cause pain. *If making amends was the answer to lifting herself out of this dead-end situation, then that was what she needed to do. It was all quite simple. If only she'd known. She would have done all this healing stuff, long ago.*

"Don't see this as a means to an end or over-simplify it, Little One. Don't reduce an action or thought that has all the power of the Universe behind it to a level that can be processed by your mind. You're only allowing yourself to remain a prisoner of your ego. You can't resolve this with logic alone. And not, if your only intention is to benefit yourself. The healing can release you from the hold of past negativity but, in order to gain access your higher Self for that purpose your intentions need to be true, and just. They have to serve the highest human value – service to others. During this process, you'll be uncovering your truth. That in itself, is far from easy. You'll be required to be honest with yourself by facing all that is dark, and hidden within you. Although you're somewhat familiar with that darkness, and in no way deny it, you don't know the full extent of it. And whatever you do know exists on the more accessible, outer layers of your conscious mind. You'll first have to get through those layers before your transformation can reach your unconscious mind - to allow you to unearth the beliefs that have been impacting your behavior, all your life. Sadly you've come to identify with those beliefs to such an extent that you believe that is your truth. But, it's not. Some of it's based on what you've been made to believe by those closest to you. Much of it relates to energies that you've picked up over the course of your life. Including, your karma – in this life, and past lives. There's no way around this process. You have to go through it - to get to your soul's truth."

She was listening intently, very much aware of her mounting anxiety. *This was completely, unfamiliar territory!* She took a deep breath. *Could she do this? It was crazy! But, nothing stopped her from trying.* Glow smiled knowingly, and continued.

"When you first encounter the darkness within you, go easy on yourself. It will look ugly; sometimes, even horrible. But, don't judge or reject it – every aspect is part of you. Removing your perceptions of self will bring you closer to compassion – something you need, for full self-acceptance. Without compassion, and self-acceptance you won't be able to fully accept others into your life. And you need others to help you actualize your soul path. In the same way that they will need your help to actualize theirs. You'll also be able to ask others for forgiveness through your higher Self. Equally important, you'll be able to grant it to yourself. If you can, ask for forgiveness in person but, it's not necessary. Healing and forgiveness can be done in the light of your consciousness. And that can be in the form of mindful thought or deed. It's the truth behind your intentions that brings about the miracle of healing" said Glow.

And she believed that forgiveness was all about the spoken word! She sighed. *Was any of this true? How was she supposed to know?* As far as she was concerned, everything was external - nothing was an inside job. She had no understanding of the process involved to heal such pain. She knew nothing about the impact of energy. Let alone, the workings of magic. *And all this sounded magical!* She frowned. *Why should she be the one doing all this healing stuff, in the first place!? What about the pain that others had caused her?* She folded her arms defiantly. *She wasn't the only one at fault!*

"And that's exactly why you need to do this, Little One. The alternative is to remain forever locked in that vicious cycle of thought that only perpetuates negativity in your life, and limits you. Having incarnated into this physical dimension, you'll be exposed to many experiences at the hands of your fellow Beings; some will be easier to accept compared to others. In all instances, however, they mirror what you most need to learn about your Self. Your focus must not be distracted by anger caused by others; that is merely how you perceive it. They're showing you the anger that already exists inside of you. Far from being a curse, those experiences at the hands of your fellow Beings are a blessing – they've been designed by your soul to bring you closer to your Self. You can transcend the experiences that trigger those base, lower frequencies, and reveal more of your soul light – to live your true purpose. That's life's real gift to you. So far, you've been subjecting yourself to experiences in this physical realm that don't serve your soul purpose. That is evident from the ongoing battle in your mind between 'them' and 'me' - the person you thought yourself to be. It has been an all-consuming battle but, you now have to move past that delusion, and face your biggest war. The one with yourself; between your ego, and soul - between darkness, and light. Others might be equally to blame but, that isn't relevant to winning this war. It doesn't matter who said what or who did what. It doesn't even matter, who started it or who was right, or wrong. This is not about 'them.' It's about you – your truth. Everyone is on their own journey to learn what's important to them, and to fulfill their individual soul contracts.

Everyone will - eventually. In this lifetime or the next. There can be no energetic vacuum in the Universe, because of unresolved karma."
"What's important now, is for you to resume your quest to align with your soul purpose. And it starts with acknowledging, and healing the pain that you carry within you. Others might never know of the healing that you've done on a physical level but, on a spiritual level, they will. All are one in the higher, spiritual realms. Whatever transpired between you, and others – no matter how long ago - is far from over. It's holding you back from realizing your full potential. Your conscious surrender is all that's required to complete this quest– it's a silent invitation to forces beyond your control, and understanding. For as long as you're caught up in this vicious void of blame you'll remain 'in the dark,' caught in your pain. By completing your quest, you'll also break the behavioral patterns that you've built up around pain, and free yourself from the burdens that you've felt throughout your life. In some cases, those burdens have extended over many generations, and lifetimes. Many don't even belong to you. You'll never be able to grasp the full extent of this with your mind. And even though you'll be conscious of some of your healing, most of it will happen involuntarily. It's only by trusting your Self that you'll be able to access the higher realms to guide you through this healing process to uncover your truth. Only then, will you be able to live the life that your soul desires."

Glow spoke with a level of conviction, and sincerity that she found hard to ignore. There were times when she'd been spurred on by various impulses, the origin of which she didn't know or understand. Was that what Glow meant by patterns of behavior from past generations, and lifetimes? If she'd previously grappled over her failure to find the necessary information to help take her life forward, then she was now at a total loss with the extent of healing that she needed to perform to get her to that point. She sighed. *There was no way that she could ever access what had happened in previous generations or lifetimes! How was she ever going to get to live the life that her soul desired?* She was devastated. And more confused, than ever. Surprisingly something within her didn't agree with that conclusion. Something was different about her. There must have been some kind of shift within her. *Did her attitude change? Or her perspective on life?* But, she refrained from clutching onto some quick-fix, rationale. Something told her to remain in that space of not-knowing. Besides, the extent of information at her disposal was minimal. And her capacity to understand this mystical experience with her mind was far too limited. Furthermore, her formal education couldn't even begin to help her fathom her soul's purpose. But, one thing was becoming quite clear – the completion of her quest wasn't dependent on the qualifications that she'd obtained in her physical world. It didn't even matter, anymore. Her insecurities were being allayed by a heightened level of awareness that was now beginning to encompass the unknown. She was beginning to feel more comfortable with the uncertainty surrounding her quest. Something told her that was of paramount importance to completing her quest. She felt that conviction vibrate through her entire body.

With her acknowledgement came the realization that there were many aspects of her previous self that no longer resonated with her. She might have been unaware of or ignored them before but, her new level of awareness refused to let her "pull the covers" over them again. She was intrigued by the ease with which she'd been able to ignore certain aspects of her behavior in her physical world and yet, within the vast ambit of the nothingness, there was no escaping her Self! She'd always tried to simplify things so that she could understand them. However, understanding based on denial that only fosters greater waves of delusion – especially, regarding oneself - was anything but, simple! It had helped her to construct a complicated web of drama in her life – with her being the only one ending up trapped! She had no proof to substantiate Glow's words. But, "right" and "wrong" were no longer strong pillars to erect a new, true foundation for her life. Not in the relentless, nothingness. Some things, however, she felt more certain about. Like the mound of emotional baggage adding to the heaviness, and darkness within her. That she could feel. And not being able to relate to her past, any longer or see a future for herself. That was irrefutable. Furthermore, she didn't feel the need to prove Glow's words or her unfamiliar insights into her situation. She knew nothing about healing and energy but, she did know that she'd previously tried a number of avenues to change her life. None of them had worked. Trusting in the unknown to help her achieve her soul's purpose was as alien to her, as the nothingness that she now found herself in. Would it help her find her way to her truth? To the life that she was meant to live? Only the silence echoed in the nothingness surrounding her. The level of dissonance was far too great. She took refuge in her thoughts.

She was very anxious. Not only about her quest but, the more rampant problems facing the world – disease, drugs, violent crime. People trafficking. Abuse against women and children. Poverty. Terrorism. Wars, and the ongoing discord between nations. The list went on, and on. The scale of human trauma was unimaginable! And petrifying! It was easier to turn, and look the other way. On another level, however, she had difficulty bridging the huge gap between her "busy" life, and not having the time to do something about the continuous onslaught against humanity. And now there was a growing acceptance that the former was futile in the context of its repetitive patterns, and mundanity – whether in a single lifetime or over lifetimes. The state of the world was testimony of that! The latter was like a red, flashing light trying to flag her attention, to get her off the "motor track" that she'd convinced herself would take her places in the world. She'd placated herself with the knowledge that things were being addressed on multiple levels - by various authorities. But, she obviously didn't accept that, because she returned time-and-time-again, to the many dilemmas of a planet in crisis. She didn't understand the ongoing delays by "authorities" to resolve these matters especially, when millions of lives were at stake! And when the very existence of the planet was hanging in the balance! Again she felt her rage but, before it could distract her, she re-directed her attention to her present space. Did she subject herself to a mediocre existence, as a means of denying what was going on in the world around her? Was the state of the world really beyond her control? If so, then who had the power to change it? Who was responsible for the lives of millions of species – including, humans? That responsibility went way beyond physical borders, and political agendas – it centered on upholding the dignity of all life forms. And supporting the planet in its efforts to nurture itself back to its original state – as best it can! By taking some drastic, sustained action against the policies, and practices that continue to destroy it. Why was the power to protect life being abused on so many fronts? Why was this responsibility being diluted by ongoing debate based on transient human preferences? There was only one essential factor that warranted any consideration – the respect for life! All these problems might be insurmountable for any single nation but, not if eight billion people spoke with one voice. It was the only "vote" that truly mattered! Her old life might have afforded some level of distraction from the daunting powerlessness that swept over her but, there was no such luxury in the nothingness. There she was once again, contemplating what she'd put on hold for so long. She hoped for some insights in the nothingness but, there were none. She looked at Glow for guidance. But, Glow was falling over itself in a cascade of stars that slowly faded as they fell.

She appreciated Glow's show of compassion but, it didn't stop her from feeling utterly hopeless, and powerless. She sighed. *This was a nightmare! Fixing the world; fixing herself!* All she wanted – all she'd ever wanted was to get on with……go to…..to…..get to the core of……of….what!? What was she searching for!? And what did that have to do with the state of the world? And Glow wasn't helping. It was quite content to let her muddle through her rampaging confusion. She was struck by a startling revelation. As much as she didn't understand the workings of world she lived in, she understood herself even less! Over the years, she'd completely lost track of what her life was about - of what she was about! And if she'd willfully pursued some direction before, she now had no clue what to do. Let alone, being capable of coming up with a plan to save the world! *And her quest was doing nothing to make her feel better about any of it! In fact, she felt a lot worse since it started! Totally tangled in all the information hitting her from every angle!* She was livid. *This quest had rudely extracted her from a way of life that made sense to her – one that was in her control! Only to find that she was now more disoriented than ever - about her past and future!* She didn't know what to do! Or who to turn to, to obtain the clarity that she so desperately needed. And it was beyond annoying to contemplate some kind of new "future" when her past was still gnawing at her insides! Surely, her past life experiences were the stepping stones to her "future" reality? Surely, she had to finish what she'd already started - irrespective, of how right or wrong it was, before she could head off in some new direction. She couldn't just leave a life that she was busy with, and chase after some harebrained scheme called a "soul path" when she didn't have a clue what she was doing! She couldn't just give up, and abandon the road that she'd been on, for so long! She realized that her situation was worse than that. She'd not only changed direction on this quest. She was on a completely, different route! Following some unknown soul "map!"

She was grappling with her quandary. She had a strong sense that where she now found herself was perfect for her - in some way or other. More so, than any other previous goal or destination that she'd set her sights on. She sighed. *If she didn't intend for this quest to happen, then how did she end up on it? The person she remembered herself to be, wouldn't have chosen nothingness over her tangible, physical world! And there was no way that she could have planned this quest in nothingness! She had no knowledge of what she was doing or where she was going!* At least, her mind didn't! Was there some other part of her that knew something about her quest? Perhaps there was more to it than met the eye. Perhaps there was more to her Self than her mind could grasp. Then again, she could be totally wrong! There was no way of knowing! All she knew was that she was dealing with the unknown. But, unknown or not, she felt as though she'd been moving towards this point all her life. Something kept "telling" her that she could no longer rely solely on her mind – it could only regurgitate old patterns of thinking. And her ego only concerned itself with her physical safety. What she was unaware of was that her new Self was serving as an invisible warrior. It was protecting her burgeoning awareness – something that she was only just becoming acquainted with. And right now, it was "telling" her that she had to reach for some other part of her to show her the way on this quest. As she contemplated what that could be she once again, felt a tingling in her chest - as if something had heard her thoughts, and was scrambling to get her attention. She recalled feeling it earlier but, it was so gentle, and unobtrusive that she'd forgotten all about it. The tingling was emanating from her chest in waves. *What was that feeling?* Was it coming from her heart? It must be! *What was it trying to tell her?* She shook her head. *But, how could her heart help her? It couldn't speak! Besides, what did her heart know that her mind didn't already know?* But, the tingling became so intense that she was forced to shift her attention from her mind to her heart space. And then, it hit her. She smiled at the sheer irony. The only part of her that could guide her on this quest was also unknown – her heart! She'd never even acknowledged its existence! She froze with this new insight. *Could she relegate her mind to the back-seat and trust her silent, vulnerable heart to show her the way on what was probably, the most significant journey of her life!?*

She sat for a long time, contemplating her thoughts in the nothingness.

What was happening to her? Why? What could she possibly achieve by embarking on this quest? There was still no one in sight. And even if there was, what would she say? She couldn't even grasp any of it herself! They would think she was nuts! And yet, she couldn't deny her inner conviction that she wasn't imagining things. As frustrated as she was by the many cross-roads that she'd encountered previously in her life, she remembered one thing – she'd always managed to find a way out of any corner. She smiled wryly as she realized that she couldn't have navigated them very well, if her old tactics had led her to nothingness! And so far, she'd failed to find a way out of it! Or around it! She sighed. Was she drawing hasty conclusions about her past life? Was she judging herself too harshly? Perhaps those experiences had served some purpose, and she needed to give herself a little more some credit. She must have learnt something. Discernment, maybe? Perhaps that learning served as a reference point of some sort - for this quest. She realized it was her discernment that was now making her distinctly aware that she wasn't at just another cross-road in her life. This was a turning point. A major one. And it wasn't a random opportunity to choose between visible paths to attain some known, objective. She had only one choice – to leave her past behind, and enter the unknown. And there was no way, other than going through with the process step-by-step – guided by the knowing in her unknown soul. She could either do this with all her heart or go back to her old way of life. There were no half measures on this quest to uncover her truth. Where she now found herself – in that single moment of knowing – was the end of life as she'd known it. And the beginning of something that she knew nothing about. Before and beyond that moment, nothing else existed.

Was that what Glow had referred to when it said she could stop her quest at any time? And do what!? Where could she go when she was stuck in nothingness!? The choice might be hers but, she wasn't willing to make it! She had to accept or decline an unknown offer. *What kind of choice was that!? It was tantamount to jumping off a cliff without any safety gear!* She was about to persist with that line of thinking, when she became conscious of it. She had to deliberately turn away from judging the situation, and focus on the choice immediately, in front of her. She closed her eyes and breathed in deeply, until she felt centered in the stillness within. It didn't take long, before she was granted the clarity she needed. Suddenly, she knew what she needed to do! She would go through with it - continue her quest! There was a clear distinction somewhere in the depths of her - stemming from her awareness - that her choice wasn't just another means of escape. It was a natural extension of her soul knowing; something that her mind had no access to. But, her awareness was making its presence felt more determinedly, with every breath that she took. She realized that despite the intensity of the feeling, there was no sense of obligation; no impetus at all behind the feeling. No mind. Just an all-knowingness surrounded by quiet, neutrality. She didn't know what it was or where this knowingness was going to lead her. Only one thing was certain. Wherever it was, there would be no turning back once she took that first step. She looked at Glow, who was watching her. It was a still, glowing mass of light. She couldn't fathom the look on its shimmering "face." All she knew was that she felt a profound sense of peace. She smiled at Glow. Glow smiled back, and gave her a nod. She didn't know how but, Glow knew exactly, what she was about to do.

She closed her eyes, and shut out the world as she remembered it. She took that single conscious "step" into the darkness, and entered a space that she'd never dared approach before - the unknown depths within herself. It looked just like the nothingness! She was sitting in exactly, the same spot! It dawned on her that she must be traversing certain psychological barriers. She wasn't going anywhere! But, it felt as though she'd travelled millennia with the release of each layer! Glow was seated right beside her; throwing little sparkles of his glowing self into the darkness, and waving them farewell as they faded away. She smiled, and marveled at its joy of being itself - wherever it was. She wondered what that level of innocence felt like. Did she feel the same somewhere in her Being? *How could she get to it?* Glow looked at her, and smiled but, said nothing. There was something about that smile - it made her "light" up. And made her acutely aware of the darkness within herself. Once again, she was overcome by a deep respect for Glow, and the nothingness. She didn't have the capacity to understand the full impact of her action. However, she could tell from the way she felt that it was of the utmost significance. If she could overcome her reticence, and somehow fully open to it, it might just help her find what she was searching for. This quest was placing demands on her that she'd never encountered before. Over and above that her awareness was signaling something. To make any kind of headway on this quest she needed to extend her "sights" way beyond the obvious. For a moment, she hesitated. She felt unsettled by what she'd just done. *The prospect of taking on more of that inner darkness was frightening! She'd never done anything like this before! The extent of all this was daunting! There was just no end in sight!* She was struck by a reassuring insight. She wouldn't be where she was, if she wasn't meant to be there. She relaxed, and inhaled deeply. She felt it light a flame in the very depths of her soul. She was overcome by humility. She felt grateful. Inspired. And overtaken by breathless anticipation for all that was still to unfold within that inner darkness.

As she sat lost in her wonder, she slowly became aware that she could access a deeper level of memory. It allowed her to recall various past incidents that had caused pain to others, and herself. The past wasn't inaccessible after all! The healing process that Glow had outlined just a little while ago, now looked so much more feasible.

"Do I have to acknowledge each one? What if I can't remember all of them?" she asked.

Glow laughed. "This process is not about quantity, Little One. It's about opening your heart. It's endless"

She glared at Glow. A tiny spurt of sparkles flew in her direction. Was Glow sticking its tongue out at her? *The nerve!*

"You just have to remember whatever you can" said Glow. "Holding your true intentions in your heart space is the most important thing in this quest. Once you surrender to the process, it has the power to work its healing magic on all levels – conscious, and unconscious. Both on you, and on everyone you include in that healing space. It is intense but, remember there are no short-cuts to this process of uncovering your truth, and aligning with your soul path" said Glow.

Glow's reproach brought her back to the task at hand. She tried recalling the people who had been caught in the cross-fire of her ego-battles. At first, it was difficult. She had to fight the tendency to place her feelings of righteousness above the healing nature of the act that she was about to perform. She also found it difficult to suppress the strong inclination to blame others for the upheavals in her life. But then, she had a significant breakthrough by simply taking her heightened emotions into her stillness, and breathing through them with compassion. She realized that the blame, and judgement were just ego-noises. And persisting with those thoughts only made it more challenging to transcend the negativity, and reclaim the lightness that was fast becoming the most precious "commodity" that she'd ever owned! So she stopped trying to import her interpretations, and conclusions about her past experiences into her current space. It was futile anyway – she couldn't get past her awareness! Besides they served no real purpose - they were only distracting her from being fully present. She'd never realized how priceless that space was! And magical. She could do things that she'd never contemplated before!

She took herself slowly through the process that Glow had described earlier - ensuring that she mindfully held each incident in the light of her consciousness by remaining present with it. At various intervals, she felt the electrical tingling in her heart space. Sometimes it spread throughout her body. There were times when it was so intense that she found herself gasping for breath but, by remaining in her stillness she was able to observe each incident with detachment. And for the first time, saw the many ramifications of her actions. She acknowledged her responsibility for each one, and asked for forgiveness through her higher Self. It was the most difficult thing that she'd ever done! But, observing her anger – openly, and without self-judgement – was liberating! She realized that she was looking at a stranger – one who was living in her body! Someone who had wreaked havoc with her life, without her being aware of it! And she was horrified at the kind of thoughts that she'd harbored. She was after all, the gate-keeper of everything that entered her mind! She was responsible for all of it - her thoughts; her actions, and her behavior! She made a silent promise to never again, be so unaware of her thoughts, and energy! It impacted others, and herself! It impacted her reality! But, as hard as she tried she couldn't forgive herself. Something within retaliated at the mere thought of it. She didn't deserve such graciousness. She was unaware that she was judging herself. The reaction came so naturally to her that she wasn't conscious of it. As she remained mindful of the process, she was drawn deeper into an ever-widening circle of healing energy. She watched in amazement, as wave after wave of negativity slowly lifted from her, and dissolved into the nothingness. She wasn't certain how long it took. When she finished, she opened her eyes to find Glow looking at her intently.

"I'm starting to see you, Little One" said Glow, gently.

She was still dazed, and battled to center herself. She felt as though she'd just surfaced from the depths of the ocean after holding her breath for an interminably long time. "What do you mean? I've been here all along."

"Yes. You've been beside me all along but, in physical form only. Your essence was hidden" said Glow, softly.

Essence? What's that? She was overcome by exhaustion, and couldn't utter a word.

"Look" said Glow, in response to her unvoiced questions.

She gazed around her. All she could see was nothingness. And Glow. And those shining specks of light in the nothingness. *What was that?*

Glow laughed. "Always looking outside of yourself. Look closer, Little One. Look at you."

She looked down at herself. It took a while for the sight to register. She was surrounded by a thin, shimmering halo. She glanced up at Glow in shock. Glow was smiling serenely, not in the least bit perturbed. *Why was she glowing?* As she gazed into the nothingness, it suddenly came to her. *Those shining specks of light in the nothingness were stars! How did they get there!? Where was she? In space!? How did she get there?* She looked at herself again. There were waves of shining colors to her halo, and they were moving…..no…..dancing…. all around her. She looked just like Glow! She was entranced. She tried touching it. Her fingers moved right through the shimmering waves. Despite her amazement, she giggled. She wrapped her arms tightly around herself, and tried to "hold" the colored halo. But, it trembled, and bounced away from her. And then, it returned to settle around her body again. She'd always loved blowing soap bubbles. And now, she was one huge, shimmering soap bubble! She burst into joyous laughter.

"What is it?" she asked Glow, feeling glad for its presence. She felt mortified that she'd wished for Glow to leave. She would be lost without it! It was the only thing helping her in the nothingness.

"It's only you, Little One" said Glow smiling. "In full glory of your true essence."

She looked around herself in wonder. She was feeling so much…… lighter. And a whole lot….brighter. Happier. She laughed. She'd never felt so full of joy. So free. And yet, there was nothing different about her circumstances. Her past was still her past. Her future was still unknown.

Her body still felt heavy, and full of pain. She was still a mass of emotion, and jumbled thoughts. She was still burdened with worry over her circumstances – over everything! She was more baffled than ever, over her quest. And Glow. The nothingness remained unfathomable. And yet, she felt totally different. She had a shocking revelation. The only thing that must have changed was something, inside of her! She'd always believed that happiness, and freedom were only possible once she attained financial success. And had freed herself of all her problems. And there she was reveling in a joy that she'd never experienced! True joy wasn't so elusive after all! And it wasn't about reaching a stage in her life when she was on "top of everything." That was just another illusion! Instead, it was about how content she felt – within herself! When being open, and accepting of everything - the good and bad; the happy and sad. Right, and wrong. The known, and the unknown. What did Glow say? That one couldn't be whole by suppressing or denying any aspect of oneself – whether through fear, pain, guilt or shame. She could add something of her own. The same principle applied to any emotion. Without the capacity to "read" her emotions she was never going to decipher her soul's map!

Despite her newfound clarity, she realized that her mind was still trying to figure out her quest. That head of hers! Why did it cling to the known? Did she derive a sense of security from the certainty conjured up by her logic? She realized just how much she'd been tricked by her conditioned mind. Everything that was visible, and tangible in her physical world was ephemeral including, her physical self! Permanent security in her physical world was an illusion! Her life essence – for all its uncertainty - was the only constant, in all of eternity! And it was invisible! Even her soul lessons – whatever they were – will never be known. They didn't even belong to her! They would pass into the Universal library of human consciousness at the end of her physical existence. All she could do was show up each day, and be present as her life unfolded. So why was her head trying so hard to hold onto a past, and a future that only existed as a mirage? It was all irrelevant to physical life, unless she remained present in each moment! And yet, all it took was a single moment of conscious breath to make her whole life indispensable to the human experience. She'd already lost, practically everything in her physical world. And she felt no inclination to hold onto whatever was left.

But, it wasn't only the material things that she had to let go off. She was also needed to let go of the identity that her mind had become attached to. All of it had served her in some way, and she felt a deep sense of gratitude for the life that she'd lived – for the person that she was. However, she'd allowed herself to become disabled by certainty, and safety. And she could now see clearly how that had limited her. She understood for the first time, how much she'd been holding onto. She must have missed so much of life, by defining her life according to her ego's limited view! And she'd always believed that she was living her best life. How wrong she was! She pulled herself sharply upright. *Did she just admit that she was wrong?* She grimaced. *She was never wrong!*

"Why is this happening!?" she cried, as she felt the anxiety slowly encroaching on her peaceful reverie. *She never did a 180 - in anything! That wasn't her! Once she made up her mind that was it!* She was trembling with pent up anger. More so, because she was becoming increasingly aware that her quest was about some inner transformation – including but, not restricted by her mind. She sighed. *Her past life was so much easier! And instantly, gratifying! This process of inner "shedding" was eroding layer upon layer of her character, and personality at a snail's pace! Leaving her with nothing for an identity but, a shifting halo of light! Was her old physical reality really just an illusion? A reflection of her thoughts - the way that she defined herself? Would her physical reality, and identity continue dissolving as she worked through her conditioning to uncover her truth? What would be left? What would she use to define herself? Who would she be?*

"Those answers will come to you as your truth unfolds, Little One" said Glow. "For now, why don't you tell me why you were constantly, on the run? What was so unsettling about your childhood?

"I don't know" she said. "I think it was normal – like everyone else's. We didn't have much but, it was enough. I've always felt like an adult, even when I was a child. The environment I was raised in didn't allow for a childhood. But, I wasn't running from anything." It all sounded perfectly rational and yet, she couldn't suppress the sadness, and a deep sense of loss over something that was gone forever.

"Leave it for now. It will come to you" said Glow.

She marveled at the way Glow dropped little hints in such a non-threatening manner – like planting seeds in the waiting-ground of the nothingness. What was going to sprout from them? Then she was drawn to an uncomfortable thought. She frowned. *She didn't want to go back into her childhood!* But, she felt a strange impulse that lured her back to another layer in the unknown, dark depths below.

She closed her eyes, and focused her attention once again on the darkness within. She searched intently, hoping to "see" something. She could only find images of the life that she'd once lived. There was very little color - only frenzied activity. And emptiness. No joy. In the past, she'd faced one cross-road after another; leading to one dead-end after another. Strangely, within her inner sanctum she now felt at ease with her empty past. And hanging out in nothingness with only the stars, and Glow felt completely, normal. Besides everything was starting to look exactly, the same. The cellar. The nothingness around her. And the darkness within her! She'd expended so much energy resisting her imaginary fears about the unknown. This quest was actually, very liberating! She didn't feel so burdened, anymore. She felt buoyant, and willing to proceed with her quest. Her past had faded somewhat into the distance. She could still see it in her mind's eye, and wanted to hang onto it for a while longer. It was all she had. All she knew. *Without it, she had no tangible proof that anything, existed in her life. Including, herself!*

She was also profoundly aware of a new perspective relating to the way in which she wanted to live her life. Previously, she'd never thought about energies. Let alone respecting, and allowing them to flow through her in co-creating the life that she wanted. Everything was due to the "power" of her mind. And she had to stay busy. It was no longer a surprise that she'd turned her life into a mere existence. Now she wanted to be the observer of her life's journey. And remain aware of her feelings. Especially, watching for inspiration so that she could direct the energy of her thoughts when making decisions. She was born with her true reality in her soul. Her true Self was part of that reality. She didn't need to make something happen in her physical world. At least, not in the traditional way that she was familiar with. To actualize her soul path, she needed to remain fully present – focusing on observing it unfold. *But, she was already doing that? Wasn't she? Why was the nothingness not shifting to reveal what was hers!?* She was confused. Maybe her journey was far from finished. What else did she have to release? Did she have to do more healing? Glow's words, slowly came back to her. She needed to observe, and learn something far more significant about her Self. Something was happening within her, on a level that she couldn't explain. If she wanted to progress on this quest, then she had to be present with her inner darkness, and remain open to everything beyond her physical senses. She sighed, wishing that she didn't feel so out of control. Then again, what did she have to lose? Everything in her physical world, other than her memory of it was already gone. What could she possibly lose by trusting the unknown to help her uncover her truth?

She felt a rebellious surge somewhere deep within. She smiled. *Her old self hadn't completely, deserted her! What was she thinking! She could trust what she did in her physical world – it was plainly visible! Tangible! And now, what could she trust? There was nothing around her - only nothingness! There was no one else around – that alone said something about this crazy quest! She should get the hell out of there! Not wait around, and watch it unfold! She didn't have time to waste! Yes – she was feeling joyous. And she was uncovering her truth. But, she couldn't just swing from one extreme to the other, and trust......trust....what? Sitting in nothingness, and chasing some invisible, pipe-dream!? All the while sinking further, and further into darkness, and talking to a ......a Glow-worm! Where was the fund in that?* She was all too familiar with that voice - it was the critic in her. *It had gotten her out of many a rough spot before. Maybe she should listen to it again.*

"Self-trust has nothing to do with where or what you place your trust in, in your physical world. Or for that matter, with the tangible results of achieving any number of your ego's goals. Real trust stems from within - from accepting your Self for who you truly are; knowing your worth, and having the courage to follow your soul path. And that, only comes with unearthing your true Self with self-love. And whatever you do, don't turn to the critic in you, Little One. It might be familiar but, it never served you before. And it definitely, won't serve you now. It's part of your old conditioning. It's not part of your truth. A 'Glow-worm!' Is that how you see me? I thought we were beginning to see things as one. Tsk....tsk.... tsk" said Glow, sadly.

She was embarrassed. She must be more careful with her thoughts. Glow meant more to her than anyone else that she'd met in her physical world. She was taken aback with her admission. They had spent so little time together! Perhaps time was of no consequence where there was a real connection between two people....between a person, and a thing. *Who – what was Glow!?*

"I'm fond of you Glow but, I don't like you! You're always in my head!" she said in a chastising tone. "I don't go rifling through your thoughts." "You sure of that?" asked Glow. And broke into small, shiny bumps – like it was mumbling something.

By now, she'd given up trying to understand everything that Glow was saying. But, she was becoming more aware of Glow's tactics. She realized that she'd been deftly manipulated into facing a much bigger challenge. Navigating through her physical life was relatively easier. Mainly, because she could relate to the workings of her rational mind. But, this quest! *How was she supposed to navigate her way through the unknown? Her rational mind didn't function in the silence of her inner sanctum!* Neither was it much help in helping her to figure a way out of the nothingness! She found it difficult to shake the conviction that she was missing something. *What was it?* Every scenario that she'd latched onto, and applied some modicum of reason to, had turned out to be nothing more than moving goalposts on shifting sands! She wished that there was someone else to talk to. Words had always helped with her reasoning. In the nothingness, she felt abandoned by everyone, and everything – including, her mind! She was struck by a petrifying thought. *She was standing in complete limbo between her shattered past and the vast, unknown nothingness - facing utter chaos!*

She sighed, mournfully. She felt despairingly close to the very edge of sanity. All her hopes for her life were rapidly fading into mist. And despite having a better understanding of her past behavior, she still didn't know anything about her true Self! Her identity was associated with her mind, and the things that she felt confident doing. She didn't like to indulge her emotions or revel in uncertainty. She now saw all too clearly, that she'd been suffering from a serious misapprehension. Everything that she believed to be of value in her life had slowly fallen apart. Her many beliefs, and philosophies were now faltering under the onslaught of her unfolding truth. The life that she remembered was no longer, meaningful. Why did she bother doing whatever she'd spent her time on? *Why bother with this quest? Nothing was going to change – she couldn't change who she was! Even if she escaped to some island, she would never be able to escape herself!* She realized that she was back where she started, at the early stages of her quest. Her joy had evaporated. She felt totally, spent. Worthless. Hopeless. Lifeless. Suicidal. She felt deceived by everything that she'd believed in. Betrayed by false hopes. Weighed down by delusions. She was devastated that she'd failed to see this mayhem coming. And yet, it had been staring her in the face, all along! *If she'd screwed everything up before, what chance did she have of doing anything differently now? She was bound to make a mess of her life - all over again.* Back then, she'd done her best to "prepare" for this thing called life – only to realize that no amount of preparation could help her deal with this quest in nothingness! She'd never felt so powerless, in her entire life!

Something within her rallied, and she felt her heart start to pump furiously. No! Whatever her past was about, it didn't define who she was! It couldn't be the sum-total of everything that her life was about. This couldn't be the end! She was still breathing! There must be more to this quest. She had to persist. What other choice did she have? She didn't want to go back to her old way of life. There was nothing pointing her in any other direction but, she wasn't stuck. There had to be some way to overcome what she was going through or move beyond it - even if she didn't know what to do. She might not know where she was but, full self-acceptance might just be the single point of entry to where she needed to be. She was overcome by a different kind of anxiety – an unfamiliar fear of the unknown. But, as much as she wanted to escape, there was a level of anticipation in her wild, throbbing heart. It was louder than her fear. Escape was no longer an option. All she could do was stay exactly where she was......and remain open-hearted about this unknown, invisible path that was making itself known to her. *Where was it taking her?*

That immediately, brought her attention back to what she was experiencing in that moment. Whether she wanted to admit it or not, she felt strangely guided by some unknown force. Previously, she'd felt challenged by her goals, and victorious when she accomplished them. In that moment, she was confronted by something startling. She didn't know what she was doing in the nothingness – there was no goal, other than uncovering her truth. And that was nebulous – she didn't know what truth even looked like! There was no challenge; no challenger. There was no direction. But, in a strange way, she felt as though she'd already reached some milestone on her quest by making the choice to enter her inner, darkness. *Did that make her a victor or loser?* And then, she was hit by a shocking revelation. This quest wasn't about winning or losing! She'd made a choice to take that one, crucial step into the darkness within - to learn more about herself. And to accept herself fully, by surrendering to her unknown, soul path. She felt like a complete idiot! *Why did she make that choice? Where was the victory in that? She couldn't blame her mind – she didn't even know what she was thinking. Or did she? If her mind didn't know, then which part of her did?* It slowly dawned on her that in order to be the "victor" she would have to be engaged in some sort of battle. And there was no one else around - just herself. *Was she at war with herself? What was the purpose of that? She was supposed to be loving, kind, and compassionate towards herself - not take herself apart bit-by-bit, for no apparent reason!* She sighed. She was totally, flabbergasted.

As she slowly disengaged from the mental battle that she was caught up in, and focused on centering herself in the stillness again, she became distinctly aware of a part of her communing with the silence within. Something was urging her to stick with her quest, despite all that was unknown, and uncertain. It was reassuring her that she might have reaped many rewards in her physical world but, she'd not as yet, experienced her soul purpose – the very reason, for Being. She sighed. There might have been reasons for her constant busyness before but, her way of doing things also distracted her from her true purpose. If she persisted with her old ways, she would have only achieved "more of the same." She would have ended up sinking deeper into that quagmire of delusion, and moved further away from her true Self. Her mind would always be ready to resume its rational role, once she integrated it with her soul purpose – presumably, when this quest ended. *If that time ever came!* She sensed that once she opened herself to trusting the unknown, she wouldn't be interested in anything as definitive, as endings or beginnings. Before she could get to that state of Being, however, she had to go through with a quest that was beyond reason – to uncover her truth. She had no idea what that entailed. She didn't even know what she was looking for. She only had a bubbling cauldron of emotions to work with. But, she could recall nothing in her past that had any of the depth, and intensity of the life she now felt pulsating in her veins as she "stood" at the very edge of this new state of becoming – as one with her soul purpose. And the calm knowing she sensed lying at the bottom of that cauldron was the only motivation she needed to persist with her unknown quest. She would have to follow a very different minstrel compared to the familiar goading of her ego. She would have to follow her heart! With many of the past barriers that she'd built around it now removed, she could feel it beating insistently, drumming out its very own melody. And it sounded deafening in the silence.

But, trust? That was a different matter. It was disconcerting to realize that what she believed to be trust was in sole reference to achieving her physical goals. It had nothing to do with trusting her Self. Was that the reason she'd found it so difficult to trust others? Could she trust herself to embark on a quest that she had no prior knowledge of? *Could she even take on something like this – something that she'd never done before?* Then again, in what or whom could she place her trust, if not in her Self - even if she had no idea who her true Self was? Again there were no answers to be found in the nothingness. It remained inscrutable. She let it be, as another revelation arose from the stillness within. She'd only just acknowledged that she'd denied, ignored, and suppressed so much of herself. In the process, she'd concealed her Self - from herself! She was now beginning to accept that the person she believed herself to be, wasn't her true Self. And as un-nerving as that was, she couldn't help wondering if her restlessness over the years had been nudging her to look closer to home for her answers. Would her quest lead her to her true Self? Who was she? *What did her truth look like? What was her true Self like? What did she desire doing? What were her likes, and dislikes? How did it behave? Who did this Self want to become?* She felt an excitement stir deep in her belly. The feeling was similar to what she'd experienced before – the hungry anticipation when she was caught in the throes of a passionate, 'love' affair. Except this time her desire was to meet this new, unknown Self that was closer to her than anyone, she'd ever known. Perhaps she would never know what her truth looked like but, she was certainly beginning to know what it felt like! A new love? Her Self? She smiled. What could be more profound? It didn't matter how long it took, she would do what was needed to uncover her truth. She could think of no greater miracle than witnessing this phenomenon of Self unfolding. She tilted her head slightly at this latest insight, and frowned. *She wasn't the type to "wait and see."* She smiled, nervously. Something about her had indeed, changed in the nothingness. And she didn't see it coming! She didn't even know it was happening!

CHAPTER 6

THE HEART'S SILENT SONG

She was awake but, she remained still - with her eyes closed. Her focus shifted between the stillness within, and the nothingness. *Could these two silent, spaces be the same?* She set herself the task of finding the differences between them. There were none, except for the stars. And they continued twinkling merrily, oblivious to her ongoing dilemma. She smiled. She couldn't help feeling lifted, even though the confusion was threatening to suck her further into that darkness within. Their constant, brilliant display gave her some measure of reassurance in a black sea of uncertainty. They were so close. She felt certain that she could touch them if she stretched her arms out. Instead she hugged herself, and marveled at her newfound joy. She felt like singing, and dancing. So she decided to "dance" with the stars. She whizzed about, grabbing a "thread" of starlight from each one. And set them alight by "touching" each one with a "magic wand" – her finger. She whirled around each star, until it sparkled brightly and then, she let go to grab onto the next star-thread. It took no time at all, before the entire sky was ablaze with a warm starry-glow. She gazed around utterly, enchanted. They were all so unique. *Why did she think that they were all the same?*

As a child, she'd looked up at the stars every night. They were her only constant companions, during those years. She recalled turning to them in moments of sadness, and always feeling cheered by their presence. And quite often, she heard them singing across the night sky – a song just for her. She would hum, and bop along to their silent melody. She was also convinced that she sometimes heard them whispering in some strange, timeless language. She'd never figured out what they were saying but, she never missed an opportunity to "join in," and tell them all about her day. One of her favorite pastimes was playing "catch" with them. As twilight fell, she would pick her favorite spot on the cool grass, and lie down – to watch them "pop" onto the night sky. She tried guessing where the next star was going to appear in the darkening sky, and pointed at each one, until both her hands were swinging wildly above her head. When she could no longer keep up she was forced to stop. She would drop her hands to her sides, and just watch them "talk." She waited for that moment when they would all burst out of the blackness, and light up the sky - just as the black night threatened to engulf them. She feared for their safety, and watched anxiously as that battle went on, night after night. She couldn't imagine anything as small as the stars holding their own against the all-consuming, blackness of the night. She dreaded the day when the blackness would swallow them all! But, that day never came. The starlight - so soft, and gentle; so unobtrusive - always won. She never understood why that made her feel happy but, she celebrated their triumph by clapping her hands, and cheering wildly. She smiled wistfully at her childish antics. For the very first time, she realized that she was looking at a miracle. And they were much more than just a source of comfort. She felt something more - an unusual affinity to them.

Her mind continued drifting back to the years spent at her father's Victorian house. It was located on a little hill, and overlooked the small town. Her room had a large bay window, with an old-fashioned iron grid that served as a security gate. There was a small wind-up lock to one side. She soon figured out how to open it to get an unobstructed view of the night sky. The lights from the town were few and far between, and did little to dull the brilliant star-light. They had no electricity at the time but, even candlelight felt intrusive. So she would blow out the candle by her bedside, and spend her evenings looking at the stars. But looking wasn't enough – she wanted to be closer to them. And the only way to do that was to hoist herself onto the rough, wooden windowsill, and slide her bottom slowly along, until she found her spot. The one that gave her the best view, and didn't have any pokey branches below it. She needed the space to dangle her legs, because it made something magical happen. She was able to imagine all sorts of things - like looking out onto the whole world! She'd often wondered what the world was, and where the sky ended but, her imagination failed to grasp such bigness. During those moments of deep contemplation she felt so drawn towards the sky that on quite a few occasions she lost her balance, and toppled headlong into the Bottle-brush tree below. And then it was a mission getting back into her room. Calling out to her sister for help was out of the question – her little escapades were her secret. The thin branches were not strong enough to bear her weight so there were a few failed attempts, before she could find the right one to give her a leg-up. And usually ended up with deep scratches on her legs. Not that she bothered with them - her adventures with the stars were far more important. Besides, she was always getting hurt. And no one said a word if they spotted a cut or bruise. So she said nothing. She didn't want to draw any attention to herself.

And now the nothingness so reminded her of those nights. She was overcome by nostalgia as she realized just how much she missed the stars. *Why did she stop looking at them?* She felt more than saw Glow's presence. She "sat" up. It was a weird feeling, because she was lying flat - floating in the nothingness! There was no top or bottom. Right or left. Front or back. "Sitting up" was about orientating herself to face Glow – it was her only point of reference. They could have been sitting upside down, for all she knew.

"Reminiscing about the stars?" asked Glow.

"Yup" she replied sheepishly. She hated it when Glow read her thoughts. It made her feel so exposed.

"I enjoyed being with them. They were my friends."

"I know. They still are" said Glow. "You must have been very lonely."

"Nope. I was alone most of the time but, never really lonely. I had so many friends." She smiled at her memories of the strange, little creatures that she'd played with. But...." she stopped. That wasn't entirely true. There was something else about those moments - a common thread linking them together. *What was it?*

"You were always searching for something?" asked Glow.

"Yes" she replied, immediately. "How did you......?" her voice trailed off.

She looked at Glow searchingly, and decided not to pursue it. Whatever this quest was about, it wasn't about Glow's behavior. She needed to focus on her own. Why did that acknowledgement make her feel so uncomfortable? Was she being selfish? But, there was no past reference point to draw on - she'd seldom paid attention to her own needs. Why did she place the needs of others above her own? Was she a "people-pleaser?" Was she afraid of being alone despite, refuting it earlier? *Whatever her motivation it had obviously, not worked! There she was once again, all alone! With only nothingness surrounding her!* Although she could now lay claim to certain traits that she'd never possessed before - a greater level of awareness, and self-acceptance. And they somehow lessened that feeling of aloneness. So she did feel alone before! Why did she deny it? That acknowledgement made her aware that it was easier to overcome her reticence towards turning inwards. And that inner stillness helped her to sift through the maze of thought, and emotion associated with some of the more important events in her life. And she didn't need to analyze anything – just sit in silence with them, until the clarity that she needed came to her. Previously, her regurgitating thoughts kept her mind in a whirl for days. Now however, her instincts were proving quite useful in moving past whatever felt superfluous. She found this newly-acquired skill quite liberating. It was helping her to maintain some perspective on everything that was hitting her at once.

It also made her starkly aware of the differences in behavior when dealing with the problems in her life. Previously, she used to be overcome by nervousness whenever facing a challenge. So much so, that the only antidote was clinging onto whatever was happening in her life. Whether it was important or not was immaterial. And whether it served her or not, even less so. She realized that "holding things together" must have given her some sense of security. And yet, she wasn't a hoarder – of physical things. Was she holding onto certain emotions or experiences? Was that "baggage" keeping her closed off from life? She wasn't even aware of it! What could it be? *Was it keeping her stuck in the nothingness? Could she remove it, and take her life forward? Where would she go?* She felt paralyzed by the lack of information. *Why didn't she know the answers to her questions? This was her life!* It dawned on her that each time things threatened to fall apart in her world, her confidence took a knock. Despite that she'd refused to relinquish her hold on anything. That was a form of defeat. And she wouldn't allow it. Let alone, admit to it. And she'd continued holding on – albeit unconsciously - until the Universe dealt her a cruel blow. Everything in her life had fallen apart within a few months. And now, when the only thing left standing was herself, she had the strangest feeling that she was also about to crumble. *Was there no end to this nightmare? Would she ever be able to piece her life together again? Would she ever be free of the past burdens that were threatening to annihilate her? Could she free herself when she didn't even know what was holding her back?*

She sighed. And now, she was on the verge of embarking on something that she couldn't even imagine - let alone grasp! She was exhausted. And shaken to her core. And yet, she'd uncovered a hidden source of strength, and capability. Each time that she was on the verge of collapsing she somehow found herself taking another step on her quest. She was still nervous. And daunted by her circumstances, and the magnitude of the many problems facing her but, somehow her curiosity outweighed everything else. She looked around at the nothingness again. What was it about this space? Perhaps there was more to it than met the eye. And yet, the more ground she covered on this quest, the less she understood. Her boundaries were being stretched to breaking point, and beyond. Her usual thinking patterns were being relentlessly tested, until they evaporated into the nothingness. And she couldn't use the technical skill that she'd acquired in her professional life, to help her on this quest. It required skills that she didn't even possess! Much to her astonishment, it didn't require any force of will, either. Or any intentional form of "doing." All that was required was her full presence – a state that she was still trying to figure out. A state that she sensed would grant her access to her soul's all-knowingness. And even though she couldn't fathom what that was, she sensed that she was being guided by it. She was also distinctly aware that her mind was often silent. For once, so out of its depth that it preferred to remain in the distant background. She was aware when it became active – by the avalanche of thoughts that hit her. But, she was also becoming more detached from her mind with each such episode. She couldn't help being surprised by her unusual behavior. Perhaps she was more than familiar with her old ways of thinking, and comfortable to leave her mind to its own devices as it unraveled itself. However, this dawning sense of inner knowing – an unknown within unknown, nothingness – utterly, intrigued her. She decided to thread gently in its presence - as though, she was approaching a sleeping child. She was hit by a startling revelation. Was this "sleeping child" her unknown Self? That shook her. She took refuge in answering Glow's question.

"I guess I've been searching for something - for a long time. But, I never found it. I thought I did – several times. But, I returned to my seeking sooner or later. I travelled a lot, and visited many beautiful places. I saw some amazing things, and met many wonderful people, from different cultures. At one point, I believed the crowning glory of that life experience would be sharing my life with someone. I looked pretty much, all over the world for the "one." And there were times when I even believed that I'd found the love I was searching for but, I was wrong. Sooner or later, things fell apart. I always wanted "more." I just wish I knew what that was. I was told once that I have the "soul of a gypsy" but, knowing that didn't make my life any easier. I never stopped looking for that extraordinary something or someone that would make it all worthwhile. I must sound like I was on some runaway, fantasy mission!" She was breathless; embarrassed at revealing so much of herself.

There was no reaction from Glow. It just continued looking at her - with its glowing waves calmly, wafting around both of them. She found that intense level of presence very disconcerting. No one had ever spent that much time with her or listened with such unwavering, attention. She took refuge from Glow's watchful "eyes" by reflecting on her thoughts. *Where were those strange thoughts coming from? For as long as she could remember, she'd never experienced such a flood of thought, and emotion! All this reflection was such a waste of time, and energy! She preferred getting things done. And the freedom to speak her mind felt weird – as though, she was hearing her thoughts for the first time!* She shifted uncomfortably but, continued to observe her trend of thought. There was a new trail of breadcrumbs, and it wasn't coming from Glow. Instead, they were being "dropped" by her awareness as she observed her emerging thoughts. She realized that she'd seldom reflected on her life. She'd needed the energy to uphold the hectic pace of it. Despite her outward dedication to the daily grind though, there was one nagging concern - her constant boredom. *Why did the events in her day-to-day, existence fail to hold her attention or inspire her?* She recalled trying to get things done, as fast as possible. As though, that would somehow negate the predictability. It never did. Sooner than expected, she always got an inkling of the outcome – of everything, including her relationships. And then, she lost all interest. She moved on, and closed the chapter. And yet, her mind and body were still so cluttered with her past! She sighed, hopelessly.

It dawned on her that irrespective of whatever she'd chosen to do, she found little or no fulfillment. Despite her achievements, the yearning for something "more" in life had always resurfaced. It added to her restlessness, and discomfort. Her interpretation at the time was that she wasn't doing her best. So she took on more. But, no matter what she did, it never quelled that desperate desire to continue searching. She was looking even when she wasn't conscious of it! And yet, she'd never got closer to understanding what she was looking for. Let alone, finding it. It slowly dawned on her that she might have controlled many things in her physical life but, there was one thing that she would never be able to control - the extent of her soul's reach! She was struck by a revelation. Her soul had continued yearning for something beyond her mind, and egotistical pursuits. What did her soul desire? On rare occasions, she recalled indulging a strange feeling that she could only describe as magical. Moments that made her stop, and wonder about life. But, what she saw in her outer world made her feel so uncomfortable that all she wanted to do was run. But, she had responsibilities. Sooner rather than later, she was forced to return to her crazy schedule. Letting go of that wondrous feeling in those rare moments wasn't easy. Each time, she felt as though a part of her had died. And she hated the lows that ultimately, followed. It made her intensify her search but, she never got closer to finding any answers. *And she was still searching!* Somewhere in the far reaches of her soul she still hoped that she would find it someday. Hopefully, before she keeled over! She wished she could be certain of that. She couldn't imagine anything more soul-destroying than not knowing her deepest, soul desires in her lifetime.

She frowned as the next thought wafted through her mind. She'd heard accounts of near-death experiences, and the images of life that flashed through peoples' minds. *If that was true, she had no intention of hanging around until then, to find out what her life was about!* And she had no interest in what happened after death. She wanted to experience life while she was conscious of it! That sentiment made her aware that now - more than ever - she wanted to live her soul's purpose. She couldn't imagine anything more futile than spending lifetime after lifetime, doing everything else but, that. That was her "hell!" And if her time on earth was the only way for her to consciously experience her soul, then she wanted to exalt in her experience of it. That would be her "heaven!" In the nothingness, her sentiments now took on a whole new meaning when they resonated strongly with her entire body. She gathered that she might never fully understand the mysteries of life but, she still wanted to explore every possible avenue to get closer to it. *Where did that thought come from?* But, whether or not she believed in her insights was immaterial. Something that she couldn't quite comprehend was eliciting a far greater respect for the unknown - by the sheer power of its invisible presence.

"Sounds like escapism to me" said Glow, provocatively. "Right up there with running from your past or reaching for that preconceived 'future' of yours. But, all this searching for something based on a 'feeling?' Quite an imagination you have there, Little One. Maybe you were running from your fears. That's why you always took on more than you could handle. But, you were only setting yourself up for failure. Fear has a way of doing that – driving you to define impossible targets and then, leaving you to wallow in self-pity when you don't reach them."

"Stop it!" she shouted. She wished they had continued playing marbles. All this stuff was annoying. And intense! It made her feel heavy; completely, drained.

"It wasn't some 'target!' It was only a feeling. But, it was real. I can't explain it. But, feelings aren't meant to be explained – just listened to." She couldn't believe those words were coming out of her mouth. *What was she saying!?* "And I never run from anything!"

What on earth did Glow mean by "reaching for a preconceived future?" She'd never heard of such nonsense! She might not have manifested everything she wanted but, she had no doubt that she would have – eventually. And yet, that thought didn't resonate with the stillness within. She just couldn't understand why there was such a difference between what she was saying, and feeling.

"Everything was fine. We were ordinary people; with ordinary lives – like everyone else in our neighborhood. Why would I run from that?

That was my home." Again she felt that dissonance between thought, and feeling!

By now, she was beyond irritated with Glow. She was also aware of feeling very uncomfortable, for some reason. And she was growing more restless with Glow's probing questions. What was bugging her?

"Perhaps you felt ashamed or embarrassed about your childhood" stated Glow. "But, were those your feelings or were you picking up on what others were feeling? Sensitive children have difficulty separating their own feelings from those around them."

That struck a chord in her but, she promptly ignored it. She wasn't the sensitive-kind! Her parents were good people, and well respected in their little community. They always welcomed family and friends into their home, and went out of their way to entertain them. But, their discomfort during such occasions was very tangible. She remembered that feeling well. So she did pick up on their feelings! What was she feeling? Did she also confuse their feelings for her own?

"That's highly probable" Glow piped in, running around in circles again, trying to catch its non-existent tail.

She glared at Glow but, didn't say anything. There was some truth in that statement – she felt it. Maybe she was ashamed or embarrassed. Or both. Was she just being empathetic? Or was she also embarrassed about their poor standard of living? Did it stem from the averted eyes, and overly polite "hellos" when people visited? Perhaps she was reacting to a whole host of unspoken emotions that she would never be able to put her finger on. *And why would she feel ashamed!? She admired both her parents.* She shook her head in frustration. *Where was all this information about her childhood coming from?* She was familiar with the memories but, the deeper insights into the silent behaviors of those closest to her was unnerving - to say the least! But, she had to acknowledge that she was gaining a completely, different perspective on her childhood. And herself. She sighed. *Of what relevance could that be, after all this time? Rehashing the past was so futile! Especially, if there was no way of knowing all the facts. And no way of changing it!*

Despite her thoughts, certain memories continued to bombard her mind. She recalled her parents being constantly at odds, about the little improvements that her mother made around the house. Her father was adamant that they shouldn't waste money "living up to the Jones's." There were far more important things to do with their limited income. She didn't understand their adult-talk back then but, she was finally beginning to understand the constant tension between them. There was a cauldron of suppressed emotion, and arguments about money were only a decoy! Over the years, she'd watched as her mother's resentment grew over her father's ongoing stubbornness. More so, because it was a trait that he exercised only on her. She also remembered her mother's silent but, very tangible anger at not being heard, whenever she spoke – which was very seldom. It wasn't customary for women in their culture to challenge their spouses or the traditional status quo, in any way. The only option for women was to suffer in silence. Her parents were never verbal about their feelings but, that didn't prevent her from being caught up in the cold, silent crossfire between them. She recalled feeling quite upset whenever she witnessed such behavior between the two people she cared for the most. And she'd often wished that she could somehow, make it all better. But, she dare not say anything. Her only outlet was to seek out her little friends in the fields.

She became aware of the painful lump in her throat. She was surprised. So many years had passed, and her reactions to those childhood experiences were still so intense! *How was it possible for her to still be carrying all that emotion inside of her?* The passive-aggressive behavior between family members aside, was it possible that she'd absorbed their energies – whether conscious of it or not? Could that past energy persist in her mind and body, and negatively impact her life – irrespective of her efforts to stay positive? Could those experiences influence her own energy levels, and make her succumb to the same behavioral patterns? Could that behavior be so deeply buried that it could make her act out sub-consciously? Could her sub-conscious behavior overrule her mind? Something told her that it did. She was horrified. She couldn't help thinking about her mother, and wondering how she'd coped with her bottled up emotions. In what ways did those suppressed emotions manifest in her mother's life – in their lives? What was the value of traditional norms, if they suppressed the truth and fostered so much pain, and resentment? What was the value of any relationship, without the freedom to express one's truth - without fear of reprisal? Those memories gave rise to the shocking revelation that she must have been prone to the same behavior as an adult. She reacted so reflexively that she couldn't recall whether she'd spoken her truth or just vented the anger within her. It was more likely the latter, for she didn't know what her truth was. But, she was beginning to understand that suppressed emotion could only be contained within the physical body, for a certain period of time. Sooner or later, it would be released, in some way or other. Did she use that anger, and agitated energy to build the life that she thought she wanted? A life she believed to be so far removed from her past that she'd never have face it again. Except for one, major oversight. Without being conscious of her underlying motivations she'd only repeated the emotional patterns that were ingrained in her cellular memory. Patterns that had kept her past very much, alive! Was her restlessness over the years trying to alert her to that oversight? And instead of heeding it, she'd buried herself in her busyness! She sighed heavily. Things were suddenly, very clear. Glow was right. Far from building the life that her soul desired, she was "spinning her wheels" in that space between out-running her past, and chasing a "future" that kept her as far as possible, from her sub-conscious conditioning!

It slowly dawned on her that whatever distraction her work provided, it was no antidote for what she needed to heal in her past. She'd avoided the emotions that consumed her as a child but, they didn't go anywhere. She still felt them! And her lack of awareness regarding her behavior led her to deny, and suppress a major part of her life that had obviously, influenced her reality! Without a diverse social circle to foster a more balanced perspective during those formative years, her parents' world had become her world. She raised her eyebrows as the extent of the challenge facing her hit home. This quest wasn't some arbitrary notion that she'd picked up somewhere along the way. It was far more fundamental than that. It was somehow allowing her to access places within herself that she didn't know existed. *What was she supposed to do with all that information? She didn't have any options in the nothingness!?* She felt utterly lost, and confused. There was no one around to help her, and Glow wasn't being very helpful although, she did appreciate its presence. It made her feel supported. *Without the usual distractions in her physical world, this quest was intense!* But, turning to some kind of distraction was the furthest thing from her mind. She had a strong sense that if she diverted her attention from her quest she would once again, be avoiding, denying or running from her past. That kind of behavior – although, familiar – now seemed out of synch with her in the nothingness. She sensed that it wouldn't serve her if she intended to follow through with this quest to uncover her truth. Again she felt her frustration rising. It wasn't just not knowing what to do next. She also had a strong sense that whatever she was reaching for to move her life forward was being blocked by her past! She sighed. She'd never felt so stuck; so utterly, hopeless!

"You tried many things to out-run your past, Little One. You can't change that. But, you don't need to change anything. All you have to do is be with yourself during this process, and own where you are right now by acknowledging the buried emotions from your past. You can only find peace by allowing yourself to be present with it. That requires you to be vulnerable but, there's no need to be afraid of the feelings that will surface in that space. If you can allow yourself to open to this emotion it can help you find what you've been searching for, all your life. Besides, the more you avoid your past, the longer you'll be caught in that in-between space, repeating the very experiences that you're so desperately trying to put behind you. And that will only take you further from your truth. No matter how many accomplishments you notch up in your physical world, nothing will be able to compensate for not fulfilling your soul purpose. There is no need to be embarrassed about your past or ashamed of it. Your past can never limit you. Neither does it define you. And thinking that it does is merely another illusion preventing you from seeing all that lies within plain sight – your true Self."

Glow's words touched her deeply. And they triggered a few more obvious insights. If her little world had been influenced to such an extent by those closest to her, what aspects of her mind – her thinking – were her own? What else lay hidden in its convoluted recesses besides, all that was so familiar? What did she use to construct her so-called identity, and reality over the years? How different was that identity from her true Self? And if her true Self was indeed within "plain sight," then what other behavioral tactics did she use to blind herself to her truth? She instinctively latched onto her rebelliousness as a child. There was now little doubt that it was a means of expressing herself in an environment that was very much an emotional vacuum in one sense, and a volcano in another. An environment that was perceived by her childish mind to be a very real threat, even though it was tempered by an innate sense of the bond that declared her to be part of a "family." Notwithstanding that, she was relegated a specific place - the "black sheep." She didn't understand it then but, she now realized that her rebelliousness as a child was in reaction to a feeling that she believed she had no control over – being constantly state of "fight or flight." To counter her agitation she'd devised a series of defenses to protect herself against an invisible, "larger than life" threat. That might have alleviated her fears as a child but, it did little to help her overcome the huge insecurity, and inadequacy of being in a constant battle against something that she couldn't see or understand. Her external environments might have changed as an adult, but, that persistent threat was already deeply ingrained in her psyche. And manifested itself in her "push-pull" attachment style. She became attached very quickly to people, and situations. And then, she pulled away for some reason, and became aloof. She'd justified her behavior on the grounds of the ongoing pressure at work. But, in the nothingness the reason for her paradoxical behavior slowly dawned on her. It had nothing to do with work - there was a far more potent volcano within her. And it wasn't just her anger. It was way more complex than that. Whatever it was, she didn't like what she saw bubbling to the surface. The identity that she believed to be her own was built on a foundation of fear, lies, guilt and shame!

"Things flowing a bit easier now?" Glow asked, softly. "After years of playing hide-and-seek with yourself, you've run out of places to hide. As frightening as that is, it's a really good place to be – even if you can't see where you are. You're making progress with your healing. And you thought you knew nothing about healing! Now that you're becoming familiar with using the inner light of your consciousness, you'll find it easier to sift through the layers as they arise, and release them. In the process, you'll be able to heal aspects of yourself that you've been avoiding for so long. That will allow you to see yourself - not as you perceived yourself to be - but, as your true Self."

She was listening intently. She felt distinctly lighter but, she was still troubled. She frowned. She'd covered more ground down memory-lane than ever before but, she was beginning to realize that there could be a lot more that she needed to unravel about her childhood. She was now desperate to move forward with her life, and the only thing holding her back was her past! She groaned. *How was she going to bring down those walls? She didn't even know what she was looking for! How could she heal, and free herself from an invisible prison!?* She also realized that as much as she wanted this to be over and done with, she couldn't dictate the speed of her quest or control the events being dragged up from her memory to be healed. She sighed. *This quest was making her feel more powerless than she'd ever felt! What could she possibly learn from her past? She couldn't even relate to it anymore – her life or the beliefs of the person that she used to be! A life that now lay scattered around her in pieces! How was she supposed to put it all back together again? She couldn't draw on any of her usual resources – not her knowledge or her mind's usual toolkit. She couldn't access them in the nothingness! And there was no one to pit her wits, and ego against to start re-building a new life. Who or what was she supposed to use as a frame of reference?* She shifted uneasily as something unexpected occurred to her. She felt no inclination whatsoever, to re-build the life that she had. Certainly not, if her memories were anything to go by! The only thing that she felt the need to do was to continue digging through the shattered remains of the life that she'd known. And yet, nothing was shifting the course of her quest in the nothingness! She remembered Glow's advice that she needed to observe the process, and remain fully present with herself as the process unfolded. The light of her consciousness would take care of the rest. She grunted. *That was easier said than done!* She sighed. *How much more of this nightmare did she have to contend with?*

Before she could stop herself, she was flung back onto the rollercoaster that was building momentum around her identity. She realized that the person she believed herself to be was curated from various aspects of the personalities she'd encountered over the years. Just like the beliefs, and behavior that were now becoming so evident – very little or none of it – could be ascribed to the identity that she prized! She'd built a life thinking that it was based on her own choices. All this time, she'd been deluding herself! It dawned on her that there might be a link between the life that she'd lived, and the identity of person she believed herself to be. She had an astonishing revelation. She believed her life, and Self to be mutually exclusive! And now that so much of the foundation of her life, and the individual she thought herself to be was in question, the image she had of herself was hanging precariously in the balance. Much worse than that was the irrefutable knowing that her false identity was also in the process of disintegrating. She was petrified. *What was to become of her?* Who was that person masquerading as her true Self? Who was the real Self behind all the masks that she'd used? She was thrown into utter turmoil. And was feeling totally lost. In the midst of all her confusion, she was beginning to understand the seriousness behind Glow's earlier words. There was only one way to get through this quest. She needed to continue uncovering her truth. *Given half a chance, she would abandon ship!* Only the realization that she was the "ship" helped her to return to her stillness, and regain focus. If her life as she'd known it was any indication of herself as a fragmented ghost of her true Self, then she'd been living a lie! As that realization sunk into her consciousness, she was struck by another revelation. She couldn't return to her old way of life – not if it wasn't based on her truth! *What was her truth? Where did she find it? Was her truth and Self, one and the same? Who was this Self?* If she'd practically destroyed herself living a lie, then what kind of life was she capable of living by standing in her truth? She turned to look at Glow who was meandering around her in reams of shimmering light. It slowly gathered into a single, glowing mass. Glow held her searching look with unwavering kindness, and silent understanding. She welcomed the embrace of its warm gaze, as her mind floundered about in the unknown territory.

"You know! You know, why I'm here" she said, softly. "Please tell me" she pleaded.

"I don't know, Little One. I can only be with you as far as you allow yourself to steer this 'ship.' Whatever you don't know, you'll have to work out along the way" said Glow, in a voice full of compassion.

She was now totally alarmed. Trembling, and gasping for breath. Finally, she understood why she was sitting in nothingness! Her entire life, and her identity were lying in a collapsed heap beside her. She was certain that remnants of that life still existed somewhere "out there" – wherever that was. But, it might as well not exist, for the reality of it was rapidly dying within her! If her life held some iota of meaning before, it was now meaningless. That explained why she could only recall a few memories at a time – those that were important in uncovering her true Self! She was "shedding" whole parts of her old self! Her physical life had fallen apart bit by bit, in the same way. And now, she was slowly losing her identity – herself! Or was it the other way round? Her outer reality had never matched her truth so it was all falling apart! *How long was this going to last? What was she supposed to hold onto? What could she turn to for safety or reassurance on this crazy quest!? Would she ever get out of it!?* She stared into the nothingness, and watched the image of herself crumble like a sand castle - washed away by waves of realization. *Would anything about her survive this quest? Who would she be?*

She was devastated by the gaping emptiness now arising within her from the loss of the life that she'd once called her own. In the midst of it, she had to face - with increasing incredulity - the false perceptions of her old self. She'd betrayed herself by ignoring her deepest feelings! And in doing so, she'd given others the benefit of the doubt - over her life! How could she have been so stupid? So naïve? Why was she so calm in all this mayhem!? Why wasn't she outraged? *That was so surprising! Why didn't she know what to do? How could she fail herself at a time like this?* She was stuck in her mind as it grappled to hold onto whatever she could, to gain some form of security in the midst of the storm raging within her. But, her efforts were futile – nothing more than a wisp of smoke against the unknown enemy confronting her in the nothingness. She realized that her mind was subdued in the presence of whatever had taken hold of her. It was still functioning but, it was losing its power to willfully formulate any thought, opinion or interpretation of her mystical experience. She was hit by another revelation. In all the chaos, she'd somehow shifted her attention from the version of herself as depicted by her mind, and entered the stillness within to be present with the unknown. *What was this space within her?* And it wasn't really empty. It was filled with something that she had no knowledge of. Was her awareness slowly superseding her mind? Was it overtaking all of her body? And then it hit her. Her true Self resided somewhere within that inner stillness! She was still in her body, although she now felt as though she'd separated from it, and was flowing with the silent, stillness within that had no identity at all! It felt vast; so deep. Completely, formless. And timeless.

"What's left now?" she asked Glow, breathlessly.

Undefined

Glow smiled. It was the most beautiful sight she'd ever seen.

"Nothing that you don't already know, Little One. You'll become aware of it soon. But, first, you have to remove a few more walls." said Glow, gently. "By becoming conscious of them."

"What walls? Why?" she whispered. What could possibly be left?

"So that you can uncover your truth, and live your soul's desires" Glow said.

"What is that?" she cried desperately. "What is my truth? What does my soul desire? Why do I have to live by that? Why can't I just get on with my life?"

"The life you had was no life at all – merely a shadow of one. Only you know what your truth is, Little One. And only your soul knows the path you're here to follow – it's in the driver's seat now. The only thing that is important right now, is for you learn how to surrender to your quest. You might not know what 'living fully alive' means but, you're beginning to feel it. If you surrender to that space it that will reveal your true reality" said Glow.

"But, I have a life. I've been living it!" she insisted.

"Were you?" asked Glow. "Is that why you're forcing yourself to endure a life where you torture yourself with doubt? Is that why you feel so un-fulfilled? So empty? Sad? Lifeless? So powerless?"

She felt herself shrink further, and further into herself as Glow drove each point home relentlessly.

"Is that why you feel no enthusiasm for the life that you're living? Why you feel like such a fraud? This 'life' you claim to be living is in every way, contrary to the very reason you have one."

"Stop" she pleaded, and held her hands tightly over her ears. "I only did what I thought was best." Her action did nothing to block the sound of Glow's voice.

"What you already know to be best for you within your soul, and force-feeding yourself a make-shift life to satisfy a self-serving ego aren't the same, Little One. For a long time you've been hearing another voice. You've been ignoring it - to the detriment of your truth. It's now time to listen to it" said Glow.

"What voice? What are you talking about?" she demanded. "Who am I supposed to be listening to?"

She was quivering with emotion. Was it fear? Anger? Frustration? Powerlessness? She couldn't tell. But, deep within that still silence, she remained perfectly calm. *How anyone could remain calm under such circumstances was beyond comprehension!* She was exhausted but, some part of her was still pushing forward- if there was such a thing as "forward" in the nothingness! Despite her insights so far, and the moments of pure beauty that she'd experienced, nothing about her quest made any sense. She was grateful for her awareness but, she couldn't ignore the confusion swirling around in her mind, and body. She'd always valued her intellect above all else. It had helped her get out of some tough situations in her life. She'd prided herself on notching up one challenge after another, and had never stopped to consider her overall, wellbeing. And now, she was caught between some kind of standoff between her mind, and something that she couldn't even name. The former a record of past experiences that offered security, comfort and certainty. It had defined, and guaranteed her success - if she played by the rules. The latter was an eternal, silence - offering space, timelessness, uncertainty, an unknown Self, and an unknown life! A life without boundaries, and rules! There was no reward. And no guarantee – of anything! *Why did it have to be one or the other!? Why did everything in her life have to be so extreme? Why couldn't she have both?* Despite her frustration, she had to smile at her ego's attempt to negotiate a way around her dilemma. It struck her that this was one situation that she wouldn't be able to negotiate her way out of. Besides not knowing the terms, she didn't know who she was negotiating with! Neither could she mold or force her quest to fit some foregone conclusion. Her intellect was her previous source of power. Now she had nothing to turn to – even her body felt paralyzed with pain! She felt completely, powerless. And daunted by the prospect of continuing with her quest under such circumstances. *How was she supposed to determine the direction of her life if her mind was in a fog, and her body useless? How did she influence the outcome of her quest? Did she even have any influence in the nothingness?* She was freezing, cold.

"What's happening?" she asked, lifting her eyes to look around her.
"What's going on?" she persisted.
"Don't look outside of yourself, Little One. Look closer. The answer lies much closer than you think" said Glow.
She looked at her hands; her arms. Her legs. Her halo was disappearing!

She hugged herself fiercely, trying to hold onto it. It was no use. It continued dissolving into the nothingness. She watched as her physical body slowly came into view again. She was trembling. *She was being separated from the nothingness!* That realization gave rise to an intense fear – one that surpassed all her musings about losing her physical life, and her identity!

"What's happening? Why is my halo disappearing? What did I say? Did I do something wrong?" she whispered, guilt tinging her every word. Despite her confusion, something still felt "right" about being in the nothingness. As drastic as this quest was to her mind, she'd never felt so calm in her whole life! Her quest in the nothingness must mean something. *She couldn't lose it! Not now, when everything else was falling apart!* As weird as it was the nothingness was her only reality. It was all she had now. And she felt closer to it than she'd ever felt to anything or anyone before. The thought of being disconnected from it was petrifying!

"You didn't do anything wrong, Little One. You just moved further away from your truth, and your soul's light is making you aware of that. As you learn more about your Self, you'll get closer to your truth. You'll see, and feel your aura shining again" said Glow, reassuringly.

"The further away I'm from my truth the darker, and heavier I'll feel? There will be no halo?" She absent-mindedly, repeated what she just heard – battling to extract some meaning from it. "The closer I'm to my truth, the brighter my inner light? My halo will shine again?"

"Yes" said Glow.

"I haven't been living my truth? Everything about my life – about me - wasn't based on my truth? Is that why I'm at such a dead-end? Why I'm feeling so…..so…..empty ….and….and…..dead?" she whispered.

"Yes. Sometimes the things that made you feel joy helped to keep the darkness at bay. Like Kitty, and your baby. Maybe one or two other experiences –like the moments you spent with the stars. That was pretty much it. But, those were all external influences – your inner 'cup' was drained very early on in life. It was never really full to begin with. As a result, you were unable to keep the negativity in your life from creating an indelible void in your psyche. Before you were able to figure that out, you were consumed by one negative experience, after another. And that took you further away from your truth – from your

Self. Before you can walk your soul path, you need to heal that void by resurrecting your truth – the light of your soul" said Glow.

If her previous life path wasn't right for her, and presuming Glow was correct about completing her quest to uncover her truth, then how did she end up on this quest, in the first place? If her old self was so caught up in illusion, then she should still be wandering around lost in her physical world! Was someone or something guiding her through the false reality that she'd created? Was there some part of her that had remained awake during her past? She shut her eyes tight, and shook her head hard. *This was all totally, bizarre! Why was she thinking about such things?* Again she reverted to the familiar territory of her mind.

"This doesn't make any sense! I'm so confused" she moaned despondently. "I've worked hard to build my life" she said forlornly. "And now it's all gone. All lost!"

"Nothing that is truly meant for you will ever be lost, Little One. It might look like that now, while you're still caught between illusion and truth but, you're not meant to remain stuck here forever. Walking any path that isn't your soul path or building a life not based on your truth, is the real loss. Your soul path offers you the experience of your best life. Living any other way is not worthy of your soul. That kind of life, is no life at all" said Glow, softly.

"But, why is this happening to me now? I already have a life! Why didn't all this happen before I established myself!? What use is this information now? I can't change anything about the past!" She felt her desperation. There was a metallic taste of fear in her mouth. *What was she supposed to do? Forget the life that she had, and start all over again?* She felt sick to her stomach, and overwhelmed by all the implications. *That was impossible! She couldn't start all over again! She refused to!*

"That's just your head, and ego trying to convince you to stay where you are. Stay aware and present, Little One. You're capable of more than you realize. You're worth so much more – if you stop trying to control your quest, and just surrender to it. Just let yourself be – let your true Self birth itself. There's no way to stop this process. You can't 'start' something that you've never even attempted. Just the way that nothing can be lost, until it's founded in your truth.

She reacted immediately. "I gave my best to everything that I did!" she said, petulantly.

"There's nothing wrong with what you did" Glow said, reassuringly.

"Then what is this all about?" she cried, agonizingly. She believed that she'd made the right decisions – wherever possible. She was certain that she'd taken the time to consider as many options, as possible. And she didn't leave anything to chance. And yet, her life lessons had been hard – each, and every time. If karma was to blame, then she'd learnt over the years that hers was instantaneous. Her "payback" wasn't only similar to the misdeed but, it was magnified a hundred-fold! So she'd tried hard to focus on what she was doing – it kept her sane. And she'd tried to keep things simple. But, in her book simple, and chance didn't equate to the same thing. That was tantamount to inviting disaster! She didn't believe in luck - she made her own way. And she couldn't afford any wrong decisions. She only gave herself one chance – at anything.

"Perhaps that was part of the problem, Little One. You didn't leave much room for the Universe to step in, and help you" said Glow.

The Universe!? She already had a mind! What did she need the Universe for!? She'd toyed with the idea that there might be some form of Divine power but, she'd never taken it seriously. *And if there was something like that, then why did her life fall apart? Why was everything falling apart in the world? Why were the poor, and innocent always hit the hardest? If she'd made a string of mistakes by following the wrong path, then why did this "Universe" not stop her sooner? Why did she have to get to the pinnacle of her career, and then lose everything?* Whenever she needed help, she turned to herself. She was the only one she could rely on. Not that she didn't need the support but, she'd learnt a long time ago not to ask. If she was really desperate, she asked her father. Yes - the Universe was magical, and mysterious. But, that belonged to the realm of fairy tales. *And there was no place for "fairy tales" in her life!* Furthermore, pinning her hopes on it was irrational - she didn't have time for that in a world that demanded she develop her mind as her best weapon. She needed to know what she was capable of. And that was what she'd focused on. It gave her the kind of security that could only come from certainty. *Simple! There was no mystery there! Her mind had helped her to build a career, and a life. Right? How did the Universe even feature in all that?*

[Like you said, it's a 'mystery']

The strange voice out of nowhere, startled her. "Did you hear that? Who said that?" she asked Glow.

"Said what? I didn't hear a thing" said Glow, sending little balls of its halo shooting into the nothingness in an attempt to light up the blackness, and reveal the invisible intruder.

She looked around but, she saw nothing. She shook her head. She was certain that she heard something. She was talking to a Glow-wor......... she stopped herself. She'd better not call Glow any names. She knew how much that hurt. And she didn't want to hurt anyone or anything. And now, there was some other "Voice!" *An invisible one! She must be hallucinating!*

"A little bit control has its advantages, Little One. But, using it to shut your Self off from the Universe is a different matter. That's the soul-destroying part in all of this. Have you ever thought that being more open, and vulnerable could turn your life around? And that not controlling or preempting the path of your soul could take you exactly, where you need to be?" asked Glow.

She looked at Glow with a bemused expression.

"I've always been open. I've taken my fair share of chances" she exclaimed, vehemently.

"Only those 'chances' that fitted a pre-determined outcome. And after weighing up all the pros, and cons that supported that perfect image of yourself, and prevented you from seeing your true Self. Life's too big for that kind of small thinking. It might have served you well in the past but, it's not the real you" said Glow.

She was about to say something but, decided against it. Glow had a point. Based on her quest in the nothingness her life was a broken mess. She was a broken mess! There was nowhere to go. No one she could turn to. No future that she could even begin to think of. *She'd lost everything! So what could she possibly lose by allowing the Universe to intervene in her life?* It was pulling out all the stops to get her to see something – even if those "stops" amounted to no movement in the nothingness! She couldn't help wondering where, and how she'd gotten it all so wrong. She'd devoted everything that she knew, and owned - every bit of money; every ounce of energy to her work, and relationships. And despite that, she'd not amounted to anything! Nothing real, anyway. She sighed. *How was her truth going to help her overcome that!? What more could she do!?* It dawned on her that she'd seldom thought about the motivation behind her choices – she'd just extended herself beyond her physical limits to achieve her goals. Being a work-horse was in her blood. And yet, she'd failed to find fulfillment in her life! She was feeling slightly warmer. She glanced down at her body. Her aura was showing again! She looked at Glow, and smiled.

"Closer to my truth?" she asked.

Glow did a sparkly smile. "You're judging yourself again, Little One. There's nothing wrong with a mess - as long as it's real. And life can be very messy at times. But, that kind of 'mess' – arising from your soul lessons – will always be cleared during your lifetime. The mess caused by your ego, however, taints everything that it comes into contact with, and takes many lifetimes to fix. The old self you're familiar with might be broken but, your true Self is untouched by the experiences in your physical world. Nothing will ever be able to tarnish it. And there is nothing wrong with hard work. However, were you inspired to make your decisions or were you motivated by other factors? It's an easy way to figure out if your choices are aligned to your soul's truth. Anyone can achieve a level of success through hard work but, that offers little or no meaning, or fulfillment – only walking your soul path can offer you that. Sometimes people stumble across their life paths, although nothing synchronous happens without the support of your soul, and the Universe. More often than not, it will elude you, until you become aware of your true Self, and your soul purpose. This world exists for you to actualize that path as a human Being. Only then will you know the power behind your creation. But, it's not out there. It still exists within you."

She grimaced. *That was impossible! How was she supposed to find her way in this crazy world if she had to wait for synchronicity! She had to get things done - by any means! And that meant following the example or advice of others.* She sighed. *She had the power to create? What? What was the use of all these distinctions? She was just getting more, and more confused!*

"Perhaps you should just throw in the towel right now?" said Glow.

"You don't mean that! Not now! Not after everything that I've already been through. I'm in the middle of nowhere! With nothing! In any case, when I start something, I finish it. And this is not over" she said, scowling at Glow. She saw no reaction. Was Glow testing her commitment?

"Are you certain?" asked Glow, not in the least bit phased by her look. "Ok. Perhaps you were looking in all the wrong places, Little One? And thinking that you know all the answers can be very limiting. And Self-defeating" said Glow, throwing out sparkly breadcrumbs again.

"Where else am I supposed to look?" she asked with a challenging glint in her eye.

Glow's provocative comments were making her bristle. She was convinced that Glow had far greater knowledge about her quest than it was letting on. She wished that it would just spit it out.

"Within" said Glow simply.

"Within where? What?" she asked obtusely.

She wasn't expecting that answer. *Glow said the weirdest things. What kind of answer was that!?* And yet, she clung hungrily onto words drenched with honesty, and depth that had for so long eluded her. She didn't know if she accepted the truth in Glow's words or whether she'd been starved of it for so long that she was ready to believe anything. *Was she that desperate to find answers? Then again, she'd always been chasing some outcome or other, and that approach had gotten her nowhere! What difference will it make to her life if she just surrendered?* She sighed. *It was hopeless!* All she knew was that listening to Glow felt so good. And real. And the space they shared in the nothingness was the most cherished space that she'd ever known. It felt endless; timeless.

"Within yourself" said Glow patiently.

She bit her tongue to avoid making the first retort that came to mind. Glow was being its usual neutral self – not authoritative in the least. She was still in the nothingness. And yet, she felt caged in, and ready to explode. She entered her stillness, and observed the rage circling around it. Where was all that anger coming from? It dawned on her that her initial reaction stemmed from thinking that some form of authority was being imposed on her. She knew she had a problem with authority. In her own small way, she'd constantly fought against it, all her life. And even when circumstances forced her to remain silent, the justifications went on fiercely in her head for days on end. There was nothing more patronizing than the enforced dominion over human beings – in any way, shape or form! How could it be justified in a species with the highest intellect amongst all species – except, for dolphins!? And petty corporate politics aside, there were many more amenable ways to protect country borders if authorities changed their policies from restricting access, to supporting the basic human right for a better quality of life! Could all those resources not be more effectively utilized to uplift the very people who labor tirelessly to uphold the systems that keep them imprisoned psychologically, and physically? To protect who - the majority who had no part in bringing on the hate crimes against humanity, or the minority in positions of power who are ultimately responsible for the poor state of international relations? Ironically, the authorities are seldom around to face the fallout from their decisions; it's the majority who are exposed to the worst forms of suffering - century after century! How many "bad" people are there in the world, anyway!? Or are the voices of the majority kept in check by the threat of "terrorism." It might be a real but, terrorism is a "two-way street!" And more often than not, those "streets" are created at "home!" Are those systems geared towards treating people the way that they have been conditioned to behave or how they could behave if guided by their innate, soul-compasses? She sighed. What could the world be without such a prolific waste of its natural resources to uphold personal, and political agendas!? Far worse was the thought of so much human potential going to waste through carefully orchestrated propaganda, based on the manipulation of peoples' fears. *Where was this information coming from? She'd never had such thoughts before!* She frowned. *Why was it so damn difficult to figure this out? And she wasn't even doing anything!*

[This is the only real work you'll ever be called upon to do in your lifetime]

"There! Did you hear it? Did you say something?" She looked at Glow intently.

"No" said Glow. "It wasn't me." And an injured look spread across its wave-like face.

And then, the most amazing thing happened. A fireworks display......or ….a…..a….star-works display. Out of nowhere! In the nothingness! It was spectacular! She'd never seen anything like it. It started slowly;

small bursts of light in a single spot - like someone had lit a few sparklers. And then, it grew at incredible speed; exploding in every direction - shooting constellations of arrows; sparkly raindrops and giant, cascading mushrooms of multi-colored stars. She was surrounded by an avalanche of glittering, rainbow-colored lights in the most breathtaking display that she'd ever seen. Nothing she saw compared to this! She was entranced as she watched the magical sight unfolding in slow motion, right before her eyes - as if the conductor orchestrating the show was making certain that she didn't miss a single iota of wonder. And then, the entire display froze around her. A giant spectacle of light, and color in a trembling, soundless halo.

"Did you see that?" she asked. Turning to Glow, and pointing a wobbly finger in the direction of the spectacle that she'd just witnessed.

"Yes. Beautiful, isn't it. So like the Universe to throw us a surprise celebration. You must be making some progress, Little One." Glow chuckled, and tried to mimic the event on a smaller scale but, failed hopelessly. It collapsed into a million, tiny sparkles. It slowly gathered itself into a glowing mass again. And started emitting waves of colored lights.

"Progress?" In the nothingness? Sure! It was the first time that she'd seen Glow chuckling. It looked so funny – without a face, and body. It was just a mass of vibrating light! She couldn't help thinking that Glow looked like a fat, laughing Buddha. She smiled, as she again contemplated her strange, and wondrous journey. She gazed wistfully into the nothingness, and whispered: "why can't my life be as wonderful as that?" She shut her eyes, and willed the magic to return.

"What do you mean? Your will is of no use here, Little One. Wonder happens all the time. But, there are no repeating patterns. You need to stay awake if you want to experience it fully – just like walking your soul path" said Glow, cryptically.

"As a child I looked at the stars every night and wondered why they were up there, and I was down here" she said, softly.

She stopped, and muddled over something. Maybe "here" was "there." She frowned, and shook her head. *She was starting to sound like Glow! She better be careful! She didn't want to become a walking, talking supernova!*

"And then, life took over. I stopped looking at the stars. And I got lost - somewhere in it all. But, I have to admit that I was never inspired by my old way of life. And yet, something within me never stopped believing that there was more to life. When I look at the stars, the sky or nature in any form – including, human beings – I feel the same wonder; see the same beauty. Each person is a creator of something spectacular in this world – no matter how big or small the act. It could be an art form; a life; holding out a helping hand; a smile; an act of kindness – towards another or oneself. Even holding space in one's heart to allow for the full expression of the other is beautiful. There must be as many creations, as there are moments of inspiration in each individual's life. And yet, I never saw it. I didn't even stop to acknowledge it." She paused. She was breathing fast. And battling to contain something that was trying to burst forth from within. "But, that kind of creation is far more than the just the art or the act – it stems from the breath of life itself. It speaks to the untapped human potential – this hidden force – in every human Being. I'm in awe of all that that indomitable power can be molded into, right here on earth. That inner creative potential is true beauty. Being one with that force is the only thing that makes me feel truly worthy of a place under these stars. I aspire to create something from that space someday – to be one with the flow of life. I often wonder why I never did before. I worry constantly that I never will. And that fills me with dread! I can't imagine anything more fulfilling in this lifetime – in any lifetime. And then, I look at my world. And go back to my ordinary existence." She shifted uncomfortably, fully aware that she'd never expressed herself so freely before.

"But, as much as I try to find the extraordinary in my ordinary existence, the restlessness continues to rage within me. I've told myself many times that my life is an amazing gift; I shouldn't waste it on the mundane. Not that there's anything wrong with mundane or ordinary. I just wish I could understand this constant, tug-of-war inside me. I thought devoting my time to building a career would be enough. But, I now know that I was never happy doing that. I don't think I was ever happy, even though I tried to convince myself that I was. And now I'm happier than ever - floating about in nothingness! Embarking on an unknown quest! To nowhere! What does that make me? A con artist? A magician? A lunatic? A destroyer of my life? An explorer of…..of….. what? The unknown? Darkness? A seeker of my Self? A seeker of the light? Perhaps uncovering my truth, and finding my soul path will help me create something worthy of - on par with - the force that created me. It doesn't make sense to be created from all this - she cast her eyes around the nothingness - only to end up, buried in illusion! And I thought being buried under-ground was bad! The gap between what I feel inside me, and what I've been doing all these years is as wide as a……a….the Grand Canyon! I claim to love my life but, actually, I aspire to a very different kind of life. I don't know what that is. And that petrifies me! But, I feel it whenever I look at the stars, and the sky; I feel it throbbing within me. Perhaps that's why I haven't looked within. As you can see, it's all stars in there." She giggled, and pointed to her chest. "Just dreams." She spoke with a faraway, misty look in her eyes. "But, something feels different now. After all we've spoken about, I'm beginning to think that there might be more to me – more to this dream - than I realized. I might no longer be the person I thought I was but, that person – whoever she was – got me here. I feel immense gratitude towards her - she must have known more than I gave her credit for" she said, remorsefully.

"But, if you feel this way, why do you ignore it?" Glow asked.

"What else can I do!? I feel it – yes. I'm in awe every time, I'm moved by those feelings. They keep 'calling' to me in some strange language. I thought that I would figure it out, someday. But, someday has come, and gone. I still have to pay the bills!" she said defiantly. "What is the use of pursuing a pipe dream, anyway? How do I even begin to unravel its meaning when I don't understand what I'm supposed to do? Where do I start?" she asked forlornly.

"You have to start somewhere, Little One. At some point. Start now - right where you are…..right here. Start with what you have. But, you can't ignore your feelings, forever."

"I'm sitting in black space, with absolutely…….nothing! Nothing!" she retorted.

"Look again. It's way more than that. It's not about where you are or what you have. Or don't have, for that matter. Neither is it about what you can or can't see. It's about what you feel deep within you. That's your soul's 'voice.' To find what you're seeking, you must start looking beyond the obvious, and pay attention to your feelings. If you don't, you'll remain stuck in that vicious, cycle of illusion" said Glow.

She didn't understand Glow at all. Again she latched onto the comforting thoughts offered by her mind.

"But, what do I do with my old life? I do want to change it, and build the right kind of future for me. How do I do that? It feels as though I've been trying to change my life, forever! What do I have to do to create a new reality?" she demanded.

"The life you had wasn't yours, Little One. And you won't be able to access your future – the one lying dormant within you - without changing what your past made you believe about yourself. It might not look like it but, you've already started that process. But, to make progress, you need to consciously stop your mind from returning to the past or yearning for the 'future' that you thought you wanted. Both are only scenarios prompted by your ego-based fears. Focus instead, on acknowledging where you are, and who you are - right here; right now. It's not easy. But, the life you desire is already within your soul. Those feelings that move you so deeply are 'calling' out to you. But, you don't have to reach for anything outside of yourself. Neither are you required to do anything to make it happen – everything your soul desires is already yours. You just have to remove everything in your past that's not your truth – it's blocking you from it. There is no 'old' you or 'new' you – that separation is an illusion, because of your mind's association with events, and timelines. Wherever you find yourself in this Universe, there's only your true Self. You're the only 'event' happening across all space, and time. You'll only be able to see that when you stop resisting and struggling, and accept your soul's calling to be your true Self over the identity that exists in your mind. It's a lot to absorb – I know. But, again that stems from trying to understand everything. Remain in your stillness - there are no boundaries within. You already know what to do in your soul – trust your Self. Take each step slowly - one breath at a time. You have to feel your mind, and body becoming one with your soul. But, tell me more about your desire to be like the stars" Glow prompted.

"I don't know" she whispered, still battling to grasp what Glow was saying. "They've always been around; always been such a comfort to me. But, down there is the world I have to live in. That's where I can make things happen - it's what I know. The sky – the stars – that's just the background scenery. Nothing more." There was an edge in her voice.

"No, Little One. You do know. You've always known. You just have to remove all the barriers to get to your soul's knowing" said Glow, encouragingly.

Oh no! Her mind shouted. More unravelling! More questions! More confusion! She buried her face in her hands, and screamed. She only heard it in her mind.

"Hush, Little One. It's going to be ok. You know more than you realize. You know where you've been. You now know, what you don't want – even if it's everything about your past. But, you also know what you do want – that which comes from your soul, and truly inspires you. I know this intense. It can be easier, if you stop paying attention to your thoughts but, we can't exclude your mind or ego on this quest. Both are an important part of your inner transformation. But, remain focused on your stillness – just observe your thoughts, and emotions. Don't identify with them. I know how difficult that is but, you'll only be able to see your true reality, once you overcome your conditioning. And as unlikely as it seems, there is no better place than the nothingness to uncover your true Self before you can co-create the life you are worthy of" said Glow, reassuringly.

"Noooooooooooooooooo!!" she screamed. "I can't start all over again! How do I do that? There is no time" she shouted.

"You follow the one thing that you've been ignoring all your life" said Glow.

"What's that?" she demanded.

"The only thing that's as close to you as life itself" said Glow.

"My heart?" she asked incredulously.

[Yes]

That voice! Again! She looked around anxiously.

"What about my head? What role does that play? Maybe I would have been better off as a jellyfish" she said sarcastically. "If I'm supposed to follow my heart, what do I need a brain for?"

"Too much head and no heart, and you end up where you used to be - stuck in the illusion of your limited self. There is no contrary view - the love flowing through your heart is endless. But, paradoxically you need to uncover your truth with self-love before you can be open to all of life; everything that is real, beautiful and free. And equally, flawed and untamed. You need to feel the entire spectrum of your emotions with unconditional self-love in order to experience the human embodiment of your soul. Learning to love your Self as you uncover your truth is no easy mission but, the process will lead you to, not only your soul path but, your unlimited potential. Until you attain Self-love, every other kind of 'love' will merely be a reflection of your ego-self. But, coming back to your mind. There has to be harmony between all parts of you – body, mind, heart and soul co-exist in the same physical body for a reason. It takes all of you as an integrated whole to be one with your Being. It serves as a channel for the Divine to help you fulfill your specific purpose in this physical world. But, you were so distracted by your ego, and your illusory reality that you placed your physical self above your true Self. To become all that you are – to feel as one with this Divine Universe – you have to become one with your Self by owning your truth. There is only one way to achieve that - you need to trust your heart, and soul. Whatever you manifested in your physical world is such a small part of life – only a drop in the ocean of your Being. You're here to observe the unfolding of your soul purpose – not chase after your ego's whims." Again she could have sworn that Glow stuck out its tongue at her!

"Trust myself? Of course, I trust myself! How do you think I got this far?" she asked in exasperation. *How was she supposed to place her needs above those around her? That was selfish!*

"Trust in your heart and soul, Little One. Not yourself. Uncovering your true Self – which is a selfless act – requires you to rise above your selfish ego to irrefutably acknowledge your true Self. And that takes a different level of courage – sacrificing your ego-self to follow the truth that lies in your unknown soul. Divine Spirit can't communicate your soul's truth through your mind – only your open heart. And you got this far, by using your anger as your ally. If you did trust your Self, you wouldn't feel the need to control your life" Glow challenged.

She flinched. She couldn't think of a response. Besides, there was an unfamiliar ring to it. Truth! And there was no way of avoiding it in the nothingness. Her anger was her ally – a very close one. And she'd used it to fuel her ambitions. Her heart had never featured in anything that she did. She didn't think it existed for any purpose, other than to keep her alive. She shook her head remorsefully. Was there more to connecting with her heart than she realized? As for trusting her heart, and soul - could she? There was nothing to base that kind of trust on, other than blind faith! Was her controlling nature an indication of how little she trusted life, and her Self? And if her ego was in control all this time, could she even call that trust? Why did she have to know the outcome of everything before she even started? That wasn't the kind of trust required on this quest! No wonder she was floundering hopelessly! She'd always prided herself on knowing the end result of whatever she set out to do. "Begin with the end in mind" was another one of her favorite mantras. It was so well honed that she'd unconsciously adopted it when making decisions for her life. She assumed that everything worked in the same way, including the future that she'd mapped out for herself. She looked for patterns in everything that she did - they informed her decisions. And the predictability of a successful outcome gave her a sense of comfort, and security. It helped her to maintain her edge – to carve the niche that she wanted in her career. At least that was her belief, until it all come crashing down on her! She had a revelation. Other than providing a means for refining her variables on how to become successful, her belief had no real substance – certainly not, where life was concerned! It was based on a sense of false knowing driven by her ego, and it had provided nothing but, empty comfort! Her edge had misled her to believe that she was making progress but, all she'd done was hammer away at the 'tried, and trusted!' She'd never ventured beyond her comfort ones. What was she afraid of? Failure or success? Did she even have to bother with such distinctions, when following her soul path was synonymous with the only real success in life? She sighed sadly. She'd never considered her true Self, and its role in the reality she was creating. She'd always looked for patterns in her external world – never in her own behavior! And far from providing 'rhyme and reason' in her life, those patterns had only perpetuated the lie she was living! She was a master at trusting her comfort zones – not her Self! And it was that kind of behavior that had brought her to a dead end in her life!

She was distraught over her insights. And daunted by the implications. Surprisingly, she felt no inclination to fix any about her past. Instead, she felt something unusual - an impetus to let it all go. *How much was there?* She was now able to discern her inner knowing from the thoughts flashing through her mind. And it was "telling" her to ignore her thoughts, and remain in her stillness. She had another insight. For what it was worth her old self had served her well, although she didn't quite know how. *She'd lost her life's work, her status and her possessions!* Nonetheless, she was grateful for her mysterious, unknown soul path. Perhaps everything that had happened in her past was necessary to bring her to this exact point – suspended in nothingness with no plan, and nowhere to go! Ironically, the only gauge for her certainty was what she'd discovered within – her silent, stillness. Something that she would never have anticipated with all the foresight that she believed she possessed! Her grit might have helped her to cross many hurdles before. But that old, hard attitude now looked out of place on a quest where uncertainty was interspersed with growing self-love, and so much beauty, and gentleness. And a deep knowing that as much as she valued her past experiences, and the people she'd shared it with, it would have no place in the rest of her life's journey.

Despite her inner knowing, an image flashed across her mind. She was frantically running around, trying to find the exit in a huge existential maze. Her instincts were telling her that there was one but, no matter how hard she searched for it, her mind failed her. She picked up on feelings of being lost, and bewildered. Eventually, it dawned on her that she couldn't rely on her cleverness to find a way out of the nothingness. If anything, her mind was more of a hindrance than an ally. If she stopped "running" and closed her eyes to focus on the stillness within, the "walls" mysteriously disappeared, and she felt closer to her heart space. She realized that it might be more effective to use her feelings to navigate the many confusing avenues in her mind. Furthermore, she liked being in her stillness. It somehow reduced the anxiety to such an extent that she didn't feel that desperate urge to escape. More importantly, she could be in her stillness, and witness herself in that maze. There was no need to struggle with her thoughts to find the "door" to her freedom. That newfound perspective led to a more mystifying revelation. There was no freedom to be found in her mind! There would always be some "wall" or other! But, they didn't imprison her Being. To truly free herself, she would have to "remove" what only existed in her mind by transcending her limiting thoughts and beliefs, and her worst fears. She took a deep breath. *How was she supposed to do that!? The very nature of her mind would be her greatest obstacle! It wouldn't allow her to see her blind spots! And even if she could, her ego would refute them!* Contrary to her stifling thoughts, she now felt more inspired to persist with her quest. Her past might still exist in her mind but, it was no longer of any interest. This new life, however, intrigued her. It was as undefined as the nothingness itself – infinite, intangible; unknown. Without any structures, systems or boundaries. *And she was supposed to find what she was looking for, somewhere in that nothingness!* She felt her heart come alive with another star-burst of energy. She smiled. Her heart was trying to tell her something.

"And that is the power of your heart, Little One. As you come into your truth, and align with your soul purpose, your heart will continue to inspire you. It will help you to find what you're searching for. Your mind doesn't know what that is but, your heart, and soul do. Getting through this quest, however, is going to be a different kind of tough, compared to what you've experienced in your physical world. Those goals were challenging in their own right, and defined the direction of your life but, this quest has no known goal - other than to align your physical self with your soul purpose. There is no map; no specific milestones. No known direction. And no one to help you make your choices. You've learnt some valuable lessons from those you've met in the past. And you'll continue to meet many 'teachers' along your soul path for the remainder of your lifetime. But, you need to complete this quest on your own." Glow spoke with a quiet strength. It moved her deeply.

This was no fun at all!

"It's not meant to be fun, Little One" said Glow, softly.

"Will you help me?" she asked. Too afraid to hear the answer.

"I'll always help you, Little One. In whatever way I can" said Glow.

"How will I know if I'm doing the right thing?" she asked, close to tears again.

"You won't" said Glow matter-of-factly. "Just remain in your stillness, and stay present."

"What am I looking for in the nothingness? What is the aim of all this?" she asked.

"Only you know the answer to that, Little One. But, don't 'aim' for anything - just be in your stillness" said Glow.

"If I carry on with this……this….. quest, where will I be going?" she asked fearfully.

"Nowhere. And everywhere. But, this isn't about going somewhere or reaching some physical destination. This is about uncovering your truth; your Self. And becoming one with your soul purpose. That is essentially, the only 'destination' in life. It's not a physical location, anywhere in the Universe. Or in the nothingness. It's that 'space' within you - a sense of knowing – from whence all destinations become possible. You won't be going anywhere physically but, you'll be moving faster than you can imagine. When you 'arrive' at this inner space, you'll know" said Glow.

"But, what is this truth? What is 'becoming' all about? How do I reach this space if it's not something specific?" she asked. She was utterly, petrified.

"Only you know the answers, Little One. All I can tell you is, don't 'reach' for anything. Be one with the silent, stillness within. Whatever you're looking for will come to you. Your soul will recognize it, even though you've never seen it before" said Glow, with a gentle smile.

She tried hard to stop the tears that were threatening to fall. *This couldn't be happening to her! It was beyond all reason! Beyond anything that she wanted or expected! No actual destination!? No one to help her!? No way of telling right from wrong!? Not changing location but, still moving? She had no idea what her truth was or what her soul wanted and yet, she knew the answers! She'd never done anything like this before but, only she knew the way! How long was this transformation going to last? This whole saga was….. was….. incomprehensible! Impossible!*

"Nothing is impossible if you follow your heart, Little One. If you agree to continue with this quest, you'll meet many old 'friends' along the way" said Glow. "Pain. Doubt. Shame. Anguish. Despair. Resentment. Guilt. Abandonment. Fear, mostly. But, there will also be moments of indescribable beauty as you come into your own – as you uncover your truth, and find the Self-love that you've been searching for, all your life. Don't be too much in a hurry to understand your quest. You'll only go around in circles. Be aware of trying to preempt conclusions, and your repetitive thoughts – that's s a sure sign that your mind is falling back into its conditioned patterning. Keep returning to your stillness whenever you feel restless. It will help you stay present, irrespective of what is going on in your mind, and body. Don't force anything – that's just your ego trying to lead you astray. Follow your heart, and soul. They know where you're going." Glow's tone was gentle. But, it held a mixture of concern, and excitement.

Great! Just wonderful! More feelings!

"I've dealt with those emotions before. Why do I have to go through all that negative stuff again?" she demanded.

"You controlled pretty much everything in your physical life, including the extent to which you allowed yourself to feel your emotions. That misled you to believe that you were coping, and living your best life but, you were deluding yourself. Your 'coping' skills kept you trapped in your conditioning. You might have been able to build your past reality by pushing through some of those psychological barriers but, they still blocked you from expanding into your soul's reality. This quest is challenging all those barriers to free your soul. You don't know what that entails but, your intellect is not a prerequisite to completing this quest. You can continue holding onto the foolish belief that you don't know anything about it but, that's not your truth. Your soul knows the way – it has always known since the day you were born. However, you need to clear all the emotional blockages relating to your past before you can fully embark on your soul path. Each memory will draw you further into the emotions that you've been suppressing all these years. You'll be challenged to re-live those experiences – to love yourself through them, and uncover your truth. In the process you'll be healing, and releasing your true Self from the density of your old wounds – in this, and previous lifetimes." Glow spoke slowly. Carefully expounding the intensity of the process lying ahead of her.

"This is crazy! I can't do this. It's impossible! What if I fail?" she cried.

"No one who is committed to finding their truth will ever fail. This has nothing to do with what your mind wants. Your soul needs to free itself to express its truth. Your mind has no say in the matter" said Glow.

She dropped her head to hide her tears.

"What's my truth? How do I find it? How will I know it from everything else?" she said in a barely, audible voice. There was a huge lump in her throat.

"Only you know what your truth is, Little One. Only you know what it feels like. It has no form or shape – it's the 'sound' of your soul's voice in your silent, stillness" said Glow gently.

She felt more stuck than ever. Totally, bewildered. *There were still, no answers! And now she was expected to go on some roller-coaster quest to …… to…… where, exactly!?*

"You're not 'expected' to do anything, Little One. This quest about your truth. You can't begin by lying or deceiving yourself about the nature of it. Neither can there be any expectations about an outcome. There is only one way to transcend your discomfort - you have to subdue your will to the 'song' within your heart" said Glow.

"Why!?" she demanded.

"It's your soul's desire. You can surrender to its call or return to the life that you had. Without being conscious of it, you expressed your soul's truth for the very first time as a child, when you wrote that poem about life. You might remember the words but, you don't remember the emotion those words evoked within you. You were silent as you wrote but, you 'spoke' straight from your heart. Those words echoed across the entire Universe. And to this day, the energy of those words are still vibrating trough the Universe, even though you've forgotten all about that poem. You can try going back to the life you had but, it will be impossible to ignore your soul's truth – not with your new level of awareness. Besides, you're becoming aware of your true worth – you won't be able to accept anything less than your soul's desires. Your previous plans for your life were always in conflict with your truth. Your old reality had to dissolve to make way for your soul's reality.

That's why you now find yourself in the nothingness - there was no other way for your soul to get your attention. Getting to this point in your life didn't have to be so painful – if you'd listened to your inner voice. But, you didn't know what that was. Now, you're becoming more aware of it. It can't help you change anything about your past but, it can guide you through your healing process, and help you to actualize your soul purpose." explained Glow, patiently.

"And the Universe always give me what I ask for!" she challenged. *What did she write as a child to have elicited such a definitive response from the Universe? It had derailed all of her well-intentioned, plans!*

"Yes. Always. It's not just about the words, Little One. It's the truth, and emotion behind each word. In the moments that it took to write that poem, your soul expressed its desires through your heart – moments without time, and space. Only one such moment holds the power of the entire Universe behind it. During the time that it took you to finish your poem, you sparked the birthing of the reality within your soul. Despite everything that you've kept yourself busy with over the years, your higher Self has actually been busy 'chipping away' at your physical self to clear your soul's way. That's what brought you here to nothingness. It's the final chapter of your 'old book.' It's now time for a new book - your soul's story. The one where you bring your whole, new world into your physical reality" said Glow.

That went completely, over her head. She preferred massaging her bruised ego. *Damn! This was definitely not going the way she hoped.*

"Language, Little One! Language! Tsk….tsk… tsk. Not becoming of you. And no, this isn't meant to go according to any plan made with your mind. Only your soul's 'plan' is relevant now. And it will be heard – whether it's silent, whispered or screamed out loud. You know what that is, even though you haven't consciously acknowledged it." Glow did his wobbly, sparkly laugh again. "Whether you want to admit it or not, you've felt this for as long as you can remember. You just never believed or trusted your Self to pursue it. Your ego convinced your mind to write it off as nothing – so it could carry on with its own designs. And those turned out to be nothing more than a wild goose chase" said Glow.

Glow was speaking strangely again. It was too much. Her mind was blanking out. *Every time she thought she was grasping some angle of this quest, it was snatched from her!*

"Oh, and one more thing" Glow's words brought her out of her encroaching numbness. "There will be significant difference about this phase of your quest."

"What?" she snapped. She was desperate to lose herself in blissful slumber.

Glow carried on without even noticing the edge in her voice. She felt the old irritation at being ignored. *Glow certainly knew how to push her "buttons!"*

"Time doesn't operate here. You'll feel stuck but, you'll be making progress - you'll be processing information at the speed of light in your stillness' said Glow, smiling his sweet, no-smile. "I'm not ignoring you, Little One. I see, and hear everything in this space."

She burst into laughter. She was wide "awake" again.

"Time never stops! Now you're really messing with my head." She tapped her forefinger on her temple. "I still have one, you know."

"Nope. Am not!" said Glow, emphatically. A hurt expression spreading across its bright, haloed face. "Time doesn't exist here. It only exists in your physical world, because you attach meaning, and an illusory value to it. It's important for your healing process to surrender your will. It's of no use, anyway - you can't influence the timing or the outcome of this quest. You'll be traversing more than one dimension – at the same time. One with time, and one without. That said, things in your physical world will carry on as usual."

"Impossible!" she said, shaking her head. But, she couldn't keep the perplexed tone out of her voice. "How can everything carry on as usual, in my physical life when I'm not there? Someone is bound to notice my absence."

"People only see what they want to. You'll be there in body but, your soul will be 'travelling' through different dimensional realms - gaining access to the various energies required to bring about your full transformation. Your soul carries the necessary codes for this process but, it's a case of Divine timing as to when they get activated. No one will be the wiser for it. Including you, until the process is completed. Your physical presence will be enough to reassure those closest to you" said Glow. "When you've completed your transformation, your physical body will be free of your past – leaving space in your cellular memory to embody your soul's blueprint. Your mind won't have access to that knowing but, because its part of this transformation, it will be able to process the necessary information to help your higher Self manifest your soul's reality in your physical world" said Glow.

"I don't go back to my old life?" she asked, flabbergasted.

Glow chuckled. "You do, and you don't. It's all magic, Little One. When you finally uncover your truth, you'll feel like you've been reborn. You'll re-enter your physical world when you've completed your quest but, you'll feel like a totally, different person. And you will be – you'll be one with your Self and your soul purpose. Your old reality will exist but, only in memory. The only reality you'll be conscious of will be the one that your soul brings forth – the one where doing, and Being are one."

"But, what about my friends? My family? Will they vanish too?" she asked, incredulously.

This was unbelievable! But, she couldn't help thinking that if it were possible, it would be super-cool. *She could erase her entire past, and create a whole new life! Amazing! What a load of hog-wash! But, she was starting to enjoy this game. She better make the best of it - it was bound to be over soon. Nothing good, ever lasted! She would play along – just to see where it all ended up.*

Glow smiled its enigmatic smile.

"This is no game, Little One. Don't demean what can't be understood by your mind. This quest is the most truthful thing you've ever done. And the most real part of your life, so far. It's the only thing that will last beyond your lifetime."

She cringed with embarrassment. Glow was helping her in its own weird way. Game or not she couldn't deny that she was having the most real experience of her life. She didn't like what was going on but, then again, that was her ego talking. Far more important, was the way she was feeling. And she'd never felt more content.

"Right now, things are in a state of flux. And the nothingness is reflecting that transition between two realities – the past, and your truth. One has crumbled, and the other is in the process of being uncovered. You'll see things differently when your transformation is completed. You might look pretty the same but, your perspective on life will be very different. The impact on your physical body is intense but, there's no other way to align its density, to bring it into the same vibration as your soul - to fulfill its mission in your physical world. You don't understand what you're doing, and your isolation is only adding to your discomfort. That is as it should be. The isolation is essential to limit external distractions – to help you attune to your silent, inner voice. In due course, you'll 'return' to your physical world. At least, that's how it will be perceived by your mind. Everything in the Universe – including, your physical world - exists in a single moment of space, and time. It's all space – nothingness – irrespective of what you see with your mind. All matter is illusory – including your body. Everything is energy. And your soul can't be seen, because it's vibrating at a much higher speed. It can travel between dimensions – it can exist 'here' (in nothingness), and 'back there' (in your physical world) in the same moment of space, and time. And you can access that moment in your stillness. Anything is possible in that single, moment of pure presence."

"As you get closer to your truth, you'll become more present - you'll be able to remain in stillness for longer periods of time. The ultimate, is to be fully present in your stillness – in your physical world. Before you can attain that state, however, you have to transcend your physical density. In the process, everything that you're familiar with will change, including the nature of your relationships. Some will fall away, and new ones will form to reflect your truth as you move along your soul path. Many are awakening to their own soul truths. Those meant to be part of your soul's reality will join you on your life's journey. There's no need to go looking for your soul tribe – you'll meet when you're meant to. And your souls' will recognize each other. For now, each person has to go through their own transformation alone. This is a multi-being, multi-dimensional transformation - across time and space. And each individual is at a different stage of it. All these changes will happen quite naturally – courtesy of the true Self that you're uncovering. And the results of all this inner work will become visible in the physical dimension, over time" said Glow. Its halo was still, and brighter than she'd ever seen it. All she saw was white light. Glow continued.

"This quest will change everything that you're familiar with - from the inside out. And you won't have the luxury of using your mind to curate a personality for your true Self. Truth doesn't require one – it is what it is. You can't change your soul or the way it chooses to express itself, through your Self. You can only accept who you truly are. There's no way to negotiate your way around or out of this, to appease your mind. And there's only one way to ensure you complete it - you have to fully commit to the process with all your heart. There's no turning back. This quest will demand all of you. It will consume the old version of you to birth your true Self. Uncovering your truth to fulfill your soul path deserves nothing less – it allows you to come into Being. There's no logical explanation for any of this. Anytime your mind, and ego try to define the experience, it will delay your transformation - you'll remain in the nothingness, until you've fully surrendered to your soul. There's no one around, because no one can help you find the answers that lie in your soul. There are many voices in your head that can distract you, and exacerbate your confusion. But, there's only one voice that has any meaning – your soul. Right now, you're feeling very alone, and distraught. But, no one is going to come to your rescue. Only you can find your way to the 'other side' of that chasm within, by giving yourself what you need the most – what you never received before – love." Glow looked at her earnestly. "Will you allow this gift to unfold, Little One?"

"Is there a short cut?" she asked.

She couldn't believe that those words had come out of her mouth! She felt so stupid! But, she finally understood why that phrase had hit home so hard, when it was mentioned earlier. She was a master at finding quick solutions to challenges that she encountered in her physical world. She realized that she'd applied the same instant gratification principle to her life. But, there were no shortcuts to uncovering ones true Self. She might have made any number of choices in her physical life, and followed many avenues to find success but, she couldn't force her soul to go in any direction - other than the one that was intended for her. Her soul was in tune with a set of Universal laws - whether she believed in them or not. And by consciously bringing her soul purpose into her physical world she would be aligning both her physical, and spiritual worlds. And be able to maintain her inner state of harmony with those laws. If not, then her physical life would continue to be a series of "mishaps" and "failures," until she accepted that irrefutable truth! She realized that she could no longer ignore her soul desires - not if the amount of suffering that she'd already experienced in her life was anything to go by! She was now getting the equivalent of a proverbial "kick in the butt"- albeit a Divine one! She closed her eyes, and bowed to the nothingness. It was her first conscious acknowledgement to a Universe that she'd never really seen before. Only felt.

Her eyes opened wide as the reality of her situation hit home. *How was she going to do this? Who was going to help her? She didn't understand any of it!* Trusting in the Divine to guide her along her quest was one thing. *How was she supposed to trust her own mind her when she now knew that it had led her astray!?* But, everything Glow said resonated with her more than anything in her entire life! She'd always gravitated towards the unknown. And she'd indulged it to some extent with her weird behavior as a child. She was often called "crazy," because of it. There was a time when that word had bothered her. But, she'd outgrown the stigma attached to it when she realized that life required some craziness if she was to survive. Maybe it was that very attitude that had prepared her for this quest. *She was being crazy - throwing every last bit of caution to the wind to follow this thing called a soul path! She'd already lost everything that she owned. And now, she was in the process of losing her identity!*

[Overcoming what you mind believes to be true is the hardest part of this quest]

That Voice again! She glanced around, and stared intently into the nothingness. There was no one around. She sighed. *Every time she thought she was getting the hang of this quest, everything shifted! And she found herself being towed mercilessly along some invisible route in the nothingness!* Perhaps that was for the better. If she even so much as got a whiff of what was going on, she would lose all interest. Whoever or whatever was behind this plan, knew her well. *Far too well! Better than she knew her Self!* As disconcerting as that was, she couldn't shake the feeling that she was exactly, where she needed to be. If only she could use her mind to help her. *It was utterly confounding to behave counter-intuitively – she felt like a ship without a rudder! And as much as she appreciated having Glow by her side, she still knew absolutely, nothing!* They were both figuring things out, as her quest unfolded. She burst into laughter. For the longest time, she'd believed that she knew everything there was to know about herself. And there she was, being confronted by her unknown Self, and an unknown soul path! Her usual senses were still functioning but, they had faded into the background. She was far more aware of the "information" coming from around, and within her. Furthermore, she was very much aware of the changes – some subtle; others not - in her thinking, beliefs and perspectives. *And now she was going to continue with her quest! What changes would that bring to her life? Was that "taking a leap of faith?" A leap from the familiar in her physical world to something that she couldn't even begin to comprehend!? Informed by no formal knowledge or plan. With no reward or recognition; no title. No companionship or guidance. How could she possibly even think about doing something so ludicrous!? If her past life was a "wild goose chase," then this quest was a trip to La-la land!* She groaned loudly. *Why her? Why now?* There was no one around to help her.

[You have your Self]

Herself!? Whoever she was, was being torn to shreds! She didn't even know who she was anymore!

[Not yourself. Your Self. You do - more than your mind will allow you to admit. You just have to trust and believe in what, and who you truly are – even though you've not as yet, met your true Self]

Trust, and believe – in her true Self? She realized that she'd never questioned whether she trusted herself in her physical world - she just got on with whatever she needed to do. *That must have entailed some level of trust! Surely!* Then again, she'd also had the benefit of visible, tangible results. *But, trusting her Self to go on with this quest? How could she trust her Self to embark on a truth-finding mission to nowhere!? That equation had two unknowns! She couldn't solve that! How could she believe in something that she'd never done before? She was the one who'd driven herself into a dead-end, in the first place! How could she embark on the rest of this quest with nothing but, an old self that she no longer trusted or this new Self that supposedly, resided within her!? She would probably make the same mistakes, and end up right back where she started!*

[All of you is not defined by what you do. Your Being is much more than anything you do in this physical dimension. You're no longer the person you used to be – that was only a very small part of you. You're still discovering your true Self but, nothing stops you from continuing with your quest to uncover your truth. Who you were, and who you're becoming already exist within you. You'll meet more of your Self as you show up to complete each step of your quest]

That made no sense at all! How could she continue something like this, when she didn't know her Self? How could she trust this Self when she had no clue who she was becoming or what she needed to do to get there? Who should she believe in? She couldn't rely on her old self, and she didn't know her true Self! How could she trust, and believe in someone that she'd never met - even if that was her real Self!?

[Your mind has no knowledge of your true Self but, your soul does. You just have to trust, and believe in your soul knowing]

As much as her mind revolted against everything she just heard, she couldn't deny that she now felt a distinct connection with some part of her – a part that she didn't even know existed. A part that felt much bigger than the person she remembered herself to be. It was silently beckoning to her in the stillness within. For some strange reason her heart was throbbing fiercely, and she was convinced that she could "hear" a beautiful symphony playing all around her but, there was no actual sound. She was aware that her mind was silent – totally, removed from what was unfolding within her.

[That is as it should be]

She was too overwhelmed by what was going on within to pay much attention to Voice. She didn't know what she was feeling. All she knew was that she'd made a commitment to uncover her truth. She'd never done anything in half measure, and she wasn't about to start now! Besides, her new level of awareness made any form of compromise unthinkable. The only person to be affected, would be her Self. And that was a price she wasn't prepared to pay. She was done with compromising! This quest was about giving her all - nothing less was acceptable. In any case, she couldn't move forward if she compromised – the next step on her quest wouldn't reveal itself. She sighed. Only one thing was certain – her deep, unbidden desire to continue with her quest. She was done with her old way of life, and second-guessing herself! She would have to learn to trust, and believe in her Self along the way. She will commit to completing her quest.

"Yes. I'll do it" she heard her heart silently, whisper into the nothingness. "I'll do whatever it takes. I'll continue with my quest - no matter where it takes me. No matter how long it takes. I'll uncover my truth, and fulfill my soul path."

She "heard" her words spoken slowly. Intently. She felt the gravity of each one. And heard them echo across the nothingness. She was petrified. Completely, intimidated. And yet, she couldn't ignore the magical feeling somewhere deep within. It was so real. So true. She felt the innocent anticipation of all that awaited her in the unknown. She'd never felt so alive in her entire life! And for a long while after her silent, heart-whispering she saw her aura glowing brightly. She felt warmer. Happier. Totally safe, in the tornado of uncertainty that raged within her. Surrounded by nothing other than, a Universe of silent, stillness – within, and without. She was glad for the silence. There was so much that she couldn't quite fathom but, instead of shying away from the feeling, she somehow instinctively knew that she needed to lean into her vulnerability - if she intended to open herself to this phenomenon called life. Whatever she was listening out for or hoping to find, lay within her. She felt the gentle vibration in her chest grow steadily stronger, until it spread across her whole body in waves. She looked down at her chest. An image of her defenseless heart came to mind, and she felt drawn to its pulsating softness. How could something so small, and fragile continue to feed her the essence of life – for an entire lifetime? She couldn't begin to contemplate such commitment, and endurance. Such power. And she was now going to follow her heart's silent, song into the unknown - to learn all that she needed to know about her true Self. *Where would it lead her?* Strangely not knowing, no longer unsettled her. She said a silent "thank you" to her heart's soulful melody; for having stuck with her through her ignorant, and foolish bravado. She felt humbled by its commitment, and strengthened by its presence. She felt immensely grateful, although gratitude failed to describe or contain all the emotion bursting forth within her. And yet, no further acknowledgement was necessary - gratitude was enough. With it, each heartbeat became louder, and stronger - bouncing of every fiber of her body, and echoing through the nothingness. Each heartbeat holding her in a moment of timeless wonder as it stood suspended in stillness. She took a deep breath, mesmerized by the feeling. She would never again, forget to listen for its silent song. Its beautiful melody was her only guide through the darkness that lay ahead. She stopped as another thought entered her mind. *She could either be on the biggest fool's errand or on the most real, experience of her lifetime!* Either way, there was no turning back.

CHAPTER 7

THE GILDED CARRIAGE

When she looked up again, Glow was nowhere to be seen. She was all alone with the stars. She started crying. She wasn't sad – just very confused. And she felt a poignant loss for the life that had been hers. Despite her recent revelations, and good intentions to stick with her quest she realized that the doubt had somehow crept back in. *Was there some way she could return to her old way of life? Perhaps she could defer this soul journey to another time. There was no reason to turn her life upside down, right now!* She caught her trend of thought, and stopped. Why did she want to go back, anyway? She frowned as she was once again, gripped by annoyance. *Why was it so difficult to make up her mind? Besides being uncomfortable this constant see-sawing between thought, and emotion was out of character! Was the discomfort related to wanting her old way of life back or her failure to figure out a new future in the nothingness? Whatever it was this never-ending, stuck feeling was infuriating! She needed to get her life back on track!* And yet, despite her best efforts to force some kind of shift in the nothingness, she remained rooted to the same spot.

She shifted her thoughts to the many times that she'd capitalized on her decisiveness. She was always on the move – making things happen in her life. *And now, not only was she imprisoned in the nothingness but, she seemed to be in the middle of an existential crisis! She could no longer relate to the person that she used to be, and neither could she figure out who she was becoming! And it all seemed to be centered on what she needed! She didn't know! She just went after whatever she set her mind on!* As difficult as it was to acknowledge, she couldn't overcome the strong feeling that she'd wasted her time playing ego games, and complicating her life. Maybe her needs were a lot simpler than she expected. Maybe she would be able to enjoy life much more without the false expectations created by her conditioning. She sighed. Who was she? She couldn't tell what she wanted - let alone needed! *If she persisted with this quest would she have any control over the new direction of her life? Why did she feel so helpless? So powerless? Why did she find it so impossible to do something? Anything!* She burst into tears when her mind refused to provide any answers. All she could do was sit in silence with her feelings of loss, and overwhelming grief.

With her mind in a fog, and without her anger to spur her on, she was buried in indecision. *Perhaps someone or something will come along to rescue her. Maybe they will tell her what to do to get moving again.* She waited with every ounce of patience she could muster. During that time, the rebel in her was tempted to find some way to force her way out of the nothingness. She still felt that urge to run but, a part of her stood steadfast under the banner of her earlier commitment. And instinct was warning her that it would be the wrong move. It was also feeding a heightened level of foresight. If she was going to get anywhere on this quest, she needed to be patient. A "path" would only emerge from the experience that she was trying to escape from! As confounding as that was, it made perfect sense in the nothingness. With that acknowledgement her breathing slowed and deepened dramatically, and she felt herself becoming more open to her stillness. Even though it was such an imperceptible process, she couldn't help thinking that her physicality was slowly being taken over by this silent, inner space. She turned to look at the stars again, and bowed her head in reverence. Her ever faithful companions. She sighed. She wasn't completely alone. She sat still. Watching. Waiting. Only to become aware of her mind finding the perfect loophole in her uneasiness. *What was she doing? How could she have embarked on a quest without any knowledge of it? Glow knew something. It was lying to her! And leading her on, by exploiting her vulnerability! How else could Glow convince her to go on this mindless, expedition to nowhere!? How could she be so gullible to fall for this hogwash? There must be someone in this hell-hole she could talk to!* She looked around. *Where was everyone!?*

[This quest is with yourself - by yourself. No one can convince your soul to do anything that is not intended for your highest interests. Playing the victim when you're feeling lost, and weak won't help that stuck feeling]

She looked around to locate that Voice. There was no one to be seen.

"Who are you? Why are you hiding? Come on out!" she demanded.

There was no answer. No one showed. *She must be hearing things!* She shrugged her shoulders. Compared to this weird quest her life actually, looked quite good. *Why did she think that life was hard?* Or did she make things difficult for herself? *Did her conditioning make her believe that things could only be a certain way? Did it also make her believe that she shouldn't expect much from life?* And yet, she'd worn herself out pursuing many avenues to find success. At the time, she believed that she was making the right decision. Those choices now looked random. And fruitless. And her paradoxical behavior was baffling. She realized that she'd wasted a lot of time looking to the outside world for her answers. It would have been far better to have spent that time working on her Self! Why did she forego her own needs to satisfy the demands of others? Did the fear of rejection play on her mind? Was she pandering to the opinions of others? Was she uncomfortable being with her Self? And if her Self, and Being were connected did that discomfort prevent her from being fully present? She realized that if she wasn't mulling over some problem or other, then she was fixating on some arbitrary point in the "future" when life would be free of problems, and stress. Was that what Glow meant, when it spoke of "reaching for the future?" Building scenarios for a future was no better than the tactics she'd deployed to escape her past! And she'd never stopped to appreciate any of it! She was overcome by regret. She should have been more grateful for the many blessings that were bestowed on her in the past. She sighed. Her lack of awareness had impacted her life in more ways than she realized. Besides being a major factor contributing to her unconscious behavior, she'd suppressed her emotions and only compounded her insecurities, and fears. And that had certainly not helped anything! Far from making them disappear, they were only pushed out of sight. And now, they were back with a vengeance!

She hung her head, and tried hard to hold back the tears. Searching for answers about life was by no means, something new. She recalled her thirst for knowledge, and the multitude of books that she'd read on various subjects. She was certainly none the wiser for it! And then she was struck by a startling revelation. She only had a conceptual level of understanding of the life lessons gleaned from her readings. There was little or no application in her life, either through lack of time or no understanding of the dynamic between body, mind and soul. Did she opt for the easy way out by sticking to her comfort zones? That approach had only left her slumbering in a false reality! But, that didn't fully resonate with her. The reasons for her life choices now looked a lot like excuses. And weak ones, at that. She was more surprised when she realized that she no longer cared so much about her past actions. All she knew with certainty was that she could no longer avoid unpacking the conditioning that had dictated her life, for so long. The full extent of the mission ahead of her slowly dawned on her. *Where did she even begin to unravel such a convoluted maze?* She smiled wryly, at the first thought that entered her mind. *She wished there was a shortcut.* But, she now had knowing on her side. It strengthened her resolve to stick with the process that was unfolding in the nothingness. Besides, there was nowhere to run; nowhere to hide. She'd come face-to-face, with her Self!

She believed that she knew how the world worked. There were certain "rules," and she'd become familiar with them, early in life. The main one - comply with the structures in place, and be accepted or reject the social codes at one's own peril. She grudgingly accepted that compromise was sometimes necessary, although she struggled to comply with those invisible boundaries. To make matters worse, she could never tell who or what she was dealing with, and felt compelled to be constantly on guard. Why did that have such a familiar ring to it? Occasionally, she rebelled in small ways against the "unknown forces" that kept her in check. Another insight flashed through her mind. She was surprised to learn that she felt a sense of satisfaction, whenever she did manage to escape from the clutches of a world that seemed hell-bent on turning her into something that she had no intention of becoming. However, such moments were short-lived, and exacted a high "price." She realized that she'd compromised to such an extent that the only means of "escape" was forfeiting the few social filters that she possessed. Needless to say, bridges were burned in relationships. The flip side of that coin was equally traumatic. Such episodes were always followed by extreme remorse. Over the years, she'd worked on modifying her behavior towards difficult people, and situations. And sometimes, the only "solution" was remaining silent. However, the feeling of being torn between her natural inclinations to challenge the status quo, and sacrificing something invisible that stemmed from her very soul when she didn't, persisted. Furthermore, the feelings of entrapment, and disempowerment that ensued resulted in extreme resentment over the social expectations to compromise herself. So much so, that she often preferred a form of self-imposed exile from the ongoing rigmarole of the social "storm." She was hit by an unnerving, revelation. There was no storm out there! It was somewhere, inside of her!

Far more visible, and closer to home were the "norms" of her restrictive culture. Her personal "favorite" – the widespread expectation that she submit to her "rightful" place in the gender hierarchy! Over the years, many legal changes have elevated the status of women. And she had to acknowledge that women were spearheading worthwhile changes in various fields - demonstrating their fortitude, capability, and creativity. However, behind many closed doors gender biases, and double standards remain embedded in the implicit nature of the cultural, and social fabric that gave rise to such restrictive norms, centuries ago! There was a time in her life when she couldn't decide between the lesser of two evils – her culture or career. She realized something that had never occurred to her before. Her career had triumphed in this inner conflict. Not because she particularly enjoyed it, as she'd believed for years but, for the outlet it provided to "escape" the cultural noose around her neck! However, they were the same in principle, despite superficial differences. She'd never concerned herself with those differences. She was too busy building her career – as a means of escaping from it all! But, she now realized that her decision process was flawed. It was underpinned by two incorrect assumptions. Firstly, that she would achieve the success she desired if she modified her behavior to suit the expectations of others - even if it meant compromising her truth! And secondly, that success in her career guaranteed her a happy and equally, successful life! She sighed. The only thing that she'd guaranteed was becoming further indoctrinated by the "norms" of an illusory world, and losing herself in the ever-confounding maze of expectations, to build a life that she felt no connection with! It was staring her in the face, all this time! How could she miss something like that!? As much as she hated to admit it, she was forced to acknowledge that she'd fallen for the "glitz and glamor" of her external world. That was the easy part. Far more difficult were the decisions that she saw looming on the horizon. Did she still want to continue playing a role in maintaining such a way of life? Did she have a solution to fight the scale of cultural and social injustices that were still running rampant in the world, and destroying lives? She sighed heavily. She'd voiced her disgruntlement over any kind of injustice, more than once. And she'd thrown down the gauntlet, and destroyed relationships in her efforts to rise above it. Including fighting those that stood in her way of claiming the life that she wanted. But, she hadn't counted on a fight that she never saw coming. One with herself - for compromising her soul purpose!

She could now clearly see, how she'd forced herself to accept the "bitter pill" she had to swallow by persisting with her ego-led life, at the expense of her truth. Furthermore, as hard as she tried to focus on building the life that she wanted, she'd suppressed another dilemma - her growing dissatisfaction over the gap between the way things were in her world, and the way that they could be. She realized that the inner conflict of fitting in with those norms, and stomaching the separation that her behavior generated was overshadowed by a more fundamental discomfort that she'd been unaware of – she didn't feel like she belonged in the world that she'd been born into! It struck her that she'd never truly belonged – anywhere! Her life experiences had made her very self-reliant, and that had no doubt, contributed to her independent attitude. But, independence didn't equate to belonging. Where did she belong? Why would she sacrifice her truth to belong? She sighed. *Where was she going with all these questions!? What did it matter anyway? She'd done her best with what she had.*

[Did you? Or did you fall into the trap of living life according to your preconceived notions?]

That Voice again! She was convinced that Glow was playing games with her. *She wasn't in the mood for such nonsense! What preconceptions!? She had none.*

[None that you'll admit to]

No! She had none! She'd always made a point of making her own decisions! And she believed her life was in her own hands. She also considered herself to be objective – a trait that she found very useful. She'd used it as the overriding benchmark to ensure that she made the right decision, for all concerned. Did she – if she was prone to allowing the opinions of others to influence her decisions? Did she make the right decisions for herself?

[Your life is in your own hands but, so far, you haven't grasped the full meaning of that. Do you understand what led you to make your decisions in the past? Do you know how you ended up here?]

How could her life be so far from where she wanted it to be - if she'd made her own decisions!? Where did she go wrong? Did her choices have any merit, if all she'd done was spin around the proverbial hamster wheel, repeating the same experiences!? What were her choices motivated by? What had prevented her from seeing the repetitive patterns in her life? Was it her ambitious nature? Fear? Ego? Her conditioning? Was it arrogance that prevented her from admitting to her blind spots? Why else would she stick to the wrong path!?

[There was no 'right' or 'wrong' decision. Every experience in your life has played a role in the evolution of your consciousness. But, it sounds as though you were lulled to sleep by an age-old illusion - feeling the life your soul yearns for but, allowing yourself to become a prisoner of social dogma in your physical world. You were so busy trying to appease your fears by meeting the demands on your time that you never stopped to consider your behavior or the impact of your decisions on the reality you were building. But, the biggest travesty in all this time is that you never stopped to honor your soul's needs]

She shook her head in despair. *Another dead end!* She felt her annoyance escalating in the face of that truth, and her tears started all over again. She'd never stopped to consider her own needs in her attempts to win the frantic race defined by origins, lost in human translation! The impact of that realization hit her hard. *What was going on with her? Why was she thinking about such things? Since time immemorial, people had been asking similar questions. If there were any answers, it would be common knowledge by now!* Perhaps the answer lay hidden somewhere in the mountains of literature that existed all over the world. But, even if it was possible to get through all of it in her lifetime, where would that leave her? At best, she would gain some understanding from an array of learned sources to guide her along this path called life but, she would never know the truth – her truth. At worst, she could spend her lifetime seeking answers, and still come up empty handed! Either way, she would remain lost in an existential wilderness at the end of her mission! Maybe that was the reason for her being in the nothingness – to find her own answers –her own meaning to life. Perhaps this quest was the "answer" to her biggest dilemma in life - who was her true Self? Her previous approach was to equip herself with as many tools as possible, by pursuing a formal education. That was her truth. It had helped in many ways to support her, and her extended family. It had helped to build the life that she wanted. And now, she no longer wanted that kind of life! *Could she do that? Could she suddenly decide to stop wanting what she'd always wanted? Could she change to such an extent?* Then again, that was only different relative to her old way of doing things. Maybe this quest was transforming her to live the life her soul desired – the way she was always meant to live it.

[Nothing happens quite as suddenly, as you think. You're always changing; always in the process of becoming the Being that you are – whether you're aware of it or not. Any changes that don't allow for the expansion into your soul's truth is nothing but, an illusion]

She sighed. *Would she ever understand any of this? She never wanted things to stay the same! What was Voice going on about!* In her confusion, she felt as though she was trapped in a volcano of thought, and emotion that was going to blow her apart at any second! She was trying her best to be patient by reminding herself of Glow's earlier words: "Understanding would come eventually, as hindsight." But, she was now floundering helplessly, and overwhelmed by a desperate sense of loss. She found it difficult to concentrate in that emotional warzone. In the midst of it all, she was aware of some hidden force propelling her along her mysterious quest. As subtle as it was, it was noticeable enough for her to pause, and shift her attention inwards. She realized that as the observer, she could maintain her detachment but, she was still aware of the practically, indiscernible momentum carrying her towards some unknown, destination. If she stopped to dwell too long on a particular thought, she stalled on invisible tracks. She groaned. *Was she going to make it through this quest? How long was it going to take?* She felt as though she was on a never-ending road, to nowhere! There was nothing as futile as churning over old memories, and behavioral patterns! Besides, whenever she'd reflected on her past, it made her feel strange. She got edgy, and couldn't breathe. She'd never gone past that point. Now for the first time, she found herself sitting in the stillness, and consciously giving herself permission to enter that uncomfortable feeling. It slowly came to her. And she shuddered as her awareness made the reason for her discomfort crystal clear. She wasn't living her truth! She was living a life diluted by the truths of others! She was astounded by the paradox between her inner knowing, and her false reality! And just how easily, she'd been duped by her ego's duplicitous nature! Besides being her biggest accomplice in ignoring her behavior, it had used busyness to misguide her into believing that she was succeeding in life. How could she fall for something like that? There was no substance to that kind of thinking! Did her conditioning give rise to such preconceptions? How could she get beyond that, to living her soul's truth? How did she align her mind to her soul? If her discomfort signaled nonalignment with her truth, then what did alignment feel like? And there she was, thinking that she'd been living her best life! All this time, she'd been caught up in dogma.

As she pondered this latest revelation, she was startled by another. There was missing an important distinction. The focus of her quest wasn't whether or not, she'd done her best. It was about whether she was Being her best! And she didn't even know what that entailed! Everything that she'd learnt so far, pointed to her being more than just mind, and body. She embodied the essence of life; she had a soul. She was part of an infinite, Universe. And her soul had a specific purpose - as opposed to blindly following her obsessed-with-doing, ego-self. What did it take to align with that soul purpose, and be the best version of her Self? If her old self was caught up in past conditioning, could she dismantle those patterns, and uncover her truth? She recalled her earlier conversations with Glow. It stressed that she wasn't defined by her past. She sighed, heavily. Why then, did it weigh so heavily on her? Why was she finding it so impossible to move beyond it? Why did she keep returning to her childhood? How far back did she have to go to break this impasse?

Her anxiety, and frustration did little to stop memories of her parents from bombarding her. They were traditional, hardworking people. Despite tough circumstances, they had done their best to provide for a very large family. For many years, there was a single bread-winner - her father.

Everyone went about their lives like worker ants. There was no time for idle chit-chat. And no emotion was expressed, other than pent-up anger when stress levels reached breaking point. Only religious occasions were celebrated. Besides there being no money for anything as frivolous as birthdays, she realized that it would have been extremely difficult for family members to express some form of light-heartedness when anger was the only mode of communication. Needless to say, there was little or no warmth shared amongst them, and there was never any mention of love. It was encapsulated in what they did. She realized that the overriding atmosphere in her childhood home was laden with tension from the daily grind of survival. In that context, it was no longer incomprehensible that her attempts at living life were, either met with anger or went un-noticed. Notwithstanding that, as an adult she went after the kind of life that she wanted with dogged persistence. She believed whole-heartedly, that she was creating a better life for herself. It came as a startling revelation that her adult life had merely reflected her family's work ethic. Furthermore, her own home had the same emotional undertones as her childhood environment. How did she miss something so obvious!? Where was her attention directed during those years? She might have consciously believed that she was doing something constructive. Unconsciously, however, she was repeating behavioral patterns that had been prevalent since childhood! To her logical mind, everything looked fine, and quite normal but, it was now painfully obvious that she'd been stuck in an impasse all her life! She sighed, despondently. *She was so certain that she'd "ticked all the boxes." Where and how, did she get it so wrong?*

[Life is way more than "ticking boxes." You can't surpass your mind's conditioning – irrespective of the level of your intellect. Neither can you suppress your soul purpose by forcing yourself to do something you have no desire of doing. Especially not, if your soul desires to live life, fully alive. The depth of passion that you feel about certain things is a reflection of what truly inspires you. It's also an indication of where your full potential lies. Do anything less than that and you compromise your true Self, and your soul path. You'll always feel as though something is missing in your life. But, if you continue looking outside of yourself for it, you'll never find it]

She couldn't deny that she now wanted to live life, fully alive. She wanted to feel its essence; feel as one with the same vibrant force that created it. And yet, despite all her efforts to get closer to that feeling it had always eluded her. It struck her that nothing she'd done was capable of filling the bottomless void within her. Was she looking in the wrong places? Did she only grasp at straws all her life? How many times did she compromise her Self by being unaware? Was that the reason she'd fallen for an illusion time, and time again? Was that why she felt so empty - to her very soul? She'd devoted so much time to her career thinking it would make her successful but, deep down, she'd always hungered for something more. And the black void was still there - she felt far from whole! As difficult as it was to admit, she had to acknowledge that all her "boxes" carried the same label - "Success." As important as it was that constricted view brought no depth to her life! Furthermore, she'd assumed that if it made others successful, and happy then it would do the same for her. But, she felt far from successful or happy! Far more daunting was the realization that she no longer cared about that kind of success. Or if it meant fitting in or not. She just wanted to be happy; free to express her Self. It was the only yardstick by which she could measure her life. And the only means whereby she could overcome the longest hurdle in her life's marathon – a constant sense of emptiness, and lack. Again, she was struck by the familiar ring to that sentiment. It echoed all the way back to her childhood. Why did she keep going back to her childhood? Could it have such a huge impact on her reality by blinding her to her truth? Was that the reason she'd never surpassed the limitations of her conditioning, irrespective of how hard she tried? *Was her conditioning associated with her culture? Her social class? Did it mean she would never rise above hers? Were some people "better" or "higher up" by virtue of their family origins or their "blood?"* Did that make their lives more valuable than hers? She sighed. Only one thing was certain. For all her independence, she'd been blind to one critical fact. She'd failed to recognize the behavioral patterns perpetuated by her conditioning, and had merely repeated her childhood experiences. Sadly that had informed the full extent of the "open" mind that she'd used to make the so-called, "right" choices in her life.

[True]

She was startled by the effect that single word had on her. It diluted any reaction that she could think of. Instead, she became fixated on the illusion that she'd referred to as "life." She realized that it was nothing more than a house of cards – with no foundation; no substance. Was that why it had all come crashing down?

[Yes]

If a career wasn't the answer to making her life a success, what was?

[You're not defined by what you do. Neither are you defined by your thoughts, emotions, behavior or your blood. The blood that runs through your veins is the same for everyone]

What defined her, then? She was prepared to do anything to fix this – to make things right! More than anything, she now wanted to change her false reality. Where did she begin?

[There's nothing to fix. Despite your childhood experiences, your soul has a far greater say in the outcome of your life. You just have to heal your past by clearing what no longer serves you – so that you're free to walk your soul path. For as long as you're weighed down by your past, you won't be able to recognize your true Self. The only way to see your truth is to clear away the fall-out from the life that you've led - all the way down to the trenches]

She was horrified. *She was twenty-five years old! She already had a life! She couldn't just discard it!*

[Age has nothing to do with fulfilling your soul path. If you choose to live the life that your soul desires, then you can change it - at any time. You're not meant to "discard" the life that you had. All your past experiences are energetic expressions of you. Those energies will remain in the Universe - in that state - until you heal yourself. You can transform the negative karma imprinted on your persona by bringing it into the light of your consciousness. By doing so, you'll be able to access more of your awareness. Your awareness isn't something that you need to strive to make happen. You're awareness itself. As you release what no longer serves you, you'll create more space for your awareness in your physical body. You can change your life - by rooting out the thinking behind your patterns of behavior. Your soul will create new patterns of thought as your transformation progresses. And being aware of yourself as an awakening soul will ensure that you refrain from falling into your old patterns of thinking. You used those patterns to build a life that you perceived to be real – courtesy of the scenarios that played out in your mind. It even felt real. However, if your life isn't based on your soul truth, it will be nothing more than a mirage. You believe that you made substantial progress in your physical life but, if you're not on your soul path, you won't move an inch spiritually. You can go back to the way of life that you're familiar with – if you so choose. But, you'll have to accept the consequences of that choice. You'll continue going around in circles and end up exactly, where you were before - feeling lifeless, and unfulfilled]

She was horrified. *She was an adult! Surely, she had her life figured out by now! There was no way that she could start all over again! If all she'd done was mindlessly chase her tail in a false reality, then how was she supposed to do any better in the nothingness? How was she supposed to find her soul path in absolute blackness?*

[You don't need to find your soul path. You need to find your truth. The rest will unfold naturally – if you allow yourself to just be. And the only 'plan' for that, is the one carried in your soul. When you were born it was as evident as your first breath but, your vulnerability left you at the mercy of your environment. Unfortunately, those first impressions were imprinted on your physical body, and became the building blocks of the rest of your 'story.' You grew up believing you are that story. But, that's not your truth. Your true story is the one your soul desires to share with you, and your fellow Beings. During your lifetime you'll come up against various soul lessons to facilitate your evolution. You are given some leeway to choose when to heed those lessons – you have free will. However, if you don't complete those lessons during your lifetime - for whatever reason – you leave your soul no option but, to choose another physical body to be its vehicle. It will actualize its mission - to unravel the layers that hold your truth hostage, and fulfill your purpose. This de-layering process is grueling. It needs to be – it's up against lifetimes of conditioning! You don't need to consciously know how you've been conditioned over time. Just be open, and non-judgmental of what comes up during this process. You'll encounter certain behaviors as you navigate the chaos in the nothingness. It's a necessary part of the process - to disorientate you. So that you can break free from your conditioning, and your expectations of life. During this 'mayhem,' you'll become more aware of your instinctive nature. And less resistant to allowing your higher Self to guide you through this transformative process. Only then, will you be open enough to receive all the opportunities within your soul. They might not look anything like the opportunities you're familiar with but, they are very real. They have been designed to support your highest growth]

[In the past, you made a number of changes in your physical life. But, you only changed what you were comfortable with. That approach might have given you the illusion of progress but, it only maintained the status quo. And it failed to appease your soul. How could it, when your efforts were constrained by your conditioning? You didn't address your thinking patterns or your behavior - not in any fundamental way. More importantly, those superficial, physical changes didn't help you to identify, and heal the root cause of whatever you've been fighting against, all your life. If you truly desire to change your reality, then you have to unravel your false sense of self by getting to the root of it. As impossible as that sounds, there's only one way to overcome the immovable - shine the light of your consciousness on it. Since you've avoided your truth for so long, you have to do some serious work to re-align to your soul. If one is already aligned to one's soul path, continued expansion of one's consciousness is a natural, instinctive process. This doesn't necessarily mean that your path will be easy but, it will be without unnecessary drama, and therefore, simpler. You won't be wasting your energy fighting battles, at every turn. Being is far simpler than doing. More importantly, you'll be at peace with yourself as you take each step when fulfilling your soul purpose. You could go an entire lifetime - many lifetimes - deluding yourself that you're living the 'dream' in your physical world. At some point, however, you'll be forced to face an uncomfortable truth - your inner world is nothing more than a wasteland]

Her reality was an illusion? She'd heard that a few times during her quest but, it failed to have any impact on her. This time, however, she felt chilled to the bone. And it was compounded by the fact that she was still floundering in uncertainty. *If the purpose of her quest was to help her create a new life, then she was making no progress at all! How was she supposed to do anything in this nothingness!?* Without anything tangible to distract her, she wasn't aware that she was continuously reverting to the past. And she had difficulty convincing herself that anything was possible in the nothingness - let alone the daunting task of uncovering her truth, and creating a new reality. *Her approach might have been different in the past but, at least her time was spent doing something constructive! That was confirmed by visible, and tangible results! She might not have given her soul path much thought but, was able to function — think, and act! Now, she felt utterly useless! She couldn't do a thing! This was the worst roller-coaster ride she'd ever been on!*

[Was the past any less of a roller-coaster?]

No! And she was battling with that paradox. She'd worked really hard, and taken the time to make decisions with one objective in mind - making the right choices for her life. *How did she end up in this nightmare? It was a complete contradiction! She'd lost everything! And she felt like a complete failure.* Was she resisting her truth? Was she looking at life through rose-tinted glasses? If so, then why were those "glasses" not working in the nothingness? *How could there be no way of putting her life back together? Surely, that was the point of it all! Why should she continue living in chaos, and discomfort?* She sighed heavily. She could never relate to the phrase, "going with the flow." It was the worst kind of cliché! To her mind, living according to that philosophy only resulted in uncertainty, and chaos. *Talk about irony! That was exactly where she now found herself!* She threw her hands up over her head in frustration. *This whole situation was such an anti-climax!* But, that wasn't the worst of it! Her instincts were now telling her to remain in the chaos, and be more open to her extreme discomfort. Furthermore, she sensed the need to refrain from using her usual tactic of fixing things to achieve some predetermined outcome. And the revelation accompanying her instincts was even more unsettling. Her ability wasn't being tested. This quest was about being with herself in stillness; in nothingness. And facing her emotions as they surfaced — without avoiding or denying them. Her mind cottoned onto another expectation. *Would she then, be in the "flow of life?"*

Her old patterns of thinking, however, weren't so easily over-ruled. Her mind rallied hard. *Why was that important?* She shook her head in annoyance. *That was no choice at all! In this cold world, that was tantamount to suicide! Yes — she'd chosen safety, and security. Everyone did! She'd made the right choices.* Only to have her instinct fight back. So far, those "right" choices had assured her of nothing but, an empty existence! To live fully alive, she would have to move towards her uncertainty. Her mind retaliated. *That was sheer stupidity! There was no form of control if she gave in, and went with the "flow." Whatever that was! There was no plan; no checklist - nothing that guaranteed success! And she would have to turn to her soul to decide what was true; to guide her along an unknown path. She didn't even know what her soul was! How could she turn the reins of her life over to it? How could she deal with whatever came at her, out of the unknown? It was called the "unknown" for a reason! And even if she did find her soul path, there was no guarantee that she would be happier, safer or wealthier. Her life would in all probability, be just the opposite! What kind of life was that? Where would she work? Who could she turn to for support? Who in their right mind, would make such a choice!?* She clasped her head between her hands, and groaned loudly. *There must be a way for her to maintain some security, and achieve her soul purpose. Why did it have to be one or the other? Was her physical life and her spiritual journey not one, and the same thing? How else could she have gotten onto this quest, if they weren't?*

She came to a surprising realization. Her decisions were not only geared towards gaining greater security but, they also fed that unconscious whim to control her life. *Only to end up losing her career, and the life that she wanted!* She sighed deeply. She felt so done in by her circumstances; by everyone, including the Universe! She glared out into the nothingness. She knew she was behaving like a child in a situation that demanded more maturity. *Especially, since this wasn't the loss of some favorite toy. This was her life's work! And now she was supposed to somehow find a way to live her life fully – by uncovering her truth, and her true Self!* She felt like throwing a tantrum, and screaming expletives at a Universe for causing such havoc in her life! She stopped. A deep frown appeared on her brow. She recalled moments when she'd done just that, and the consequences had been far from pleasing. There was always a backlash, of some kind or other. At the time, she'd put it down to mere coincidence. Now, however, she felt there was some deeper meaning to those strange occurrences. *What was she missing in all this?* During those moments of outrage, she believed that she was talking to herself. Now she was no longer, so sure. Was the Universe actually, listening to her? Who was she speaking to? She shook her head to banish the thought, and brought her attention back to her current dilemma. *Besides not knowing how to go about finding her truth, just spending this much time with herself was selfish!* But, if her life was anything to go by, without Self-knowledge serving others - or herself, for that matter - was analogous to filling water into a bucket full of holes! She sighed. *How was she supposed to figure out the "holes" in the nothingness? That was impossible!*

[Anything is possible with awareness, and staying present with your Self. The alternative is to continue living a lie to convince yourself of your mind's version of the 'truth.' But, that would be the 'bucket' you're referring to. And you've already been down that road. You only have one 'road' left – the one leading to your truth. Those fears that exist as satellites around your core fear are psychological 'walls' that you built to protect yourself from perceived threats. That doesn't make them any less real or intimidating but, you no longer need them. They're blocking you from you're your soul's gifts. You can heal those fears – by transcending your past patterns of behavior. This is not something that you can do all at once – it's a conscious, step-by-step process. Guided by your soul. You have to focus on the emotions that arise within you as each layer is revealed. Only once you've healed that, will the next layer be revealed. When you've completed the process, you'll know – you'll feel free of your fears; whole again. There's no risk of repeating the past, for you'll be one with your higher Self. One with your soul, and Being. Oneness is love – it transmutes any emotion that isn't in alignment with your soul purpose. For as long as you're driven by your fears, you'll always be looking for the security of your material possessions to provide some sort of emotional insurance. You'll always expect some kind of guarantee from life. Life offers no such thing. Nothing stops you from maintaining that physical 'security' throughout the course of your lifetime but, that doesn't make it any less of an illusion. Not if it projects a false reality to help you feed your fears. It was all bound to collapse sooner or later, because you're not living your truth]

[The real question, however, is why you've made certainty the foundation for your life? So much so, that you defined your life around it. And yet, there's nothing to uphold it – other than your fear of losing it. Irrespective of how much you believe in the certainty of your physical world, it's one illusion that you can't afford to have – not if your soul desires to experience its full potential. By its very nature, your soul path is uncertain. And living your soul's purpose demands awareness, open-hearted vulnerability, and courage. That courage isn't a factor of your material worth but, of other qualities – your joy, self-worth, and self-love. Innate qualities that can't be derived from or sustained by any external source. Innate qualities that might appear to be nebulous when compared to the grit required to build your past reality. And yet, their absence keeps that void within you alive, and gives your ego carte-blanche to reinforce your false identity. It's a vicious circle - the more you're defined by what you're not, the emptier you'll feel. And the greater your predisposition towards your outer, material world. Even if you could obtain everything that your ego wants in your physical world you'll eventually, realize that it's not enough for what you truly need within your soul. And nothing will live up to your expectations – nothing is as insatiable as your ego]

[You're looking to your physical world to provide a formula to live the greatest 'mystery' ever created – life itself. There is no formula. To live fully alive, you have to first and foremost, acknowledge that you embody that mystery. Embrace it. Immerse yourself fully in it. By doing so, you get to participate in the most magical, adventure ever created – life. There is no greater feat; nothing more memorable. It must have taken a lot of energy, and courage to fight for what you wanted in your physical world. But, it takes a different kind of courage to fight for your unknown, soul path. You have to choose your silent, truth over the constant, screaming of your ego. More so, if the only 'mirrors' helping you to find that truth are the closet relationships in your physical world. This is the work of your soul – your spiritual journey to uncover your true Self - as experienced through your physical self. Your spiritual, and physical paths are one, and the same. To access that inner knowing, you have to 'see' past your mind. Past the illusion of separation created by your polarized thoughts]

What was she supposed to have done? What should she do now? She hung her head in confusion. She had no tolerance for mistakes. She'd experienced failure many times but, she'd lifted herself up after each fall, and pushed on to the next goal that she'd set her sights on. *But, she was now talking about writing off her entire life! With no new goal in sight!* She felt inadequate. Worthless. *So much time, and effort.......wasted. Where did she go wrong?*

[Making mistakes is part of life's journey; part of fully accepting your humanness. And you'll have many opportunities during your lifetime – over many lifetimes, if necessary - to clear the lower layers of your physical self, to embody your soul purpose. However, you'll be required to be aware, and remain focused on the highest values of your soul. It's your 'north star.' It will never fail you]

Her spirits lifted. *She could still find her way out of this darkness?*

[Not 'out of' but, through - yes. Call it by any name but, this is as real as it gets. All you need to do is listen to your heart. Your inner voice - your soul - speaks through it. And trust that you have the courage to help you face what lies ahead. Stay humble with each step taken into the unknown. Above all, remain in stillness, and stay present. Trust the process. You'll find what you seek. It lies within – not anywhere, outside of you. Whatever you've done, until now is not 'wrong.' Honor your feelings but, there is no need for regret. You haven't failed. You have actually, learnt a lot from your life experiences. There are many unacknowledged, blessings – even in you darkest moments. And as unwieldy as this nothingness seems, it holds an even bigger blessing. You just have to continue with your quest - listen to your inner voice, until you find the 'gold' behind the pain, and fear]

To uncover her truth, she needed to listen to her inner voice? That was so self-serving!

[Living your soul purpose, is not being selfish. It's your highest calling. It's only by being selfishly true to your path that you'll fulfill your soul purpose. And in doing so, you'll not only serve your Self – you'll serve all of humanity]

That went completely, over her head. She was so petrified that she once again, turned to her familiar comfort zone – her mind. *How could she use her inner voice as a reference? As a child she'd followed her parents' advice, and deferred to them in all matters, until she was older. She'd applied the same principle later in life, to all other role players who had molded her character. Without them, she would never have gotten anywhere!*

[Different people define success, and find meaning in their lives in different ways. But essentially, it boils down to a choice between exploiting every opportunity in your physical world, and graciously allowing your soul path to unfold. The former is based on fear and ego, and is dictated by physical time. The latter is guided by Spirit, and is dependent on Divine timing. It requires trusting that the life you were born to live will serve your highest intentions, and will unfold at the right time - in the best possible way. By all means, follow the advice of others wherever necessary but, don't deny your inner voice when doing so. And be aware of your ego's flirtation with every 'new' idea that it encounters. There are none, in the domain of egos. And as enticing as it might be to pursue, no idea is worth destroying this planet for. If you remain aware of your thoughts, and what drives you, you won't succumb to being baited by your ego's competitive urges. Your Being has no such inclination. If it did have a desire, it would be for this planet to support all life forms, and for everyone to hold space in their hearts for their fellow Beings to reach their highest potential. Contrary to popular belief, one's highest potential doesn't equate to financial wealth but, to abundance in all its forms. You'll discover that there's no lack of resources to attain one's highest potential - souls' have their own means of natural selection]

[Striving to be 'on top of everything' is another illusion driven by your ego. It only feeds your penchant for perfectionism. Again, your Being has no such need – its perfection, personified. It doesn't require you to know all the facts, and have the perfect plan within your soul. You'll always have what you require, at the time when you need it – that is the power inherent to your soul purpose. You get to co-create that purpose with the Universe. Your physical self – whatever its form - will accomplish what your soul requires you to do. And it will be perfect – whether or not, it meets the 'standards' in your physical world. This is all part of your life path towards greater Self-knowledge, and higher consciousness. It requires self-acceptance, and self-love. And it's never completed, until your soul's time here is done. Every conscious step taken in instinctive harmony with your soul, will be a moment of pure bliss. If you believe that you worked hard previously, then you'll have to work a lot harder, and dig much deeper before you can uncover your true Self. Your soul won't let up until you do, either in this lifetime or over as many lifetimes as it takes. You don't need to feel daunted by the unknown. It only feels that way, because you believe you've lost control over the 'future' that you wanted. You've lost nothing – not if that 'future' was based on an image in your mind to give you the illusion of security, and certainty. That kind of 'future' doesn't exist. That is another wicked ploy of your ego. By keeping you locked in by fear, it's easier to make you believe that it has the power to give you what you want, at some 'future' point in time. It keeps you looking away from the only source of your true power – the present moment. Its control, and power over you are nothing more than extensions of its own self-importance. Or rather, lack thereof. As for the knowledge required to walk your soul path, you possess far more innate soul knowledge than you could ever imagine. Open yourself to that truth by acknowledging the limitations of your mind in this, and surrender to the unknown. Embrace the uncertainty. Feel how your Being resonates with it, and allow yourself to become one with that feeling. You'll discover that the unknown is nothing to fear]

She'd never stopped to consider her soul purpose. Neither did she have any idea of the potential embedded within it, to help her achieve that purpose. She'd always aimed high in her career – she knew she was ambitious. She'd always assumed that she was utilizing her full potential. And yet, she'd always fallen short of attaining her most cherished goals. If she did achieve one, then it ended up falling way below her expectations. She sighed. It was such a double-edged sword – her ambitious nature on the one side, and constant disillusionment on the other! Was that an indication of not being on her soul path? Were her fears at the root of her decisions? Where was her heart, all this time? She covered her face in dismay, as the full extent of her ego's deceptiveness dawned on her.

[Ego - yes. Little or no heart, definitely. But, both are underpinned by something that had a far greater impact on your false reality – your lack of Self-knowledge. You're now acquainted with your heart's song, and more accepting of its role in helping you uncover your truth. However, you still have some way to go before you can interpret the 'language' of its silent melody. When you're able to do that then it will mean the end of life as you know it, and the beginning of life as you're meant to live it – standing in your truth. For now, focus on the feelings that surface in the nothingness. What was behind your choices?]

As hard as she tried, she couldn't come up with an answer.

[Were you seeking approval? Did you feel obligated to meet the needs of others? Did you eventually, become complacent?]

Did the trajectory that she'd defined for her life become so predictable that she'd switched to auto-pilot? Was that the reason for her constant, boredom? For how long was she asleep – just as an adult or from childhood? For the first time, she stopped to reflect on her decision to take care of her parents. She felt honored to have fulfilled that role. And was grateful for all the sacrifices that they had made over the years. But, she never felt obligated to them in any way.

[There's a fine line between caring, and duty. And your cultural conditioning would have made you more inclined to react out of fear]

That made her feel very uncomfortable. Recollecting her earlier conversations with Glow, she was astounded to realize that most of her life had been spent feeling insecure - about everything. But, she'd cottoned on quite early that there was no place for any kind of weakness in her physical world. Especially, not in her career. So she'd watched, and learnt what worked for the role models around her. And strong, and independent did. It didn't take long to convince herself that she needed to adopt those traits. Now however, she saw how the portrayal of a false image of herself had been met with a string of experiences that "tested" her truth – including, the subtle forms of rejection that she'd encountered along the way. Why did she expect that others would accept her when she didn't accept herself? Why would others want to know her, when she made no attempt to know her true Self? She sensed that this dilemma had nothing to do with whether or not, she was strong or confident. There was a big difference between the innate qualities of one's true Self, and a false sense of confidence shielded by bravado that only served as a coping mechanism. She had a startling thought. Why did she feel the need to constantly protect herself by wearing a mask of bravery?

It struck her that in a similar vein, most of the other personality traits that she'd associated with her personality couldn't be called her own. The qualities that she'd adopted from others were probably not even innate to them! Was everyone flouting some image or other to survive in this crazy world? Was the cost to one's Self, worth it? Why couldn't she just be herself? Why were the "masks" necessary? What was behind those masks? Those traits now looked like nothing more, than a grey sludge of mixed up wants, desires, expectations, and fears. And they were only "walls" that she used to protect herself. It was all in support of the bluster, and grit to pit her strength – or what she perceived as strength - against the competition! She might be independent but, she was also hiding something! She frowned. What!? Was her caring nature masking co-dependency? She'd never lived on her own so she was none the wiser. And her 'confidence' was derived from doing things for others, and being acknowledged for her efforts. Other than giving herself a few luxuries in life, she'd never done anything purely for herself – not anywhere near bringing forth her soul purpose! What level of confidence did that require? How strong did she need to be? She had no clue. *How was she going to get through this quest?* She sighed. But, whatever traits she was familiar with were not going to serve her in the nothingness. It was no longer surprising that she'd failed to find meaning or that her whole life had fallen apart. The caliber of one's traits could only be an extension of one's true Self. Any other version was purely an attempt to hold a false sense of self together in the face of whatever her ego felt threatened by!

[What are you afraid of?]

Nothing! She got out there, and made things happen in her life! She was responsible for holding everything together for herself, and her family. Her life was everything that she wanted. She stopped. Was she speaking her truth? Why did her life fall apart then? Or was that just a reflection of how fragmented she was? Was the control of her outer world an indication of her efforts to hold herself together? Why did she constantly, feel torn apart? *And yet, she would never have thought that she of all people, would fall apart!*

[You might not have acknowledged your fears but, you manifested them, nonetheless. You were so engrossed with protecting yourself from threats you perceived coming at you from your outer world, you never anticipated that the biggest threat was within you – your own fears. And it's only by 'falling apart' that you'll see what's real about you]

Whose voice was that? Who was speaking to her as if they knew her? No one knew her! She didn't even know herself!

She was startled by that admission. *Why did she say that? Where did it come from?* But, she became caught up in a new quandary. Something was nagging at the far reaches of her mind. *What was it?*

[Doing all the 'right' things failed to give you the life that you yearned for, deep within your soul?]

She gritted her teeth, and groaned. Whatever avenue she tried on this quest only led her to another dead-end! She shook her fists at the nothingness, and screamed: "God, what do you want me to do?"

[You believe in God?]

She flinched. She didn't – not in the traditional sense. *But, unravelling what she believed in could take forever! There was no time. She wanted to get out of the nothingness, as fast as possible.*

[You don't have the luxury of deciding what's necessary here. Forget about your notion of physical time. Time is an illusion - it won't serve you here. Your conditioning led you to believe that if things went according to plan, you were 'right.' And if they didn't, you were 'wrong.' That worked for a long time. It underpinned your confidence. But, it also reinforced the illusion of control, and safety in your physical world. Persisting with your of preconceived thinking won't help you to open yourself to the wisdom that already exists within your soul. Here everything is, exactly as you see it – empty, nothingness. There is no 'plan'; no 'right' and 'wrong' way. Nothing needs to be done in this space – only undone. And the key to that is self-love – accepting yourself fully as you uncover your truth. Without judgement or criticism. Only then will you feel truly safe, and confident in yourself – to allow yourself to be with your Self. Only then, will you feel the endlessness of your Being in this space - in any space. And be able to grasp eternity in a moment]

She sighed. *How was she supposed to simply, be? There was nothing simple about that! To her mind that was the equivalent of doing nothing! And if her time in the nothingness was any indication of that, then a lifetime of just Being would drive her insane! It was boring! And utterly, futile! Irrespective of what she tried, nothing happened! Whichever way she strung her thoughts together to shape her understanding of events in her life, she failed to gain any kind of lasting clarity. If self-love was the "key" to this quest, then it was the furthest thing from her reach! There was no way she could go on. Her nerves, and patience were stretched to the limit!* To make matters worse, she was now having difficulty suppressing the feelings of shame, and guilt that were bubbling to the surface. She tried accepting the emotions for what they were, and grappled instead, with the underlying causes. And then it struck her. *Her entire life was a failure! She was a failure!* She hung her head in shocked dismay. *Everything that she'd done was a complete waste of time, and effort!* Her life was built on the premise that decisions were, either "right" or "wrong." With the logical extension that a greater number of right choices equated to a higher probability of success. She was convinced that she'd applied that approach to the best of her ability – she'd always been her strongest critic. *To negate that premise now, would be threatening a fundamental belief!* She sighed. *There must be some way to fix this mess!*

As she plodded on with her quandary, she was again drawn to the deep silence in the nothingness. It intrigued her. It felt so complete; so content. It was bursting with some mystical, invisible energy. And by virtue of it being everything that she wasn't feeling in that space, it was affecting her in the strangest of ways. It dawned on her that whatever she was experiencing on this quest was unfolding within her but, it was also outside the storm raging in her mind. Furthermore, it had its own pace, and was impervious to the workings of her mind. What was the source of it? What was directing it? As nebulous as this new form of inner knowing was she felt drawn deeper into it. And she was now beginning to feel safe with her uncertainty - in a similar way that she'd accepted her body being suspended in nothingness. She still felt as though she was cocooned within a warm embrace – no matter, how cold she became when her aura disappeared. And as mindboggling as it was, the longer she remained in the nothingness, the greater her awareness of being connected to everything through her throbbing heart. She realized that she had to overcome her reticence, and open herself to being guided by it. Somehow she had to find the courage to follow her heart for as far as she could tell, her mind was taking her nowhere! And her instincts were warning her that if she clung to her old conditioning, then she would only end up chasing a different mirage. If she focused on her heart center, however, there was one thing that she could be certain of. The only "compass" that could liberate herself from an invisible prison lay somewhere within her. Until she found it, she would be tossing about aimlessly in any space that she was in – be it in her physical world or the nothingness! And that didn't appeal to her.

As simple as her decision was, her body refused to acquiesce. It retaliated with such fierceness that she felt as though, she was kicked in the stomach! She bent over with her arms around her, and gently rocking herself to ease the pain. It was the only thing she could do in the face-off between a false identity, and her true as yet, unknown Self. She had a startling revelation. Even though her inner knowing was slowly filtering into her conscious mind, and helping her to process aspects of her quest, her body was still catching up. *Why didn't she see this coming? How could she fail to recognize how out of balance she was within herself?* She'd prided herself on her astuteness. Then again, that was another attribute that she'd capitalized on in her career – not her life! *When did her career become her life? When did her mind become her master? Why did she correlate wellbeing with making choices for her life based on the highest probability of outcomes in her physical world?* Again, she sighed heavily. *Why was she sighing so much? Why was she having difficulty breathing?* She shook her head to clear the fog but, it was no use. There was nothing or very little that was real about her life! Or about herself! She was on the verge of continuing with her barrage of negative thoughts when she recalled something Voice said. She shouldn't judge herself. There were no right or wrong decisions in her past. She needed to focus on loving, and accepting herself. *Could she fully accept herself – warts, and all?* Her life might not have been everything that she'd hoped for but, it was still a part of her Self – perfect or not. Perhaps loving herself meant accepting her imperfections. Maybe through self-acceptance she could open herself to see what lay beyond the conditioned beliefs about herself. If she'd been living an illusory life, with an unreal self then there must be something real behind all those "walls." She could take her life in a whole new direction by uncovering it. And she didn't have to figure out the direction - her heart, and soul would lead the way. All she had to do was stay aware. And be present.

She slowly straightened her back, as a new insight hit home. She should give herself some credit. After all, she'd recovered from some pretty hair-raising stuff in the past. Whichever part of her had been responsible – old self, new Self; mind or soul – was irrelevant. She was there now. *Wherever that was!* She'd taken herself to her limits in her physical world, and had probably done what she needed to do. She might have not achieved much but, it was still way more than she ever thought possible, given her circumstances. For the first time, she felt a sense of pride for what she'd accomplished. She'd made her fair share of mistakes but, she was now certain of one thing – she'd done her best. And if it was not for her quest, she would have continued doing so in her own off-beat, rambling, kind-of way. But, she was now beginning to appreciate her quest – it was teaching her some valuable, new perspectives. She could now see some of the vicious patterns that she'd been caught up in. Even if she could go back in time to fix the glaring "holes," she wouldn't make any progress. She needed to change the whole "bucket"- namely, herself! She also had to admit – albeit grudgingly - that a career alone, couldn't help her live the life her soul desired. That was her all-new, benchmark for success. Engaging her mind in the rollout of some logical plan in her physical world was a very small part of her full potential – if anything, at all. And she now had a burning desire to become acquainted with her true purpose, and that potential. Her previous approach might have helped her take on many challenges but, realizing her full potential was the ultimate challenge. And there was no way of knowing for certain, if she possessed any kind of knowledge to help her access it – none at her beck and call, anyway. Her formal education might have equipped her with some academic knowledge but, it didn't provide much in the way of Self-knowledge, and wisdom.

She was struck by a daunting revelation. She actually, knew nothing about her Self! She'd groomed an identity around labels associated with her deeds, titles, accolades and other peoples' opinions, and expectations of her capability or lack thereof. She smiled at her naiveté. She had no idea of her real capability! She knew one thing, though. She always delivered. Somehow that didn't ratchet up many points on her own opinion poll! Did she devote so much time to her career, because it was the only place she received some kind of validation? Why didn't she feel as validated in her personal relationships? And then, she was shaken by a jolt of anxiety. She'd seldom if ever, contemplated her close relationships! Outside of her career, she really had no idea of the meaning of those relationships! Who was she, outside her family name? Or her marriage? She was distressed by those insights. She must have been asleep her entire life! If she felt lost over the dissolution of her material world, then she was now teetering on the very edge of sanity at the realization that she'd lost touch with the only person who knew anything about her. Her Self!

She centered herself in the stillness once more, and looked at the full ambit of her frightening conundrum. *How was she supposed to find her true Self in the nothingness?* Her old self was rapidly disintegrating – in the same way that her physical world had fallen apart! And even if she could find some way of holding herself together, she doubted it would be of much help on her quest. She was now in uncharted territory. Her travels in her physical world had somewhat, satisfied her desire for adventure. But, that didn't do much for her pioneering spirit. She realized that going on some expedition or other, seeking out new vistas in her physical world didn't do much to inspire her. She sighed. Well, she'd now stumbled on one that did! She was sitting on the threshold of a whole new frontier – one poised at the very edge of reason between the person she believed herself to be, and her true Self! She felt a tremor pass through her entire body. She was about to embark on the ultimate expedition – to uncover her truth, and her Self! Something that she had absolutely, no clue how to do! She shifted uneasily, as a strange emotion started bubbling somewhere within her. She couldn't describe it - words failed to describe the depth of emotion cascading through her. Only one thing was unmistakable. This was no ordinary quest. It might be incomprehensible, because it was shrouded in mystery but, with every breath she felt herself being drawn further into its unknown depths.

She felt a familiar stirring in her heart as it shivered gloriously in the echo of her silent acknowledgement. She felt the anticipation towards the unknown with her entire Being. She felt inspired, and was actually, feeling.....hap...hap....happy. No. It was more than that. It felt like joy – a never-ending, fountain of it! And there was no basis for it. The anxiety was still there. As was the uncertainty. She had nowhere to go. Nothing to do. And she still had no answers. But, she felt invigorated. Full of joy. Hopeful. She lifted her head to ponder her weird; magical quest. Everything was disappearing – her material world, and the self that had constructed it. She had nothing, anymore. She was starting to suspect, however, that the silent nothingness, and the stillness were far from nothing. There was something special - almost reverent - about both. And it was probably, the most important "something" that she'd ever encountered. She might not be able to define it but, all her senses were beginning to attune to it. She felt awake for the first time, in her life. The purpose of that awakening, however, still eluded her. She felt as though she was being presented with a whole new "canvas" for her life, in the nothingness. One that had always belonged to her but, one that she'd never been conscious of. She didn't quite know what to do with this….this….gift. *Was it real? Was it another illusion?* She felt completely, overwhelmed. *If it was a gift, how could she possibly, accept something so priceless? She wasn't deserving of it! What was she supposed to do with it? Could she do it justice?* She was petrified. At the same time though, she felt very blessed. Grateful. Shivering with anticipation. And as light as air. Her initial reaction was to look around her. She expected closure with that revelation. That she would miraculously, find herself back in her physical world. She frowned. Everything looked exactly, the same – black, never-ending nothingness.

[You don't have to change locations to find what you're looking for. You can exceed all your boundaries - physical, and psychological - from where you are now. In this moment]

She was contemplating the meaning of that when she became aware of something so profound, her breath caught in her throat. An invisible curtain between her mind and another layer slowly lifted, and floated away in the nothingness. She couldn't tell what lay beyond it. *What aspect of herself was this? Why didn't she know it was there?* What had prevented her from being aware of its existence, for so long? The realization that this hidden part of her existed, however, left her shaken. She realized that during the course of her quest she must have cleared away some of her false beliefs. She must have also removed some of the social constructs that were limiting her. She was also aware of the labels that she'd used to define, and constrain herself in her physical world. And hidden beneath those layers was yet, another layer! Did she have to heal, and release it to get closer to her true Self? If her physical world was founded on old conditioning, and if its demise was destroying everything that she'd built over the years, then what of her inner world? *If her identity was also destroyed during this quest, then what would be her fate? Would she still exist?* Was she as "together" as she'd always believed or was that belief just another illusion? *If she entered this layer, would she know what was real about her, and what was false? How long would it take to heal, and uncover what was lying beneath it?* What would be revealed about her inner world? Was this layer part of her false identity? *She'd felt pretty real throughout her life! That was, until she ended up in this circus!* What was this unseen force that had destroyed the life she was familiar with, and was now threatening to do the same with her identity? Was all of this turmoil, in honor of her truth?

She recalled that her life had become increasingly grim, over the last few years. She'd seldom given much thought to the heaviness – it was always there. She just got on with each day. She did experience the occasional bout of depression but, she'd lifted herself out of it by staying busy. That gave her some kind of control over the negativity that seemed to follow her around, wherever she went. She never expected life to be smooth sailing but, she firmly believed in a positive attitude to get through the dark times. During the last "dark night of the soul" however, something within her "snapped," and she'd never been able to lift herself out of it. She tried everything to get back the life she was familiar with but, things just got worse until eventually, she dropped into a darkness that she'd never experienced before. First, she lost her father. He was her rock, and meant the world to her. He still did. She dealt with his death in her usual pragmatic manner but, she now sensed that she'd probably started to shut down when he first got ill, years ago. Watching his slow suffering was excruciating. She felt his pain. She often wished for it all to end – for both of them. And then, she was wracked with guilt for she knew that letting go was the hardest thing for him - he was holding on with every ounce of life left in him, for his family. Eventually, he did leave her. It felt like such an anticlimax after so many years filled with pain, and heartache that she had extreme difficulty coming to terms with the sudden emptiness that opened up in her life. In the midst of it all, she had to find a way to cope with the family drama that became a predominant feature in her life. She recalled pondering the dynamics of the various personalities, for the first time. She realized that as the head of their extended household, her father had somehow kept everyone together. He'd also served as an invisible buffer for years – preventing any major disruption to the family values. As a result, tempers simmered for long periods of time, before flaring out of control.

When they did he had some power that miraculously re-established peace in the troubled household. The shock of his death, however, disorientated everyone. They reacted in strange ways, probably in an attempt to regain some form of control over their individual pain. Except for her. She stood by watching everything and everyone, and felt completely, removed from it all. A few months following his death, she lost her job. And then, the few closest relationships in her life, also fell apart. All that remained was the emptiness. And the numbness.

Now she could see certain behavioral aspects that were becoming increasingly apparent in the nothingness. Why was she always haunted by feelings of discomfort when it came to her family? Besides her father, did she have any connection with any one of them? She started to compare some of the experiences in her life and was taken aback by the similarities between her professional, and family lives. In essence, she'd never fitted in - in either one! And both were fundamental in molding her behavior, and identity. How could she miss something so obvious, for so long? She was very unsettled by her insights. More so, by the power of her perceptions - they had led her to view life one way, when the reality of it was completely, different! What else did she miss about herself during those years? Her acknowledgement made her more vulnerable, and open to her truth. The hard façade that had been built over years of conditioning suddenly, shattered to reveal a blinding clarity. She might have been aware of the cultural, and social restrictions over the years but, she'd overlooked how well indoctrinated she'd become as a result of her exposure to them! She'd strived to fit in to such an extent, that she'd become dutiful to the point of self-sacrifice! And she'd fallen into the trap of being the "good-girl." But, her conditioning had failed to make her completely, submissive! The rebel in her had made certain of that!

Again, she was surprised at her calmness in the face of her revelations. She continued taking refuge in her stillness, while being buffeted by waves of emotion. Regret being one of them. As overwhelming as it was she held steadfast, until eventually, she came to rest in her silent, center again. It helped her to realize that any regrets were superfluous. And that the insights that surfaced above the regret were far more important. If she'd spent so much time pandering to the needs of others, what did she do for herself? Where did she feature in her own life? How did she take responsibility for herself? She'd lost sight of that need, until everything in her world had crashed! And yet, despite the turmoil leading up to that crash she'd muzzled the fighter in her, and accepted her fate with as much grace as she could muster. *That kind of behavior was completely, out of character!* Was it a defense tactic, because she was on the back foot after losing everything? Eventually, it dawned on her that she'd taken some kind of sabbatical - from her life! Was that the different "avenue" that Glow had alluded to? She sighed. She was grappling to understand her life - herself. Over the years, the "cracks" in her life hadn't completely, bypassed her. On quite a few occasions, she'd painstakingly tried to "fix" them. It wasn't the first time that she'd lost her job or experienced hardship, of any kind. If the events leading up to her current crisis had occurred sequentially – like they usually did - she would probably have dealt with it in her usual way, and would have been back-on-track, in no time. She'd become so good at applying the "plasters" that she could tell where the next "crack" was going to appear, way before it did. It was repaired before anyone noticed anything, and life went on its merry-way. Or so, she'd thought. What she failed to realize was that any attempts to superficially address flaws in character would only become undone, as fast as they could be patched them up. As became evident, when her usual tactics failed to resolve her most recent crises. And everything that she'd attended to so diligently over the years was swept away in one fell swoop by a force beyond her understanding, and control. Nothing was left in its wake. And now, she felt as though her identity was about to follow the same fate.

She sighed sadly. It dawned on her that when her father died, she could find no resources within herself to cope with the magnitude of emotions bombarding her, all at once. Without being aware of it, she'd shut down. Now however, within the embrace of the nothingness, she found that she had the strength to revisit that time of extreme pain in her life. She closed her eyes, and took a deep breath. She had to face what she could no longer avoid. She was sucked into a tidal wave of fear, anger, and loneliness. She stood her ground as she watched herself slowly being torn apart by a grief that she'd refused to acknowledge. She thought that she would never be able to lift herself up from the full burden bearing down on her. She'd always considered herself resourceful enough to overcome anything. However, being hit by one painful event after another, during such a short space of time was beyond anything that she expected. Rationalizing her experience to gain some sort of perspective, failed to ease her misery. There was one overriding question burning a hole in her mind at the time: *"Why me?"* She went about her days like the "living dead" as everything that she'd worked so hard to build, slowly fell apart. And she didn't lift a finger to try, and stop it. She was buried under her pain, loss. And the betrayals along the way. Her anger over the finality of death; her anger at her father – for leaving her. The anger, at not being able to control her anger! She re-lived her overwhelming heartache time, and time again. And when her world eventually, caved and was blanketed by darkness, she'd felt strangely relieved. And had welcomed it with open arms. She opened her eyes, and looked at the nothingness; overwhelmed by gratitude for its warmth. Why did she do nothing? Who was that "other" Self who had stood by, deliberately watching her life fall apart? Or was it she, who was responsible for destroying her own life? Why? What would make her do such a thing? *What was she supposed to do with her life now?* She was even more bewildered when she realized that she didn't feel like doing anything at all!

[So everyone.….everything, including life.……conspired against you?]

Was she playing the victim? Did she look at her life – herself - objectively enough? Over the years, she'd interrogated every situation from as many angles, as possible. But, she wasn't so sure, anymore. Perhaps she'd over-deliberated, and tied herself up in knots! Maybe she didn't consider her options, carefully enough. She must have missed something. As much as there was betrayal from others, she'd also betrayed herself. For all the lies that others had spoken, she'd also lied to herself. *Was there some way she could determine how much of this mess was circumstantial?* How much of it was brought on by herself? Did she set herself up by making choices that didn't serve her highest interests? Why would she treat herself so disrespectfully? So unlovingly? Why would she devote time, and energy building a reality so full of holes that it eventually, collapsed? *Why did her life fall apart when she'd relentlessly pursued the exact opposite? Why was her life so beset with negativity, despite her trying so hard to maintain a positive mindset?* If that was her reality, what was it saying about herself? What role did her past, and her bottled emotions play in defining the reality that she'd experienced? She shivered as another revelation struck her. If Glow was right about one's outer reality being a reflection of one's inner world then hers, must be in tatters!

She sighed. She was so exhausted that all she wanted to do was get away from what was now facing her. That dark, inner void was threatening to swallow her whole! It felt worse than the nothingness outside of her! She had this hollow feeling deep in the pit of her stomach. She was falling..... falling into something that she couldn't see or name. And she felt powerless to stop it. *That was it! She was finished! Her life was over! There was no way out of the nothingness, and the darkness that she'd fallen into.* Just a little while ago, she was on a high - in great anticipation of her expedition into the unknown. She was hopeful that it would lead her to some better place. She was exhilarated by the magic, and willing to embrace the challenges of her unpredictable, quest into the unknown. Now, however, she felt utterly devastated. *There was no way that she could handle this kind of darkness! As difficult as her physical life used to be, she was the one in control. She knew what she needed to do. But, this? This was impossible! How did she go about navigating the unknown, and the unseen? How could she cope with all this uncertainty? Without any instructions or help?* She felt sick with fear. Her belly was cramping so badly that she wrapped her arms around her midsection to help ease it. She gritted her teeth. She was expecting more joy. Some form of reprieve or breakthrough. And renewed enthusiasm. Perhaps a new lease on life. But, there was none of that. Instead, she found herself hurtling through the nothingness on an endless pendulum of emotional highs, and lows.

Again, she was struck by how much this reflected her old way of life. There were spurts of determined effort for long periods of time; interspersed with sparks of enthusiasm. Her stress levels were always high but, for some reason, she'd never bothered with that. Each opportunity was grasped with the belief that she'd found what she was looking for. It convinced her that she was on her way to achieving her "dream" life. She believed that all her sacrifices were finally, paying off. That spurred her on, to work harder. But, her feelings of success invariably, plateaued. Despite that she'd hung on, until eventually, she couldn't deny her disillusionment. She was forced to accept that the opportunity wasn't exactly, what she was looking for. And then, she descended from her high hopes with a crash, and was buried in disappointment. But, before long she was at it again - looking for that "new" opportunity. Accepting her losses, and lifting herself up each time was excruciating. But she'd never lost hope, and she returned to what she knew best – her work. Only to have the same experience repeated. The highs. Followed by the inevitable lows; the feelings of failure, and disillusionment. All leading her.... nowhere. She found it hard to believe that the same pattern had repeated itself so many times, during her lifetime. Perhaps she'd been caught in the same pattern, over many lifetimes. So it was no surprise that over time, she'd forgotten her life's purpose! She sighed heavily. She realized sadly, that she'd subjected herself to the most futile way of finding meaning in her life. Time and time again she'd defaulted to the familiar, because of her age-old, conditioning.

And so, despite all her efforts she'd taken her life exactly, nowhere! She thought she'd wizened up over time. That she'd figured out what she wanted, and where she was going. She'd hoped that her restlessness, and the continuous uphill battles would cease. She'd hoped that life would ease up, and give her a break someday. She wanted nothing more than to feel happy, and to cease her endless worrying about everything. But, life continued with its relentless pummeling, and she'd persisted with her efforts to stay on "top of everything." Only to come to the realization now - years later - that she'd been suffering from a major oversight! She would never get to her planned success no matter how hard she tried, because she'd overlooked a critical piece of the puzzle. She didn't know who she truly was! She didn't know her truth! Things were never going to turn around, even if her father had always said they would. She smiled sadly as she remembered his gentle smile, and the warm, glow in his eyes. She so missed that look, and the unspoken love in everything that he said, and did. She recalled his favorite words of encouragement whenever she faced one of life's hurdles: "Make the best of it." She uncurled her arms from her mid-section, and straightened her back as the memory of his voice triggered something deep within her. She couldn't give up. She was her father's daughter. It would all make sense someday. She was convinced that it would.

[You'll only continue ticking boxes if you try to solve this with logic]
That's what everyone did! What else was she supposed to do?

[You're now an authority on other peoples' lives? What about your own?]

She sucked in her breath as that comment found its mark. Was she an authority on her own life? Could she make such a claim when she was no more than a puppet, hopping to some random tune? She was so busy searching everywhere for the right answer that she'd built a semblance of a life, based on what? And that outward search had made her an authority on what? Geography? Cultures? Cuisine? Airports? That experience might have given her the ability to converse on various subjects but, none of it allowed her to claim knowledge of Self! How could she have been so ignorant? She shivered at the realization that all she could lay claim to was being a builder of illusions. Her life wasn't the solid structure she believed it to be. It had no substance; no foundation. Her mind had used its conditioning for a blueprint; her ego was the master craftsman. And her anger had been used for bricks, and mortar! She was no authority on anything. Least of all, her Self! She was having trouble grasping the volume of revelations bombarding her. However, as shocking as they were, she was fascinated by the paradoxical nature of her life. An entire life defined by everything that she could no longer relate to; as a persona that she felt no connection to. No wonder she'd hit so many dead ends along the way! Each one was trying to point her in a different direction. And she'd ignored the warnings, thinking that she knew best. That she knew what was right for her. She'd survived those years but, at what cost? She'd traded in the right to her life for a glory ride to nowhere! That's why everything had fallen apart – there was nothing real about her! Her external reality was merely a reflection of her inner world - a broken, empty, shell. And her ego had blinded her with rose-tinted glasses - making her believe she was on the right track. She was shocked by the realization of just how broken she must be, to be so out of touch with her truth! And she was running around her physical world, looking for the pieces to make herself feel whole again. Completely, unaware that what she needed to piece herself together could only be found within.

It was too much. She couldn't take anymore. She was feeling light-headed, and nauseous. Her physical body felt like it was about to explode. She looked at the nothingness. It was still; peaceful. Get a grip, she told herself sternly. She focused on her breathing, until she calmed down. Again, she looked intently at the nothingness; hoping to find some way of breaking the stronghold of uncertainty that had engulfed her, since her quest began. Only to find, that even the nothingness now looked different. *Did something change in the nothingness while she was preoccupied with her thoughts?* She looked long, and hard to see something. But, it remained impenetrable; silent, blackness. Perhaps something had changed within her. She was very felt cold; every part of her felt raw, and exposed. Whatever it was, she'd never been so close to breaking point. *She wanted.... needed....to get away from there! To run ....as fast as she could....somewhere! Anywhere! She just wanted out but, she couldn't move!* There was nowhere to go. No one to turn to - other than inward. *She'd never felt so alone. So completely, out of her depth as she found herself on this quest; trapped nowhere in the vast, immovable nothingness! She'd never felt so helpless!* But, for the very first time, she was in awe of the Self that she was slowly becoming more aware of. She'd never realized that there was so much to her Self – a Self that chose to reveal itself in small glimpses whenever she was the observer. She felt as though she was seeing herself, for the very first time! It dawned on her that she'd been suffering from the biggest delusion of all. She believed that the attributes for her accomplishments in the physical world, equated to Self-knowledge!

[You'll be able to see more of your truth without that self-righteous clutter]

If only she could see who that Voice belonged to! Self-righteous!? She?

['I've better things to do with my time;' 'I can do this faster on my own;' 'I'm right;' 'this is beneath me.' Sound familiar? Those are just some of the misconceptions that your ego feeds you. It blocks you from expanding into your soul. There is so much more to the Universe - around, and within you. But, your old way of life had to be disrupted to shake those limiting beliefs – to allow for your truth to emerge. For as long as you remained unaware, nothing was going to get past your ego. And nothing would have changed - within you or in your reality]

She raised a single eyebrow. *So this was all, because of her ego?*

[Sarcasm – like an unchecked ego - will only impede your quest. This transformation isn't a test of your beliefs or intelligence. You're in the process of unravelling both. Life isn't a logical series of events that add up to some pre-conceived outcome. It's not a linear, one-dimensional experience across a horizontal timeline. Life - as you're meant to live it - is everything but, that]

Her defensiveness immediately, kicked in. *Life demanded that she work on as many scenarios as possible! Her survival depended on it! And pre-empting outcomes was her way of ensuring that she fitted everything into each day. "Wanting it all"- a successful career; a successful relationship; a happy life - exacted a heavy price! She already knew that! Her life experiences had prepared her for that!* And yet, she didn't feel very successful! In the same instant, she realized just how heavily conditioned she was by that kind of thinking. It had turned her into a robot! Everything was acceptable, as long as it fitted the same pattern of doing things – even if the result was ongoing stress, and strife. And unhappiness. And she was never aware of it!

[You compartmentalized your life, relationships, and career. You saw them as something outside; separate to your Self. You split yourself into so many different pieces as a coping mechanism but, you fell apart, anyway. Your busyness was just a shield - to protect you from your pain. And your resistance towards all aspects of your character shielding you from it, only attracted more of the same into your life. You continued running, until you ended up here. And now, there's nowhere else to go. You have to face your pain]

She couldn't handle any more of this nonsense! She was getting nowhere!

"What do you want from me?" she screamed into the nothingness. "I've already given you everything! I want this to end! Now!"

She slumped into a small ball, and sobbed uncontrollably. *What was she doing in the nothingness? Was she doing any of this correctly? She should have been out of there by now!* She shook her head for the hundredth time. *This couldn't be happening to her! Her past experiences didn't prepare her for this!* No one she knew had spoken of this kind of quest. The endless spirals of thought, and emotion that took her nowhere! And the daunting uncertainty of it all. *The very reason for all her hard work was to counter all this uncertainty!* Things in her life worked out. They progressed according to plan; logical steps. And she followed them; she always knew what was going to happen next. She knew where she was going. She was familiar with the many clichés about life: "Fail to plan – plan to fail;" "Life is what you make it;" "Make each day count." But, she'd sought more than mere platitudes to live her life! She didn't want to survive. She wanted to thrive.

She wanted to experience the joy held captive in each breath. She wanted to feel life radiating through her - she could feel herself coming alive with just the thought of the power inherent in it! She could now hear life's essence running through the layers of the earth - just as it flowed through her veins! It existed in every natural creation on the planet. The same essence flowed throughout the Universe. It made her yearn to make visible that ocean of life's essence, and to ride each wave with carefree abandonment. And she wanted – more than anything else - to experience all this, while she was still alive! She was breathing fast, and could barely contain the feeling of exhilaration within her. She realized that contrary to the emptiness that she'd experienced in her physical life, this feeling was the only fulfillment she needed. And she'd found it in the nothingness. After searching for it her entire life, in her physical world! She felt warm, electric waves pulse through her body in response to her sentiments. She didn't have to look at herself. She knew her aura had re-appeared, and that she was glowing brightly.

[It will require a lot more inner work, and healing to uncover the self-love necessary to open your heart to live life this way. Perhaps you've set your expectations too high]

She closed her eyes to tap into that inspiration bursting within her. And then, slowly opened them to look at her aura. She lifted her love-struck, gaze towards the nothingness. Not expectations - her feelings were on point. She had nothing else to go on. She'd already been down that wasteland of compromises in her physical world. She'd lowered her standards on more than one occasion. That just made her feel more disempowered, and resentful. She realized some time ago, that lowering her standards wasn't only appealing to the lowest within herself – it lowered those whom she engaged with. That was the highest form of insult – to both Beings! She encountered yet another, paradox. She could continue lowering her standards in her physical world but, she would be denying her truth. She would lose her Self in the process – a Self that connected her to something far greater than anything that existed in the physical world. Furthermore, by continuing with her quest to uncover her truth, she would lose those around her who weren't in alignment with that truth. The choice wasn't easy but, it was obvious. The price of any further compromise was way too high. She would end up living her life in the shadows of a disempowered self, and not in the light of her soul.

[So why did you give so much of yourself to others? What were you hoping for in return?]

She'd never thought of doing things to elicit favors in return - she just did whatever she needed to do. She paused. Did she? There must have been something behind her actions.

[Those circular patterns of behavior were feeding aspects of your shadow self – no matter how noble your intentions. On a macro-level, the existence of harmony in the Universe revolves around balanced energy flows within, and between everything – be it matter or life form. To sustain that balance, there needs to be an equal exchange of energies – between giving, and receiving. An imbalance of any kind will give rise to some form of disruption – its magnitude being an indication of the extent of that imbalance. The same principle applies on a micro-level. Give as much as you can – of yourself and your possessions but, you also need to be open to receive. And you're not]

She was puzzled. In her book, giving and receiving was about showing up - no matter what. And she always showed up! Things didn't always turn out the way she anticipated but, that never stopped her.

[You showed up to meet the needs of others. You never showed up to honor your own. When you sacrifice your wellbeing, you create an imbalance of energy within you. If you did practice some form of self-care your inner 'cup' would never have run dry. You put in a lot of effort in your relationships. But, why did you give of yourself, until you were depleted? Why did you think that you had to make all the effort? What about allowing others to step up? Were you helping or enabling those around you? The former can uplift whereas the latter is a factor of ego – it weakens, and controls people. Don't you believe that you deserve a life that includes, not only material comforts but, love, respect, and kindness? Sometimes you have to say 'no' to honor your truth, and the truth of another - no matter how difficult it is for both concerned]

She'd seldom said "no" to anything asked of her. On more than one occasion, she'd intuited the needs of others, and met their expectations without being asked. And she'd persisted with the many demands on her time, believing that she had no choice. Now she wasn't so sure, anymore. How was it in her best interests if she'd allowed herself to be taken advantage of? Did she really love herself if she continued to place herself in toxic situations? Did being committed to something or someone mean compromising her truth? Why did she attach so easily - to the extent of sacrificing her needs? Why was she so insecure? But, there was something else that weighed heavily on her. Why didn't she recognize such behavior when she was subjected to it? Why didn't she remove herself from people, and situations that didn't serve her highest interests? Whether she was deserving or not had never featured in her thinking. Her life was about doing, and her focus was always on "the other." Why didn't she feature in her own life? Did she deserve a better life? Did she deserve love, respect, and kindness as well? She'd always believed that she needed to earn respect in her physical world. But, that was her physical world. Didn't her Being deserve respect, irrespective of the roles she could perform in her world? She had an epiphany. She didn't respect herself if she'd subjected herself to such inhumane behavior! That's why it was so glaringly absent in her life! She bent her head in shame. She was responsible for what she allowed into her space! And for the way she got treated!

[Your life is so much more than doing. And it's not the relationship with 'the other' that you should concern yourself. In your life, you are 'the other.' Your relationships with others merely reflect the relationship that you have with yourself. Why were you constantly trying to prove your worthiness?]

What was self-worth? What more did she have to do to get it? Surely, her good deeds so far, entitled her to it? Did she give enough? She was struck by an insight. Why did she go on giving without setting some boundaries? Again, she found herself feeling confused. *When was enough, enough? Did this quest involve removing boundaries or putting them up? Did she need new boundaries? What was wrong with the existing ones? Why did she feel so awkward, whenever she received something – to such an extent that she preferred avoiding receiving, altogether!? If this was about energy flow, then why was she the only one giving!? Why did everyone else just go on taking? Why didn't they stop?* She had another revelation. Why didn't she say "stop?" That was her responsibility! Was this dynamic an indication of her low self-worth? She sighed. She felt as though she was being tossed about in a

Undefined

whirlwind. Only to be hit by another revelation. She might have showed up but, her old self wasn't "open." Was this what becoming open entailed? She was horrified. She was being stripped of her defenses! And there was nowhere to hide; nothing she could do to protect herself! Her curiosity got the better of her. What would it feel like to be open?

[This quest isn't a negotiation. Self-worth isn't something you buy or receive in exchange for your 'good' deeds. Giving is noteworthy but, you're not required to deplete yourself, and sacrifice your soul's growth. Your high levels of resentment were an indication that you were taking on far more than you needed to. And those constant niggles when lowering your standards were pointing you in the direction of your Self. By continuously ignoring your needs, you denied your soul's desires, and shut yourself off from your instinctive nature. You left yourself no choice but, to be defined by the standards and practices prevalent in your world. To prove yourself 'right,' you even tried bringing others around to your way of thinking – thereby disrespecting your truth, and the truth of others. That egoist attitude only added to your burdens. You're responsible for your soul – for maintaining the vibration of your physical body in accordance with your soul's purpose, until you fulfil it. You're not responsible for the way others choose to live their lives. Your self-sacrificing beliefs stem from your conditioning, and far from securing you some heavenly place in the 'afterlife,' it's sabotaging your souls' growth. You do have a rightful place in this world, just as you are – from the moment you were conceived. You have nothing to prove. You owe nothing - to anyone - for being here. And in the same way, no one owes you anything. That is the premise of true giving, and receiving. Be kind, and generous by all means but, you're not expected to be anyone other than your true Self. No one can judge you for the Self you embody or for not being whom they expect you to be – that's on them. And self-judgment is unfounded. It also stems from your conditioning - of how you should behave. You – more than anyone else – needs to accept your Self for who you are. Your relationships with others – no matter how good - won't cover up a sense of lack or keep your fears at bay. Your physical world has groomed you to believe that your worth is defined only in financial terms. But, those terms won't sustain your soul. Looking to your external world to provide

sustenance for your soul is the real poverty in your life. It's the real poverty in the physical world]
[It's the same with love. You don't need to do anything to secure or earn the love of another. And you don't need to prove your love. Love isn't a transaction. It doesn't require compromise or self-betrayal. It's not about control or ownership - love doesn't need a contract to define or validate it. It's a mutual exchange of energy built on a foundation of self-love, respect and trust. It allows for two people to inspire and nurture love for themselves, and each other. As opposed to playing on ego-based fears to force, demand or exploit it. It's a connection between hearts that reflects the love that already resides within each Being. Each individual holds the space for the other to express the relationship that they have with themselves. And if nurtured, it will support the continued growth of each individual to fulfill their respective soul paths. Unnecessary complications arise, because of power struggles that focus on playing each other's weaknesses. Resist any tendency to gain control or power over another by compromising or lowering the other – that's the domain of ego. And you'll only end up lowering yourself, and feeling smaller for it. True love can't exist in the same space as ego. Ego fosters entrapment, and co-dependency in the web that is woven around the question: 'Am I enough?' And that is evident in a physical world that is run by social constructs that only feed the ego's fears, and weaknesses. There is no such question between two hearts in the presence of unconditional love. It doesn't necessarily mean that such a relationship will be easy-going. If anything, true love involving souls can be messy. And painful. But, the process to get there is necessary for two people to overcome their egos if they desire true intimacy – not just physical intimacy but, the intimacy that comes from being vulnerable with each other. It's only by being aware of the ego, and being willing to overcome its self-obsessiveness that each individual can give, and receive love unconditionally]
[The experience of true love in the physical dimension is unsurpassed for that very reason. But, you already know that – you've been seeking it all your life. If you must classify it in terms of a 'trade,' then the one for your heart is simple - love for love; in the presence of truth. And if it's absent in your life, then look within for the reasons. Being 'enough'

isn't the defining criterion for a love that's unconditional, and mutually fulfilling. Self-worth, and self-love are. No other aspect needs to be defined to hold true hearts together. There is no need - unconditional love encompasses them all. And if you do find it and then, have to let your beloved go because, either one or both of you no longer respect each other's truths, then do so with love, and kindness – no matter what your ego demands of you. For during the time that you shared together, you inspired the best in each other – you created a timeless beauty in the eternal light of your love. Letting go isn't the end of love – endings, and beginnings only exist in the realm of ego. True love - in any relationship - is the only eternal form of energy in the Universe, whether you're physically together or not. Pain, and suffering only arise when you hold onto someone who no longer serves your soul's highest path]

Was she trying to secure love? To prove her worth?

[Your behavior is partly due to a lack of self-worth but, the absence of self-love played the leading role in your self-sabotaging behavior. And what you believe, and allow yourself to accept under the banner of 'I am deserving' is determined by both. Both are a reflection of how you treat yourself - and by extension - how you treat others. With self-love, you can overcome low self-worth. Without it, you'll be your worst enemy. You came into this world as a Being of love. Somehow you lost your way - your connection with your Self, and your soul. And you've been floundering in the dark, ever since]

She shifted uncomfortably. She had no self-worth? She didn't love herself?

[Do you know how to love yourself? Can you freely express the light within your soul? And share the love within your Being?]

She didn't – not after what she'd just heard! To her, love was just another word - with far too many complications. And any mention of it made her feel uncomfortable. It put her on guard. She didn't like any emotional ties. She preferred things to be simple; straight-forward. And based on past experience, that was never the case where love was concerned! *Besides, life was way too short. Why waste it on something that never lasted, anyway? Nothing ever lasted in this crazy world!* She paused – becoming aware of her thoughts. What was she thinking!? Why would she think like that? Her mind was back in the driver's seat before she could stop it. *How could true love be eternal? Why was it important, anyway? It could never save the world!* She sighed. *All this stuff was way too complicated! But, she was getting older. Maybe she should reconsider. She didn't want to be alone for the rest of her life. Maybe some love in her life wouldn't be such a bad idea. Was there some way she could get her hands on it? What did she need to do to achieve it?*

[There are many things in your physical world that you can rationalize, and control - love shouldn't be one of them. If you do, you'll deny yourself the experience of something truly unique, and wonderful - the expression of the ageless beauty of your soul. Love is your soul made visible in your physical world. It can't be imported into your life from anyone or anything outside of you. And you'll find fear – not love - if you react from a place of fear. It's not a 'goal' to be achieved; there's nothing you have to do. You're love; it's the natural state of your Being. But, before you can share the love of another you have to uncover your self-love by removing all the barriers blocking you from it]

She felt herself bristle with irritation. *More barriers! More work! More questions! She was just going round in circles! Where was this quest taking her? When would it end!?*

[Further away from who you thought you were. And closer to all that you truly are. There is no ending. And no beginning. There is just your soul expressing its light in human form - in a single moment of physical time. Outside of that experience you're an infinite, Being of love]

Closer to who she truly was? Who was she becoming on this quest?

[You're not 'becoming' anyone. You're already who you're meant to be - within your soul. You just have to remove all the layers blocking you from your truth]

She let out a long, frustrated sigh. *So her life was in her own hands! What else was new? She'd always believed that! And look where that belief had dumped her – in nothingness! Talking to a glow-worm, and an invisible Voice!*

[There is a key distinction. You believe that your old reality was the expression of your true Self. It wasn't. It was only an illusion manifested by a false sense of self]

She was having difficulty grasping the many nuances that were being revealed. She didn't realize that the rigid black, and white borders underpinning her old conditioning were slowly disintegrating. Neither was she aware that her discernment was being refined in the process. It was becoming more difficult to hold onto her old image of being "together." And without the familiar, mental structures that upheld her illusory reality, she believed that she would never reach her destination - finding this elusive, true Self. It dawned on her that she was now caught up in another in-between, phase. The one between unbecoming, and becoming – her true Self. And the tug-of-war was excruciating. *There was no respite from the unknown forces that seemed to be hell-bent on ripping her apart! How was she supposed to make any sense of something as abstract as her true Self? Did it even exist? There was nothing to go on – she was floundering around in inner, and outer darkness!*

[Uncovering your true Self isn't a 'destination.' It's an ongoing process that lasts for an entire lifetime. And your soul awakening is only a continuation of the journey that started when you were born. But, unlike the previous phase of your life, you won't be able to understand this part of your life's journey with your mind. Your existing thought patterns will only regurgitate the same old, familiar stories. And your ego won't allow you to think of yourself as anything, other than 'together.' It ruled over every aspect of yourself to such an extent, that you believed you were walking your true path. But, its 'power' is limited to its reflexive urges, within the constraints of physical time. Your heart, and soul know no such constraints. They both play the long game – spanning lifetimes, if necessary. Besides, you wouldn't have been able to avoid the stark difference between your false reality, and your unknown soul reality, for much longer. Very little about your physical reality was an extension of your truth - it wasn't created by your true Self. The result was all the heartache, and suffering in your life]

If she was living life as her authentic Self there would be no suffering?

[Don't over-simplify things to placate your ego - it's only trying a different escape hatch. That won't work here. And using ridicule to cover up your denial won't work, either. Life is characterized by a whole spectrum of experiences, and emotions – good and bad. You've done your Self a major disservice by curating an identity through polarizing your experiences into either/or categories. Life can't be constrained within the linear, logical constructs of your mind. Furthermore, choosing an illusion of the 'good life' by fostering denial of the full human experience is self-defeating. That approach only allows you to experience a small, limited version of your humanity. And you'll only encounter the same 'walls,' until you awaken to your truth. Chasing the type of 'success' that your ego wants, and walking your soul path provide two very different experiences of your time in this physical dimension. The first will provide the illusion of success in your physical world. It will be as fleeting, and fickle as the desires of the society dictating it. Only the second offers you the guarantee of fulfillment – it has your soul behind it. There's a fine, invisible line between them – easily overlooked if you persist with your unconscious way of life. Once you awaken, however, you will be able to discern at what 'points' you need to 'step' across it to realize your soul path in your physical world. The distinction is really, quite simple when you're in touch with your emotions. When you're out of alignment with you soul path, you'll feel depleted. Joyless. You'll feel separated from Source. And you'll treat yourself in unloving ways. Walking your soul path won't be without its share of challenges but, you'll be on an ever-evolving, upward, energetic spiral – always in touch with Divine Source. You'll feel an unrivalled sense of love, and joy. You'll feel empowered. As opposed to the downward spiral that you've been on thus far, in every aspect of your life. Feeling both joy and insecurity during times of uncertainty are only mutually exclusive to your mind - the result of it polarizing your thoughts, and emotions. It's counter-intuitive but, remaining with uncertainty is the only way to surpass your mind. Once you uncover your truth, and align with your soul path you'll also be closer to the natural state of your Being – which is love. And there are no mind-induced, polarized thoughts, and emotions in your Being. It's all love. Oneness with everything, and everyone]

[But, you still have a long way to go before you can attain that level of consciousness. In the meantime, you can help yourself by identifying the barriers that you've used to mold your false identity. In doing so, your truth will slowly 'break open' your old self – layer by layer. And reveal those aspects of yourself that need healing. Trust your inner voice - it will help you to find your way past those barriers. The process is not easy – it's not meant to be. But, now that you've shaken your mental constructs you're more open to uncertainty, and the unknown. Without realizing it, you've also become stronger during this quest. You'll be able to strip your illusions of self, even further - to uncover what lies at the core of your fears, and limiting behavior. Try not to worry about what comes next – it will only add to your confusion. Your mind will calibrate a new way of thinking as you become more integrated with your Self. Again, don't concern yourself with how or when that will happen. Trust your soul's knowing – not the noise in your mind. It won't be necessary for you to start from scratch to create a new reality – it already exists. You just have to focus on uncovering your truth. And release, and heal whatever reveals itself to you, until you're all emptied out. Your soul's light will expand into that spaciousness – to guide you along your true path. There is no more meaningful way to experience life – no matter how many lifetimes your ego-mind makes you go around, to prove otherwise]

This was starting to make some sense. But, how did Voice know all this? Was Glow, impersonating Voice? She scoffed. *She wasn't about to fall for that scam!*

[You're allowing your ego to distract you. There is no one around to fool you. Your thinking is only highlighting your lack of trust in your Self. And you won't make much progress here, without it. You need to trust your soul's knowing. And that you'll find what you need - when you need it. As you continue with your quest, it will become easier to discern the many ways that your ego has misled you in crafting a false identity. And as more of your truth is revealed, you'll be able to focus your energy more effectively, on what's essential for your soul's growth]

She raised her eyebrows. *She'd focused on non-essentials?*

[Yes. Because you've been trapped in a maze of illusion defined by your mind. You're much more than your mind. It does have its uses in your physical world but, your mind serves your soul. You can't force your soul to be subservient to your mind. It's an essential distinction to help you dislodge your ego from the pedestal that you've placed it on, before you can see yourself for all that you are. A Being without fear, judgement or lack; without desire or ambition. Your Being isn't separated from your physical body or your soul. There is nothing for you to attain; nothing to reach or achieve. There is nowhere to go – you are the 'destination' that you've been seeking. All that your soul desires is already yours – it lies within you. And you possess all that you need in this lifetime to fulfill your soul desires. Your Being isn't caught up in a quagmire of distracting, and destructive thought or emotion. It's one with the flow of life; one with the entire Universe. You've always felt its power but, you rejected it, because you couldn't explain that feeling with your logical mind. But, the full depth, and breadth of your Being will always defy any rational explanation - your mind won't be able to do it justice. It doesn't speak to you in any of the languages in your physical world. Love has its own language – it's silent, wordless; toneless. And yet, once you attune to its vibration you'll never again, mistake the 'sound' of its 'voice.' All you need to do is honor it with integrity, and you'll always 'hear' its timeless wisdom. All this time, you've been fighting to build a life, because you didn't know your truth or trust in the timing of the Universe. If it's not based on your truth, any kind of life built by an ego will fall apart, for nothing can subdue the ego's sense of lack, and fear of physical time. It's only by embracing your truth to remain in resonance with the love within your Being that you'll be able to witness the unfolding of reality within, in your physical world - not by doing or through force]

She shook her head vehemently. *Wonderful! Perfect! But, how was she supposed to find an unknown path in nothingness? How would she know if it was the right path? And if she ever got back to her physical world, how was she supposed to navigate her way across some "invisible line" to stay in her truth, and walk her soul path? And she didn't have a clue how to transform her old self into this new Self! How could both be a part of her? Surely one had to die, before the other could come into existence? That wasn't possible in the course of a single lifetime!* She threw up her hands in frustration. *This whole thing was utterly, ridiculous! She'd never been so confused, and frustrated in her life! Why did she commit to this – it was impossible!* With each moment she was becoming more horrified, and short of breath.

[Stop resisting the process by trying to grasp this quest with your mind. It doesn't have the answers – not after years of conditioning. And you can now control your anxiety by detaching from your thoughts, and emotions. Your ego has been silenced to some extent but, don't be fooled. It will rear its head at some point. Right now, it's busy grappling with the decline of its power. You might not be conscious of the energies bringing about your transformation but, your mind is still functioning - to help you process aspects of the transition between your old self, and your true Self. You don't need to concern yourself with the changes happening on an energetic level – that is out of your control. The only indication of their presence will come from the pain in your physical body. Listen to it, and take care of what it needs. And remain aware of your thoughts. Your ego can still access the information in your conscious mind, and mislead you. The same applies to whatever is made conscious as it surfaces from your sub-conscious mind to be released, and healed. Don't think about what you know or what's right – it will only add to your confusion. Let the process unfold naturally – free from your mind's interference. Focus on staying present with what's unfolding within your expanding heart space, irrespective of your discomfort, and the uncertainty. Stay vigilant – remain in your stillness. You can trust your heart to guide you through the process - only the heart is removed from control by the mind, and ego]

So her mind didn't have a clue how to go about this quest! Glow did warn her about that - it did say that she would have to turn inward.

[All of you – in a state of Being – is much more than your human form. It holds parts of your Self which you're not as yet, familiar with. And parts that you became acquainted with in the past. But, your truth has been forgotten during cycles of conditioning through the ages. Your Being belongs to something far greater than your physical self. It has been guiding, and protecting you throughout your life - without you being aware of it. As you uncover your truth, you'll become re-acquainted with your true Self. At the same time you'll be opening your physical self to your Being – creating a channel for more love to enter, and heal you]

She was totally, bemused. *Her unknown destination was being guided by her unknown Self! There was some kind of invisible channel between her Self, and her Being – another unknown! And all of her was part of a much bigger unknown – a mystical, infinite Universe!*

[Everyone has access to guidance from their higher Selves. And everyone can choose with every decision to, either get closer to Divine Source or move away from It. And therein lies the experience of heaven, and hell during your lifetime]

She sighed. *This was totally, beyond her! She knew nothing about this stuff! How was she supposed to know if any of it was true?*

[Don't discount what you perceive as unknown, in favor of what you think can be understood by your mind. That is a classic misconception. Life's biggest questions remain inaccessible to those who remain caught up in the illusion of the physical world. However, the answers that you seek are far from unknown - they're readily available to anyone seeking their truth with an open heart. You're fooling yourself if you believe that what you understand with your mind is all there Is. Whether you admit it or not, it's easier to define your world, and yourself within the domain of your five senses. It also helps that those thoughts can be manipulated by your ego to suit whatever fantasy you choose to become attached to. The certainty makes you feel comfortable. So far that age-old, belief system hasn't turned out the way you expected but, you continue to cling to it. However, your soul has a different knowing. It seeks to expand your consciousness - to help you actualize your life purpose. It desires a true expression of Self. If you doubt that in any way, then look around you]

[Everything - across all dimensions - is energy. There are various forms, and in some cases, they are inter-changeable but, the total amount of energy in the Universe is constant - at a specific level of consciousness. At the higher levels they might not be visible to the human eye but, you're quite familiar with one of the more prominent forms of energy in the physical realm – white light. It touches everything that you see with the human eye. But, what you 'see' is not all that Is – the human eye can only see within a certain band of frequencies. That limits your sight in many ways, and leads to misconceptions. For example, you perceive all tangible structures as fixed. However, everything possesses energy, in some form or other, or a combination thereof. And everything is in motion, including the most dense, inanimate objects that don't contain the essence of life. Everything is always changing, even though it's at such a low vibrational level that it can't be discerned by the human eye. The human body presents an interesting anomaly. It's perceived as solid, and tangible in its physical state, and you're able to move it to comply with the bidding of your mind but, even when you're still, and unconscious of it, your body is in motion. Your entire Being, is in motion. Every cell is alive; vibrating with the essence of life – which is another form of energy. Remove that life essence, and you might as well be an inanimate object. The best way to appreciate this phenomenon is to imagine yourself deconstructing into a mass of individual cells. If you could somehow reconstruct yourself using exactly, the same pool of cells you'll no longer be alive, because that invisible, life essence is no longer present. That same essence exists throughout the Universe. Its power remains undiluted no matter the form it embodies. That same power is inherent to your Being. It connects you to the entire Universe; to all Beings. Your uniqueness, however, comes from your soul; it's your Divine purpose. And only you can fulfill that purpose in this world]

[Many are capable of accessing aspects of this energy in various ways, and to different degrees. Some have even learnt to manipulate forms of this energy for self-gain. However, the highest form of this energy – love - will always remain elusive to those whose intentions are driven by ego. The more emphasis you place on manifesting the dictates of your ego, the further removed you'll be from your soul's truth, and the less your ability to access your full potential. Even if the physical reality that you build is considered to be a momentous feat in your physical lifetime, it will be meaningless to you if it's not based on your truth. You have nothing to fear. The more aligned you are with your truth and allow your soul's reality to unfold with an open heart, the greater the ability of your inner light to protect, and support you through any challenge in this physical dimension. Although you live in a physical world defined by time, your soul path will not be dictated by it. Your path will unfold in accordance with the natural laws of the Universe. And in Divine timing - over a single lifetime or over many lifetimes. The realization of the reality based on your soul's truth might not be considered a legacy by worldly standards but, you're not here to comply with those standards or limit your Self to an age-old, definition of 'legacy.' You're here to fulfill your soul's evolutionary path of realizing higher levels of consciousness. Each individual who follows the path of truth, lights the way for the evolution of all human consciousness. That is the only timeless legacy you participate in co-creating. You diverged from your truth when you ascribed a higher value to matter, as opposed to fulfilling your soul purpose. In doing so, you exchanged your life essence for something as superfluous as your ego's fixation on material gain. Your Being is connected to the infinite; the eternal. And you're trying to force it to fit your understanding of existence in this physical realm. That is the source of the imbalance you're perpetuating within you. That is the imbalance you see reflected all around you, in the physical world. And that imbalance is the root of your ongoing unhappiness, and feelings of lack. Only by healing yourself will you begin to open to the fullness of life, and be able to embrace the abundance that exists within you, and in the Universe. Only then will you stop destroying the planet in an attempt to find the harmony that only comes from being at peace with your Self. Everything in your world begins, and ends with your healed Self]

Those words sounded completely, foreign to her. However, she couldn't deny that she felt alienated from her life, and Self. The way Voice explained things was comforting enough but, comfort was no longer a drawcard. Instead, her attention was focused on the extent of the discomfort between herself, and her truth. She might not know what her truth was but, she felt it in the extreme dissonance that arose from that separation, and the extent of the lie that she'd been living. Finally, she understood why her entire life's work had to be destroyed. And why the identity of the person she remembered herself to be was also being annihilated. None of it was true! She recalled that she'd always been fascinated by light. It was the one constant in her life, since her childhood love affair with the stars. In later years, she'd learnt that it was around since the dawn of time. She was enthralled by the wonder, and magic of the rainbow of colors that comprised white light. And yet, each color possessed its own unique, beautiful hue. It traveled at speeds beyond anything that she could comprehend and despite such power she could stand in the sunlight, and feel it caress her skin. She could feel its warmth and taste it in the food, and water that nourished her. She inhaled it each day, with every life-sustaining breath of air created by the plants, and trees after they'd consumed the sunlight. She played a part in that process with every breath that she exhaled. And yet, the space around earth remained shrouded in blackness – the light from the sun travelling straight through it, and lighting up the planet like a magnificent, blue sapphire in an ocean of stars. Her breath caught in her throat as she realized for the first time, the wonder of the planet that she was living on. And the glory of a Universe that stretched far beyond her imagination. It was daunting to think that she was a part of that miraculous, mystical creation. But, the longer she spent in the nothingness, the more inclined she was to believing just that.

[You are a part of It. You've just forgotten your soul's truth. Doing something – anything - was far better than doing nothing. Even if it took you further away from your truth. And yet, what you perceive as 'nothing' is actually, everything. But, you failed to look beyond the obvious, because it's easier to stick with the familiar - even if it takes you round in circles. Some realize that they're caught in an illusion, and break free from the shackles that bind them to a futile existence. Others continue to wander aimlessly in this physical dimension, trusting the illusion more than themselves. Just the way you did]

As difficult as it was to accept, she couldn't deny the truth in those words. What she'd viewed as success before, now looked nothing more than organized chaos! Over the years, she'd convinced herself that everything was fine. She even believed that she was fine - even though there were times when she felt like she was going insane! But, she believed that she could fix anything, and the more chaotic her life became, the harder she tried to make it work. She was struck by a revelation. The only way she could have become blindsided to pursue such an existence was if she'd been denying her truth! And that kept her completely, out of harmony with her Self! Achieving some of her goals might have given her the illusion of success but, she couldn't have been living her best life if she wasn't fulfilling her soul purpose! And she'd continued trying to fix everything, and everyone - without realizing that she was the one who was broken! No matter how difficult her life was, she'd been taking short-cuts all along! And despite the 'realness' of her physical reality, she'd been riding a "gilded carriage" to nowhere! Her life looked, and felt real. She even thought that it was real! But, it was only an illusion! She'd never felt so devastated by anything, before! What was the root cause of such an imbalance? It had made her accept an illusion as a fair tradeoff, for the life that she truly deserved! No small wonder that meaning had eluded her – she'd sold herself way too short! As was evident from the false reality that she'd created by betraying her soul's growth. Her ego might have considered that a fair enough exchange but, her soul certainly, didn't! It never had! As evidenced by all the pain in her life. She was struck by another revelation. Irrespective of how much effort she'd devoted to an illusory reality, she would never be able to trade her soul's truth for something that wasn't worthy of her highest calling.

[Discerning the meaning of 'fair exchange' in your physical world is itself an illusion. But, you'll continue to be diverted from your true path by any number of external factors, until you possess the inner conviction that comes from embracing your truth. Once you uncover that, you'll be able to manifest your soul's reality with instinctive harmony. Be aware that the odds will be stacked against you, because of the few who benefit from imposing the systems, and structures that have become the perceived reality of the majority. A 'reality' that conforms to the same limiting cycles, day-after-day; month-after-month; year-after-year; decade-after-decade. Century-after-century. As horrendous as that sounds it's acceptable, because it's 'familiar.' It's 'known.' But, it only continues to exist, because it leverages the ego's weaknesses, and suppresses the truth of souls. Sticking within the confines of those systems makes you believe that there's only one kind of success, and that the only way to achieve it, is to overcome your weaknesses. But, you're not weak - you're more powerful than you could ever imagine. You're made to believe that you're smaller, and weaker than the 'powers' you're trying to overcome, because your social conditioning keeps your ego's biggest illusion intact – a false sense of identity born of separation from your fellow Beings, and the Universe. That false notion has another effect – one that's far more treacherous to attaining your full potential. You've been conditioned to believe that you're powerless to change it. Your belief in the 'system' is so strong that despite all the pain, and destruction you see around you, you continue to uphold it in all its forms. The system has to be 'right' even if longevity – and not humanitarianism - is the only yardstick by which it can be measured. However, that isn't the world you wish

Undefined

to live in. That isn't the level of human consciousness desired by your soul. But, the world you desire does exist. The life that you deserve is real. There is only one, true reality - it lies within you. You have the power to co-create it. And your heart, and soul already know the way]

She felt her tears burning in her throat but, her anger helped keep them at bay. So much wasted time, and effort chasing an illusion built on fear! So many sacrifices for a life that she believed was her own but, all this time she'd been living a lie! And denying her one, true calling – her soul purpose! She might not know how to find her way out of the nothingness but, she was now determined not to be ruled by the fear of an illusion! Her physical world might continue being dictated by those who held it hostage by feeding on the fear, and pain of the innocent. She might not know how to change the world but, she refused to be a part of an illusion, anymore! And if it was within her power to free herself from a self-perpetuating form of defeatism then that was what she would focus her energy on. There must be another way - a better way - to live her life. Her soul guaranteed her of that! If she'd succumbed to a false identity through ignorance and naiveté, and if that left her separated from her truth wandering the outer limits of her soul, then she had only one, essential choice. She had to uncover her truth, and live her soul's purpose – her best life!

Again, she was struck by self-doubt. *This was way too big! Could she succeed on this quest? Could she give up everything that was known and familiar, and change her life mid-stream? Could she trust.....the unknown over the known.....uncertainty over certainty......the intangible over the tangible ....a silent inner voice, over her mind? Could she change old belief patterns with her soul's knowing? Could she surrender to faith and trust, and forego certainty? Could she heal and transform herself with unknown, invisible energies, and allow her true reality to unfold? Could she make something intangible, tangible in her physical world? That was impossible! She couldn't make something out of nothing! What if she gave up everything that she knew to co-create this unknown reality, only to discover that she didn't like the way things turned out? She was trading everything that was familiar; everything she knew for....for....what? This quest had already pulled the rug out from under her! She had nothing more to give – to trade! What was she supposed to do? What kind of result could she expect if she persisted with her healing?* She sighed, and shook her head. *She couldn't just hand over whatever control she had, and pursue some whimsical notion to nowhere!*

[You're assuming that the knowledge, and experience gained in your physical world allows you to do everything that you're capable of. Whatever existed in your previous reality might be familiar, and tangible but, it's far from what's possible using your innate potential to fulfill your soul purpose. Perhaps the biggest hurdle you need to cross before you can grasp the full extent of the limitless possibilities available to you in this Universe, is to ask what you possess without your true Self? By your own admission the harder you strived to reach your egotistic goals, the further removed you felt from your life essence. If you stand by your conviction that you tried your best and yet, still failed to attain what you wanted, then you must have been missing the most important attributes needed for the life you deserve – self-worth, and self-love. Without those qualities, actualization of your soul path will remain a myth. And inner peace will continue to elude you. And yet, you persist with the delusion that you were living your 'dream' life in your physical world. The life you deserve, and the life you desire in your soul are one, and the same. Everything that inspires your soul is pointing you to what it desires, and the limitless possibilities available in the Universe if you own your truth. The main reason you haven't been living fully alive is your belief that nothing is possible outside of your mind. You'll get to the root-cause of that problem by continuing to unravel your old patterns of behavior. The process will help you to see how you made choices that didn't serve you. Learn how to better serve, and honor your Divine Self, and everything becomes possible in this physical dimension, including co-creating your soul purpose with the Universe. By letting go of the life you expected to have, you'll create the space within to receive the life that you deserve]

[However, the extent of healing required to open yourself fully to receive your soul's gifts is far from over. You need to go the rest of the way to uncover your truth. And that will require every ounce of Self-love. You can choose to stay within the confines of your old conditioning, and relegate yourself to a certain station in your physical world but, you'll be betraying your soul. And you'll have to accept far less than you're worth, because of that. Your soul will continue

Undefined

to remind you of your true calling in this lifetime. And the next, if you continue to ignore it. It will continue to remind you, until you heed its call. And that will be more difficult to bear than completing your quest. You're making this quest more difficult than it needs to be, because you're trying to understand it. Your soul already has the knowing - it chose this path before you were born. You encountered certain life experiences after you were born, and now you're going through a kind of death before you can fully awaken to the life that you deserve. In the process, you'll learn to discern the workings of your ego to a far greater extent. If you remain centered in your stillness, you'll be able to recognize it coming from a mile away. And your increased awareness will negate your ego's intent, thereby ensuring that its only role is supporting your soul path. So whether you 'like' your newfound reality or not is unimportant, because you ego will no longer be in the driver's seat. Your soul's light will be guiding you in the creation of your true reality. You can trust it will be more than anything that you ever thought possible, because it will be in harmony with your truth. You've been grappling with this dilemma for many lifetimes. It's the reason you're still alive – to find that place of silent, stillness. To bring your soul purpose into reality, and finally, feel peace. Your soul purpose might not bring you fame or fortune but, it speaks to the Divine essence that you embody to make it possible. Without it your physical world will continue to feel like a desert. It's your choice]

And her past life now looked like an endless desert that she'd been wandering around aimlessly, for years. For all her efforts, the life that she'd built resembled a steel tank buried somewhere beneath it. There was nothing about it that she could relate to anymore. She could pass her time sticking pictures of her ideal life on the walls to disguise where she was but, makeshift changes no longer appealed to her. She realized that she wasn't even sitting in a corner - she could always get herself out of one. This was a self-imposed, prison! How was she supposed to free herself!? The walls were invisible and yet, she was the one who had erected them! She could feel them slowly, closing in on her! She couldn't bear the pressure but, all she could do was sit with her eyes closed, and face the onslaught of the thoughts that emerged. What purpose would be served by returning to her old way of life? She might have nothing more to lose by the standards defined in her physical world but, if she returned to her old way of life she would lose everything that she was beginning to learn about her Self! She felt an icy chill creep into her heart. She didn't know what to do. *Did she have to move to some monastery to live out the rest of her days?* Some part of her retaliated fiercely. *She didn't want to live like a monk! Why was she still alive? Why couldn't she find the answers to help her get out of the nothingness?* For whatever reason, she was still breathing. And she was still stuck in the middle of nowhere! How could she change her life from there? How could she change her life by doing nothing – by simply Being? How could being her true Self, transform her life? How did she connect with her Being? What did it mean to begin where she was - with her Self? Was there a way she could go deeper into herself? She had no idea. But, she was still there – not certain, where "there" was supposed to be! She couldn't bring herself to go back, and the only way forward was to go deeper within herself. She sighed, hopelessly. *What could she possibly learn about herself that she didn't already know?*

She smiled at the irony. She'd always, steered away from anything that she considered mundane. She wanted her life to be a marvelous adventure – to experience something new, every day. Over the years, she'd continuously challenged herself with one objective in mind - to "do it all" before she died. And she'd made certain that nothing deterred her from that single-minded, focus. Until now. And there she was, caught up in some weird, quest that she never saw coming! It wasn't like anything she expected. It wasn't the corporate ladder that she'd hoped to scale in record time or all the wonderful places that she'd hoped to visit. It wasn't a house or any of the other physical assets that she'd accumulated over the years. It wasn't a relationship with 'the one." It wasn't any lofty ideal or belief; or some grandiose plan. Instead, it was something that she'd never given a second thought to – staying present, with the birthing of her unknown Self! Throughout her life, she'd never thought that anything important existed within her - other than her mind! In the silence that consumed her, some of her childhood memories surfaced, and she again recalled her fascination with the sky. She'd often toyed with the idea of "diving" into its vastness, and bouncing merrily on the clouds. She was convinced that if she looked hard and long enough, she would become one with it, and make the infinite distance between them melt away. It never occurred to her to question

Undefined

whether there were depths within herself that were as infinite as the sky. She smiled at her childish memories but, as crazy as they were she now suspected that they held some hidden power. In some mysterious way, this entire quest was very much what she'd created during her silent, wishful thinking when gazing at the stars. She breathed in deeply, and unconsciously held onto it as she contemplated the power behind those long-forgotten, musings. Well, she was now experiencing something that she would never have thought possible. She realized that as much as she hated the mundane, it was more the ordinary that riled her. Whether she wanted to admit it or not, her life epitomized ordinary! And now, she was confronted with the most unexpected adventure in that very "ordinary" life – the birth of her true Self. Something that she never even thought existed. She realized that her ordinary self was actually, quite extraordinary – it had led her to her quest; to uncovering her truth, and her soul purpose! She felt something stir deep within her heart, and rise whole-heartedly to embrace that unfamiliar sentiment. Her mind might not know what to do but, that feeling must be her soul's desire to explore the unknown within her. She'd never felt all of herself rise so intently to act as one body, mind, heart, and soul. And even more surprising, there was no intention or will behind it. It was based purely on inspiration to rise to the unknown challenge beckoning her. It was petrifying, and exhilarating at the same time. She wanted to stay immersed in that feeling - that magical, throbbing, aliveness beating in her heart. She felt as though all of her was resonating with the entire Universe.

[Remember that feeling. Therein lies the 'future' that your soul has been yearning for; the only one worth living. However, you've only completed part of your quest. You need to go back to your past to uncover all of your truth]

It took a while to register what she'd just heard. Then, she reacted fiercely. *No! Never! She'd already gone back. She was done with the past! None of it was real! She wasn't real - she wasn't her true Self! Whoever that person was, she no longer existed! She had no intention of wasting any more time. She wanted a whole, new future.*

[There are parts of you still trapped in that 'steel tank'- locked away somewhere in your past. There's nothing to fear. You've discovered your stillness. It will help you to remain detached as you unearth the untruths lying buried beneath the invisible, steel walls of time.

Carrying all that pain no longer serves you. You might think that you don't remember anything hidden beyond your conscious mind but, you will - once you surrender to the expanding space that's opening up within you. Whatever lies behind those 'walls' defined your old self - in some way or other. Only by re-living your unconscious pain – by witnessing it with the light of your consciousness will you be able to free your Self from that invisible prison. Nothing is as impossible as you fear in the nothingness. But, using your will in the nothingness to reach for a 'future' outside yourself is futile. Your future lies buried in your past – in this very moment that you find yourself in. By going through the pain that you've been trapped in for lifetimes, you'll be able to transmute it and create the life that your soul desires]

Where did she start? This could take forever!

[Your understanding of 'forever' is limited to physical time. It has no meaning here. But, if you're still caught in its illusion, then know that you do have time - all the time you need. In the nothingness, you're in an endless, moment of time. You'll encounter many 'beginnings,' and 'endings' in this single moment. Don't allow yourself to be distracted by such illusions. Your thoughts are only misconceptions prompted by your ego to make you believe that you can control the outcome of your quest. There will be times when you feel you're going nowhere in the vortex of emotion that threatens to swallow you whole. Be aware of your thoughts, and emotions. Observe what happens to your physical body with each one. More importantly, does your energy expand or contract around your stillness? Trust in your soul's wisdom, and the unmoving, momentum of your Being. Your body might be immobile but, the transformation you're undergoing to bring you into alignment with your soul's truth is occurring at the speed of light. Don't be concerned over your foggy mind. It exists so that you can access your instinctive nature again. Surrender to your discomfort, and acknowledge the fear of not knowing. If you can, you'll make an important discovery - how to stay centered in the chaos. Ignore your isolation - the silence is necessary to teach you how to tune into your inner voice. Most of all, remain open to your stillness - the silent, voice of your soul echoes through it. Only your heart understands its language. It will lead you to where you need to be]

CHAPTER 8
LET IT GO

She drifted in, and out of deep sleep. Each time that she gained some semblance of consciousness, she tried lifting a thread of reason from the convoluted thoughts in her mind. But, it was hopeless. Despite the length of time that she'd spent in the nothingness, and the insights gained, she seemed unable to break its relentless grip. She felt as though she was being pushed further, and further into some dark corner of that steel tank. Except the 'walls' were now starting to push back. The relentless pressure of dealing with the torrent of memories, thoughts, and emotions was unbearable. She was overcome by claustrophobia as she felt herself being engulfed by the darkness within. Without much bidding her ego came to the rescue. *What was so difficult about this quest, anyway? There must be some way to free herself. She needed to re-think her options – she must have missed something.* She couldn't tolerate that sense of endlessness that surrounded her not knowing. And she was becoming increasingly uncomfortable with the vicious tussle going on between her ego, and the extreme inadequacy that was now at the forefront of her mind. She felt as though she was sitting precariously atop some invisible fence. On the one side she saw her past, and the identity that she associated with herself. On the other side was everything unknown - her true Self, and her soul's reality. And yet, she couldn't help being lured by the promise of a new beginning within its boundless, unknown depths. *Why did she doubt that promise? Why couldn't she enforce her will to accept it, and get on with her life? She couldn't just sit there! She had to do something!*

She visualized her past as a ball of sand. She imagined crumbling the 'ball' between her hands, and letting the sand slip through her fingers. She repeated the process a few times. With each attempt, she willed her past to release its hold on her. And watched as it floated off into the nothingness. All to no avail. Eventually, she gave up in sheer frustration. *Something was blocking her way! Why couldn't she see it?* What was she resisting? *Surely, she was open enough by now! Why couldn't she use her mind to figure anything out? She needed to know what was happening to her! What or who was controlling the timing of the information that she so desperately needed?* Why was she reticent about forcing an answer? Was that a form of resistance? She sighed hopelessly. *Not being able to do anything was frustrating beyond measure! And not knowing was haunting her to distraction!* It wasn't a matter of will or choice. She was already an outcast - caught in the nothingness between two worlds. *Why couldn't she let go of one, and grab the other? It was so close. She could feel it!* And yet, she felt frozen - torn by anxiety, and indecision. *This quest was beyond anything that she knew or had experienced! Nothing that she'd done before, had prepared her for something like this! Was this what her life was going to be like now – all alone, and buried in blackness!? She might as well be dead! She couldn't live with constant uncertainty!* She sighed. *Why couldn't life be easier? Why was there always some hurdle or other?* She felt like stamping her foot, except she was "sitting" – suspended - in nothingness! With only the stars twinkling their eternal light. She fisted her hands, and let out a blood-curdling, scream. But, she was greeted with silence. There was no sound in the nothingness. *Did the stars know something about her quest? They were the only witnesses to her past, and present. Did they also know what awaited her in the future?* But, she couldn't think of any way to ask, demand, influence, bargain, blackmail, threaten or flatter them into revealing their secret.

She was struck by a revelation. She'd spent most of her life using those very tactics to achieve her empty success! If she was honest with herself - it wasn't only hard work that was responsible for her progress in the physical world! Drawing various tactics from the bag-of-tricks in her mind had no doubt, also played a part. Except she'd overlooked a critical caveat, until now. "Progress" as she knew it was nothing but, an illusion! At that point, she was struck by the stark difference between her past life, and her quest. It wasn't just about the nothingness. The very nature of her quest was unlike anything that she'd encountered in her physical world. She was experiencing something totally, foreign to her. And it was non-negotiable in raising her awareness of herself – of aspects that she'd never used before. Making one thing evident - her unethical behavior had not served her. And neither will it serve her on this quest. Besides, it was getting harder to access her usual thinking patterns to attain any kind of success. And then, she was hit by a startling revelation. There was no form of success in the nothingness! Neither was there failure! *What was she doing there!?* There were no goods to trade or markets defined by some arbitrary, value system. There was no one to compete with; no one to pit her will against. There were no discussions, negotiations or comparisons. There were no decisions or actions to be taken. Nothing to convince her of anything! No wants or desires to pursue. There were no expectations to satisfy or egos to pander to. There was no idle, chit-chat. No banter. No entertainment. No physical destinations to travel to. Not a single, known distraction! Not even a sunset or sunrise; or any beautiful vista to admire; to take her mind of things. And yet, for everything that it wasn't, something told her that the nothingness was about to change her life forever.

It dawned on her that her familiar mental frameworks must be disintegrating. She was dumbfounded. *Why was this happening to her!? How was this happening? What or who was orchestrating such mayhem!?* Was she responsible for it? She was aware of certain aspects of her transformation but, things were also happening on a level that she didn't - couldn't - understand. *Was this quest helping her to re-define herself? As who or what? Her Self? What was that? What was her role? What did she have to do to make it happen? How could she make certain that this "new" Self had all the necessary attributes to achieve the kind of success she wanted?* She frowned. *What did that kind of success even look like? Could she define it?* Success was relatively easy to identify in the past but, in the nothingness there was no system by which she could define or attach a value to the kind of choices that she associated with becoming successful. And without a value system, she couldn't identify or define the goals she needed to pursue. Neither was there some kind of qualification to prove or acknowledge the achievement of her new Self! *How was she going to prove to the world that she'd attained it? What would she be qualified to do? What would her title be? What office would she hold? Who would she be…… exactly?* This entire process was between her and....whom? Or what? Again she was met with nothing but, silence.

The only feeling rising above the mass of thought, and emotion was that she needed to find the strength, and courage to continue with her quest. Something was happening to her - whether she understood it or not. She couldn't turn back – even if she wanted to. That insight somehow, made her feel better. It was inspiring to think that she could still make some choices in her current circumstances! She felt another electric sensation charge through her body. *What was that strange feeling? What was causing it?* She'd never experienced anything like it in her past. So she distracted herself by turning to another relatively new, sensation within her body. She was feeling happier with each breath, and her physical body felt lighter. She realized that she wasn't as troubled by the presence of the nothingness, anymore. She sighed, and felt her body relax. As soon as she did she felt another release – further opening her to the unknown depths within. Again, she felt that sense of oneness with the nothingness. But, it was no less disconcerting this time around. She swiftly moved her hands over her body – to make certain that she was still intact. She heaved a huge, sigh of relief. *She was still in one piece!* She looked at her hands. She was glowing again! Only this time, she was bursting with some kind of new emotion. She'd never felt so much......what? *What was that feeling?* She smiled as she watched her aura dance in slow rhythm to a silent melody.

[It has always been there. You were just never aware of it]

How could she have missed something like that? It was magical. Why did it appear, then disappear? Was it reflecting her emotional state? Her inner transformation? *Why couldn't she hold onto it?*

[Too many things were blocking you from it in your physical world. You've cleared some of those barriers but, you need more healing before you can free yourself. When you've completed your quest, you'll be aware of what affects your aura, and be able to protect yourself from any negative influences in your physical world. You can't 'hold' onto your aura – just be aware of what affects it. Ownership is the salve for your ego's fears. Hence, its constant focus on safety. But, amassing material wealth won't fill the void within or ease your restlessness. There's no escape from your fears – they will be a feature of your physical reality, until you transcend them. You own nothing in this Universe – not even your soul. You can experience what your soul desires in your lifetime but, you'll never 'own' anything. Realizing your soul purpose isn't due to your mind – that's a very small part of it. It can only be actualized by surrendering your will to your soul's knowing. However, you first need to uncover your truth, and open your heart – to help you decipher what that purpose is. And only your feelings can help you get there. Know that nothing desired by your soul is contrived. It's illogical to your mind but, your inner knowing is real. It's as real as that weightless, endlessness arising within you. Being present with that space - without expectations of any outcome - is 'being in the flow.' That spaciousness is all there Is. It has always been present within you - even in your physical world. But, you were far too consumed by your fears to recognize the behavior preventing you from accessing it. That's daunting in itself. Remove all sources of attachment, and you would have had to face your ego's extreme discomfort with mortality, lack, non-identity, insecurity, uncertainty, and the unknown. Your fear of fear underpinned your constant need for distraction – you had to soothe it somehow. However, once you've healed yourself, and refocus on your soul purpose you'll also free yourself from the illusion of safety. And without any disturbances arising from your psyche, you'll be able to stay fully present with that space within you. You'll be open to the flow of life – to access your full potential, and realize your soul purpose]

There was more healing to be done!? She let out a long sigh. *What more did she have to do? How much more healing did she have to do? She'd already let go of everything – physical, and emotional! How would being more "open" allow her access to life's flow? That was such a contradiction! Surely, she could only gain access to it by using her will? And what on earth was all that about "limitless potential"* She sighed. *What was that "space" within that Voice kept referring to?* That word in the context of a physical body, and world baffled her. *And how was she supposed to heal her psyche!? Besides, if she removed all the barriers that she'd built up to protect herself, she would be exposing herself to more pain, and betrayal! That made no sense! She needed to protect herself! How could an open, vulnerable-state serve her better than her ego-state? Why should she give up everything that she knew…?*

[Think you know…..]
…..everything that she was…..
   [….think you are….]

…..whatever she still owned…...to become… what? More open? What did that even mean!? She would have nothing to her name!

[Who are you without your possessions? Without your mind's knowledge? Without a name? In your physical world, you believed your deeds added up to something 'concrete,' because of the material value attached to it. That kind of value has no significance to your soul. Everything that you experience on this quest, however, is fundamental to actualizing your soul purpose in your physical world. No value can be placed on that. However, before you can acknowledge that, you need to shatter all preconceptions of the 'value' you ascribed to yourself with a false identity. It only masked your feelings of worthlessness. And prevented you from seeing who you truly are. Your soul won't be contained within the boundaries of anything – physical or otherwise. Let alone a price tag, irrespective of how high it is. Your true Self is connected to your soul; to all of your Being. Neither your soul nor your Being can be defined by any label. Opening yourself to access your full potential means removing all your limiting beliefs]

That was crazy! What would become of her if she gave up her value system? How would she get paid for her work? Where would she live? How would she survive? She couldn't see herself living like a hermit on some mountain top! Then again, neither did she want to go back to the life that she had. She sighed. *What did she really want?* Or need? What did her soul desire? *She had no idea!* She just knew that she wasn't ready to give up her past existence. *It was familiar; known. It was everything that she knew!* She recalled that not too long ago, she was prepared to do just that when she lost her father. She didn't want to go on living. And now, it dawned on her that some new spark of life must have been ignited within her in the nothingness. She wanted to try again - to explore life in a way that she'd never done before. Except for one, small bit of detail. She didn't know what she needed to live her best life!

[You'll remember - soon enough. But, first you need to let go of your past, and the 'future' you envisaged for yourself. Those 'stories' are ingrained in your psyche. They're preventing you from experiencing your soul's reality. You need to transcend your limiting beliefs – to allow for the full expression of your soul's truth. You might have convinced yourself that the past was the life you wanted but, it never inspired you.

Own that truth. In no way is that being ungrateful or disrespectful of your past. But, denying your soul's truth will be. Besides, it won't let you - your soul is ruthless in fulfilling its purpose. The only thing stopping you from living a life of limitless possibilities is your mind. Before you can conceive of such a life you need to uncover your truth, and accept your Self fully. The process is necessary to create that inner spaciousness to allow for your soul's expansion into your physical body. Only truth can open the way to your infinite Being. Without your soul's wisdom, you'll remain susceptible to your ego's whims, and continue seeing yourself as separate from the Universe around you. Your Being knows no such separation – even in the physical realm. You've already experienced that oneness in the spaciousness within. It's far from empty – it is the birthplace of all creation. In your physical world nothing is, nothing. In this space, nothing is everything. It's all there Is. All there ever was]

She could still live her best life? She could co-create everything that her soul desired by uncovering her truth? And everything she needed to make that a reality – her full potential - could be found in that spaciousness within her? Despite her skepticism, she was intrigued by a single thought. *She was familiar with what her ego wanted but, what did her soul desire?* She held her temples, and pressed them hard in an attempt to relieve the tension. The light-headedness was seeping in again. And as hard as she tried, she couldn't shake the exhaustion. She felt a familiar sensation in the pit of her stomach - it lurched, and knotted painfully. She remembered that feeling well – even though she had no idea what had caused it. It made her feel strangely, relieved. It was something familiar - a form of certainty in the nothingness. She recalled using it often enough, when working on her physical goals She sighed. At last, something she could use. Maybe she could get something done!

However, what she didn't count on was the extent to which she'd already transformed in the nothingness. Fear might have been a familiar emotion in her physical world but, she'd never acknowledged it. It never existed. It was nameless. And over the years, she'd come to believe that the reactive behavior stemming from it was just part of her nature. She'd never questioned herself or her behavior. What she didn't know, however, was that the nothingness would bring her face-to-face with her fears. She watched in horror as her aura rapidly faded, and before she could do anything to stop it, she was engulfed by the black void that existed within. She couldn't think. She was gasping for air. And trembling violently. The knot in her stomach twisted, and grew tighter as she caved into herself. She was falling faster, and faster. Deeper, and deeper. She felt weak. Nauseous. Dizzy. Powerless. She couldn't think - her mind was in a daze. There was a dry, metallic taste in her mouth. And she felt a hard, coldness seeping through her - like she was freezing from the inside out. Her arms were waving around her as she desperately tried to grab onto something to break her fall. But, there was nothing to stop her descending into that merciless, black void within.

[Brrrreeeaaaathe........brrrreeeaaaathe......s...l...o...w...l...y......S....L....O....W...L...Y. Breath out....very....very.....ssssllllooooowly. Breathe in, again. Aaaannnnnddddd.....out. Again. Feeling better? Stay within that spaced-out feeling. Let yourself expand into it. Going deeper into yourself to uncover your truth is not easy. Especially, when there's nothing but, the unknown facing you, and your mind is pushing you for answers. But, there's nothing to fear. As difficult as it is, it's far less painful than sitting on the fence between illusion, and your truth]

She did feel spaced-out. And annoyed. She wasn't the type that sat on a fence! She recalled many occasions when she'd deliberately taken on challenges to push her boundaries. However, she had to admit that those were visible challenges; with tangible outcomes. She had no idea how to deal with the unseen; intangible aspects of her psyche. They were proving to be more challenging than anything that she'd encountered in her physical world. She sighed, and brought her attention back to the emptiness of the space within. With her ego sulking in some corner and her mind still frantically sifting between her fading past, and unreachable "future" she realized that she had very little energy to deal with anything, other than the present moment.

[We're talking about your attachment to your material world - the things you used to curate an identity]

Her career?

[A good enough place to start]

She'd devoted her life to building one. It gave her a feeling of accomplishment. And a sense of tangible progress.

[Did you define yourself by it? Was it the basis of your self-worth?]

Of course! She lived for her work! It was her income source. And by extension, it gave her the freedom to make choices in her life. It gave her life purpose. Without it, she was nothing!

[Why did you change jobs so often?]

She smirked. *Was that question still relevant in this day, and age!?* Nonetheless, she decided to follow that "breadcrumb." There must be a reason for this mayhem - even if the answers continued eluding her! She cast her mind back to her teenage years. It dawned on her that she'd wandered into her career for various reasons - financial security being the major consideration. But, there was more to it than that. The female role in her culture was firmly entrenched, and receiving an education was a privilege - not a right. She only became aware of that when her father breached all customary norms to give his daughters a tertiary education. There was such an outcry from family members that she became aware of a shocking reality. Her role in society was already dictated by cultural, and gender stereotypes in an age-old, patriarchal system! If she wanted to achieve anything, other than what was already decided to be in her "best interests" she would have to work harder than anyone else. Not only to secure a place in the "game" but, to also prove those stereotypes wrong! At the time, she didn't quite realize what she was up against. But, she made the best choice for that "future" of hers. Happiness wasn't a consideration. There was only one motivating factor. If her father could bear social ostracism with dignity, then the least she could do was support him by making something of herself.

In the nothingness, she became aware of some of the other circumstances that had influenced her uninformed decision. She might have grabbed the opportunity but, she was too emotionally immature to realize that the decision wasn't based on her truth. She soon discovered – much to her surprise – that stereotypes weren't limited to their small community. They extended much further. And were impacted by a host of other factors that she wasn't even aware of. Like the limited avenues providing "career counselling." Essentially, they reinforced careers earmarked for females – like education, and nursing. Or other careers modelled around the role of women as the care-givers in society. Law, and medicine were available but, only to the fortunate few. And there was no guarantee of being accepted at any of the recognized, tertiary institutions in the country. Entry for "Blacks" was restricted by a "quota" system. Which was somewhat redundant in a financial system that didn't provide loans to Blacks without some form of collateral. And that was a moot point in the context of the legal prohibition to land or any other resource – natural or otherwise. Anything published in the media was controlled by the ruling political party. And more often than not, it was left to international media to highlight the appalling state of affairs within the country. Any other literature in segregated libraries was pretty much redundant – it was long, outdated. There was no access to female role-models who had risen above their restrictive conditioning. And male role-models expounded the virtues of a patriarchal system to such an extent, that women believed they had to behave like men in order to succeed. All institutions were modelled around upholding the status quo of cultural, racial, and societal "values," either through preference or fear of incarceration. There could be no "mixing" between the races – through marriage, geographical location or education. It was the "law!" It was necessary - to maintain the "superiority," and "purity" of the "bloodlines!" And it was "written" by God!

There was little in the form of entertainment – only community-funded, sport. Television had just been introduced but, it would be decades before adequate strides could be made in local, educational content. There was no internet. And the decades-long, sanctions on the country had a more dire impact on its people than on the government policies that it was designed to target. The very people who were expected to "benefit" from it continued to suffer the negative impact of such measures, long after they were lifted. She sighed heavily. Those years had blanketed an entire nation in darkness, and suppressed the potential of many generations of people. She had a startling revelation. The saga was far from over. It was still playing out on another, hidden level that was seldom spoken about. Those sanctions had not only impacted the economy. They'd reinforced the existing cultural, racial, gender and societal conditioning, and left a deep, psychological chasm in the minds of all its citizens - black, and white; male and female; young and old; rich and poor. And for as long as it remained unhealed, it would fester. The full potential of the nation's 'reality' will

Undefined

remain hidden. For no nation's "reality" can surpass the collective truth of its people. Neither can the planet's.

She sighed, and continued with her earlier trend of thought. It was no longer surprising that once qualified, her life didn't go quite as she expected. There were a number of factors leading up to each job change but eventually, she had to admit a hard truth. She didn't like the career path that she'd chosen for herself! She didn't even like what she was doing! Furthermore, none of her choices had inspired her. She realized that she must have known that on some level, because she started looking for the next opportunity the moment that she took up a position. Still she didn't wizen up when she hit the same "walls." She regarded it as a challenge, and only increased her determination to achieve her goals. She suppressed her frustration, and boredom by telling herself that she had no other option but, to stick with her choices. Besides, she was no quitter. But, her decision didn't do much for her inner conflict. It only increased. It never occurred to her that her conditioning was the basis for the many decisions that she'd made over the years. It was far too ingrained in her psyche. She was also unaware that her inner turmoil was being overshadowed by a false belief that she was achieving the "success" she'd always planned. She was struck by another revelation. It didn't matter that she didn't know what her truth was! The many "obstacles" that she'd encountered over the years were highlighting one thing - she wasn't living it! And her awareness was offering her some kind of "saving Grace." Those "obstacles" were not real. She could still change the direction of her life. Except, she didn't know what that direction was!

[Why did you ignore your soul's calling? Did you ever consider that you were born to follow a different path in this physical dimension?]

What could she possibly do, if she gave up her career? She didn't have the time to start something new! And she needed an income to survive in this world!

[Time isn't a deciding factor on this quest. The expansion of your consciousness is - as determined by your soul. If you continue resisting it, you'll only encounter more obstacles in this physical dimension, until you surrender. Life gives you all the time you need to figure this out - in this lifetime or the next. Far more important than anything you've given up in your physical world are the limiting beliefs that continue to starve you of the happiness you deserve. Hammering away at something, because it's familiar is no justification for sacrificing your happiness. Your conditioning made you betray your Self, and every other aspect of your life. Each day you died a small death by settling for less than your true worth. Is that how little you value, and respect your Self? Is that meagre offering of self-love deserving of the soul you embody? And you question whether to stop this living death to uncover your truth, and live the life that you deserve! You're only subjecting yourself to the same cycles of illusion if you continue with your limiting beliefs]

She sighed. Yes - her choices were dictated by financial gain! Everything was about money! It had been drummed into her since childhood. Hardship, and strife wasn't restricted to her family. It was the reality of many in the small community. And in no time at all, it had become hers. The solution was well known – work harder, and earn more. She didn't know any other way to survive. It was compounded by how much she earned. It made her like she was worth something. And for as long as she had something tangible bolstering her self-esteem, there was never any reason to question the basis of her self-worth.

[So your career defined you?]

She guessed so……..

[Yes or no?]

She frowned. *Was this a trial? Where was the court? Who was the judge? Where was the jury?* She scoffed. *Yes! She was nobody without her career! What else was she supposed to believe in a world where "doing" was the sole basis to attest one's worth?* And yet, something about her reasoning didn't resonate with her. She dropped her head in her hands as she grappled with her confusion. Eventually, she cried out feverishly into the nothingness: "Who am I!?"

Despite her angst, she was feeling much lighter after her mini tirade. She realized that whether she was conscious of it or not, her transformation was continuing on another level - beyond her mind. She might not know the full extent of it but, some unknown part of her was very much, aware of it. *What was driving it? Her soul?*

[Who you are……your true worth…..will all become part of your consciousness once you get past those inner 'walls' by trusting your inner knowing. Right now, you just have to focus on surrendering to the present moment. Where were we? Aaahhhhh……yes. Your achievements made you feel successful. And worthy]

She was about to react. Then, stopped herself. Yes. It afforded her some form of status in the world. She was struck by a strange thought. She wasn't looking for status! She felt even more confused. For so long, it was the means by which she'd measured her worth. It had given her life meaning. And it wasn't what she was looking for! She looked at the nothingness, and shook her head hopelessly. *Was there nothing good about her past choices? Was there anything good about her life or herself?*

[The nothingness is completely, neutral. It's only reflecting how you feel about yourself. Do you believe you're a 'good' person? So your worth was based on value judgements derived from your physical world. And that was the benchmark you used to determine whether you were happy or not?]

Of course, she was good! What was all the fuss about happiness? It had never featured in her life! She believed in making sacrifices for the life she wanted. If "happiness" was the price she had to pay, then so be it! It was small enough! But, she found her line of thought very unsettling.

[Was it 'small' or easy to betray?]

That hit a nerve! If she'd discounted her happiness so easily, and sacrificed it time-after-time, she'd betrayed her Self! How could she respect herself if she treated her Self in that way? And she wasn't even aware of her behavior! Then again, she'd never experienced much happiness to know its true value. There was nothing to compare her trade-off against. It struck her that she given up more than she realized.

[Your joy is an indication of what inspires you at a soul level. It's the 'fuel' that sustains you during your lifetime. It feeds the trust needed to live life openly - with love. As opposed to shutting yourself off, because of your fears. You're no victim. You're the creator of your life experience. And self-love, and joy are priceless to fully embrace your human experience in this dimension. Both form part of the only 'currency' that your Being 'trades' with the Universe, to help you co-create the life that you deserve. Anything less is beneath your soul. It will deplete you, and have you constantly reaching externally for something that resides within you. If you didn't feel joy, then you were caught in a vicious cycle of negativity, in spite of your efforts to maintain a positive mindset. Nothing outside of you can make you feel joy. True joy comes from within – from fulfilling your soul purpose. To continue searching for it in your external world will only add to your disillusionment, and victim-mentality. And you know that feeling well – you kept it alive by continuously setting yourself up in circumstances that didn't serve your highest interests. But, the Universe is neutral. It's abundant. The potential for creativity is limitless. You embody that same life essence. And you were born to fulfill your soul purpose – only you can bring it into this physical realm. Your soul guarantees that every step will be a joyous celebration. Nothing can deplete your joy. It will always be present – even in times of loss, and sadness. Your joy isn't something that anyone or anything else can provide – it's a gift from your soul for doing what you came here to do. Living according to your ego's mandate has made your life far more complicated than it is, because you traded your joy for less than your true worth. The only way to remember what joy feels like is to transcend the pain, and anger blocking you from it by healing yourself. There were only a few occasions when you felt joy – correct?]

Yes.

[Throughout your entire life?]

Throughout ....her.....entire...life. She repeated the words several times. Very slowly. And realized for the first time that she was talking about her life! Even then, she found it difficult to believe the gravity behind those words. Why did she feel so little joy? Suddenly, everything that she believed to be important – so right about her life - now felt like a waste of time, and energy! Her achievements might have boosted her self-worth, and given her a sense of identity. But, could she claim to have any self-worth if she'd only repeated patterns that kept her going around in the same negative cycles? Why did she forsake her own needs, and betray her Self to such an extent? The guilt was more than she could bear. She collapsed under the burden of it. Once again, her ego came to the rescue. *Why was she being punished? And her joy was the litmus test? That was so lame! So self-serving!* Although the nagging thoughts raged on, she found it difficult to ignore the chasm emerging between her illusory reality, and her truth. She was transfixed by the paradox.

Undefined

[Watch the ego. It's feeding you the victim-card. There's nothing 'wrong' about your past]

Could she fix this mess?

[It's not a 'mess' if it brought you here. Your past has served you in many ways – even if you're unaware of it. The nothingness might not look like much but, it's a lot more than you think. And it's all you have - right now. You might be unable to keep track of your inner transformation but, it's well underway. If you desire to uncover more of your truth, then you have only one choice – continue to unravel your behavioral patterns. It will require courage to stand by your Self as you observe the unfolding of your truth. Your ego will try to override your commitment at every turn. But, you need to remain present with each layer as it reveals itself, and observe your reactions. Whatever comes to the surface now, serves only one purpose – to teach you the power of self-love in healing your past. Without self-love, you won't be able to complete this quest. Trust the process – trust where you find yourself in each moment. Any self-judgment is an opportunity to observe those negative patterns, and love yourself through your pain. The more out of balance you feel, the greater the conflict with your ego. Despite the level of discomfort churned up by your memories remain in the chaos, and focus on observing your emotions. As you hold each layer in the light of your consciousness, you'll release more of yourself to expand into the spaciousness that is unfolding within you. There's nothing to fear – you're safe. Your memories can't hurt you. They're only surfacing to be acknowledged, and healed. To fully accept your truth - to see your Self as you are - you have to let go of the fears that bind you to a false sense of self]

She wasn't paying attention. She was bristling with irritation after what she'd just heard. *She'd always been true to herself!*

[Only partly so. Your 'truth' was processed through many unconscious filters. So much so, that your reality resembled a mirage. Each time you latched onto some aspect of 'truth' believing that you'd found what you were looking for, it slipped right through your fingers. There is no truth to be found in fear-based decisions. Your past behavior stemmed from your conditioning and consequently, you've never been able to walk your life's path with conviction. And with your truth so deeply buried under it, you've yet to experience your full potential. It doesn't stem from your mind, although your mind can help you process the experiences that will unfold when you fully embrace your soul path. However, using your conditioning to formulate a 'future' only resulted in you looking behind you, and creating one that was never more than a stone's throw away from the past you were so desperately trying to escape. Your full potential will only come to the fore when you're fully aligned with your soul purpose. Your life path – the only future that your soul is here to create – will naturally unfold in each moment that you remain present with your truth. Your soul will be guiding you – not your mind. It's the only part of you that's connected to your Being - untouched and unfettered by the trappings of your mind, ego. Your Being is part of the unknown - it defies worldly definition. And yet, you can feel it in that inner sanctum of silent, stillness. It connects you to all that Is. But, it's far from nothing. It's everything. By surrendering to this process of uncovering your truth you'll gain access to it. And there is nothing – no one – to fear once you're standing in your truth]

As much as she hated to admit it, she'd deferred to the so called "authorities" in her life when making her most important decisions. She'd even regarded their truth, as her own. And now, she realized that she'd misled herself by denying her own truth - the only real power that belonged her. No wonder she couldn't lift a finger to stop her life from falling apart! Her higher Self was fully aware of her mind's game of charades! She sighed. Why did she ignore her deepest emotions? All this time, she wasn't only suffocating her joy but, giving away her power as well! She was still uncovering her true Self but, she realized that she was the single-most, important authority in her life. She groaned when she realized that her ego-self had kept her transfixed on the illusion of quantity, and speed in her physical world. She'd never given any consideration to the quality of her life – to its depth or meaning. And by denying her deepest emotions she'd suppressed her soul's desires, and remained nothing more than a passenger in her life. She'd never stopped to consider what made her feel joyful; what she needed or who she truly was! That explained why every so-called "success" felt so empty - why her life felt so barren. It was her misguided belief that life was somewhere "out there" in the physical world. She'd made it her life's mission to find it, even if it killed her! Ironically, that was exactly what she'd achieved – bled away her life essence in exchange for a meaningless existence!

She felt a piercing pain in her chest as she was gripped by another revelation. If that was true, then who was she!? Who was her true Self!? Was she feeling lost, because she was in the process of losing her old self? Or was she afraid of allowing this unknown, Self to emerge? She'd never thought of herself of being afraid of anything – let alone, change! She'd always welcomed it, and adapted as best she could. Why then, did her soul feel stymied by a lack of growth? What did her soul seek? How could she fulfill her soul's desires? Did she force change in her external world to distract herself from the fear of the unknown? Then again, perhaps change within the same paradigm of illusion wasn't real change – not if she'd been living a life of repetitive patterns! But, changing herself – unveiling her true Self - what did that entail? *Did she have to release, and heal all the blockages within herself before she could uncover this true Self? Was that possible? She didn't even know enough about her old self – let alone, her true Self!* And if she intended to make any kind of headway on this quest, she would have to be the observer of the process - to allow for the necessary healing to occur. She would have to remain in the observer's seat, and not take anything personally. *How was she supposed to remain objective about her personal experiences!? How could she step out, and away from the self that was as familiar to her as breathing?*

She shook her head - trying to clear the fog. Whatever the answers, she was now on her soul's quest – something that she had no knowledge of! It dawned on her that she'd been avoiding her truth under the pretext that her choices were necessary for survival. All she'd done was keep her shadow self buried! She'd avoided dealing with anything that she didn't like - her emotions, thoughts; people. Memories. Uncertainty. The unknown. Again, that truth was difficult to concede. Her mind reneged, and she took refuge in her ego. *Surely, her past experiences had taught her everything that she needed to know about herself? There was nothing else! She could move forward with her life if she really wanted that. But, she couldn't go anywhere if she was stuck in nothingness! Her life philosophy was based on "doing." She couldn't just shelve it, and change her focus to Being! Where would that take her? What kind of life would she have? What would she use to define her worth? The world she lived in required that she perform at her best. Without a means to support herself what would become of her? How would she survive? What would her identity be based on? Nothingness!?* She sighed in frustration. *She refused to do this, anymore! She was exhausted. And bored with coming up against one wall after another. Everything in the nothingness was worse than before. And she thought that things were bad when she first started on this quest! At least, she had an identity back then! Now she had nothing! No Self. No self-worth. No self-love. Everything that she owned, including her identity - everything that she valued - was disappearing into nothingness!*

[You wouldn't have been able to sustain anything in your physical world - for as long as you remained untrue to your Self. Besides, nothing can prevent the birthing of your true Self especially, something as fragmented as the illusory reality perpetuated by your ego]

If it was possible to sit bolt upright in the nothingness, she would have. Was that it? Was that why she felt like such a fraud? She wasn't true to her Self? Was that the source of her constant uneasiness? Was that the reason she found it so difficult to believe in herself, because nothing she'd done was based on her truth? How could it? With all the walls that she'd erected to hide her insecurities, and fears. The walls were so effective that she'd failed to see her true Self! She shivered. And despite the confidence her physical life had helped her cultivate over the years, she didn't know the answer to the most critical question in her life: "Who am I?" Despite the inner chaos, and uncertainty she felt relieved. She'd finally uncovered a truth that was hidden from her, all her life! She ran her fingers through her hair. *Now what? She could spend the rest of her life trying to find her true Self. Was there anything, real about her? How could she determine what was real in the nothingness? Surely, she needed to be in her physical world to get to know her true Self? Why was she isolated from it?* Despite the confusion, she realized that she now had a better understanding of the walls that she'd built around herself. Her time in the nothingness had helped her to discern, and release some of them. She also suspected that she'd uncovered certain aspects of her true Self during her quest, even though she had no image of this Self or couldn't relate to it with anything other than her feelings. However, if she used her current surroundings as a gauge, then she was still stuck somewhere far, and beyond the reach of anything familiar in her physical world. She sighed, hopelessly. *When would things be normal, again? When would she get her life back? This was the most arduous, and unrelenting process she'd ever experienced! Were there more walls to be released? Was that the reason she was still stuck in the nothingness? What could they possibly be?*

[Be patient with yourself. Trust the process. You're still uncovering your truth, and learning how to love yourself. But, you need to look at your self-worth more closely......]

She sighed. *She wanted this over, and done with!*

[......and some of your other self-sabotaging patterns, besides your busyness]

What do you know! Self-sabotage! It would never have crossed her mind......

[Your ego would never have allowed it to]

......her career was everything to her. She couldn't afford to turn down any opportunity that came her way. Something within, however, wasn't convinced. The only thing that was glaringly obvious was her proneness to the same patterns in the relationships that she exposed herself to. How could she have missed it?

[You weren't aware of the triggers driving your behavior. And without that awareness you remained unconscious of your patterns. You saw it mirrored by some of the experiences in your external world but, you were too busy blaming others to pick up on it. But, that outwardly directed energy also pointed to an imbalance within you. So much so that you were constantly trying to prove your worth. But, no amount of external validation is going to appease your low self-esteem. And nothing in your physical world will compensate for a deep-rooted, sense of lack. You'll only attract more experiences that leave you feeling empty, and worthless. And you'll continue over-compensating for your shortcomings by seeking outward recognition to make yourself feel better. Every experience in life will mirror some aspect within you, until you find the courage to seek your Self in those 'mirrors.' Your true Self seeks no external validation. It knows its worth – it's based on your truth. But, you need to remove all the smoke screens that reinforce your false sense of self before you can see that]

She grimaced. *There was no way out. She might as well get on with it.* She closed her eyes, and sat quietly, until she felt herself drop into the silent, stillness within. Did she peremptorily judge the situations that she'd encountered? Instead of reacting in anger, and viewing delays as an unnecessary hindrance to her progress, could she learn something new by taking a "bird's-eye" view of some of her past experiences? The answer was slow in coming. When it did, she inhaled sharply. Her progress wasn't being stymied – she was being re-directed to reflect on what triggered her behavior, and ask herself some life-changing questions! Needless to say, she'd avoided that! And subjected herself to a life of illusion! Why was her anger triggered so easily? What was it pointing to, within herself? Was she judging herself? Why? Did she not believe in her own goodness? If her Being was all about love, how did she come to be her own worst enemy? Once again, the onslaught of questions turned her rigid with anxiety. She found some relief in sarcasm. *Funny! She'd always thought that hard work opened "doors!"*

[It does. But, there are no 'doors' for those aligned to their truths. The Universe offers you a blank canvas to realize your soul purpose. Your conditioning only fostered choices that were a means to an end. Nothing more. And those choices didn't serve your highest interests. You might not have been aware of your behavioral triggers but, the consequences of your actions were very evident from your false reality – in the form of various energies, and how you felt. But, that energy wasn't from your external circumstances – it emanated from within you. By not being aware of that you only added to your 'walls.' And became the single, biggest factor keeping the Universal 'doors' of opportunity shut. Irrespective of the behavior of others, you're still responsible for your own actions. You might not have been conscious of it before but, you've been reacting out of fear, all your life. And anger is your first line of defense. That kind of behavior only generates more negative karma, and keeps you trapped in your illusions. However, now that you're aware of it, you won't be repeating it. And your existing negative karma can be can healed. You can transcend your past, and focus on co-creating your soul's reality. You'll discover a whole, new world inside of you]

She was the one standing in her own way?

[Yes]

She was familiar with that expression. And yet, it had never occurred to her that she'd fallen prey to it. She considered herself too smart to fall into such an obvious trap. Her intention was to live her best life. It still was. That was the only reason she'd extended herself beyond her physical, and mental boundaries. So why did it feel as though she was still locked inside that steel tank!? It slowly dawned on her that she couldn't persist with logic if she intended to "escape" the nothingness. She needed to surrender to the 'walls' holding her captive. She had to transcend them by using a very unfamiliar trait - self-honesty. Only by being true to herself could she find her way to her soul purpose. Anything less would lead to more failure. Yes - she had to fight to survive in her physical world. But, what was a more worthwhile use of her energy? Realizing her one, true soul path or resisting her Self by persisting with many arbitrary roads to nowhere!? Besides, fighting to survive was the way of the physical world – it wasn't the way of the Universal laws that supported her soul purpose. Still her mind was far from convinced. She sighed. *What was the point of going on with this quest? She didn't know the answers, and there was no one around to help her! Even if there was, how was she going to explain her predicament?* Without being conscious of it, she fell into her usual patterns of victimhood, and avoidance. *There was only one way to solve this! Take it head on!*

[Now that you can no longer fight your physical world, you believe that turning on yourself is your only choice? Is that how you express love towards your Self? This quest is unlike any battle that you've fought before. It's a 'war' – against yourself. Your usual defenses aren't available to you, and neither do you have access to any ammunition. Even the world's largest army won't be able to help you now. Self-love is the only 'weapon' you can use to win this war. Just focus on observing the illusions that have held your true Self captive. Hold each one in the light of your consciousness, and let it go with love, and compassion in your heart. Fighting is your mind's way of resisting. It will not serve you - you're only fighting your Self. And you'll continue feeling stuck. But, even if that feeling is an illusion, it serves as an important marker. It's highlighting the extent of the conflicting energies within you that are keeping you away from your truth, and your soul purpose. You're still trapped in that black void within. To be fully alive you have to open fully to the present moment – to access the flow of life. It can only be accessed in the present moment – nowhere else. It's your 'door' to all the opportunities in the Universe. Feel into those energies – don't be distracted by the push-pull effect of the storm in your mind. Trust the process – stay in your silent, stillness. Your heart can access your soul's knowing in that space - it will guide you along your true path. You can never lose your way in the silence - even in your physical world. Focus your energy on being the observer of your life as it unfolds around you. This isn't being passive. That silent, stillness is the most active state of Being – you can access all of the creative force of the Universe. There is no 'plan' that you need to concoct to make this happen - the masterplan to co-create the life that you deserve already resides within your soul]

Another open-ended placation! Would she ever make any sense of all this?

[Not if you're looking for the proverbial 'bottom-line.' It doesn't exist. This is your life. There are no beginnings, endings or outcomes. And drawing conclusions or having opinions that stem from your old thinking patterns are futile. Your path can only be what your soul knows it to be. None of this will make 'sense,' until you're standing in your truth. By then, nothing about your past life will matter, anyway. For now, surrender your ego's need to know. And stop resisting by trying to understand it all. You'll only go back into your mind, and keep your past alive. For now, focus on remaining in your stillness. The next step will be revealed to you when you've released your notions of a past, and future. You'll recognize it when your soul reveals it to you]

Letting her future go was easy enough – it was nothing more than a plan. But, how could she let go of her past? "Letting go" was just another worn-out, cliché. And her understanding of it was totally, inadequate to help her action her intention. How could she let go, when her past, and identity were part of every breath that she'd taken? Even if she wanted to let go of it intentionally, her physical body was holding onto every shred of it! And it was consuming every ounce of energy, to hold herself together in the face of everything that was hell-bent on destroying her! Her mind had always been her safe-haven whenever life became too much to handle. Once again, she allowed it to assume its position of power - believing that it would help her to create some order in the chaos. *If she could just formulate some understanding of it all, then she could work out a way to fix this madness! How could she leave the past behind without some indication of what to expect for her future?* She felt the onset of another panic attack.

Undefined

[Take a deep breath……hold it. Release it…..slowly. Let it all go. You're not in control]

Not in control! The full impact of those words struck her with the force of a tornado. *Her identity was being eschewed from right under her! The entire foundation of her belief system was in the process of being ripped apart! Everything that she valued was being destroyed! She no longer had any semblance of a life!* She could no longer tell what was more excruciating - the lost time, and effort that she'd spent building a life or watching it all disappear in an instant! She had no known means of dealing with her quest on a rational level. Neither did she have the self-worth to cope with the magnitude of the mental, physical, emotional and spiritual upheaval that she was experiencing. *And now, she had no control!* She had to "let it go" or risk losing something that she didn't even know existed – her true Self! She breathed in deeply. And then she exhaled….. very, very slowly. *Nothing was more impossible than acceptance, and surrender under her current circumstances! If anything, the unfathomable nothingness was all the more reason for her to hold on as tightly as she could! Her life had never been the same from the moment that she entered it! She felt as though she was being torn to shreds by some unknown, invisible force! And she was supposed to focus on her breathing, and let it all go!*

[Yes. Let go of everything, until you're as empty as the nothingness. Your past no longer serves you. Feel yourself expanding into that inner space with each breath. It might not seem like much but, it's the only thing you do have control over]

Despite her reservations the slow breathing quietened her mind, and helped her relax. She couldn't remember a time when she'd done nothing but, focus on her breathing. It made her aware that she'd always had difficulty breathing. For most of her life, she'd held her breath for intermittent periods of time. She recalled that whenever she travelled, she was able to breathe more easily. Why would her breathing improve when she was away from home? Away from her family? It dawned on her that there were also times when she found it necessary to make some excuse, and disappear for hours at a time. The long drives, and wide open spaces somehow made her feel better. She explained away her behavior on the grounds of stress, and convinced herself that nothing was wrong. And driving at high speeds was the only way to make herself feel like she had a grip on life. In that moment, an image of her daughter came to mind. At last - she could see what her baby looked like! She was the reason she'd always come back home! Her child had somehow, given her the strength to return to the one place that should have made her feel safe. And yet, she'd never felt safe at home. She came to a shocking realization. She'd never felt safe, anywhere! And she'd never had a "grip" on life! All she'd done was escape for a little while, in an attempt to patch-up a broken life. But, the guilt every time she looked into her child's eyes was unbearable. Each time, she promised herself that she would never give in to her craziness. But, it didn't take very long before something triggered her. And she'd never figured it out. She again became aware of her labored breathing. Why did she have difficulty breathing whenever she thought about home? Was there some latent, fear that she was unaware of? For the first time, it became glaringly apparent that the life she'd lived, wasn't her best life. Her body made that evident – with every breath! She raised her eyebrows at her admission. It was the first time that she'd acknowledged it. What was so drastic about her past that she preferred blocking it out? Whatever it was, she had to face another truth – the nothingness had no tolerance for her lies. It was after all, the birthing ground for her true Self. She wouldn't be allowed to move forward if she repeated any self-betrayal patterns, and put herself in situations that didn't serve her! She sighed. All along she'd firmly believed that life was going according to plan – her plan. *Where, and how did it all go so wrong?*

[Perhaps by thinking that you could live life according to a 'plan.' Or allowing your mind to delude you into believing that you could out-maneuver your soul purpose. But, you can't avoid the responsibility for your soul's growth. More often than not, everyone does what they think is 'right,' until they wake up one day, and realize that they're not where they would like to be. Then we have to choose between our truth, and continuing with an illusion. If it's the latter, we remain lost forever]

She was baffled. *Her equation for life was so logical. So simple. Hard work equaled success. It didn't require "passion" or "soul" or any of the other mysticisms that were threatening to swallow her into unknown depths!* However, her usual pragmatic approach also didn't allow for taking things at face value – it required that she do her research before choosing the best option. *Except, doing any research in the nothingness was impossible! And even if her philosophy didn't allow for synchronicity, she was in control. And for so long, things had progressed the way that she wanted. Why did everything collapse, despite her best intentions? She might not have been following her soul path but, she'd always believed in her choices. Right or wrong, doing was the only version of truth that she'd known at the time.* In hindsight, how did her life turn out to be so complicated? Did all this chaos have something to do with her soul purpose? She sighed. *Why was that so important!?*

[You did whatever you could, based on your conditioning. It wasn't your soul's truth. By making your life about doing, you only resisted your truth]

She sighed hopelessly. *How was she going to fix this? And if the precursor to that was fixing herself, what more did she have to do!?* She was distraught. It wasn't about getting her life "back on track." It looked as though, it was never on track!

[You've already started the process of 'fixing' this – by embarking on this quest. And by challenging your old beliefs, you'll continue to subvert your ego's demands, and uncover your truth. The conscious acknowledgement of your past behavior is opening you to accept yourself for who you truly are. As you progress on your quest, you're creating ever-widening circles for your soul to expand into your physical body. You're well on your way]

Well, it certainly didn't feel like that! She was overcome by exhaustion, and wallowing in self-pity. She was on the verge of collapsing. With only shreds of her identity left, and without access to many of the old, obsessive patterns to occupy her mind, she felt utterly lost. She didn't know what to do, and that was very unsettling. Perhaps she should just end it all. It wasn't the first time that she'd contemplated suicide. Each time, however, she'd talked herself into waiting, until morning. And then, by some miracle she always found the strength to continue. This time, however, was different. She'd never before felt this sense of finality about her life. She'd lost everything in her physical world that was so painstakingly built over the years, including her identity. Her past only existed as some rapidly, fading mirage. Only that black, void inside of her still existed! She couldn't help wondering why she was still alive. *This must be some kind of cosmic joke. She must be already dead.*

[You're far from dead. But, you're experiencing a form of death so that you can live, fully alive]

She started crying. For someone who hated crying she was certainly, having more than her fair share of it in the nothingness! Her body shook with sobs that seemed to come from the very depths of her soul. She cried for a long time. For all that was lost. For all that could have been. For all the wasted years. Most of all, for the life that she wanted - which had never quite turned out, the way she hoped it would.

[Nothing is lost. You've travelled far, even though it doesn't look that way to you. Nothing that truly belongs to you is ever lost. You still have time to do what's important for your soul. Your foundations have been shaken but, not your roots. Not yet. You've removed some of the biggest obstacles to co-creating the life that you desire. This is a good place to be – even though your ego will try to convince you otherwise. But, you now have one up on that ego of yours. You're starting to understand where, and how it has controlled you. You're also becoming more aware of how you've been avoiding, and suppressing your pain. It made you run from your Self, all your life. But, your past was only reflecting the pain already within you. Furthermore, you're now aware of the disrespectful manner you've been treating your Self. All because of your low esteem, lack of self-worth, and self-love. You've given away your power by feeding your negativity, and allowing yourself to remain trapped in the same patterns of thinking. And no matter how positive your intentions, you now know that the outcome of your actions will never rise above the lowest belief that you have for yourself. You've taken some huge strides in facing your false identity, and the role it played in constructing the house of cards that you built around you. In doing so, you've destroyed many of the illusions you had of yourself, and the life that you built over the years. Now that you're conscious of all this, you'll be able to take responsibility for your thinking, and change your behavior. That's the kind of progress you're unfamiliar with, because it's intangible, and invisible to your mind. But, it's real for your soul. That's the only thing worth worrying about. After all this time, your soul's reality still awaits you. Your mind will never be as powerful as your heart and soul. They have the entire Universe behind them]

It certainly didn't look or feel anything like that to her! Why couldn't she see her soul's truth? Where was it taking her? Was this what it took to align herself - her life - to her soul purpose? A complete destruction of her old self!? Of everything that she knew, and had worked so hard for all her life? If it wasn't based on her truth, then she had to let it go or continue with a mere existence!? Was there no middle-ground in the nothingness? As distraught as she was, she became aware of some unknown force spurring her to carry on with her quest. Despite being faced with a level of physical destruction that she'd never contemplated, some part of her was still holding space for the unknown to unfold within her. Her mind was still processing as much information as possible but, she'd come to accept that she wasn't aware of all aspects of her transformation. In the midst of everything, she was also trying to remain present with her Self. She knew that she was still seeking refuge in her old behavioral patterns but, she sensed that it was only an illusory safety-catch by her ego to distract her. Mostly, she was relieved that she was miraculously developing a greater ability to remain detached from the hurricane raging within her. The conviction that she was somehow being protected from the full impact of it as she trundled towards some unknown, destination was beyond comprehension.

And yet, she still found herself wishing fervently for her old way of life. However, no matter how hard she tried to manipulate her thinking to find an outlet, she remained in the nothingness. As motionless as she was, she couldn't deny the feeling of being escorted along a mysterious railway. She could see herself watching her past life flash by outside the windows of her carriage. A destination had already been decided upon - although not by her mind. The further she travelled along this unknown track, the further removed she felt from her past life. What was far more incomprehensible was how unreal, the familiar felt. It was being replaced by more of that expansive, spaciousness within. Mysterious, and unfathomable it held her suspended in anticipation for an unknown life that was yet, to unfold. A life still to be co-created by a set of Universal laws that were upheld by an infinite wisdom that she'd never encountered before. And yet, a life that beckoned with more realness compared to anything that she'd experienced before. Based on the insights she'd recently uncovered that "rulebook" lay dormant somewhere within. Something told her that if she hoped to find it, she was in the right place.

She might have avoided dealing with a lot in her past. Now that she was more aware of her behavior, she felt sufficiently "armed" to continue with her inward search. Irrespective of what she found or where she ended up. But she became aware of her restlessness again. *Was she unsettled by the admission that she'd failed to find any answers to help her out of her dilemma?* That set her mind off, doggedly re-tracing what she could recall of her quest. She couldn't help thinking that she was missing something. *The answers had to be there – somewhere!* But, she kept on hitting one blank wall, after another. Despite her reticence she had to dig deep to uncover an unfamiliar trait – patience! *Whatever this quest entailed, it wasn't going to reveal itself to her. Not yet, anyway. Which pieces of her life were still missing? Or was she playing mind-games with herself, and avoiding what was in plain sight? Was she making any headway, at all?* She recognized that she was still toing-and-froing with the conflicting thoughts in her mind but, she felt helpless to stop it. *There was no way of knowing anything, for certain, irrespective of what Voice said!* Again she rubbed the tears from her eyes. She couldn't help feeling overwhelmed by desperation, and confusion. Somehow she had to endure with her quest. It was the only thing still present in her current reality. Her acceptance slowly replaced her despondency with a calmness that helped her to step back from the storm, and into her role as the observer. She had a sense that she was "doing" something, although there was nothing visible to support it. She turned to look at the nothingness around her. It didn't take long before some clarity took hold. She was excavating that void within, even though she could only sense an impenetrable, blackness. *Where was she supposed to direct her efforts in all that blackness!?*

[At your roots]

She didn't understand what that meant but, she was forced to close her eyes as the words sent a piercing pain through her heart. She waited for it to subside before opening her eyes to stare into the nothingness. She felt uncontrollably, drawn to its omniscient beauty. How was it possible for something without any form, color or texture to look so beautiful? How could something so unfathomable make her feel blissful, in the midst of the hurricane she was experiencing!? *If she were ever to leave the nothingness, could she hold onto that feeling? She was happy to stick with her quest, and learn whatever she needed to know in the nothingness – if it meant that she could somehow lock onto that feeling. She was loathe to lose it.* She sensed that if she could somehow get past that stuck feeling, she would be able to experience more joy, and peace than she believed possible. And now that she'd encountered her inner darkness she wanted only joy, and peace in her life. *Life would be ideal, if she could maintain that feeling in her physical world – she could get through anything. Would the attainment of that ability mark the end of her quest?* Would she feel whole again? Her instincts were warning her that she was allowing her ego to become attached to a different kind of illusion – some kind of reward for working on her Self. *Perhaps at the end of her quest, she would find herself settled back into her old way of life.* But, she could now recognize the inner shifting between her awareness and her mind. She remained in her stillness and ignored that thought. She realized that she was still scouring the patterns of her old conditioning seeking some form of comfort; some certainty. And yet, in the stillness she was fully aware that her attempts were futile. As difficult as it was she needed to remain focused on her silent, stillness. Whatever she needed to know would emerge from there. She sighed, as her eyelids drooped. Without a second thought, she succumbed to the infinite spaciousness that spread through every fiber of her. And drifted off into a peaceful, dreamless sleep.

CHAPTER 9

MIRRORS OF LOVE

She woke to an even deeper, stillness within. She was very grateful for the presence of this unknown force in the face of the never-ending, chaos. Although that still didn't explain the nothingness. She couldn't help thinking of the maxim: "As within - so without." Was Voice right about the nothingness reflecting her inner stillness? She found that hard to believe. *If her physical world had disappeared, why was she still caught in the throes of chaos? Why didn't it disappear along with everything else in her life? What was the source of it? It couldn't exist just in her head? She'd lived through her past experiences – not imagined them!* Her mind grappled with, yet another paradox. Her old life seemed to be riddled with them! And the nothingness was only accentuating that! In the past, everything made sense! She was clear about her life - her shit was "together!" She'd been composed as she went about her hectic life. She'd often congratulated herself on that trait – it was one of her "strengths." It gave her the reassurance that life was going exactly as she wanted it to. *And now, her "perfect" life was being flipped on its head in the nothingness!* It dawned on her that her composure might have been comforting but, it was nothing more than a security blanket. Another illusion! She sighed. Why the need for a forced façade? What was behind it? What was she denying? She had a shocking revelation. Far from being something new, the chaos in her life had always been there! Her denial that anything existed beyond her false reality had prevented her from seeing it! Just like the stillness. And that made her starkly aware of another paradox. Why was she unable to feel the stillness in her physical world if it was within her?

It slowly dawned on her that the nothingness was serving as a "mirror." Except, there was no physical world to reflect her mind's projections. Instead, the "mirror" was turned inward - to reveal the state of her inner world. In addition to making her intimately aware of her denied emotions with each disruptive memory, it was also giving her the opportunity to "see" her past in a very different light. And she didn't like what she saw. She was far from the composed! Her life wasn't as perfect as she'd made it out to be! And now, it looked even less so. And her refusal to acknowledge her past was keeping her from her truth! It was keeping her trapped in an illusion! She sighed. *Which world was real? The silent, stillness of the unknown reality within or the tumultuous, whirlwind of screaming thoughts in her head that were pointing to her past?* Why were there so many stark paradoxes coming to light now? As disconcerting as it was to encounter ever-evolving, depths of the unknown with her revelations and insights, she was having greater difficulty accepting that her past was so flat – so one-dimensional. So black and white. Either-or. Right and wrong. That linear perspective now looked limiting. And it no longer resonated with her. Could her conditioning confine her perspective to such an extent? Was there a different way to live life? Could she surpass the safety and comfort of the familiar and open herself to discover more depth, and meaning to life? Or would she merely re-create another illusory future, because of her dualistic, polarized mind? The only way she was going to create her soul's reality was by freeing herself from her conditioning, and building new neural pathways! *How was she supposed to do that!? If this quest was helping her to transform on that level, how would she know when it was completed? And whether she was successful or not? If she could somehow free her mind of old patterns, she would have nothing to think about!* Was a free mind, and soul synonymous with true freedom? What did that feel like? What was her mind capable of thinking in that state? What would her life look like? *And if she had to open herself to this unknown way of life, how much longer would her quest last? Was she chasing yet another, empty rainbow?* Was she allowing herself to be distracted by her conditioned thoughts? Could her awareness help her control them?

She realized that she was still clinging to certain thought patterns as a form of security against the unknown, and the uncertainty facing her.

Her instincts were urging her to go beyond her past illusory reality but, she was ignoring them, because they were being held hostage by a fear that she didn't even know existed. A fear that had her unconsciously reaching for the safety of her familiar thoughts, and ignoring the feelings in her heart. *What if she let go of everything, and embraced her unknown soul? Would she subject herself to a reality that looked like the nothingness? Who would she be? Who was she becoming?* She felt a surge of anger. *Why was she born into a physical world if her life was supposed to resemble the nothingness!? What would she be expected to do in this new kind of world that required less mind, and more heart?* Was she still caught in her linear thinking? Maybe she could attain a state of wholeness that would allow her to act from a place of heart-mind, harmony? *Was that possible? Did such a state exist?* What did being in that state feel like? She sighed. *Exactly, where was this new world!?How did she get there?* It was beyond her imagination that a whole different reality already existed within her. And that the only way for her to see it was to remove the conditioning that bound her to her past.

Her anger sparked a greater awareness of her thoughts, and emotions. She tentatively shifted her focus towards the stillness within. Immediately, she encountered a very different dimension to her experience. She felt as though she'd stepped into another world. It was so startling when compared to the mayhem in her head that she felt a strange inclination to bow her head. *Why was she doing that?* Was it reverence? Humility? Both emotions were new to her. She wasn't religious. She'd never acknowledged any power greater than her mind. It didn't require reverence or humility – any emotion, for that matter - just work. She respected all religions but, believed that their underlying philosophies were the same. And she had no inclination of dwelling on the superficial, differences between them. Some of the insights gained during her quest made her question her perspective. If there was a Divine power would It create anything or anyone, less than Itself? Did it distinguish between Beings - in any number of ways? Did the Divine have the intention of discriminating between the spiritual Beings that are separated by the different religions in the physical world? Would It acknowledge only one religious group, and hand out a "reward" - when all human races were protected by the same Divine power? If It did, then the Divine must have an ego! And she doubted that – not if all forms of life emanated from the same Source, and contained the same life essence! She frowned. So why the ongoing battle for religious supremacy that only perpetuated polarization, and separation of humanity? Surely, the fundamental purpose, and philosophy of any belief system should be uniting humanity to fight the scourge of crises threatening its very existence! Like all nations uniting, and combining resources to save the planet. And uplifting the billions of people subjected to living in the most undignified, and inhumane conditions around the world. Our only chance of saving the planet, and all its life-forms lies in going beyond the separatist views promulgated by "world powers" that these crises will somehow be resolved by the individual efforts of nations, while maintaining domain over their political beliefs – let alone, religious ones!

As for humility, she'd never felt it. Not until now, anyway. The only other time that she'd felt anything close to it was whenever she looked up at the sky. As a child she'd been fascinated by that immense space and all that lay hidden within its blue depths, and beyond. She was more intrigued when she later learnt that the blue color was only an optical illusion - it was all blackness beyond the earth's atmosphere. Then again, space might only appear that way to human eyes restricted to vision within a limited range of frequencies. Over the years, she'd often pondered the meaning of infinity. Especially, when it contrasted so starkly with her own mortality, and the transitory nature of everything in her physical world. Whenever she felt her world caving in on her, she would look up and feel strangely comforted by the never-failing, presence of the sky, and stars. She would close her eyes and revel in that feeling as something within her reached up, and out of herself. For a brief moment, she felt free from the boundaries of her physical existence. She felt the presence of something bigger than herself; something larger than all the pettiness of her day-to-day existence. There was never a need to define what she felt or question it. She had a sense that a label would somehow limit, and spoil the sheer wonder of it. It now dawned on her that those moments were filled with inspiration, and had provided brief periods of respite from her mundane life. She recalled that she'd often wished to live her life free from the many restrictions of her physical world. For the first time, she became aware of just how strong that feeling was. Was the intensity of that feeling an indication of her soul's true desires? She'd never realized that her soul felt so restricted by the life that she was living! Why did she feel that way? What was limiting her from freely expressing her soul's desires? *How could she free her soul?*

Reflecting on her earlier interactions with Glow, she realized that most of her adult life was devoid of the usual forms of support from those around her. *What happened to Glow?* What had made her turn away from the norms proffering safety and support, and become so self-reliant? If she valued safety to the extent that she'd molded her entire life around it, why did she look to herself to provide it? That contrasted sharply with her wanting validation from the very people who threatened her sense of safety! What about validating herself? She massaged her forehead, and sighed. *This was all very confusing!* And if she possessed so little Self-knowledge, then she'd effectively turned to her estranged Self to provide what she most needed! What had prompted her to behave in such a contradictory manner? Was it instinct? Was she being guided by her soul's wisdom? How could her unknown soul's wisdom guide her towards her unknown truth? Was her inner wisdom separate from her mind? Was her wisdom and this so-called, Divine power one, and the same thing? If they were, how was she able to access it in the physical realm? Were they connected in some way? She sighed. *What would a Divine power want with someone as un-religious, as herself!?*

She realized that her feelings for the Universe around her were pointing her towards the existence of some kind of Divine power – even if her mind had never been able to accept the unseen, and the unknown. Why did she now feel so strongly connected to this strange force? How could she connect to something unknown? And yet, doubt did little to prevent her from experiencing a palpable sense of its presence. She looked around her. What existed in the nothingness? She shook her head to clear the mugginess, and promptly latched onto her earlier trend of thought. What had caused her to become so self-reliant, in the first place? She scanned her adult relationships as far back as she could, and realized that she'd always steered away from any form of close contact. She also realized that she'd seldom admitted to needing help or support – even when she needed it the most. She put it down to her independence. But, her own separatist view was now at odds with the feeling of oneness in the nothingness. Why did she behave in a manner that reinforced her separation from those around her? Was it her ego? Why was she so uncomfortable whenever anyone got close to her? Did her childhood have something to do with her getting easily attached at the early stages of a relationship? She realized that she drew people in, and then pulled away when she felt herself growing close to them. But, thoughts of her childhood had seldom featured in her adult life - she was more than happy to leave that time in her life behind her. And she had no recollection of whether her family had played any major role in those early, formative years. But, she'd always felt something missing. She was constantly searching! For….. what…..!? And she was always in a rush to get somewhere or other. Where exactly, was she going!? For some reason, she felt very uncomfortable and completely, at odds with her past behavior.

[Did you believe that you could out-run your childhood?]

She raised her eyebrows, and tilted her head slightly as she mulled over that question. She didn't know! It dawned on her that her childhood wasn't just some distant memory. It felt more like she'd never had one! She'd always felt like an adult – even as a child! She realized that she, was the only person she felt comfortable turning to, for support. And for whatever reason, she'd painted all her relationships with the same brush – she separated herself from "them." Why was she so uncomfortable in her relationships? Was it her low, self-esteem? Although that rang true to some extent, it didn't resonate with her fully. Her resourcefulness had helped her overcome many of life's challenges. And that, together with her penchant for getting things done, boosted her confidence. She had a startling revelation. Her focus was always directed outwards! And on satisfying needs of others. Only to be on the receiving end of abusive or narcissistic-type behavior that ended up destroying her confidence! To add insult to injury, she subjected herself to extreme self-criticism, and judgement when doing a post-mortem of the incident. Why was she prone to such disempowering behavior? What could she possibly have gained by subjecting herself to experiences that were so devoid of any love? If she truly loved herself would she expose herself to such people? Why didn't she recognize the signs of such behavior? Or see it coming? Was she that desperate to gain the approval of others that she would betray herself!? Was she that insecure that she hid her weaknesses by overcompensating in her relationships? She realized that she'd never been aware of her ego before but she was starting to understand how effectively it had blindsided her! And then she had the strangest revelation. Why did she always feel so small in her world when her soul could touch the sky, and the stars!?

She shook her head despondently. Whatever it was, she now clearly recognized how her egotistic behavior had turned into a double-edged sword. Not only did it serve as a barrier that kept people at a distance - it had also driven her to over-extend herself in her relationships. And more often than not, it was to her detriment in the toxic relationships that she'd habitually fallen prey to! Until now, she'd never factored any weaknesses into her character. Her entire focus was on shielding herself from being constantly hammered by the external world. She wasn't aware of being triggered by her own pain, and fears. At the time, she'd focused on what was uppermost on her mind – protecting herself from feeling hurt by the ongoing abuse. Sooner rather than later, her tolerance levels hit a maximum. At which point, she forcefully broke away from such relationships, and isolated herself. Promising herself that she would never expose herself to such abusive behavior again. Only to find herself drawn into another similar, experience!

[Your physical reality was a combination of experiences that arose from your karmic patterns, and soul contracts. Ultimately, it's a reflection of the love, and fear that already resides within you. Since there was so little love, you must have been ruled by fear. And the repetitive nature of your experiences were highlighting aspects within you that need your attention before they can be healed. Once you've healed yourself, the karmic patterns will stop – unless you create more by being unaware of your behavior]

She scoffed. *She wasn't afraid of anything!* She was just about to reinforce her opinion with further justification, when she was hit by a revelation. Why was she always trying to be nice to people, including those who'd hurt her!? And why was she striving to fit in with the expectations of others – at the expense of her own soul growth? She didn't need to fit in! There was no such thing as a social equation! It was another linear, construct! How did she want to live her life? How could she lead a happy, and fulfilling one? How did she define success? What kind of reality could she build with her truth? She was taken-aback by the 180 degree shift in her thinking. It wasn't common – not once she'd made up her mind about anything or anyone! Far more surprising was her persisting with this new line of thought. Perhaps she was trying too hard - at everything that she wasn't supposed to do! Did she really want the kind of life that she'd lived before? What was true for her? What was her soul purpose? Her whole life suddenly, felt like an anti-climax! The pressure that knowing elicited within her, didn't prevent her from becoming hyper-aware of the number of ways that she'd disempowered herself by trying to gain approval from others. Not only were her efforts futile but, she'd limited her growth within the infinite, expansiveness of life! All those years, she'd been dancing to the same tune – in the same small, world of her conditioned self! And all the while, her soul was trying to lead her towards a different reality - without any limitations.

She sighed heavily. All this time, she'd been receiving "impulses" from her soul to raise her awareness, and change her behavior. It needed her to decide whether to stick with her old, restrictive thoughts or move beyond them. And she'd ignored her soul's calling, and stuck with the familiar – time, after time! She was flabbergasted by her denial to accept what had clearly been visible for years. She no longer fitted in with her illusory reality. She never did! As crazy as this quest was, the real madness was persisting with a way of life that wasn't based on her truth! And despite her discomfort, she felt surprisingly OK about her newfound insights. Instead of freaking out, her acknowledgement had the strange effect of grounding her. She couldn't recall, ever feeling that way before. She was always on edge! Was that what it felt like to be in one's truth? Her next thought was more surprising. There was absolutely, nothing wrong with her if she didn't fit in with her world! There was nothing wrong with anyone, who found themselves in a similar situation. And she was under no obligation to edit her truth to make others feel comfortable! If she felt judged by others then she must be judging herself! If she felt uncomfortable in the presence of others, then she must be non-accepting of her true Self! If her experiences were fraught with pain, there must be pain within her. And if her life had collapsed, then she must be rejecting her truth! She'd curated an identity for herself based on the opinions of others. She'd subscribed so fully to that belief, that non-acceptance was translated as not having a "place" in the world! But, she did have a place – in her unknown soul! Her eyes welled with tears. She had to accept responsibility for the consequences of her past thoughts, and actions – as reflected by her old reality. Her conditioning did play a role in her behavior but, she didn't know any better at the time. Now, she did. And her only role now, was to undo what no longer served her – which was pretty much everything, and everyone! She'd created so many "stories" in her head about herself, and her life. *Which ones were real? How did she recognize her truth as she sifted through them to uncover her true Self?*

Her acknowledgement opened the doorway to her Self by another fraction. What she saw astounded her. There was nothing wrong with her life – other than a lack meaning! Her acknowledgement helped her take back some of her power, and she felt an instant shift. And another layer of false logic keeping her from her truth was revealed. What was the foundation of her life after all this time? She'd often espoused the value of principles in simplifying life. Why then was hers so unnecessarily, complicated! Did she have to adopt new ones to live a life of meaning? Were these new principles her own or determined by the world at large? Who was ultimately, responsible for giving meaning to her life? The general populace or herself!? She sighed. Perhaps it was a combination of both – in an ideal world. But, the world was far from ideal! And she wasn't perfect! How did she go about finding the meaning to sanctify this gift of life? She stared into the nothingness for an interminably, long time. She realized that she had very little control over the state of the world. She did, however, have control over her mind, and the way she decided to live her life. If her conditioning had resulted in a life of no meaning, then it was well within her power to change it – by aligning with her soul purpose. Except, she had no idea how to access the unknown to achieve that! She'd changed her external circumstances so many times before - all to no avail! It slowly dawned on her that she did miss something. She'd never before, extended her attempts to include the behavioral patterns that had arisen during childhood. Could she still create a life of meaning by unpacking the childhood experiences that formed the foundations of her conditioning?

That thought was far too alienating to contemplate, any further. She buried herself in her distress. She couldn't believe that she'd spent so much time, and energy living her life for others! And in the process, she'd lost sight of what she needed for her own life! She'd also expended so much effort trying to uphold a system that she had so little regard for that she didn't realize her soul had no desire to be a part of it, in the first place! Now, she saw all too clearly that as disconcerting as society's non-acceptance was, it had another far more significant impact on her psyche that she was unaware of. It had afforded her a different kind of "escape" hatch. It made her conditioned way of life relatively easy, compared to the effort required to surrender to a far bigger, unknown - her soul's true purpose! And trying to prove herself to others helped her to ignore taking responsibility for her own life. How could others accept her, when she didn't accept her Self!? How could others see her, when she didn't see her Self? Where did her disempowering behavior stem from? What was it covering up? Pain? Fear? Insecurity? Whatever it was, it was an insatiable monster! Despite the daunting implications of her new-found insights, she heaved a huge sigh of relief. She felt as though she was finally, making some progress on her quest. She felt elated. Maybe now, she could get back to her life, and focus on the two most important people in her world - her father, and daughter.

[Careful about drawing any foregone conclusions on your quest. That won't help you overcome your entrenched conditioning to change your behavior. Focus on being present with each layer as it opens within you – it's revealing aspects of your Self. Feel into the spaciousness as each layer is healed - become one with the emotions arising within your body. It will help you to integrate your soul's expansion with your physical body. One of those layers, deals with the denied grief over your father's death. He passed away two years ago]

She felt a cold, steel-like fist clench at her heart. She buckled under the piercing pain. As hard as she tried to stop them the tears once again, blinded her. Two years! She still found impossible to accept his death. How could she? He was the only person she'd felt close to – her entire life. He was an indomitable force in her life! And he was interested in everything that she did – no matter how small or insignificant. He especially, loved hearing about her travels around the world – he had done so little of it himself. She realized how torturous that must have been for someone with such an adventurous soul. She sighed sadly. He was the only person who listened to her – who made her feel truly heard. She missed him so. Her heart ached terribly just thinking about him. His passing had left an irreplaceable space in her heart. She felt his presence all the time, and often spoke to him whenever she was alone – something that she'd also done when he was alive. He had to be alive! He couldn't be gone! But, she felt her aching heart break through the shield of denial that she'd used, for so long to protect herself from the truth. She sobbed uncontrollably as the long-suppressed, memories of her father flooded her mind.

She recalled the slow decline of his health, over many years. Her heart ached for him. He'd worked so hard his entire life, and when he retired he was too ill to enjoy it. She'd stood by, watching in silent agony as his life slowly ebbed out of him. She recalled her reticence every evening, before visiting him. But, she knew how much he looked forward to seeing her. So she suppressed her dread, and went anyway. She hated seeing him lying there, with that resigned look on his face. He used to be so vibrant – constantly, doing things. So much so, as a child she believed that he could be in more than one place, at the same time. She'd never seen him falter or succumb to the heavy load that was his daily life. Just his mere presence filled her with so much hope, and motivation. Whenever she sat by his bedside, she was careful about her choice of subject matter for their conversations - she didn't want to upset him. But, he always knew what was uppermost on her mind, and got straight to the heart of whatever she wanted to avoid. But, showing any kind of emotion was out of the question. She sensed that he somehow needed her to be strong - for both of them. And despite being worn out by tearless grief, she refused to let him down. He was a pillar of strength in her life – even on his sick-bed. She would have endured anything for him - his love was the most precious thing to her. It still was. She smiled sadly, as she recalled how invincible she'd felt whenever she was with him. Did she do enough? Did she bring just a little bit of love, and happiness into his life? In that instant, she realized just how little she knew about her father. He'd never spoken about himself or shared his feelings.

That thought set in motion a cavalcade of memories. They lured her even closer to a place in her childhood that felt alive with his presence. She recalled some of the things that he used to do – repairing anything from appliances to cars; building things; art; playing musical instruments. She was in awe of him. To her child's mind, he was a living testament of the 'magician' that she'd heard about in fairytales. He did all kinds of wonderful stuff – like building an indoor toilet so that no one had to leave the house at night to use the drop-toilet outside. He even installed plumbing to bring water into their home, and a geyser when electricity finally, got to their neighborhood. As much as she enjoyed roaming around looking for firewood to heat water for their evening baths, having a geyser made life a whole lot easier. And a lot more fun. She still remembered her first shower. It was heavenly. She loved the rain, and couldn't believe her eyes when she first saw the odd-looking, contraption spouting water in the bathroom. She eventually, got the hang of it, and firmly believed that he'd built it just for her - to feel the "rain" on her face every day. Occasionally, he went into the cellar to store odd bits of stuff, and she followed close behind. She remembered how afraid she was when she first saw that dark hole in the wall. The sunlight hit the entrance, and then was rapidly swallowed up by the cold, black tunnels. She was convinced that something terrible lived inside that drank the sunlight, and ate little children. But, when he emerged safely one afternoon - after she'd spent an eternity outside the entrance picking at the grass - she suppressed her anxiety, and went in after him.

She also enjoyed watching him draw the designs to renovate his Victorian house. She didn't know that he wasn't an architect. And she was too little to understand what he did for a living. The entire household was abuzz with excitement over the extended living space. It was such a luxury in their lives. But, it was more than that to her. It was another opportunity to spend time with him and create something new, and wonderful. He did everything with such mastery, and turned odd pieces of nothing into amazing pieces of something! The process was pure art. More so, because everything he did was self-taught, and made by hand. She was fascinated by his ability to focus on the task at hand, and became equally engrossed in whatever he was doing. Sometimes, he asked her to fetch some tool or other. She didn't know the names of the tools so she would scamper around, holding up one tool after another for inspection, until he gave a nod of approval. Then she would race to his side, and hand it to him. She remained by his side, until he looked at her, and smiled. That smile was always worth the wait. It was soft and gentle, and so full.... full.... of something. It made her feel as though nothing else existed in the space between them. Occasionally, he held something up, and asked for her opinion. He always waited patiently for her to find the right words to express herself – even though she didn't have a clue what the object was.

She realized that her answers must have sounded very inadequate back then but, he used to listen so intently that she felt as though the successful completion of his project depended on her every word. When he completed his task, she remembered standing beside him, and mimicking the serious look of contemplation on his face as he scrutinized his craftsmanship. She often peeked at him while waiting for his slight, distinctive nod of approval. It signaled that he was finally, satisfied with his efforts. More importantly, it meant the beginning of another project. And a brand new, adventure.

Climbing the roof to repair the aluminum sheets that repeatedly came lose after a bad storm was another one of her favorite pastimes with him. But, she knew that she wasn't allowed on the roof. So she snuck up the ladder behind him, and stayed just out of his line of sight. She didn't know that he was only pretending not to be aware of her presence. She was always surprised that he somehow knew exactly, in which direction to look whenever he spoke to her. She put it down to his magical powers – she felt it every time she was close to him. That alone was worth the risk of seeing the warm look in his eyes replaced by a withering frown whenever she displeased him in some way. Eventually, she cottoned onto his game when she realized that he always shouted "watch-out" whenever she got too close to the roof edge. The tone of his voice was enough to stop her in her tracks; backtrack slowly, and then, make her way down the ladder. She usually, spent the rest of her time waiting patiently for him to come back down. He always smiled, and acted as though the incident never happened. Neither did her reprimand nor forbid her from joining him on the roof. Her little escapades remained their little secret – something that made her feel closer to him. She hated having her fun spoilt by another lecture to stop being a "Tom-boy." Not that she understood what that meant as a child. But, she decided that if Tom-boys had more fun, then she had no problem being one.

She suddenly remembered why she liked going up onto the roof so much. She used to sit on one of the levelled out spots, and gaze out at the little town. And marvel at how different everything looked during the day. Only one thing was the same - she felt on top of her little world when sitting so close to the sky. It didn't matter whether it was the blue sky or the star-studded, night sky. She felt her happiest, whenever she lost herself in its vastness. It always elicited a strange feeling within her – like she was lifting out of herself, and flying like a bird. She had no concept then, of just how far the sky was from earth or the full extent of the planet that she lived on. No one in their family had ever travelled out of the small town, let alone visited another country. The only thing that existed in her physical space was their house. And school. And neither one of them made her feel the way that she did whenever she looked at the sky. It was her entire "world." She smiled wistfully, as she watched that memory slowly waft across her mind. Once again, she felt the lightness, and expansiveness that she'd felt as a child. She was struck by another revelation. She was experiencing the same feeling in the nothingness!

That thought startled her back to the nothingness. How was it possible to remember so much when not so long ago, she was convinced that her childhood was long-forgotten? Now, not only were her memories more accessible in the nothingness but, she seemed to be re-living those childhood experiences! This time however, she was looking at them through a completely, different "lens" - granting her new insights into those early years. She realized that her father, and herself must have been very lonely. As the eldest, he'd become the sole breadwinner of a large family, after the death of his father. At the time he was no more than a child himself. He must have assumed the role quite naturally, because for as long as she could remember he was regarded as the father-figure in their household. He had a natural air of authority - not that he ever enforced it - his presence always spoke louder than words. She'd never seen him lose his temper but, she instinctively knew that she should never challenge him on a matter of principle. He always wore a stern countenance and yet, he was also the gentlest person she'd ever met. Whenever he did smile or laugh she was mesmerized by the way his face softened, and his dark, brown eyes sparkled. She admired his quiet strength, and even though he didn't have an ounce of pride, he always carried himself with an unmistakable air of dignity. She felt as though the very air moved whenever he entered a room. He shouldered his innumerable responsibilities with such grace, and there was never a hint of resentment about anything. There was only his unfailing dedication, kindness and patience. And a great big heart, with an immense capacity for love. She realized that she couldn't imagine how he'd become the man that he was under such burdensome, circumstances. The death of his father must have hurt him deeply. And yet, she'd never heard him speak of his own loss or pain. She wondered whether he'd shared his feelings with anyone. Was he ever truly, happy? Tears filled her eyes. She assumed that he was. She'd never asked him.

She recalled how much she missed him whenever she was away from him. She made every excuse to be with him - even if she had to raise hell to get her way. Her behavior obviously, didn't engender much support from anyone else in the family. She smiled when she remembered the tantrum she threw when she first heard about going to school. The mere thought of being away from him was terribly unsettling. Then she learnt that she would be travelling with him each day. And then suddenly, everything was fine. Each morning, she drew her strength from his silent presence in the car. In the afternoons, she waited impatiently for him to get back home. Whatever had transpired at school was miraculously forgotten, as soon as she heard his footsteps on the wooden, passage-way. Then, there was dinner – another favorite time of her day. She always chose her favorite spot - the seat right next to him. She didn't bother much with what was going on at the table. Besides, no one spoke at dinner. Not that she minded - she was too busy following his every move. She even mimicked his slow chewing – just to remain at the table, as long as he did. And she was usually, lost in her head in some silent dialogue with him about the events in her day. After dinner she excused herself, and dragged herself off to bed without saying a word. She hated leaving him but, she'd never heard him complain - about anything. Neither did she.

However, she didn't understand at the time, that she'd begun to internalize a more subtle reaction to her home environment that would have far-reaching, implications on her life. She wasn't aware that she felt "invisible" to everyone, except her father. A feeling that now, spread slowly throughout her body in the nothingness. It made her conscious of her entire world turning to color whenever he was around. And feeling so happy, and safe. For the first time, she realized that the light shining in his eyes must have been his love for her. She choked with tears. Perhaps he'd wished to open a world of opportunity for her; for her to succeed at everything that he'd never had the opportunity to do in his own life. She'd never again, witnessed another gaze filled with so much love, hope, belief, and trust. It had nourished, and inspired her throughout her life. As she was lost in the memory of his gaze she was struck by the realization that she'd spent most of her life living up to that look in his eyes. Did she succeed? She hoped that she did - even in some small measure. The thought that she might have hurt or disappointed him in any way, felt like a physical blow. He must have sacrificed so many dreams of his own to ensure that the entire family never went without anything essential. Finally, she understood why every bit of progress in her life was a moment of quiet celebration between them. It further cemented the bond between them. A bond that even now, made her feel as though he was still a part of her life. She guessed that she could have gotten away with anything - not that she tried. She never felt the need to test the love that was so openly visible in his eyes. Her heart stopped briefly, and then started thumping wildly as she realized how precious those moments were. She'd experienced a love that was as timeless as eternity itself. She couldn't define, let alone begin to fathom such a feeling - it extended to every part of her small world. She still felt it.

With the feeling of his love still lifting her from within, she allowed more of her sub-conscious to filter through to her conscious mind. She realized that life during her childhood was far from easy. Adversity was the order of the day. And yet, she'd barely noticed - his silent love had cocooned her from it all. His love was the source of her joy wherever she went, and it had become her armor against a cold, frightening world from her very first encounter with it. Whenever she doubted her ability to succeed at anything, she would think of the love glowing in his eyes, and that always gave her the courage to push on. Without him knowing it, he'd helped her through the most challenging times in her life. For the first time, she was struck by something she'd never thought of before. Did her life choices make her happy or was she trying to make her father happy? Or was she using her achievements to secure his love? During those early years, she couldn't recall being conscious of her life or what she wanted to do with it. Did she live her life for him? Was that the reason she felt so removed from her truth, and her life? What did she want for her own life? What did she need? What made her happy? She was so thrown by the resultant turmoil in her mind that she was momentarily distracted from the pain that she'd avoided since his death. Before she realized what was happening, some unknown force sucked her straight into it.

She saw herself standing at the foot of the hospital bed looking at him while he slept. He'd never looked so peaceful. For once, the stern crease on his forehead was gone. She smiled as she recalled his stubbornness over the last few months. He'd refused to succumb to his condition. He insisted on managing his affairs, even though his health had deteriorated quite badly. Death itself must have been sent packing a few times, because of his refusal to accept his mortality. She took a step closer to his bed, and then stopped. Something was wrong. His eyes didn't open. His eyes always opened the moment he sensed that she was close by. She tentatively reached out to touch his hand. There was no movement. And his eyes didn't open. She froze. She lost track of how long she stood by his bedside, looking at him – willing him to open his eyes. She heard nothing; saw nothing. Not her mother sobbing by her side or the medical staff who came running in, shortly afterwards. All she could think of was that she would never see his smile again. Or see the love shining in his brown eyes.

She never realized the full extent of her love for him, until after his death. She avoided the full impact of her pain by taking care of his funeral arrangements. She remembered nothing about the actual events leading up to it. The day itself was a blur, except for the sight of his face as she drew the lid over his casket, just before the cremation ceremony. She insisted on performing his last rites, although women in her culture weren't permitted to do so. She firmly believed that he would have wanted it that way. She now realized that her selfishness was behind her insistence. On some level, she must have believed that it would bring her closure. After all, it epitomized the final step in letting him go. Instead, she was trying to sooth her own fears of a life without him. A life that she didn't have the faintest idea what to do with. All she knew was that she desperately needed him - his silent, acknowledgement of her decisions; of her very existence. Taking her life forward was dependent on it! She was struck by another revelation. There was no closure that fateful day. Instead, something had also "died" within her. Whatever dreams might have survived her non-existent, childhood disappeared with the sight of his coffin as it was consumed by the searing flames. She bent her head as she allowed her grief to flood her body, for the first time since his death. Somewhere in the far reaches of her mind, she realized that she had no idea what being an adult, actually meant. She still felt, very much like a child – without a childhood. More than anything, she remembered that feeling of being trapped. There was nowhere she could go; no one she could turn to. All her life she'd never had to turn to anyone. He'd taken care of all her needs - without being asked for a single thing. It dawned on her that she was familiar with the world's coldness from childhood but, for as long as he was alive, she was afforded the luxury of turning a blind eye to it. Well the Universe had eventually, collected on that privilege. It had taken the one person she loved most in the world. For a second, an image of Kitty flashed through her mind. It had also taken Kitty.

She sat staring into the nothingness for a long time. She was distraught over the intensity of her suppressed emotions. She'd denied her loss and grief by allowing herself to be distracted by the gross injustice of his death – the finality of it. She realized that months had gone by in a blur of anger, and self-pity. And her conflicting emotions of guilt, and self-recrimination for failing to save him. She was convinced that she could have delayed the inevitable – somehow. She should have spent more time with him; taken him to seek different medical opinions. There must have been someone out there who could've saved him. His death wasn't just about him losing his battle with life. She'd also lost – by failing him. She refused to acknowledge her feelings – the way she'd always done. As far as she was concerned, he was still alive. Still with her. There was no need to mourn him. But, her mind felt like it was in a constant daze. She saw nothing of the world around her. She stopped eating. Her work suffered. She lost track of everything going on around her. She remembered the long, soulful looks in her child's eyes whenever her mother turned away from her, and left her in the care of others. The only thing that she couldn't get enough of was sleep. It was her only form of escape; her only solace. At some point, she did lift herself out of her daze to get back to the life she remembered but, she'd already completely, lost touch with reality. But, she was unaware that her denied grief was very much alive.

As difficult as it was to face her buried emotions in the nothingness, she miraculously managed to stay within her stillness, and keep herself open to the pain unfolding within her. She realized that on some level, she must have known that something was wrong but, she felt helpless to do anything in her distressed state. Eventually, she forgot how long she shut herself off from the world. And herself. She went through her daily routine in a trance-like state. Perhaps that had given her some semblance of control – of still being a part of her world. Being in control made everything looked "normal." She recalled at some point, starting to feel more like her old self. She remembered how relieved she felt. She regained some of her drive, and started the long haul of trying to put her life back together again. But, it didn't take long before her faltering marriage fell apart. At around the same time, she suspected that there was something afoot at work. But, no matter how hard she tried, she just didn't care. It felt as though everything was happening in another place, and time - to someone else. When she lost her job it didn't matter, as much as she thought it would. In fact, nothing mattered. Not even the family ties that perished with her father at the funeral pyre. She now realized that her denial had come at a cost. Her suppressed grief, and burning anger over his death might have served as a safety net at the time but, it had also prevented her from becoming aware of her own unloving, behavior towards herself. She'd abandoned herself at a time, when she most needed herself!

She realized that about the same time, something about her world no longer felt the same. She felt increasingly, uncomfortable with every attempt that she made to reinstate the life that she was once familiar with. It slowly dawned on her that many of the illusions supporting her old reality when her father was alive had started to implode - as though an invisible hand had flicked some invisible switch. She recalled that it began with some very strange thoughts. Mainly that she was attempting to re-build a life by perpetuating the naïve expectations stemming from a cognitively, starved childhood. It was accompanied by another niggling thought - as much as she believed her father's love had supported a solid foundation, nothing about that life felt real anymore. But, she'd disregarded her instincts at the time, and forced herself to fall back in line with her "normal" routine. For all intents, and purposes life looked the same - the same people, and places; the same routine. And the same rhythm of day and night – for days; months; years. It was all very reassuring. But back then, she wasn't aware of her conditioned attempts to force outcomes in her external world. There was no quest in sight; no awareness of the subtle, unconscious changes that were triggered by her traumatic experience. Only to find herself unraveling on a level, and to an extent that took her completely, by surprise! The behavioral armor that she'd used to shield herself from the world also failed to protect her from being bombarded by conflict, and disruption from every angle. To make matters worse, every attempt at finding some means of financially supporting herself ended in failure. She was forced to sell her material possessions just to survive each month. Eventually, there was nothing of value left, except the memories of a life that once was. As difficult as it was to suppress her pride, and ego she had no option but to turn to family, and friends for support. Still, she persisted with the belief that she would get herself out of the mess that she was in. Even with her entire world blown to bits, the ongoing circus in her mind convinced her that she still had some semblance of a life. With her physical life, went whatever confidence she had and she was left feeling more alone, and exposed than ever before – in a world that looked more unfamiliar, and frightening than ever before. And then, she discovered she was on some quest! And that the disruption wasn't limited to just her physical life - it was destroying her very identity! And nothing was as petrifying as the complete, stranger that she kept running into, in the nothingness – herself! Someone who had never really existed except, in her father's eyes.

[Was that how you felt when you lost Kitty?]

She remained silent.

[What happened the night Kitty died?]

She couldn't remember - no matter how hard she tried. She went back to that house – eventually. But she never went back to the cellar after that night. She must have left Kitty there. And she refused to think about him, ever again. It struck her that Kitty's death - whatever had transpired that night - must have had a far greater impact on her than she realized. She couldn't put her finger on it but, Kitty's death seemed to also be part of the dark, void within. She shook her head. *What was she doing there!? She couldn't feel a thing! There was nothing left of her; nothing to go back to! She didn't even want to be alive!* She shook her head morosely. *It made no sense. Nothing did. But, there she was - still breathing!*

[You haven't said much about your mother]

There wasn't much to say. She'd always thought it strange that she had no special childhood memories with her mother. She'd never felt any kind of connection with her. Neither was there any inclination over the years to build or maintain a relationship with her. For as long as she could remember, there was always a distance between them. She smiled wryly, as she recalled her childish attempts to bridge the gap between them. She used to get a pittance for pocket-money, so buying gifts for special occasions was out of the question. However, that didn't stop her from secretly laboring over hand-made cards, and gifts. Her father loved her childish attempts at poetry, and took his time when reading the verses out loud. She loved it when he did that - he had a beautiful voice. There was always a pause when he finished, as he contemplated the meaning of her message. And then, he would look at her, and smile. He never expressed his feelings – he didn't need to. His eyes glowed warmly with love each time. It was all the appreciation that she'd ever needed. But, she was disheartened by her mother lack of interest, and absence of emotion. She stopped her little creative pursuits. She was struck by a revelation. That's it! That decision had cast a long shadow over her life! She stopped doing what she loved most – writing poetry.

She was so excited with her insight that it took a while for her to center herself. She realized that her inability to understand the people closest to her had remained a burning obsession throughout her life. She'd tried on many occasions to quell it by learning whatever she could about her parents' childhoods. However, neither one of them were open to sharing much about their lives. It was only as an adult that she came to know that neither of them had experienced much of a childhood. Her father was already the head of his household as a young boy. Her mother was orphaned as a child, and raised by relatives. She could only imagine, how painful those early years must have been for both of them. They married very young – as was the custom in those years. Neither one of them spoke of love but, she was certain that they loved each other in their own special way. One surmised that hard work, and their unfailing dedication to the family was their way of expressing love. And as children they never thought to ask for anything, over and above the small comforts of food, shelter, and clothing. She never realized that there were other "gifts" that they could have shared – laughter to lighten the load; somewhere soft, and warm to land, whenever "life" happened; an outward display of compassion. As well as a whole spectrum of other enriching, emotions associated with the journey called "life." That would eased the constant tension in an environment that was so devoid of any color, and warmth. And that left her with an aching hunger for connection in her heart that remained with her, all her life.

[Sounds like you have it all figured out]

She might have silently bemoaned the sad state of their lives countless times but, she firmly believed her parents had done what they knew best – as had the generations before them. But, back then, she didn't count on a quest in the nothingness! Her blind acceptance was being replaced by something stronger – an awareness that was giving her access to greater knowing, and the ability to gage the truth of her old perspectives against her unknown Self. She couldn't change her past, and no one was to blame for anything. But, something didn't feel right. She still felt burdened by that past. She couldn't understand it. That was then; this was now. Why couldn't she move forward with her life? Her "life" didn't even feel like her own!

[You were never aware of the extent of its hold on you. But, it blocked you from your true Self, nonetheless. However, every experience in this lifetime – over lifetimes - is valuable. They've all played a part in getting you to this point in your soul's evolution – experiencing this transformation from self, to Self. However, you'll move beyond your past only when you lovingly accept all of you; when you own what you've been denying about yourself. Don't allow yourself to be distracted by non-essentials – like the differences between your physical world, and the nothingness. There are none - they're one, and the same. Neither are you required to do anything to achieve this transformation. You don't have to understand how it works or set out to find what you're looking for – your transformation is already underway. Only you can uncover your truth, and heal yourself to live the life that your soul desires. Your soul's reality will be birthed from the ashes of your past. As will your true Self. You just need to center yourself in your stillness, and observe your truth unfolding - without judgement or the need to embellish what is revealed to you]

She reacted instantly. *What did her past have to do with her truth!?*

Besides, how was she supposed to delve into things that were forgotten a long time ago!? She believed in the social construct of a "family." It was an inseparable bond in her mind. More so, because it encompassed the histories of both her parents — stories that extended over many lifetimes. She was part of that history. And that bond meant everything to her, even if she could never fathom the Universe's motive for bringing them together! *She could think of so many alternative scenarios that would have served her much better.* Nonetheless, she'd decided to make the best of "the cards" that life had given her. *Her heritage must have impacted the choices that she'd made over the years. There! It was all very simple. Done, and dusted.* But, her over-zealous conclusion felt completely, out of place in the nothingness. She still needed to know what her truth was. This awareness-thing was a funny! Why were her old thought patterns no longer resonating with her? Something told her that her heritage didn't define her Self. Neither did it define her soul's innate potential. And the concept of a "family" now extended way beyond just her heritage. It encompassed everyone; every living thing — the whole planet! Harming one living thing - in any way — meant harming all of life! She sighed. *How was she supposed to achieve that!?* There was no answer. She turned to her stillness. Her past might have impacted her old reality but, if her soul held the only real blueprint for her life then her past was only the tip of the proverbial, ice-berg! She needed to witness her soul's reality if she wanted to experience her limitless potential. And the only way to do that was to dive deep into that ocean within her — whether she wanted to or not! *How was she supposed to work with a metaphor? How was she supposed to extract something tangible out of the intangible!? Make something visible that was invisible! That was impossible! Her identity, past, and future were all decided by her heritage! She couldn't do anything to change that. There! Simple. There was nothing more to it.*

But, her conclusion didn't resonate with her. She still felt uneasy. She sighed. *Another dead-end! Why couldn't she just get on with her life!? She couldn't change her past or her beliefs! What difference would digging around in her past make, anyway - to the present or future? This quest was a circus! A....a.... complete, waste of time!* She was probably doomed to carry on living life the way that she'd always done — the way her family had done before her. Maybe everything was decided the day that she was born - as she was told as a child. Maybe that was all the "truth" there was. She should stick to it. After *all, she'd tried her best to make her life what she wanted. And she'd failed, hopelessly. She should just accept that her life would never change. There was no use trying to escape a destiny that had already been cast in stone by her heritage.*

[That conclusion might be simple enough but, it won't absolve you of the responsibility to walk your soul's path. That's exactly why you need to persist with your quest. Your past influenced you to a far greater extent than you're aware of. But, it doesn't define you. You came into this world with your own destiny – your soul's Divine purpose. Honor your parents, and family by all means but, you're solely responsible to bring that destiny into the physical realm. Nothing is 'decided' – not until, you align with your truth. Your destiny is in your hands – it still lies untapped within your soul. But, your human form also possesses free will, and that is dictated by your ego. And it will remain so, until you heed your soul's calling to align your physical body with your true purpose - by surrendering to Divine will. Living your soul purpose isn't easy for someone at the mercy of their old conditioning. It's even more difficult when you take into account the burden of inter-generational, conditioning of your body's cellular memory. It's a long, and arduous journey to free yourself from that but, it's by no means, impossible. Your soul already carries the wisdom to help you bring about your transformation – by making the unconscious, conscious. This is your soul's 'work' – not the mind. If you can trust, and surrender to the process by letting go of what you think you know, you'll discover access to another source of intelligence - an innate wisdom that will help you find your way through your inner darkness. Trust your soul's wisdom. Listen out for its voice – your truth. Listen to your heart – it will help you to discern it from the multitude of superfluous 'noises' that your mind has become conditioned by, in your outer world. That conditioning only feeds the doubt that constantly plagues you and promotes feelings of disempowerment, and inadequacy - robbing you of your innate power. And those thoughts only reinforce your old conditioning. It's the vicious cycle of your physical existence. You can only free yourself by transcending it]

She sighed heavily. She was getting nowhere. There were no areas of common ground with her family. She'd always felt uncomfortable around them – except for her father. Then again, she felt uncomfortable around everyone! She wondered if the conflict that she'd witnessed during her childhood had somehow become ingrained in her personality. There were many occasions when the conditions under which they lived proved to be a catalyst for acrimonious outbreaks amongst family members. As a child, she was always told to leave the room whenever an argument broke out. But the walls didn't protect her from her senses! She might not have understood what was going on but, she was very much aware of the rife tension that went on for days afterwards. Did those experiences affect her in some way? Did that kind of environment make her more prone to conflict in her life? She recalled how difficult it was to accept something as simple as doing her daily chores. She'd constantly fought against it. Her ire wasn't helped by the double standards when it came to the boys in the neighborhood. They were allowed to continue playing, while she was confined to the kitchen for hours at a time! As she grew up, she saw other gender inequalities being perpetuated in many ways, and that only made her more disgruntled. Instead of grooming her for a life of domestication, those glaring inequalities made a career look far more appealing. And the stress associated with it was a small price to pay compared to a lifetime of drudgery that accompanied an imposed role that was ascribed to her, because she was a woman!

She soon realized that gender inequality wasn't just an aspect of her cultural conditioning. It was prominent in every corner of the world, including the workplace! Except, there was an interesting twist to it. She was more highly rewarded when she adopted the traits, and working habits of her male counterparts! As soon as she became aware of it, she'd voiced her dissatisfaction to fight the injustice of it. The ensuing backlash from her peers came as a surprise. And when she refused to back down it wasn't long before she was shown the door for contravening some corporate code or other. And then she was hit by another astounding revelation. Those experiences might have been hard to swallow but, there was something worse that she'd remained unaware of. The impact of her dualistic charade – wearing a mask in society, and disowning her true nature – resulted in an inner conflict in her psyche that was far more detrimental to her soul's growth. Over the years that conflict had made it impossible to be at peace with herself. To add insult to injury, she'd allowed her experiences to dictate her behavior, because she didn't understand the impact of social prejudices on reinforcing her separatist views. She became even more separated from her feminine nature, until she was unable to relate to it at all. If anything, she preferred to keep it well hidden to avoid being preyed upon by cultural, and societal "norms" that she'd developed no tolerance for. To her it was the ultimate form of waste - both from a human potential, and economic perspective! And gender had nothing to do with her viewpoint. That restrictive thinking impacted negatively on both sexes. It confined the feminine nature that existed in both women and men. And the converse was equally, devastating for the masculine nature in both sexes. For a planet in a state of perpetual crisis – generation after generation - any form of restriction, and discrimination that confined the evolution of humanity was an unaffordable luxury!

She shifted her focus to observe her rambling thoughts. She had to admit that the boys in the neighborhood did add a whole different dimension to her childhood. It wasn't acceptable in her culture to date before marriage. There were all kinds of repercussions from parental castigation, to outright social ostracism. As a child, she'd never understood what the fuss was all about. She didn't find boys appealing at all. She was only interested in playing sport with them – something that she loved. However, none of the other girls in the neighborhood shared her interest, and that meant further ridicule. Not that she minded, because the only alternative was playing "house" with papier Mache dolls, and cardboard boxes that served as makeshift kitchens! Where was the fun in that? Besides, it looked so obviously, like the real chores that she was expected to perform that it made her suspicious – even if it was called a "game." It was only later in life when she realized the more serious implications of that "game" in perpetuating the psychological stereotypes that restricted more than half the human population. That together with the practices, and rituals commanding everything from body mutilation to marginalizing the full rights of women left her disillusioned with the social constructs that continued to be upheld, after centuries of dehumanizing, and disempowering treatment of women.

She returned to her stillness. And recalled the time when some invisible barrier came crashing down on her fun-filled, sporting afternoons. It was about the same time that her boobs came onto the scene. The boys started behaving strangely, and she noticed that none of them wanted to select her for their team. Nonetheless, she went to the sports field every afternoon to watch them play, hoping that they would change their minds. Eventually, she stopped – there was no point in being a by-stander. Other than her mother's repeated instructions to stay away from "those boys" no one offered any explanation for their weird behavior. That did very little to alleviate her confusion, and sadness at losing her best playmates. She was left to ponder how two bobbing pieces of anatomy could change her whole life. It made it all the more difficult to accept, since it was so insignificant compared to the many fun times that they'd shared. Needless to say, their rejection made her very self-conscious, and the only outlet was to direct her frustration towards her changing body. Since she didn't own many pieces of clothing to hide behind, she preferred being alone. The damage, however, was done. Her mind took over playing the same scenes of rejection that continued feed her insecurities, and fears.

Thankfully, time raised its masterful hand - and took over her life. She became more interested in her studies, and spent less time playing. Thereafter her life was all about building her career. And soon enough, everything fitted into a progression of some sort that was considered "normal." It was reinforced by the many looks of approval that were flashed in her direction. The little rebel had finally grown-up, and was behaving like a "good" girl. She was convinced that she heard a distinct sigh of relief from her mother. She'd often wondered about the reaction to her change in attitude. It made no sense to her. After all, she'd fallen into the same routine as everyone else, and nothing she did was in the least bit interesting. She spent many an afternoon pondering the "future" that everyone was so hell-bent on chasing, and questioning what she had to do to join in that race. Any thoughts about her purpose in life, however, were taken over by the comfort of being accepted by those around her - after what felt like an extremely long exile. She couldn't believe how much easier things were. So much so, it convinced her that she'd finally "come into her own." As the years passed she became more "successful" with each passing day that she implemented her people-pleasing, formula. The fact that she'd fallen for a red-herring, and that her life purpose might be something completely, different to her career never occurred to her. Neither did her happiness. Life as she'd known it in her childhood home – cold, hard, empty, uninspiring, conflict-ridden – became her "norm." She didn't even see the signs or notice the pattern.

She came back to the nothingness with a start. She now understood the deeper impact of those experiences on molding her personality. Far from giving her the freedom, and independence that she so desperately desired, her "play it by the book" mentality had compromised her ever reaching the doorway to her true Self. Furthermore, it had misled her to believe that she – as in her mind – was in control of the direction of her life. She sighed as revelation hit. Effectively, all she'd done was move into adulthood with the same pair of blinkers that she'd worn as a child! Her life might have taken on a different hue as a result of different circumstances but, nothing had fundamentally changed in her life over the years, because nothing had changed within her! The barriers that she'd built up as a child were firmly entrenched in her psyche by then, and further reinforced by the same pattern of experiences in her outer world. As real as she perceived it to be, her identity was as fragile as the illusions that had helped her manifest a sand-castle for a reality in her physical world! With her lack of awareness of the interplay between an illusory reality, and a false sense of self she was far removed from anything real, including her true Self! Until now – in nothingness – she was completely, unaware of the extent of her conditioning.

[How you did handle the ongoing rejection?]

She came out of her reverie with a jolt. Not well. It hurt. Terribly. Her defense tactic was to stay, as far away as possible, from everyone. And besides, there was no time. She was far too busy with building her "successful future." And when the baby arrived, there was even less time to dwell on her past, and something as nebulous as her life purpose.

[Denial is one way of coping. Avoiding your Self by running away from it, is another. Whatever your justifications, you resolved nothing – you remained a prisoner of your past]

Running! She? Not a chance! She'd never run from anything in her life! She did what she had to do. And went after what she wanted. But, she never abandoned any "ship" that she was on! It was always "all or nothing" with her.

[You showed up to honor your responsibilities towards others but, you never showed up for your Self. To honor your Self - by being fully present. You're so used to running that you're not even aware of it but, you feel it in your separation from Self. You're all too familiar with putting as much physical distance between yourself, and your pain. But, you were unaware of suppressing it. It's easy to overlook that kind of behavior. It's very subtle, and it doesn't interfere with the belief that you're committed to seeing your battles through. But, you're only avoiding what you need to face within you. You were so focused on your external world that you failed to notice your increasing numbness. It might have been your preferred survival tactic but, it also prevented you from fully engaging with your Self - and life. Consciously, you gained a false sense of control by bottling everything up but, you became so far removed from your true Self that you were never fully present. Sub-consciously, however, you continued to grapple with your world – to force yourself to feel something. Because of your limited awareness, you failed to recognize your soul's impulses to help bring the truth of your behavior into consciousness. That truth hasn't gone anywhere. Until such time that you heal the root-cause of your pain, you'll only be lying to yourself, and others. And you'll continue to keep your past reality alive - you can't change what you resist. Each soul comes to earth with its share of challenges but, no purpose is a constant, battlefield of bleeding effort. If it is, know that you're resisting your truth, and living contrary to your soul purpose. There's no honor – no self-love - in suffering or martyrdom. It's only an indication of the extent to which you're resisting your truth. Your soul will continuously remind you of that, until you get the message - to align with your purpose. This could take any number of forms - a self-sabotaging mishap, an illness or an accident. Losing your job; a loved one. There are many examples in your world - it's one huge, vicious circle of suffering. Staying committed to your battles is admirable but, it takes self-love to set boundaries that serve you, and that purpose. Boundaries that help you know when to let go – to free yourself from limiting patterns or toxic relationships. Until you learn to love yourself, you'll only add more pain to an emotional-body founded on pain. Your soul is ruthless in its efforts to awaken you to your purpose]

And she could no longer deny that there was a lot of pain - in every area of her life. Even if she tried avoiding it, it followed her around relentlessly. It was easier to just accept it as her "lot in life." For the first time, she asked herself: "What was the root cause of all that pain?" Some part of her must have been aware of her self-deceptive behavior, because on more than one occasion she'd made a concerted effort to choose happiness. That ability to see some light beyond whatever pain threatened to pull her under had helped her through many a dark night of the soul. After the most recent avalanche of events in her life, however, she'd somehow lost that ability. She was puzzled. She waited patiently in the silent, stillness for some clarity. She had no problem with pain but, there was something about the ongoing pain in her life that felt, unnecessary. It struck her that this was the first time that she'd given so much thought to her life experiences. She was completely, unsettled by how close she felt - to herself! Or was she now experiencing more of her Self - as the layers of deception were being unraveled, and released? She'd always believed that she was aware of what was happening in her life. But, she now realized that she'd made a serious assumption. Her physical reality wasn't something outside of her - it was reflecting what was inside her! She was so wrapped up in her physical world that she'd lost track of a host of things. She sighed. It was actually, much more than that. She'd lost her connection with her Self, and her soul purpose! If she was that aware, she would have picked up on her deceptiveness a lot sooner. And stopped trying to force her life into some kind of conditioned mold!

[Don't be so hard on yourself]

That was the kindest thing anyone had said to her – in such a long, long time. It made her heart swell with emotion. It was so strange that she brusquely, pushed it aside. It didn't have any place in the negativity that held her captive.

[So you're ready to acknowledge that you were avoiding the negativity in your life?]

Definitely not! She'd always maintained a positive attitude! She owed her progress to that trait. It had helped her lift herself up every time that she landed in a rough patch. She didn't know where she found the strength to get out of bed every morning. She only knew that she refused to give in to the spasms in her stomach. Her single, most prevalent thought was: "Get through the day." And then, she would crawl back into bed at night, too exhausted to think.

[There were many such times – when you needed to 'lift' yourself up?] Countless.

[Sounds like a joyless life. Why didn't you acknowledge how you were feeling? Why did you cover it up by staying busy? Did you ever think that you were going against your truth?]

She smiled wryly. No. She looked around her again. She was glad that she could share this conversation with someone, even if she couldn't see who it was. Despite her efforts to shape her life according to the advice from a host of role models, she had to admit that she never felt inspired by what she saw in the world around her. And since no one shared much of their personal lives in their small community, she assumed that everybody used a similar approach when it came to life. Besides, it all looked pretty "normal" to her. There were the many, larger-than-life characters that she saw portrayed in the occasional movie but, she'd always discounted that - it was only entertainment. To her way of thinking, dreaming of another life or wishing hers away, did nothing to change the stark reality that she woke up to every day. She was taken aback by that thought. If she had the ability to recognize that about a movie, why was she unable to make that distinction about herself!? Her conditioning had turned her life into one! And she didn't even write the script!

[You don't have any frame of reference for 'normal.' You only know what you've been conditioned to believe]

True. And in the nothingness, one thing was becoming increasingly apparent about one aspect of her conditioning - the labeling. She'd heard it throughout her childhood. Every antic of hers was, either "bad" or "crazy," until she believed that something seriously wrong with her! It made her try desperately hard to do things as she was told – to be as "normal" as everybody else. But, no matter what she did to fit into that mold, it only ended in disaster. Eventually, she reached a damning conclusion - she was born at the wrong time, and place - in the wrong world! She looked at the nothingness, and couldn't help thinking how right it felt to be there. Something about it made her feel like she belonged - like she was home. She'd never felt like that in her own home! Her heart exploded with gratitude, despite there being nothing to substantiate her thoughts, and feelings. And then, she was struck by another revelation. It didn't matter what others thought about her - they were only reflecting a fundamental truth. She might have been spurred on by external impulses to think positively about her life but, that was another cover up – she didn't think much of herself. She'd never thought that anything good existed within her. Everything, and everybody else was better than she was. Her first recollections went right back to her school days. She'd emulated the behavior of the other kids, and so began the game of "copycat." And then, something unexpected, happened. The more effectively she played that role, the more she was accepted by others. At first, she was confused. Why was she being accepted, when she was pretending to be someone else? But, she downplayed her instincts, and suppressed her concerns. It was so much nicer having friends - she didn't feel so left out, anymore. And so, her adopted versions of self became her "normal" in the life of pretend that she'd lived thereafter. For some reason that realization now made her feel sick to her bones. It struck her that that feeling had always been there – she'd just never been aware of it. She was horrified at her lack of awareness. There was only one thing to do. She closed her eyes, and rested in her stillness, until clarity dawned. What she was conditioned to believe as "normal" wasn't normal for her! It wasn't her truth! Her truth was something, altogether different. She didn't know what it was but, she felt it in the nothingness. And then it hit her. She might have found various ways to be accepted by others but, some part of her had refused to accept the false version of herself! She didn't even like herself!

That insight gave her a very different perspective of her behavior as a child. It made her different - even strange. But, there was nothing wrong about climbing trees; keeping weird creatures as pets; playing cricket with the boys or spending afternoons in the cellar. Or the myriad other things that she'd done during her life while meandering through the "human condition" – like preferring her alone-time. And yet, she'd gotten into an awful lot of trouble for her "bad" behavior. She was constantly reminded that "good" girls don't behave the way she did. Only the "devil" behaved like that. As a child, she didn't know what that word meant but, based on the stares, and whispers from those around her whenever she made an appearance, she gathered that it was something terrifying. Suddenly, so many missing puzzle pieces fell into place about her childhood. The way people treated her; avoided her, and the many accusations of wrongdoing – even when she wasn't to blame. It made her hyper-alert, and defensive in the company of others - even as an adult. And despite her belief that she always put herself "out there" there was some latent fear that she'd always denied. She didn't engage fully with life – she always held herself back. The pain in her stomach was always there, because she wasn't living her truth – she was resisting her Self. Finally, she understood some of her contradictory behavior as a child. She was afraid of being alone, despite her preference for spending time with herself. She was petrified that the "devil" inside of her would capture her! That's why she felt safe whenever her father was around – he was the only one she could rely on to protect her. She might have become more adept at wearing her social mask as an adult but, she'd never overcome that inner conflict from being constantly in flight-fight mode. But, where could she go? There was no way she could out-run her Self! And not understanding her behavior made it difficult to express her innermost thoughts, and feelings. She'd become more silent, and withdrawn - locked inside her fears. She felt constantly alone, even in the company of those closest to her. And then, she had a flash of insight. Whether she was "bad" or "crazy" didn't matter. By remaining open in the nothingness to face her inner "devil" she'd somehow laid that skeleton to rest. How did she know to keep herself open under such circumstances? But, she became aware of a different feeling. A whole new spaciousness was replacing her fear. She realized that her childish escapades were the only fun times that she'd experienced in her life. And they were what any childhood should be about - carefree, fun-loving, and full of adventure. From the way her heart was beating, she gathered that she'd just resurrected a few long-lost, traits of her true Self.

She got back to her memories with greater enthusiasm. At some point, she started devoting more time to her schoolwork. She discovered that it was somewhat comforting to take refuge in her studies. The improvement in her grades was just a bonus. She noticed that she also received a lot more positive attention than she was used to. More importantly, this development made a stronger association in her mind between working, and receiving validation. Especially, from her father. He beamed with pride, each time she brought home her report card. She sucked in her breath as she realized that she'd just reinforced some of her earlier insights about being motivated by him when making many of her life decisions. She was never really interested in what she was doing. It was all done to secure his love.

[Why do you believe that you needed to 'secure' his love? Do you not consider yourself worthy of love? That you deserve love?]

Worthy of love? Deserve love? Love was like trust – it had to be earned! And she could only consider herself worthy when she earned it! Anyway, her father loved her as a child. That was the most important thing in all this rigmarole.

[And when you matured into a young woman?]

Her mind immediately, turned to the afternoons that her father spent working in the dining room. She sometimes sat on the stairs just outside the patio-doorway, and watched him out of the corner of her eye. She often wondered what he was thinking, as his pen moved furiously across the pages in front of him. She wished that he would share his thoughts with her but, she also knew that her childish chatter wouldn't be encouraged - this work was important. It wasn't one of his DIY-projects. She had to be content with running up to the table whenever he left – to admire his hand-writing. She couldn't read the cursive script but, that didn't stop her from running her fingers over the page in sheer wonder. It was beautiful! That feeling had the strange effect of lifting her out of her troubled little world. She'd always admired his dedication, and realized that she'd seldom seen a lighter side to him. But, there was another quality of his that she'd never appreciated before. He'd lived his life with a gentle air of respect for everything, and everyone. He had a quiet acceptance about him - a surrender to life. And there was so much power in his presence – a power that he'd never enforced. Her eyes misted over as she realized that she now respected him, more than ever. For the first time, she marveled at the blessing of sharing her life with someone who was so generous of spirit that he could alter a person's attitude the moment he entered a room. She recalled helping him with his chores on a number of occasions. She even mowed the lawn, and washed his car on weekends. It was no easy task for a little girl, and as much as she loved that old Chevy, it was a monster to keep clean! It took her an entire day! Not that she minded. She knew how much he loved his car - the only time that he showed any kind of emotion was when sitting behind the wheel of one. There was always a little smile at the corner of his lips. And for some reason, seeing him smile always cheered her up. But, she remained silent whenever they were together. She sensed that he needed this time for himself. It was more than enough to sit by his side, and share the ride with him. She couldn't wait for the day, when she would be able to drive on her own.

And then, she recalled the day when she'd done just that. She slid onto the driver's seat of his car, and started the ignition. Then she positioned the gear lever next to "D" – just the way her father had always done. All the while, blissfully unaware that she wasn't allowed to drive as a child. She slowly eased the car down the driveway, and stopped at the gate. She turned her head a few times to make sure there were no other cars on the street before pressing the accelerator, and turning the wheel. Soon, she was slowly weaving down the road; her head barely topping the steering wheel as she stretched to work the pedals. She drove around the empty streets in the small neighborhood for a short while, and then made her way back home. Only to find her father standing on the front porch, with an anxious look on his face. She didn't take her eyes of the road but, smiled nervously to let him know that she was fine. He waited for her to maneuver the car safely between the gates, before going back into the house. She parked the car, and switched off the ignition. She sat, and slowly ran her hands over the steering wheel while savoring her big moment. Their big moment, because he never said anything to spoil it. And that was the beginning of her life-long, love of cars. Many an afternoon was spent doing her homework on the huge, one-seater at the back. Sometimes he joined her, and took her with him to the grocery store. As soon as the car pulled up outside the small, local shop she would jump out, and run ahead to pick out the few items on the list. Her father stood by the counter, chatting to the owner. Then she waited impatiently by his side as the items were rung up, and paid for. She knew it was only a matter of time, before she received her favorite… choc…choc…late. Her stream of thoughts came to an abrupt halt. She paused, and shifted uncomfortably.

[Yes……..?]

She hesitated. For the first time, she realized just how strong her resistance was towards her past. But, as much as she tried to stem the flood of memories, they continued to filter into her mind. She recalled the day when she had her first period. At first, she told no one. She was too scared. She didn't know what was happening to her. She'd experienced her fair share of serious cuts and bruises, and the sight of blood didn't scare her. But, this was different. The bleeding went on all day. Then, another. And another. Even though she didn't want to, she raised it with her mother. Her mother looked at her for a second, and then gave her something called a "pad." She was told how to use it. And that was the end of that. To her the silence signified that there was nothing to worry about. The knowledge that it was a monthly occurrence, and would result in a number of changes to her body wasn't shared with her. Neither were some of the implications to her emotional body that would significantly impact the development of her sexuality. That information she had to figure out for herself – further down the line. She managed to overcome her concerns about her physical body when she saw some of the "accidents" that happened to the other girls at school. She also figured that it was something that only affected girls. She was just grateful that her "accidents" happened at home. It spared her being ridiculed by the boys. And like most things that she didn't understand during those years, she just learnt to live with it. Silently. It became her modus operandi when dealing with any set of circumstances. In the nothingness, she realized how that approach had taught her never to acknowledge her true feelings - even to herself. No matter what the challenge, she had no choice but, to "get on with it." She felt a piercing pain in her throat, and realized that for all her outspokenness there was a history of suppressing her voice. And that had only compounded her inner turmoil. She sighed. How many other acts of unloving behavior did she subject herself to!? Why did she willingly accept treating herself that way? Why didn't she question it? She returned to her memories.

She was tall for her age with a thin, boyish frame. The first thing that became noticeable, were her breasts. At around the same time, she spotted her pubic hair but, that was too terrifying to think about - let alone, mention to anyone. She stuffed her fears into a box labelled, "Later." No one had ever broached the subject of the "birds and the bees." She had no knowledge of sex or how babies were conceived. She didn't even know that breasts were used for nursing them. She'd once almost witnessed piglets being born on a farm but, the children were ushered away from the scene before they saw anything. She only had an image of this strange pink, mass protruding from the mother-pig. For years she thought that they'd left that poor pig to die! But, she knew not to ask any questions about the incident. On that terrible day, she was so sore and miserable from her period that she could barely walk. But, she couldn't suppress her craving for chocolate. To make matters worse, it was a blistering hot day, and she was already tired after her long walk home. The idea of walking to the store didn't occur to her. She changed into a pair of shorts and a T-shirt, and didn't take notice of her tiny breasts. Her father was already home - working in the dining room. She went to ask if he planned on going to the store that afternoon. She hoped that he would leave a bit earlier. She wanted that chocolate.

Reflecting on that afternoon in the nothingness, she realized that her father had reacted very strangely. He glanced at her when she entered the room but, instead of smiling, he looked down abruptly. She must have known something was wrong, because she hesitated, and stopped a short distance from the table. She waited, and then took a step closer. Before she could speak, he instructed her to change, immediately. His voice was stern, and he didn't look at her when he spoke. She was surprised by his manner. And confused. He'd never spoken to her in such a harsh tone. It left her frozen. But, more than anything, she felt an overriding sense of shame. She looked to him for some kind of reassurance but, he ignored her. Eventually, she walked away. As soon as she reached the passage-way leading to her bedroom, she stood against the wall, and waited. Hoping that he would call her back; say something. But, he carried on working, even though her breathing was loud enough to make her presence known. It took her the longest time to cover the short distance back to her room. She never left it for the rest of the day. They never spoke about the incident but, for some reason, she never went to the grocery store with him again. Something changed between them that day – she was just never able to put it into words. He continued buying her chocolates but, she'd lost all desire to ever eat them again. The strange sensations in her body brought her back to the nothingness. Every cell was screaming for her to think of something else; do something else! But, she remained in her stillness, and ignored everything, except the tornado of emotion within her. She eventually, found some of the missing pieces to understand the intensity of that day. He must have noticed that she was no longer a child. And that she'd turned into a young woman without either one of them noticing. It explained why his attitude towards her changed completely, after that day. But, it also changed her entire world. She realized that that afternoon he'd stopped being her best friend, and had become the protective father. But, there was something more. She'd never overcome her feelings of shame – about her body.

[What else did you feel?]

She knew that he loved her but, she couldn't understand why she felt so rejected, and abandoned. It dawned on her that the inexplicable distance that developed between them had left a yearning emptiness within her. She'd never acknowledged it until now, because she'd never paid any attention to her feelings. Especially, when her feelings oscillated between sadness and ……..more sadness. Pain …….and more pain. Tears ……and more tears. There didn't seem to be much point. So she remained stuck in her emptiness. As painful as it was, it was associated with the only love that she'd ever known. She was only now beginning to understand the depth, and meaning of the ocean of emotions flowing within her. Perhaps her emotions had had a far greater impact on her mind, and body than she believed. Perhaps they were more than just random triggers of chemicals coursing through her veins. Why did she suppress them for so long? If the recollection of this single incident had provided her with so much insight about her past, were there other experiences that she'd lost track of that could enhance her knowledge of Self? Could she use her feelings as a kind of roadmap to go deeper into her past to reveal her truth? Maybe her past was more important than she realized. There must be more hidden truths in the silence of that emotional vacuum of years gone by, than she'd previously thought. She'd spent all her time fighting to move on from it - to "turn a new page." She was shocked to realize that she'd not turned any pages at all! She'd not even moved beyond that first chapter of her childhood! And she couldn't move on, until she went back, and unearthed whatever was blocking her! She might not be able to change her past but, she still owed it to herself to understand how those years had impacted her behavior, and created a self that she could no longer relate to. It was the least she could do - for her Self. What other "pages" did she have to revisit in her childhood? Would that help her close that chapter, and move on from a past that had unknowingly, overshadowed her entire life? She had a burning desire to find out.

She closed her eyes, and let the stillness within carry her back to that afternoon. She remembered going to her room, and crying all afternoon. The initial hurt was obviously caused by her father's reaction, and his harsh tone of voice. But, she realized that her tears were for something, far more precious. Something major had transpired in her life that day – something that defined how she felt about herself. Her special relationship with her father had received a catastrophic blow – one that was beyond her control. And she could never fix it. She was no longer his "little girl." She'd grown up. It had all happened so fast….so unexpectedly. Both of them were caught completely, off-guard by that thing called "puberty." There were probably a whole string of thoughts going through his mind that afternoon. Perhaps he was worried that……

[….How did you feel….?]
…..that she would meet someone……
[…How…. did…… you….. feel…?]
…….get married …….
[…How…. did…… you….. feel…?]
…..and leave him…….
[How did you feel?]
Each time she ignored that question, she felt her stomach lurch with pain - taking her closer to that dark pit of emptiness that she'd blocked out, for so long. Each time she got close to it, she did her usual mental flip to ignore it but, the feeling only became more intense. It rose to her throat, and blocked her air passages, making her gulp for air. Then the feeling turned…..dove….squeezed out all the air in her lungs, and left her gasping from the piercing pain that erupted in her chest. Before she could take another breath, she felt the next attack slowly building, and rising to her throat. She froze, as she waited for the pain to hit. *What was that feeling?*

[Answer the question]
"I don't know how I felt. It was a long time ago!"
[You do]
"I don't!"
[Answer it]

"Why don't you tell me? Why are you trying to break me down!?"

[You have to speak of it – to transcend its hold over you. Only then, will you surrender completely, and be open to fully accepting yourself. And in breaking the walls down – in breaking your heart open – only then will you be able see what you've been denying, all this time. It will free you to see your Self – for who you truly are]

Those words had a strange effect on her. She felt something deep within her belly give way, and she was plunged deeper into that black void. Before she could figure out what was happening, there was a flood of tears, and the insights seemed to come out of nowhere. She felt powerless to stop them. Speak of what? The resentment of being caught up in a body that she didn't want, and couldn't escape from? A body that had caused her the loss of the most important relationship in her life! Her shame of being a female? Of becoming a woman? An experience that should have been revered, and celebrated. Did she have to speak of how much she wished to forever remain his "little girl?" How much she wished that their special bond was never broken by something as stupid as puberty? Did she have to mention that since that day she'd unknowingly focused on developing the masculine side of her personality – just to make him love her? Although she'd never allowed herself to think it, something about that incident led her to believe that her father wished she was a boy. No matter the silence – his feelings that afternoon were loud enough to be "heard." They were transferred to her, and she'd carried the burden of it all those years. Those suppressed thoughts might have upheld her false identity before but, she now realized that she felt like a fraud for denying her true nature. She wasn't a boy. She wasn't a man. And behaving like one, didn't change her truth. She was a woman, possessing all the attributes of a one - physical, and emotional. Including, an intuitive nature. A voice. And the power to create. She possessed a masculine, and a feminine energy. And she had no idea of the kind of life she could have created if those energies were in balance. She only knew that her past reality was anything but, balanced. She remained silent for a long time completely, overwhelmed by her insights.

[What else?]

What else? Wasn't that enough?

[You're not done…..yet]

She swallowed hard. Not through fear but, because of the huge lump in her throat. It was a familiar pain - not one that she indulged. She hated crying. Girls cried! Even through her pain, she was struck by the strong rejection of her feelings. She took a few deep breaths, and tried to extricate herself from falling deeper into that black void but, she was already in it - way too deep. And she sensed she still had a long way to go before it bottomed out. There was nothing she could do, other than face what was in it. She might not be willing but, she could no longer ignore her feelings – she would only further suppress her feminine nature. No matter her tears; insecurities or that hitherto unknown fear of being vulnerable. And whether she liked it or not, she had to feel her way towards her Self, even though her masculine mind was rejecting that thought. Furthermore, she was sensitive to the feelings of others – to the whole world. But, she wasn't sensitive towards her own feelings; her own needs. And right now, she needed to honor her feelings.

She opened herself to that black, void. She realized that she'd turned to her father for the first time, in a moment of complete, vulnerability. She'd expressed a need to someone she loved, and trusted. Instead, he'd turned away. And rejected not only her need but, her physical person! That hurt more than any verbal refusal - more than a slap on the cheek. It sent a strong message to her child's mind that her needs weren't important - to ignore the feminine in her. A straight "no" would have been better - the silence wouldn't have been left impregnated with emptiness. It struck her that the silence that afternoon was far from empty. Besides her father's fears about her budding woman-hood, it was filled with his sense of loss; loneliness, and sadness – all at once. And in addition, to the burden of her own feelings of shame, and guilt, she'd felt all of his pain. And she'd unconsciously modified her behavior, and her life - to stop him from feeling it. She sighed heavily. She realized that they had both lost something precious that afternoon. Her father lost his "little girl," and she'd lost the ability to connect to her feminine nature. She smiled, wryly. That afternoon had nothing to do with chocolate.

She'd never expressed any of her needs after that. To anyone – including, herself. Although his behavior was unintentional, it left an indelible mark on her psyche. Perhaps denying her femininity had helped her to maintain the illusion that nothing had changed between them. And not accepting any form of support from others was her way of avoiding her vulnerability. Her self-reliance was the tower that she'd erected to protect herself – against ever needing anyone. What saddened her the most was the insight that she'd turned on herself that day. Never mind the rejection from others for being a false version of herself – his rejection of her had dealt the first blow. Followed by her own – of her femininity. And her ego had railroaded her into proving him wrong about wanting a son! She intended to be better than any son of his could ever be! Before she could prove anything, she married while still quite, young. It didn't take very long before she realized that she'd made a mistake. But, there was nothing she could do. Divorce was forbidden in their culture – the word didn't even exist in their Holy book! So she took on the only role that she'd always identified with – the "fixer." And set about fixing everything in her life. Except, herself.

The false premise underpinning her decisions was now glaringly obvious. Without knowing who she truly was or what she wanted for her life she'd bought into yet, another social construct. And no matter how "rock solid," compliance to social and cultural norms didn't solve anything real for her – not when those norms only reinforced her conditioning. She had a shocking revelation. She didn't know what "real" meant! She sensed that it had something to do with her soul purpose. Neither did she know what "role" she needed to play in her life - beyond those dictated by cultural, and societal norms that she'd become indoctrinated by since childhood. She realized that the only role she could accept was the one required to fulfill her soul purpose. What did her soul need? What was her purpose? Whatever it was she was worthy of it – she was born to live it. That was the only real thing about her. Who was she born to be, before her conditioning made her adopt a false identity? How did she make herself whole again, and resurrect her true Self? If this was all about energies, how could she bring her feminine nature back to life? How did she heal generations of suppression, and abuse against the feminine? How did she heal her predisposition towards masculine behavior, because of the unbalancing effect of societal conditioning on her energies? Could she bring those energies into balance to create the birthing ground for her whole, true Self? She frowned. *What did any of this mean? She understood none of it!* For the first time, she fully understood the intricate nature of the new boundaries that she needed to establish if she wanted to meaningfully, take her life forward. They couldn't be "solid walls" that kept her trapped in her fears, and barricaded from the Universe. Instead, those "walls" needed to be words of love – gentle, and yet, firmly spoken in truth while she remained fully open, and vulnerable.

She turned her gaze once again, to the nothingness. She'd always looked outward for her answers but, it dawned on her that her more fundamental needs to live the life that she truly deserved – peace, joy, self-worth, and self-love – couldn't be supplied by another person or obtained from her external world. Looking to establish a sense of Self, relative to any aspect of her physical world was futile – if what she saw was merely a reflection of her lower mind. She'd grabbed onto everything like a starving maniac in an attempt to fill that empty void within her. For years, her perceived success had allayed the concerns that were being repeatedly flagged by her deeper instincts. But, she was now beginning to understand just how empty she was. And the black void within, was far from gone. It was still there somewhere, deep within. She might have been distracted by the illusion of her false reality but, she was now fully conscious of it. There was no hope of denying or ignoring it any longer. And there was no escape from it - in the nothingness. It was all she was aware of; the only thing she could feel – the absence of her soul's light in the blackness. And that void refused to be filled by her old self or some kind of success, as defined in her physical world. It needed her true Self. And she had no idea who that was.

CHAPTER 10
MIRRORS OF FEAR

She was petrified by that thought. She sat amidst her memories trying to figure out for just how long she'd been deceiving herself. For years, she'd been stuck on compulsive achievement in her physical world. She'd regarded herself as just another cog in the wheel of "progress." Notwithstanding that, her drive was relentless - marked by an intensity that rattled her sometimes. Very little thought had gone into the motivations behind her actions - let alone, her soul purpose. She became aware of her awareness, slowly superseding those thoughts. Why was she born in this world? How could she best use her time while she was alive? She might not be defined by her heritage but, her birthright must serve her purpose somehow. How did it serve humanity? She realized that for all her "progress" she'd merely maintained the status quo in her physical world. And the unconscious, mechanistic workings of her conditioned mind had only aided her delusion. She'd been fast asleep - her entire life! And she'd believed that subjecting herself to the same mindless routine each day was being awake! She felt an unusual urge to laugh but, was hit by another revelation. Without the emotional maturity to discern the implications of her conditioned personality she'd honed a skill that was detrimental to fulfilling that purpose - the denial of her emotions.

She stared into the nothingness, and trembled from the icy coldness seeping through her body. She didn't have to look at her body to know that her aura had disappeared. She wrapped her arms tightly around herself, in an attempt to retain some warmth. All she wanted to do was curl up, and sleep. She quickly unfolded her arms, and took a few deep breaths. She couldn't sleep – not now. She felt she was on the cusp of a breakthrough. She just had to stick with her quest – no matter how uncomfortable it was. Besides keeping her awake, the coldness was giving her an indication of just how far removed she was from her Self. She frowned. *She'd never thought it necessary to be close to her Self!* It struck her that she couldn't recall having close feelings towards anyone, other than her father, and daughter. Her view of the world was based entirely on the reality that she encountered, each time she walked out the front door. She had one intention every day – to get through everything. All she had to do was shovel through her tasks, as fast as she could. Not all of them were pleasant but, that was life. Any understanding beyond that would have required the ability to reflect – a skill that she'd never acquired. She didn't even know it existed. Every situation was viewed through the limited lens of her mind's conditioning. There was a beginning, and an end. There were inputs, and outputs – all within a specified time, and cost. And that process determined the "value" of the outcome. And her worth - for delivering it. Nothing else was allowed in her "space." And that kind of thinking had informed her reality. She was hit by a revelation that shook her. There was no room for creativity in such a low-vibrational, perspective! She'd been on the same treadmill - reacting to situations – all her entire life! That couldn't be the sum-total of her human experience! How did she stop reacting, and start creating her life? How could she align herself with what her soul wanted to experience during her lifetime? For so long, it had been trying to "tell" her that there was more to life. And yet, she'd ignored those niggling "reminders." She'd been given so many "opportunities" to change her reality. Those were the real "opportunities" that she'd missed! She sighed. Life could have looked, and felt very different. And yet, she'd stuck with a false reality that only left her feeling more powerless with each passing day. Why did she choose to live a lie, instead of her truth?

    She grappled with her latest dilemma but, could only come up with more questions. Why was she so shut down, and reactive? Why did she believe that life was out to get her? Life wasn't vindictive! She was created for a reason! She had a purpose! And such a Divine Universe didn't exist to merely pass her time on a limited, physical existence! *There must be much more out there!* She shifted to her awareness. No! There was much more within her! If she could somehow tap into the innate gifts of her soul could she change life as she'd known it? She sighed. And felt her frustration rise sharply at her mind's failure to find a logical outlet. *Why couldn't she get out of this nightmare? Why was she stuck there?* Only to be hit by a revelation. She wasn't stuck. Nothing was keeping her there – other than her stubborn defensiveness! She shifted her focus to the stillness within to observe that impenetrable "wall." Why was it there? What was lying behind it? It looked completely, incongruous in her silent, stillness. She had the irrepressible urge to tear it down. She had to see behind it; see herself without it. Then, she was struck by a weird insight. There was no wall! There was nothing physical to be broken down! It existed only in her mind! *How was she supposed to remove it? Surely, her ongoing presence in the nothingness was proof of her commitment.* She grappled with her quandary.

[You're not present when your mind is resisting]

She sighed. She had to find some way of transcending that inner resistance. It was so damn subtle! She couldn't detect it with her mind! Could she overcome that stuck feeling by surrendering to the unknown power of her awareness? She had to try staying completely, open. Her instincts were pointing her in that direction, even though her mind didn't approve. And her instincts were real – even though they were invisible! She needed to trust them. She'd learnt that much on this quest! She needed to uncover something in that void – she could feel it! She closed her eyes, and turned to her stillness. She slowly "approached"– settled into - her defensiveness. She felt her anxiety escalating as she got closer but, she continued focusing on her slow breathing. She gently told herself that this was an opportunity unlike any other - to love herself through whatever experience would be unearthed from that void. Very slowly the wall "crumbled," and faded into the nothingness. She was taken aback by the "force" behind her gentle, loving intention. *How was she able to destroy the invisible – the intangible!? She'd done nothing!* Suddenly, the answer to her dilemma became crystal clear. Her past reality was an illusion. Every experience was merely a reflection of her unauthentic self. If she wanted to get closer to her true Self, she had to remove every "story" that she believed about herself - with self-love. Facing that truth was excruciatingly, uncomfortable. Nonetheless, she sat in the stillness for a long time, just being present with her uneasiness. Once again, she was confronted by the elusiveness of her truth. And thrown headlong into a more difficult conundrum. *Where could she find her true Self, if not in her physical world? There was nothing she could use to define herself in the nothingness!! How was she supposed to find her Self in complete, blackness!?And yet, all she'd known in her physical world was a false reality, and an illusory self! She was stuck! How was she supposed to uncover her soul purpose without her true Self!?*

She hugged herself. Her mind was in a daze and she felt utterly lost, and alone. She remained present with her feelings. She became aware of a different kind of "thought" – something rising above the myriad other thoughts in her mind. It was a silent, sense of boundary-less knowing that took over all her senses. It didn't feel like an instinct. *What was that feeling? An extension of her awareness? Her soul's knowing?* As impossible as it was to comprehend, it was "telling" her that the only place she could hope to find her Self was in the silent, stillness within. She needed to surrender to the process, even if her mind was still caught in its chaotic, rambling. Furthermore, she couldn't deny or avoid her anxiety – she needed to hold it in her awareness. She recalled that whenever she was within the stillness, she could detach from both mind, and emotion. She closed her eyes, and felt the storm in her mind slowly fade away as she once again, turned inward to embrace the stillness. It was a lot easier this time around. She realized that she was more open – more allowing. She had a sense of being absorbed within this unfamiliar, spaciousness unfolding within her. She was still battling to understand why she felt no emotion in the stillness - not even fear. She was more aware of the different, boundary-less "thoughts" once she was immersed within her stillness. *Where were those "thoughts" coming from? How was it possible to know fear in her mind, and not feel it in the stillness - if all of her was contained within the same body? Why did the stillness look, and feel so much like the nothingness around her?* As she battled to grasp some form of understanding, she felt a familiar urge slowly invade her mind. *Run!* Her eyes flew open, and her connection to the stillness was immediately, broken. Before she could stop herself, she was firmly ensconced in the realm of her mind. *She looked around, and fervently wished for some magic path to appear in the nothingness. A path that would take her away from this madness! It didn't matter where she went. She just wanted out!*

As she gazed into the nothingness she had an image of herself as a young girl, running through her neighborhood streets with her pet Alsatian. She was often warned against running alone but, she refused to let that stop her. It now dawned on her that whatever was driving her at the time was far greater than any fear of being attacked. She ran as if the devil itself was behind her! She caught herself smiling at the thought, and wondered why she didn't feel the usual resistance towards that word. She was struck by a thought that took her by surprise. *Perhaps the devil was within her – like her mother had always said.* This time her breath caught in her throat. And she became aware of the tumultuous emotion rising within her. How could something said so long ago, still have such a profound impact on her? She felt something surge deep within her in response to her question, before waves of pain pierced her belly. She gasped for air a few times but, somehow managed to remind herself to breathe through the pain. Slowly, sanity prevailed. *Surely everything she now knew about her Self was enough to get rid of the void within her? Why couldn't she get out of the nothingness? She wanted to get on with her life!* She looked around desperately but, she remained exactly, where she was. Something told her that her quest was far from over. Did she discover just the outer layer of that void when she'd processed those memories of her father? Were there other layers that she needed to unravel? She was struck by a thought that made her tremble. If she'd been busy all this time with only the outer layers of that void, what lay at the core of it? How much more did she have to purge before she reached it? Despite her extreme agitation, she detected a newfound level of curiosity. Would her efforts help her gain a deeper level of Self-understanding? This time, she didn't wait for any answers. She sensed a different kind of motivation spurring her on to quarry through the layers. She realized that it wasn't being directed by her will. Instead, it was coming straight from her heart. It was responding to something that stemmed from the very depths of her soul.

It dawned on her that she'd kept her childhood in a box – tightly sealed, and out of sight. What she didn't count on was becoming increasingly intolerant of her avoidance tactics in the nothingness. Despite its blackness, it still managed to cast a "light" on areas within her that she didn't even know existed. All she could do was observe as one memory after another, bombarded her conscious mind. It was a time in her life when she'd lived in a structure that looked like a house but, she could barely remember the personalities that she'd shared it with. Why did she feel so removed from the people she was supposed to feel closest to? She could recall their physical appearances but, they were no more than strangers. She was also puzzled by her extreme emotional reaction to a word that she thought was long forgotten. Why did it still affect her so? Perhaps her turmoil had nothing to do with that word. *What then? Surely, she was over all that childhood stuff by now?* She sighed. Her mind hit another blank as she was denied access to the usual benchmarks that she'd used for evaluating anything. Then again, that was in her tangible, physical world. She had no clue what was happening to her on an emotional scale! Besides, whatever her rational mind could conjure up was powerless to suppress the depth of emotion now welling up inside of her. Was there something more to the relationship with her mother that she wasn't aware of? The pain in her belly was all the confirmation she needed to continue following that breadcrumb. She realized that she'd never had any kind of relationship with her mother. That insight was so alienating that she quickly closed her eyes, and dove straight into the calm ocean of the stillness within, leaving her mind to pick through the thoughts that made absolutely no sense to her. In the stillness, she felt safe again. And her entire body relaxed. She breathed a huge sigh of relief.

With her eyes still closed, she felt herself being immersed into something warm, and soft. She was flowing into it - becoming one with it. For a brief moment, she hesitated. And then, she let go of her apprehension to embrace the strange sensation. It felt like water. She was confused. Another memory surfaced. She was swimming! Her face broke into a broad smile. She'd forgotten how much she loved swimming! She recalled the major, fund-raising event at school to build a pool - a first, in so many ways for the small community. After innumerable cake sales, and sponsored sports events the exorbitant sum of money was finally, collected. And after what seemed like an interminably long wait, and many furtive glances out of her classroom window, she got to see what the fuss was all about. An air of excitement pervaded the entire school as the children waited impatiently for their turn. The first time she jumped into the water was beyond anything that she imagined. She took to the water quite naturally, and learnt the basics quite fast. More than anything, she loved diving into the pool. And she over the moon when she mastered the art of it. It became the "doorway" to a whole new world - a blue haven. A wonderful, magical realm where only she existed. And she didn't have to think about anything or anyone. Only the audible sound of her heartbeat drumming through her entire body, and echoing way beyond the walls of the pool.

One hot afternoon, she struck out to the far end of the pool. And then, she stopped for no apparent reason. She looked up at the sky, and the white, puffy clouds. She tried to duck, as a swallow swooped right above her head. But, she'd misjudged her speed, and the distance that she'd covered. She was already in the deep end of the pool! That understanding only hit when she tried to stand, and watch the amazing acrobatics of that bird. There was no floor! Her head dipped below the surface, and she swallowed so much water that she couldn't breathe. She splashed around furiously to get above the water level but, once again, she sank below the surface. The last thing she remembered was a weightless, sinking feeling as she watched the sky slowly moving out of sight. She remembered thinking how beautiful it looked. And then, everything went black. When she regained consciousness she was lying on the floor alongside the pool, coughing her lungs out. There was a burning sensation in her nose, and throat. She tried opening her eyes but, then quickly shut them. The sunlight was way too bright. She had a bad headache, and her head felt as heavy as a boulder. She saw the hazy outline of someone kneeling beside her. He was saying something but, she couldn't understand a word. There were a few children standing around, and looking at her with strange expressions on their faces but, she didn't recognize any of them. Eventually, someone helped her up, and walked her to a nearby bench. She found herself holding a glass of water. As she sipped slowly, the whispers turned to loud chattering. Someone asked how she was feeling. She opened her mouth to speak but, couldn't utter a word. Her throat felt dry; raw. She wondered why everyone was staring at her - it was unnerving! So much so, that her near-fatal experience didn't register. She shifted uncomfortably, and grasped the towel wrapped around her. She was freezing, despite the hot summer sun. Sometime later, she recognized her teacher by her side. She saw him pointing towards the pool, and nodding encouragingly. It dawned on her that he wanted her to get back into the pool. She shook her head fiercely, and pushed herself against the back of the chair. But, he gently persisted, until she decided to follow his instructions. She had to get away from all those prying eyes! He held her arm, and slowly walked her to the pool. And then, stayed by her side, until she was calmly swimming across the length of the pool.

When she reached home that afternoon - after what felt like the longest walk - she couldn't remember how she got there. It only registered that she was home when she spotted the boy next door hanging over the fence; waving at her. He walked alongside her as she made her way up the driveway to the back entrance. She remembered looking at his mouth moving, and his arms gesticulating wildly but, nothing he said made any sense. She heard the words "drown" and "lucky" but, she just continued staring at him blankly, wishing that he would go away. As she approached the house, her eyes darted nervously to see if anyone was around. There was no one. She heaved a sigh of relief, and snuck into her room as quickly as she could. Her whole body felt as heavy as lead – like she was lugging around all the water in that pool. As she changed out of her school uniform, she thought about going to her mother for some reason. But, she quickly dismissed the notion when she saw the scars on her legs. They were a stark reminder of the number of times that her jaunts in the field had ended in some mishap or other, and she needed to be patched up. Her pain was pushed aside, because she needed to bolster herself for what would happen, as soon as she mentioned she was hurt. She didn't know what was worse - the treatment being administered in silence or the hard slaps across her head. Crying was out of the question, because she'd been warned repeatedly, to stop her recalcitrant behavior. But, as painful as the experience was, she refused to cry. She hated being reminded that she "deserved it," and had brought the whole thing on herself for being such a "wild thing." But, that didn't stop her from going back to the fields. In her defense, she did try really hard being the "good girl" that her mother insisted she be. And her ongoing disobedience was the cause of much conflict between them. So much so, that even as a child she knew not to expect any understanding or sympathy for anything that went on in her life. She was always the one at fault.

That afternoon, however, she didn't feel like herself. She felt weird. She had the strange urge to be near people. But, based on the reaction of the kids at school she also knew that what had happened in the pool was somehow different. She guessed it was more serious than any other scrape that she'd gotten herself into. She decided not to mention it to anyone. She didn't want to be the cause of "trouble." Again. So she decided to hide out in the cellar – it was the best place to be. Just as she was about to leave her room, she heard voices in the garden. She stopped, and glanced out one of the windows. She dropped to her knees when she spotted the boy next door chatting to her mother. She crawled towards the nearest door, and scurried outside. After everything that had happened that day, she welcomed the cool, silent darkness of the cellar. She needed to think. What was she going to tell them? She was overcome by guilt. And shame. Why did she always do things that none of the other kids did!?

However, not even her experience of that near-tragic, event had as much of an impact on her as the silence during dinner. No one said a word. She wasn't certain what she expected – everyone was behaving the way they always did. But, on that evening, the silence was nerve-wracking! All she felt was an overwhelming desire to speak to someone – about anything. She didn't know what was going on with her - she was more restless, than usual. And for some strange reason, she wanted to hear the sound of her voice. But, she remained silent. After finishing her meal, she went straight to bed. When she pulled the covers over her head she couldn't help feeling relieved. But, that did little to prevent the frightening thoughts from popping into her head. She shut her eyes tight, and made her body as unmovable as a wall to ward off the scary, floating images. Eventually, she fell into a fitful sleep by holding an image of that flying swallow, at the forefront of her mind. She turned to look at the nothingness, and could still feel the confusion over everyone's silence. She recalled learning a few years later that no one had mentioned the incident to her father. Somehow that made her feel better - he would have said or done something to make the whole incident go away. But, she'd never broached the matter with anyone – then or since. As an adult, she made peace with that incident by telling herself that her family had dealt with it in the best way possible. There was nothing more to be said.

In the raging storm now escalating within her in the nothingness, she realized that day was a major turning point in her life. The little girl who stayed out of everyone's way suddenly, had a lot to say and do to counter the silence of that night. She became rebellious, and prone to fierce outbursts with other children. And she challenged the patience of the adults with her outrageous behavior - just to irk some kind of reaction from them. Any reaction, even conflict was better than the loud, silence that stalked her wherever she went - day in and day out. As far as everyone else was concerned, she was a "typical teenager." And she willingly subscribed to that cliché. It gave her the license to do as many "crazy" and "wild" things as she could think of. Over the years, wherever she went her relationships had a strange way of mirroring those that she'd experienced as a child. It didn't take long, before she started using some of those defense barriers to protect her adult-self from the world - even when there was no threat. She'd come to expect conflict in her life as the "norm." But, she'd never picked up on those old, relationship patterns. And neither was she any wiser about the ways in which her behavior perpetuated her subjective reality. Her whole life was one, never-ending battlefield. So she continued fighting it - with every ounce of energy that she could muster. Nothing in her outer reality gave way. So neither could she. Needless to say, her attitude didn't engender much popularity. But, popularity was a distant thought to something else that was constantly, eating away at her. She'd never figured it out. And after all this time, she was still nowhere close to finding the answers that she so desperately needed. Only one thing was certain. The battle within her still raged on. And she had no idea who or what she was fighting. Or why.

    She choked back the tears as her heart went out to the little girl who had unknowingly, borne so much on her own. She might have rationalized her childhood fears but, she didn't outgrow them. How could she? The silence surrounding her near-death experience had echoed through her psyche over the years - feeding a devastating conclusion by her child's mind: "It didn't matter whether she was alive or not." Was that the stage in her life when she'd shut herself off from her Self? Was it guilt, and shame that had prevented her from seeing past her many childhood barriers? Could she still carry those emotions when she was in no way responsible for what had happened on that day? Her mind went back to her experience at the dinner table that night, and her heart trembled with a strange coldness. She realized that her experience in the pool probably made every other life experience – good or bad – irrelevant. As a child, she'd faced her biggest fear – death. She didn't know anything about death at that stage of her life but, on some level, she'd been aware of the finality of it. And the only thing that mattered was that she'd somehow, escaped it. Or so, she'd thought. What she didn't expect was that her life would end up feeling like a living death! It slowly dawned on her that life, and death had somehow merged into one that day. And after that, both had lost any significant meaning to her. She couldn't recall fearing anything or anyone after that.

The first person to teach her that there was an entire spectrum of emotion that could enrich life with meaning was the smallest human being she ever suspected of such a feat - her own child. From the moment of her birth, she realized that something was different. Everyone was in a good mood - in honor of her child. But, she didn't mind – she was bursting from a strange emotion herself. It took her while to figure out that it had a name - happiness. She smiled. The baby must be about a year now. The child's angelic smile was so out of place in that dark, somber household that she was constantly on edge. So much so, that whatever happiness she felt was reserved for those quiet moments when she was alone with her baby. She would often play, and talk to her well into the night; delighting in the soft, gurgling sounds that she made, and the way that her eyes lovingly followed her when she moved. Eventually, they both would fall asleep, with the baby tucked close to her mother's side. Each day was filled with amazement as she witnessed some new development in her child's behavior. But, she couldn't stifle her uneasiness. How could her baby be so happy in the same household that she'd grown up in!? She'd often thought that she was in the wrong house - with the wrong family!

She recalled watching her little miracle with a mixture of wonder, and bewilderment. How could she have given birth to such a child? It felt as though her own dark, silent world was struck by a sliver of light that was too bright to imagine. Let alone, look upon. And she found it difficult to overcome her skepticism that people could change so dramatically, in such a short space of time. And yet, with each passing day there was no denying the light-heartedness that had taken over their lives. People smiled more often, and looked at each other when they spoke. They started saying things that she'd never heard before, and cooed at the baby in soft, gentle voices. The baby was unaffected by the unusual behavior around her, and her laughter continued working its magic on everyone's lives. Her voice rang throughout the house, and lifted their spirits. And her smile cast its light in all the dark corners of their hearts. When the baby was only a few months old, she started hugging everyone – including, strangers. For some reason, she felt very uncomfortable with this intimate form of physical contact. But, she couldn't bring herself to deny her child, and hid her discomfort whenever the little arms were wrapped around her. It was a small price to pay for this phenomenon in her life. And for being able to feel her heart-strings tugged at – something that she'd never felt before.

One afternoon, after returning home from a long drive with the baby she laid out a blanket under the huge Jacaranda tree in the front garden. She must have dozed off, with the baby playing quietly by her side. When she awakened, she found her father sitting beside them. He was murmuring softly to the child. She watched them through half-closed eyes, and was drawn into the love flowing between them. She smiled, and wished nothing more than for her daughter to experience many wonderful moments with her grandfather. In the midst of her daydreaming, she heard him whisper something to the baby. She listened carefully, and heard the words: "I love you." At first, she thought she was dreaming. But then, he repeated the words. And for the first time in her life, she experienced envy. Perhaps it was outright jealousy. She didn't know what was worse – the pain that she'd never heard him say those words to her or the shame of feeling jealous of her own child. Her eyes must have opened, because when she looked at her father again, he was smiling at her. In his eyes she saw only love – for them both. She regretted her thoughts, and smiled back at him. He held out his hand to help her up. And they stood side-by-side, looking at the baby sleeping soundly under a shower of purple blossoms in the evening breeze. She was holding one in her mouth, and gently sucking it like a pacifier. They both laughed at such innocence, and she turned without much thought, and hugged her father for the first time in her life. In that moment, she knew never to question the love between them - it flowed like a silent, endless ocean.

She was confounded, however, by her reaction whenever her mother was close to her baby. She watched her mother openly express her love towards her grandchild but, the words, and actions left her completely, numb. She'd known for a long time that things were strained between them but, she'd grown accustomed to the heavy silence that was only broken by the odd, perfunctory comment. But, she couldn't ignore the total absence of emotion whenever she saw her mother, and child together. And for some inexplicable reason, she watched them all the time - albeit surreptitiously. Not out of fear - she had no doubt that her child was safe. She just couldn't put her finger on it. Besides, the baby openly returned her grandmother's love, and the thought of denying her that experience was instinctively rejected. Strangely, there was some part of her that respected the bond between them. Perhaps because she'd never known her own paternal or maternal grandparents. She was now well attuned to the silence in the nothingness. To such an extent that the dynamic between her mother and herself caught, and held her attention. It struck her that more often than not, they were no more than an arms-length away and yet, the distance between them felt like a chasm! That sent her mind into turmoil. Did something happen between them before that incident in the swimming pool? She'd always believed that had caused the rift between them. Then again, that incident might have only cemented something that already existed between them! Immediately, she felt her anxiety escalate, and her breathing became more labored. She shifted uncomfortably, and again looked for some kind of escape route. But, there was only nothingness. She had to remind herself that she was safe – a few times. She relaxed.

Again, that was the catalyst for a flood of long-forgotten, memories. There was a time as a little girl, when she was always playing outside. She had so many pets – rabbits, dogs, cats, a lizard; a tortoise. At one time, she even had a chameleon. In sharp contrast, there came a time when she never left her room. What had caused such a drastic change in behavior? For the first time, it struck her that she'd stopped doing the things that made her happy. Why did she remain in her room, and forgo her adventures in the field? The only time she left it was to go to school. And that experience was harrowing in itself! She often rushed back to her only refuge – her bedroom. She recalled choosing a book from the bookcase, and then reading for the rest of the afternoon. An image of the old, wooden bookcase came into focus. It was her father's - he'd built it with his own hands. And she'd watched him labor over it. At some point, it was moved into her bedroom. Before that, it was.....in....in.....his......

bed….bedroom. Again, she felt the sharp pain in her belly as a memory stirred from its deep slumber, and seized her insides.

Despite wanting to suppress the feeling, she closed her eyes, and gently submerged herself into it. She was probably around eight years old; still reveling in her tom-boyish antics, and getting into all kinds of trouble with everyone. She'd tried to be on her best behavior but, when that failed, she spent much of her time alone, sitting under the trees at the far end of the school playground. However, that only gave the other kids more reason to taunt her. More often than not, she ignored them. She knew that things would only get worse if she retaliated. So she often consoled herself with thoughts of running away. Not that it helped much, because she knew that at some point, she would have to go home. And that thought only made her more anxious. For a long time, she'd believed that her punishment at home was for her bad behavior at school. But, she soon realized that that wasn't the case, for there were many occasions when she got "what she deserved," for no apparent reason. There were no warnings or explanations. And she never asked any questions – she knew she wouldn't get an answer. In her quiet moments, however, she'd often pondered her "bad" nature. And then, the beatings stopped. She frowned. She'd forgotten all about that. Until now.

On that day, she couldn't recall what she'd done or whether, she'd done anything at all. She only knew that she blanked out, the second she heard her name being called. It wasn't hollered but, there was something about her mother's tone of voice. She didn't delay. She'd given up a long time ago, trying to avoid the inevitable – it only made things worse. So she capitulated – just the way she did that afternoon. She walked behind her mother as she strode into her bedroom, and locked the door as she was instructed to do. She already knew what was coming - it had happened, often enough. Not that she'd ever mentioned it to anyone. So she just shut her eyes when it started, and waited for it to be over. She preferred thinking about the fields; the bright, blue sky, and playing with her little friends. On that day, however, something unexpected happened. Her mother started to hit her. Usually, she would run and hide under the dresser – while dodging the objects being hurled at her. More often than not, it was a book from the bookcase, standing next to the bedroom door. On that day, however, she didn't run. She just stood next to the bookcase, with her head bent. She was struck a few times, quite hard on her upper body – not her face. Never on her face. Her mother was so angry that it took her a while, before she noticed that the child in front of her was standing still. Her mother's arm rose, and then stopped mid-air. There was a long pause. She slowly, raised her face to look at her mother's. She had to blink a few times, before the face looking down at her became visible.

In the nothingness, she remembered the thoughts that had flashed through her mind, as she stared at her mother's flushed face. It wasn't so much the pain - she was used to that. But, she was too young to understand the words that were being thrown at her. And confused as to why they were only used on her. She only heard them when she was alone with her behind closed doors. And she'd heard them so often, that they were synonymous with her name. She centered herself in the stillness, and re-lived the emotions coursing through her body that day. She remembered standing there for what seemed like an eternity, looking at her mother. And then, she inhaled sharply as she recalled what happened next. She took a step backwards - very slowly. But then, she felt the door behind her. She panicked but, stood her ground. For the first time, she found herself looking directly into her mother's eyes - eyes that showed nothing other than, a fiery anger. Something stirred within her - something that she'd never felt before. She heard herself saying: "Hit me." Her voice was so soft that she didn't hear it. When her mother didn't react she spoke, again. This time, her voice was louder; the words more emphatic: "I said…..hit me!" She was shocked to hear the sound of her own voice. At first, she thought that there was someone else in the room but, she dare not turn around. Her eyes were glued on the face in front of her.

She was trembling. She bent over, and hugged herself in an attempt to find comfort from the suffocating memory that threatened to undo her all over again. But, there was no stopping it. In her mind's eye, she heard the slap on her right cheek. Her head swung hard to the opposite side. It was the first time that her mother had struck her face. She was reeling from the slap but, somehow she managed to stand her ground. Something told her not to run or show any fear. She slowly straightened her back, and shoulders. And once again, lifted her head to look directly into her mother's eyes. Her mother lifted her other hand, and she received a hard back-hand on her left cheek. Her head swung around, and the corner of her left eye bashed into the door handle. Her head exploded with pain. She felt something spurting from the side of her face, and slowly drip down her left cheek. She stumbled weakly, and almost fell but, her left hand reached out blindly and she caught, and held onto her father's bookcase. She held onto it as she slowly lifted herself, until she was standing upright. But, her gaze remained fixed on the red splashes on her legs. She felt her mother's shock. And then, felt her hand on her face as she yanked her face closer to get a better look at the wound. It wasn't the first time that her mother had drawn blood but, the sight of the open wound so close to her eye, must have momentarily shaken her out of her blinding rage.

She couldn't stand the closeness between them. She stepped back – without once taking her eyes from her mother's. She stood looking at her, for a long time. Neither one of them, said a word. She slowly lifted her left hand to unlock the door. It was an awkward movement – the key was positioned above her left shoulder, and she was right handed. But, she couldn't bring herself to turn around. She felt as though she was being watched by some wild animal that would pounce on her, if it so much as got an inkling of her intended escape. She searched her mother's face for something, while slowly turning the key. Perhaps a memory of a happier time together; some spark of remorse. Maybe an inkling of hope of better times to come. She felt an urge to find some shared moment between them that she could justify holding onto. There was nothing. There were no "goodbyes" spoken that day but, on some level, she knew that it was a final meeting of sorts. It signaled the end of something that could have been so special. And in its place was an empty longing for all that they would never experience as mother, and daughter. She turned, opened the door, and walked out. Her mother never said a word. She never touched her, ever again.

Over the years, there was no inclination on either side to address the impenetrable "wall" that had sprung up between them. There was no need - everything appeared quite "normal." They didn't question the palpable tension between them – no one did. But, she knew that something was no longer the same – she felt very different about her world. She realized that as a child, she'd seldom paid much attention to the family drama. But, after that day, she started observing the dynamics between the various personalities, and gained a deeper understanding of their family politics. Her mother was obviously unhappy, and chats between family members were one-sided or limited to monosyllables. She also realized that a large part of her mother's behavior stemmed from her own feelings of victimization. Her mother's only source of comfort were the rare visits by members of her own family. She had very little contact with them, because they lived very far away. And no one was able to afford a telephone. The only other means of communication was a hand-written, letter. She was shocked to learn a few years later, that her mother had never gone past first or second grade. She was practically, illiterate! She remembered being overcome by remorse, and guilt. They weren't accustomed to any form of luxury but, just being able to read, and write had added a whole different dimension to her own life. She found it difficult to imagine what her mother's experience of the world must be like. She could only think of it as being so much darker than her own. And that made her feel terrible. Without being aware of it, her empathy made her a willing victim – at home, and in her outside world. Instead of standing up for herself, she ended up tolerating the abuse of others, by making excuses for their behavior. And without proper boundaries to protect herself, the volatility of other people's emotions – silent or otherwise – made her a willing sponge for everything that was going on around her. As the years passed, she became firmly ensconced in a "prison" of her own making. After withdrawing from everything that she loved doing, the only "safe" haven was spending her afternoons alone, reading. That way at least, she could stay out of everyone's way, and couldn't be blamed for anything. She wasn't aware that she was reinforcing barriers that would keep her from her true Self. Neither was she aware that she'd turned a blind eye to the volcano lying dormant within her.

Initially, her numbness was just a form of armor at home. Until, she met up with the outside world. And encountered similar experiences, either through projection or naiveté. As a result, she and her invisible armor soon became inseparable, wherever she went. However, instead of feeling protected by it she found herself on the receiving end of more slight, and ridicule. It didn't take long before she started believing that life was unfair, and cruel. She couldn't believe her luck! She'd managed to stop such episodes at home - only to find that her outer world was no different! For a long time, she held her own amidst the name-calling and bullying at school. Her experiences at home had hardened her, somewhat. However, when the verbal abuse turned physical, she found it difficult to hold herself in check. One violent clash led to another, with some of the girls at school. And after being a victim for so long, she easily stepped into the role of aggressor. One afternoon, after a particularly violent clash with another pupil, she was told to report to the principal's office. She remembered entering his office, and standing in front of his desk. It was her first time in his office - she didn't know what to expect. He lifted his head, and looked at her. She returned his stare with expressionless eyes but, she sensed his annoyance. She re-assured herself that nothing could be worse than what she'd experienced at home. She was wrong. He informed her that he'd spoken to her father about the incident, and that he needed to take steps to protect the other kids at school. The slight intake of breath belied the fact that she was shaken to her core. The last thing she wanted was for her father to be informed of her behavior! She was mortified. So much so, that she didn't feel the six lashes on the palms of her hands.

She reached home that afternoon, filled with anxiety. She had no problem dealing with anyone else - no matter what. But, facing her father about her misdemeanor made her feel physically ill. She had no reason to fear him. He'd never used the parental "power-card" before. But, her little world was divided into "good" and "bad." And everything good was associated with him. She didn't want to cast a shadow over that special place in her heart that she'd set aside - just for the two of them. Furthermore, she hated being the one to drag him into something that she considered beneath him. Besides, any risk of losing his love was too terrible to contemplate. She spent the afternoon in her room, waiting for him to come home. When she heard his footsteps on the wooden floors she immediately, stood up. She expected him to shout out her name. He didn't. She stood with her ear glued against the door; listening as he went about his usual routine, before heading to the dining room to work. She hesitated at first but, then decided to go to him. She walked slowly down the passageway, and stood at the doorway taking in his bent head as he concentrated on the task in front of him. He looked up, and smiled at her. She smiled back, and looked searchingly at his face. She saw nothing, other than the usual warm glow in his eyes. Then, he carried on with his work. She walked past him, feeling relieved. And very confused. She spent the rest of the afternoon with the creepy-crawlies in the cellar. Life was so much simpler down there!

Later that evening, just as she was about to excuse herself from the dinner table he glanced at her, and told her to wait for him in his bedroom. She looked at him, and nodded without question. She felt her mother's reaction, before turning to see the surprised look on her face. It was obvious that her father hadn't mentioned the incident to her. She left the kitchen, and in spite of her anxiety she smiled - for some unknown reason. She went to his bedroom, and waited. After what seemed like an eternity, she heard his footsteps outside the door. She stood up. He entered the room, and sat down on the bed, facing her. He looked into her eyes. She held his gaze, and then turned to look at the open door behind them. Still, he made no move to close it. Again, she looked into his eyes - which were at the same level as her own. His eyes continued searching hers. She saw a glint of something but, it was quickly forgotten when she detected his move to reach for her hands. She yanked them away but, he continued looking at her calmly, until she slowly removed them from behind her back, and placed them into his - never once taking her eyes of his. He looked down at them. The lashes had left their mark. There were red welts on her hands, and a few blue spots where the blood had started to clot. He held them gently as he looked at them, and then raised his eyes to look into hers. She felt more than saw his pain, and her heart went out to him for being the cause of it. He calmly asked about the incident at school. She was struck dumb by the question, and just continued staring at him. No one had ever been interested in her side of a story before! He continued watching her patiently but, didn't insist on an answer. From a distance, she heard him ask: "Will you do that again?" Without a second thought, she shook her head. He looked intently into her eyes for a second and then stood up, and left the room. She slowly walked out of his bedroom, and went outside. She sat for a long time on the verandah, looking up at the sky, and feeling the cool, night air on her skin. After everything that had happened that day, she'd never felt…..felt…..so…..She couldn't find the words to describe it. But, she remained true to her word, and refused to be drawn into retaliating whenever she was bullied at school. Instead, she buried herself in her schoolwork, and made every effort to behave according to that unspoken code of impeccable conduct that she'd witnessed in her father.

She sighed heavily. It was now evident that her numbness had given her a sense of perceived control over a world that she felt powerless in. Unintentionally, she'd become a master at hiding from everyone, including herself. Outwardly, she presented herself to be a picture of togetherness. So much so, that over time she came to be regarded as the epitome of strength by many around her. And for as long as she lived up to that expectation, no one bothered with what was actually, going on with her. Neither did she. She thought she detected a sigh of relief from many around her. The fierce little tigress from years gone by had finally, been tamed. And life went on "smoothly." Unconsciously but, smoothly. Before long, it became the "norm" with her – ignoring her needs, and lying to herself about her true feelings. And for as long as she could remember that was her "peace" – not knowing, and not feeling. Except, on those odd occasions when the rage buried deep within her erupted, uncontrollably. Just like her mother.

A shiver ran down her spine as she recalled something in the nothingness that she'd kept hidden from her conscious mind. One evening, after a particularly hectic day, she threw herself into her chores as soon as she got home. She prepared her child's bath, and then went to find the baby. She found the child playing with her grandmother in the garden, and stood for a while, watching them. The baby looked so happy, and she felt a twinge of regret for missing out on the best years off her child's development. She called out her name enthusiastically, and made her way towards them. Seeing her baby after a long day was the best part of her day – no matter how exhausted she was. She knelt down with outstretched arms, and waited expectantly. Usually, the baby was happy to see her mother, and would hop-crawl towards her as fast as she could. That evening, however, she refused to leave her grandmother's side. With her mind on the hours of work still ahead of her she got up, and walked briskly across the lawn. She bent down, and roughly took the child into her arms - ignoring the shocked look on her mother's face. Then she turned, and marched into the house but, instead of stopping by the bathroom, she went straight to her bedroom. Without a second thought she shut the door, and started hitting the child on her little bottom. She must have given her a few spanks, when something caught her eye in the dresser at the far end of the room. She stopped, and looked up. She saw a reflection of her own face in the mirror. She froze. For a second, she thought she was looking at her mother. She continued staring at herself completely, shocked. She didn't even notice the baby scrambling from her lap, and heading for the far end of the bed. She grabbed one of her teddy bears, and whimpered softly into its fur – too afraid, and confused to cry. She just huddled behind her teddy, and peeped at her mother.

She couldn't bring herself to look at her child. She was horrified at her behavior. How could she treat her own child that way? How could she behave like her mother? She wasn't her mother! Whatever she'd gone through was forgotten – a long time ago! She never wanted to treat anyone the way that she'd been treated – least of all, her own child! She was so shaken by the experience that it placed her on high alert. She promised herself that it would never happen again. It didn't. But, the sword of guilt was already lodged deep within her heart. She covered her face in the nothingness as she felt the depth of her grief. Why did she suppress the memory of that incident? If her experience in the nothingness was anything to go by, her child had never forgotten it! Even if she did, she still carried the pain of it! The way she'd carried her own pain. And now after so many years, those memories were back to haunt her! *What was she supposed to do? There was nowhere to go; nowhere to hide! How much more of this quest did she have to endure? She couldn't take it anymore!* But, as overwrought as she was she knew that she had to continue with her soul's quest in the nothingness. She was determined to face whatever she'd buried, and heal it. She just wished that she knew what it was. All she knew was that she had to continue digging through that childhood void. She could still feel the piercing pain in her belly. And for as long as it was there, her healing wasn't over. She couldn't stop the trembling. She was ice-cold.

Her recollection of that incident was enough to trigger a host of other suppressed emotions. Yes – she was angry with her mother! *But, so many years had passed. Surely, she was over all that stuff! She'd made every effort to understand the people in her life. All was forgiven. What more was she expected to do?* Her mother had seldom spoken about her own childhood but, she was certain that her mother's latent pain had been re-enacted on her. What's the big deal!? Everyone must be caught up in some form of inter-generational maze – consciously or not. And she had no intention of remaining a victim of something that she could never fathom! She was convinced that she was free of her past - free of her mother's hold on her. *The past was just that – the past! She couldn't change it. And it was a complete, waste of time to even try! It was out of her control. And no one was to blame for what happened to her. She'd brought it on herself.* She heaved a sigh of relief. Clarity! At last! But, she could still detect a level of discordance that kept her apart from being fully present with her stillness. And her heart still felt heavy. *Why did she still feel caught up in a vortex of emotion? Why did she still feel trapped? How did she free herself from something that she couldn't name - let alone, see!?*

[By being patient. And loving yourself through the emotions as they surface. Don't pay heed to the conclusions being drawn by your mind. It's only resorting to old, thought patterns to feed your ego. All it wants is to impose a timeline on your quest – to know when it will step back into power. It can't; it won't. Having empathy, and sympathy for others are good qualities. However, not extending those same qualities towards yourself won't help you to heal the pain that imprisons you. Neither does forgiveness of others, free you of the responsibility of fulfilling your own soul contract within your lifetime. What about forgiving yourself - for being there for you, all those years? For bearing all that unnecessary guilt, and shame? As a start. Considering the needs of others is important but, so are honoring your own. And fulfilling your needs is an act of self-love. Guilt, and shame were not the only 'swords' that you turned against yourself. Your experiences also gave rise to feelings of extreme inadequacy, and self-doubt. Those negative emotions lowered your self-esteem, and perpetuated your false reality. But, in order to see that, you have to uncover more of your truth – by further unraveling the layers of your most traumatic experiences. And learning to forgive yourself for being a 'failure' - for not being the person that others expected you to be. You're not here to fulfill the expectations of your outer world or your ego's expectations, for that matter. You're not defined by what others think of you. You're much more than that. First, however, you need to remove the limitations that those expectations have imposed on your thinking]

[One of life's conundrums is that you can't survive as a child without those who bring you into this world. However, as much as you respect, and remain loyal to those dear to you, you're also responsible for remaining true to your Self. And you'll never be able to live the life that you deserve, until you understand who you truly are without succumbing to everyone's notion of who you should be. Once you uncover your truth, and own your sovereignty by separating yourself from your illusory reality - based on your need for acceptance - only then, will you discover your unique, soul path to co-create your true reality, in harmony with the world. And instead of fear, lack and separation you'll find that your truth is synonymous with oneness - with everything, and everyone in the Universe. What is past, is past - yes. Within the context of linear time, in your physical world. But, you still carry your past pain in your body – it houses your soul. And both are a part of your multi-dimensional, Being. For as long as that pain remains unhealed, the burden of it will prevent you from loving yourself unconditionally. It will keep you trapped in your past, and hinder your soul's ascension. And without ascending to a higher level of consciousness, you won't be fully present with your Being - to access your true potential, and co-create your soul purpose. Furthermore, without your truth, you'll always doubt your worth, and question whether you're "enough." You'll continue with your small, limited experience of life. The real question, isn't whether you're "enough" but, whether you love yourself unconditionally. You'll never be "enough" in a world that is seen through the eyes of billions of subjective realities. Only you can uncover your true worth by freeing yourself from your conditioning. Only you'll know the meaning of "enough," when you can serve humanity by offering them what lies in your soul. What you see around you, isn't the world as it's meant to be. It's only what it has become, because people have been conditioned to believe that they're not powerful enough to create their own realities. And for as long as that illusion exists, you'll be blind to the Universe of potential lying within you – to make this world a better place. There is a better world. It exists – within you. To create it, you need to understand who you truly are - without your past. Not by running from it but, by accepting and loving yourself through the experiences that have kept you trapped, all your life. Only then, can you can heal the past, and unlock the true reality within your soul. And only self-love can help you surrender unconditionally, to your unknown Self. To become the sovereign of your soul's destiny. It's in your hands]

She was dumbstruck. *Self-love? Self-forgiveness? She had no time for all that!* How was she supposed to understand herself as a multidimensional, Being – with her mind? A mind that was the product of her conditioning in a physical, one-dimensional world! She sighed heavily. *She so desperately wanted to be free of whatever was making her feel so heavy - so stuck!*

[You only have a conceptual understanding of forgiveness. It might have helped you believe that you've forgiven others but, you didn't take into account how you were affected by your past. At no point, did you deal with your pain. Neither are you aware of the victim-mentality and anger that was transferred to you during childhood, and instilled in your psyche. You've only just started to heal the negative emotions relating to your childhood experiences but, you're still a captive of your childhood fears, and insecurities. You still have some way to go before you can forgive yourself, and others. That is the reason you're feeling so stuck. It has nothing to do with your physical world or the nothingness. No one; nothing has that kind of power over you. You're being held back by your own fears. Without purging your mind of its old conditioning, and healing your body you'll remain stuck in that old paradigm of limiting yourself through fear. And you'll carry it into your next life - keeping yourself in survival mode in a world that you're meant to flourish in]

[Survival is the domain of your mind, and ego. It lurks behind the self-fulfilling prophesies that you've used to convince yourself of what lies within, and out of your control. You would have transferred the same conditioning to your daughter, either unintentionally through your cellular memory, and auric field or intentionally, by imposing it on her verbally. But, she was born with her own soul purpose. And she has her own soul knowing to help her achieve it. Your only role as her mother is to guide her without succumbing to your ego's desire to control her life path. Let her go when she's ready to walk her own path. There's no way you'll be able to determine what that will be - in the same way that you're unable to determine the outcome of your own path. Whatever form it takes, you're only required to observe and trust in her ability to walk her own path, and fulfill her destiny. Any form of attachment only exists to satisfy your ego's desire to feel needed. Your realities might intersect from time-to-time but, even if they don't, you'll always remain connected to each other. Nothing needs to be forced in the realm of oneness. Your only responsibility now is to heal yourself – if you desire access to your soul's birthright. If you don't, then you'll forever remain trapped in the illusion of a false reality that isn't yours to begin with. If your true intention is to align with your soul and free yourself, then you need to continue uncovering your truth from all the behavioral traps that you've used to reinforce your illusory reality. Only then, will you know true freedom - as free as you were on the day you were born. How far you're willing to go on this quest to achieve that is very much within your control - by surrendering your will to your soul's calling. When you do, the true reality that you're meant to co-create with your Being will naturally unfold. There will be nothing for you to "do" per se – only observe. You'll be led by your heart, and soul]

She watched helplessly as the remaining "dominoes" that she'd so carefully laid out to map the trajectory of her life started to collapse in the nothingness. Her conscious will was powerless to stop it. And whatever stories she'd tucked-away between the spaces revealed themselves, one-at-a-time. Like word cards. Only this time, the cards were being held up in front of an invisible teacher called "Awareness." She realized that whenever she didn't feel right about a course of action in the past, it was her awareness trying to "flag" her attention, and re-direct her towards her truth. She would have seen the obvious if she'd taken the time to be more present. But, not knowing her truth, only made her select the very first "domino" that she could lay her hands on - hoping that it was her "once-in-a-lifetime" opportunity. And her anger had provided the fuel to stick with her egotistic intentions, even when she realized she was going nowhere. She sighed. She recalled her awareness revealing itself at odd moments - when she least expected it to. If only she'd not ignored it - she would have saved herself being stuck with more cycles of pain! She realized her awareness, and instinctive nature were the only innate "skills" she truly possessed - as opposed to every other skill that she'd acquired through formal study. She'd never placed much emphasis on them before but, she now sensed their power in helping her get closer to her truth. After all, both had played a distinctive role in her life – even if she wasn't conscious of it. What other aspects of her unknown Self lay dormant within her? She hesitated. She felt very uneasy. Was she afraid of that power? Why? How could she be afraid of a part of her Self? Was her old conditioning so strong that it could make her turn away from her truth in favor of an illusion? Something told her that it was. And yet, she didn't feel angry. She frowned. Where was the all-consuming anger that had wreaked havoc in her life? Why didn't she feel it in the nothingness?

She reflected on some of those past experiences. It surprised her to realize that in the majority of instances, there was nothing about the situation that warranted any anger. Neither could she recall intentionally, provoking it. And yet, she kept on encountering situations that triggered her anger! She deliberately shifted her attention from her thoughts and once again, tuned into the stillness to observe her thoughts, and feelings. It helped to remove herself from the various stories that she'd associated with her anger, and focus instead, on the feeling itself. The emotion somehow, looked very different. It wasn't at all like the volatile side of her that had become almost second nature. It looked like another mirage. She could still relate to the emotion, and there was no doubt that she'd felt it but, it wasn't a part of the stillness within. In the same way that all her other thoughts, and other emotions were apart from it. She was intrigued. Although she'd seldom indulged them, she was now beginning to suspect that her mind had played a more integral part in helping her construct a false reality in her physical world. And if she was angry all the time, it made perfect sense that she'd manifested more anger in her life! Why was she consumed by anger? Was it another defense mechanism? What was lying beneath it? Was she in the process of releasing all the emotions that she'd become attached to, as she uncovered more of her truth? What was to become of her when the process was completed? Would she be left with her awareness, and her stillness? What was the purpose of her stillness? Could it help her fulfill her soul purpose? Would it help her stay in her truth as she walked her soul path? What happened to her soul when she died? Would it merge with the silent, Universe after she'd fulfilled her last soul contract? Was her stillness the only real, true aspect of her? Was it the only part of her that was immortal? *But, there was nothing in it! She felt nothing, when she was within it! It looked exactly like the nothingness around her!*

She was so astonished by those thoughts that she immediately pulled her attention away from her mind, and turned towards her stillness. How was it possible for her to discern different aspects of herself? Who was thinking? Who was observing? Who was aware of her, observing herself? How was it possible for her to be aware, of her awareness? How could she be conscious of what was going on in her mind, and be aware at the same time, of other "information" that was emanating from her Being? She'd always regarded her physical body as the form that separated her from the outer world. Was she only deluding herself by drawing conclusions based on what was visible, and tangible in her physical world? Was there any separation between her inner Self, and the Universe? Or was her tangible, physical body – for all its realness - merely another illusory form that existed in her mind, to help her during her earth-bound existence? If so, were there other aspects of her invisible Self, and Being that she would be able to discern through energetic resonance, even though her mind had no prior knowledge of it? Would those cosmic energies also transform her mind to align with her new way of Being? Who or what was this Being? Who or what was directing its thoughts? Did it even need any direction or was it part of the Universe's plan – a part of which was already carried within her soul? She was awed by the insights that were flooding her awareness. She felt more inspired than ever. It was mind-boggling! Unbelievable! And yet, for as long as she remained within her stillness, she remained calm; centered. Non-attached to everything going on in her mind, and body. She'd always believed that her physical world was the only world that existed; the only one that she needed to pay any attention to. And yes – there were a whole host of physical bodies in the Universe awaiting discovery. But, this was the first time that she acknowledged the existence of another world – many worlds - within herself. It was the first time that she acknowledged a connection that she'd never contemplated – one between her Being, and all other life forms on the planet; with all the Universes around her. If her external world had only revealed a limited version of herself, what could she learn from her Being, and its seamless connection to her inner, and outer worlds? She was fascinated. But, she didn't need to concern herself with any external world – only her inner worlds. Without hesitation, she dove back into the silent, stillness to discover what else lay in its hidden depths.

She immediately, crashed into another layer floating around the core of her stillness. *What was it?* She decided to focus on what was as familiar, as breathing – her anger. What was the basis for it? Why was her anger triggered so easily? Were her experiences as an adult triggering the wounds imprinted on her mind during her formative years? Was she using it as a decoy? What was lying behind the anger? Was her anger related to feelings of regret for missing out on her childhood or was it an accumulation of resentment over the years, because of her ongoing failures? Was she angry about messing up her life? Was it messed up permanently or was this quest – as unlikely as it seemed - an opportunity to uncover her truth, and still create the life that her soul desired? Was all that emotional baggage hers or did some of it belong to others who were in close proximity to her? Were other emotional experiences of her family transferred to her in some way? Was it possible for their conditioning to be transferred to her as a child – energetically or genetically? Was that the "cellular memory that Voice had spoken of? Did the principle of energetic transference also apply to other relationships? The implications were far too numerous to contemplate. How could she keep her energetic aura clear of the energies of others? Could she reach a zero-point, energetic field - where she didn't have to concern herself with the energies of others - by healing herself? *How would she know when she reached such a state? How was she supposed to continue with this process? Was self-love the answer?* She felt daunted by the barrage of strange, questions. *She'd never thought about such things. Ever!* It didn't help that she also felt completely, inadequate for missing so many cracks in her life. *She was falling apart! How was she supposed to put herself back together again? Could she heal, and integrate the lost aspects of her Self into wholeness, again?* She sighed, hopelessly.

Again she felt the stirring of a deep, discomfort. She knew by now that it was pointing her towards something that she'd missed. She realized that she might have uncovered some level of understanding of her Self through her childhood-based, behavior but, she was now more concerned with her tendency towards self-criticism, and self-judgment. Why was she so hard, and unkind towards herself? Why did she treat herself in such unloving ways? Despite her opinion to the contrary, she realized that more often than not, her emotional state had detracted her from making sound decisions. And yet, she was averse to her sensitive nature - it made her feel uncomfortable. She realized that if she wanted to transcend the discomfort of her latent emotions, then she needed to get closer to them – not suppress them! Did the lack of nurturing as a child have something to do with that kind of behavior? She realized that she didn't know what "nurturing" entailed. And then, she was hit by another revelation. There was no role model for her to turn to, to help her understand her behavior, and use it to establish healthy emotional boundaries. Instead, whenever she felt overwhelmed by any strong emotion, she dismissed it. She wasn't composed at all! It was merely a catch-all for a grey mass of emotion that she was too afraid to feel! Furthermore, if the one person closest to her had found her lacking in so many ways, then that was the "mirror" that she'd used to build another one of the "pillars" to her character. The only difference was that the image wasn't as transient as some reflection in a mirror - it had left an indelible, imprint somewhere on her psyche! No wonder her world had fallen apart! She was overcome with gratitude for the love of her father. She realized that she wouldn't have survived without it. But, a part of her had always yearned for her mother's love. It was different. It spoke of a bond between mother and child that existed from conception, and extended way beyond birth. There was a depth, and closeness to that connection - a promise of indestructibility in the face of any kind of separation. It was a soft, warm, loving embrace - no matter the "distance" between mother, and child. In the midst of the sharp pains threatening to pull her apart, she realized that she'd never known anything like that with her mother.

 Her ego retaliated strongly. *She was mistaken. Her mother loved her! She'd given birth to her! The nothingness must be making her even more delusional!* But, she was unable to suppress a nagging question. Why did that love manifest as blatant anger, and hatred towards her? Why did her mother withhold love, and nurturing towards her youngest child? The pain became worse when she realized how her child-self would have translated her ongoing rejection: "There must be something wrong with me." It dawned on her that her "punishment" didn't end there. Over the years, every slight; every failure had chipped away at what little self-esteem she possessed, until she reached a damning conclusion: "I'm unlovable!" And there was no achievement big enough that could break her out of that prison! Suddenly, she understood the absence of love in her external world – her experiences were only reflecting the lack of love at the core of her beliefs! As difficult as it was to acknowledge, she couldn't ignore the piercing waves of pain in her chest, and the truth that she now found herself staring at. Her childhood experiences might belong to the past but, they had left a wide, gaping wound that was visible in the "reality" she'd watched playing out in her life - in every relationship; in every set of circumstances. She saw with blinding clarity what she needed to do, although she had no idea how she was going to go about it. Her mother's past and her reasons for treating her the way that she'd done were far less significant than acknowledging her own feelings, and healing herself – to bring herself to a place of wholeness. A space where she - her Self - could blossom. Something told her that it still existed somewhere within her. Without it, she would never fulfill her soul purpose.

Her heart heard her silent commitment, and she witnessed another layer slowly lifting from the void. She saw her buried guilt, and shame for not being the person that her mother expected her to be. She saw the hidden anger towards herself, for being so inadequate that she'd continuously failed to win her mother's love. The self-hatred, for not being worthy of the one person's love that she so desperately yearned for. She relived the years of anguish when she'd wished to be someone, other than herself. She couldn't imagine another thought that was more un-loving than that! It served as the ultimate barrier - preventing any part of her true Self from shining through. And to top it all, her anger had served as a red herring. By allowing herself to be continuously distracted by it, she'd avoided her pain. As far as she was concerned, it didn't exist. And her denial made her oblivious to the kind of behavior that was birthed in the fertile ground of that pain. The closest she ever got to being reminded of it was on the rare occasions when she reached out to someone. She realized that some part of her acknowledged the need for love and nurturing but, she hated letting down her guard. Her inner conflict made her resort to the only familiar outlet for expressing that need - lashing out in anger! In doing so, she childishly believed that she would receive the love that she yearned for.

But, she'd only invited more conflict, and separation with that behavior. She was struck by a revelation. Her pattern of behavior had re-created the "love" that she'd known with her mother – a "love" that only served to reinforce her worthlessness. It struck her how torn she was by the love-hate dynamic in her relationship with her mother. It was the most vulnerable phase of her life - when she'd experienced home, and love for the first time. And she'd never thought to question her warped association with either - it was all that she'd ever known. But, that association helped her to perpetuate the same negative experiences of her childhood "home" in every other relationship. The tears ran down her face. It wasn't her qualifications; her title, status or material wealth that had defined her life. It was love. Or rather, the lack thereof.

She stared into the nothingness for a long time. And was startled out of her reverie when she realized that she was more protective of her pain than her anger – it defined her. She'd kept it well-hidden from everyone, including herself. It was even more disconcerting that as much as she was familiar with the word, she had no idea of the full extent of her pain or the depth of it. She sighed as insight dawned. If she was going to attempt healing herself in any way, then she had to get closer to it. She felt utterly daunted by that thought. And yet, she knew that there was one thing that she needed to do – whether it changed her life or not. She had to find a way to heal her pain. It was the key to unlocking her purpose, and her full potential. And that was the only way she could honor her true Self – overcoming her discomfort to heal her pain. She didn't know how to go about it but, she couldn't stand the thought of delaying, any longer. She realized that hard work was only partly responsible for her constant state of exhaustion. Suppressing, and denying her truth was far worse. And lying to herself had taken her life nowhere - other than, going around the same circles. Lifetime, after lifetime! This time, if she wanted to get closer to her truth she had to go beyond her fears. She could hear it calling out to her, from somewhere deep within. Her knowing was unmistakable. Uncovering her truth was her only priority now - it was her only reality, in that moment. Whatever her life turned into after that, she had no way of knowing. It didn't matter.

With her surrender came the feeling of expanding, spaciousness within.

She felt as though layers of something were slowly being drawn out of her, and scattered into the nothingness. She held her breath. She knew that something else was about to come to light. *How many more layers did she have to clear? How much longer was it going to take?* There were no answers. All she knew for certain was that the nothingness had a strange way of making her see things differently, by removing layer upon layer of delusion! She slowly exhaled, and waded into her stillness. Her patience wasn't in vain. She became aware of a more subtle – far more dangerous - form of unconscious behavior. She'd turned her anger on herself by pursuing relationships, and situations that didn't serve her highest interests! She might have practiced some restraint in her relationships with the outside world but, she hadn't shown herself the same mercy. And over time, she'd slowly let her soul drip out of her by failing to protect herself from physical, and emotional abuse! She was the only person in closest proximity – to herself! And by not understanding her Self she'd only attracted more pain into her life. There was no other outlet - she couldn't direct her anger at her mother. In that relationship, she didn't have the capacity to behave in any other way but, as a child still yearning for its mother's love. And even as an adult, she was always reduced to one in her mother's presence. Her mother's absence didn't afford her much relief either, for she carried that lack of worthiness with her, wherever she went. She was no longer surprised by the self-criticism, and -judgement. That was only her mother's voice in her head.

And she'd been countering that voice ever since, by constantly trying to prove her worth. The world around her might have been unfair in many respects but, she could now see how unfairly, and unlovingly she'd treated herself. She'd set herself up by using the most unfair benchmark of all – making herself believe that she was someone other than her Self. To prove that she was lovable. She'd buried her insecurities, and doubts under another inculcated belief - a sense of duty. That made her the "good" daughter – if only in her own mind. But, her denial also kept her in a state of blissful, ignorance. And without the validation she craved from the one person who refused to give it to her, she caved with severe guilt each time she thought that she'd failed to live up to that title - which was all the time! Never mind the inscrutable mask that she'd shown the outside world to make others believe that she was "together." Whenever she was alone, she was racked by remorse over her ongoing failure to be loved by others. Only to go back the next day, and drive herself relentlessly to prove that she was a "success." She believed it was her only way of securing what little love she had in her life. And earning it. Occasionally, she crumbled under the pressure but, she always found a way to lift herself up again. Her sense of duty made certain of it. Acknowledging any limitation or making an excuse was a major weakness that she refused to tolerate in herself. *After all, if she couldn't be a success, then who was she? What kind of life would she have? Who would love her?* She might have forgiven her parents for their shortcomings but, she'd never forgiven herself for being so undeserving, and unworthy of her mother's love. Unconsciously, it made her feel unworthy of receiving anyone's love, including her own. The thought of love existing within her never even occurred to her. That was the real punishment of her childhood conditioning.

She was overcome by grief. She'd always believed that life was a gift to be treasured. And yet, she was so buried in her pain that she'd overlooked something critical. She was the gift! She was the embodiment of life itself! She was dismayed at having treated herself with so much disrespect; with so little love. *What was the power behind this thing called "love" anyway? Was she forever, doomed without it? And if it had been absent all her life, how was she supposed to know what to look for in the nothingness!? How was she supposed to nurture something into existence that was as unknown, as self-love!? Was there some way to work around it? How could something as nebulous as self-love be her biggest obstacle to uncovering her true Self? Without it, there was no hope of co-creating her soul's reality!* She sighed hopelessly. *If her physical world had reflected only a false sense of self was that the reason for her life falling apart? How was her quest in nothingness supposed to help her rebuild a life for herself? Why did all of this have to happen now!? She still had so much that she wanted to do with her life! She might have had a proclivity towards drama previously but, this kind of "drama" – the destruction of a life built on a false sense of self was something that she would have never anticipated! How was she supposed to take her life forward after an experience like this? Would she ever recover from something so drastic? Would her new reality have to be founded on her truth for it to survive in her physical world?* She couldn't even begin to comprehend a life lived according to such terms!

She shook her head, sadly. *How did she get herself into this mess!? How was she going to get herself out of it!?*

She rubbed at her throat impatiently as she fought back the tears. As difficult as it was to admit, a part of her was glad for the insights that she was gaining in the nothingness. For years, she'd been lugging around unnecessary baggage, and based on her limited understanding, not all of it was hers! Without any other source of love, and support to draw on her childhood experiences had cast a shadow of powerlessness over her entire life! It slowly dawned on her that by only using the mirror of her parents' eyes to define her identity, she'd never actually, known herself. After so many years of living an illusion, she had no idea who she truly was! The irony was that she prized her independence above all else and yet, a false identity had denied her that. By failing to understand her Self she'd never been able to differentiate her soul purpose from all the distractions around her. All she'd effectively done was appease her ego's fears, and define her life according to two main criteria - securing her father's love, and rising above the invisible barre that she'd consistently fallen short of, to earn her mother's love. She might be an adult with a child of her own but, she was no more than a child herself! For a long time, she believed that becoming an adult gave her a license to leave her past behind. But, nothing was behind her! Her childhood had been front, and center – her entire life! It defined her - by keeping her locked in the same conditioned thought, and emotional patterns. All she'd done was play her longest game of pretend! And her lack of awareness resulted in a level of self-deception that had taken her exactly – nowhere! All those years, she'd been on a round-a-bout, powered by her projections. Each time it stopped, she'd been looking at the same scene - albeit from a different angle. It pointed to the strength of her belief in the dogma that she'd been indoctrinated by. But, those "stops" were her ques to wake-up. To get off the "wheel" that was slowly wobbling to a halt with the demise of a defunct, old system. To stop reaching outside of herself, and look within to find her own truth. But, she'd ignored the repeated calls - dulled by her illusory reality, and its false sense of security.

The tears ran slowly down her cheeks as the significance of that "call" slowly dawned on her. She didn't understand its meaning or the implications. Strangely, she didn't doubt herself. Was that an indication that she was now more open - more trusting of the unknown? She no longer felt so anxious about the uncertainty facing her. In fact, the more she embraced the unknown the less her anxiety. She smiled as she recalled a time when she'd worked so diligently to build a life according to the plan in her mind - an approach that now seemed a life-time away. Not only did it constrain her in her physical world but, she'd also defined herself, and her potential by it. And yet, she'd known no peace. On the contrary, each day she awakened to an un-named fear knotting her insides. It had kept her in a constant, distracted state of anxiety. She sighed. The only thing that she now felt comfortable doing was to remain in the silent, stillness. Again, that voiceless voice; that unfeeling feeling; that unknown knowing - helped her realize that there was something special about the nothingness. She was beginning to see herself as she'd never done before. Far from being free, she'd been trapped by her conditioning throughout her life. If she desired to free herself, she had to embrace everything about herself - the good and bad; old and new; the light and dark. All of her was contained within one, single breath - the past, the present, and her unknown soul's reality. And all of it was her truth - her Self. She had to stop limiting herself based on roles stipulated by her physical world. She had to let go of the "plan" for her life, and trust the wisdom of her soul – despite the uncertainty and her rampaging mind, and ego. She had to trust in the unknown, mystery of life to reveal the path that she would have to walk in co-creating her "future." It wasn't one in the proverbial sense – rather it was unlike anything that she'd ever thought possible. Her future lay within each moment – a moment that spanned an entire lifetime. It was one that required no thought or plan - only the surrender to every breath; with self-love. And without any thought of the outcome. To access that timeless moment of full potential within her, she had to uncover her truth, and trust her Self, unconditionally – to guide her through every aspect of her soul path. She had to remain committed to her quest – no matter what obstacles her mind threw in her way. The obstacles weren't real anyway - they existed only to keep her awake, and aware under the constant threat of being lulled to sleep by her mind with its predilection towards results, familiarity, and safety. She had to find the courage to trust only in her truth - to deny all else but, her truth. Most importantly, she had to consciously choose her truth when co-creating her reality. It was far from lost. It still lay untouched within her, and her self-love was the key to accessing it. Paradoxically, she didn't have to bother with building her soul's reality as an act of will – just abiding in oneness with her Being would help her actualize it. She hung her head in regret. If only she'd known all this sooner. She'd lost so much time chasing worthless rainbows. The saddest part was that she had no idea who she truly was. Without her awareness to keep her present she'd unconsciously, pretended herself right out of her life! With her eyes wide open!

[But, with your heart closed]

CHAPTER 11
THE CALLING

She looked at the stars, and wondered for how long people had turned to them for guidance on their physical, and spiritual journeys. They were an enticing invitation to the mystery of the infinite beyond. She was fascinated. More so, because it contrasted starkly with her obsession with everything ephemeral in her physical world. Whatever had preoccupied her in the past now looked so inconsequential compared to the potency of the mystery beckoning her. It filled her with hope, and inspiration – feelings that she'd seldom experienced in her physical world. She was enthralled to be in the presence of such timeless beauty, and majesty. For a while, she allowed her imagination to freefall into a whole different world built on nothing but, love. Was such a world possible? What would it look like? Would all the walls, and borders still be necessary? Would exorbitant sums of money still be spent on defense budgets? Would there be a need for ammunition? The death penalty? Would there be a need for a monetized financial system? Or any of the current systems, including governments? What would the people be like? How would they treat each other? Would there be more kindness? More compassion? More brotherhood? More love, and no fear? She sighed. *Maybe in another time, and space! Besides, whatever "treasure" lay out there was beyond her reach!* She stopped as she was struck by a revelation. Was it? Why did she feel so close to it? Could that "treasure" be real? Or was it something she would only know, and feel in her soul?

Another insight emerged from the space created in her mind by stopping her superfluous thoughts. She wasn't interested in the physical proximity. Her desire was to share in life's eternal mystery – the "treasure" – roaming freely across time, and space. It was all around her. She embodied it in every cell. And yet, she couldn't see it or fathom its enigmatic presence. But, she could feel it! And by some miracle, that Universal mystery continued to thrive in abundant creation, whereas everything in her physical world kept falling apart! What held that great, mystery of life's creative power together? How did it sustain itself – in complete nothingness? And in circular rhythm - outside the constraints of linear, man-made time. The Universe operated according to a very different "clock" to realize its objectives! Objectives that were effortlessly achieved in perfect harmony with nature. Sadly, the biggest threat to all that natural creation was mankind itself! Regarded by many as the most evolved of all living species! Would the planet, and every living creature stand a better chance of survival if mankind lived in harmony with those Universal Laws? Perhaps it was arrogant to think that man could determine the fate of the Universe! It existed before mankind, and would prevail long after the demise of humans at their current level of consciousness. For all she knew, the Universe must have already instigated a whole new "design" for a higher level of human consciousness. She bowed her head in shame. She was equally responsible for the declining state of the planet. And it was going to take much more than the current, efforts across the world to change that. The only way was to align herself with the design of this infinite mystery.

She sighed deeply. How was she supposed to get to the bottom of world crises when she'd lost the plot of her own life! She'd taken refuge in the short-sighted, egoist constructs of her mind to validate her existence, and lost her connection with a Universe of limitless possibilities! She'd seldom considered the wider implications of her actions, let alone the purpose of her life. She found the paradox startling. Without access to something as intangible as her truth, all she'd done was erect sandcastles in her physical world, irrespective of how tangible they appeared to her mind! Each time that the walls of her "castles" collapsed, she'd forced herself to start over. And ended up building the same illusion! She'd refused to give up in the face of the "external forces" threatening her. Or rather, that her ego felt threatened by! And that willfulness had kept her going against all odds. In private, however, she wracked herself apart trying to figure out why she felt like such a failure. The last string of events in her life, however, had occurred in quick succession over the course of a few months. And the trail of destruction left her so traumatized that she found herself incapable of thought or action. All she could do was stand by, and helplessly watch her life fall apart. She realized that the only constant underlying her past decisions was the presumption that she was in control of her life. And yet, year after year, she'd continued making the same mistakes! How conscious was she, if her thinking patterns had made her believe in an illusion? Did her conditioning only allow for a constricted, superficial grasp of the Universe? Was that the reason she'd focused on her material world, and allowed no space for the limitless opportunities available to her in the Universe? What was behind her small, hoarding mentality - her fear of mortality? Far from providing a sense of security, her possessions only left her feeling more trapped! Could the fulfillment of her soul path provide the meaning that she'd so desperately been seeking in her external world? It dawned on her that the "opportunities" she'd pursued in her physical world were nothing more than straws to someone who was already drowning! They were merely an extrapolation of her childhood conditioning!

She returned her gaze to the stars with a very different perspective. Did she limit herself by pursuing goals constructed by a one-dimensional, mind? Perhaps she should have looked to the sky more often, and given more thought to achieving something of greater substance! If there was no separation between the Universe, and her Self then her soul purpose must already be aligned to the great mystery of life itself. An image of the stars came to mind, and she recalled her star-gazing as a child. She smiled. They were the only constant in her life. She couldn't remember the last time that she'd stopped to acknowledge the magic that lit up her world, every single night. Was she really a part of all that wonder? Was she a part of the same force that created the stars; the entire Universe? Was her life essence, as timeless as the stars? Then her life must be nothing less than Divine! And that Divine essence must be present in everyone, and everything around her! She closed her eyes as she felt herself expand, and lift out of herself into the immensity of the nothingness. True or not, she was in complete, awe! And she detected a single "thought," connecting her body to the wonder of the expansiveness surrounding her. How could she best live her life on earth, and serve all aspects of her Being - the physical, and spiritual?

That thought weighed heavily on her shoulders. It felt as though she was shrinking, and falling back into her physical self. And being sucked right back into the black void that she was so intent on avoiding. She sighed. Each time she thought she was making some kind of headway, along came that sinking feeling, and derailed her! She wished that she could get rid of it permanently! And then, she had another revelation. If that feeling still existed after so many years, then she must have been using the wrong approach! Perhaps the only way to rise above the void was to surrender to it – not avoid it! She lifted her eyes to the glittering stars. No matter how deeply engulfed she was by the blackness – outside or within her - the stars were always close by to comfort her. She was overcome by reverence, and gratitude. It reassured her that she hadn't completely, lost her mind.

Glow's words slowly wafted back to her. What did it say? Something about time standing still, and that she shouldn't be deceived by the lack of motion. She would be moving, despite all signs to the contrary. She bowed her head to acknowledge her wise friend. Its words now resonated with her strongly. That was exactly how she felt! Time had ceased to exist in the nothingness. And even though her past hadn't changed, she felt very different. Something within had shifted – without her being aware of it. But, as far as she could tell her quest was far from over. Those inner shifts must have gained momentum in the nothingness even though she was rooted to the same spot! And she didn't feel a thing! But, she did feel further away from her past, and that "distance" was replaced by a sense of increasing spaciousness within her. At the same time, she felt as though she was slowly disappearing into the nothingness. She was only able to grasp the immensity of it in her stillness - not with her mind. She was astounded by how real her quest was beginning to feel. More so, than anything that she'd encountered in her physical life! *What was happening to her? How could an entire lifetime disappear before her eyes? She'd sacrificed, and denied herself so much to build it. It meant, everything to her!* And now, it was nothing more than a meaningless blur – like a passing dream. Only to awaken, and find that it was replaced by a very different reality – black, nothingness! Despite that, the nothingness felt more real than the life that she'd lived – in all its multi-colored, glory! As she pondered that thought through her tears, she was hit by another revelation. Why was she so grief-stricken, if she felt no connection to the life that she'd lost? Was she mourning the loss of her material possessions? The time, and effort that she'd dedicated to building it? And if none of those things had any meaning in the nothingness, then what was the true measure of her loss? The meaningless life that she'd lived? How could she use something as intangible as meaning, to measure the intense loss for a life that she could no longer relate to!? What did living a meaningful life entail!?

She sighed heavily. She'd never expected her life to remain stagnant; she was well acquainted with her adventurous spirit. She knew she wanted to devote her life to her career but, that didn't preclude wanting a life of meaning. Instead of applying meaning to arbitrary goals based on conditioned benchmarks for success, would it have been better to surrender to life, and accept her calling – whatever that was!? Was that the reason she'd failed to find any meaning, at all? Did life have any meaning or was it some abstract notion to placate a small, and fearful ego in the face of this infinite phenomenon called life? Was it even possible to live a meaningful life in a world that was starved by the illusion of "progress?" Perhaps life was a game as suggested by some, and best lived without meaning. Perhaps searching for meaning outside her Self was the "game." Maybe uncovering her truth, and fulfilling her purpose would give her life meaning. She trembled. She felt totally, lost.

[Your sense of loss is understandable. After all, you spent many years building a life. And it collapsed right before your eyes. And the identity you associated with that life is also in the process of dissolving. Soon, neither one will occupy any space in your body, and mind. Twenty-five years – all gone in a flash. Without conscious, awareness. The only evidence of that life being the material gains along the way – everything that you've lost, since your quest began. You can't change any of that but, you'll be able to discern more of your truth by accessing greater levels of your awareness. And discover more of your Self to understand what your soul purpose is]

The rebuke found its mark. The life that she mourned was treated casually, and she'd used her lack of time to justify her behavior. Her life didn't have any meaning, because she was only interested in one objective - material gain. That wasn't just disregarding her inherent potential - it was also disrespectful of her Self; her soul! How could she have found any meaning living by that code! And she'd never bothered questioning her actions, because she was a hypocrite! She balked. *Where did that come from!?* She would never have admitted that! Then again, she'd never encountered the nothingness before. She was unable to escape anything about her personality in the nothingness – not if it was her truth! As confounded as she was by her past behavior, and the way her truth was unfolding in the nothingness, she had to admit that the approach was sheer mastery. She would never have embarked on it willingly, and even though she was firmly on her way – to who-knows-where - she was still resisting by turning to the familiar patterns in her mind. Who was responsible for engineering this quest? Who knew that she would succumb to her ego, and take her life in every direction but, the one designed for her? She could see no other avenue to pursue with her reflections, other than the one pointing to a mind, and ego limited by her conditioning. That approach might have been relevant in the past, and it had no doubt, served her well. But, she now realized just how constrained she'd been by her conditioning. Her life was much more than her past; the sum total of her old perceptions, insecurities, and fears. If she wanted to live a life of meaning, then she needed to transcend her limited, conditioned mind.

She felt mortified. *This couldn't be happening to her! She was smart. Why didn't she see this coming? Why didn't she see through all the red herrings!?* She couldn't remember a time when she'd let her guard down. She was always watching – everything! *Was that not evidence of her consciousness? And her level of awareness?* She was baffled. She'd had her fair share of doubts about her life but, at no point, did she ever think that she was on the wrong path! Everything was so real!? If her physical world had disappeared, because she wasn't living her truth, then which parts were real? Was any of it real? And if her identity was dissolving, was there anything real about her? She felt as though her heart stopped beating at that point. Her eyes darted around, looking…....searching….for something. She shifted, uncomfortably. She felt the onset of a panic attack. Invisible walls were closing in on her. And she was once again, battling to breathe. *She had to get out of there!* Previously, she'd had access to any number of "escape" routes. When she reached a ceiling at work, she changed jobs. When the town became too small, she re-located. When she was bored she travelled or read a book. Or she would get into her car, and drive at break-neck speeds for hours on end. The high speeds calmed her frazzled nerves, and helped her to forget her anger. When she returned home, things felt "normal." At least, they appeared that way, until the next time. And the next. Now, she was caught up in that same feeling. Only this time, there was no escape!

Just as her anxiety was about to spill over, she was hit by a shocking revelation. Even if she could, there was nowhere to run to – not in the entire Universe! There never had been! The only thing that she'd been running from was herself! She sighed, mournfully. What did she find so impossible to face in herself that she preferred living an unconscious, meaningless existence? Through her confusion, she felt her heart's soft, flutter. It reminded her that underpinning her behavior was a desire that she'd never acknowledged. All she ever wanted was to find the "love of her life." She'd travelled all over the world searching for "the one." But she'd never found him. And although, she'd visited many amazing places, and seen many wonderful things, she'd never felt at home. Anywhere. She was always restless – no matter where she went; what she did. Or whoever she was with! What was the reason behind that underlying restlessness? *Her fear that she would never find the love she was searching for? Was she chasing an illusion?* Until now, she'd never been aware of herself living in a perpetual state of distraction. *What was going on with her?*

[You were looking in all the wrong places. You should have spent more time getting closer to your restlessness, instead of avoiding it. You've attached the wrong connotation to your discomfort. It was pointing you towards the fears that kept you running, all your life. Until you face them, you'll remain where you've always been - nowhere. However, staying close to your discomfort will serve your soul growth in many important ways – both physically, and spiritually. Be aware of your restlessness; be present with it. Become one with it. There's nothing to fear – its part of the process to create more space within to hold your awareness. And with greater awareness you'll be able to overcome your aversion towards uncertainty. The extent of it is symptomatic of your ego's fears. If the core philosophy of life revolves around uncertainty, why do you pursue a mind-numbing, illusion? Why do you identify with such a limited expression for your life when you have access to unlimited possibilities? Why are you attached to the illusion of permanence? That attitude doesn't serve your soul's growth, for you'll associate the absence of certainty with some form of lack or failure on your part. And you lack nothing. You haven't failed – no matter what your past has led you to believe. There's no chance of failure when you're walking your soul path – only growth. And you have everything that you need to fulfill it. As for love, you seek from another what can only be found within you. Until you do, you'll never know your true home. Each event – every person – is only a reflection of who you are in that moment of time. And the nature of every experience offers you the opportunity to learn about your true Self - by highlighting the extent of your self-love. Once you realize self-love, you'll free your soul to live its desires. Including, being open to receive the love of another]

Another paradox! But, she was intrigued. And it resonated with her deeply even though, her first reaction was to deny it. She'd always viewed her relationships as difficult. And unfulfilling - in many instances. Things just never added up. But, as keen as her "nose" was she realized that she'd missed something fundamental. Her relationships were only reflecting her resistance towards acknowledging flaws in her character! That had never occurred to her! She'd devoted all her time to learning about the world that she was living in but, had never included herself in that mix! As for self-love – she didn't have the faintest idea what that was or how to show it to herself. How did it feel to love oneself? Her life was about doing anything, and everything to build that "future" she wanted. And she was determined to reach that "destination" whatever the challenge. No sacrifice was too great, and she never acknowledged any limits. She drove herself to distraction, trying to fit everything into a single day. She ignored her feelings of dread, and focused on her goals – even though she was constantly, exhausted. At best, her life was an array of planned events to accomplish more than one goal. At worst, she was a terrible juggler - always choosing more "balls" than she could handle. It never occurred to her that the biggest obstacle to living the life that she desired was her mind. It dawned on her that the discomfort she'd felt throughout her life had nothing to do with other people. Instead, she was uncomfortable about herself. The obvious reason being that she was denying her truth. But, she'd ignored the warning signs, and continued forcing her life into some conditioned mold! And for as long as she could remember, her life had gone anywhere - other than in circles around her fears! She realized that she'd not only been deluded by her definition of progress but, she'd also used her busyness to block her inner voice.

As the years passed, her dilemma over the incongruity between her feelings, and her outer reality became even more glaring. So she tried harder. She took on more responsibility in every area of her life. Her efforts with each passing day being matched only by her growing desperation. On more than one occasion, she felt dejected by her continued failure to achieve the life that she wanted. Even more disconcerting was her inability to make any sense of her failures. It certainly, wasn't through lack of trying. The obvious interpretation was that she lacked knowledge. So she studied further. *There had to be some information out there that would help get her out of the hole that she was in!* Except, she was digging her own hole! One simple question would have changed everything: "Does this feel true to me?" By doing so, she would have shone that first ray of conscious light onto her inner darkness. And taken her first step out of that hole towards her Self! But, she'd never asked the question - through fear, pride, arrogance or ignorance. Instead, she'd powered on with a life that had no meaning. And failed to understand something critical. No amount of effort could help her, if she wasn't living her truth!

She sighed. That explained why she now found herself in nothingness - facing the reality that she'd built! To own it; own the self who had created it – warts, and all! Based on her logic, her quest was insane. Unreal. And yet, despite feeling deserted by her vigilant rationality, and overwhelmed by uncertainty, she felt safer than ever before. The nothingness felt more real than anything that she'd experienced in her physical world. She held her head between her hands, and massaged her temples to stem the flood of thoughts suffocating her. *None of this could be right! Just allowing those strange thoughts to enter her mind, turned her whole life into a farce! Her life couldn't just disappear, because of a new perspective! There had to be some explanation for this madness. There must be some way to control it. Who had flicked the "switch," in the first place? There was no one around! Maybe it was she? She did have a warped sense of humor! But, there was nothing funny about this quest!* She was once again, consumed by anxiety. *She must have overlooked something. And yet, she was certain that she'd thought of every scenario to manage her life. She knew herself well!*

[Do you?]

She trusted herself!

[Do you?]

She was certain that her approach was right. She didn't allow for any mistakes. Nothing should have gone wrong!

[And yet, it did]

And how! She was still reeling from the onslaught! Nothing about her past or herself, for that matter, made any sense! Neither could she envision any kind of future in the nothingness. As weird as it was, the only thing that made any sense at all; the only place that she wanted to be was exactly, where she found herself - in the nothingness. And doing exactly, what she was doing – taking her life, and herself apart! *Maybe this quest was just a figment of her imagination. Or the latest escape hatch, in a long line of failures! For all she knew, she was probably back home - fast asleep in her warm bed.* She blinked rapidly, and stretched her arms a few times. She took a few deep breaths. She even pinched herself! All to no avail. If this was a dream, then she felt more awake than she'd felt in her entire life! *Well then, she would just have to hang around, until something gave. It was bound to. At some point. Things couldn't stay this way, forever! She wouldn't give up. She would get on top of this weird quest.* She waited; drumming her fingers on her knees, and stared into the nothingness. Nothing happened. The nothingness endured. As difficult as it was, she had to admit that the stubbornness, and willfulness that had helped her to push her way through life in the past had absolutely, no impact on the nothingness.

Despite her frustration at not being able to control the situation she found herself in, she couldn't help feeling a huge measure of respect. Whatever this quest was about, the nothingness was certainly, not going to give in to her manipulating tactics or childish tirades! *She'd never encountered anything like it before! Whatever "it" was!* For someone who had placed so much reliance on her mind, she was slowly beginning to accept that her mind couldn't help her on her quest. She had no means of fast-tracking her soul lessons – whatever they were - to attain her goal. *Wherever that was!* The exact nature of her quest - the reason, and the duration of it - continued to elude her. She was, however, very conscious of her heightened level of awareness as she sat in the nothingness, observing the multitude of thoughts tumbling around in her head. She just didn't know what she had to do…..or say….or look for. All she could do was sit in the nothingness. And feel her anger, and confusion. Be with herself, as her truth unfolded - at its own pace. She was hit by another revelation. Perhaps this was no ordinary quest. Maybe…..just maybe…..this was the mystery itself! She was hooked.

Just then, she was distracted by memories of her usual behavior whenever she'd tried fixing some situation in her life. She'd tackled each one with zeal. Although, she had to admit that there was nothing exciting about the task. It was almost as though she'd tried to counter the things that she couldn't control - by controlling everything that crossed her path! And whatever approach she'd conjured up to deal with a particular scenario, then became part of the "toolbox" she used to plan, and structure everything else in her life. All her efforts were focused on the end result. There was little or no time for emotion – other than the occasional, passive-aggressive outburst. It dawned on her that on the basis of that behavior alone, she must have felt very much, out of control! Somewhere – somehow – she'd developed the belief that structure was a good thing. It probably was - at certain times; for certain things. She realized, however, that the adoption of that coping strategy had led her to believe that she could plan her life. She could now see how ludicrous that belief was! In the nothingness, her life looked immense - infinite. And there were no borders - of any kind. She felt innocent and free - like a new-born baby lying peacefully asleep, in the midst of a jungle full of wild creatures. The vastness of her life undulated within her in waves; a distant melody echoing through the nothingness, and holding her lovingly in its symphony. The symphony was mirrored by a kaleidoscope of colors, flowing around her in sweeping rainbows that occasionally, merged in glorious, white light. Every note hinted at a rare, and meaningful soul experience just waiting to be discovered. As scary, and mysterious as the calling was, she felt drawn to its loving, soulful embrace. It was mesmerizing. Uplifting. Inspirational. She felt it resonating through every fiber of her body. It was everything that she could never have imagined. She thought she caught glimpses of her as yet, unborn Self. A Self still, unknown. Undefined. And yet, she sensed a close affinity to this stranger that she'd never experienced with anyone before, including the person that she believed herself to be! Her old self was the outsider now - observing something from afar. Something that she knew instinctively, to be her authentic Self.

She desperately wanted to know more about this part of her that had remained hidden, all her life. She felt as close to it as the breath that passed through her body. And yet, she didn't know how to reach... her Self! Somewhere she'd learnt that the best way to achieve her goals was to define a plan of action to achieve them. But, if that goal was to reach one's true Self, how did one go about doing that? Without any other form of knowledge, besides her formal education, and her limited life experiences she'd never thought that the meaning of life extended to unknown shores within herself! And that the only "boat" that could reach it was an invisible one created by aligning her mind, and body with her soul purpose! She felt daunted by the thought that if she wasn't pursuing her soul purpose, then no amount of planning or effort would get her to where she needed to be in her lifetime. She might have achieved some of her goals in her physical world but, doing so didn't afford her the luxury of escaping a downward vortex of disillusionment. And she must have instinctively known that on some level. Why else would her soul send her repeated 'wake-up' calls!? She sighed morosely. Why did she ignore her deepest instincts? Why did she ignore her soul's calling?

She again turned her searching gaze to the stars and couldn't help feeling sad that she was so close to them and yet, she would never be able to touch them. Did they hold the key to her dilemma? If she could somehow communicate with them, would they reveal the secret to opening the "door" to her hidden Self? Why did she feel such a close affinity to them? She again felt the frustration at her inability to find answers to anything! She tried placating herself with the knowledge that some things would remain beyond her understanding but, that failed to appease her. *She was still desperate for answers! If her past had led her to nothingness, then she must be there for a reason. She had to figure it out! Maybe the answers lay in the nothingness.* Perhaps she should let go of the desire to find answers, and just be with herself in the nothingness. She cringed. *That was impossible! She had to know! She couldn't just surrender to the "unknown!"* Once again, she was brought face-to-face, with controlling nature. And that begged a question: "What did she control in life?" There seemed to be some sort of order to the Universe. Except, whenever nature disrupted the status quo. But, even though she didn't have a clue about the intricate workings of the Universe, she suspected that those natural "disasters" weren't as random as they appeared. They must be prompted by some form of energetic imbalance or other. But, if she looked beyond the necessary changes designed to restore harmony on the planet – apart from the unnatural disruptions caused by global warming - then everything in nature remained essentially, the same. It had done so, for millennia. And she was a part of that natural order. What if the purpose of her quest was to disrupt her status quo – the inertia that she'd fallen into over the years? And if that left her hanging in limbo between her physical world, and an ocean of nothingness then where did she actually, belong? Where would she find harmony – her home - when the dust settled? *What would become of her, if that didn't happen? Would she remain stuck in limbo, between two worlds?* She doubted very much that she could go back to her physical world. Even if she could, she no longer wanted that kind of life! Definitely not, after her sojourn in the nothingness! That basically, left her homeless! *Where was she supposed to go? She wasn't just a physical body. Neither was she a part of the etheric realm – yet! Where did she belong? What was her natural state? Who was she?*

She sighed. *She wished that she could be a part of the stars permanently but, it wasn't her "time," yet - whatever that meant!* But, her birth, and death were the only aspects of her life that she was willing to concede to Divine timing. Everything else was in her own hands. So why did she shrink her life to fit in with her limited beliefs? She'd often wondered whether each individual had some higher purpose but, hers had always eluded her. Whenever she thought about it, there was such a major disconnect between her physical life, and the promise of potential she felt when looking up at the sky that she preferred not thinking about it. And yet, she was now beginning to wonder if her Being possessed the same imitable power as the Universe. She felt a sense of conviction, and saw a purpose to everything in Its timeless, creations. She gazed lovingly at the stars. And realized for the first time, that if there was one gift she would like to bequeath herself, it would be to live a life that rivalled the limitless, potential of the Universe. Was she being idealistic? Unrealistic? Naive? Probably! *And plain, downright crazy!* But, the small life that she'd already encountered in her physical world was such a futile existence! All her life, her conditioning had dictated what she'd done; what she believed, she was capable of doing. What was capability anyway but, a way of doing something that was already defined within the context of worldly success or failure. To her mind, that was still playing the game of copycat. She would never know the mystery of life if she lived a million lifetimes but, she was certain that everything she thought herself capable of doing, wasn't anywhere on par with what she now felt bursting forth within her. This space somehow, made her aware of a very different kind of potential. It made her feel something so much more; it inspired her. And alluded to a kind of power that she'd never encountered before – the power to create something different; something greater than anything that she'd ever contemplated before. It "spoke" to her soul, and even though she couldn't hear the words, she felt certain that she was beginning to understand the meaning in some strange way. If she could just extract a single thread of meaning to the life she was there to live, then it would be worth all the sacrifices that she'd made in her life. It would make her entire quest, worthwhile. Priceless.

Did Divine timing also apply to finding one's soul purpose? Would she know when she found it? How? Would things change in her outer world? Would those changes be right for her? It did nothing for her curious nature or her ego to leave everything in the hands of some Divine force! But, if she could see the stars from earth, and still feel so close to them, then perhaps that Divine force was far more omniscient than she'd previously acknowledged. Perhaps she was a part of all that Is - with every breath that she took. And the reason for every breath was to allow her to breathe life into her soul purpose, in the physical realm. That made far more sense than hanging around consuming, procreating and then, not only returning to but, adding to the earth's carbon footprint! *How did her mortal life, and soul purpose fit into this Universal design? Would she ever understand it? Could she surrender to the unknown design in her soul, and forgo the desire to understand it?* Was understanding even necessary, when she was one with the flow of life? Or was this a test of her trust, and faith? *In what? In whom?* She stared into the nothingness, willing it to provide the answers that she needed. It stared straight back at her, relentlessly – without revealing an inkling of its eternal secret. Eventually, it struck her that even if this was a contest of wills, she wouldn't stand a chance against such a Divine force! And she would stand even less of a chance against it, with her mind! As difficult as it was to accept, she had to acknowledge that there was something far bigger, and greater than herself. All she could do was bow her head, and be grateful to be in its presence.

It was such an unfamiliar feeling that it took a while, to feel her way through it, and surrender. She was expecting to experience some sort of closure as a result of that act but, she realized that she was expecting too much with her head, and heart still at polar extremes about her quest. The only indication that she was where she needed to be was based on instinct, and......and....feeling. And then, she had another revelation. Whether she cared to admit it or not, she controlled absolutely, nothing about her life! Nothing of real significance, anyway. She'd filled her time with any number of activities to give meaning to her life but, the meaning of her life would only unfold in tandem with her soul path. Her soul might be at peace in the nothingness but, her quest was excruciating to her mind! And her ego was in a flat spin! *What if her soul path turned out to be boring, and uneventful? She couldn't bring herself to accept that her existence in the physical world was ordinary.* And yet, ironically the life that she'd lived so far, smacked of mundanity! Talk about a self-fulfilling prophecy! She sighed. *She was going around in circles, again!* There had to be some other reason for this magnanimous gift called life. There had to be some other purpose for her existence. *She might not have thought much about her soul purpose before but, she'd put her soul into everything that she did! She believed that was enough but, somehow she must have gotten it all wrong to have ended up in the nothingness!*

She sighed in frustration. Something was missing. She shifted, uncomfortably. This time, instead of letting her thoughts run awry - something she was learning to be an egotistical ploy to avoid her feelings - she remained focused on her discomfort. She allowed herself to get caught up in the throes of it - to discover what was lying beneath it. Slowly, and with imperceptible ease, the discomfort gave way to a startling insight. Whatever she'd done using her intellect had kept her boxed in a one-dimensional, reality - separating her from the magical splendor of the Universe around her. That splendor was now evident in the nothingness by the vibrations passing through her body in electrical waves, even though she couldn't see a thing! She realized that what she was feeling was by no means, absent in her physical world. She'd never felt it before, because she was never aware of herself as a Being – one with her Universe. To live fully alive, she had to open herself to her Being! It connected her to the entire Universe - wherever her body might be located! And the only thing standing in her way from experiencing that oneness was her mind! She was flabbergasted. *What now? She couldn't separate herself from her mind! If her past was a series of repetitive behavioral patterns, then where did those patterns originate?* The product of those patterns – her past life – was now swirling around the periphery of something she believed to be far more fundamental to her human experience on the planet - her Being! Her past life had served her well - for most of her life. But, as much as she was her parent's daughter, she was first and foremost, her own person. She had her own purpose to live - her own path to follow. Somehow she had to free herself from her conditioning – it was preventing her from becoming one with her Being; one with the Universe. And she had no other choice but, to do it in her human body! Her death wasn't a prerequisite to becoming one with the Universe! She had to experience herself as a part of its never-ending mystery, while she was still in the physical realm! Besides, she'd already experienced that feeling of oneness in the nothingness, earlier on. But, it didn't go anywhere – it was still there. She just had to tune into it, in her stillness. She realized that as weird, and whacky as her quest appeared to her mind, she was making some kind of progress. She wasn't going around the same conditioned patterns anymore! She was moving in ever-widening, circles of rising energies in the nothingness. She frowned. She had to continue with her healing, until her mind, and body were fully aligned to a soul that already knew her purpose. She was startled by the huge question that suddenly, loomed in front of her. What was blocking her from her soul path? What did she have to do to remove it?

[The conceptual understanding of a soul path, and opening yourself to the knowing in your soul to realize it, are two very different things. Your quest will test your openness to receive your soul's mandate. If you don't complete your quest for whatever reason, you might be able to continue existing as you have in the past. However, your soul won't absolve you from your truth - you'll find yourself in a state of perpetual conflict with it. Nothing you do in your physical world will ease the restlessness that will stem from that inner conflict – something you'll have to endure for the rest of this lifetime, and carry into the next if you don't surrender to your soul's calling. However, as impossible as it seems to align your physical self to your soul purpose, it isn't improbable. Heart, and mind can be merged in your heart space – by following your soul's wisdom. Only your heart can understand the silent language of your soul to help you fulfill your purpose. It requires all the qualities that you've learnt so far, on your quest – vulnerability, kindness, gratitude, gentleness, endurance, patience, humility, acceptance, surrender, trust, faith, and belief in yourself. Most of all, it requires self-love to release yourself from your ego's grip. You won't fully understand the unnecessary burden you've been carrying, until you free yourself from it. And in doing so, you'll redeem your self-worth to live life as your soul intended you to do. Your quest is teaching you how to direct your energy inwards to discover the love that you have within. That love will allow for the natural unfolding of a much more important channel that has always been available to you - the one between your Being, and the Universe]

Was that what this quest was about? Releasing, and healing the energies that no longer served her – from people, places; the conditioning of her mind, and body? And increasing her awareness to reach a higher level of consciousness? To help her discover self-love, and uncover her truth - to realize her soul purpose? She was overcome by gratitude. Why did she become so attached to everything in her physical life, in the first place? Was it, because of that inner void? Did her constant busyness distract her from her anxiety over life's uncertainty? Did that behavior lull her into a false sense of security by making her believe that she could control her life? Strangely, she no longer felt a part of those fears in the nothingness. Did those fears belong to her ego? *If so, she had no problem having one! After all, surviving in her physical world was tough. How could she survive in a constant state of Being, without some means of bolstering herself against the competition? She didn't have the patience to trust that she would always receive what she needed - when she needed it? From where or whom would she obtain it? From a benevolent Universe? That was utterly, crazy*! But, she was still haunted by why she'd done things in the past, if they were so out of alignment with her truth. It was becoming more obvious that her soul desired a different path – a different way to express itself. She clearly recalled her heartache over losing everything that she'd worked so hard for. It had all happened, so fast. It felt as though some "hand" had descended on her life, and wiped everything away - in one fell swoop! She felt the anger over her failure to save the life that she'd built for herself, and her family. *Did she have what it took to start all over again?* She felt the sobs rising in her throat as doubt flooded her mind. She combed her hands roughly through her hair; digging her nails into her scalp, and swallowed hard. *Best to forget about a whole new life. She couldn't do it all over again! She was a failure.*

[You are who you've always been - from the moment your soul entered your body. But, you're only familiar with a limited self, because of your conditioning. Nothing is further from your truth. You're so much more than your past – so much more than anything you believe possible or could ever imagine. You've lost nothing. Nothing of real value, anyway. This is difficult for you to accept, because you haven't as yet, encountered your true Self. But, you need to gently, feel into your resistance. Your old self, won't be able to take you further on your life path but, your true Self can]

She didn't know who her true Self was but, it was becoming more evident that her quest was about uncovering her truth, with self-love. She realized that her conditioning might be more of a hindrance to her truth than she'd anticipated. Did that include her perspective on the life that she believed was lost? If her loss related to the illusory reality that she'd seen through the eyes of her old self, did she really lose anything, if her truth was still undiscovered? If her true Self still lay dormant within her, then her true reality was yet, to unfold. Nothing was lost – it couldn't be! Not yet, anyway. But, in order for it to unfold in her physical world, she had to let go of everything in her past that she was attached to – material possessions; outdated thought patterns and beliefs; memories. And as heart wrenching as it was, the relationships that no longer served her true Self, and her soul purpose. That involved unpacking, and releasing layers of her emotional, and physical bodies that no longer served her truth – something that she would never have thought impacted on the evolution of her consciousness! That was the realm of her mind. Or so she'd thought!

She felt overwhelmed by the daunting mission ahead of her. She might have already covered some ground on her quest but, the fact that she remained steadfastly held within the nothingness was a clear indication that she still needed to do more work on herself. Much to her surprise, the most difficult part of letting go wasn't the loss of her material possessions. Instead, it was letting go of how real her illusory reality was in her mind! Why did her mind still cling to what had no meaning to her? Did her mind perceive the familiar as a form of security, even though her conditioning no longer served her? Did her inability to let go of her past have something to do with her low self-worth? Or her lack of self-love? Based on the limited knowledge she'd gained during her quest, she gathered that living her soul purpose would serve all aspects of her life in her physical world. She just couldn't figure out how or in what way it could do that. Something told her that she was still attached to some kind of outcome to her quest. She had to let go of it. Was her previous lifestyle geared more towards her ego-based wants, as opposed to her real needs? Could she live more simply? Could she survive on less? Perhaps she was making an assumption - that living her soul purpose meant a life of impoverishment. Was she afraid to embrace life fully, because of her near-death experience in the pool? Was that the reason she became so easily attached to everything? Was her childhood so deprived of love, and nurturing that she'd tried to fill the emptiness within by hoarding everything that she could lay her hands on? Did her low self-worth explain her lack-mentality? She frowned. That contrasted sharply with the feeling of such abundance in the nothingness! She had a revelation. Lack must be her ego-state. And abundance must be the natural state of her soul! How could she bridge the gap between the lack in her mind, and the sense of abundance in her soul? Perhaps there was nothing to bridge - the gap probably only existed in her mind - courtesy of her conditioning! Could she overcome it by aligning with her soul purpose? Why would she devote a lifetime to forging a path of make-believe when the only true reality resided within her soul?

> [There were many reasons. Beginning, and ending with the conditioning that spanned generations; interspersed with a whole spectrum of low-vibrational thoughts that fed your ego's fears. With a single objective in mind - to fill that void within. But, a void can never be satiated by your ego - no matter what you fill it with. Not, until you get to the core of it, and heal it – with self-love. The distractions

in your physical world only helped you to avoid your pain – thereby, adding to the emotional debris in your pain body. That compounded your inner conflict, because your soul knows that you were fighting your Self. Consequently, you were never fully present. And the degree to which you can be present with yourself, and others will impact your life experience in this third dimension. You can, either live in harmony with all life forms on this planet or wreak havoc on it. Your patterns would have been easy enough to recognize - if you allowed yourself to work with your awareness. Instead you persisted with the same mindless behavior, until your soul had no option but, to step in. But, your emotions are not the problem – your mind, and ego are; with their predilection for attachment. If anything, acknowledging your emotions in your stillness will free your soul to live fully alive.]

Something within her stalled. Those words resonated with her as strongly as the chords of a brass band cutting through her senses. What she was missing all along was now, glaringly obvious. She gasped. What she was holding onto had very little to do with her attachment to material things. She was devastated by the loss of her home, and livelihood but, somewhere deep within, she knew that she would rise again. But, now that everything, and everyone familiar was absent from her space, she saw what was hidden beneath the frenzy of activity in her physical world. Her pain! She was hanging onto it with every fiber of her body! She'd identified with it so strongly that she'd become her pain! Without it, she didn't know who she was. And by not being aware of it she'd only attracted more of it into her life! Why was her life riddled with the one thing that she could do without!? What was at the core of it? She realized that whenever she pondered over the "story" of her life, each incident was analyzed as a separate event. And she'd overlooked something important by adopting that approach. All her experiences were joined by the same thread of pain! If she wanted to transcend it, she needed to look beyond each event - to find what was lying at the root of her pain. And if her adult life was only a reflection of that pain, then it must lie somewhere in her childhood. She'd already gained so much insight about her Self, and her childhood on this quest. She sensed that in doing so, she'd accessed certain experiences in her life that had significantly impacted her behavior. But, those experiences were the off-shoots of the void within her – they weren't the root cause of it! She sighed. She desperately wanted to move on with her life but, she suspected that would be impossible, without revisiting in her childhood. There must be something else that she needed to heal. Could she go deeper into that void to reclaim the lost part of her Self when the information she required was buried beyond the walls of time?

[Time is another illusion in your physical world. In the nothingness, time has no relevance. Your Being is infinite. You can go back in time by turning within, and being consciously present with the lost aspects of your Self. There are no barriers within your Being - of any kind. There is nothing that can prevent you from finding what you seek - not if it's your truth]

She struggled to grasp the meaning of that. It was so profound to someone who had monitored life by measuring every passing minute, of every day. She was so intently focused on time that she'd missed that life had a rhythm all of its own – totally, unconstrained by physical time! Again, she felt a sensation that she'd only recently, become acquainted with – the electric tingling in her heart. She was drawn to it, and quickly abandoned the avenue of thought that she wanted to pursue. Instead, she closed her eyes, and focused on the feeling in her heart space. With that acknowledgement, she felt her heart rejoice, and expand in ever widening waves with each breath. Eventually, it exploded into a million, little electric waves that spread throughout her body, like a wild fire. She felt as though her entire body was ablaze. And yet, she'd never felt so at peace; so full of joy. It slowly dawned on her that whatever she most needed to know about her past would come to her - if she remained in her stillness, and listened to her heart. She now knew without any doubt, what that feeling was. It was love. She smiled, and turned within to enter the soft, quivering vulnerability of that space. She had the distinct impression that she was approaching a sleeping child, and her smile broadened. She was amazed at the sense of beauty she felt, just to be in that silent, inner space. She felt so exposed and yet, completely safe. And then she was hit by a shocking revelation. She was that "sleeping child!"

She stared at that open space around her heart in awe. She felt as though she recognized a long lost part of her – even though, she was facing a total stranger. It was such an astounding thought that she was immediately, filled with doubt. But, she couldn't deny the feeling in her heart. She might be an adult but, if that was how she felt in her heart – a lost, hurt, and vulnerable child - then somewhere within, she was still holding onto the pain of abandonment. She realized that by following through with her instincts, she'd just experienced trusting her unknown Self, for the first time. She might classify herself chronologically in her mind as an adult but, her truth wouldn't permit her the luxury of ignoring a part of her that still needed to be heard - even if that voice belonged to her child-self. And if she'd never known nurturing as a child, then she needed to learn quickly how to nurture herself – even if it meant, just listening to herself. She was captivated by her access to this new-found, fountain of wisdom. She dove into it willingly, without questioning what would be required of her or where it would take her. If she could reach across space-time in her stillness, to learn what she most needed to know about herself, then she would embrace that possibility, irrespective of how crazy it sounded! With most of her inner barriers already removed, she detected no resistance within her physical body towards her decision.

    She braced herself, and mindfully released herself into the soft, slumbering, heart space within. At first, she couldn't discern much. It appeared to be just another world as black, as the nothingness around her. She sat quietly. Respectfully. Waiting. She lost track of just how long she sat still. Silent. Focused only on her heart-felt, intention to lovingly connect with that sleeping child. And then, like a flower slowly unfolding its petals, she saw a glimpse of another world opening within her heart space. She was mesmerized, as she felt an irresistible, force drawing her closer. Each step that she took was welcomed with an indiscernible kiss, as she was embraced by layers of unfolding petals - each one accepting her without question. And then, she stopped. She was standing right at the core of that space. She was stunned. It was unlike anything that she'd seen before. A place of such untouched beauty, and innocence; such infinite love that it took her breath away. It was so magnificent in its purity that she froze in reverence. Her eyes blinded with tears as she battled to comprehend the depth of what she was feeling. *Was it real? Could something like that exist within her, after all the darkness in her life? Why did it remain hidden from her for so long?* There was no space or time associated with her feeling. There was no shape or color to it. There was just a profound sense of all-encompassing, love - of being touched by her very Being. In that moment, she felt as though she ceased to live the life that she'd known, and was held in an unknown space to await the birth of a completely, different world.

When she opened her eyes in the nothingness, she felt as though she was gazing at her life for the first time - through the eyes of a newborn child. Her body was the same but, nothing else about her felt the same. She was aware that her physical world existed somewhere but, this silent, inner heart space was now her world. She was entranced by the feeling. And then, she felt the "child" stir. She quickly closed her eyes, and observed the "child" slowly, opening its eyes - fully aware that someone was in her presence. She felt the "child" beckoning her to come closer. She acknowledged the gesture with a gentle smile. The "child" was obviously curious at the approach of a stranger but, showed no signs of fear. She heard herself whisper a silent "hello," and was greeted by the sweetest smile. She reached out a hand to touch her, and felt a bolt of energy surge through her. She was afraid but, she stood her ground – she couldn't lose the connection with her inner child. When the energy subsided, she "looked" at the space again. There was no one there – only a soft, warm vibration that started in her heart and slowly, reverberated through every fiber of her Being. She returned to the silent, stillness once more, and held that "child"- a feeling of the most profound love - for the longest time. She realized that she was feeling true love – for herself - for the very first time! She let herself bathe in it, until she felt herself come alive - every cell within her body was caressed, and awakened by love. Eventually, she felt herself let go, and surrender completely, as it touched places within her that she never knew existed. She felt her entire body slowly settle into a love that she'd never known. And she remained in it, until she was consumed by a lightness that was beyond anything, she believed possible. She felt no pain, anywhere in her body. Awareness struck. That must be the healing power of love.

And then, in that single moment of self-love - when she allowed herself to feel raw, and vulnerable she saw what she'd been holding onto, her entire life. The actual event eluded her but, all the pain, and sadness that had plagued her physical body for so long came gushing out. She saw fragments of the "love" that she'd latched onto during her adult years with a force equal to the loveless years of her childhood. After all the years of being invisible in the eyes of those closest to her, that vault of pain had given her the validation she needed – albeit a false one. She inhaled sharply, as she realized that the depth of her pain was related to her constant yearning for the love of another. She never imagined she would find all the love that she needed within her Self - "contained" within her Being. An empty space as far as her mind was concerned but, once all the cellular structures of her physical body were removed, a space filled with energy that resonated with the entire Universe. She sat basking in the warmth of her love – for her Self. And she felt time, and space fall away in those endless moments filled with an indescribable beauty. It brought back memories of the way she felt in her father's presence. She might have lost him but, she'd finally re-discovered the love that she'd seen in his eyes – within herself! In that moment, she felt herself lovingly let go of the memory of his death. And for the first time in her life, she felt herself stand alone, and tall in her own person.

She reluctantly withdrew from her warm haven to process her insights. Although her mind was in turmoil, and she was trembling, she remained centered in her heart space. All the pain of having her physical world ripped out from under her was nothing compared to the startling realization that she'd been separated from her inner world by that black, void of pain. And her openness to life was limited to the extent that she engaged with herself! And that small, broken self was the "foundation" of her make-believe, reality. Suddenly, her broken past made perfect sense. Her physical self was in pieces! It was pieced together from anything, and everything - as long as, she didn't have to face her pain. And that she was living a lie. But, as real as her past reality was, she could no longer deny that she felt no connection to it. Neither could she relate to the identity of the self that had created it. She had another revelation. That identity was nothing but, an illusion! The destruction of her past was merely reflecting just how false it was! She tried ignoring her newly acquired insights but, it remained the main feature playing out in her stillness - courtesy of her awareness. She sighed. There was no way of getting back to the time when she was blissfully, unaware! *What was this awareness-thing!? Where was its source? Why couldn't she locate it in her body?* It wasn't a thought that she could control, alter or suppress. Her awareness felt like a constant, omniscient presence. Did it have access to her soul's knowing? It was acting like a filter of some sort; sifting through and transforming old thought, and emotional patterns as soon as they were detected - keeping her stillness untouched. And as soon as her old, conditioning was removed, the increased spaciousness was rapidly filled with greater awareness. And yet, it wasn't separate from her body – her awareness was an integral part of her. She felt as though it connected her physical body to all of her Being – with no beginning or end; no past or future; no life or death. Just total, presence. Something happened in that moment – she felt as though she could "hear" her soul! And her awareness was the "antenna" that transmitted the energetic "messages" to her heart. As gentle as it was, she felt her soul's voice reverberating throughout her Being - to the ends of the Universe!

She still didn't have any idea of the extent of her transformation. She couldn't tell what she was becoming or if she was becoming the Self that she was always meant to be. Her non-active state was still a huge concern. *What was wrong with her? Why wasn't she doing something!? How could she remain so calm in the face of everything that was going on?* Just a short while ago, she was living a completely, different life! She might have believed that she was given a "raw" deal but, it was a life, nonetheless! And now there she was, not only accepting her mistakes but, also learning how to be compassionate, forgiving, and loving towards herself! She could even think about her "failures," and not feel small! It made her realize how much she'd judged, and criticized herself. And how liberating it felt to release the burdens of her old self, and accept all of her. Every experience - every thought and emotion; every choice was a part of her. Whatever had happened in the past had nothing to do with life. And nothing to do with her soul. She could surrender to it. Her soul had her back; it knew her path, and had the knowing to help her fulfill her destiny. She sensed that this lifetime was another "chance" to heed her soul's calling. It wasn't important for her to know what that purpose was – just accept that she was an irreplaceable link in the human chain of consciousness. And the fulfillment of her purpose, either strengthened or weakened the evolution of consciousness. She might be an individual, and responsible for her life but, the fulfillment of her purpose – as the fulfillment of every other individual's purpose – somehow, contributed to the Universal design of creation. There was no place to hide at any point in linear time - from her Self or the millions of species on the planet. Or from the planet itself, for that matter. Neither could she hide as a Being – she was connected to all Beings outside of time, and space. And everything she did, whether in this lifetime or over lifetimes was universally known – by virtue of the energies contained in all that Is. The illusion of separateness was her wounded self – using her mind, and ego to protect itself against anything that she perceived as a threat. Now that she had a better understanding of its effect on her behavior, she was also beginning to understand the choices that she'd made. And she didn't have to worry about making the same choices, again. She was no longer the same person! She was becoming her Self! She didn't know how it was happening. She only knew that it was unfolding in the midst of the blinding light of her awareness.

In the same breath, she realized that becoming her Self also meant the birthing of a whole new life. Far from feeling daunted by the thought that had so recently, filled her with dread she was overcome by gratitude to be blessed with another opportunity to live the life that her soul desired. *But, where did she start? With what? What choices did she need to make? What were her options? What career should she follow? She grimaced. That would probably mean starting at the bottom, somewhere!* Where was "bottom" anyway, when she felt so elevated by a heart filled with inspiration? Where was the "top," when one resided in the humility of one's ego-less, Being? Did she need to bother with choices when her soul was now in charge? Did any of this matter when her soul had already made the most important choice in her life – to be born at this time, in this world. What transpired along the way, and what the outcome of her life would be was as big a mystery, as the nothingness itself. But, if she wanted to witness her true reality unfolding in her physical world, then she needed to stand in her truth, and live her soul purpose. Exactly, how she was supposed to fulfill her soul lessons, and attain the level of consciousness that she needed to within her lifetime was beyond her comprehension. But, understanding was not a pre-requisite to fulfilling her soul path. She recalled Glow's words: "Understanding will come as hindsight," as she took each step on her soul path. She trembled. She was exhilarated, and petrified! *That was a 180 degree-shift in her usual way of thinking! She couldn't live her life that way! It was impossible!* She paused, and shifted her focus to her stillness. Was it? Then again, why not? If she had access to everything that she needed - within her Self? She had nothing to lose. There was nothing to stop her. She didn't need anyone's permission. And she didn't need a "plan."

With her anxiety now under the umbrella of her awareness, she no longer felt the need to define her life by any choice or decision. She felt confined by the mere thought of re-defining a life that she was so painstakingly taking apart. Besides, her soul didn't need to make choices – it already knew her purpose. It struck her that even her awareness had different levels. She was conscious of it on one level but, the change in her neural pathways, and physiological functioning was also occurring on other levels. And she couldn't keep track of or control it – she had to trust in her soul to take her through her transformation. Her perspective had also changed in ways that she couldn't fathom but, one thing was certain. She no longer felt so buried under a huge burden. If anything, she felt stronger - lighter. Free. And she felt more open to uncertainty, and the unknown. If she was in the process of discovering her true Self, then she needed to trust her heart, and soul to lead the way. Her neural pathways might be changing to align with her path but, needed to watch her ego. She needed to remain in a place of no-mind, and be fully present with her unfolding Self. And when the time came to act, she would know. She sighed with relief. She realized that most if not all the barriers in her physical life that had compromised her truth, were now removed. And in its wake was an immense spaciousness. The space within, merging with the nothingness around her. And she had no idea what to fill it with. The only thing she knew with certainty was that she no longer desired a life without her truth. If the life she had before was acceptable, then it was no longer so. She reached a shocking conclusion. It no longer served her soul purpose – the life that her soul desired. That statement didn't stem from arrogance or ingratitude. It was simply, her truth. She felt it with all of her Being. And that feeling was all the "understanding" she needed. There was no greater responsibility towards the gift of life that had been bequeathed to her, other than living it the way that her soul desired. It didn't matter that she had no idea what to do or where to begin - she would be guided by her heart, and soul. She felt elated. *She was finally, getting somewhere!*

Even as the truth of those electrically-charged "thoughts" registered somewhere deep within, her mind couldn't stop switching between the "then" and the "now." *She might have been granted a bird's eye view of her physical reality collapsing, because it clashed with her truth but, she still needed to understand what was lying at the core of her pain. Everything else, was irrelevant - not if it had already ceased to exist in her outer reality. But, if she could understand the root-cause of the disparity between her inner, and outer worlds she might have a chance to free herself from the past, and get out of the nothingness. How else was she supposed to fulfill her purpose, and find meaning? Without meaning, she had nothing.* She was certain that she'd given enough consideration to the direction she wanted to take in life. She'd always found a way to obtain the information needed to solve any problem, and had found a way over......out of......under......or around any obstacle. As a result, she considered herself to be very resourceful. And at times, very clever for overcoming the challenges that she'd encountered. Now, however, she could clearly see that was playing cat-and-mouse, games with her life. She raised her eyebrows at extent of her ego's deception. *She couldn't believe it! And she'd taken her responsibilities, so seriously! She'd given her all to make things work out perfectly! And she'd achieved anything but, perfection!* Her life was one, huge mess! For a moment, she dwelled on that shocking realization. It was followed by another shocking insight. She was an even bigger mess! But, she was amazed at her response. It was ok! She was ok! Everything was......absolutely......ok! Just as it was. She felt happy! She was dumbfounded. The person she used to be, would never have accepted that perspective! She would have berated herself no end, for being such a failure, and would have attempted all avenues to regain her lost status. But, that person was only familiar with the old avenues of rationality, and she was rapidly fading away into the nothingness. And in the process, she was becoming more, and more present with her true Self. The "unknown" no longer felt so daunting. Self-acceptance had somehow taken precedence over understanding. And her sights were no longer set on a "perfect" life. She only wanted a life where she got to live every moment, fully alive. She closed her eyes, and reveled in the silent spaciousness within her. *What was happening to her?*

[Escapism has various aides – being distracted by too much choice is one of them. And for as long as you remain ignorant of how your behavior impacts your energy, you'll remain out of alignment with your truth, and soul purpose. And continue feeling stuck. The only way to free yourself is to heed your soul's calling. There is no way to deny or avoid your true path. You've removed many of your barriers so far but, you still need to free your Self – the light within you. By facing your fears - not with quick-fix escapist tactics but, by feeling your way through your pain with conscious awareness. There is no need to force a breakthrough - your soul will endure, and lead you to your purpose. Don't focus on the completion of your quest will be completed or any outcome. There is nowhere to go; no 'destination' - anywhere in the Universe. You're not 'broken' - nothing needs to be fixed. Everything happened exactly, as it was meant to happen. To bring you to your real home – self-love. It's the natural state of your Being. Your life path will unfold synchronously in your physical world - once the vibration of your physical body is in harmony with your soul. That is the 'ending' in all this. It also heralds a whole new beginning – the fulfillment of your soul purpose in your physical world. Savor the experience of your quest - celebrate it Even though it doesn't look like one, it's the opportunity that you've been waiting for. It has taken you lifetimes to get here]

She'd never questioned whether or not she trusted herself. Then again, she believed that she had her life figured out! *And yet, she'd failed to see this rollercoaster coming! She couldn't even say that she needed to get her life back on track. It looked as though it was never on track!* And even if that was an option, it made her cringe. She didn't want to go back to the way things were! That way of life felt heavy; lifeless. It contrasted with the increasing feeling of lightness within her body. It dawned on her that her transformation was somehow healing her physical body by removing her conditioned patterns. And the memories that were surfacing were the catalysts for each phase of the process. Once each phase was completed, the thoughts, and emotions associated with that memory were no longer triggered. She realized that the spaciousness within was also an indication of how far she'd come on her healing journey. She might be in the same body but, she was no longer the same person! With every new phase of healing her old self was becoming fainter, and fainter in her mind. She was petrified. *Who was she, if she was no longer the person she used to be!?How was she supposed to define who she was becoming!?*

[Your mind won't help you find the answers you're looking for]

She shook her head in frustration. Why was it so difficult for her to accept that? She already knew that her mind couldn't help her and yet, she kept turning to it to find answers! Her doubt gave her ego the loophole it was waiting for. *But, she had to turn to her mind! There was no other way in the nothingness! Besides, she would never survive in her physical world without an identity.* If she felt lost before, then now she felt more alone, and uncertain than ever. She flung her hands over her head in exasperation. *It was no use! She was getting, nowhere!* It was somewhat bearable to have lost her tangible, physical world but, to have her thought patterns unravelling, and her beliefs destroyed was excruciating! Every aspect of her identity was being shredded! *Her very psyche was being attacked! This can't be happening. It wasn't normal!* It was somewhat easier to release control of the changes happening to her body – she couldn't see that. But, she was battling to understand what was going on with her mind. She was aware that her perspective was changing with each past experience that was being pulled up for review. *And it was petrifying!*

[You can't keep 'track-of' or 'understand' what is happening to you during this transformation. And you can't use any of the approaches that you're familiar with - you'll only remain stuck in that prison of your own making. The only way to make progress on your quest is to trust the process - have faith in your soul's guidance to get you out of this in-between time. Be present with your discomfort, and uncertainty. You're not familiar with those feelings but, be patient with yourself. Your resistance comes in many forms. Be mindful of it especially, that endless feeling of waiting for something or someone. That's another expectation – you're waiting to be rescued from your 'dilemma' by your outside world. That won't happen. This is your soul's quest – to bring your physical self into alignment with your purpose. You won't be able to make any other choice or act in any way contrary to what it desires by using your mind. Focus on your stillness. Feel your feelings. They're in a state of flux right now but, stay present with that inner chaos. You're now looking to master the ability of remaining in that state of inner harmony, in spite of all the chaos. You'll know when you attain it – it's unmistakable. And you can only get there by feeling your way to it. For now, just stay with the chaos going on between your heart, and mind – its part of the alignment process. Don't judge what you feel – things are as they're meant to be. You're in the process of aligning with your soul - becoming one with your Being. There is no 'plan' for that. All you can do is observe your Self becoming]

Once again, she turned to the nothingness. It felt more familiar than the mayhem going on in her physical body. She felt even closer to it. As though there were now fewer barriers separating her from its vastness - all wiped away by life's invisible hand. She felt totally exposed, and vulnerable. She'd never felt so completely, at odds with any situation. And yet, in a strange way, she felt more aware of, and closer to her unknown Self than ever before. Unconsciously, the heart space that still held her captivated in its loving glow had unobtrusively, started to consume the empty void within. That knowing slowly seeped into her conscious mind. She realized that her transformation must be happening on multiple levels, and that she wasn't consciously in control of any aspect of it! Her frustration gave way to wonder. Again, she turned her attention to being the observer of her thoughts, and feelings. That gave her the distance she needed to gain some vital perspective. Her Being didn't concern itself with her earthly existence – with thoughts, opinions, conclusions, judgements or stories. It wasn't concerned with anything, other than its true state – which was love. It was free, and neutral towards any of the beliefs or emotions that she'd come to associate her identity with. An awareness of her thoughts, and emotions still existed to help her process some of the information about her quest but, her level of awareness was also changing. As soon as she transcended a past experience, her awareness also expanded. She realized she was more open – many of the things that used to consume her with anxiety, no longer mattered. And contrary to her expectations, she felt more present; more in her own skin. She no longer needed to worry about keeping track of her physical transformation – the unravelling and transfiguration was happening on a level, and to an extent that she would never be able to grasp. She needed to focus on her discomfort, and trust her Self. Perhaps that inner tension could be used as some sort of gauge of the level of trust, and acceptance of her truth. Maybe it was also an indication of the level of intimacy with her Self. Those thoughts resonated with her strongly. And the only way to achieve that new state of Being was to remain focused on abiding in the silent, stillness within.

She looked at the nothingness with a new level of respect. It struck her that as unnerving as it was, the nothingness was the only space she wanted to be in. She was starting to relax around her new-found sense of non-attachment. All the usual feelings of angst over any number of irrelevant choices to get her life up, and running in her physical world were still fighting for center stage in her mind, and wreaking havoc with gaining any clarity. She realized that at some point, something amazing had happened to her in the nothingness. She was now able to abide in her stillness in the midst of the mayhem of her past life. At the same time, her unknown Self was unfolding within her. She just knew it - by the burgeoning sense of oneness with herself; with life, and the entire Universe. That feeling of freedom contrasted so sharply with her usual urge to run that it took a while before she realized that that urge had miraculously faded away into the nothingness. She'd never known her life without that feeling. She smiled. She felt so light; so free. She was overcome by gratitude towards her unknown Self for making her persist with her mysterious, quest. It made her appreciate just how profound her experience in the nothingness was. She closed her eyes, and embraced the stillness within. In that moment, she experienced something that she'd never felt before. A feeling of celebration for her Self, and her life.

For as long as she could remember, peace was just a word. It was something that she'd often thought about but, it had always eluded her in her physical world. The only thing she could recall was a brief childhood and then, a clumsy, hurtling - straight into the phase referred to as adulthood. She didn't even realize that she'd become one. There was no transition phase; no rite of passage to mark such a significant turning point in her life. She didn't even expect one. She only knew that she needed to be ready - to confront whatever life threw at her. Accompanied by an increasing anxiety with each passing day spent in a strange world that she never could relate to. She thought she was doing fine. Until the day, when everything fell apart. That was something she never thought would happen – not after she'd intentionally set out to make her life a success. Nothing had prepared her for that traumatic turn of events. Somewhere, she'd read about a "Saturn return" but, judging by the typical experiences that marked such a return, she considered her entire life one! So she'd applied herself to doing something constructive with her life - like building her career. She was so intent on achieving her goals that she believed a successful career would make her feel successful in herself. But, the nothingness made her realize that she was suffering from a major misconception. A successful career didn't equate to a successful life!

She sighed heavily. *What was this phenomenon called life?* She'd never before tried to fathom its unknown depths. *Where did it come from? What was she supposed to do with hers?* For so long, she'd believed that she was doing something worthwhile with hers. Only to find herself on this rollercoaster of a quest and discovering that there was a big difference between doing life, and a life of Being. Perhaps there was no difference. Maybe the "difference" only existed in her mind. She was probably caught in another illusion of separation between the physical, and spiritual! Nonetheless, she was now faced with the task of bridging the gap between the two. With the hope of having that oneness reflected back to her, in the new beginning that she sensed somewhere within her. There was no other way out of the nothingness. *How did she align what she needed to do in her physical world with her soul's expression, and her Being? Doing was confined to her physical world, and her soul belonged to the spiritual realm.* She sighed. *It made no sense! Why was she born in a physical world, if her life's work entailed bringing the spiritual into the physical realm? It would have been far easier to remain in spiritual form, and continue floating around in the heavens!*

Then again, she was never the type that took an easy way out. And she would never have accepted a spiritual explanation for her existence. Perhaps the physical world was just a playground to exhaust her dualistic mind games, until she embodied her true nature – her spiritual Being. Perhaps life was foremost about Being, and the natural extension of that was the expression of her soul purpose - the spiritual - in her physical world. It wasn't one or the other. It was both! And fulfilling her true purpose was the thread that held them together. It didn't matter what form her purpose took or if its value could be pegged to some arbitrary monetary system. Its value was already pre-determined by virtue of its origin – Divine Source. As such, the spiritual, and the physical must both be part of her human experience - in the physical realm. *If her mind perceived them as separate aspects of herself could she bring them together? How? Who could help her find the answers to her dilemma? Who was the authority in such matters?* She paused. Who could tell her how to move beyond mere existence, to living fully alive? Who could tell her right from wrong? Positive from negative?

Real from false? Truth from illusion? What had value, and what didn't? Good from bad? Happy from sad? Success from failure? Dark from light? Divine from human? The difference between herself, and her Self? Who could help her discern between the myriad choices available to her, to live her soul path – her best life? Would that give them authority over her life? Was that authority justified, looking at the calamitous state of the world? And when existing authorities only reinforced separation by feeding peoples' fears. And there she was falling into the same trap by her polarizing mind! There was only one choice – to follow her soul's path by using her truth as her guide. That perspective would require making some tough choices to purge her life of anyone, and anything that no longer served her highest interests. Essentially, clearing the canvas of her life, for a whole new beginning. *Could she do that? Did she have the power within her to bring about such a drastic change in her life?* If using her mind had resulted in her becoming tangled in knots, could her emotions help her to understand her Self better? And help her uncover her truth to realize her soul's highest desires in this lifetime?

Again, she was overcome by frustration at her inadequacy to deal with everything coming at her out of nowhere. *How was she supposed to find the answers to her questions? Why did she not think about such things before? Why was she thinking about them now? Was anyone else having a similar experience?* Could others help her understand her quest? Could she help them in some way? Perhaps the only significant aspect of life was the mutual sharing of knowledge when crossing paths with other people in life – the so-called "school-of-life." Perhaps the institutions of learning in her physical world served to educate people in their chosen vocations. But, over and above that, the people with whom she strongly connected during the course of her life were also teachers – on her spiritual path. She sighed. She was beginning to see just how small a life she'd lived. And she was starting to accept that there must be so much more to life in her physical world, if she could open herself fully to her Being. If her physical world reinforced separation on the grounds of race, gender, sex, religion, culture, status, class, and material elitism, then her spirituality was pointing in the opposite direction - towards oneness of all life-forms in the Universe. There were no distinctions; no separation – of any kind. As such, it afforded her many avenues – together with her fellow Beings - to explore their life paths whenever their paths crossed. And to support the realization of the full potential of each individual's soul desires on this planet. She had no idea what those avenues were. But, she had no doubt that people were born with the capability of creating them, if they didn't exist. Maybe the answers lay in the Universal laws themselves. Maybe the old ones had served their purpose. And new ones needed to be embraced, to take humanity forward into a new world. However, relying on her egotistical, one-dimensional mind to frame any kind of concept in that regard would defeat that humanitarian objective! To turn it into reality, she had to explore her new belief within her heart-center, and her dimensionless Being.

She'd always believed that each individual walked their own path in life. But, she now realized that her belief was only partially true. Each person was indeed, on a different soul path but, everyone was ultimately, heading towards the same "destination" – higher consciousness. And levels varied for different individuals over the course of a lifetime or lifetimes, until their souls' attained full enlightenment. And honoring each person by being fully present allowed for the mutual sharing of soul knowing, thereby helping both on their respective paths. Neither individual needed to be conscious of the soul knowing being shared or the reasons for it. Understanding wasn't essential - mutual respect was. The process didn't detract from or hinder the progress of any individual. If anything, it was enhanced. It was nature's way of "leveling the playing fields" for the real progress of humanity after generations of separatist, limiting, man-made ideologies. That kind of conditioning only perpetuated the illusion that peoples' worth was determined by their heritage or class. And that one gender, sex or race was superior to another. She cringed at the underlying connotation - that some people were more important than others. She grimaced. Nothing felt further from her truth in the nothingness. Each individual might be walking his/her own path but, they were part of the energetic system, within an expanding Universe. She frowned. Was the Universe really expanding? Or was that "expansion" a reflection of human consciousness? Perhaps more of the Universe becomes visible as human consciousness evolves to higher frequencies of energy. And all the resources being utilized to find another planet or other galaxies was just another wild "goose chase!" If everything was energy then everything "out there" could be accessed from within the physical body; by raising energetic frequencies, and transcending our physical limits! Her breathing slowed as she was struck with another revelation. Perhaps every form of energy in the physical realm - since the dawn of creation - still existed the Universe. There was nowhere for it go, until humanity collectively, transcended the dense form of those energies to vibrate at higher frequencies of light. As improbable as that sounded, she sensed that every human Being was an energetic representation on a micro-level, of the potential that existed on a macro, Universal level. And if light, the highest form of that energy could travel across space then lower, physical energies could be transmuted to reach that level of vibration! Anything within or between dimensions could be transported to any other dimension through thought alone – in a state of Being.

She sighed. Man had become so self-obsessed by perpetuating separation on a physical level that a critical, Universal law had been overlooked. Outside physicality, and time everything was part of the same Universal, energetic design. Nothing – no one – could energetically exist, apart from anything or anyone else. And according to that energetic principle, every individual within the human race - since the dawn of time - had contributed to every phase of our collective ascension or declension. In the cosmic "race," humanity could only "win" or "lose" as a collective. But the conscious choice to be part of that evolution rested with each individual – to continue replicating the small existence expounded by generations of egoist, power-struggles or rise above that limited past by embracing their true power - the unlimited potential residing within each, and every individual. She gazed at the nothingness for a long time. That explained why history repeated itself! Humanity was trapped in a limited cycle of perceived "progress" by promoting separatist ideologies that suppressed the full, innate power of human potential! If such restrictive behavior had been promoted over generations then something must have shifted within humanity - and the Universe. The chaos on the planet – within individuals or in nature - was at an unprecedented high. She frowned. Was that symbolic of the disruption within humanity to bring about the evolution of a higher level of consciousness? Was the old reality of the planet not reflective of humanity's highest vision, and values? She sighed, and shook her head. How could it be? With all life-forms, and the planet under continuous threat! And where, with the exception of a few, the majority were still subjected to a form of modern-day, slavery through a host of crimes against humanity, including poverty. Such an existence wasn't aligned to the soul of life or the Universal principle of oneness! Not if "progress" was being promoted by the centuries-old, illusion that one could attain success by sacrificing one's truth! Was the planetary "chaos" a reflection of the energetic shifts within humanity to raise levels of consciousness, by returning to their truths? Were those shifts contributing to the rise of the empowered sovereign? She raised her eyebrows as she was hit by another revelation. Would the existing "reality" of the planet continue collapsing in the face of growing waves of sovereign individuals rising to create a new planetary reality? A hopeful smile spread across her tense features. She wished for nothing more than a more dignified life for all - equality, and justice to conserve not only the rights of all life forms but, the rights of the planet, as well. After all, it was a living entity in its own right – a truly Divine mother that continued to sustain life, despite the ongoing ravages by man. It had "voiced" its discontent for generations. But, alas to no avail. It was time to heed the call to save each other, and the planet!

The limitations of a poverty-stricken life on one's physical and psychological wellbeing were plainly evident on a global scale, and her heart ached for the many who had sacrificed their soul light over the centuries by holding onto the limiting beliefs that were enforced onto them. There was no doubt that a re-distribution of global, country wealth would ease the burdens of billions of people. However, even if the "powers-that-be" released their hold on their coffers, she doubted it would result in any permanent changes to the archaic structures that were founded on entrenched practices, and policies that only compounded the humanitarian crises across the world. And with that kind of mindset, it would be practically impossible to convince the power-mongers that there was something far greater at stake that required a revolutionary change on a world-wide, a-political scale – the evolution of human consciousness, and the survival of the planet. The only solution is to hold a loving heart space that allows for the expression of truth, and the fulfillment of each individual's soul purpose. And to stop all practices detrimental to sustaining life on earth – including, stripping the planet of its natural resources to support egotistic "progress." That approach, together with clean, minimalist living will give Mother-earth a fighting chance to restore herself to her natural state. Contrary to the general view that our worldly "progress" is necessary for human survival, our current global practices, and policies are only hastening the very annihilation of the only planet that sustains all life forms – not just humans.

After a lifetime of determined effort to make her own way, and battling egos –including her own - to secure a place in the world, she couldn't believe the new insights bursting forth from her. It was near impossible, to contemplate an inter-connected thread between herself, and other Beings to fulfill her soul purpose. Her ego was completely, at odds with that perspective. It was engaged in a furious battle with her mind to reinforce the separatist view of maintaining her individuality, as opposed to surrendering to the unfamiliar Universal principle of oneness. *How could she have a "place" in the world, and still be her own person within the human collective? That was a contradiction!* Then again, did she need all the external trappings of her ego-self to distinguish herself from others when everyone was the same, as a Being? Surely, the only significant thing was whether her soul was at peace. What if she could look beyond time? What if she removed every structure in her mind's eye that separated her from every other life form in the Universe, including her physical form? Then there was only space - only nothingness – within her, and between everyone, and everything! And that's exactly where she found herself now – in nothingness! And yet, despite the oneness - the inter-connectedness of all Beings, and the Universe - her soul was still unique! She was enthralled. That was all the individuality she needed! Perhaps the only way for her to accept this truth was to first destroy her physical reality, and the identity that she'd come to associate with it. And observe her limitless Being, in the nothingness. She recalled an old adage: "As within – so without." She couldn't imagine anything simpler and yet, it had taken years – probably, lifetimes - to obtain some inkling of the depth of meaning behind such simplicity! She sighed. She was so exhausted that she could barely keep herself upright. *Was she any closer to her truth?* Then again, why did she think that she would recognize her truth using her old, thought patterns? Surely her truth would emerge naturally in her outer reality, once she'd removed all the layers that she'd covered it with? She would most probably, only recognize it when she was looking at it. If it was still not visible then something must be blocking it. She sighed. *How much longer, before she removed everything that no longer served her?* Her mind remained silent. But, her heart was racing with anticipation.

[Your mind has served you well but, it won't help you to comprehend this quest. This is something that can only be "understood" with your heart. That is as it should be. This isn't a quest of the mind. It's a quest to uncover your truth through the healing power of love; to help you realize your soul purpose. Whether you feel ready or not, is unimportant. As is evident from the space that you now find yourself in. Your soul desires a very different reality to the one you forced upon yourself in the past. But, before you can observe your soul's reality in your physical world, you have to honor its call. There's nothing for you to do; no special talent required to manifest it. It already exists within your soul. You just have to surrender to your soul with an open mind, and heart. Don't worry about your mind, and body. Both will catch up - eventually. Your transformation is occurring at a pace, and at an energetic level that your physical self won't be able to control. The process will take care of itself – just remain present in your stillness.]

She was experiencing a strange emotion. She'd never felt it before. Whatever it was, it was giving her the ability to move through unchartered territory by granting her access a wisdom that was completely, beyond her mind. And then it struck. It was humility! She was very familiar with using her intellect in her physical world. Her mind, coupled with her ego and arrogance had led her to believe that she knew whatever was necessary about her world, and her life. And if she didn't know, then she would educate herself. Humility didn't feature in that mental construct. And now, she found herself accepting that the answers to life's most critical questions would never be known. She'd done her best – with what she knew. Now she had to surrender to the unknown. It would mean walking her life's path blindfolded - with her open heart to show her the way; with trust, and faith as her only companions. But, she no longer had any doubt that there was something much bigger at stake, than anything her mind could contemplate. To even begin to fathom something on that scale, she would have to acknowledge her ignorance. And be open to the invisible forces guiding her. That left her feeling more vulnerable than she cared to admit! But, she'd ridden her ego's "high-horse" long enough. And attained nothing of real value in the past. Her experiences were limited to acceptance or rejection based on a false sense of self - which was constantly held in check by her fears. The disintegration of that illusory self had resulted in the destruction of her old reality, and her identity. She had nothing anymore - other than humility, and her unknown Self to take her forward on the rest of her life's journey! She sighed. *What now?*

[If your choices aren't based on your truth, nothing created in your physical world will stand the test of time. But, that is nowhere near as devastating as losing your sense of Self, and the connection with your Being. You'll always feel the void within you, and be limited by it. You'll feel separated from humanity; from the Universe itself. And you will never know self-love. You'll continue searching for love, and a 'home' outside yourself. The only 'home' you'll ever need - all the love that you seek - lies within you. That doesn't mean you have to forego all relationships, and become a hermit. Only that you'll no longer succumb to the old patterns of relationships that reflect your unhealed self when you project your unconscious fears, and needs onto your world. By healing the separation within you – by healing that void – you'll become one with your soul, and Being. One with the Universe. You'll know when this happens - your relationships will only reflect your soul's light, and the essence of your Being – love]

"That's impossible" she screamed. *"I'm a physical body in a physical world! Not 'love, and light!' Even if I was, I don't know how what to do! I've never done this before!"*

[Your mind doesn't know but, your soul does. It already knows what is required of you to reach a higher level of consciousness. You might not have been responsible for everything that led you to this point, but you're now more aware of your unconscious behavior, and your truth. And you're more open to your heart – to your soul's knowing. You were never alone, at any stage of your life. Your soul chose the external circumstances best suited to bring about your awakening - family, places, and experiences. All this time, you were being guided by your higher Self, and now that you're awakening to your truth, you won't be able to go back to a lifeless existence. Your quest will continue to awaken you, until you've completed your transformation, and ready to take that first step of co-creating your soul's reality in your physical world. Your level of consciousness, and your soul's reality are by no means separate. They're one, and the same. If you truly desire changing your past reality, then you have to trust your soul to take you further on your quest. Ultimately, you have only one responsibility. To free your Self to achieve your soul's most important Universal objective - actualizing your highest level of consciousness. And the only way to realize that is to shine the light of self-love into all the dark places within you. That's the real work you're here to do. Therein lies the alignment of 'doing' with your soul purpose in your physical world. Everything else that you choose to do in your physical world is subservient to that purpose]

She was free!

[Only as 'free' as your conditioning allowed you to be. You've been repeating the same restrictive patterns, all your life. Like everything else in your life, freedom is an illusion]

She glared into the nothingness, and looked around for Voice. She was bristling with anger.

[Your anger has been triggered, because you still haven't broken free from some of your old patterns. You've used them so often that you don't realize when you fall into those traps. But, making excuses will only keep you from your soul purpose]

She didn't make excuses! She showed up!

[You showed up for others. But, remained within your comfort zones. You've yet, to show up for your Self - fully opening to the unknown, and surrendering to your purpose. Your reaction is only one in a long line of excuses designed to resist your truth. Would you have willingly embarked on this quest if you knew that you couldn't control it? You're still caught in a web, trying to understand it - so that you can pre-empt your next move, and figure out the outcome. How do you know if what you've achieved before, is everything that you're capable of? You've no idea what you're capable of as a free soul – present with your full potential. Check-in with your stillness - you'll feel your truth]

She didn't. But, she was certain that she'd tried whatever she could - to the best of her ability. Although, she had to admit that despite her efforts, she'd never felt fulfilled. If anything, she'd felt inadequate, and more demoralized with each passing day. She was only now beginning to see that she was the one, standing in her own way. For so long, her soul had been trying to lead her onto a different path, and she'd ignored it. Did that explain the lack of joy in her life?

[Yes]

Could she change her behavior?

[Yes. By continuing to release what no longer serves you, and surrendering to the Divine will of your soul. There is only one state of Being – love. And only one emotional state, once you attain it – joy. Happiness, and unhappiness, like every other polarized aspect of your physical and emotional bodies are constructs of your ego, and symptomatic of a dualistic, polarized mind. Once you've healed yourself, you'll be free of such distinctions - separating you from oneness; from joy. You already know what that feels like. Be patient as your quest unfolds. Stay present, and observe your Self coming into Being]

She sighed. *But, she'd already dismantled her old patterns! She'd acknowledged her limiting beliefs! What else did she have to do? She would happily, give up all her comfort zones if she needed to. She was exhausted. She'd had enough! She wanted out! Nothing that she did was getting her out of the nothingness, anyway. How could she bring about a new reality, if she remained stuck in it?*

[You don't need to be anywhere else, right now. There's nothing for you to do – other than remain in your stillness, and observe yourself. You're exhausted, because you're resisting your truth. There's no 'in' or 'out,' of the nothingness. This is where you – your life essence - has always been. Since the dawn of time. There's nowhere else to go - you're here for all eternity. Your human experience is just that – an experience in a single moment of linear time, in the third dimension. There are many other experiences awaiting you in the Universe]

She grimaced, and covered her face with her hands. *She knew nothing about this stuff! How was she going to find any answers on her own - stuck in the middle of nowhere?*

[You're not alone. You're being supported by the Universe on your quest. And you'll be supported as you take every step along your soul path. However, if you choose to continue looking at it through unseeing eyes, you'll be convinced to stop by your mind. And you'll have to contend with feeling 'stuck' for the remainder of your lifetime. But, if you open your heart, you'll see a very different world beginning to reveal itself - within you]

In that moment, all she could think about was being back in her old world. *She would get into her car, and drive at breakneck speed, until she made sense of all this madness!*

[And end up where?]

Exactly, where she'd been before. Nowhere! Suddenly, another old pattern became crystal clear. All this time, it was staring her in the face, and she never saw it! As much as she hated it "up-there" in the nothingness, she detested even more, being "down-there" in her physical world! And if It was all nothingness, then the only differentiating factor between those two dimensions was her truth. She couldn't believe that she'd been deceiving herself, all this time!

[You were called, a number of times. But, you didn't stop to listen]

Words failed her. She draped herself in the soft, comfort of silence.

She recalled her conversations with Glow. It was all starting to make sense. The pattern of her life experiences was pointing her towards something. *Was something wrong with her?*

[No]

Something, must be missing........

[No.......]

Was she so shut off from herself that it prevented her from being fully open?

[That's one way of looking at it]

Was there another way?

[You did what you thought best, until your soul was ready to reveal your purpose to you. A major part of your healing requires that you learn discernment - to recognize what no longer serves you. So that you can own your truth without any fear. And you can only do that, once you feel unconditional love for yourself. Without it, you won't be able to let go of a centuries-old past, and heal yourself – to reclaim your innate power. And without your sovereign power, your ego won't allow you to choose the life that is rightfully, yours. You would have reached here much sooner, if you'd learnt to listen to your inner voice.

But, your quest didn't start in the nothingness; your awakening has been in progress for many lifetimes. You've only just become aware of the process, because your soul has designed a whole host of factors to shake you from your slumbering existence. Perhaps this time, you'll heed your soul's calling]

She sighed. She wasn't paying attention. The only thing reverberating through her mind was that she must be her own worst enemy.

[Pretty much]

She groaned. Why!?

[Any number of reasons. Generational conditioning. Ego. Ignorance of how your shadow effects your behavior. Fear of lack. Fear of failure. Fear of success. Fear of the unknown. Lack of Self-knowledge. It kept you asleep for many lifetimes. But, for everything that you perceive you lack, you possess one quality that made you embark on this quest]

What's that?

[Your naïveté]

She almost choked. Her secret was out! She'd kept it well-hidden. But, she'd paid dearly for it, because it made her see the best in people. And now, it was that very trait that had led her blindfolded to this quest! She groaned. There was only one thing to do - continue with it, as best she could. She turned her attention to a burning question. *Why wasn't she living her full potential? She'd always given her all – to every situation. She held nothing back.*

[Suppressing your fears with compulsive doing isn't living at your full potential. The continuous disruptions in your life were attempts by your higher Self to shake you from your complacency – to make you aware of your behavior. The intensity of each event only increased, every time you ignored your soul's calling. No life path is free of its share of challenges but, if your vibration is never raised above your lowest experience, and the beliefs that it fostered, then those beliefs will show up in your physical reality. You can't outrun your shadow side. At some point, you'll have to face your truth. That holds for every limiting belief that you have, including abundance. If the belief underpinning your noblest intentions is founded on lack, then you'll only generate more lack in your life, irrespective of how far back in time that belief arose. Until you heal yourself, you'll remain locked in your limiting beliefs, and never be open to seeing your inherent abundance. Nothing is lacking in your soul - your life in the physical dimension can only be abundant. And you already have everything that you need to live your best life]

[Granted, it can be difficult to discern your life purpose while being caught in the throes of illusion. And many have lost themselves while uncovering their truth - just the way you have. Unfortunately, it's only when your world is disrupted and you're pushed into a corner to face your fears that you will awaken to the illusion, and surrender to your soul's calling. And only then, will you acknowledge a greater power within you than your ego, and fulfill your soul purpose. You've often referred to it as the 'the flow of life' but, you've never been able to grasp the fundamental meaning of that phrase. There is indeed a flow; a synchronicity to life. It contains all the natural power inherent in creation itself to support the realization of your soul's highest, selfless intentions. You're in the process of discovering your true values, and your life purpose on this quest. Once you do, your Being will naturally support you in fulfilling that purpose by allowing you access to your full potential. You don't have to do anything, other than surrender to your soul by feeling into that spaciousness within – that's the flow of life. And self-love is the 'key' to accessing it]

She groaned. *That was impossible!*

[Just continue removing whatever is standing in your way. Let's start with why you persist with treating yourself in unloving ways – you're only punishing yourself]

She was so engrossed in her conversation with Voice – calm, and still - that that statement took her by surprise. She was jolted right back into her body. *For some strange reason, she kept on letting her guard down in the nothingness! She needed to be more careful – lest she reveal too much of herself!* But, her intention was quickly, forgotten. Her old neurological patterning of putting up barriers to perceived threats was rapidly disintegrating. Without her being aware of it, parts of her brain were being transformed to align with the changes to her emotional, and physical bodies. But, her healing was far from complete. Once again, she found herself facing certain memories that popped into her mind, out of nowhere. It dawned on her that for most of her life, she believed she was being punished. But, she'd never admitted it to herself. She realized that it was another untruth that had become ingrained in her psyche. To such an extent, that she continued to subject herself to some form of punishment or other - her un-gratifying work ethic; her toxic relationships; the way she treated herself. Including, the self-inflicted abuse to her body. But, that was the easy part. That was within her control, and she knew what she was doing. She had a high enough pain threshold, and always stopped hurting herself when the physical pain got greater than that nagging, nameless feeling that refused to leave her alone. Far more difficult to acknowledge was the part that she'd remained unaware of. Until now. Unconsciously, she'd inflicted more pain on her adult self by repeating the same experiences of her conflict-ridden, childhood. It had never occurred to her that she was repeating a pattern of abuse. Neither did it occur to her that she deserved better. And she was unable to grasp that her worth extended beyond the worthlessness that she'd come to accept as her "truth" from childhood. Despite that, she believed in what she did, even though she wasn't aligned to her soul path. She'd put every ounce of energy into her career, and relationships. It slowly dawned on her that her penchant for over-extending herself in every aspect of life had nothing to do with attaining success. She was trying to overcome her pain-ridden, life! Except, without understanding the root cause of it, she'd only ended up chasing rainbows! How apt! There was nothing real about her life. In the same way that there was nothing real about herself!

[You succeeded in one thing - keeping yourself occupied to the point of distraction. It kept you from doing any real work - on your Self. And in the process, you put up enough barriers to protect yourself from the outside world but, you couldn't hide from your Self. However, once you consciously align with your soul purpose, there will be no need to put up barriers to protect yourself or hide, anymore. No one has the power to stop you from realizing your soul purpose. That belief was another limiting projection that kept you locked behind your fears, and insecurities. Until you own your truth, any reality that you chase or become attached to because of your ego, will only reflect where you are in your life's journey of becoming your true Self. You'll have countless battles to fight. And encounter various 'obstacles' - delays, heartache, lies, betrayal, and failure. Or rather, what you perceive as obstacles, since they are attempts by your soul to wake you up. But, fighting to overcome failure is the norm in your physical world. And what is perceived as failure by your ego-self is, more often than not, success for the actualization of Self. Not betraying your soul - your inner light – requires awareness. For your soul path, and inner light are synonymous with each other. If you're feeling depleted of vitality, check if what you're doing is aligned to your soul purpose. You'll invariably find that your head, and heart are at odds with each other]

Aha! So once she was on her soul path, life would be a breeze! Wonderful! She wished she'd known all this sooner.

[Your soul path will have its fair share of challenges but, none of them will be insurmountable if you're standing in your truth. All your life, despite your best intentions, you always chose a path that made you feel less than your true Self. Without being conscious of it, your higher Self was asking you to turn to the one place you would never have expected to find it – within. That was the gift of your past experiences – they kept breaking your heart, until it opened to the purest form of love there is. Self-love. It's the most important distinction between the way that you approached life previously, and walking your soul path. It will change everything about the way you see yourself. And consequently, the reality that you co-create in your physical world. Instead of being the driver navigating the many routes chosen by your ego, you'll now be the observer of your soul journey. That in no way implies being a passive, by-stander in your life. A state of Being is the most active form of presence to manifest your soul desires in your physical world. You'll be aware of everything around, and within your Self. And instead of chasing every perceived opportunity in your external world, and depleting the resources of the planet, you'll keep your attention focused on your stillness, and observe your soul's truth unfolding in your physical world. There's no reward for completing this quest is – only self-love. That's the equivalent of every other 'reward' in your physical world. You'll feel inspired to take each step, and whatever you create in your physical world will be soul-gifts to be shared with others. Furthermore, you'll feel empowered by the challenges that you encounter. You'll feel strong, and vital – not depleted at every turn. Most of all, you'll be at peace. And you'll stand in the glorious light of your Self, instead of being a greyed-out, image of the personalities that your ego wishes you to adopt]

[You'll recognize your soul path by the synchronicity of events surrounding it, and the support you receive from others – some of whom will be complete, strangers. Synchronicity doesn't imply the absence of challenges but, for as long as you remain in your truth, you'll always be able to overcome them. At any time that you feel separated from your sense of inner harmony, look inward to feel your truth about the person or situation. In this way, you'll be able to discern when you're centered in the flow of life, and when you're not. Eventually, you'll master the feeling of having your energy in alignment with it so that there's no separation between life, and your Self in your physical world. That is your 'work' in this physical dimension – to stay centered in your truth, and in the flow of life. Whatever unfolds in your physical world as you walk your soul path will be a reflection of who you are, in that moment. There is no need to force or rush anything – physical time is of no significance to your soul. It will reincarnate as many times as needed, to help you achieve your ultimate state of Being – love]

[Your life thus far, has been entirely focused on your external world. This is of secondary significance to your Being. It's only interested in the full expression of your soul's truth – not your mind's expression of its conditioning. That's the reason you've never felt fulfilled. And why you felt so confined by your old reality. Your soul is very much aware that an entire Universe of possibilities exists – something your mind will never comprehend, and your ego will never accept. You were always aware of it but, you still settled for your mind's small, limited view of life. Living with all of your Being – with an open heart - allows you to engage fully with the Universe. You'll feel as one with the essence of life, irrespective of how chaotic your physical world becomes as other subjective realities crumble. You'll no longer feel separated from your Self or the Universe. The realization of your soul reality will feel like an extension of your Self, - your physical life will be an expression of all that you truly are. You'll still feel your emotions, and process your thoughts but, you'll no longer be identify with them. More importantly, you'll no longer feel afraid. Your fears were only an indication of your limited self, and an expression of an ego that wanted to control the outcome of everything in your physical world. But, you're much more than your body, mind or ego - or any other aspect of your physiological, and neurological make-up. You embody the spirit of life itself. You are limitless]

[Your soul path will challenge you but, it will also inspire you. Each life experience is designed by your soul to elevate your consciousness, and support the achievement of your highest values. This process isn't at all, like the achievement of your ego-picked, goals. And your soul path can't be managed like a career. There is no beginning, middle or end. You don't have the luxury of stopping or reneging on your purpose or choosing a different soul to the one that you were born with – no matter how much you prefer a different, more palatable set of life lessons. And neither do you get to choose the final outcome of your life path. All you can be sure of is that by taking each step with love, your soul path will be beyond anything that you could ever imagine or plan. There is no 'retirement' from your soul path. Your physical body might slow down over time but, the essence of life remains unaltered, throughout your lifetime. You can be healthy throughout your lifetime by being aware of what affects your energy. Again, you've allowed yourself to be limited by the phases of life in your physical world – birth, middle-age and old-age. Your essence isn't defined by such labels. Life is an ocean of colors, and your soul has access to the entire palette when expressing itself on the blank canvas of your physical life]

[You don't need to master-mind a plan to fulfill your path - you soul already has one. Every experience is designed for the highest expression of your Self – as you are. There are no strengths, and weaknesses to fulfilling your soul purpose. Neither is there constant security or comfort but, you'll always be safe. For far too long, you've avoided, denied, lied, and cheated yourself out of everything that your soul desires - by making choices from a place of fear. That's tantamount to strangling your soul to death, every hour; every day. You'll never be anybody else in this lifetime, other than the soul you were born to express. Stop running from your Self, and give your heart permission to lead you. It's fully committed to your soul's calling. Your purpose in this physical dimension, is not to amass whatever material wealth you can to satisfy your ego's insecurities. That behavior stems from a sense of lack and is based on your low self-esteem, and poor self-worth. Lack might have dictated your behavior before but, once you transcend those negative thought patterns you'll have access to all the abundance that lies within your soul. As unknown as it is, your soul will lead you to an incomparable, life experience. Whatever is true for you in your physical world will unfold when you surrender to what lies within you]

Sounds like heaven on earth!

[There is no separation between heaven, and earth. The full expression of your soul purpose is your heaven on earth. Sarcasm is a form of judgement. It won't help you to surrender to your quest. And without surrender, your heart won't be fully open to experience your Divine purpose]

She sighed. That sounded simple enough, compared to the chaos that she was caught in. And she was desperate to find some way of solving her never-ending, conundrum. *But, how!? The logic of it continued to elude her!* Strangely, she wasn't so aggravated by that anymore. She realized that if the only thing going for her in that moment was the nothingness, then logic must be overrated! And she was slowly opening to a new neural pathway - that to get through her quest she needed to adopt an approach that was polar opposite to her usual way of thinking. Perhaps the only way of getting out of the nothingness was to stay present with herself – not look for a path outside of herself. Whatever she needed was within her. It will reveal itself – she just needed to be patient with the process. *Besides, she might gain something from her weird experience.*

[Your mind is doing what it has always done - deluding you that the only way out of the nothingness is through understanding. This quest isn't a 'User's Guide' for your escapist tactics or a means of satisfying your ego's motives for self-gain. And you don't need mind-power to convince yourself to complete it - your heart, and soul will continue to guide along your path if you remain in your truth. There's nothing to 'figure out.' Your soul took the decision to embark on this quest before you were born. Your mind has no recollection of it, because it was never part of it. Your soul already knows the 'agenda' for this lifetime. You can rest assured that this one has your best interests at heart. It always has. It always will. If you choose to heed your soul's calling, that's all you'll hear. You'll recognize it by the force, and conviction with which it resonates with every heartbeat. Once you tune into it, you won't be able to live your life in any other way]

[There is another distinction between walking your soul path, and your previous existence. In the past, your ego made you believe that your efforts would get you to a prescribed destination in your physical world - one that can only be reached by competing in man-made, hierarchies. That approach might have kept you in the 'game' that has been played for eons in your physical world but, it no longer serves you. It won't help you to uncover the new beginning that lies within you. To realize that you need to master your ego – to completely uncover your truth, and align with your soul. The objective of your quest isn't to rid yourself of the ego – you still need it to fulfill your soul path. However, your soul will be in 'control' of your purpose – not your ego – once you surrender your will to Divine will. Only then, will you be able to access your full potential to realize your soul purpose. Your soul knows that there is no 'destination' in the physical world. All possibilities within your lifetime lead to the realization of your full potential; your 'final destination.' Ironically, you concern yourself with only one dimension – your physical world. And you've succumbed to the many choices that you were inundated by in your physical world. But, you've only squandered your priceless energy, and the planet's resources by pursuing them all. You have but, one purpose to fulfill during your lifetime – the level of consciousness desired by your soul]

[Your innate potential won't serve you in the ongoing destruction of the planet – even if you believe that your only salvation lies in finding a new 'home' on another planet. Finding another planet to merely repeat mankind's collective conditioning isn't the answer to humanity's ongoing crises. The evolution of consciousness to embrace oneness, and live in harmony with all life on earth, is. It's the only way to overcome resistance towards working together as a collective to solve problems of this magnitude. Many have been trying for decades to promote practices for a greener earth; many more have awakened to this life-threatening need. And yet, interminable debates still circle around maintaining policies, and trade agreements that uphold destructive industry in the face of the ongoing threat to all forms of life, including the planet. What you see around you is only a reflection of multiple, subjective realities based on a single belief throughout human history - that people are separate from each other. Besides the psychological barriers, various physical structures exist to reinforce that belief - country borders; walls; fences. And astronomical defense budgets to ward off any threats to that belief. But, all of mankind exists as the single manifestation of one essence – life itself. Destroying a single life to perpetuate the illusion of separation impedes the evolution of all of humanity. The opposite, is equally true. Uplifting one life, uplifts all of humanity]

[Similarly, pain or any aspect of the lower physical bodies aren't confined to just the individual feeling it. On an energetic level it's carried, and felt by humanity as a whole. And the power of a loving heart space doesn't just heal the person who strives to open to it - it heals all those who come into contact with such an individual. It's based on a simple principle. There can be no energetic vacuum - of any kind – in the Universe. Be it on a micro- or macro-level. Any imbalance of energies will be restored to counter this. The 'future' of the human race isn't dependent on finding another planet. It's dependent on grasping a simple energetic principle. All of humanity is part of one, life essence. And the collective human experience at any given moment in time, is visible in the projected macro-experience of humanity at that time. The same principle applies to the individual. There is no 'better future' out there. The only future is the one lying within. But, nothing is lost. Each individual can still create their true reality by healing the illusion of separation within - by healing their past conditioning, and embracing the innate potential lying within each soul. You can change the outer reality of this planet, and co-create the better world that you each desire in your soul. It's real. It does exist]

[When you uncover your truth, and use it to navigate your way through your soul purpose, your inner reality will naturally unfold in your physical world. For a long time, you believed that your thoughts manifested your reality. That is only partly true. No amount of positive thinking will attract what your soul desires - not if your conditioning is standing in its way. And no matter how good your intentions are, you won't be able to suppress your soul's truth. If the human 'playing-fields' were level for all that would be plainly evident. But, the 'reality' you see in your physical world is the imbalance caused by an age-old system that has survived by making you believe an illusion – you're only worthy if you subscribe to the systems in place. But, not only have the 'goalposts' shifted in the 'game' of life - the game itself, has changed. You can no longer manifest anything in your physical world, if you're not aligned to your truth. Furthermore, it's no longer about 'manifestation' but, actualizing the unique, soul purpose within you. And your soul will circumnavigate many lifetimes – any number of physical bodies - to fulfill its true calling. Sometimes, that purpose might be too large for one person to achieve, so a few people are born in the world to realize it. Although the realization of one's soul purpose may be seen as the effort of an individual, it impacts on all of humanity by contributing to a more significant goal - the elevation of collective consciousness. There is no 'first' or 'last' in this evolutionary process. It isn't a race. But, there is a 'finishing line' – a higher level of consciousness. And there's only one way of reaching it – together with your fellow Beings]

[All this time, you believed that finding meaning was the equivalent of attaining success in your physical world. Your belief was based on the usual benchmarks, and reinforced by the 'value' that you could attach to it. But, that belief no longer serves you. No man-made system can place a value on your truth, and worth for they don't exist to uphold any system or structure in your physical world. They serve you, and all of humanity. If you must ascribe a value to it then, let that be in accordance to your self-worth. You're the only judge, and jury of your soul's expression in this physical dimension. It's when you deny yourself your truth that you rob yourself, and the rest of humanity of your light. The chaos in your life is only a reflection of the chaos within you, and arises when you're separated from your truth - your light. The same principle applies on a global scale. All the unnecessary conflict, war, and suffering you witness around you is a reflection of that separation. Unnecessary, because no death inflicted through war, genocide or any other means is an isolated incident on this planet. It will impact on all of humanity - leaving behind a feeling of bereft emptiness, across the length, and breadth of physical time. There are no wars to be fought with other Beings on this planet. The only war that needs your attention is the ongoing war within you - if you can bear to be alone with yourself long enough, to confront it. You've punished yourself long enough, for not living up to the expectations of others - for not being the perfect person you thought you needed to be to 'earn' your place in this world. It's now time for you to acknowledge, and accept your Self for who you truly are. There is so much more to you. So much you've yet, to discover about life, and your Self. You'll only find peace in loving, Self-acceptance. There will be no peace in your physical world, until you do]

[So far, most of your challenges in life have been ego-battles. And your ego's only objective was to differentiate itself from everyone else using material worth as a measure. But, as you've discovered, irrespective of how much you chase those goals in this third dimension, you'll only go around in circles. However, heeding your soul's call to walk your true path will open you to a very different experience of life in this physical dimension. Your mind will be the servant to the true master – your soul. And only by listening to your heart as it follows the inner knowing of your soul, will you be able to stay on your true path. Sounds simple enough but, it won't be easy. However, once your mind, and body have completed this transformation on a cellular level, you'll be able to maintain your center through any external discomfort. As your old conditioning unravels, the confidence based on your mind's penchant for the familiar will also fall away. Insecurity will become your new confidence. And uncertainty will be your new comfort zone. Only by trusting in your Self – something far bigger than your ego self - will you be able to stay in your truth. With each step, you'll embrace more of your Self as it unfolds to bring forth the gifts that lie within your soul. And with each step, you'll be co-creating a new reality, free of illusion - just by Being]

[And remaining true to your soul's reality by making it conscious will be the one, and only war throughout your lifetime. But, it's the only one worth fighting for. Winning this inner war negates all other battles for it's a spiritual rite of passage to regain your sovereignty. You'll need to take each step with conscious intention, as your heart follows your soul's knowing. 'Doing' is not the way to create your new reality - Being is. But, don't underestimate what will be required of you. It's a process that will accept nothing but, your full presence – all day, every day. Throughout your lifetime. And your highest intentions - not according to anyone else's standards but, your own. And in return you get to live your best life – fully alive. There will be mistakes along the way but, each day will bring another opportunity to start with a clean slate. All that will be required of you is to remain centered in your truth, and witness your soul revealing itself in the experiences that unfold around you. Have no expectations of yourself or others. Remain non-attached to everyone, and everything that you encounter along your path. Refrain from trying to figure out the final outcome or destination. It's not important to fulfilling your soul path. Stay focused on the limitlessness within your heart space. Your mind will follow your soul's lead. That's the only intention you need to be mindful of. Be kind to yourself along the way, and lovingly accept all that you learn about your Self. Trust your Self to do what you need to do, even if it seems strange. Don't bother trying to understand it with your mind – your soul is in charge. To succeed on this path, you have to remain present as the observer. Remain in your integrity, and always fight 'the good fight' – at all costs. Be conscious of each step – you're creating your soul's reality. That's true freedom. There is no one to judge you. No one will be watching you - other than your higher Self. And despite the uncertainty, the outcome of this quest lies fully in your hands. The logic of it will always elude your mind - to protect your soul purpose from being derailed by your ego]

[Walking your soul path in your physical world isn't dependent on your mind. Although you'll still use your mind to process what you observe along the way. The formal knowledge acquired in your physical world has served you well. However, you'll need to tap into your wisdom to complete your soul path. There is no external source that can provide it – written or otherwise. Your soul's wisdom stems from something far more omnipotent than anything you can imagine. It has a depth and breadth that has been birthed in infinity itself – it's connected to the same Source as the entire Universe. And that connection gives you access to all forms of wisdom across space, and time. It spans past, present, and future by cutting across linear time barriers in your world. You can transcend all limitations to co-create your best life in this lifetime. Nothing can hold you back from accomplishing your soul purpose. Everything that you've experienced on your quest so far, has arisen to make you aware of those limitations – so that you can heal yourself. Release your past – feel your soul expand into the spaciousness within you. Don't rush to fill it with some thought or deed. That's just your ego trying to manipulate you through fear. There's nothing to fear - you're in the process of transmuting the very foundation of the physical self you once thought you were, and liberating yourself by embracing your truth. In the process, you'll transcend your ego-self and embrace your true Self, and your limitless Being. That is surrendering to the great unknown]

[It's the most difficult part of your quest. You'll feel exasperated and constantly, exhausted. And it can be very confusing if you approach it with your mind. As you release more layers of your false self you'll feel more lost, and alone - caught between two worlds. A physical world that holds no meaning, and a new world that you're unable to see. And an old self that you can no longer relate to, and a true Self that you're still uncovering. Only when you've completely, transcended your existing conditioning - only then will you reveal your true Self. And when you humbly acknowledge all that you are – nothing in this Universe - only then, will you fully surrender to the unknown. Only then, will you be free to take your first step onto your soul path. It takes love, and courage to see your Self for all that you truly are – empty, nothingness. But, nothing else you do will be more fulfilling or rewarding – you'll be in the full power of your undefined Self. No other experience is more real – it's the foundation of your true reality. Your intellect, and physical body will continue to be challenged along the way but, nothing will break your stride for long. Your soul path might be invisible but, you'll know it by the peace that resides within you, as you take each step. Remain in your stillness, and keep your heart open to the world around you – it will translate your soul's messages, and help you to co-create your true reality. There might be other soul lessons to be learnt, and other paths to be followed in other lifetimes. But, this moment – here and now – is all you need to fulfill your purpose in this lifetime]

She started laughing. Hesitantly, at first. And then, uproariously. *She must be completely, insane!* She continued laughing, until fear caught her off-guard, and yanked her back to the nothingness. She was trembling violently; ice cold. *Was any of it true?* It was beyond anything that she'd ever encountered before! And yet, it resonated so deeply with her that she didn't have to analyze it. In fact, the less she thought about it, the more open she was becoming towards her quest in the nothingness. It felt as though she was moving further away from her old reality, and touching the outskirts of some new invisible, world. She still couldn't see it. She could only feel it. And her transformation in the nothingness was making her feel closer to it. Her analytical mind was processing some of it, although she was still at a loss as to what was actually, happening to her. She became aware of the throbbing in her heart. Why was it sounding wilder, with every breath that she took?

[Your head won't help you with those answers. Only your heart knows what you're seeking. You've been so intent on barricading it that you haven't learnt to detect when its rhythm changes to the call of the Universe]

Barricading it from what!? She got the pain part. What else could there be? She wasn't afraid of anything!

[You suppressed your much of your fear but, you're still carrying it in your physical body. You don't remember the exact nature of it but, you're getting closer to the core of the removal of each wall]

She didn't like that. A part of her still believed that she could determine the direction of her life, by controlling her emotions. With her acknowledgement came the realization that she'd made another incorrect assumption – that if she didn't feel anything then her emotions didn't exist. She'd always denied her emotions, and yet unconsciously, her suppressed emotions had still affected her behavior. What purpose did her emotions serve? Were they important? By suppressing them, did she limit the fullness of her life experiences? And reinforce the illusion of her physical reality by removing herself from her truth? She felt ripped apart by her questions. She wished she could stop them but, the emotional rollercoaster she was on had a momentum all of its own. And its course was already set. If there was a power switch, then she didn't even know where it was located. *Who switched it on? What or who was controlling it?* Her soul? She swallowed hard to control the lump in her throat.

The rollercoaster stopped. She realized her periods of isolation over the years had had an unexpected benefit. It wasn't a conscious choice but, the silence had given her a reprieve from the constant "noise" in her world. She'd spent her time reading or traveling but, her sub-conscious must have been processing her experiences. She'd never really understood her behavior, and was very much aware that those around her, understood her even less. But, their discontent or ostracism was easier to deal with. Not only did she hate explaining herself – anything she said only aggravated the situation! It dawned on her that she might have tried her best to "fit in" but, it wasn't something that went down well with her. There was an ongoing battle with herself – she didn't agree with society's code for acceptance. Especially not, when the "goalposts" for that code were shifting all the time on some whimsical notion or other! The power of her awareness became evident. Whenever she'd gone against her truth, whatever she hoped to accomplish was steamrolled in some way or other! Far from being an "obstacle" her external reality was flagging that she was betraying her soul! She might have complied in various ways but, her awareness didn't allow her to stay committed to any kind of double standard or majority view that she didn't subscribe to. She was being steered towards committing to one thing – her truth!

Just then, the rollercoaster started moving again. She gathered that she was being given glimpses of her conditioned behavior – it was helping her discern how her true Self contrasted with her old self. She realized in every instance, her reticence was signaling that she was out of alignment with her truth. She sighed. Why didn't she acknowledge her true feelings? *And now, she was moving away from her old self towards something that she couldn't begin to comprehend! If she was unraveling her conditioning to leave the past behind her, what was she supposed to use to create her new identity? Did her true Self have its own identity?* She was sidetracked by the recollection of the many risks that she'd taken during her lifetime. She dove into a situation and stuck with it, until she emerged battered, and bruised from the experience. It took a while to lick her wounds, before she could pluck up the courage to take on the next one. The next insight took her by surprise. Monetary gain wasn't the motivation! Instead, she was playing some kind of Russian roulette with herself – gambling with the emotions that held her hostage! She smiled wryly. For someone who made a point of suppressing her emotions, she certainly had a strange way of bringing them to the surface! The balancing act that she'd instinctively performed – often with painful repercussions - was now very apparent. She realized that her awareness had always been by her side – even if she'd only become conscious of it during her quest! Why was she so uncomfortable about her feelings? Why was avoidance so 'normal' that she'd failed to notice it before? Why wasn't she open to receiving anything, other than pain in her life? Did she believe that she only deserved pain? She felt an immediate reaction to that question. Why did she believe that? It was such a weird paradox. She'd attracted exactly, what she was intent on avoiding! It was only when she started gulping for air that she realized she was holding her breath. She closed her eyes, and took a few deep breaths. Slowly, she felt herself settle into her stillness. She breathed a sigh of relief.

Only to have the rollercoaster in her mind screech to a halt at another trait - the number of times that she'd tried to prove her worth. She realized that the more she modified her behavior to accommodate the demands of others, the less she respected herself. Why was it acceptable to her, to be less than her true Self? That attitude was limiting on so many levels! More so, because that behavior had done little to prepare her to face the one thing she couldn't avoid in this war – her truth! And nothing more was more dishonorable to her soul! She saw all too clearly that there was only one way to redeem herself - not betraying her soul to make herself feel less than, her true Self. She was the only one who needed to look into her eyes - each day, of her life. She needed to know that she was equal to the soul looking back at her. The existing standards in her physical world were less important than those required by her soul. And they were relentless. She knew instinctively, that her awareness would make it impossible for her to betray her soul again. She might have possessed the grit to rise above the many challenges that she'd experienced in her physical world but, none of those challenges required her to journey within. For that she needed her awareness. And wisdom to fulfill her soul path in her physical world when she completed her quest. But, for all her past mistakes she'd never been far away from her Self. She might have set out to achieve various goals but, throughout her life, her soul's truth had taken precedence – without her being conscious of it. Was her physical life separate from her spiritual path – like two railway tracks that ran in parallel, throughout her lifetime? Did they only come together intermittently or was she the victim once again, of her dualistic mind?

[The challenges you faced in your physical world were demanding, and you always went the extra mile but, your ego made you settle for less by playing the fear-card. Whenever something got too close to those inner barriers, you caved. But, despite your unconscious state you were always toddling alongside your soul path - nothing can separate you from your truth. Furthermore, self-doubt was the reason you never committed to your goals in your physical world. But, it existed for a reason – to steer you from what you didn't want to get you to your truth. Your experience of the world - everything in pieces – emanated from the projections of your unconscious mind. And it occurred in so many different ways, and so often that it only reinforced your poor self-worth. In your mind, you saw yourself as committed, but, you were never aligned with your truth – a part of you was always holding back even though you went all out to achieve your goals. If nothing else, this shows you the extent of your soul's desire to realize your purpose in this world. This quest will heal your physical self to support you on that journey. But, despite what you think, you're not 'broken' – just separated from your Self. As a Being, you're completely whole – you've always been whole. And there's only one 'track' to live a life of meaning – your soul path. Outside your mind there is no separation between your soul path, and your physical reality]

Again, she failed to grasp that. And the mention of "settle" hit a nerve. But, she was now more open to any emotion triggering her – being present, until it cleared. She was also very curious about her true Self. And as far as this quest was concerned, she was way out of her league. She might have pushed her external physical boundaries but, her transformation was revealing inner limitations that she'd never been aware of. Conquering them, required a very different approach – a totally, unfamiliar one. She shifted, uncomfortably. *Did she really have the soul knowing to deal with this?* She sighed. *Perhaps the only thing she could do was indulge the process.*

[This quest requires you to face your pain and fears, until they no longer trigger you. You always have a choice - you have free will. But, exercising it requires that you accept the consequences of sacrificing your soul's growth, and your happiness. Indulgence is another way of avoiding your discomfort. You're sabotaging your truth by trying to make your reality something that it's not. Take a moment to feel into your discomfort; become acquainted with it. It will help you to recognize your lower vibrational thoughts. There's no turning back – your awareness won't let you. The only way to move forward is to recognize when you're out of alignment with your truth, and navigate your way back to your true Self. The process will teach you trust, and faith in your Self. And raise your inner vibration to think higher thoughts, until you become one with your soul. You already possess the inner knowing to align your physical body with your soul purpose. Your mind is too fickle to make choices that serve your Self. And full acceptance of your Self can't be dictated by what you think will please others. Hence, your higher Self has access to your soul to ensure the actualization of your purpose. Be gentle with the pain that surfaces within you now; love yourself through it. You can't uncover your truth by only acknowledging the emotions that make you feel comfortable. You can't be open to joy if you shut out pain. You can't acknowledge your good traits, and malign what you consider bad. And you can't seek out the light within by denying the existence of your shadow side. Every aspect of you is an integral part of your Self – to realize your purpose in this physical realm]

[By pouring the light of consciousness onto the darkness within causing your separation, you can integrate body, and mind with your soul purpose. That is a tall order but, there are no quick fixes to completing your quest. You can't confine your soul within the realm of intellect. That is the equivalent of living blindly - with your eyes wide open. Your eyes can only see through the existing patterns in your mind but, your soul has access to wisdom way beyond the mind. Your soul is connected to your Being – to the Universe. It sees everything; knows everything - across all dimensions. But, opening the channel between your Being, and the Universe requires alignment with your truth, and full surrender to your soul path. Over time, you became blocked from receiving your soul's gifts by the many negative experiences in your physical world. Healing your pain body is necessary, before you can free yourself to live fully alive. And unapologetically. Being open requires you to be vulnerable but, you won't be putting yourself in harm's way. On the contrary, living with a heart wide open allows your soul light to shine through – to keep out any darkness. Stay centered in your stillness; feel into that vast, empty spaciousness within – it's all of your Being. Release your need for control, and give your heart permission to voice your soul's truth. You're safe in the loving embrace of your Being]

[This is difficult to believe when you're blinded by confusion, and pain. If you can stop resisting your pain body, you'll be able to stay present with it, and make the breakthrough you need. You're not your thoughts or your emotions. Your Being is completely, neutral. You can continue avoiding your pain if you choose but, your feelings provide the 'map' to help you uncover your truth. Emotion in its energetic form is passed between generations through cellular memory, and will continue being mirrored in your life experiences, until you become aware of your unconscious behavior. Going through this healing process to get back to your neutral Being is necessary. There's no other way to make your ego surrender to your truth - that even as a mere mortal, you're a Divine creator of your life. Your confusion, and physical pain is the result of your mind resisting to let go of those old cellular memories. This transformation is being driven by your higher Self, in accordance with your soul's blueprint. There's nothing you can do, other than stay present with your pain as your physical body 'grows' to accommodate your soul's expansion. The pain will be extreme at times but, that is due to lifetimes of repression. And as ethereal as your soul is, it will relentlessly persist with each layer of energetic expansion, until it has worked through the density of your physical body. Because of density, your mind and body will be the last to release what no longer serves you. Your thoughts might emanate from your mind but, they're also forms of energy that add to your pain body. The intensity of your healing process is due to your physical body holding onto those painful experiences, long after they've left your mind – sometimes for years or lifetimes. As overwhelming as this part of the process is, stick with it. You have to heal your emotional body by processing, and releasing the thoughts that have given rise to your pain body, before you can free yourself from your past. There is no way to skip this part of your quest] [As you heal the layers of your physical body, you'll open yourself to more of your soul light which will repel the lower frequencies of energy from your body. And since, there will no longer be anything blocking your inner light, you'll find it easier to tune into, and resonate with the higher frequencies of energy. That is all the protection you need against any form of lower energy. This shift will make you more receptive to receiving all the gifts that your soul has eagerly been waiting to share with you, for such a long time. You won't be able to foretell what those gifts are but, you can be certain that your external reality will shift to reflect them once you align with your truth. And you'll know that true reality by your joy. There is no way of predicting how long this healing process will take - each person's journey is different. All you can do is be patient, and stay lovingly present with your body as it releases the pain that it has hung onto for generations. Continue to direct your attention inwards, until you find what has been holding you back all your life. It will require immense courage, and patience. Wishing for this process to be different will only cause further delays. Trust the healing process that your soul has designed for you. It will lead you to your truth, and your purpose in this lifetime. This is one war you can only conquer with self-love. And only love can heal your physical self to increase the soul light that your body can hold. Empathy comes naturally to you but, it's only by nurturing yourself through your pain that you'll learn kindness and compassion towards yourself. It's only through lifting yourself out of the hole that you've been buried in for so many lifetimes that you'll learn to respect your innate gifts, and embrace your worth – to unapologetically accept what you truly deserve. It's only by facing the disillusionment of losing what you wanted that you will surrender to what your soul needs. And it's only by letting go of your ego's desire for the love of 'the other' will you allow yourself to be vulnerable enough, to transcend your fear of loneliness with self-love]

[As frustrating as your mind perceives this quest to be, your heightened level of awareness won't allow you to go back to your old way of life. Celebrate where you are now - you've travelled far to re-claim your sovereignty. Stay in your stillness – follow the silent echo of your soul's calling. It will lead you the rest of the way on this quest. As far as your mind is concerned, things only become worse. But, ignore your mind – your ego's battle becomes more intense as you get closer to freeing yourself. Sometimes you'll think you're going backwards or spinning in circles. Don't become despondent. Your spiritual path is circular - not linear like your experiences in your physical world. Sometimes, you'll feel as though you're falling deeper into the void within. Let yourself 'fall' – just stay centered within your stillness. It's the only way to transcend the darkness within. As you become aware of it, refuse to judge anything - where you are; who you think yourself to be; what you're feeling. You're not your thoughts or emotions. Let them play out in your mind, as you open to greater waves of your soul's expansion. Eventually, when your healing is complete, your mind and heart will be one - bringing an end to the separation within you. You'll be one with the full power of your Being. But, this isn't a matter of power. It's a matter of love - for your Self. And faith in your unknown soul as it prepares you to fulfill your life purpose]

Again, she found herself wondering who or what she was talking to. And why she was being so tolerant with something that she couldn't see or understand. *It was totally out of character!* The character she remembered, anyway. But, as confused as she was, she was more intrigued by the stillness within. With each moment, she was becoming more aware of her inner world; of being the observer of her experience in the nothingness as opposed to, being distracted by her outwardly, directed thoughts. She realized that her awareness was helping her navigate past and present timelines; and the physical, and spiritual realms. But, she was still unable to fathom the nature of the transformation that she was undergoing. She realized that she was now able to switch with greater ease between the thoughts in her mind, and the stillness within. She also discovered that she could discern "messages" streaming into the stillness from around her. The process was happening quite seamlessly, with no specific decision or action required on her part - just the instinctive shifting of her awareness to focus her attention on whatever she was "called" to focus on. She could locate no central point for this ability - this form of non-doing, action. It seemed to be emanating from all of her, and culminating in the stillness within - which felt connected to her soul; her Being. To the entire Universe. Her mind was still foggy but, she was no longer concerned. The 'fog' represented the mass of old thoughts that were slowly fading away. She didn't need to process them – they didn't belong to her truth. And she needed to accept that there were no new thoughts replacing them. She needed to abide in her spaciousness. Despite her exhaustion, her body felt a level of alertness and connectedness to everything within, and around her that she'd never experienced before. *What was she connected to? Why couldn't she see it? She couldn't even feel it – it was just a knowing. What purpose did it serve? What did she have to do, to stay connected to it?*

[Nothing. You've always been connected to all that Is – always will be. You just have to stay within your stillness, and be present with your Self in your heart space]

She bristled with irritation. She hated repeating herself. "I don't know what that is" she shouted.

[You do]

"I don't" she screamed.

[You will, if you stop resisting, and allow yourself to tune into it by abiding in your stillness]

So where was it hiding all these years? She put her hand on her chest in a gesture of defiance. There was nothing there; just the usual beating of her heart against her palm. *There! She'd proved her point.*

[Who would you like to prove that point to?]

She inhaled sharply. She'd forgotten that small - significant - detail. There was no one around! She sighed. *What now? There was nothing "out there!"* Her hopes were in vain. She buried herself in her thoughts to avoid the fear that burst into flames, and zig-zagged painfully across her belly. Her attention was distracted by another puzzling thought. Despite her dedication to her career she'd never been fully committed to it. She'd disengaged during the early stages of every assignment. And she'd never challenged the decision to continue pursuing opportunities in her chosen field. She justified her behavior by telling herself that she didn't have a choice – she had to earn an income! This time, however, she couldn't suppress her awareness from rearing its head. Was her heart ever fully engaged in anything that she'd done before? Or did she make herself a willing slave to her conditioning? That explained her constant boredom! And then, she was hit hard by what Voice had said a short while ago. She'd settled, because of her fears! And on some level, she'd known that she was disempowering herself! She might have pushed her boundaries by striving to reach one ambitious goal after another but, she'd remained confined to the same limited beliefs, because she didn't want to face the root cause of those fears! Effectively, all she had done was marginalize herself by making choices that didn't resonate with her truth! Not owning her truth had made her succumb to her weaknesses – it kept her small. She'd repeatedly settled for the familiar, instead of pushing herself to embrace her unknown soul. Why did she continue betraying her true Self? That kind of behavior in no way, demonstrated self-love! She wasn't born that way! Did something happen during childhood – perhaps even in previous lifetimes - that made it second-nature to undermine herself to such an extent? Or was her past symbolic of an ego that had led her horribly, astray? Perhaps it was a combination of both. And yet, despite the great odds, her awareness was still hanging around! She would have to leave the healing required for previous lifetimes in Divine hands but, healing the wounds of her current lifetime was very much in her power on this quest! She could trust her soul's knowing. Her acceptance was supported by another wave of electricity that passed through her body. She was struck by another astounding revelation. She realized that there was a correlation between the intensity of the electric waves passing through her, and how open she was becoming. Was her quest also removing her ego from the pedestal that she'd placed it on? And assigning her awareness the leading role so that she could align with her soul purpose?

Strong on the heels of those insights came another. With the exception of her parents, she'd seldom sought validation from others. She frowned. *Why did everything in her life begin, and end with her childhood!?* She was grateful for the recent insights into those early years - they had helped her understand her Self better. *But, she'd had enough! She was done with that old story! It was time to move on.* Just then, she felt something else stir within. She couldn't put her finger on it. Previously, she would have been irritated by any interruption to her intended course of action but, she no longer felt the need to power on, and ignore her feelings. She turned her full attention towards that feeling. She realized that it went far deeper than she suspected. She sat with it for a while. It dawned on her that she'd been resisting something else by constantly, reaching outside of herself - something that she'd never before acknowledged. It was once again, seeping into her awareness, and making itself known to her conscious mind as some kind of imbalance. She realized that she'd always turned a blind eye towards it. Now, she could no longer ignore it. It was the ongoing dilemma of the impassable chasm between the "haves," and the "have-nots." She groaned. *Why was she thinking about that again!? There was nothing she could do about it!* But, her discomfort only increased with her attempts to shrug it off. It dawned on her that she was avoiding taking responsibility for her contribution to that inhumane reality. Whether she acknowledged it or not, her non-action, and silence condoned it. The injustice of it now hit her like a thunder bolt. The majority who upheld such systems, weren't even being served by it! Certainly, not in any dignified way! What was more frightening was that there was no real basis for it - other than maintaining the wealth in the hands of the few who had put those systems in place eons ago! And the longer she contemplated it, the more it looked like another mirage – created by manipulating peoples' fears. She suddenly understood why she didn't seek validation from her outside world. Why seek validation from a patriarchal system that didn't respect her gender or sex? And was driven by perceptions of value that not only marginalized her worth but, also required her to prove it constantly!?

That revelation shook her, and for a long time she sat contemplating the fallen state of her past life. And yet, she couldn't deny being inspired by the new insights being gained on her quest. It contrasted sharply with her constant anxiety in the past. And yet, the new beginning inspiring her couldn't emerge, without the demise of her past! She sighed. *Nothing was adding up! Her thoughts were saying one thing, and she was feeling something completely, different!* Despite the immense, infinity of the Universe, and the obvious power latent in every atom, there was a simplicity to nature. But, nothing was as random as it appeared. There was an invisible "order" to the perceived chaos. And remarkably, there was nothing at the core of every atom except, empty infinite, timeless space. And more space, surrounding every particle within each atom, vibrating at breathtaking speeds in an electromagnetic field that echoed the same essence of life present throughout the Universe. And yet, when anything was subjected to scrutiny at a point in physical time, everything appeared motionless. And structured. Controlled. Even more remarkable, was that notwithstanding the nothingness at a microscopic-level, everything in nature was bursting with endless, abundant creation. If so much could be created from uncontrolled nothingness in the Universe, why was her human existence so unnecessarily complicated? Why was it impossible to meet the most basic of human needs in a physical world controlled by man? Granted, there was some progress over the centuries. But, how much of that "progress" was essential to sustaining, and supporting life on the planet? And compared to the natural order of the Universe which selflessly, supported all life, man-made "progress" depleted, and hastened the planet's demise with the deluge of toxic waste generated each year! Who was responsible? Those in positions of power who continued abusing the trust of billions of people? Or the people themselves, who continued to put their trust in those who continued to destroy life on this planet? How was it possible, for such systems, and structures to continue on the grounds of market demand when that "market" wasn't even a true reflection of what was needed to sustain all life forms!? Who decided to keep such systems, and structures operational? Who decided that upholding a farce was more important than life itself? Was any one life more important than another's? Based on what belief? By what right? How did the simple right of all life forms sharing this planet become so convoluted, because of an insatiable desire for more power, and material wealth? She groaned when she realized that she'd fallen prey to the same mentality. Why was she blind to her behavior for so long? How much of her life was lived by her soul's blueprint, and how much of it had been decided for her by her conditioning? How could she break those destructive patterns, and fully align herself with her truth? After all, it was the only "plan" being directed by her soul, and supported by the Universe.

[A critical question. It's not that you didn't see it - you refused to acknowledge it. And the refusal to accept the greater wisdom of your soul is the reason for your inner conflict. Remember that feeling - it will keep you moving closer to your truth. For now, let's stay with you. Turn your attention inward. You still need to heal the separation within yourself]

She could relate to what Voice was saying. On more than one occasion, she'd felt that urge of being silently drawn towards something. She didn't know what it was so she'd ignored it. It was just a……..a…..feeling. She believed that it had no substance, because she couldn't identify it. It had no name or origin. And she had no time for fanciful notions. It didn't pay the bills.

[And everything that you did in your physical world had substance? It gave you the meaning that you so desperately desired in your soul? Nothing built on fear will ever be a suitable substitute for what truly inspires your soul]

She sighed and bowed her head. Fully aware that the reality she'd devoted so much effort to constructing was slowly dissipating around her. It was easier to acknowledge now, with the insights that she'd gained so far. She realized that her newfound awareness of her truth had shattered a belief that she'd used to hold her past reality together. She now sat facing the mirage that she'd slept through her entire life - thinking that she was wide awake! She no longer felt any inclination to hide or avoid what was staring back at her. Could she uproot her conditioned self? Could she change her life? What would she gain if she did this?

[Nothing important by your previous calculations. But, you'll gain the one thing you need to live the life you deserve - your truth. You've never known your true Self although, you've encountered glimpses of your truth during moments of inspiration. There's nothing - no one - to compare your true Self with. There's nothing against which you can reference the value or worth of your truth. It's priceless, nonetheless. It offers you a way of life that you've never experienced before. A life of inspired choices, powered by your full potential]

Voice was still not listening to her. She'd never done anything like this before! What did she have to do to get there? Where did she start?

[Your excuses only make you own your limitations, and make you feel less than your true Self. You're keeping your physical body in a lower sate of vibration. You'll be able to better discern that by focusing on how your thoughts are affecting your feelings. You're already 'doing' what you need to do. Continue listening to your soul's voice in the stillness within; tune into the silent, melody of your heart. There's nothing to be gained by reaching outside of yourself. However, everything becomes possible in each moment that you choose to be present with your Self. No decision or deliberate action, is necessary on your part. The only thing required, is your presence. There is no 'right' or 'wrong' way to accomplish this; just follow the knowing of your soul. Trust that; trust your Self. It's not easy to let go of your past but, there are many changes occurring throughout your lower four-body system to bring it into alignment with your soul purpose – even though you're not aware of it. Eventually, when you least expect it you'll transition from your old self to your true Self. No part of you can be left behind - you're in the process of calling all the lost parts of your soul back to you. Irrespective, of how long ago you lost touch with them. Trust your Self, even if you don't fully understand what you're doing. There are no signposts along the way; take heed of your feelings as you make your way through this quest. There's nothing of value to be gained - as defined in your physical world - by doing this. There will be no accolades, if you complete it. You'll only transform yourself into your true Self - the person you were born to be. That will be your only "reward"]

She rubbed her hands roughly over her face to brush away her tears. For the first time in her life she found herself wishing that someone would rescue her. Without being aware of it she once again, gave away her power. And her mind took the opportunity to regain control. *A silent call? What was that? No known goals!? On her way to some unknown, destination? No reward? No map, other than her emotions! And a silent, inner voice that only her heart could interpret! What was she supposed to listen out for? What did a "silent voice" sound like!? She wished that there was some way of dealing with this situation. Once, and for all.*

[This isn't something you 'deal with' or negotiate your way around. You need to stay present, and heed your soul's voice. It's not something that you 'hear.' You'll 'feel' it in your heart space. Your heart will help you to interpret your soul's messages, to get you through your quest. It goes beyond logical understanding, and the power of your will – you can't control it. But, you already know how to go about doing what you need to do - you have access to a wisdom outside the limitations of time. You aren't required to prove anything, least of all your worthiness. Nothing needs to be forced. Living life at your full potential has nothing to do with the results that show up in your physical world. Now it's about releasing your expectations of any outcome. Whatever your path is, it will naturally unfold in your physical world – by standing in your truth. You don't have to think about becoming someone in your world – you already are who you need to be. Everything you're doing now, is in preparation for walking your soul path. You'll always know what to do - you're never alone. You'll be guided by your soul - it's 'voice' is always present. Tune into it with your open heart. This might be difficult for you to comprehend now but, you'll remember it when you 'hear' it. There's no way you can miss it - it's unmistakable. You've heard the call before but, you ignored it. If you continue ignoring it, whatever you manifest in your physical world will only be a shadow – a pseudo-reality flirting with the borders of your consciousness. An enticing game for your ego but, it will never satisfy your soul. However, if you embrace the calling, and trust in it implicitly, you'll merge with the miracle of life that flows through you. You'll transcend the borders of your previous reality, and enter a higher level of consciousness to co-create your true reality. It's excruciating but, let go of your past. Trust the space that you're now in. You're connected to all that is Divine within you; in the entire Universe]

She recalled many an occasion when she'd felt that invisible, tug-of-war within herself. Generally, it followed those rare moments of solitude, when she was forced to down tools, and remove herself from her physical world. Despite her best efforts to suppress it that inner war persisted, and had found some way to spill out of her, and mess things up. As was evident from her past reality. How could she have ignored something so obvious?

She recalled trying to counter her inner turmoil by burying herself in something else. *What was it?* She paused. And then she was struck by the memory of a long-forgotten, pastime. Her poetry! She smiled wistfully as she remembered some of the poems that she'd written over the years. She'd felt truly inspired during those moments. She tilted her head to the side, and gazed thoughtfully into the nothingness as she tried to dislodge some memory tickling the edges of her mind. She drew in a sharp breath. She recalled a poem that she'd written as a child. It had no title. In it, she'd described a force, far bigger than anything she could imagine. The words had been discarded as mere fantasy but, every living thing reminded her of it. She felt it touching her skin in the rays of sunlight dancing through the leaves of the eucalyptus trees that lined the road she used, on her way home from school. She was struck by a revelation. Despite the prominent focus of other events over the years, she'd been unknowingly, moving towards the reality of those words. Did that poem have something to do with her soul path? Was that the reason the truth of her words had remained alive over the years, even though she'd never given it a second thought? She raised her hands, and crossed them over her heart to express her gratitude to her unknown soul for guiding her towards her truth. She felt so guilty; ashamed of the arrogance that had blinded her to the Source of the very meaning that she'd been searching for. And yet, in the same breath, she couldn't help feeling exhilarated. Suddenly, there was an unrivalled sense of anticipation for all that she didn't yet know about her Self, and her true purpose. There was so much more to her Self – so much more to her life! She would never have believed it possible. Whatever she thought lost was actually, not lost at all! Her soul's purpose – her true reality – still lay within her. She was trembling with anticipation at the thought of finally, living her truth – living a life of meaning. She felt as though she was going to burst from joy. Her heart was pumping furiously - overflowing with love, and inspiration. A love that she'd searched for, all her life. Only to find it within her Self! And despite the odds, she'd found an inner sanctum that remained connected to her unknown soul – this life essence that was every bit a part of her, as it was of the entire Universe. She sighed. Such a gift - she could now live her life free of the shadows from her past.

With this new perspective, her illusory past was further dismantled. She realized that she'd acted out her life as though she was in a theatrical drama of some kind. There were so many masks that she'd used to fit in, manipulate or control any number of situations. All the time, keeping her thoughts, and feelings safely hidden from view. Those masks might have helped her survive in her physical world but, not one of them had survived the onslaught of the truth that she was uncovering in the nothingness. It dawned on her that irrespective, of what others saw or whether they knew of her deception was unimportant. She was aware of it! Her soul knew! If she wanted to change her life, then she had to drop the masks. Her physical self had to first, and foremost be aligned with her truth. She didn't need to act out some role - she just needed to stay in alignment with her truth. Suddenly, all that appeared so wrong about her quest now felt very right. As unbelievable as the nothingness was, it now looked more real than her old reality. She still had no idea where she was or where she was going but, she now knew that she somehow had a hand all those years ago, in creating her quest when she'd silently, communed with the Universe with her poem. How she could have lived a life interwoven between her old self, and true Self was beyond her comprehension. One helped her build an illusory reality, and the other had slowly directed her towards her unknown truth. She would probably never understand it. But, understanding was no longer important. All that mattered was that somehow in all the chaos, and uncertainty - in the endless nothingness – she'd found her stillness; her peace. She felt happier than she'd ever felt before. She felt safe. She felt loved. She smiled. This must be what "home" truly, felt like! And she was, nowhere! With no one – just her Self! Her past lay in tatters - strewn all along the memory lane that she'd travelled, thus far. She could no longer relate to it. Neither could she relate to the person that she used to be. And yet, in the nothingness she felt more her Self than she'd ever felt!

And then she had another startling revelation. The more open she became in the nothingness, the more real she felt. She could now recall aspects of her life at will, while remaining in her stillness. She didn't have to expend any effort on ignoring her thoughts or emotions. Neither did she have to shut herself off from them. She could just be present with whatever she was thinking, and feeling, and not get caught in the maze in her mind. She sighed with relief. She felt as though, a huge burden was lifted off her shoulders. She felt exhilarated. She'd never felt so free; so fully alive. It contrasted so sharply with the way she remembered herself that she could now clearly discern how far removed she'd been from her soul's light. Again, she wondered what could have caused her to dissociate from life to such an extent that she'd existed as a mere shadow, of her true Self. Whatever had caused it, must have happened quite early in childhood for her to be unaware of it. She couldn't help feeling saddened by everything that had gone on in her past. And yet, she was overwhelmed by how blessed she felt. Truly blessed. For somehow, despite everything, something or someone had helped her release her illusory life, and take that invisible, step towards her true path. Had that something or someone been outside or inside of her? Was there an "outside" or an "inside?" Probably not – not if the essence of life flowed freely through everything. Perhaps there were no boundaries – physical or otherwise. If there were, they existed only in her mind. She might have lived the life that she thought she wanted but, her soul had guided her onto the path she needed to follow. Even though, she had no idea what it was.

She realized that whomever or whatever she'd anguished over before, no longer served her highest path. But, every experience, either good or bad had something to teach her - about her true Self. And experiences were repeated, until she learnt the soul lessons that she came into this physical realm to learn. She realized that she'd attained exactly, what she set out to achieve in her physical world - a meaningless life, because she wasn't in her truth! And she'd gone on with her unconscious outward search not realizing that what she was looking for, could only be found within. And because she'd never loved herself, she didn't know that she was, enough – just the way she was born. Her experiences not matching her expectations was purely a case of a bullying ego, and her low self-esteem. It meant that she would have to admit that she was wrong about what she wanted. She didn't think her ego had the stomach to admit that! Now she saw with blinding clarity that her physical life had turned pear-shaped, because it was the furthest thing from what her soul desired. She sighed. *Writing a poem might have led her closer to her truth but, where to now? What was her purpose? How did she fulfill it?*

She frowned. She detected that she was feeling lost, and overwhelmed. She turned inwards, and centered herself once more, in her stillness. She felt totally, at peace! And there was no underlying anxiety about her "future." For some reason, that word now jarred her senses. She realized just how indoctrinated she was by time. She'd either ruminated over some past event in her life or worked on some scenario for a future that stretched interminably in front of her! She'd never been present! And she'd always thought of past, and future as distinct, phases in time. Now however, they felt anything but, separate. Both were swirling around the exact moment, in which she found herself. She felt a profound sense of oneness with her Self – in the same way that she felt with the nothingness around her. She felt as though she was floating……no…..flying! Encompassed in that oneness was a silent, open invitation to be all that still lay undiscovered within her. Without further thought, she closed her eyes and "launched" herself into the nothingness, and whirled about fearlessly. Her body felt light; she felt so free. She could barely contain the joy emanating from her entire Being. She felt as though her body disintegrated into a billion stars that shot off into a myriad, different directions! Within her stillness she could feel all of her flying to the furthest reaches of the nothingness; sparkling, and shining her light into its blackness. And then, she was hit by a blinding clarity. She was everywhere, and nowhere - all at once! She reveled in her knowing, and laughed from somewhere deep within her soul. She "heard" the sound echoing across all of eternity. She smiled. She was home - at peace. She'd never felt so whole - as one, with her Self. She felt as though she was standing at the very edge of unbecoming and becoming, at the same time. She felt totally, alive. She wanted to stay there, forever. She felt like forever! She shouted out into the nothingness: "I am forever. I am all that Is." All billion pieces of her, scattered across the infinite nothingness heard her at the same time, and twinkled gloriously to the "sound" of her voice.

[Now that you've discovered your true home, it's time for you to go back]

All of her froze instantly, in mid-flight. *No! No! Never! Why on earth must she go back? She'd found everything – her home - in the nothingness. There was nothing for her in the physical world. She would never leave the nothingness. Never! It was the only place that she wanted to be. Always! She would never give it up.*

[You have to go back, one more time – to reclaim a part of you that's still trapped in darkness. Without fully integrating all the lost parts of your soul, you won't be able to live a life embodying your full potential in the physical realm, and achieve your purpose. Your physical life is far from over – you can't live it here. But, no matter where you are, what you've discovered here will always be with you. You'll always be one with the nothingness – in your stillness]

She was trembling with rage. *She didn't want to go back! This was home now.*

[Your home will always be within you. You'll take it wherever you go. But, the human experience of your soul can only be fulfilled in your physical world. There can be no compromises with your soul's truth – in any dimension. Your rage has nothing to do with going back. It's an indication that you still have something to heal within you. All the barriers that you've used to shield yourself from your core wound have been removed. It's now time to face it]

No! There was nothing more! She was done with this healing stuff!

[That's your ego talking. Your truth can be found in the stillness within]

She turned inward. And immediately, felt her resistance to what she heard Voice saying. Something was still there. That void was not gone!

[You must go back to release yourself from its hold. If you don't, a part of you will forever, be lost]

Something in what Voice said resonated strongly with her. She was aware of a distinct niggling - something in her past was still holding her back. She took a deep breath, and closed her eyes. She felt into her rage and resistance, and gently breathed into her heart space to embrace her emotions. It wasn't long, before she felt herself open to her fiery anger. And felt all billion pieces of her floating amongst the stars, die a billion deaths! She couldn't believe that she'd descended into darkness again! She collapsed into an exhausted heap. Yet another "road" that ended up nowhere! She realized just how strongly she was attached to some kind of outcome. But, there was no change! The nothingness endured. *What next? She was desperate for a visible shift - for closure with the old, and a brand new beginning. She wished for all the twists, and turns to stop. She wanted some certainty; some stability. Some reassurance. This quest was an ongoing rollercoaster of endings, and false beginnings! Would she ever find some security? Could something lasting come from all this nothingness?*

Undefined

[Your need for security under the current circumstances is understandable but, nothing in your physical world is meant to last. Your only safety zone is your inner light – it's the only constant. And you're close to fully uncovering it. What you see around you now, is all that Is. When you manifest your purpose in your physical world it will be a part of this space - always. You'll feel 'forever' – limitless - in whatever you create from your heart space. That feeling will outlast your physical existence - it's outside time and space]

She felt flat. Joyless. Empty. From feeling as one, and dancing with the stars; feeling love, and joy……feeling inspired……feeling the kiss of eternity…..coming face-to-face with her immortal soul ….. she was now back to ……to ……living the rest of her life, in her physical world! She felt like she was drowning in heartache, and disillusionment. *How could she let go of the only real home she'd ever known? What was her truth, anyway? What was her purpose? She didn't even know what she was going back for!*

[Your truth is the inner light that guides you throughout your lifetime. It's the highest form of your energy - your soul vibrating at your unique, frequency. Light is the only aspect of the Universe that has been constant, since the dawn of creation. But, it's also present within you. You'll always know when you move away from it - by the way you feel. Stay true to it. Create your true reality by using your inner light to guide you, and you'll always carry with you what you have now. Irrespective, of where you find yourself in your physical world. Your physical life is about maintaining your inner harmony through non-attachment. But, your inner light is the essence of life itself. It's part of you. It's indestructible]

The little "stars" that had broken away from her to light up the nothingness just a short while ago, now "gathered," and merged with her body once again, as though beckoned by a silent call. It was time. Except, she didn't know for what. She'd already committed to this quest, and had come a long way, even though there was no way of telling how far she'd travelled. She only sensed that she was light years away from the person she used to be. How hard could going back be, after everything that she'd already been through? Besides, what did she have to lose? Whatever or whoever she was now must be very different. She needed to trust that she was ready to face the last remaining thread of her past, and free her Self.

Despite her anxiety, she now wanted more than anything to complete her quest. If that was the only way she could fully embody her soul's light, then she had to persist. If she needed to reclaim the last part of her soul before she could create the inner reality lying dormant within her, then there was only one thing to do – go back. Why settle for a small, limited life when her soul desired a more fulfilling, heartfelt life? She felt her heart leap with joy. She filled with a yearning to fully live her soul's desires in her physical world – whatever they might be. After all, she was separated from the Universe by her birth into this physical realm, with only that purpose within her soul. Whether she had other lifetimes was immaterial. She wanted to reach her highest potential, and live fully alive in this one. And she would be true to it – even if she had to devote her last breath to it.

[You will - eventually. It's the only 'trade' that the Universe will accept in return for the gift of life; the last breath from that inner sanctum of truth, that unites your soul to all that Is]

"I'll go back" she said.

[Mindful intention meets with your soul's truth in your heart space. And so it is. You won't be alone – not if you remain within the love, and light of your soul. You'll always be home]

"I know that now" she said. And she felt her heart burst into a billion stars as it danced to hear her speak her truth for the very first time.

CHAPTER 12

THE CAVE

She turned her longing gaze to the stars, and drew their comforting embrace tightly around her. She couldn't grasp her state of mind or her feelings. Thoughts, and emotion that had been suppressed for far too long, collided within her with all the force of an erupting volcano. She realized that she was in the midst of something profound and yet, she couldn't suppress her annoyance at failing to make any sense of it. Her continued isolation wasn't helping - or so she thought. And she suspected that Voice, like Glow were somehow colluding to confuse the hell out of her! But, despite the chaos in her mind, and the pain in her body she couldn't ignore her awareness of the expanding stillness within. It convinced her that she was exactly where she needed to be. And that she'd been moving towards this quest all her life. Irrespective of where her unconscious meanderings had taken her in her physical world. There was no defining moment for this new belief. Somehow, all the pieces of her past had collapsed, and landed exactly where she now found herself. For someone who had defined life by action, and rationality alone this quest defied all logic. But, she was no longer phased by that. Her only focus was on remaining centered in her stillness. And feeling grateful. That still, silent space was miraculously holding all the shattered pieces of her past life together.

She also discovered that within the stillness, she could easily connect with that sense of oneness. *Was it outside or within her?* Was her heart opening a little more, as she transcended each layer of her past in the nothingness? She couldn't help being entranced by its lack of boundaries. There was nothing to do or see and yet, she had a sense of wholeness, and fullness; a sense of abundance encompassing everything in the Universe. She couldn't even begin to imagine a Universe of unlimited abundance. And everything was part of that unknown mystery of life – a single, seamless, invisible ocean, including herself. And something magical was unfolding in that mystical space. She didn't know what it was but, she couldn't help feeling that she was partaking in something Divine. She inhaled that amazing feeling slowly, and felt every part of her awaken to its epic wonder. That sense of wonder felt like everything that she'd described so many years ago in her poem without fully comprehending the magic behind her words. And now, she was living it. She was humbled by the profound power of her innocent words. What had inspired her to write about something that she had no knowledge of? How was it possible for those words to manifest as her quest, above everything else that she'd willfully set out to achieve in her life? She could find no answers. The only thing possible in that moment was sitting completely still, and allowing her gratitude to flood every fiber of her body. As broken as she felt, she couldn't deny the sense of being wholly contained within that empty spaciousness within. She felt so at peace. So fulfilled. There was no urge to look for anything; go anywhere or be anyone else. For the first time, she felt utter contentment. She sighed, blissfully. This feeling of home within herself, felt so good! So safe. She felt as though, she'd come full circle in her quest – her broken, painful past helping her to find self-love by uncovering her true Self. *Reaching this sense of knowing must be the reason for her return. She'd attained her ultimate goal of finding the home that she'd been looking for, her entire life! Finally!*

[Your soul's quest is not over - yet. And for as long as you hold onto a specific outcome, you'll remain separated from your truth, and full alignment with your soul purpose. Your quest just marks the 'end' of your conditioned way of existence, and the 'beginning' of life as an awakened soul. But, there are no 'endings' or 'beginnings' for your soul - only an endless now. Don't waste your time trying to figure it out. Just be present with your feelings right now. Feel into the infinite, spaciousness of your opening heart; feel into the oneness with your Self, your soul – all of your Being. That feeling is the ultimate form of power that flows throughout the Universe. It's not at all like the horizontal form of power that you're familiar with in your physical world. That only entails exercising your will, and strength to move along a linear path in your physical world. The power that you're feeling within your stillness, travels across all dimensions - across time and space. It's limitless - it spans all Universes. But, it can't be accessed or understood by your mind. It can only be accessed when the channel between your Being, and the Universe is opened to actualize your soul purpose. To access it, you need to fully release the impact of your past conditioning on your lower physical body, and abide fully in your Being. You'll know it by the way you feel – there'll be no boundaries between your physical body, and your Being. Remain in your stillness – as the observer. No matter what's going on in our mind, and body. When you're fully present, your physical body will be in resonance with your soul. And when you become one with your unique level of vibration, you'll be able to access the true reality within your soul. That's the 'key' you've been seeking for many lifetimes. Your old reality no longer exists. Whatever remnants of memory remain will eventually, fade from your conscious mind. And your physical body will be the vehicle to manifest your soul purpose - marking the dawn of your new beginning. Except, there's nothing new about it. You've always had access to it. You couldn't see it, because you were blocked by your illusory reality]

[Where you find yourself now - in this space spanning the almost ended, and the almost new – you have to make the ultimate, choice to free yourself from the shackles of illusion. Consciously. You have to take a leap of faith - into nothing. But, it's far from nothing – it's the opportunity you've been waiting for, for lifetimes. It's the nothing that connects you to your soul purpose, and your limitless potential. It can't be defined by rational thought – no matter how liberal your thinking. Your mind will always be confined by its need to understand. As demonstrated by your past. As much as you believed in how 'right' your approach to life was, you merely conformed to the conditioned stereotypes in your world. Pursuing your ego-based goals did give you a certain degree of satisfaction but, brought you no lasting fulfillment. Your old identity suppressed your uniqueness. And your ego helped you to deny your true worth. Your conditioning blocked you from your true purpose; from accessing your full potential. You were always searching for something more, because you were being called by your soul fulfill your purpose. So the harder you tried to defy your truth by holding onto your illusions, the greater was your loss, and suffering. Don't waste your time trying to build a legacy in the physical realm – that's your ego's desire. If you want to leave a timeless, legacy then walk your soul path]

She lowered her gaze with embarrassment. She'd always considered attaining her goals, her top priority. And they might have been but, any goal that compromised her truth could never compare to realizing her soul purpose, and feeling fully alive - even if that feeling lasted a single moment. She didn't need a lifetime of meaningless events – only a single, moment of being one with all that Is. She shook her head morosely. She could have had a very different life experience. Instead, she'd wasted her time, and energy on the small, limited existence offered her conditioned mind. She'd been re-living the same experiences, and fighting the same battles! Now she could see how much easier those battles were, compared to the real challenge of living with an open heart, and being the conscious observer. It wasn't only about trusting her Self but, trusting life – a force as powerful, as it was unknown. It struck her that such an approach defied any form of control or prediction. The unknown would always be, unknown. And yet, it held the secret to living the life that her soul yearned for. She could do any number of things in her physical, human existence but, whatever she chose to do couldn't be at the expense of her truth. That revelation shook her. But, there was no reprieve on the rollercoaster careening through her past. She was hit by another revelation – just how predictable her life had been. She knew the outcome of every challenge that she'd undertaken, before she even started! And the consistency with which she attained her expected outcome had no doubt, contributed to her arrogance and complacency.

Her head dropped in shame. She knew absolutely nothing, about anything that truly mattered in life! She realized that complacency had kept her in auto-pilot mode. And that explained why nothing she'd done, truly challenged or inspired her. What did she gain from such haste, besides the adrenaline-high of chasing one arbitrary goal after another!? And repeating the meaningless, round-a-bout ego trip that kept her fixated on the illusion of success! She realized that always choosing to do something with her life – anything that came to mind – had lulled her into believing that she was manifesting the "plan" for her life. All she'd done was suppress the anxiety that she didn't have a clue about what she truly needed to live her best life! How could she be so dumb? Although, she had to admire her conniving ego for promoting its own interests! To such an extent that she'd remained lost in Self-denial! But, life certainly had no intention of complying with her ego's plan or indulging the maze of delusion that she'd become lost in. Acknowledging her complacency triggered greater clarity. She could now see the many loopholes in her logic. They were openly visible - if she'd taken the time to look at her behavior. Instead she was too busy congratulating herself on her "progress!" She'd believed that her plan was simple. And foolproof. In reality, all she'd done was maintain the status quo of her childhood conditioning! She wondered to what extent her conditioning had influenced her thinking. Going by the insights that she'd gained in the nothingness, she'd been triggered to react in certain ways by her conditioning. She sighed. It struck her that pursuing that line of thought was a further waste of her energy. In that moment, she was certain of two things. Her old way of behavior no longer served her, and she was responsible for her choices - conditioned or not. The only important thing was that she was now aware of it. And that she could now see straight through any attempts by her ego to deceive her.

    With her new-found insight came a deep compassion for herself. She now knew that the only thing she could do was accept the choices that she'd made, and the self who had made them. She might not be able to relate to that person anymore but, her old self and the new Self she was in the process of uncovering were somehow all wrapped up together, in a single soul. Resisting to recognize either one was futile – her inner world would always be at a deficit. She sighed. *Was it possible to integrate all of her, and live a different life? Could she still transform into her true Self, after all this time?* Perhaps it wasn't about changing herself but, allowing herself to embody her true Self. Besides, now that she was aware of her past behavior, she could no longer bear the thought of going back to the life that she had. And the "future" that was curated by her past conditioning no longer had any meaning, in the light of that knowing. Her soul was now, her only north star. If returning to her old way of life meant that she would continue running around the proverbial hamster wheel, then she had only one choice - she had to complete her quest. Nothing else, felt relevant within her heart space. She heaved a huge sigh of relief, as she felt the burden of doubt lift from her shoulders. She felt different - something had shifted with her decision. *What now?* She still felt a strong urge to continue digging through that black void within. *Which parts of herself did she have to discard? Which parts did she need to keep? She couldn't just throw it all out! This was her life! How could she stop mid-stream, and expect to change everything about herself? Did she have the time, money, and energy to start all over again?* For a moment, she indulged her mind. *There were an endless number of scenarios for the kind of life she would like to have - once her quest was over. If only she had the financial means to achieve it. But, she had nothing to her name, anymore. Life seemed determined to punish her or teach her a lesson! Or both! Why was this happening to her? Why now?*

She again sought refuge in the familiarity of her thoughts, and labored over the sequence of life events that she'd been bombarded with over the past few years. She recalled the escalating mayhem, until she could no longer think straight. She realized that some part of her must have recognized that her life was in a mess but, denial was far easier to accept than acknowledging she was fallible. So she'd focused on reinstating some semblance of normality in the physical life that she felt slipping from her grasp. But, no matter how hard she tried or how tightly she held on to any person or circumstance, each willful attempt ended in failure, and misery. And the more effort she put into finding new opportunities, the faster they slipped through her fingers. At some point, it dawned on her that her situation was worse than anything she'd encountered before. Still, she persisted with her efforts. But, despite giving it her all, her life continued to fall apart. Finally, she gave up. And fell apart. It wasn't just a case of feeling beaten. For the first time in her life, she found herself without hope. Far worse, was the utter lack of motivation to do anything. To someone who had always fought so hard to build a life that feeling was tantamount to death itself.

She closed her eyes as an avalanche of memories threatened to overwhelm her. She reached into the loving embrace of the stillness within. It gave her what she was looking for - the strength to continue digging through that black void. She recalled that she'd resorted to the one thing that she was familiar with – her unloving behavior. And directed her anger, and frustration towards the person closest to her – herself! She hacked away at the life choices that she'd made. She was adamant about finding answers for a life that had gone so horribly wrong. But, her usual approach only led to more locked doors, until finally, she was left facing her victim-mentality. At some point, she stopped digging through her experiences out of sheer exhaustion. She sighed. She was going around in circles! Again! But, she consoled herself with the knowledge that if she still felt so strongly about her past, then there must be something more to heal. She allowed her memories to resume. She recalled the strong feelings of hopelessness, and powerlessness - feelings that were alien to her. And then, she remembered doing something that she'd never done before. She unconsciously stopped resisting her feelings, and sat with them - her sense of defeat, her only companion. She shivered, as the full weight of that memory hit home. But, that wasn't all of it! She was given a front-row seat - to watch her life falling apart! She was petrified as the destruction of her life continued without reprieve. She'd never felt so alone – so small - in her entire life.

She returned her gaze to the nothingness. Again, she was struck by the thought that for all her attempts at a happier life, her actual experience was a far cry from that. She felt like screaming! *She'd been down this road already! What more did she have to gain by revisiting it? Why was she stuck there?* She was hit by a weird insight. Why was she resisting the one thing she wanted to change about her life – the pain? If nothing existed in her outer reality anymore, perhaps she should turn towards it! Counter-intuitive? Yes! *But, what else could she do? Nothing was shifting in the nothingness!* She was again, caught in that empty space between two worlds. She sighed. The only way forward was to go back. She felt the stirring of a strange emotion deep within. *Why not? What did she have to lose?* She had nothing to her name; no title, no home, no car, no money, no partner. No future. No past. And no identity. With the acknowledgement of her truth, something slowly gave way inside of her, and she felt herself drop into another layer deep within her. The black void went far deeper than she suspected. It sucked her mercilessly into the depths of a darkness that she'd never encountered before. And she'd experienced many dark nights of the soul during her life! She felt herself freefalling - drowning in her powerlessness to control any of it. She watched helplessly, as a life that was held in such high regard flashed in front of her - crowned by so much pain, defeat, loss, and betrayal. The remnants of memory over the emotional turmoil of each experience swirled around her, as she hurtled through the darkness. At the "end" of each event she'd miraculously surfaced, believing that she'd survived her ordeal. She realized, however, that she'd only distracted herself from the reality of her circumstances by doing what she'd always done – directing her attention outwards, to force some change in her life. The only exception to the number of scenarios that she'd conjured up to deceive herself was the death of her father. Then her life, and the world as she'd known it did change. Suddenly. Everything ceased to exist. It dawned on her that despite the changes to her external world she'd remained in a kind of "bubble" throughout her life. All she'd done was move around in it, accumulating more pain and grief, until there was no more space to contain her. Clarity slowly surfaced from the murky depths below. Her father's death was the catalyst that had pierced that bubble.

The sudden jarring pain in her chest made her realize that she'd drifted back into the realm of her mind. She was still desperately trying to connect all the dots. And still trying to make some sense of the life that was the closest thing to her and yet, after all this time, she was forced to admit that she was still unable to gain any substantial insight into the soul that took every breath – just for her. It was all the more frustrating, because the answer she was looking for was probably staring her in the face! She loved a challenge. She knew that much about herself. But, this quest was something, totally different. The challenge facing her now wasn't something that she'd encountered in her external world. It was her Self! And despite her being the only embodiment of that Self, she had yet, to understand or fully uncover it. Even more confounding was her recent insight that she was the only one who could solve the conundrum presented by her quest. She was now convinced that whatever she was going through wasn't some random coincidence. Her quest couldn't have just "happened" to her. She didn't believe in coincidences. And she didn't do complicated. But, more than anything, she hated loose ends. She was hell-bent on finding an explanation or a solution to get her out of the nothingness. She might not have seen the loose thread before but, she couldn't help thinking that her father's death had yanked it loose from the carefully crafted tapestry that she'd called "life." While she was performing his last rites, she had the distinct impression of the "threads" slowly unraveling, until they lay in a mottled heap at her feet. She sighed. *She was going around in circles! She needed answers! Voice did say she had to return. But, for what?*

[Why do you think that you need to connect the dots? You've contained your life within so many physical structures, and defined it by a man-made system that dictates the order of everything. Do you believe that approach will help you fulfill your soul purpose? Those structures, and systems might have helped you before but, they no longer serve you as an awakening soul. Your soul already knows that. It's the reason you started withdrawing from your old way of life. Your mind would never have given you the space needed to pursue your quest. Your isolation is part of process. It's the only way the Universe can support you on your quest. You're being forced to limit distractions from your outside world - to allow you to access the volume of information from within, and around you. You're moving away from the worldly 'order' of things, towards a very different order - one that you can't control or decipher with intellect alone. You may refer to it as 'Divine-order' if you must but, this isn't an order from something or someone outside of yourself. It's coming directly from your own soul. And only your heart can help you translate it, in any meaningful way - if you have the courage to trust, and follow it. But, don't try to understand it. After all, it takes the part of you that has always been a mystery, to help you live the ultimate, mystery – life itself. By surrendering to the unknown – becoming one with it. Only then will you allow for the opening of a channel that connects your heart, and soul to your Being - to the entire Universe. You can choose to access that channel in your physical world at any time - through your open heart space. That channel has been blocked by your conditioning. And it will remain so, no matter how many iterations of a false reality you force-feed yourself in your physical world. You can break that cycle by uncovering your truth, and fulfilling your purpose. Your soul's reality is your one true reality, after you've awakened from the dream – the illusion of your physical world]

[This doesn't mean that you should deny yourself any of the experiences in your physical world but, let those be experiences that nourish your soul. You can no longer deny one, for the other. Your physical life isn't the playground for your ego's desires. It exists to help you realize your soul purpose in this physical dimension. Your ego keeps your mind locked onto illusion – on all that you can define using logic. However, once you learn how to harness your ego in service of your soul purpose, it plays a critical role to help you actualize it. It will help you process what you observe as you walk your soul path in your physical world. Your many attempts to define, and confine yourself with labels to fit into a false reality are only indications of the extent of your ego's control over you. Ultimately, that causes an imbalance within you. The pendulum of your emotions, and thoughts will continue swinging between extremes – exposing you to a host of experiences that leave you feeling more hurt, and confused. But, you now have the knowing of your stillness. And of being the observer of your life experience. You are that still, nothingness – not your feelings, thoughts, beliefs or any aspect of an identity that you can attach to. Your truth, and stillness are synonymous with each other. Attachment only leaves you embroiled in convoluted scenarios of manifesting your ego-reality in your outer world. It abandons you to an ever-increasing vortex of self-doubt, and negativity; it makes you believe that you're a failure. In doing so, however, you negate an obvious truth. The ego-reality you're pursuing is not real for you. As counter-intuitive as that sounds, you need to fully let go of your past before you can awaken to your truth. It's all you need to manifest the reality that you've been searching for. The life that you desire is far from lost. It still exists within you, and you can access it within that silent, stillness – nothingness - within you. Stop hoping for your life to be anything other than a reflection of the Being that you are. There are no labels in your physical world that can contain or define your Being. And the fear that it will unfold in your physical world, as anything other than the love and light that you are, is unwarranted. Trust, and believe in your Self. Have faith in the unknown; in the nothingness. Nothing exists outside your truth – your stillness. And nothing else is required to facilitate the transition from your old self to your true Self; from the past to the future that you're worthy of]

[Your inner dissatisfaction stems from the fact that you've always been aware of your soul purpose and yet, you persisted in pursuing a life that is so much less than your truth. You dug yourself into a deeper hole by over-compensating for your perceived 'smallness.' There's nothing small about your true Self but, your ego would like you to believe that - so it can feed your insecurities with delusions of progress. But, in all of this, you didn't do anything 'wrong.' The only 'scenario' you didn't consider was that your soul already knows you weren't living your truth. It knows that you've been sabotaging yourself. Denying your truth has kept you going around in circles all your life - over many lifetimes. You can make any number of compromises or excuses in your physical world to deny your true Self but, eventually, you will come up against that Self. However, if you truly embody your soul purpose, there will be no need for compromises or excuses. All dimensions will converge within your Being to help you realize your purpose. For all worlds are one within you, and accessible through your truth. Your human experience isn't a separate part of you or confined to your outside world. It's an extension of your soul – of your life path here on earth. Your physical and spiritual paths are one, and the same]

[You might be able to create any number of false realities in your physical world by wearing various masks but, you can only create your true reality by aligning with your soul purpose. And that's only possible, once you drop all the masks that you've been wearing over the years. You became so entranced with your ego's many plots, and sub-plots for a life that you completely, lost sight of the real show - the realization of your soul purpose in your physical world. This physical dimension exists to help you witness the manifestation of that purpose, and to experience your true Self through your human eyes. Your soul already knows who you are. Your mind, however, has no idea. It can only give meaning to something that it has already experienced within the boundaries of your five physical senses. And it does so by using its existing patterns to frame your perceptions of the incident. If your mind is averse to accepting your sixth sense, it would be near impossible for it to accept your Being or a form of potential that extends beyond its capability. Especially not, with an ego standing guard at its doorway. However, whether or not your mind accepts who you truly are, there's no amount of money that will assuage the inner conflict within you if you continue ignoring your soul purpose] [The ingenuity of the mind is important in your physical world. But, you are so much more than just your mind. And you're far more than anything that your mind could ever conceive. The magic of life only really touches you when your mental prowess is in service of your soul purpose. That purpose, not only supports the elevation of your individual consciousness but, it also contributes to the elevation of human consciousness. Don't delude yourself that you're separate from the rest of humanity or that the world's challenges will get resolved by ignoring the very essence of who you are – a human Being. You won't be able to resolve anything on this planet, until you admit to being a part of the problem. And you're a fundamental part of the solution, irrespective of the illusion of physical time or location. The soul you embody in this lifetime has been around for many lifetimes. It has participated in, and witnessed many events – whenever or wherever it occurred. And if that isn't enough, your cellular memory carries the collective history of your lineage. Your soul won't be confined within the ambit of your physical world - no matter how far into the 'future' you're capable of extending your mental prowess. You'll continue to encounter the same problems, wherever you go on this planet; or any other, for that matter. You can't outrun your humanness - no matter the number of worlds you attempt to find to avoid it]

[You believe that you spent your time building the life that you wanted but, you've been caught in a time warp of your history repeating itself. The irony is that you see your physical time on earth as limited, and drive yourself relentlessly to achieve your goals. And yet, you refuse to see the endless cycles of repetition that are self-imposed, and a waste of the very time that you claim to value. You attempt manufacturing more time – by any artificial means - to do what you've always done. And you continued to synthesize any number of variables in your physical world to bring about some kind of 'breakthrough' from your limited existence when essentially, each variable was extracted from the same limited conditioning. Things might have appeared to change on the outside but, nothing of substance changed within you, for the illusions that have their foundations in the familiar are far more acceptable than facing your perceived fears of the unknown. You wanted to construct a 'fairy-tale' experience in your world using your imagination and yet, you denied acknowledging the one true wonder – your unique, soul. It's the only fairy-tale worth living. Your life essence is already abundant - limitless; infinite. You're timeless, and capable of spanning multiple dimensions to realize the magic of the true reality within you. You can free yourself from the illusion of time in your physical world whenever you choose - by embracing, and living your soul purpose. Eternity can be found in every moment that you live by your truth. There's nothing unknown to your soul. That's another illusion born of your ego's desire to label only what fits within the limitations of rationality. Your fear of the unknown is nothing more than an illusion]

[Your ego's fear that you won't have enough time to achieve everything you want within your lifetime is also unfounded. You can exercise free will to do many things with your life but, you're here to accomplish only one – the fulfillment of your soul purpose. There's no getting around that. But, following your soul path is not as dire as it sounds. Within that purpose lies the entire spectrum of human experiences in this physical world. The constant urge to succeed at a multitude of things is only driven by your fear of death itself. And death is just another illusion. Your body might perish but, there's no end to the life essence within you - only the beginning of consciousness at a different level of vibration. Hopefully, a higher one. However, without transcending the soul lessons within your lifetime to fulfill your soul purpose, you'll subject yourself to an existence at the lower levels of consciousness, until you awaken to your soul. Delude yourself by all means with any kind of 'success' in your physical world but, without fulfilling your soul purpose you won't make any real progress in the annals of human consciousness. Your physical body won't survive eternity but, your soul's light will. And you get to witness whatever form that light takes by allowing your soul's truth to unfold during your lifetime. You might perceive that as only a fraction of time and space but, your lifetime – every moment of living your truth – is eternity made visible. Just look at any of the examples of human accomplishment that have withstood the test of time in your physical world. They continue to inspire love, and beauty against all odds. You have access to that same creative power. All you have to do is trust in your soul - it holds the ultimate, vision for your life. More so, than anything that your mind could ever conceive. It allows you to see beyond the separateness of physical form, and it rises above a mind that keeps you trapped in a maze of familiarity. If you can surrender to that shift in perspective happening within you, you'll be able to participate in the one true miracle of life - the evolution of your consciousness, and that of all humanity]

She felt dazed, and exhausted to her bones. It dawned on her that she was still trying to keep a mental note of everything that was happening to her. And failing miserably! She was falling apart – layer by layer. And each layer felt as though it was holding a mountain of physical pain. It was too much to bear. She felt as though she was on the brink of death. She felt a surge of anger and immediately, countered it with a defense tactic. *She'd done her best. It wasn't as though she'd arrived on this earth with written instructions!*

['Best' as defined by your mind or by your soul? Your mind doesn't have the 'instructions' but, you already have all the information you need. It's 'written' in your soul]

She stifled a scream of frustration. *"Where is my soul? How do I access it?"*

She'd never professed to know anything about the esoteric world. But, neither was she ignorant of it. But, it was unknown. So she preferred devoting herself to a life of doing. *Surely somewhere in all that knowledge, and experience were the answers that she needed to crack this thing called life - mystery or not! How difficult could it be? People have been doing it for eons!* She recalled the times when she'd refused to stop - for fear of sinking under the sheer weight of everything that she needed to accomplish. She remembered the constant anxiety. For years, she'd hacked away at her usual routine convinced that the success she desired was just beyond the next goal. Over time, little cracks had appeared in her enthusiasm from sheer exhaustion but, still she fought on. By then, she was so caught up in the existing structures that she'd used to build her life that she fell into an invisible trap - she felt obligated to continue with what she was doing to maintain her stronghold over the anxiety that was slowly eating her alive. The only salvation from her anger was to take on more - as fast as she could. She froze as she was hit by a revelation. She'd lost "hold" of her life by the very act of controlling it! And the only thing forcing her to do that was her ego!

[Completing this quest successfully, isn't a factor of your intellect or physical effort. Besides, you don't have access to either - your brain is foggy, and your body is practically, immobile with pain. Fortunately, soul work is different – it requires that you work on your relationship with your Self to actualize your Divine purpose in your physical world. And you've only just started learning about both. This quest is about learning to love yourself unconditionally, as you uncover your true Self. That can't be achieved by holding onto the false identity of person you used to be. Before you even get to the starting line to start your purpose you have to un-become everything that you believed yourself to be. It requires you to be still and quieten your mind to 'hear' your inner 'voice' - the vibrations from your soul that reveal your truth. You're dealing with many emotions in this process. Feel your feelings but, don't engage with them. Just observe yourself in the face of your fears, and insecurities. And allow yourself to feel into the uncertainty. Surrender into the unknown. There's nothing to fear. If anything, celebrate yourself for taking on this quest]

[As difficult as your past was, and despite the feelings of failure to achieve the plans that you had for your life, everything conspired to bring you to this moment. It might not look like much but, it's exactly where you need to be right now. You might have previously believed that you were on your chosen path but, your soul didn't lose sight of your truth. It still directed you here. And the 'obstacles' you encountered in your physical world were 'signposts' that guided you here. Contrary to your belief, most of your past experiences were chosen by your soul - they offered the path of least resistance in getting you to this point. You might have believed that you were 'living' by expending all your energy to achieve your goals but, you were never present while pursuing them, because of your unconscious inclinations. Without being aware of it, your higher Self was always directing you towards your soul purpose. That split within you is another reason for the feeling of separation from life. You were also processing a lot more information than you were aware of through all your senses including, your sixth sense. Your perceptions of failure in your physical world actually, served a very important purpose – the pain of each experience kept jarring you awake in the false reality that you were attached to. Despite what you currently think about the life that you previously led, it served you in one critical way - you didn't totally succumb to the illusion of your physical world]

[But, your soul purpose won't be distracted by anything – which is why you felt constantly restless. You should have delved deeper into that feeling, instead of being incited by your ego to go after every challenge. Your ego is insatiable when it comes to latching onto all the things that starve your soul, for it can't exist in the same space as your truth. It's constantly, on the rampage to maintain its position as 'master' of your life. More often than not, it's an easy win, because of a lack of awareness. Your ego goes on promoting its own interests by helping you to deny your weaknesses. And it thereby, reinforces your illusions of the physical world. But, you're becoming more aware of its tactics as the spaciousness within you increases with the release of each layer of trauma. Eventually, your ego will lose its hold on you as your true Self rises. However, as you get closer to your truth, you can expect that your inner war will become more intense. And you can be assured that before your ego succumbs, it will take you around in circles, lording itself over your fears, and insecurities. Again, don't be distracted by your anxiety; don't give in. Your ego will never win the war against your truth. And once you've gained Self-knowledge your mind, and ego can serve as useful allies to manifest your soul purpose in your physical world. For your Being – the channel to access your limitless potential – doesn't recognize the ego. It simply Is]

[Of all the options that you've considered to live your best life, there is only ever one path for you to follow – if you're willing to subvert your ego to achieve your soul purpose. And therein, lies your glory - without the need for recognition or validation by another. You delude yourself if you believe that you can reach anything higher in your physical world, than the highest values within your soul. And you can't fulfill your only 'role' as a human Being by suppressing your true Self. You won't get anywhere, in any dimension - physically or spiritually. To experience true freedom, you have to consciously transcend the illusion that entraps you from one lifetime to the next, and walk your soul path in your physical world. It exists purely, to reveal your soul to you. A new world doesn't exist outside of you. Once you transcend your physical experience you will be able to access the new world within you. The experience of walking your soul path, and living your truth will help you learn from others, as they will learn from you - to do all that is necessary in the highest interests of your Selves, and this planet. Each soul has its own wisdom to achieve this. The mind exists to help process, and navigate the experiences during your lifetime. The full extent of your soul's wisdom will remain forever hidden from your mind's grasp - to protect you from your ego which will always be lurking in the 'wings' to take back control of your life. The biggest 'sign' that your ego is back in the driver's seat will be your mind's attempts to formulate outcomes for your soul path. Paradoxically, the more uncertain you are on your soul path, the greater your chances of fulfilling your purpose. Your soul path is not meant to be 'figured-out.' Besides, you don't need to if you fully trust the truth that lies within you. It's only in hindsight – when you've completed your life's journey - that you'll be able to fully understand your purpose. While you're walking your path, you'll have glimpses of your purpose - trust your soul's 'eyes,' and your heart to guide you. Stay open to your thoughts, and emotions but, don't identify with them. All your physical senses will help you process your life path, and translate who you're Being as you take each step along your life's journey. Your touchpoint to this connection is your open heart space. Only your heart can understand the Universal language of your soul to actualize your soul's desires in this third dimension]

The truth of those words resonated deeply with her. She now understood that busyness was her way of maintaining control - to escape the unknown. She realized what a great aphrodisiac it was – for numbing her to her emotions, keeping her oblivious of her truth. How could she take any responsibility for her life, without fully engaging with her true Self? She was amazed at how much lighter she felt by simply acknowledging those truths even if she couldn't as yet, fathom their meaning. Each one was a revelation of Self – as though she'd found a sparkling gem in all the darkness that she was buried in. She clung to them – their light shining on her newly acquired understanding of Self and offering a modicum of relief, and validation in a sea of uncertainty! She realized that there would always be unanswered questions. But, she didn't need to know everything about her outer world – she needed to know her Self. And if greater Self-understanding was the key to realizing her purpose, then life might actually, be a lot easier than she envisaged. She sighed. The truth really was very simple. *Why didn't she think of it before?*

[Still trying to find a logical way out? Your soul path isn't about making life 'easier.' Neither is it about ascribing any other adjective to it that will allow your ego to become attached to it – to regain control. Your soul path is about fully expressing your truth during your lifetime. You can only achieve that by being present in your heart space – with each breath that you take. That is about as difficult, and as simple as it gets. You create each step by being aware of all that you are in that stillness. And whatever the extent of the interplay between your conscious, unconscious, and sub-conscious minds in that moment, that's what you'll see mirrored in your outer reality. As you become more aware of your role as the creator of your life experience, you'll be able to bring forth your full potential in that inner spaciousness to realize your purpose. That emptiness holds your past, your present, and the only future that you're meant to experience in this lifetime. Your ego kept you in a constant state of dissatisfaction, and always had you reaching for more – taking you out of the present moment. That attitude was compounded by your ignorance of your true Self. However, that's changing now. You're slowly beginning to accept that you're far more than anything you could ever imagine. That isn't something your ego will accept - it prefers keeping you in a state of denial of your true essence, by replaying old patterns to convince you that you're nothing without it. The irony is that your ego is correct - you are nothing. But, your nothingness is far from nothing – it's everything. And you don't have to do anything to earn it – it's already yours. It's always been yours]

[Your ego blinded you to that truth. All this time, you've been scrambling around, hunting for something that already lies within you. Your desperation only manifested those experiences that reflected your constant state of lack, worthlessness, and pain. By feeding your disillusionment, you continued to betray your soul. And you kept wondering why nothing you did ever lived up to your expectations. Nothing will – against that backdrop. The blueprint for the life that you deserve still lies within you. You see yourself as a failure for losing everything that you worked so hard for but, your real journey has yet, to begin. Right now, that spaciousness within might not look like much but, it's the opportunity that you've been waiting for, your entire life. It will help you to transform your life into all that your soul has been silently yearning for. Neither your mind, nor all the other voices in your physical world will ever be able to suppress the silent voice of your soul. It will be heard – if not in this lifetime, then in the next. By becoming aware of your ego's game plans, and being the observer of your life, as opposed to being constantly busy, you'll give your inner voice a platform to be heard. It's the only voice that you need concern yourself with. Your soul path will never be free of challenges for its purpose is to continue expanding your level of consciousness - over lifetimes, if necessary - until you reach the highest possible frequency of light that your physical body can hold within a given lifetime]

[Just how easily you tune into your inner voice and surrender to your soul path is dependent on the outcome of that internal war being waged between your ego, and truth. Not that there is any contest. The former will always lose, because of its fear of mortality, and obsession with competitive advantage, at any cost. Your soul has no such obsession for it knows its true worth; it's always connected to the infinite flow of life itself. You don't need written instructions to decide which one to follow. But, don't expect your soul path to be similar to the linear path that you're familiar with in your physical world. Following your soul path is like swimming in an ocean - with no land in sight. But, don't concern yourself with the 'ocean'- your physical location. Geography is irrelevant to your soul. Neither should you worry about the 'tides'– mass opinion. No one has the power to prevent you from fulfilling your soul path. You'll always be safe. Many souls on their true paths have lost their lives when attempting to change the course of human history. But, their soul missions have always been fulfilled – no matter how many lifetimes it takes. Wherever you find yourself; with whomever enters your space, you're there to gain Self-knowledge. More so, if you keep getting caught in the same 'currents.' Your natural instinct is to fight against the current – don't. Instead, focus on the underlying motivation for your decisions - are they prompted by fear or love. You'll know by the way you feel. Fear makes you contract into your lower self; love allows you to expand with your Self - way beyond your limited, physical self. But, none of those 'tides' can exist without you – you're the ocean itself. The ocean of life is using those 'tides' to reflect what is out of balance within you – what you're denying; suppressing or hiding from – for life can't be out of balance. Over time, you'll become more aware of the way your energies are being affected by the external energies. You'll be able to discern any imbalances, and by using your inner stillness as a gauge you'll be able to bring yourself closer, and closer to your inner peace. Eventually, you'll be able to maintain your physical self in harmony with the outer world without excluding, any part of your Self. You'll find yourself making choices with love in your heart that support your soul's growth, whereas decisions based on fear have kept you trapped in smallness. Your only role in all of this is to remain in stillness, and observe your Self. There is no 'role' in your outer world that can replace living your truth to actualize your soul path. You can't achieve this anywhere else but, in the physical dimension. But, the physical, and spiritual dimensions are not separate – they're one. All dimensions are one. But, before you can 'see' them you need to be open to your infinite, Being by raising your consciousness. That is the only way to birth the new beginning within you, and change the course of this dying planet. It's more imperative than ever to change the human 'tides' that have been the same since the dawn of time by elevating human consciousness. The current state of the world is not sustainable – the existing energies are totally out of balance with the mass of new energies being birthed by those at higher levels of consciousness]

[If you consciously focus on being present with your quest, you won't be disappointed. Your physical world will still unfold in parallel with your soul's growth, and the evolution of your consciousness. Although your primary focus will be observing who you're being - not what you're doing. Progress will be about acknowledging, and accepting who you are as more of your Self is unveiled. Every step will be surrendering with love, and gratitude for the many gifts that you receive as you move through this lifetime. Your soul path will have a multitude of forks, loops and any number of twists, and turns. It will also be marked by many occasions when you'll be able to exalt in your freedom – your true power. However, in life there is no final destination. Your soul path is designed to lead you to a very different 'place' - one that lies within your physical body and yet, lifts you up, and out of your physical world. For all its uncertainty, your soul path is the most enchanting journey you'll ever undertake in this physical realm. Only your mind can overshadow this experience by casting fear, doubt and judgement by defining each experience as either 'good' or 'bad;' 'right' or 'wrong;' 'successful' or 'unsuccessful.' No such labels or distinctions exist as a Being. You're undefined]

[If you find yourself being triggered in your physical world, know that those experiences are trying to help you consciously move through your emotions, until you reach a place of neutrality. That's when you'll know that you've freed your soul from whatever is hindering its full expression. It's only when you've completed your healing, and can be fully aware of your Self – no matter how far the emotional pendulum swings between the extremes of your experiences - will you be able to abide in the full presence of your Being. In this state, you'll be able to easily discern any form of manipulation by your ego, because denial will keep you locked in a repeating reality. By turning inward whenever it rears its head, you'll be able to discern your truth, and uncover deeper knowledge of your Self. This invisible, intangible process of uncovering your true Self is without any pomp, and ceremony but, it's key to actualizing your soul's reality, and living your full potential. Your conscious acceptance of all that you are - not rejecting aspects of yourself through judgement, rejection or fear of ostracism – allows you to fully accept your Self. It's the ultimate form of acceptance. You'll be free to own your truth - your life. And that gives you the freedom to express your soul's truth in this physical realm, without any fear. That is fundamental to your inner joy and peace, and the realization of your purpose]

[Anything that doesn't stem from your soul purpose, isn't your truth. Nothing in your physical world – no form of illusion - will be able to suppress it. Your insistence on retaining your 'place' in the illusion is the root cause of all your pain, and suffering. And your fears keep you caught up in those battles. However, uncovering and owning your truth will give you the courage to confront your fears. You'll never fear anything or anyone, ever again. As counter-intuitive as it sounds, your open heart is all the protection you need in your physical world. All matter, including your body will be destroyed over time. Whatever physical reality your soul will manifest after this quest, will also fade in time. That is the nature of the physical dimension that you exist in. Living your truth and your soul purpose, however, is about elevating your consciousness in your physical body, whilst being on this planet. It's the closest you'll ever be to knowing the Source of your life essence – the light - that created you. You've always believed that you're separated from that essence but, you're the light – here in your physical world. Your soul embarked on this quest so that you can remember your truth]

The level of cognitive dissonance was too great. She dialed out, and latched onto the first thing that crossed her mind. *Was she afraid of dying? She'd never thought about it – she was too busy trying to survive.*

[Not physical death - no. However, there are other kinds of death. Like the one you're most afraid of - a living death. It became your reality when you suppressed your truth, and denied your true Self. Truth was nothing more than a word that you bandied about, and sometimes practiced in your deeds. Being your true Self was never considered important to your survival in the physical world. However, it's fundamental if you desire thriving in it. As nebulous as it sounds, your truth is very real; with a real impact on the type of reality that you co-create in your physical world. By uncovering it, you're offered the infinite potential of your Being - in every moment that you chose to be present with it. And in return, you can actualize a life experience that is the polar opposite of your past existence]

She raised a single eyebrow in surprise. *She possessed power?*

[You possess your soul's truth. That's your power]

She was fascinated. She still didn't understand her truth. And the only association to any kind of power was the willful determination that she'd used when pursuing various avenues for success in her physical world. *How did owning one's truth give one access to one's full power? How did one's truth allow one to experience a life of unlimited potential?* She'd always believed that success was directly related to hard work. To her way of thinking that was evidence of her potential.

[Only partly so. What you accomplished through hard work was only an indication of your mind's capability. However, that is not an indication of your full potential. Neither does it touch on the full extent of your authentic power]

With those words she was struck by the realization that she'd never been interested in the many faces of power in her physical world. And she believed her personal power was related to her intellect. She'd exercised it on more than one occasion by placing herself in situations that challenged her mental, and physical boundaries. She'd often wondered about her uncharacteristic behavior. Was she more comfortable living life on the edge? Was her true Self more open to uncertainty than her ego-self? Why did she only feel that she was making any kind of effort when she was going full throttle trying to achieve something? Success, and exhaustion were synonymous to her. But, there she was utterly spent – practically, lifeless - without any sign of the success that she'd strived for all her life!

[You only ever concerned yourself with two things – money and love. And you pursued both from a place of lack; fueled by your poor self-worth, and fears - the two traits that your ego leveraged to its full advantage. You're instinctively aware of your innate power – so you never paid much attention to it in your physical world. Besides, your ego would never allow you to acknowledge your authentic power. That would deny it the very place it has usurped to gain control over your life. And so far, it has ruled your world. But, with its gaze firmly fixed on your external world, it never counted on being hit by something truly invincible from within. The infinite capacity of your Being to bring forth its natural state – love – to heal, and open you to your truth. Owning that consciously is your true power. Your previous experiences in your physical world demanded a certain level of bravery. However, your fear of lack was driving your choices. And everything that demands pushing your mental, and physical boundaries to achieve a tangible outcome are not the only challenges that require courage. That's very much part of the conditioning that rendered your masculine energies out of balance. This quest demands a very different kind of courage – getting closer to your feminine nature. Your soft, vulnerable, intuitive nature. And that requires a different kind of 'work' compared to the physical effort that you're used to – being aware, waiting without expectation of an outcome. Your exhaustion is symptomatic of the burdens you're clearing as you heal. Once this process is completed, and you fully embody your soul purpose you'll feel very different - lighter, and more joyful. Free]

She sighed, hopefully.

[There is more. By becoming more open to your feminine nature, you'll also surrender your attachment to outcomes in your physical world. As a result, any form of control will no longer be an option when fulfilling your soul path. Your ego will only function to realize your soul purpose. However, you'll be able to observe the essence of your Being through various forms of love that become visible as your soul's reality manifests in your physical world. It will be present in your endurance of situations that appear to be beyond your control. You'll encounter it when your patience is tested. It will be present when expressing deeper levels of compassion towards and acceptance of yourself, and others. It will be evident when you can be fully present with yourself, and others without judgement. It will take the form of higher levels of tolerance when you work with others to resolve challenges – without pushing your personal agenda or resorting to conflict. You'll experience it each time you lovingly surrender to the guidance of your higher Self. It will support you, and give you strength to surrender to the unknown. It will be felt in the silent wisdom of your soul, and the absence of the constant craving for external validation. Your Being doesn't require validation – your ego does. It will be known through self-respect for what you need to do without constantly, comparing yourself to others. It will be felt in embracing each day with gratitude, irrespective of the external circumstances that you're faced with. It will be visible in the loving relationships that enter your life. This quest to uncover your truth requires the courage to love yourself unconditionally, and to trust that who you are is exactly, the person you're meant to be. Your external circumstances will change – they must. That is the very nature of life in this physical dimension. But, for as long as you're separated from your truth, and continue to fall under the dictates of your ego nothing in your physical world will satisfy you. And you'll find that nothing about yourself will be worth loving]

She felt herself bristle. *She did love, and trust……*

[Then why are you so easily triggered whenever you hear something you don't like. Or rather, that your ego doesn't like. Surrendering to the love within your Being is being open to give without expecting anything in return, and to receive without attachment to a specific outcome. You're very familiar with giving but, you've always had difficulty receiving. Granted that some of your life experiences have been challenging but, the barriers you erected to protect your heart also prevented you from feeling any love towards yourself. And even though you claim to have loved before, you can't openly give or receive what you don't have the capacity to feel towards yourself. This quest requires trust, and unconditional love - for yourself. Your understanding of both have been defined, and limited by your past experiences. You have to undo whatever you've come to believe and learn how to love yourself again to complete your quest, and walk your soul path]

She couldn't deny that she had no clue what self-love entailed. As a result, she'd easily succumbed to the systems, and structures in her physical world. Far more critical were the unconscious restrictions imposed on the expression of her truth. Quite early in life, she'd become aware that those boundaries spanned various social, and cultural norms. And although she resisted them, she'd also known instinctively not to challenge them. Not directly, anyway. There were all kinds of implications, and it was way too complicated to figure them out. Whether she understood the reasons behind their existence or not, it was relatively easier to tolerate, and abide by them to some extent. After all, they offered some sort of protection, although she wasn't certain from whom or what. She was struck by the realization that that sense of safety was another illusion! If her acceptance of those norms, and stereotypes had engendered any feelings of safety before, she now felt smothered by the very thought of it. That sharp contrast in her emotions sparked a tirade of thought. If she was the one being controlled by such systems then who were its beneficiaries? Why was it being upheld in the face of ongoing global crises, and suffering? For so long, she'd been occupied by the injustices in her own little world that she'd completely missed the injustices on a global scale. Thinking small didn't only keep her grappling with her own demons but, had blinded her to the gross injustices being perpetrated against the majority of people, and the planet itself! To add insult to injury, her blind compliance with that covert form of conditioning had resulted in resentment not only towards others but, towards herself! During her lifetime, she'd witnessed many positive changes in the world but, many of the atrocities – mainly, against women and children – had been going on for centuries! It was mindboggling that those practices still existed across the world! How something so glaringly visible, and obviously wrong could be allowed to continue for generations was beyond her. The injustice of it all not only impacted those in direct contact with it but, also left a gaping wound on collective consciousness, as a whole. She realized that very little had changed over the ages. Certainly not to the extent that could be ascribed to the "progress" so widely promulgated for the twenty-first century! And certainly not, when compared to the investment in every other economic sector, in what was considered the most "advanced age" of human evolution! She sighed. Why was it so much easier to engage in endless power struggles for supremacy, rather than wage outright "war" against the structures that marginalized human dignity? Are the "problems" that plague humanity really so much bigger than the combined efforts, and resources of all the countries, and people on the planet?

She brushed aside her tears as she was overcome by a vicious anger. Was she playing the victim again? Or was she connecting to a much deeper wound? What was the origin of it? She was centered in her stillness. She was feeling her emotions but, she remained unattached to them. It dawned on her that the wound was part of her psyche but, she was also sensing something much wider in the energies around her. There was also a deep wound in the collective psyche of humanity. How was that going to be healed? She realized that there was no form of overt pressure that could be applied to change individual thought, opinion or motivation. Not for as long as people were in denial of, or felt powerless to change their circumstances due to their unvoiced fears - courtesy of generations of conditioning. In the same breath, she was struck by just how much she'd been consumed by her false reality. So much so, that she was unable to distinguish herself from the world around her. She was fickle, and wore as many masks as were necessary, to comply with any number of situations. In the nothingness, she became starkly aware that a large part of her discontent with her previous way of life could be attributed to feeling imprisoned. She might have acted out her frustrations in her immediate surroundings but, the microcosm of her life experiences was merely a reflection of what was happening on a far larger scale, everywhere else around her. She didn't know what was at the core of it. And that, petrified her! She was allowing the one life that she was now conscious of to be dictated by some nameless system - the origins of which were long lost in the annals of human history! And yet, its daily impact on her and the world at large was very visible, and tangible - it was the enforced reality of billions of people, and thousands of other species on the planet. She remained in her stillness, and observed the overwhelming rage without any origin. Slowly she became aware of another strong emotion that had defined the meaning of her life for so long - a sense of powerlessness to help herself or anyone else. It struck her that she'd been embroiled in this battle on some level, throughout her life. It was only when she was exhausted from her many failed efforts to change her old reality that she'd turned the mirror on the one person who had suffered through cycles of the same behavioral patterns – herself!

And now, she saw all too vividly the impact of being caught in her illusory reality – as though she was perched on a high window ledge between the life that was, and a life still to unfold. She now had no doubt that she'd contributed to the crafting of that illusion. But, the extent to which it had detracted her from her truth was frightening. And heartrending. This quest - whatever it was, and wherever it was taking her - had provided her with some insight into everything that she no longer wanted for her life. That left her with a burning question that she'd never given much consideration to before: "What do I want for my life?" Her quest so far had taken her beyond the usual frames of reference that she'd used to perceive her life. Despite the chaotic state of her mind, she'd never before seen her behavior with such clarity or felt closer to her Self. Then again, she'd never known such inner peace before. And that had nothing to do with her strangely absent external world - it emanated from the silent, stillness within her. Something that she could carry within her, wherever she went. Her acknowledgement made her see herself for the first time, through the haze of self-delusion fostered by an adopted reality. It wasn't only about the way that she'd perceived her physical world. It was equally about the identity of the person she believed herself to be. Her true nature extended beyond a certain "type" of personality. She was capable of a vast spectrum of behavior between good and bad; right and wrong; positive and negative; light and dark. Someone capable of greatness, and also a level of mediocrity that previously, would have horrified her. Someone selfless to the point of self-sacrifice and yet, also ruthless when her boundaries were infringed beyond her tolerance limits. Someone who reveled in expressing her mind with rational conciseness. And now, she was beginning to grasp that reason wasn't the only quality by which her life could be judged or the only means of understanding the vastness of the Universe around her. Far more important was the revelation that followed. She could adopt various roles in her physical world but, she wasn't defined by them. She'd always believed that there was some method to her madness in her physical world but, that again was only an extension of logical thought. To open herself fully to her Being - to "hear" this silent, Universal language and "comprehend" it, there was no logical method. Only the complete surrender to a random kind of madness within a stillness that required no mind. Only a heart open to a Being filled with love.

She realized that her past attempts to make sense of her life had left her more confused than if she'd simply let it be - let her Self be. She'd made a few good decisions. Mostly, she'd royally screwed up her life! Most surprising was that somehow, despite all the failure, heartbreak, and darkness - despite how imperfect everything was, it was all good. It was perfect exactly as it was, because she was starting to see her truth. And her insights were allowing for Self-acceptance, and facilitating her soul growth.

Ironically she'd always questioned whether or not, she was doing the right thing. And yet, her soul's growth had stagnated. She was hit by another revelation. Whatever she'd attempted to do in with her physical world wasn't wrong – it was just wrong for her! Her choices were not aligned to her truth. If they were she wouldn't be in a state of constant fear. If they were she wouldn't have been riddled with self-doubt. She inhaled deeply. And then, slowly exhaled. She felt relieved; so much lighter. So free. Was that what real freedom felt like? Perhaps it was her new found Self-knowledge. Perhaps the veils behind which she'd hidden for so long, had finally lifted. Whatever it was, she now felt free of a huge burden. *Was she?* There was nothing else she could think of, that still bound her to her past. It had become a mirage – like the identity of the person who had built it. She couldn't get over how neutral she felt over the catastrophe that had transpired in her midst. Where was the anger? The sadness? Strangely, none of it mattered – it didn't touch her stillness. The only thing that mattered in that moment was being present with her Self; more open to a whole new way of life - a whole new reality. One that was still invisible, although she could feel its presence with every breath that she took. Whatever shape her reality took now, and whomever the true Self to co-create it, both lay unexpressed within her.

She turned to her stillness. There was only a serene, silence. And her unknown Self. She was unable to discern any kind of identity for that Self – only a burgeoning sense of presence. She was happy to let it be – to allow it to unfold. There was no sense of urgency to make something happen, and she knew enough by now to surrender her expectations of a specific outcome. She turned her attention once again, to the nothingness. She felt so much closer to it. She mindfully surrendered to the uncertainty of being in a space that she couldn't fathom. It somehow reflected her inner stillness but, despite its monotone blackness it now looked distinctly, different. The nothingness had an intense presence that contrasted sharply with the meaningless life that she'd known. She was astounded. A life that was so all-consuming, and somewhat impressive now looked lackluster. She was even more fascinated by the different hues of light that she could see glimmering in the nothingness. She could also feel waves of heat, as invisible streams of energy surged through her. Again, she felt humbled, and bowed her head to acknowledge the magnanimity of the mystical space around her. Despite her anxiety over facing the unknown, time-and-time again in the nothingness, she realized that was the only space she really wanted to be in. She felt held in a cocoon of love; all of eternity stretched before her as she uncovered her truth. She realized that the only way to do justice to her quest was to complete it by honoring the space she was in with her full presence. Despite all the weirdness of the unknown, she felt safe – safer than she'd ever felt in her physical world. Besides, she had nothing left to lose. But, her conviction was interrupted by something that stirred deep within. She felt so at peace that the tinge of discomfort somewhere within her sounded like an alarm. *What was that? Why was she feeling that strange restlessness, again?* Was her instinct guiding her to uncover something that she'd overlooked in that void within? Was it blocking her from fully aligning with her soul's truth? She sighed. *Would this quest ever end? It was relentless!* All she knew was that she no longer felt anything like the person she used to be. And despite the uncertainty she was convinced of one thing. If her soul desired a whole new vision for her life then she was willing to do anything to align herself with it – even if she had to put her faith in something unknown - way beyond her mind. And she would purge whatever obstacles remained in her way, to open herself fully to it.

That acknowledgement was the que for what transpired next. Calmly, and with more gentleness than she was familiar with she watched as a few more veils relating to her old identity gradually lifted to reveal more of her truth. Some traits were quite obvious, and easily released. Others were practically, indiscernible. She had to labor at unbundling, and releasing them with acknowledgement, and forgiveness. Staying present with her awareness was no easy task! Before she got side-tracked by deciphering the many implications on her past life, she intentionally focused on how much lighter she felt as each veil drifted away into the nothingness. She lovingly observed her stubbornness, and codependent tendencies without judgement. And her passive-aggressive tendencies whenever her ego didn't get its way. Although those experiences belonged to her past, she sensed that she still needed to feel aspects of her shadow self, and honor them with her presence. In some peculiar way, she felt as though she was becoming whole again by integrating all aspects of herself. She realized that she didn't need to suppress the shadow aspects of her personality. Now that she was aware of them, she could transcend them. And when she finally, slumped to her knees feeling depleted after purging herself, she realized that her unknown Self was much more than she'd ever anticipated. *Who was this new Self? How did she go about figuring out which traits best served her? Where did she start? She didn't want to risk taking back on board all that she'd just released.*

[There's nothing you can control about the process of rebirthing your Self. It lies outside the ambit of your mind, and ego. There's nothing for you to 'figure out.' Your true Self already possesses the traits that best serve the highest interests of your soul. And there is only one place to 'start'- stay present with your awareness]

How did she do that? She was being swallowed up whole in this interminable process! Nothing that she did yielded any results or opened up a path – anywhere! She was in the dark about everything! When would she see some light?

[Be patient with yourself. Try to relax. There's no 'result' or 'path' outside of yourself. There is no light 'out there' – it's unfolding within. Stay centered in your stillness, and observe what's happening within you]

It was all too much to bear. She experienced something that she'd never felt before - her body shattered from her heart outwards. She did what she'd never done before – she caved. Her sobs wracked her body. And again, she felt that fierce pain in her chest. She clutched at it frantically, and massaged it in an attempt to ease the spasms. She felt ice cold, and was gasping for breath. She'd never felt such pain or grief before. She was petrified that she was having a heart attack. She raised her eyes, and searched the nothingness for help. But, there was no one. Only nothingness holding her in its loving embrace. She was more desperate than ever. *How could she possibly feel safe under such circumstances? She must be deluding herself!* She reminded herself that the only thing she could do was stay present with her heart-breaking pain. The tears continued falling as she gently rocked herself. She started humming a strange tune. She stopped. *What was that tune? She'd never heard it before and yet, it sounded so familiar.* But, she couldn't take her mind of the pain in her chest. *Was she dying!?* The fear was quickly suppressed by the anger that surged somewhere in the depths of her. *Why was she going through this? What was the meaning of it all? Why was she all alone in the nothingness? Why was there no one around to help her? This must be some kind of sick joke!*

[You're receiving all the support you need. Your aloneness is just an anomaly created by your mind. You're being guided by various energies on your quest, although they are invisible. Feel your feelings. Stay with your pain. Witness your thoughts. Whatever you need to do next will come to you]

She was trying! G*ddammit! How much more of this was she supposed to take? She was done! Enough was enough! How was she supposed to focus when she could barely breathe? What was she supposed to hear?

[Witness who you are being in this moment. What are you feeling?]

She felt livid. Lost. Afraid. Abandoned. Wandering the desolate desert of a self that she thought she knew. *How could she now let go of the only life, and self that she'd ever known? How could she abandon herself? Whatever lay ahead, surely she could still get there – with her old self? Why did she have to give up everything? Why was she the only one going through this mayhem? Why should she change? She'd done enough already! It was time to end this nightmare!*

[Let go of your ego's need to control the timing of your quest. Get out of your head, and stay in your heart space. Remain in the stillness within. Breathe….]

She closed her eyes, and reached for the stillness within. Slowly she became aware of her breath. Without being aware of it, she'd moved into the raging storm in her mind. She continued to take deep breaths, and watched as her mind slowly receded. She was able to center herself, once more. She sighed, and relaxed into the peace that flooded every fiber of her. She marveled that she could remain non-attached to her fears, and insecurities within the stillness and yet, still feel her emotions. Her stillness was one with the all-encompassing, force of her Being. Her eyes flew open to check if she was still in the nothingness. She sighed with relief. A word flashed across her mind's eye: "Victim." She ignored it. It continued rummaging through her mind, until she had no option but, to be present with it. But, it was too late. Her ego was triggered. Her defenses immediately, came to the fore. *Was she not entitled to feel like a victim under the circumstances?*

[Try not to be drawn into judging what you feel. Just be with whatever shows up in your heart space. Feeling entitled, and victimized only disempowers you. No one is going to rescue you from yourself. Neither does anyone, owe you anything. However, you're still responsible for showing up on this quest - for your Self. Only you hold the key to creating the best life that you deserve. But, you have to recognize, and change the neural pathways of being a victim]

She felt winded by how hard that hit home. She wasn't even aware of her victim mentality! That realization shook her even more. What other traits she unaware of? How often did she compromise her truth, and disempower herself?

[Your low self-worth made you desperate to prove yourself – everything else in your life took the backseat. You weren't aware of compromising your Self by betraying your soul. That's the hidden cost of a lack of self-love]

That rattled her. She battled to regain her equanimity. *What was she trying to prove? That she had a place in this world?*

[That is your soul's birthright]

Then why did she always feel impelled to prove her "place!?"

[That's an age-old, conditioned belief. One that was reinforced by the financial rewards you received in your physical world. And that, eased your discomfort by reaffirming your 'place' in this world. Feeling comfortable is a powerful aphrodisiac – it numbed your sense of not belonging. However, you do have a place. One that is real - where you've always belonged. Always will. You'll find it on your soul path. But, there is no recognition or reward for fulfilling it. Your 'reward' is this quest]

Those words sparked a whole new perspective. Why did she have to "know her place," and be rewarded by a system that pre-determined her worth? Based on what value-system? Who determined what was best for her life? What was the value of any form of recognition if the only benchmark against which she could be judged was the way things were done before? Were the history books a good enough testimony for that benchmark when they reflected the biases of the reigning authority, during a particular historic period? Even though many changes in the world are noteworthy, fundamental change that alleviates poverty remains painfully slow. And the longer that disparity is allowed to exist, the greater the threat of drugs, abuse, disease, and malnourishment in such communities. What would the world be without enforced exclusion based on elitism? Could a better world be created by a process of organic evolution that encompassed the inherent potential of all individuals? Would that result in true freedom or anarchy? Or is that merely an illusory "stick" to maintain control within a system that is geared towards protecting the interests of the few, at the expense of the majority? What would a free community of human Beings uphold as their highest soul expression? A holographic bubble that suppresses, and divides people? Or an open human "landscape" of Beings that supports and nurtures freedom built on mutual growth, and prosperity? What would the world be like, if its original state could be restored – one without borders? Why were borders even necessary on a planet populated by a single species of human Being? Weren't they superfluous in a Universe where all Beings could access the pool of human consciousness? Is it possible to embrace human and cultural diversity, and celebrate it? Instead of judging, and fearing it? If there was a map depicting human consciousness as a whole, what would it look like? Would it depict those living in first world countries as having a higher level of consciousness, compared to those in third world countries? What kind of indicators could be used to assess the levels of consciousness? Would there be as many claims to "progress" if one considered the catastrophic impact of corruption on millions of species, and on the planet? The fact that life on this planet has been written-off on some arbitrary scale in man's race to find another planet for human occupation, speaks volumes of the warped rationality that perpetuates the illusion of "progress." And prevents us from fully acknowledging the dire state of life on earth, and taking collective responsibility to change that reality.

She sighed. Did she seek a "place" in such a world? Did she recognize any kind of "value" ascribed to herself by the systems prevalent in such a world? The tears flooded her eyes as her rage mounted. It was superseded by an overwhelming feeling of powerlessness. She shook her head in disbelief. *This couldn't be happening to her. If that was the state of the world, what chance did she have of taking a stand against it? What could she do?* So much in the world around her was already crumbling. That in itself, must be an indication of a form of Divine intervention, and Universal justice.

Undefined

But, where did she fit into all of it when her own life had fallen apart? She recognized that on a personal level, her external reality was only a reflection of the extent of the destruction of her inner world. Was the external realities of others also crumbling around them? If the news in the media, and the many personal stories were anything to go by, then yes, there was some kind of mass purging going on. *But, for what purpose? To what end?* She sighed. *She didn't understand any of this! Where to, now? There was no place to hide. She couldn't go back to a life that held no meaning to her! Neither did she have any kind of future to pin her sights on.* All she had was a burgeoning desire to live her life fully alive - to co-create her new reality, and observe it unfolding in her outer world. And she only had this lifetime, and the help of her fellow human Beings to fully express that purpose. Never mind what had transpired in the past or in previous lifetimes, for that matter. Only this lifetime mattered now - by virtue of her being conscious of her truth. *How could she make it count?* Her mind was unable to grasp this new perspective. She bowed her head, and felt herself drowning in bewilderment as her ego retaliated viciously at being ignored.

[That's a good place to be – a sure sign that you're allowing yourself to move beyond your conditioning]

It slowly dawned on her that many of her thinking patterns had emanated from her old way of life. Her ability to achieve most of the results that she wanted in her career had led her to define success in terms of specific outcomes. She also believed that she was invincible, because she'd cottoned onto a "formula" – one that provided a track record of her success. And it was all the more appealing, because she was in control. Now she saw all too clearly that she'd been playing herself – courtesy of her mind, and ego! She might have been successful in one area of life but, that didn't translate to feeling successful within herself. How could it, when she'd based that "success" on a false sense of self!? If she'd only trusted what was within her control in the past, then what else was needed for her to open herself to trust the flow of life? *Did she have to relinquish control over her life? That was easier said than done! How could she place her trust in the unknown? Did she have the courage, and discipline to uphold her truth?*

Now that she'd experienced a fleeting glimpse of what her life could be – filled with love, joy, abundance and freedom - she was impatient to begin her new path. That was what she'd been searching for, her entire life! She hoped that there would be enough time to fulfill her soul purpose. And then she cringed with embarrassment. Her ego! It was still pursuing an outcome; still fixated on time! She acknowledged her mind's brief glitch, and breathed slowly, until she felt herself drop into her stillness. One thing was clear. Whatever time was left would be enough. She only needed one lifetime to experience being fully alive; to be one, with the essence of life itself. Nothing else would silence her soul's voice. *If she was bound to a physical existence, and had failed to find her purpose in her material world thus far, then where else could she look? Did she have to give up everything that she was familiar with, and widen her search by looking in every corner of the world!? Would she ever find it? Could she live with the uncertainty of not knowing what to do next or when she was supposed to do it? If she decided to surrender to her soul purpose, where did her need for security feature in such a life of uncertainty?* She shivered as awareness hit. She didn't know the answers! She would never know the answers!

The pain in her chest was excruciating but, she took heart from the fact that she was still breathing. She turned to the only thing that she knew would make her feel better - her ego! *She already knew that she didn't control everything in her world but, it was mayhem out there! She needed to survive! And yes, she'd lived her life according to a "formula." She was a control freak! So what!? It had worked for her!* She scoffed. *All this wishy-washy, soul-stuff was insane! Completely ludicrous! There was no proof that any of it worked! She was born; one day, she was going to die. End of story! She could find meaning in whatever she did. At least she could make sense out of that! Who knew what was real, anyway? Everything was going to crumble at some point, anyway – no matter what she did or didn't do. She just had to do the best that she could. And not take anything too seriously. There was no meaning to life. She could ascribe whatever meaning she could to her own life. She just had to stick with what she already knew. It had never failed her before.*

[That attitude might have helped you to survive in your physical world but, it won't help you live the life that your soul desires. You might be able to achieve some target using your mind but, it will be one dictated by your conditioning. Your mind has no concept of what you're truly capable of. It can't take you beyond your limits, into the unknown where you can tap into your unlimited potential. That is the domain of your soul, and Being. Whatever you chose to do is your prerogative. But, don't use your intellect as the only basis to make this crucial decision. No matter how far-reaching your goals might be, your mind can only operate within the framework of your past conditioning. Listen to your heart; it speaks for your soul. Your soul is connected to life's infinite wisdom. A wisdom that can be accessed by you – and every other Being. The only real indication of your soul purpose is what inspires you, and brings you happiness. And you've always been inspired by something very different to what you've confined yourself to doing in your physical world. And you can fulfill your soul purpose, in spite of the constraints that you're now aware of. You can transcend your limitations; nothing can hold you back from your soul purpose. You might have extended yourself to achieve your goals but, your physical self was in opposition to your truth. And the extent of that inner contradiction is the reason you've never felt fulfilled by what you chose to do. Furthermore, there will always be a limit to how far you can push yourself to achieve them. And you won't be able to tap into your full potential if you're forced by your conditioning to be less than your true Self. Truth requires you to be present with your Self – not sabotage yourself with mindless activity. Your lack of energy, and focus were symptomatic of how far you were from your truth. However, if you can surrender your will, and allow your mind to come into alignment with Divine will, then you'll have access to the ultimate "formula." You'll also discover many avenues of support - the entire Universe exists to help you achieve your soul purpose. You refer to it as 'synchronicity'- something that you've never been open to. But, it's real. It's part of the flow of life. And when you've completed your quest you'll be one with the flow of life's energetic force – a magical melody in the never-ending, orchestra of creation. And your Being is your soul's conductor. All you need to do is stay tuned into your soul with your heart. 'Listen' to its voice –align with its vibrations. Your heart will help you understand your soul's messages]

The chasm between her worldly achievements, and her deepest feelings was all too familiar. It had always riled her. But, she'd ignored it - repeatedly. She wanted to be a "winner" – her world only recognized winners. And she believed she could only accept herself if she was one.

And being one, didn't allow for any weaknesses or excuses. She'd lived by that credo. Now, she wasn't so certain, anymore. And her awareness of not being on her soul path was weighing heavily on her. She would never know what she was fully capable of if she didn't fulfil her soul purpose. There was a huge difference between what she'd forced herself to do in her physical world, and abiding in her Being – being in the flow of life to co-create her purpose. *What was her true purpose? What was she meant to do with her time on this planet?* She had no idea. It struck her that, until she figured it out, everything that she tried her hand at would be a waste of time. And her life. And despite her ego pointing to everything familiar in her physical world, the answer that she was looking for couldn't be found there. It lay somewhere within her – in her soul. And by listening to its voice, she would be able to tap into her full potential, and co-create her true reality. She sighed as she took in the vast nothingness. Her Being was connected to all of that!? She didn't know where to focus her attention – on her feelings of awe or the fear of the infinite, unknown that was threatening to overwhelm her.

It dawned on her that she'd compromised herself all her life by ignoring her deepest feelings, and reaching for only what her mind could grasp. She'd consistently mistaken her ego-driven enthusiasm for intelligence. And far from having boundless energy, she'd been driven by anger, and fear. And an addiction to the adrenaline-highs that came with pursuing one goal, after another. But, each time that she reached the end of a goal-line, she'd collapsed from exhaustion. Only by grabbing onto the next goal was she able to get back onto her "progress-horse." Not only did it give her a sense of purpose but, it also provided her with much-needed motivation. And her goal-orientated life had given her a sense of self-worth - albeit a false one! In that moment, she was struck by a revelation. There was a vast difference between the decisions made by a self-serving ego, and those that could be made using her innate soul wisdom. She shook her head hard to clear the mugginess. It was all too much – caught in the constant war between her limited old beliefs, and the limitless potential of her soul's wisdom. She felt as though she was being pushed to the very edge of reason. She couldn't take it, anymore. She buried her head in her hands, and wept.

[Those superficial judgements, and limitations are the domain of your mind, and ego. They're part of the burden you've been carrying for so long. You're in the process of releasing them. But, you haven't reached - your breaking point. Not yet]

She shifted uncomfortably, as she felt the grip of some unknown fear. But, she quickly distracted herself with another thought. She couldn't help comparing her old life with her experience in the nothingness. Milestones defined everything in both her career, and relationships. Those milestones defined her life! And yet, all of it had translated to a limited expression of Self. A Self that could expose her to a new way of life that was completely, beyond her imagination – a life of love, freedom, joy, inspiration, and limitless potential. With one proviso – she had to be in alignment with her soul's purpose before she could access her life's blueprint. And following her soul's vision for her life didn't require her to make any plans. There was no map to outline the specific route that she needed to follow; there was no known destination in her physical world. It will unfold naturally, once her lower physical body was aligned to her soul. All she needed to do was remain present with her quest, and respect the process.

[Again, this quest isn't within your control. And there's nothing here to limit your thinking. This space holds your physical self, and your limitless Being. The nothingness is reflecting all of you as each layer is healed. Your past reinforced your belief that you needed to 'fit' in with the existing systems, and structures of your physical world. But, your soul purpose doesn't comply with a 'one size fits all' formula. The unravelling of your old way of life doesn't translate to loss, chaos, madness or any other adjective that your conditioned mind is inclined to latch onto, to console your fearful ego. On the contrary, liberating your mind from that stifling conditioning to pursue your truth is the greatest gift that you can give yourself in the third dimension. And as painful as this transformation is, it's the most self-loving act you can perform. It's the hidden blessing in all this. The suffering in your life is merely a reflection of the disharmony within you - caused by forcing yourself to act out of fear, as opposed to extending the love within your stillness when you're inspired to act. Following your soul path won't necessarily be easy but, neither will you feel the need to fulfill it through incessant strife. Self-sacrifice or martyrdom doesn't serve your soul purpose or your fellow Beings. However, irrespective of the challenges that you encounter, and the state of the world around you, you'll know when you're on your soul path, because of your inner peace, and joy. There will be multiple realities playing out at any point in time in your physical world but, for as long as you remain in your heart space, you'll always be able to find your way through the unknown. Your true work is to maintain your physical state in alignment with the unique vibration of your soul. By doing so, you'll co-create your true reality in the physical realm - your very own heaven on earth. You won't want for anything. Have no doubt that it will demand every ounce of your energy. But, following your true path will feel effortless. All you need to focus on is celebrate each step of your soul path with gratitude]

How was she supposed to express gratitude for what didn't even exist!?

[It exists – you just have to bring your physical self into alignment with it. That's what your quest is helping you do – helping you feel your way to your soul path. You'll know when you're in harmony with it – you'll feel like you're at the very center of the Universe. That's your destiny– the choice to fulfill your soul purpose. Whether you make that choice or not, is in your control. The rest is a matter of Divine timing]

She was trembling. *It sounded…..so….so…..simple. And too good to be true! As much as it resonated with her, she couldn't deny her skepticism. This had to be one of the most fantastic dreams that she'd ever had! If this was the kind of illusion that she could conjure up in the nothingness, then she wanted to stay there forever!*

[You've always tried to control what you don't understand. But, your logic will never define your Being or the Universe. Both will continue to defy any logic. This is indeed a fantastic dream – the only reality worthy of you if you can free yourself from that prison that holds you captive. You've already started to experience the wonder of this space - you can feel the realness of it, even though you can't see anything around you. But, don't be sidetracked by what you think you can or can't see – your mind is still playing games with you. You'll gain more clarity as you get closer to your true Self. There are still some blockages within you that you have to remove, and heal. Before you can co-create your soul's reality, you have to fully surrender - let go of all the fear that separates you from it]

She felt the familiar thrust of her chin. *She wasn't a control freak!* Once again, she became aware of her inner calmness as she was consumed by indignation. Her mind registered that paradox, and she realized that it was about to rebel. After all, it was used to fielding endless criticism whereas no justification was necessary for her Being - it remained at peace. She turned her attention to the stillness within – it was starting to feel like an ever-present, faithful companion. She closed her eyes, and gently allowed herself to settle into her feelings. It felt as though she could "hear" them. It took a while but, eventually, she detected another layer of darkness deep within the void. *What was that?* It felt heavy – solid as that steel box that she'd "seen" earlier on. But, this wasn't her imagination – it was real. She could feel it! She realized there was something else that she needed to bring into the light of her consciousness; something that needed to be healed. And the only way to uncover it was to lovingly hold the intention to go deeper into that black void in her stillness. And trust her heart to lead the way.

[Each person born into this physical dimension can continue to exist within the conditioned existence inherited at birth or choose to create the life from the unique blueprint that lies within their soul. More often than not, it's difficult to break social and cultural ties, and many stick with what is 'known.' As you did. There are various reasons but, that attitude originates from your innate ability to mimic others right from birth. And as a child those behavioral patterns got reinforced by energetic transference from those closest to you. However, before becoming aware of the impact of your circumstances on your development, you ended up perpetuating the same behavioral patterns of earlier generations, as an adult. Add inter-generational cellular memory, soul karma and egos into the mix, and you found yourself trapped in an ongoing war with yourself. It left you feeling constantly confused, afraid, and lost. Notwithstanding the odds against them, a few have risen above their circumstances, and manifested success in the physical world. Consequently, many of their tactics, and behaviors have become the sought after success-numerators by which many define their lives. Only to discover that they don't quite achieve the same 'success' as their icons. For the most part, the only experience of the vast majority will be entrapment in a vicious cycle of behaviors that they've mimicked; behaviors that have led to consequences that are difficult to understand. And even more difficult to break free from - leaving nothing but a sense of deep alienation from Self. For it's easier to perpetuate what is known – no matter how disillusioning or destructive – rather than face the unknown. Ironically, you fear something that is your essential nature – you're the unknown. And therein lies your biggest conundrum. In striving to gain Self-knowledge, you'll grow closer to the unknown. And by surrendering to your transformation, you'll reveal more layers of your consciousness; each one taking you closer to your truth - closer to nothingness. You're the 'key' to overcoming your fear of the unknown – by becoming one with the nothingness – one with the Universe. And despite re-living the trauma reflected by the nothingness to get you back to your truth, it's the only space where you'll recognize it]

[However, don't expect your Self to mimic the self that you're familiar with in your physical world. Your Self knows no such limitations. Once you uncover your truth, your Self will become one with your soul. And your Being is the bridge that will channel the limitless potential of the Universe to help realize the purpose within your soul. That's your highest calling - to free yourself from your illusory self by uncovering your truth. What that is, only you will know. Each person has his or her truth, for no person is born to exist in the shadow of another – no matter how long or prominent that shadow is. Each person's reality is their own. But, as real as it feels, it's still subjective, until each individual uncovers their truth. The meaning that you seek, is your truth. The physical world only serves to reflect each individual's state of consciousness, for each phase of evolution. Once it has been fully attained, there will be no reflection to contend with. There will only be nothingness – that which existed since the beginning of all creation. Think of your soul calling as the ultimate rite of passage – one that integrates all aspects of your physical body with your soul. And when you're resonating – fully present with that truth – you're one with all of your Being. One with Divine Source]

[This isn't something new to your Being – it has always been connected to Source. It's your ego that reinforces your separateness - to keep you from your truth. But, your soul calling overrides the ego's false sense of power by bringing the eternal knowing of oneness into the consciousness of your physical body. Your Being has no form, mind, will or ego. It's pure love – energy in its highest vibratory state. And there's no distinction between the energies of love between different Beings. It's a single body of energy – connected to a single, Divine Source. By becoming attached to your physical existence, and using labels to define your life's meaning, you've reinforced separation from your true essence. And forgotten that all consciousness is oneness. Your soul's growth during your lifetime – over lifetimes – is an ever-evolving cycle towards enlightenment. The highest form of evolution - the 'final destination' if you will – is to become light itself. And only Divine Source can determine when you attain that state. Your physical self is only the 'vehicle' that facilitates the evolutionary process of your consciousness. Exactly what that evolution is, is directed by your soul, and life itself. Your responsibility in this lifetime is to heed your soul's calling, and to trust it as your path unfolds. Your Being already knows that all consciousness forms a single body of light in the Universe – across all Universes. It's tuned into the call, and will always respond – with or without your consent. Your mind can't suppress what it's not attuned to hear. Hence, the confusion over your current situation. Know that your ego will fight every attempt made by your soul to divert any attention away from its physical agenda. The only way to fight it, is to remain in your awareness – no matter what is going on in your mind]

[This never-ending, push-pull between your mind/ego, and soul will remain your single, biggest war during your lifetime. And for as many lifetimes as it takes, for you to become one with your true state of Being - one with the Source of life. But, the call will be heard. It can be within your current physical body or your soul could take on another to fulfill its purpose. Don't take this personally – this war isn't about your body or mind. It's about the evolution of Universal consciousness. You don't get to have a say in the physical form your soul embodies at birth but, you can trust that your soul will choose the best version of you to co-create your highest purpose. Heeding your soul's calling is your choice but, you're under no obligation to do so, because of free will. However, 'free will' comes at a price - you'll perpetuate your limited self, and remain stuck in a pseudo-reality. It might be enticing but, it's still an illusion. You can choose to step out of it at any time to begin the life that you deserve – there are no walls that can imprison your soul. All that's required is for you to take that first 'step' towards the unknown by heeding your soul's call. But, it's not 'out there.' The unknown lies in the spaciousness that you feel opening up within you]

[By being unaware of the void within you, you became more entangled in the drama of your physical world. As a result, you forgot your true nature, and lost the very thing that you came into this world to express – your individuality. You adopted many 'faces' to express that individuality but, you've always felt like a 'fish out of water.' And you'll continue to feel like one for as long as you remain caught in the grip of your fears - it separates you from your true Self, and the oneness of the Universe. To heal that black void that consumes your inner light, you'll have to do the one thing that you've always avoided – to turn towards it. Remain centered in your stillness, and observe whatever surfaces from that darkness. You're not being punished – it's an opportunity to love yourself; to reveal the light behind your darkness. Once you do, you'll become one with your soul; one with your Being – wherever you find yourself. You'll be able to remain in your heart space in your physical world, and observe your life as it unfolds. For once you're aligned with your truth, you'll never have to venture from your inner sanctum to become someone or achieve something. You've always known what to do from the moment you took your first breath. You just needed to transcend your past – to level-up with the vibration of your soul to see what's already yours]

[Your Being belongs to an infinite ocean of possibilities and potential across all time, and space. By aligning all aspects of your physical self with your soul purpose when you surrender to Divine will, your Being becomes the bridge between many dimensions. The lowest, and densest is your physical state, in the third dimension. The higher dimensions are lighter; more fluid. Connected to oneness. You refer to them as 'spiritual,' and consider yourself apart from them. You're not. You can ascend with your soul to experience them all – they can all be found within a single moment. Your Being spans all dimensions – the physical, and spiritual. It connects your physical body to all that Is.

It's only in your physical state that everything is perceived as separate. But, before you can experience the other dimensions, you need to fulfill all aspects of your soul's human experience by transcending your dense, physical-state. And that process is nothing like your linear, physical existence. It's circular - like walking around a high mountain. You'll encounter the same 'views' – the same patterns that keep you trapped in your lower-level, dense vibration – until you raise your consciousness, and transcend them. As you do, you'll go through a process of 'levelling-up' – integrating, and balancing the higher energies within your physical body. With each rotation, as your physical body increases its energetic vibration to hold more of your soul light, you'll 'see' more of your true Self. The process will continue, until you reach the level required by your soul in a specific lifetime. Your 'progress' is determined by the extent of your ascension – the resonance of your consciousness with the soul that you embody at birth. Compromise your soul's truth in any way, and you'll only place obstacles on the path of your own ascension in a given lifetime – you'll remain stuck, 'looking' at the same 'view.' Keep denying your truth, and you'll be forever lost in the illusion of separateness. Rise with your soul; overcome your fears of the unknown, and become one with all of eternity]

She'd spent so much effort trying to fit in with her physical world that she'd seldom questioned her experience of it. She'd assumed that the way she encountered the world was the way it was meant to be. That small mindset had become her entire Universe! She never expected that her reality could be any different; that she could experience so much more of life. It never occurred to her that she wasn't living the life that she deserved – the one in her soul. Neither did it occur to her that she could make different choices for her life - other than those that kept her within the constraints of existing structures, and systems. She never dared think that she possessed any kind of inner power to create a better life for herself - one that transcended the visionless existence of her conditioned self. She never believed that she was capable of healing, and transforming herself. She never imagined a better world – one that she would be proud to live in as a human Being. Between her conditioning, and the multiple layers of her false identity, she never once contemplated that there might be a distinction between the person she believed herself to be, and her true Self. With this latest revelation, she somehow felt stronger; more confident. She felt the grief associated with the loss for her old self and the life that she used to live slowly lift, and fade into the nothingness. It was replaced by a sense of wonder, and veneration for this magical, invisible life-force, within her soul.

Only to have that inspirational perspective immediately rejected by her mind. As she pondered the strange dichotomy of her mind, and its penchant for complexity, she watched in growing amazement as she started to discern two distinctly separate parts within herself. The silent, formless, omniscient observer - at one with the nothingness around, and within her. And another frantic, wisp of something that looked like an emaciated, gnarled form that vaguely resembled a human skeleton. It looked so frightening that she recoiled when she first became aware of it. She reminded herself that there was nothing to be afraid of, and relaxed. In that instant, she was struck by a realization. That must be her ego! For so long, she'd only had a conceptual understanding of it. For the first time, she had a real sense of its existence. She remained in the loving warmth of the stillness, and watched as her ego ranted, and raved at this new perspective of Being – of oneness - that was slowly birthing in its very presence. She sensed its fury at being ignored by the observer in her - in favor of something else. Something that was regarded as far more important, despite it being unfamiliar. She could feel her ego's perplexity, and fear as it realized that this unknown "something" could very well mark the end of its supreme reign over her life. She stalled. She sensed her ego's remorse, and almost capitulated. She wanted to comfort it - reassure it that everything would be fine in this new, unknown reality that she sensed unfolding within her. But, in the stillness, something made her stand her ground. Eventually, it dawned on her just how critical that decision was. Her ego was in no way concerned with her wellbeing. It was solely focused on the fear of its own demise. In that exact moment, she realized how much of her old life had been ruled by it. Despite her growing discomfort at having lived in the same body with something that she'd been unaware of – other than in name only - she was fascinated by her ego's subtle manipulation of her mind. It had consumed her with so many false notions – all keeping her from her truth! She realized that her ego had constantly played on her fears. In stark comparison, if she remained centered in her stillness, she was aware of the fear but, felt totally, at peace. She realized why she didn't feel any kind of emotion in her stillness. Love, and fear couldn't reside within her Being! But, fear did exist in her physical body. And she could heal herself from the root cause of that fear to get closer to her soul. She shuddered. What was the basis of her life decisions – love or fear? What lay at the core of her fears?

She found herself lost in a maze of conflicting thoughts between her old desire to make her life a success, and her Being's irrefutable sense of its own fully accomplished state, with her simply abiding in its presence. Her ego's fear that there would never be enough time, and the calm surrender of her Being to its infinite, timelessness. Her ego's compulsive attempts at doing everything, and her soul's wisdom that she existed for a specific purpose. Her ego's grasping behavior, because it could never get enough of everything that it obsessed over, and the abundance she felt within the expansiveness of her Being by feeling as one, with the whole Universe. Her ego's fear of its annihilation, and the deep peace within her Being from knowing that it belonged to all of eternity. She was very aware of her ego's refusal to acknowledge a Being that was already one with the Universe. After all, its validation could only be obtained through competition. How else would it prove its superiority!? She was hit by a startling irony. After all the effort by her ego to reinforce her individual status, she'd only been following the worn out tracks of her conditioning. Where was the originality in that!? No matter the number of routes that she took to create something new in her life, she would find no meaning! She stared into the nothingness, drawing some comfort from it in the throes of her inner turmoil. And yet, there was a growing sense that not all was lost. She was still receiving the guidance that she needed to uncover her truth. She just had to stick with her quest.

[You structured your physical world around what you could conceive with your mind. You applied that same principle to your life purpose – all neatly boxed into body, mind, and soul. That also formed the basis for your individuality which only perpetuated the notion of survival through competition, and separation – from your Self; everyone around you, and the Universe. It might have been the only way for you to make sense of your world but, you were unable to suppress your wisdom that life is only worth living by expressing your soul's truth. Your physical body merely exists to help you observe this experience in human form – not to separate you from humanity. As an individual you have the freedom to express your truth, and still remain connected to all of humanity. Your individuality is based on your soul purpose. Your uniqueness stems from your soul's expression of Self – not from your ego's attachment to people, places, possessions or roles that define an identity. You aren't required to perform any overt acts of 'doing' to make your Self known or visible to the world. Your presence in each moment is all that is required. That's your highest form of doing]

[In spiritual terms everyone is created from, and contains the same life essence. It's only your mind that perceives the physical, and spiritual worlds as separate, because that's what logic dictates to understand what can't be seen. However, all that you see in your mind's eye, isn't all that Is – either of yourself or the Universe. The same principle applies to the other senses interpreted by your mind. You grapple with understanding life, and the mysteries of the Universe in the same way that you grapple with the immensity of your Being. But, you can't grasp infinity using your logical mind. You can only feel it. More importantly, the physical and spiritual aren't separate - they are one, and the same. And understanding your Self will lead you to your infinite Being, and the Universe. There's no mystery. Everything becomes 'visible' when you're open to your Being - not with your eyes but, with your heart. Your soul has been trying for a long time to lead you to this wisdom but, you were unable to connect to it, because you're so disconnected from your Self. But, nothing and no one is capable of preventing you from accessing your truth. You just have to hold that intention within your heart space, and listen to your soul's guidance. It's not more knowledge you seek but, a certain feeling of fullness; completeness that arises when you surrender to the stillness within. It houses the 'silent voice' of your soul. It's the only part of you that speaks to you outside, and beyond the reaches of your mind. It's not easy to heed your soul's timeless wisdom in a world that places so much emphasis on your physical senses but, learn to attune to its 'silent voice.' It will introduce you to all aspects of your Self that you've been denying for so long. And in honoring it, you'll be honoring life itself] [In your physical world, the mind can very easily succumb to acting out of alignment with your soul purpose. That can continue for many years within a single lifetime or over many lifetimes – depending on how strongly you resist your calling. It's what you experience as separation from your Self, and all that Is. It's also evident on a much larger scale. Collectively, humanity has persisted with the notion of separateness for centuries. But, that isn't your natural state of Being. Hence the chaos within you. And that chaos, is reflected in the world around you. The longer you maintain the familiar structures of your conditioning, the more suffering you'll experience. At some point, something will give – first within then, outside of you. As is evident, from your quest. However, there's nothing to fear. You're safe. Becoming aligned with your soul purpose doesn't present a stumbling block to the progression of your physical life or detract from it, in any way. On the contrary, your transformation will carry you to that space within you - from where all things become possible. It only appears as if you've lost time but, you've lost nothing. Nothing real or meaningful, anyway. The door leading to your soul path has always been open. It will remain so - waiting for you to take that first step through it, with an open heart. The only challenge in getting to it lies in healing your biggest wound – your perceived separation from the Divine. Again, that separation is an illusion - compounded by the duality that arises from existing in your physical world. Once you merge fully with your Self, you'll release yourself from that 'steel tank' to hear your inner voice. It will guide you to the 'door' that lies in plain sight, and within reach. But, there's no need to unlock or reach for it. By abiding in your stillness, you'll feel it. It will 'open' when you fully resonate with it - opening to a Universe of unlimited potential. Your truth is the 'key' that unlocks the new reality within your soul. You can't create all that your soul desires in your physical world without first becoming whole within yourself - by merging with your true Self. All it takes trust. And self-love]

Of course she trusted herself! She wasn't fragmented! What nonsense! She looked down at herself. Her body was whole. It looked the same. As always. Despite her defensive attitude, she couldn't deny the truth of those words as they nudged at the corners of her consciousness. She was in pieces. She felt torn; scattered – right down to her core. She felt completely, alienated from her Self; from the natural state of her Being. And from the Source of all creation. It slowly dawned on her that that alienation was the real cause of the lack of depth, and meaning in her life. Could she heal that separation within herself? What did that kind of healing entail? How could she integrate all aspects of herself to become one – to resonate fully - with her Being? She'd already felt the oneness in the nothingness – she knew what that state oneness felt like. It was magical! *But, how could she attain it?* Her ignorance sparked her frustration. She'd never felt so incompetent before. *What was she supposed to do? Was that what was so wrong about her life? She felt broken? Why?* What was the cause of it? When, and how did it happen? Was that void within her related to that feeling of separation from Self, and Source? Was her past life built on a shattered sense of Self? No wonder she was falling apart!

As pulverized as she felt, she couldn't help noticing how much lighter she felt. Almost imperceptibly, her lightness gave rise to another strange insight. What would it feel like to be whole - one with her Self? One with her soul? Based on the all-encompassing oneness that she'd experienced in the nothingness, there was no separation or difference between the essence within her, and the Divine essence of life. Was she really a human representation of Source itself? Was she as infinite as the entire Universe? That meant every human Being on the planet – every life form – was also Divine! She was awestruck. It took her a long time to come out of her reverie. When she did, she felt very different. Closer to the nothingness; closer to her Self. What could she co-create with a Self that felt whole - one with the very essence of life itself? What would that soul-reality look like? She knew that the inscrutable nothingness would provide no answers but, she smiled at it with all of her heart. In some bizarre way, it was providing the answers that she needed. Although not in a form that could be interpreted by her mind. She had to listen with her heart. Voice was right after all. Her heart could decipher the silent language of her soul. She crossed her hands over her heart as she was enveloped in a love that had no beginning nor end.

[Trusting only what you can control within the confines of your mind isn't everything that there is to you. You've been limiting yourself]
Limiting herself? That "limited" self had achieved a pretty successful life! Real or not! She realized that she'd just been triggered again. The lapse into her ego-state was so imperceptible! If it were not for her awareness she would be none the wiser! She sighed. Her healing was far from complete!

[You achieved many of your goals but, you've never been anywhere near your full potential. The benchmark for your success was based on achieving or exceeding what had already been done in your world - not on actualizing your soul purpose. Without fulfilling that, you'll never know your true power. The power of co-creating a better world for yourself, and others by speaking your truth into existence. You've always sensed that unknown power and now, you can feel it moving within you. Embrace that feeling; it will bring you closer to what you're seeking – oneness with your Self. Contrary to your belief, it's not out of your reach. To move beyond your limiting beliefs, you have to remove not only the illusions that have held you captive throughout your life but, also overcome your illusory identity caused by that false reality. The former is relatively easy, because you've witnessed your physical reality crumbling around you. Overcoming your illusions of self, however, is far from simple. Besides being intangible, they're also invisible – they're embedded in your psyche. You've already experienced aspects of that process on this quest – by becoming aware of your old thought patterns, beliefs and the personality traits associated with that identity. But, you're far from finished. And you won't be - not until you've become one with your Self. A process as imperceptible as being sucked in by your ego. The only difference being the nature of the energies of your Self, and ego]

[You might be aware of some aspects of your transformation but, you don't know the full extent of it. Your mind hasn't gone through this process before. To bring you into full resonance with your soul, there are changes to your physiology on a metaphysical level - to allow more healing light into those unknown dark spaces within you. Your old physical self is going through a form of death to bring about the alignment with your soul - to birth your true Self. When the process is complete, you'll look very much the same physically but, nothing else about you will be the same as the person you used to be. You'll shed every ounce of the identity that you once associated with yourself – both in body, and mind – to allow for the fully embodiment of your soul's truth. Consequently, you won't be able to remember much of your old self or the life that you used to live. Your soul won't entertain any form of compromise with your truth. You'll never fully comprehend the extent of that truth but, you'll always be able to feel it as you take each step along your soul path. And you'll be able to observe it unfold as the new reality in your physical world. A reality that reflects the co-creation between your Divine soul, and the Universe]

[Right now, you're still caught up with some of your old beliefs. And you're still grieving for what you perceive to be lost. Your mind is in turmoil, because it's trying to process the changes between your old and new perspectives but, it has no frame of reference to monitor or control any of it. You're experiencing intense pain in your body. And you're battling to understand why you're still breathing, when every fiber of your body is telling you that you're dying. You're exhausted from fighting this war on various fronts. But still, you go on. Besides the trauma of loss experienced in your physical world, your stress levels continue to rise, because on a soul-level you're aware of the death of your old self, and the re-birthing of your true Self. Your soul understands this process but, your physical self still has to bring your body into alignment with the energetic changes that you're going through. While this is happening, you have to contend with your mind rejecting this quest; it prefers to deny what is happening, because it won't accept what it can't comprehend. Your mind still remembers aspects of your old self and it will continue with the same old neural pathways, until the process of inner transformation is complete, and new pathways are created that align with your truth. It will continue to reject each phase of this new frontier opening up within you, for as long as those old pathways exist. And while all this is going on, you still have to confront your ego - it's still vested in your old self. More so, because it sees this quest as a major threat to its power. It won't support this transformation in any way, so it will take you to the very edge of sanity to convince you to stick with the old self that you're familiar with. But, don't give up. Trust your soul – stick with the process. This inner conflict will only go on, until your healing is complete. By then your mind, and ego would have also transitioned to serve your soul purpose. No matter what your mind would like you to believe, this quest is necessary. You've outgrown your old self - it can't help you fulfill your soul purpose. You have no control over any of the processes during this inner transformation – you're in the realm of your soul now. All you can do is trust and love your Self unconditionally – notwithstanding the discomfort, and uncertainty. Surrender to it. There's no turning back now. Whatever you need to know will come to you – when you need it. You already have all the soul-knowledge you need – trust your Self. Believe in your Self. To complete this quest, you need to uncover the truth behind your biggest fear. What caused you to lose the connection with your Self? What shut you off from the light – the love – of your Being?]

She had difficulty pinpointing what bothered her more – that she never realized the depth of her fears or that she knew so little about her Self. As infuriating, and exhausting as it was to be pulling apart the very threads of her existence she couldn't help but, be amazed as each thread revealed some hitherto, unknown aspect of Self. She felt as though she was seeing herself for the very first time! She'd never thought of herself as a perfectionist. She knew that she had high standards but, she demanded them of herself. And she'd never given much thought to whether or not, she trusted or loved herself. She only knew that she could always rely on herself to get things done. *Surely that meant she trusted, and loved herself?* And yet, the very qualities that she'd placed so much reliance on, and which had come to her aid so involuntarily in building the life that she wanted, now seemed to have also contributed to her downfall. And notwithstanding her good intentions, her past looked like one huge contradiction! With one major caveat - she didn't believe in contradictions. *There had to be a reason why her life was being turned upside down! And yet, no amount of logic, and none of her usual mind games seemed capable of solving the mammoth puzzle that was her quest! The very pieces of it seemed to belong to different puzzles!* She was even more petrified, because this was no game. This was her life! *How could her life be in pieces? How could she feel so broken?* Putting it down to a self-fulfilling prophesy felt as though she was resorting to another escape hatch. She groaned in frustration. *Why did life have to be so damn complicated!?*

[Life is actually, very simple. You just have to align your mind, and ego to your soul purpose. There's no end to the scenarios that you could conjure up to satisfy your ego's hunger to be right. That's your 'complicated,' right there. You're a complex, multi-dimensional Being but, life itself is simple – if you allow it to flow through you, and not force it to fit a contrived illusion. Life doesn't require you to think about living it – it requires your surrender to its flow. That requires trust, and self-love - for life is unfaltering in its promise to lead you to your highest path. It asks for nothing in return, other than bringing forth your soul purpose into this physical dimension. But, you've chosen to live a linear existence driven by fear. A great approach if you're a machine but, you'll never be that. No matter how advanced technology becomes, and how many programs you write to design life according to any number of variables, you'll still be confining your Self, because you'll always fall short of actualizing your soul purpose. Nothing will be a worthy enough substitute for living the life that your soul desires]

She sighed heavily. She always believed that she was doing everything possible to make her life a success. She'd been busy practically, all day - every day.

[Being busy doesn't translate to a life well lived. If anything, you're using your busyness to distract you. You've been on the run for the longest time - from life; from yourself. What are you so afraid of?]

She felt the familiar stirrings of a deep annoyance. The composure that used to be such a prominent feature of her old self seemed to have completely, deserted her! She'd never thought about any of this before, and that made her feel very unsettled. She was forced to admit that even if she had, she wouldn't have been able to come up with any answers. Nothing in her past had prepared her for this quest. She'd never felt as inept as she did, in that moment. She deflected her frustration by turning her attention once again, to Voice. *Who did it belong to? Why was it speaking to her? Who did it think it was? It just went on and on with its barrage of criticism, and she was certain that she'd never met it before. And yet, it seemed to know more about her than she knew about herself! Why was it hiding? Why didn't it just come out, and face her?* She looked around again but, she saw no one. She did, however, feel its omnipotent presence.

She slumped back under the full weight of her powerlessness. But this time, instead of resisting it, she opened herself to the feeling, and surrendered to it. She felt its edges slowly dissolve; she felt herself becoming lighter. And in the process, a deeper insight was revealed. This kind of trust in life; her Self – wasn't something that she was familiar with. Self-love, even less so. And that, made her more uncomfortable. She believed that accomplishing whatever she set out to do was an indication of trust in herself. *As for trusting life – how could she? How could she hand over the reins of her life to something unknown? The closest that she'd come to allowing it was pegging her trust on the way things transpired in her world. And that only served to reinforce her mistrust!* It dawned on her that third-party, information, and information manipulated for a variety of reasons provided no basis for trust in her Self. Certainly not the kind required to complete her quest! As for self-love, how did one love oneself? Her reality – her life - was based on whatever was happening around her. She was suddenly struck by how misguided she'd been. Her life was much more than her perceptions from the many subjective realities projected around her – including her own! Life didn't just happen to her! She was no bystander! She'd always set out to create her own reality – even if all she'd done for years was bumble her way through it! However, there was one underlying thread throughout - she'd always believed that somehow, she would find her purpose. Now the life that she'd built, no longer existed! And she was rapidly un-becoming the person that she believed herself to be! If her old self had any notion of trust or love then that too, was fast disappearing with everything else that was part of her old, illusory reality! What or who could she trust now? What was there left to love in her fading self? There was only nothingness. If trust, and self-love were necessary to walk her soul path then where was she supposed to look for it, if all that was left of herself was nothing!? How could she find her inner light in all of the darkness within her? Was there still some inner blockage that was preventing her soul light from shining through? Could fear do that to her?

Her sub-conscious mind immediately made her go on the defensive. *She wasn't afraid! She'd never been afraid of anything, her entire life!* Was she in denial? *No! She'd come a long way on her quest. And she was now familiar with the tricks in her old "toolkit." There was no need for denial. And……* Something made her stop, and turn inward. She became aware of another invisible layer slowly unveiling somewhere deep within. Without the usual distractions of the outside world, she was beginning to appreciate that there was an entirely different world within her. And this quest was intent on making her intimately aware of every aspect of it! She could now discern many layers within herself – layers within which she'd hidden certain life experiences, and the emotions relating to them. Emotions that she'd suppressed for so long but, they were now rising like a tsunami - threatening to destroy her! And she knew that there was no escape in the nothingness. The only thing that she could do was get closer to it. She needed to keep digging through that void. She sighed. *It was tantamount to digging a bottomless pit! And it was sheer hell! What was she looking for, anyway? Would she ever find it? She'd never attempted anything so futile before! She was used to her efforts yielding results. Not this endless type of non-doing; with nothing to show for it! What did any of this mean? What lay within her that could help her understand her life – her Self - so much better than all the knowledge that she'd obtained in her external world?*

There were no answers in the nothingness. She let her exasperation be. In the space that arose from surrendering she realized that the extreme discomfort was a precursor to another layer becoming visible. To deny or avoid it was futile. There was no escaping herself! She continued observing, and acknowledging more layers as they were revealed. Her only responsibility was to stay fully present with the process, and observe without judgement what was being uncovered. It dawned on her that her openness somehow increased her detachment, and lessened the pain. Until eventually, each layer that revealed itself dissolved of its own accord. *How much more did she have to endure? How much further into her past did she need to go? Was she lying to herself about something? Was there something in her past that she didn't want to face?* She recalled her conversation with Glow about relationships mirroring what was within her. She closed her eyes, and surveyed the flood of emotions within. She was able to discern two strong reactions elicited during her interactions with others – irritation at any sign of weakness, and a lack of trust. Why was she intolerant of weakness? Was she afraid of being seen as weak? Did she really trust herself?

[There are no degrees to love, trust, and integrity as far as your soul is concerned. Only absolutes apply to your truth]

She was feeling increasingly edgy. The fact that she'd been lying to herself about her fear was painfully obvious. She just couldn't figure what it was. She breathed into her discomfort, and slowly allowed herself to be present with that truth. The thought that she was weak, however, didn't sit well with her. She considered herself to be strong - she'd overcome so much over the years! Mental, and physical strength, however, were only part of life required of her. She realized a long time ago, that there were other "tests." Unknown tests - by some invisible examiner. Were those experiences teaching her a different kind of strength; a different level of trust? Were they testing her faith? She'd never understood any of it. So she'd just continued applying the same mental grit, and super-human effort to her inner battles as that used for overcoming the challenges in her physical world. But, that approach had obviously not worked! Not if all that effort had only brought her face-to-face with nothingness! Was she approaching herself in the wrong way? Why was she always so hard on herself? There were times when she was practically, ruthless! Would she treat herself the same way if she loved, and respected herself? If being hard on herself didn't give her the life she deserved, could a gentler, more loving approach be the answer? If anything her tough, uncompromising approach now felt completely foreign to her in the nothingness.

[You'll be amazed if you could see what gentleness, and love can accomplish. Why did you feel uncomfortable about feeling weak? Why did you want to cover it up? It's part of who you are – your humanness. Just like all your other traits. The key is to be aware of your emotions in each situation - not avoid them. The same applies to your thoughts. You have to feel the emotions relating to your thoughts – to be one with your Self. No matter what they are. What are you hiding from? Whatever it is, it's also blocking the feelings that you're most afraid of facing. And that is blocking you from your truth?]

Be herself? In this world? She would be eaten alive!

[You've already been gorged, and spat out many times by the illusions that fed your self-deception in your physical world]

She was now very much aware of that. She'd fought as hard as she could. And lost. Everything! Her relationships…..her possessions….her money…..her time…..her pride…..her dignity. And her energy. She didn't take losing lightly but, she'd tried everything to hold onto what was hers. Everything allowed by her integrity, anyway. And that she refused to compromise - for anything. Did her refusal to compromise mean she was weak?

> [Survival in your world might be associated with physical, and mental strength. However, 'failure' in your world doesn't make you weak. That's a misnomer stemming from your fixation on all things physical. And that stems from your conditioning. You can be forgiven for thinking that only a gladiatorial effort will help you achieve your soul purpose. After all, that's the stuff that world history holds in such high regard. But, you're now fighting a different war. It calls for a very different approach. There are no opponents in this war – other than your ego. No battlefields, except your mind. There are no weapons at your disposal other than self-love, and an un-flailing conviction of your worth. There will be no medals for what you accomplish – you don't even know what the outcome will be. And no amount of physical strength or mental prowess will help you win a war against your soul's truth – it will always triumph. Your refusal to compromise your integrity isn't a weakness. If anything, it's one of the values fundamental to completing your quest, and your purpose. You were vehemently protecting something else. Your vulnerability, perhaps? You fought very hard to hold your life together. But, you don't need to fight for what already belongs to you. It points to a lifetime of feeling threatened - you always came out fighting whenever you felt the need to protect yourself. Why?]

Vulnerable? She? She scoffed. *She'd never felt that way.*

> [Never? What about when you found Kitty? Or when your baby was born?]

She felt an instant shift through another layer, and fell deeper into herself. She smiled as she felt the warmth flood her body at the recollection of those tender, long lost memories closest to her heart. She could still hear her heart pounding when she found Kitty. She was overcome by a tangible sense of childish delight. She couldn't remember the last time that she felt so charged with enchantment in the presence of another living thing. It was the first time that she'd seen a kitten, and she was instantly drawn to it. In some strange way, it reminded her of herself. She frowned. That thought had never occurred to her before. She now realized that even as a child, she could relate to how lost, and abandoned the kitten must have felt in that vast field. She was surprised. She'd never associated those feelings with herself. She felt an ache, deep within her heart with the acknowledgement of that denial. Whether she wanted to admit it or not, some part of her certainly, felt that way. Things were different when her baby was born. Her life was complete, madness. And she was overwhelmed by all the turmoil. It was made worse by the fact that she didn't feel ready for motherhood. When she saw her baby's face for the first time, something changed within her. She didn't know what it was but, she was keenly aware that she'd entered another phase of her life. Whether she was ready or not, wasn't up for debate. She was now a mother – with the responsibility of raising another human Being. The full extent, and implications of that responsibility terrified her. She recalled the overriding thought at the time. *Was she even capable of being a mother - let alone, a good one?* But, her life was of secondary importance to the one that she held in her arms. It was replaced by a burgeoning desire to protect this little miracle that had been entrusted to her. She recalled how uncertain she felt. And weak. Her feelings of inadequacy were overwhelming. *How was she supposed to raise a child? She didn't know the first thing about taking care of a child's needs or nurturing one, for that matter. She could barely take care of herself!* All she wanted to do was run away as fast as she could. But, something held her back. She felt worse when that small titbit of human treasure looked up at her with such adoration, and trust. In a strange way that look in her child's soft, brown eyes gave her the courage that she lacked. She remembered her grit rearing its head, and she shoved her insecurities back into some dark corner. She made a promise to herself. Somehow – whatever it took - she would rise to those unspoken expectations in her child's eyes, and be the mother that she needed.

[So you saw your vulnerability as a weakness, and covered it up with bravado? The same bravado that you used to protect yourself in your physical world - with disastrous consequences. There are various kinds of weaknesses - many of which you've never permitted yourself the luxury of succumbing to. And your denial only kept your barriers firmly in place. But, whatever form your defenses took, they only existed to protect your vulnerability. A trait that you perceived as a weakness when actually, it's your biggest strength. It's the 'bridge' that keeps you connected to self-love, once your lower body becomes aligned to your soul purpose. For love, and ego can't co-exist in the same heart space. Accessing that bridge though, is a case of Being - not doing. And it requires a very gentle approach to abide in your stillness, until you start to resonate with it. Imagine a ball of mercury in the palm of your hand. Any attempt to grab or hold onto it tightly will cause it to slip through the gaps between your clenched fingers. But, if you allow it to rest gently in your open palm, you'll always remain connected to it. Your 'palm' is analogous to your heart, and 'mercury' to your soul. Your vulnerability is the bridge – the skin - that connects them, and allows your heart to 'hear' all that your soul desires to bring forth into your world. Despite the suffering in your life, your true power lies in transmuting those experiences through your heart open in your physical world. And that needs you to be in touch with your vulnerability. Believe in your open, vulnerable heart to help you achieve your soul purpose, and you'll have access to a kind of power that you never thought possible - to create the life that you could never imagine. You'll never be able to claim ownership of what you co-create, for you're only the physical vehicle to manifest your purpose in this physical world. Your desire for ownership stems from your ego's powerlessness when it's not in control. And that only results in you amassing more stuff in your physical world to suppress its fears, and insecurities. The irony is that you remain feeling powerless, because that very desire feeds the illusion of lack that keeps you separated from the true source of your power – your open, vulnerable heart]

[Despite your doubts, an open heart won't cause more suffering. Standing steadfast in your truth with an open heart space keeps you in harmony with your Being. It keeps your lower body in a state of love. And by remaining present in your heart space, you'll be able to recognize, and transcend any threat in your physical world. You'll be centered in the stillness within you - the only real thing about you. The only real thing in the Universe. There will be no more suffering. Once your healing is done, the past will be no more. If you do experience any pain on your soul path, then as the observer in your life you now know that you've wandered from your truth. It's a trigger pointing to a recent issue – not one in your past. And it's an opportunity to turn inward - to check in with your Self. You also know that self-love is the key to surrendering, and healing yourself. Surrender isn't simply resigning yourself to whatever comes your way. It's the very seat of your soul from where you abide in harmony with your true Self - without any emotional extremes or thoughts, including separation or lack. You lack nothing. You'll still encounter various emotions from the experiences that form part of your soul path but, you'll behold them through the eyes of love, and that will allow you have a very different life experience. More importantly, you'll no longer be distracted by any of the stories that your ego throws in your way. Unfortunately, you erected so many barriers, so early in life that you've never known anything, other than being a prisoner of your mind. It kept you in a constant defensive state, making you believe that you were protecting yourself. However, without being aware of it, you were so entrapped in the prison of your own making that you couldn't access your soul's desires. The only way to get you to heed its call was to break open your heart. It was the only way to get you to be vulnerable – to feel what you've been avoiding. And open you to surrender to a very different kind of transfiguration process - the death of your old self, and the birth of your true Self]

As she listened, completely dumbfounded by what she was hearing, she became aware of another shift within her. She felt as though she was floating. Flowing all around, and into herself. Her body felt free from the confines of her skin. She felt as though she was slowly dissolving, and once again, becoming one with the nothingness. She glanced at her body. She was still very much in it. There was a warmth in her chest and stomach, and an electric current was pulsing throughout her body. She had a sense of being released from the past and at the same time, she could feel the increasing spaciousness within. She had a fleeting thought of what would replace that space once she was free of her past. It was such a weird thought that she immediately pushed it away. She felt no inclination to force an understanding – she was happy that it remain a mystery. For now, all she wanted to do was embrace the spaciousness, and peace within her. There was something else – a sense of the amazing liberation that awaited her on the other side of that wall, once she broke through it. She hugged herself, and giggled with a sense of carefree abandonment. It was another one of those emotions that she'd never felt before. She savored its soft, girlish sweetness. Girlish? She? Amazing! She felt like an idiot! Something that she would have been horrified to admit before. And yet, her heart didn't mind.

[You wouldn't have felt that – not after your first experience of becoming a woman was unknowingly snuffed out by your father. You've been caught between two worlds ever since - a child in one, and an adult in the other. And not belonging to either one]

So she'd denied any feelings associated with her changing body, and suppressed her feminine nature. She tilted her chin towards the nothingness – she'd made quite a habit of getting caught in-between time. There she was hanging in nothingness, caught between her past, and a new life - caught between different worlds. And she'd spent her whole life so far, caught between her lost childhood, and adulthood. What was she during those in-between years? She couldn't bring herself to ask "who," because she couldn't ascribe any identity to the person that she used to be. She realized that she'd never given any thought to what those changing phases in her life would mean to her cognitive development. The extent of her understanding was limited to the physical changes to her body. She'd never contemplated the impact on her psyche. She'd felt like an asexual, empty vacuum all of her life! Her physical body might have changed to resemble that of an adult but, she'd been separated from her Self! She never realized that it even existed; it was as though she'd fallen through time! It struck her that she'd been wandering that nowhere-land for years - as a lost child, in an adult body. Why did it take so long for her to see it? An image of her father came to mind, and she recalled the look in his eyes whenever he gazed upon her. That was it! She was trying to capture the way he made her feel! And be that person she saw in his eyes. She sighed. She didn't know who that person was but, she did feel loved. But, she could look to an external source for love. Neither could she rely on such a nebulous image of herself to build the new foundation for her soul path – even if it was in the eyes of someone she loved with all her heart, and soul!

[You're never an 'image' of yourself when the reflection comes from a place of love. Your father was only reflecting the love that already exists within you. And don't fall into the trap of your old mindset - thinking that you need to curate an identity before you can have all that rightfully belongs to you. You already have an identity - your Self. And your only real future lies in surrendering to your soul path]

She could feel the tears threatening to burst through the constricting walls of her throat. The pain of loss, and sadness was excruciating. What did she miss in life by being so unaware of her actions? What did she lose by not fully embodying her true Self? So much precious time lost! So much energy wasted! *Where would life have taken her if she'd remained true to her Self? Who was she in the first place?* She felt devastated. *Would she ever be able to get back what she'd lost?*

[Nothing that belongs to you will ever be lost. You still have all the time that you need in this physical realm to actualize your soul purpose. And you have everything that you need within you to realize it. You are everything - just as you are right here; right now. Even if the unveiling of your purpose takes a lifetime, you'll discover an eternity in every moment that you surrender to your soul's truth. All you are required to do is stay present with your Self. And trust. You're exactly where you need to be. Part of this quest involves transcending the stereotypical roles assigned to you in your physical world, before you can merge fully with your true Self – which is both masculine, and feminine. None of those linear, dualistic definitions that you've been conditioned to believe in, apply to your Self. You're first and foremost, a human Being – irrespective of age, sex, gender, religion or custom. Before you can take that first step onto your soul path, you have to grasp the full measure of its meaning. You're far more than you ever thought your Self to be. And you're enough – just as you are. You're timeless; limitless. You've lost nothing. Nothing of real value, anyway. Only when you fully surrender to that knowing, will you be able to break out of an identity formulated around lack]

[It made you view your Self within the context of the roles that you attributed to yourself. It's time to free yourself from such limitations. Any role that demands a denial of Self doesn't serve you. Neither does any form of ego-attachment or assumed status to prove yourself. You're not required to prove yourself equal to any other. Equality is a misnomer when applied to your Self. The Self can never be 'equal' to anyone else – no one else carries your soul. And only you can fulfill your unique, soul mission. As a Being, equality is a non-issue. Everyone is equal - everyone emanates from the same Divine Source. If you can only validate yourself by adopting any number of roles to prove your worth and identity to society, then you're truly lost, and you serve no one. Least of all, yourself. Neither does society serve you – if it requires you to be anything less than your true Self. Your truth stems from your soul purpose. And only by owning your truth, will you become visible to your Self. Every other version of you will be invisible in this physical world. Continue working on identifying any resistance to the unveiling of your true Self. Celebrate it - for everything else that needs to happen to move you into your true reality follows from that]

She closed her eyes, and turned inward. She felt drawn to a sense of something within – something that she'd never felt before. She felt an unusually, strong connection to it – like she was meeting a long-lost friend. Despite her anxiety, she remained present with that strange feeling. With that acknowledgement, she felt herself release her resistance to an inner softness – nothing more than a sweet, whispering thread of vulnerability. It felt as though something was about to burgeon forth from the spaciousness within – like a flower, the instant before it burst into bloom. She had the distinct impression that her Self was about to be revealed. She was in awe of the wonder transpiring within her. There was no fear. Neither did she care about hiding or protecting herself in the midst of this unknown phenomenon. And yet, the scale of what she felt as her heart, and soul were completely revealed to her must have been the equivalent of some cataclysmic event. This hitherto unknown, invisible Self didn't feel so insignificant anymore. It felt limitless, as though it extended to the very "edge" of the Universe – if there was such an edge! She really was connected to the infinite beyond. All of this, must be part of her Being. She crinkled her forehead as she tried to fathom the magnanimity of what she was feeling. Then she hunched her shoulders, and hugged herself fiercely. She didn't know how else to express the wonder seeping through her body. The image of a flower came to mind again. This time with its open petals held in the loving gaze of the sun's rays. Each petal was being gently kissed, and caressed by the warm sunlight. Each petal quivered with fear knowing that once it revealed itself, its beauty could catch the eye of some passer-by.

They could pluck it, and destroy its beauty before it was shared with the Universe. And yet, it bloomed anyway - unable to stop itself from being enticed by the glory of being one with the light. She was so mesmerized by the thought that she could feel each unfolding "petal" with every breath that she took. Until she – her new-born Self - was dancing in the light of her soul, and showered by the love of her Being.

In that moment, she became aware of her breathing. She stopped - afraid that her breath would waken her. She didn't want to awaken from such a wonderful dream. But, she wasn't dreaming! She was fully awake, and conscious of each breath as it gently wafted through her body. She relaxed, and took long, deep gulps of air. She relished the headiness as it swept through her like a conductor's wand, slowly coaching the chords of the various instruments - the emotional energies - in its wake. Each chord was moving to its own rhythm at it coursed through her veins in a silent symphony, until they reached her heart in one, resounding crescendo. She closed her eyes, lifted her arms, and breathed out what she felt within her. She'd never before, felt so light. So unburdened. So vibrantly alive. She realized that this was probably what it felt like to be a child bathed in the warm glow of its mother's love. But, that feeling of joy didn't emanate from some external source – it was within her! She paused, and took a deep breath. Finally, she had some clarity about her arduous quest. Everything that she needed was within her! And the only way for her to see that was to remove everything that was standing in its way! She felt overcome by gratitude. And liberated from her constant wanting of love, and validation from 'the other.' In the freedom, and expansiveness of her Being she realized that she wasn't just a daughter, a wife, a mother or a woman. Neither was she defined by titles, qualifications or any of her material possessions. She was – had always been – a ray of light; made of the same Divine essence as life itself. She was a Being – an infinite energy field of love. It wasn't just a thought but, a deep, silent knowing stemming from an unknown, inner well of wisdom. It dawned on her that her Being required no definition. Neither did it require any walls or barriers for protection. It needed absolutely, nothing. She was safe. And loved. She didn't have to be afraid of anything or anyone, anymore.

[So you are afraid of something?]

That question! Again! She didn't want to deal with that. Not now – when she'd discovered so much love, and light within her.

[Now is exactly the right time – in the presence of such love. It can never be lost but, you won't be able to step onto your soul path, until you confront what you fear the most]

She hated being pressurized! Especially, when there was no point to it.

[What you think is unimportant. Your thoughts only serve to placate your ego. Stay present within the space of your Being, and observe your thoughts, and feelings. Nothing can hurt you any longer]

She stuck out her tongue at the Voice.

[I'm aware that you don't think highly of me]

She grimaced. And once again, looked around. But, there was no one to be seen. *How could Voice know that? She wasn't even aware of it! Was it one of those unknown truths that she needed to become conscious of?* She sighed, and turned to her only companions in the nothingness – her memories. She vaguely remembered the standoff with her mother as a teenager, and the deafening silence between them that went on for years. Her memory of Kitty was as clear, as the first day she saw him lying in the field. She recalled playing with him in the cellar. And then, nothing. For the first time, she became aware of the underlying restlessness whenever her mind wandered too close to that night. She frowned. What happened that night? She'd always considered her childhood to be uneventful - downright boring most of the time. All she wanted was to grow up as fast as she could, and get away from that hell-hole! She sighed. *There was no reason to labor over things that she would never know the truth about. It just made her angry and sad, and there were more important things to do. Like finding a way out of the nothingness, and making some money. Money gave her more choices......*

[.....to escape. Except there is no escape from the fears that are holding your Self captive ....no matter how much money you make......]

......and now that she knew herself better, she was going to make as much of it as she could.......

[.....you've already been down that road.....it took you nowhere]

She ignored Voice. *She would get through this quest in the same way that she'd always done things in her life – with willful intention, and sheer grit.....*

[Good luck with that]

......Life was a series of events – nothing more. Some good; some bad.

There! It was as simple as that. She could handle it. There was no need to go around in circles, trying to understand something that was lost in time……

[….you need to heal, and transcend your past – there's no other way to get to your true Self. But, first you have to face your biggest fear, and uncover the truth buried under it]

…..and the less emotion involved, the better. Her approach was simple; it had always worked for her. She could count on it – like she'd always done. Her fear couldn't stop her! She would deal with it as she'd done before – just ignore it! Besides, it was useful. It kept her anger alive – it was the fuel she needed to accomplish what she wanted in life. It kept her motivated and…..

[…..running from your Self. Without fully embodying your Self you'll never be in a state of inner harmony. And without inner peace, you'll never be able to be present. Return to your stillness. Stay in your awareness, and observe your thoughts. You're drawing on old patterns that still exist in your mind but, they won't work for you anymore – they are out of alignment with your soul purpose. You've healed many of your past traumas, and shifted a number of times during your quest. You've transcended many of your painful experiences. But, your inclination to run still remains your strongest trigger - the fear at the base of it still has to be healed. Your restlessness is caused by your resistance. You have only one option – face it. What are you so afraid of?]

She wasn't afra……

[….denial is resisting. But, there is no way around it. Sit with those feelings – they will lead you to what you fear the most. It's so deeply ingrained into every fiber of your body that you can't see your Self apart from it]

She felt goaded. *How many times must she repeat herself!? Voice wasn't listening to her!*

[Do you listen to your Self?]

That hit a nerve! And completely, deflated her anger – distracting her from her original trend of thought. She reacted immediately. *She always listened to herself!*

[You're not listening now. You're still acting out from that place of fear. And for as long as it remains you won't be able to hear your inner voice clearly. You've been repeating the same patterns partly, because of your anger. But, that emotion is merely a trigger, because you refuse to acknowledge your latent fear. It 'motivated' you all right – to deny your feelings. You might not have been aware of your inner voice before but, now you are. And it won't stop, until you hear what it has to say]

Something about what Voice said caught her attention. She'd accepted the daily grind as her reality. But, she couldn't deny that she'd always yearned for something more – specifically, to feel more of life; to be one with it. A desire to live fully alive - beyond anything that she could possibly imagine or anticipate. It had very little to do with material gain although, her past actions contradicted that. Was that the reason she'd never felt inspired by what she did? Now she felt a desire unlike any other. It felt like something so much more – more than anything that she could do by willfully motivating herself. It was coming from somewhere deep within her – without any external motivating factor. Was that what inspiration really felt like? It must part of the life force that was her very essence and yet, she'd seldom felt so close to it. She recalled feeling that way when she'd written her poem. At the time, her vision of being one with life seemed like an impossible fantasy, compared to everything that she had to contend with in her outward reality – real or not. For some reason, she'd given up living life with such fierce, single-minded passion, and fearlessness. She was suddenly struck by something that she'd never thought about. What was she doing with her life, if she wasn't living it that way? Why was she even alive if she'd compromised her soul's truth? Was her life a product of love, and inspiration? Or fear? Again there were no answers. She realized that it didn't matter - she knew what she had to do. She sat silent and still with her eyes closed, as she poured the love of her Being into the chasm between the life that she'd lived, and the unknown life that her soul desired. If love and light were all that she had, then she would use that power to heal her separation, and bring her soul's reality into the physical realm.

But, logic was still the most predominant pattern distracting her from being fully present. She tried hard to center herself - to observe the thoughts that were now confronting her. She felt as though she was watching herself, see-sawing between two lives – the past and the new, vast, unknown spaciousness within her. The past life of the person whom she believed she knew and yet, that identity had separated her from her Self; from all of life. And the spaciousness of her Being made her feel as one with all that Is. The past life that she believed to be so real now felt cold, and empty. Lifeless. And yet, as empty as the unknown spaciousness within her appeared to be, she felt inescapably drawn towards the invisible, intangible force within it. She felt more alive than ever before, by just being present with it. And it felt more real, compared to anything that she'd experienced before. So real that she felt an intimacy with her Self that she'd never known before - a bond bathed in a timeless love that could never be broken. Her restlessness had disappeared. In its place, she felt only peace. Warm. Safe. Filled with love. And fully aware of the fear that still existed in that dark void within her. She was amazed at her steadfastness, as she sat with that knowing. She didn't feel the need to run or suppress her discomfort. Within her silent stillness, she came to a startling revelation. Her past was Ok. And she was Ok - with surrendering to the life that was still to unfold. In fact everything looked, and felt perfect - in all its imperfection. She felt whole; complete – in spite of all her broken pieces. And she felt so very real – for the first time in her life! She realized that every part of her was an irreplaceable aspect of her humanness - to experience life, exactly the way it was. In whatever way her soul presented it to her. And not to make it something that it was never meant to be. She sighed blissfully. Life in all its infinite, unknowable essence had never felt so good. For the first time, she was utterly in love – with her Self! And the life that was hers – only she could make it everything that it was meant to be.

In that state of no-mind – just Being - she observed the contrast between aspects of herself that held widely, differing beliefs. A past marked by persistent planning, and drive to maintain momentum. There was an ongoing, romance with new ideas, and a frantic pursuit of new opportunities - rivalled only by an extreme urgency to get them under her belt. Coupled with the constant anxiety over the lack of time to accomplish everything that she wanted. Back then, the life that she'd planned for herself was so clear – it only took intellect, will, and physical strength to make it happen. And of course, her ego - in control of it all. And yet, in spite of all that super human effort, she'd felt constantly disempowered. The inner spaciousness to co-create her soul path, however, felt totally different. Yes - it was beyond logic. And it existed in the realm of the unknown - she would never have control over the way that it unfolded.

And yet, she felt at peace. She felt present with her Self – centered in her silent, stillness. There were no goals that she needed to pursue to force her new reality – only the conscious surrender to the purpose that lay dormant in her soul. There was no urgency – just the calm knowing that she would complete whatever she needed to do in her lifetime. Time wasn't a factor – being present with her truth was. There was no fear or desire; no motivation - no emotion at all in the peaceful neutrality of her stillness. There was no need for competition – only she could fulfill her soul purpose. There was no need to prove anything. She just felt an unquestionable sense of her own limitless potential to co-create a life as yet, unlived – feeling fully alive. There was no need for compulsive reasoning or innumerable scenarios for the outcomes she desired - her soul already carried her life's blueprint, and the wisdom to help her accomplish it. The exact nature of her purpose was unimportant. Far more important was her state of Being – her presence. And being inspired to act from her heart space. This wasn't an abdication of responsibility. On the contrary, it was the certainty that arose from fully surrendering to something far greater than herself. And taking a blind leap of faith by consciously committing to her soul's reality, even though it was unknown, and uncertain. And trusting her Self to see it through. Her physical form only existed to observe, and support the unfolding of her soul path. That was her only "role." That was the real work that she needed to do during her lifetime. As for the rest, the Divine essence of life residing within her would lead the way.

She again bowed her head in reverence to be in the presence of such Grace. She realized that she'd always been her worst critic. Never mind what lay at the root of her fears. Her self-doubt, mixed with anger made her hack away at herself, until what little self-esteem she possessed was ground to dust. Her childhood might have been the catalyst for her destructive nature but, her lack of awareness had made her inflict the same behavior on herself. She'd never known much compassion or patience. She might have been generous with her money but, her imbued sense of lack sabotaged her good intentions, and kept her spirit small. As for love? It had seldom featured in her life. She'd never considered herself worthy of her own time, and love – let alone, anyone else's. Her low self-worth made her a bottomless pit - for experiences that showed it up. She'd strived to compensate for what she believed she lacked by giving and yet, she was unable to receive any form of love, affection or support from anyone, other than her father. Her past was nothing more than a financial transaction. And her reality had merely reflected that. No matter the number of variables factored into it, she would always be in the red. There might very well be enough material wealth in her physical world to compensate for such a 'deal' but, it wasn't one that her soul would even consider, let alone accept. The repetitive nature of her painful experiences weren't the actions of a vindictive Universe but, an invitation to awaken; to elevate her consciousness. To help her move into her true reality in the world. And everything, and everyone in her past existed to support her awakening - that was the gift of the soul that she was born with. Her past reality was merely symptomatic of a life lived in fearful slumber, and her fears will continue to be triggered if she didn't get to the core of it. And since she'd paid so little attention to her emotions, she'd probably missed some vital clues along the way.

She was having problems breathing again, and the pain in her chest was excruciating. Moreover, she was overwhelmed by a feeling of entrapment. *What was happening to her? Surely she'd made enough progress on this quest to be granted some respite?* She sighed. *When would it all be over? What more did she have to do?*

[Who are you bargaining with? There's no one coming to save you]

She felt mortified. She realized that somewhere in the recesses of her mind she still believed that she was waging a war between "right" and "wrong." *And that making the right choices would bring some kind of reward ……*

[This quest is your 'reward']
That she would be saved……

[By whom? Throughout your lifetime you're the same soul that you entered this world with – in a physical body. That's all you are. And being born into this world doesn't entitle you to anything]

She massaged her battered ego with the fantasy that she could now escape from Voice. She had the know-how. Her excitement grew tangibly as she contemplated just how she was going to go about it. Her breathing became faster; shallower. The change in her breathing, signaled that an emotion was reaching a crescendo within her but, she wasn't in her stillness. She was consumed by thoughts of escape. *She now knew how to enter the stillness within, and become one with the nothingness. And if anything was possible in that space, then she could escape from this quest at any time.* But, the instant that she indulged those thoughts, something within reneged with such ferocity that she stopped, and turned inward – to observe her thoughts. She was able to recognize her ego's conniving attempt to lead her astray. She realized that she was embattled with a much deeper level of deception. But, this was Self against self; truth against ego! And that, was no contest at all! Her truth slowly revealed the clarity that she needed. She might be able to entertain any illusory thought in her mind but, her truth now provided her with an invisible shield of integrity that protected her stillness. And nothing that compromised her truth, would be allowed to get through it. It was no longer necessary to concern herself with the integrity of her actions. As long as she had that inner shield upholding her integrity towards her Self, she could trust that she was behaving with integrity towards those around her. Sometimes, her truth might be ugly but, it was essential for her to speak it - with love. Furthermore, it gave her the assurance that any decision made in the presence of her higher Self would serve both her interests, and that of others. She was being observed – by her higher Self. Her pact now was to be in service of her soul purpose. In doing so, she would serve the highest interests of her Self, and humanity. There was no escaping her soul purpose; no compromise would be worth it. As daunted as she was by her revelations, she felt extremely humbled, and blessed to be re-connected with her Self. Things were so much simpler. She bowed her head in gratitude.

In the openness of her gratitude, she remembered that she'd agreed to revisit her past. She grimaced. *Each time that she felt as though her past was behind her, something else reared its head to suck her into that black void! All she wanted was for this quest to be over so that she could get on with her life!* But, that would only be possible once she cleared whatever was still keeping the light of her soul from fully embodying her. She sighed heavily. *What was she going to do? What would it take to get herself out of this void?* Although her patience, and knowing had grown since the start of her quest, she couldn't help wondering why so many answers still eluded her. Perhaps the answers weren't meant to be found. And surrendering to not knowing was wisdom in action. Just as her mind resumed control, she realized that her new-found vulnerability had deserted her. She was back in her body again, feeling heavy and frozen. After experiencing so much love, and lightness in the nothingness the feeling of being swallowed by darkness again, took her by surprise. But, the contrast between the two states that co-existed within her, jarred something else in the depths of her. She sat with her discomfort, until clarity dawned. She realized that she was very familiar with that feeling - she'd felt frozen throughout her life! It had never occurred to her before, because she'd never known that any other state existed. Certainly, nothing close to the depth of love, and expansiveness that she experienced within her Being. Now that difference was glaringly evident.

[Why did you not trust the feelings evoked by the poem that you wrote as a child? Why did you choose to exist in smallness when you could have experienced life as it was meant to be lived in all its infinite glory - in love and light?]

She grunted with irritation. *Wasn't it obvious!? She didn't know any better at the time. Besides, she was just a child. And then, she was too busy to worry about anything else. It's not like she had a choice!*

[That's just the victim in you talking. You always have a choice - in any situation. You can stand in your truth or turn away from it. And that choice will determine the nature of your life experience – acting in alignment with your truth or continuing in a numbed state of existence. The former supports you rising into expanded levels of consciousness, and unlocks your limitless potential. The latter reinforces your smallness by making you believe in your limitations, and confines you to a world of illusion]

She sighed. She'd focused all her energy on resolving the ongoing chaos in her life.

[Did you?]

Yes! And yet, there was never a time when she'd had a "smooth ride." And over the last ten years or so, everything had spiraled out of control! Now she was nowhere - sitting in nothingness! She probably would have had better luck if she'd devoted her time to pursuing her soul purpose! If only she'd known!

[This quest isn't a game of chance. Neither does your mind get to choose the timing of your soul's lessons. You've spent many lifetimes chasing outcomes in your physical life. You might have missed the opportunities to fulfill your purpose but, you also gained invaluable wisdom from your soul lessons. That wisdom is still available to you, although your mind doesn't remember it. You can now use it to fulfill your soul purpose in this lifetime. The only constant over all your lifetimes, is your soul. And it led you to exactly, this point – to heal yourself, and reclaim your sovereignty. Whether you realize it or not, you've come very far on this quest. There's just one, last hurdle for you to cross]

She was tempted to react but, she now knew better than to deny facing the huge, invisible wall confronting her. She just wished that she knew what was lying behind it. She sensed a whole new world waiting for her on the other side of it – one that she couldn't see! *What was blocking her? Why was she still playing the victim? Surely she'd won that battle a long time ago.* For years, she'd blamed everyone around her for the ongoing drama in her life. When she was older, she realized that she was caught in a vicious cycle. Any negative thought or behavior towards others had a strange way of ricocheting back to her. As a result, she'd diligently worked on freeing herself from the negativity plaguing her life - or so she thought. That approach might have helped somewhat, to counter her victim mentality but, it was now obvious that she'd never really resolved anything. She felt weighed down, and horribly confused. Was she going around in circles trying to circumvent the real problem? What lay at the core of her fears? Why did she repeat the pattern of pain in her life? For the most part, she'd come to grips with the limitations of her conditioning. But, why did she succumb to it in the first place!? It slowly dawned on her that as much as she'd used her career to reinforce her notions of success, she'd led herself down the garden path with ill-informed choices, and knee-jerk reactions stemming from her easily threatened ego. Yes – she'd refused to give up, and had picked herself up on numerous occasions. But, despite her efforts, things in her life just never went as intended. Nevertheless, she'd persisted with her attempts to become the "success" she'd always envisioned for herself. And when she didn't, she'd ascribed her failure to her shitty luck. But, even at the height of her success she was never able to overcome her restlessness. It slowly dawned on her that in her private moments, she'd indulged her thoughts of her sorry lot in life. She sighed. She'd reinforced the pattern of victimhood, without even being conscious of her thoughts!

Furthermore, by indulging in self-pity she'd reinforced those behavioral patterns. That only further compromised her soul growth! And she'd been doing that for lifetimes! An image came to mind of her soul as a funnel - reaching outwards from her body. In the presence of the nothingness that 'funnel' now looked minute. Inconsequential. Was that the state she'd enforced onto her soul!? Was that the result of her conditioning? She stared at it for a long time, wondering what her soul really looked like, outside the barriers that had confined it for so long. She became aware that her soul was grappling to free itself from something holding onto the base of it. What was that? That constricted stem looked completely, out of place in the presence of her infinite Being! Then again, the entire image looked foreign in the nothingness! She sensed that by getting past this last constriction – another inner, invisible wall - she would somehow, free her soul. She sighed. Why did she never see this before?

['No time?']

She sighed. Those were her words, all right! And she hated being reminded of it! *Almost as much, as she hated all this digging! Her emotions just tied her up in knots! Like always!* So she'd kept her gaze firmly fixed on taking her life forward.

[But, you didn't move 'forward.' You were so hell-bent on out-running your past that you never stopped to check in with your Self. Neither did you question what kind of life you were creating by skirting around your fears. To your credit though, you showed tenacity in driving yourself to get 'there.' But, nothing much changed. How could it - when nothing changed within you? You're still buried under that fear that you've been lugging around, your entire life. Your life purpose can only really start when you free yourself from it, and take that first step from your heart center to consciously create it. Your quest is giving you the opportunity of a new beginning - to realize your soul purpose. But, you're still holding onto something; your mind is still resisting. The only thing preventing you from fully surrendering is the fear that you've been holding onto, all your life. You can't surrender conceptually or through healing alone – you have to consciously enter your fear, and be present with it. You've now found the love within you to face it. And heal your pain]

She groaned. She realized that that feeling of being stuck didn't arise in the nothingness. She'd felt stuck, all her life! Every time she found an opportunity that she believed would take her life forward, she hit a wall. And as relieved as she was at finding what she wanted, she'd never managed to overcome the nagging feeling that something was wrong. She barely escaped one battle, before she went hurtling into the next! And despite all her efforts, she only ended up in the same hole that she'd spent so much time, and energy digging herself out of! She often wished that there was some other way to live life but, she'd just never figured one out. Over time, she'd come to accept her circumstances as her "lot in life." And just soldiered on. She was hit by a revelation. Without knowing any better, she'd capitulated to the same behavioral patterns, because she was being driven by her fears!

['Soldiered on'......to where?]

She was about to react but, then she paused. Where did she think she was going? Her decisions weren't motivated by visions of success! On the contrary, her ongoing attempts now looked filled with a desperate fervor - like she was trying to escape from something. If she'd never seen it before, it was now staring her in the face! Was fear at the center of her behavior? Why was she blind to it? What was the belief that was so much stronger than her fears that she preferred being its captive instead? She winced as another revelation came to her. She'd seldom asked much of those around her but, the demands of herself were relentless. What was she trying to prove? To whom? Herself? But, that didn't resonate with her. Her poor self-worth might have impacted negatively on her career but, that was only secondary to its impact on her life. She felt strongly that the pull was coming from something or someone other than herself. Her father? But, she'd seldom felt any pressure to prove anything to him. And reveled in his quiet pride whenever she accomplished something.

[Was there anyone else that you sought validation from?]

No.

[Did you treat yourself with self-love before?]

No.

[Why not?]

She shrugged dismissively.

[Never mind. The answer will come to you. What about your mother?]

She hit another blank. For as long as she could remember, her mother never really featured in her life. She was physically present but, that was all. She could just as well have been on another planet! And there weren't many childhood memories of her mother. Before she could figure out that relationship, she'd become a mother herself. And thereafter, the only priority was her own child.

[What about taking responsibility for your own life? Or did you think you could forfeit that responsibility by focusing all your attention on others?]

She sighed. How was she supposed to fit that in? There were always so many demands on her time; everything was a priority.

[Right here; right now, you're the only priority]

That made no sense! What did that even mean? She didn't know how to prioritize herself! Besides, she was a mother! She had only one responsibility - her child!

[Your conditioning smothered your feminine nature to such an extent that you believed forsaking yourself for others is noble. You don't have to sacrifice yourself to serve others. Your discomfort about receiving is the other side of that coin – you feel guilty. You don't believe you deserve to. So you gave, until you were depleted. Being in service is a mutual exchange of energy between people. Both the giver, and the receiver are uplifted, and strengthened by their respective actions. And if lack underpins the act of giving, you'll only perpetuate lack in your life. Whenever you give, there is a fine line between uplifting, and enabling. But, there is a critical difference - enablement does nothing for your soul growth or the growth of others. It perpetuates a victim-mentality, and entitlement]

Her body stiffened. *She was done with this madness! She was getting nowhere! She had to find some way out of there. There was nothing more to do or say. She'd stuck with this quest thinking that it would take her somewhere but, it was only a wild goose chase!* She paused. It was strangely wonderful – she had to admit that much. She'd never experienced anything like it. And she'd learnt a lot about herself. *But, enough was enough! She'd probably conjured up some mind-game to distract herself from something or other, in her physical world.* She smiled as she recalled her fascination with magic. *This was exactly what a magician would do – conjure up some fantasy to escape reality! But, she was exhausted. And bored. She'd had enough of this* never-ending, emotional rollercoaster! It was time to move on. There! It was a done deal. With that forced summation of her quest she looked around expectantly – thinking that she would find herself back in her physical world. Everything, however, remained exactly as it was – nothingness! She felt utterly gutted by her lack of power to change her circumstances.

[Be kind to yourself. You're not in control of this quest. It falls outside the ambit of your mind, and ego]

She groaned while clenching, and unclenched her fists. But, no amount of angst changed the reality of the nothingness. She remained in it - held by nothing other than the Divine Grace she sensed all around her. As difficult as it was to shake her disbelief, she was grateful that she wasn't alone. Only to have her worst nightmare rear its head. She was dumbfounded. *It had been years since she'd felt like that!* Her first reaction was to resist it. It took every ounce of energy to surrender to her stillness. She observed her anxiety as it slowly clawed its way from her stomach to her chest. And before she knew what was happening she was gasping for breath. Her hands were waving frantically, searching for something to hold onto but, her efforts were futile - her body remained rooted to the same spot. Her throat was on fire, and her mouth was so dry that she started to retch. She broke into a cold sweat as she fell into the grip of a fear that she'd refused to permit into her space. She rubbed her chest to ease the pressure, and nausea. She was distraught over the flurry of thoughts whirling about in her head but, acknowledged them. *This quest was a nightmare! A huge mistake! There was absolutely no reason for her to be there! She had to get out! Where was her daughter!? Where was everyone!? WHERE WAS SHE!?*

She pressed her temples – hoping to stem the tide of emotion sweeping through her. She felt as though she was going to implode from the sheer intensity of it. She grimaced at the irony. There she was surrounded by all the space that she could ever need and still, the "walls" were closing in on her! She felt - more than saw - the nothingness moving closer, and closer. She looked up to see what was happening, and realized that the stars had disappeared. She gasped. *She was in utter blackness! Where did the stars go? She was all alone!* Despite her extreme fear, she noticed that her breathing had eased. She realized there was something different about this blackness – it didn't feel at all like the nothingness. She trembled. Why did the air feel so cold? And it smelt dank, and musty - like a space that had been enclosed, for a long time. She wished that she was still in the nothingness - floating amongst the stars. But, they were nowhere to be seen. She shifted uncomfortably, and winced – her legs scraped against rough earth. Her heart stopped beating. There was only one place in the whole world that smelt like that! The cellar!

She looked around nervously. There was a strong metallic taste in her mouth, and the waves of fear in her stomach were threatening to drown her. She continued breathing deeply, and remained in the stillness within – feeling her fear. She instinctively knew that if she succumbed to the alarm bells ringing in her head, she would be lost forever. She needed to face that black, void within. One last time. She could no longer avoid it. She was aware of the frantic thoughts in her mind, and her ego's rampant efforts to attach to them – for security. But, she stayed in her stillness. Finally, she understood why she'd endured the unfolding of each phase of her quest. She thought that she'd reached her breaking point at various stages but, each time, she was being dragged beyond her limitations to transcend the fears, and insecurities that she didn't even know existed. And by grappling through the ocean of emotion, and thought she'd somehow managed to find her way to the eye of the storm within her. And when she looked around her, she could see her entire life swirling around her in a mass of chaos, and uncertainty. But, she was at peace - she could stay present with it. All, because of self-love. Once again, she felt a wave of electricity surge through her body. She smiled. She knew that she was ready to face whatever lay ahead of her on her soul path. And what was lying in that void. So that's what true power felt like!

And then, she was hit by a barrage of thoughts. *Why was she back in the cellar? How could she be a child, and an adult at the same time!?* Her mind raged on in disbelief and yet, within her Self she felt only peace. And a loving surrender to that moment – filled with nothing but, fear. She realized that she was once again, observing her mysterious experience. And not identifying with the stories in her mind was such so liberating! Her instincts told her to just let the story unravel – it was leading her closer to her fear. She sighed. *For everything that her old life wasn't, it used to be quite predictable. And according to most accounts, quite normal. She missed the reassurance that accompanied that level of control. Would things ever be the same again?* Did she even want things to be the same? After her so-called "normal" life lay in tatters around her, could she even claim to know what normal was? She felt the tears rolling down her cheeks as her confusion mounted. She was ice cold, and shaking violently. *Was she going mad?* How could she be thinking "mad" in her mind, and still feel so centered within her Self? Could someone be so ripped apart in body, and still be alive? She was horrified at the thoughts, and emotions clamoring for center stage in her mind and yet, within her stillness she felt only peace. Love. Oneness.

She gently brought her attention back to the cellar - to her long forgotten hideout. It still looked the same – after so many years. She recalled how much she enjoyed playing within its cool walls. It was her only haven. And now, she felt nervous; very uncomfortable. *She had to get out!* She shifted onto her hands and knees, and turned instinctively towards the exit. She gingerly placed her knees wherever her hands felt soft patches of earth. Her fingers brushed against something. She knew what it was, the instant her fingers grazed the soft, furry coat. *Kitty! He was still lying there! After all this time!* No! She was in her stillness! Time didn't exist in the nothingness. Again, the dissonance was too great. She stopped breathing. *This couldn't be happening. Not again! Not after so many years! It was all behind her! A long time ago!* She felt as though she was caught in a time-warp. *This was crazy! Time never went backwards! It never stopped! How else could she know that Kitty died of starvation? And that she was an adult with a child of her own? None of those things would have happened if time stopped! But, if that was true, why did she still feel like a child? How could she still be in a child's body?* Her reverie was cut short by the commotion coming from the floorboards above her head. What the.....! Whatever thread of reason remained totally, evaporated. She succumbed to the void. And she found herself back at the point in time, when her worst fears had taken her captive.

They were looking for her! She trembled, and pushed herself further into the corner. The shouting voices, and running feet got louder and louder, until her brain felt like it was going to explode. She squeezed her eyes shut, and held her hands tightly over her ears but, that didn't work. She caressed her beloved Kitty; wishing that he would wake up. She was cold and hungry. And even though she didn't want to, she had to go to school the next day. She hoped that her bedroom window was still open. She could sneak into bed without anyone suspecting a thing. She looked at the unmoving body of her little friend – she so wanted to take him with her but, she knew that he would be safer in the cellar. She made a silent promise to return the next day, and play with him when she got home. And then, she made her way to the exit. There was still a faint light coming from the small opening in the outer-most wall, even though it was well after mid-night. She moved towards it as fast as she could. In the darkness she felt the heat from the hand reaching for her, before she felt the painful grasp around her wrist. Her mournful daze did nothing to dull her reflexes. She knew what awaited her on the other side of that wall if she got caught. She managed to wriggle free from the tight grip, and tried scrambling back to her secret hideaway. But, she was too cold, and stiff to move fast enough. She felt the hand grab her foot, and she was dragged out of the cellar. When she landed on the cool, dewy grass outside she felt a familiar cloud of resignation descend on her. It was too late. She closed her eyes, and just lay there. She heard the snarling, and hissing words but, refused to look up. She was yanked upright to her feet but, she kept her face tucked in towards her chest as the hard slaps rained down on her head, and shoulders. She heard herself humming something but, it was lost in the weird sounds that thundered all around her. Now in the stillness within, she realized that she was humming one of the tunes that she'd made up. In some strange way, it had helped her shut out the whole experience. It must have been her way of soothing herself. Tears blinded her as her heart went out to the little girl who had tried so stoically, to protect herself from the ongoing abuse. But, the odds were far too great. It dawned on her that with every beating, she must have taken refuge in her numbness. Until eventually, she'd remained forever lost in the black void of her pain.

She shook herself out of her daze. But, now she was awake, and very much aware of her Self. She recalled rationalizing the experience by blaming herself. She must have made her mother very angry by staying out late. She was the one at fault - she deserved the beating. As devastated as she was by the memory of that night, she was more taken aback by her behavior towards herself. She realized that over the years, that kind of self-talk must have compounded her guilt, and unworthiness. She'd remained on the defensive, and apologetic towards everyone – for everything. She bore the blame - even when she wasn't at fault. She centered herself once again, and continued observing the silent "movie" flashing in her mind while her emotions as a child played out in her body. That night her tiny, humming voice failed to drown out the strange words that were spewing from the gnashing teeth. She'd never heard such words before. And she thought that they were long forgotten. But, there was no mistaking the sound of her mother's voice as it blasted through the walls of the black void, into her consciousness.

"Look at me" her mother hissed. "Look at me when I'm talking to you."

She knew she was only a short distance from her mother – she could feel her breath on the top of her head. But, she couldn't bring herself to lift her head. She felt her mother's nails digging into her face, as her bowed head was forced upward. Her eyes flew open from the pain. The sight before her was so terrifying that she stopped breathing.

"How many times must I tell you to behave? Why don't you listen to me you devil, bastard child? I'm going to kill you one day. Do you hear me? I'm going to kill you." Each sentence was punctuated with a hard slap. She just stood there – too petrified to say or do anything. But, the thoughts running through her mind were loud, and clear – louder than the thumping sound of her mother's hands against her head. She was very bad. She was the "devil." Her mother was right - she should be "killed." She didn't know what that meant but, whatever it was, she deserved it. And she knew that "one day" was bound to come. Maybe then, she would be with Kitty. Would she be as still as Kitty? Would she be all alone in the dark? She couldn't recall what happened after that. She must have blanked out. And remained in trapped in that fear, all her life.

She was sobbing so hard, she could barely breathe. In the stillness she was finally, able to grasp the full impact of that dreadful night. Those words, and her mother's chilling tone of voice had become the "voice in her head." It continued to break her down long after the beatings stopped. She was shaken by the animosity that was directed towards her as a child. The physical wounds might have healed over time but, she'd never gotten over how petrified she was that night. And how bereft, and powerless she felt. She'd felt that way her whole life! She was hit by another revelation as her mother's face flashed large, and ominous on the invisible screen in her mind's eye. It wasn't only the words, and the beatings that had crushed her.

It was the sight of her mother's face! She cringed as she braced herself to look at the face that had so filled her with dread, that she preferred blocking it from memory. Her mother's face was a snarling, roaring grimace. Her teeth were clenched, and the words were being spat out from lips that were pulled tightly across them. Her hair was undone, and hanging loosely about her face – practically, covering her features. She only caught a glimpse of her mother's distorted features that night but, what she saw was so terrifying that she feared her more than anything or anyone else. That terrifying image and her mother's words had remained the single, biggest threat that kept her constantly on the defensive, and expecting the worst at every turn. It made her cower in her mother's presence, even when she was standing upright. Over the years, she might have recovered somewhat, by re-gaining some self-esteem but, nothing was able to prevent her from dissolving into a puddle every time she felt afraid – which was all the time! Living with that inner conflict of protecting herself from, and yet, still desperately seeking the love of the woman who wanted to destroy her, was soul-destroying! She realized that her experiences as a child must have driven her away from her mother. And yet, her need for love, and nurturing kept her returning to the one person who refused to give it to her. That emptiness left her feeling constantly, restless and abandoned. And she tried to ease it by repeating the same "push-pull" pattern in all her other relationships. Was that the reason, she fluctuated between behavioral extremes? She recalled how she'd rebelled against the "power" that her mother had exercised over her as a child. After each incident she'd withdrawn for long periods of time, in an attempt to draw her out to express some kind of concern. But, her mother never capitulated or showed any remorse. She finally, understood the self-inflicted abuse, and the abusive relationships that she kept returning to, time-after-time. It was the only kind of "love" she was familiar with. In her mind, that was "home."

 She was shaking, and crying uncontrollably. That was not only the worst night of her life – it was also when she reached her breaking point! That was when she put up her biggest wall against any kind of relationship, including the one with herself! That was why nothing or no one, had ever been able to get through to her. She realized that even losing Kitty had never fully registered. She must have buried her grief under her fear. And there was never an opportunity to learn how to nurture self-love or self-worth in the painful experiences that kept popping up wherever she went. Her fear, and underlying abandonment issues were constantly triggered – so much so, that she could never bring herself to trust anyone. She'd learnt very early in life that she wasn't worthy of being treated with love, and kindness. It made her always settle for less, because she believed that she didn't deserve any better. And she had difficulty receiving, because she never considered herself worthy. Her inclination to give was reflexive – driven by her fears of being unlovable. And without self-love, she'd never known any better. Seeing her Self as a Divine conduit in a benevolent Universe that was capable of supporting her to actualize her soul's gifts was totally, beyond a mind incapacitated by fear. That was the night she stopped crying. And stopped hoping for any kind of reprieve from the outside world. She only knew that she had to protect herself from it, and fight for what she wanted. It made her defensive, and desperate. And made her stubbornly cling to whatever kind of "love" she could find. But, the only true love she'd ever known was for Kitty, and her father. And losing them had led her to believe that she'd forever lost their love. But, by some miracle she'd re-discovered their love, and the love for herself in the nothingness. It still existed. And now, in the stillness, she realized that true love could never be lost. It existed in every fiber of her Being. It was all around, and within her. She was love.

In the arms of her re-birthed Self, she became aware that there was another truth that she needed to acknowledge about that night. Her mother had never treated her sister or any other child, in the same way. She encountered another, deeper layer of pain. Why was she singled out to be punished, over and over again? For so many years, she'd believed that there was something terribly wrong with her! And she'd strived tirelessly to prove herself worthy of her mother's love. All her efforts though, were in vain. She returned to her stillness. Eventually, she gained the clarity she was looking for. She was battling with an ego! And her mother's never relinquished the stronghold it had over her youngest child, until she'd plucked up the courage to stand up to her as a teenager. That must have shaken her mother to such an extent that it made her somewhat aware of her actions, and she stopped physically abusing her youngest child. But, it was too late - to save her, from herself. She was shaking with grief but, she was close to making a breakthrough - she could feel it! Something told her that it would get her to the "other side" of that chasm of separation that she'd known all her life. She was exhausted right down to her bones. She could barely breathe. She felt death just a whisper away. She so wished that she could succumb to its final blackness but, there was still a sliver of light shining somewhere in the darkness. She sighed. It had taken so long - probably, lifetimes - to get to the level of awareness of being one with her Self; with her Being. She couldn't give up now! The cost was far too great – to her soul! She closed her eyes once again, and entered the stillness within. This time, it looked like a lake. The "movie" continued playing on its shimmering, misty surface. She was still humming the same childhood tune. The mist lifted, and she saw something on the glass-like, surface. She stared at it for a long time, trying to figure out what it was. Slowly, revelation dawned. It was an image of a face! She continued staring at it, and realized that the face had no eyes. And then, what she'd been struggling to understand all her life suddenly, became very clear. She'd never seen her mother's eyes - even when she was looking directly at her face! She burst into tears as she realized the full meaning of that symbolism to her child-self. Without her mother's love to mirror anything good back to her, she'd never seen herself as anything other than, the hateful words that were always thrown at her. Never mind all the positive affirmations that she'd used over the years to boost her confidence. She'd never risen above the belief that she wasn't worthy of being alive. She'd just bided her time – waiting for the day when she would be killed by the woman she loved most in the world.

The full impact of her childhood experiences on her behavior was suddenly very clear. Over the years, she'd re-enacted the limited emotional spectrum that she'd experienced as a child – the anger, pain, guilt, shame, abandonment, grief, hopelessness, and powerlessness. For so many years, she'd carried the heavy burden of being unworthy. And unlovable. Her fears, and insecurities made her avoid relationships. Even when she was with others, she preferred to remain in the background. In some strange way that made her feel comfortable – it validated the kind of "love" she was familiar with. And in some paradoxical way, it also made her feel closer to the childhood that she'd never had. It was her only memory of "home," and she'd clung to it with every fiber of her body. And as painful as that memory was, she felt even less without it. As grateful as she was for her father's love, "home" and "love" were never synonymous to her, because of the separation caused by pain in her psyche. That explained why she never felt at home – anywhere! As a child, she didn't know that her mother was running from her own demons. All she knew was that she deserved to be punished. And she found it difficult to accept that her mother had any conscious knowledge of the burden that her behavior had placed on her youngest child. *Why did her mother treat her that way? Was it a karmic relationship from a previous lifetime? Was it due to a lack of awareness? Did it give her mother a sense of power over her own dysfunctional life?* She sighed. She would never know the answers to her questions. She only knew that such a lack of awareness had exacted a heavy price on a child's sense of worth, and the ability to love her Self. She sighed. She'd forgiven her mother, a long time ago. But, she'd never acknowledged her suppressed resentment. There was only one thing left to do. Acknowledge her feelings, and release it. Love herself through her pain, and heal herself.

She realized that since that terrible day, she'd never seen herself as worthy of being alive – let alone, deserving of love. Furthermore, she'd reinforced the way that she was treated by denying herself any form of compassion, patience, kindness or gentleness. In fact, anything "good" was in opposition to the death sentence that she'd been dealt. If she did encounter anything positive or uplifting in her life it never registered on a conscious level. She didn't exist - even in her own eyes. Whatever she experienced in her life was secondary to the emptiness within. She realized that during the course of her life, she might have wanted to express herself in many different ways but, the pain, and hatred in her childhood was so strong that those emotions found a way of overshadowing her best intentions. It dawned on her that as much as she revered her father's love, it wasn't enough to save her from the void within that was like a growing vortex of negativity. It fed on itself, and had left her starved of love. And she'd projected those feelings onto others, throughout her life. But, her mother's "story" wasn't her "story". It was in no way, associated with her truth; with the love within her. She might have been invisible to her mother but, she wasn't invisible to her Self. If she hadn't come to the nothingness, and discovered self-love she would probably still be acting out her unconscious pain in her physical world. And believing that there was something wrong with her. But, that wasn't her truth. There was nothing "wrong" with her. She wasn't "bad" or the "devil." And even if she was, there was nothing to fear, anymore. Nothing, other than the Divine hands that held her had the power to destroy her.

What happened in the years between that night outside the cellar, and the standoff with her mother as a teenager? She shrugged. Probably, more of the same. But, somehow none of it mattered, anymore. It had all mysteriously dissolved in the light that was now shining so brightly within her. Contrary to the belief that her emotions were temporary chemical reactions that could be controlled by a flick of a switch, they were actually, very real. With real implications on the kind of life experience that she manifested in her world. She might not have understood the impact of her emotions before but, her emotional body had contributed to building her past reality – a false reality that had reflected her false self, and her fears. She sighed. Despite all the destruction in her midst, she felt different. Relieved. Unburdened. Happy. Free. For the first time, she felt as though she was fully in her own body. Her instincts told her that she'd already gained the insight she needed – an understanding of the fears that had held her captive, for so many years. She might have found the courage to stand up to her mother as a teenager but, she'd never acknowledged her fear of her or her own fear of being unworthy of love. She sighed with joy. She was finally, free of her past! Free of her fears! She'd uncovered her true Self. She was now fully open to receive the light of her soul. She could now fulfill her soul's purpose. It was the only answer that was worth anything.

The movie stopped. Was that it? Was there anything else in that black void? Then again, how would she know? There was no finish line - no visible proof. All she knew was that she felt hugely, unburdened. She felt warm, and as light as air. Full of joy. And very much at peace with her Self. For the first time she felt completely, free - to express her true Self. Finally, she understood why she'd felt so haunted over the years. It was her life and yet, it wasn't. She was there and yet, she wasn't. She'd lived through her experiences and yet, she didn't. She realized that as a child, she had no way of identifying the various emotional nuances that she'd experienced. Neither did she have any way of differentiating her truth from a false reality. Her fears, insecurities, and conditioned behavioral patterns had become her reality. At no point did she question it, and consequently, she'd never changed it. After all, that was "love." It was "home." And now, she knew that nothing was further from her truth. In uncovering her truth she'd birthed her unconditional love for her Self, and her true home. She'd purged her life of anything, and anyone who no longer served her truth. She'd removed the beliefs that had kept her small, her entire life. She'd destroyed the "stories" from her past that had no place in the new life that her soul desired. More importantly, she'd learnt to respect, and love her Self. It made her more discerning about the people she chose to associate with in the life that she was still to co-create. She was worthy of that life. She deserved it. If this was what she'd come back to heal so that she could take her own life forward from a place of love, and light then her quest was worth every second! She could now lift herself from any threat of darkness, by shining her soul's light onto it.

It dawned on her that self-love came with its own gift - it made everything remarkably simple. Finally, she understood why her life had never felt like her own. That wasn't about passing the blame – she no longer felt like a victim. It was about using her wisdom to discern her Self from everything, and everyone else around her. It was her soul's desire to walk its own path – not be trapped in the darkness of someone else's shadow or the shadow of her conditioning, for that matter. She might be a small part of a much bigger Universal plan but, before she could do any justice to her part in it, she had to be aligned with her true Self. For therein, lay her true power. And once she co-created her true reality, it would be the single-most, important puzzle piece to the only kind of work that truly mattered - the one that contributed to the beautiful tapestry of human consciousness. She shivered as she realized that she'd assumed her old self to be her true Self. It was no more than the sum total of a few experiences that she'd repeated over time - experiences that now all looked the same in the nothingness where the illusions of physical time, and separation didn't exist. She slowly wiped away her tears, and lovingly turned to embrace the child within. She felt an outpouring of gratitude towards her child-self for lovingly, patiently and courageously standing by her, for so many years. She would never have made it without her. She sighed. Why was she not angry? Where was the hatred towards her mother or any of the people who had caused her so much pain? She scanned her inner world. There was nothing. Only a deep contentment in her silent, stillness. An image

Undefined

of her own child came to mind. She smiled, and her heart lifted as she was finally, able to see what her child looked like. Memories of their days together, slowly filtered into her mind. Her child was the only reminder of everything that had to be left behind as part of a life that no longer served her. One that she'd believed to be real, and true. Now, it no longer existed.

She suddenly realized just how much had changed in the nothingness – without her lifting a finger. How it actually, happened was beyond anything that she could ever imagine. She had a strong sense that whatever was behind her was gone forever. Whatever her new reality was, she had no clue. All she knew was that she had everything she needed in her soul to co-create her new life. Again, she bowed her head to the Divine Grace that had been by her side throughout her mysterious quest; throughout her life. The only meaning she could attribute to the life that she had – one that had to be destroyed by her own hands - was that it no longer served her. And the power to uncover her soul's reality already belonged to her. For no reason other than, the courage to own her truth in each moment, with her vulnerable, open heart. Of all the places that existed in the Universe, her stillness was the only place that she needed to abide in. She sighed knowingly. Her mother might very well have been both antagonist, and protagonist in the "story" of her life. With her, all she'd come to know was a broken existence; lost and separated from her Self, and from the world around her. And yet, without her, she would never have found her way to her true Self. Perhaps her mother had loved her on some level, after all. For only love could grant such a gift of light - to show one the way through all the darkness to one's Self. And home.

She turned, and stared into the nothingness for a long time. She smiled joyously. The stars had suddenly re-appeared! She wasn't alone, anymore. She realized that she'd never been alone. Without her knowing, another Divine Mother had been by her side – watching over her every move. Perhaps whatever had gone on in her life previously, had happened exactly as it was meant to happen. It was all necessary to help her awaken - to remember her truth in this lifetime. She felt so grateful; so very Blessed. How else could she explain where she now found herself, despite everything that had transpired in her life? She might not have acknowledged the existence of the Divine before but, she now felt Its presence all around her. And she felt a profound connection to It - emanating straight from her heart. She smiled as she realized that she'd remained visible to something or someone, after all. Something or someone had never lost faith in her; had never stopped loving her.

[And never will. Love is the only thread that connects you to the Divine - to the entire Universe]

Did she have that much faith in herself? Could she walk her soul's path with such unwavering, conviction in herself? Did she have the capacity for such unconditional, Self-love?

[Self-love is synonymous with owning your truth. For as long as you remain present in self-love, you'll always remain one with your Divine Self. And one with the Divine Universe]

She sighed as she drew in a deep breath. As though she was taking her very first breath. And reborn into a whole, new world - not her external world but, the one within. She closed her eyes as she focused on her breath slowly entering, and awakening every fiber of her physical body. And then, when she could no longer hold onto it, she slowly exhaled. All that was left in its wake was empty, spaciousness. She remained present with that feeling; savoring its vast, fullness. Allowing herself to become one with its infinite, eternal reach. And then, she felt a shower of electrical impulses pass through her, as her soul light slowly expanded into her whole body. She felt her body, and mind slowly become one with her Self; one with her soul. One with all of her Being; one with love. One with the nothingness; one with the Universe all around her. She became what she'd been since the dawn of creation. Nothingness.

CHAPTER 13

COMING HOME

She sat with closed eyes, and took in the timeless, vastness within her. Doing nothing, other than absorbing its sacred wonder, and allowing herself be lost in the love that she'd been ignorant of for lifetimes. She was aware of the conflicting thoughts floating aimlessly in her mind but, she remained in the observer's seat - non-attached, and non-reactive. She felt completely, weightless – there was no sensation of her body. She was only aware of the unmistakable oneness with her Self; with the whole Universe. Was that the unknown she'd avoided her whole life? She might have had many experiences during her lifetime but, nothing compared - would ever compare – to that feeling of oneness! Why did she believe in avoiding the unknown? Why was she afraid of anything black? Those beliefs had only helped her manifest a reality that reflected what she was resisting in herself! A dualistic reality split into black and white; male and female; good and bad; light and dark; positive and negative; physical and spiritual; life and death. Heaven, and hell. From her vantage point in the nothingness, she could now see that such duality only existed in her mind. She was an embodiment of all those aspects – it was all part of her human experience! And there was nothing to fear - inside or outside of herself. The blackness – nothingness - was only a reflection of her infinite Being.

She realized that her conditioning had made her delineate choices along the lines of what she should pursue or avoid – giving rise to a polarized perspective of life. Furthermore, she'd associated the former with "right," and the latter with "wrong." And she'd believed that a predominance of "right" choices would lead to happiness, and the "wrong' ones to some kind of living hell! It dawned on her that all forms of behavioral fragmentation originated from her polarized mind. And were reinforced by her ego's misguided fixation on a separate identity to make her feel superior. And over time, that lower perspective had consumed her entire lower body making her feel heavy; joyless. However, there were no such distinctions within her Being. In the absence of her conditioning, her natural lower-body state was joy, and that of her Being was love. And being aligned with her soul purpose allowed her to move between her physical state, and the other dimensions accessible to her Being by holding her soul-felt intention within her heart space. All the while, remaining in her awareness, and present - firmly ensconced in the observer's seat. The same principle applied if she wanted to witness her soul's reality unfolding in her physical world. Her physical body would be host to a myriad thoughts and emotions but, she needed to remain centered in her stillness; feeling the love within her Being.

She sat back, and took a deep breath as her insights slowly permeated her mind. Gaining access to that sense of oneness must have been the result of her healing - not only the physical and emotional pain but, also that invisible divide in her psyche. That was the "bridge" she needed to cross between her illusory self, and her true Self! That clarity was affirmed by a familiar sensation - waves of electricity moved through her body. But, this time it didn't just flash through from head to toe. It continued moving up, and down her body for an interminable time! And the electrical impulses grew in intensity; she felt as though she was being burnt alive! And she could do nothing to stop it! She had to muster all her inner resolve, and courage to remain in the stillness, and focus on her breathing as the energies surged through her. Eventually, the waves and searing heat subsided. She slumped over her knees, totally exhausted. Her body was drenched in sweat. She must have passed out, for when she regained consciousness she felt extremely, weird. Totally, different. In her body – her Self. And yet, part of that oneness – not just feeling it. She slowly opened her eyes - not knowing what to expect. She felt something. She closed her eyes again, to connect with her open heart in that wondrous, infinite space within. What was that feeling? Peace? Love? Joy? It extended to every cell within her body. Until that moment, she'd never experienced anything like it! Although her physical body felt weightless she felt completely, contained in its lightness. She felt utterly, free, and whole – in all her emptiness! And yet, she had a sense of her Self as a real, distinct part of that infinite; eternal oneness. She sighed blissfully. Whatever it was, she knew she was home. She was safe. It would be with her, wherever she went; with whomever she was with. She would feel it with every breath, and watch it take form in everything that she co-created with her soul in her physical world. She opened her eyes once more, to rejoice in her new-found knowing. A flash of light caught the corner of her eye. She turned towards it, and saw a familiar sight.

"Glow!" she shouted. She launched herself at it. And again, received a painful thud on her head as she passed through the glowing mass, and hit the wall behind it. She sat up feeling dazed, but, still managed to make the shadowy outline of a familiar sight. She was back in the cellar – as her adult self! But, there was no fear. No emotion, at all – just an overwhelming sense of her presence. She turned to face Glow with a broad grin on her face. Its glow was brighter than she remembered.

"You ok?" Glow asked, softly.

"Where have you been!?" she demanded with mock anger. "Why did you leave me!?" Her heart made an unusual flipping motion, and she felt it shooting "sparks" in all directions. It made her realize just how much she'd missed Glow.

"Did you miss me?" Glow asked, pulling a funny face.

"Nope," she said with an impish grin. "You should have stuck around. I've had the weirdest…..most wonderful…..experience. And you missed everything!" She half-mockingly, chastised Glow. What was up with her? She was behaving like a kid! But, she couldn't help herself. She felt as though she was going to burst from child-like enthusiasm.

"I know" said Glow, with a swirling curtsy that sent sparkles flying everywhere.

"No, you don't! You weren't here" she said, waving an accusing finger at Glow.

"I've been with you all along, Little One" said Glow, gently.

"No, you weren't! Don't lie! You…..you….. vanished into the nothingness" she exclaimed, with annoyance.

"I'm not lying. I couldn't – even if I wanted to. Not to you. I was with you, all the time. You were so focused on your healing that you didn't see me. Look......" said Glow, pointing a shiny finger in her direction.

She turned to look behind her. And then, stopped. She looked at her Self. She took in a sharp breath. She looked, exactly the same as Glow! She turned to Glow with a bewildered expression on her face.

"What happened? Where am I" she whispered. "Am I dead?"

"You were 'dead,' Little One. You were 'asleep' your entire life - for many lifetimes. Now, you've awakened to a life of conscious, soul living" said Glow gently.

There was something about Glow's voice that warmed her heart, and soul. She could listen to it forever.

"Where am I? Is this what I'm going to look like now?" she asked.

"You were, where you've always been, Little One – trapped inside your mind. And now, you'll always be where you feel one with your soul, and your Self. You don't 'look' like this - it's how you feel when you're standing in your truth. Your physical appearance hasn't changed" said Glow, with loving patience. A smile shimmered, and bounced of its light-body; lighting up the cellar.

She didn't understand any of it but, the words resonated with her strongly.

"But, who am I?" she cried desperately. "What do I do now? Where do I go? How do I live my life?"

"Whoa! Slow down, Little one" said Glow. "You already know the answers to all those questions. The past is no more. Whatever you need to know will come to you – as, and when you need it. Your world is still very much the way you remember it – for now. Many things have changed. And there are many changes still to come. But, you're no longer your old self; you won't behave the way you used to. And neither will your experience of your world be the same. You're now the co-creator of your soul purpose in this third dimension. You won't be able to grasp the meaning of any of this right now. That's OK – let your soul's reality unfold as it's meant to. You've completed your healing; you're whole. You've aligned your mind, and body with your soul purpose. Don't think about doing anything, until you're doing it. Don't reach for anything – just be present. You've integrated all the timelines – past, and future. By remaining in your stillness, you'll always have access to the wisdom of your soul - you'll be able to take whatever action is necessary; at the right time. You'll feel it - inspired action from the heart will bring you closer to oneness; your ego will take you away from it."

"During this quest you became acquainted with your true nature – love. It's what you're feeling, and seeing in the aura around you. You still have a physical form; it's just not visible right now, because you're focused inward - on your Being. And that can't be seen with your mind's eye - it can only be felt with your heart." Glow's eyes never left hers as it spoke. "Be patient; kind, and loving towards yourself as things unfold. Take it slow - feel your way as you move along your soul path. It won't make sense. In fact, nothing will make any sense, from now on. That's what true freedom feels like – being present with each step of your soul path; not the mindless, functioning based on a role. Be foolish; indulge your child-like spirit. Let your heart guide you; feel your joy. Trust that whatever you do in your physical world is an extension of your soul. Your mind doesn't possess your soul's knowing, although it will help you process the experiences along your soul path. Have faith that everything will fall into place – as it's meant to. Just remain present in your heart space, and observe the miracle of your soul purpose unfolding in the physical world"

"But, how do I survive?" she demanded. "How do I earn a living?"

"You don't need to 'earn' anything. You've already earned it – by virtue of the soul that you carry. You just have to be true to it in your physical world. And by doing that, you'll do more than survive, Little One. You'll be fully alive."

"Will you be with me?" she asked, hopefully.

"Always, Little One. I can be nowhere else - with no one else" said Glow.

"What do you mean?" she asked. A deep frown creasing her brow.

"I am you," said Glow.

Before she could process what she'd just heard, Glow started to disintegrate once again, right before her eyes.

"*Where are you going? Don't go!*" she shouted, desperately. "*Don't leave me. Not now!*

Please don't leave me here on my own. Take me with you."

"You're not alone, Little One. You're home now – with your Self. And I've always been with you; always will be. Your reaction is pointing to your ego – it's still around. It needs to attach to something to feel secure. Remain in your stillness – you'll find all the security that you need." She heard Glow's voice slowly fading into the distance.

"Don't go! Please Glow, don't go! I need you now, more than ever. Please! You can't leave me now! I don't know what to do! I have nowhere to go; no one to turn to. Voice also left me! Please don't go!"

She was so distracted by Glow's leaving that she didn't register what Glow said about being her. She was sobbing. Again! Not that she cared! For some inexplicable reason, she now felt at ease with her feelings. She felt like crying - so she did. She felt angry that Glow had deserted her – so she allowed herself to feel it! But, she no longer felt that urge to run. She was able to stay present with her discomfort. She turned to look at the cellar. It was just that - a cold, dark, smelly cellar! She had no idea what lay out there in the world but, she sensed that her life would never be the same when she left her small hideaway. And even though she couldn't deny the suspicion that her quest had taken a long time - in a physical, linear context - she couldn't ignore the awareness that in some other realm, it had all occurred in the flash of a moment! Even more surprising was the knowing that physically, she'd gone nowhere! She must have been in the cellar, all along! And she'd not moved a muscle to make anything happen! But, her spiritual quest in the nothingness was more transformative than any action that she'd taken in the past. It had all taken place somehow; somewhere – perhaps in another dimension. And even though she would never be able to grasp it with her mind, the spaciousness within told her that every cell in her body had been part of that transformation. It was real. She knew it by the way she felt – about her Self. Was she ready for the beginning of a whole new life experience? She detected no fear to face whatever awaited her, in her physical world. There was just a strong knowing that her new Self wouldn't repeat the past. She realized that if she was different before then now, she was unrecognizable! After spending a lifetime defining herself in relation to doing, she would now be required to use a very different "toolkit" to the one that she'd used before. It didn't contain anything tangible - just her soul. She was awareness, in an open heart space. With no mind – just soul knowing. Within a physical body - to help her observe, and process the unfolding of her soul path in her physical world. There was little doubt that she was a novice, as far as that was concerned! She would have to practice a lot before she could master her new way of Being. But, it was essential; the only thing worthy of her time. *Phew! That sounded like a lot of work! "Doing" absolutely nothing - other than being aware of, and present with the unfolding of her soul purpose in the physical world?*

[Why do you think of Being as 'doing nothing?' It's not the passive state that you believe it to be. On the contrary, it's the most active state of your Self. Taking your life forward now, is about being your Self - expressing your truth. Unapologetically. Now that you've released everything that held it captive, it will unfold - as it was always meant to unfold. Irrespective of whether your mind thinks you're ready or not]

"Voice? Is that you?"

She looked around. *Those two! They were bound to be close by - she could feel them. If she ever got her hands on them…..! What on earth did they think they were playing at?*

"Voice" she demanded. "Is that you?"

"Yes" But now, Voice sounded, exactly like Glow.

"Come on out. Show yourselves! I'm tired of this stupid game."

She hoped that she sounded fierce. She wanted to put an end to this drama.

[We're not hiding from you. There's only ever been one person on this quest]

"Voice!" she exclaimed, without thinking. And smiled to herself as she looked around with high anticipation. *Glow left but, she could still walk her path with Voice by her side.* She felt like a kid playing hide-and-seek.

"No." Now it was Glow's voice that she heard.

"Glow?" *It had to be one or the other! There was nothing more boring than the obvious!* She grunted impatiently.

[No]

"Then who is this!? There's no one else here!"

[You are]

It took a while for that to register. She was bewildered. *That wasn't possible! She couldn't be the only one there. Not after everything that she'd heard, and seen!*

"It's been you, Little One. All along."

"*That's ....not..... possible.....*" she heard herself say. And then, she heard "**Yes it is.......**"

But, her lips weren't moving! The words were emanating from all of her – within, and without. Silently. She'd been by her Self, all this time? She felt her disbelief give way to an outburst of emotion. She was laughing, and sobbing between intermittent gulps of air. *She must be crazy! She couldn't be two different ages; in two different places - at the same time! Maybe she'd suppressed everything for too long. That explained everything! She had to face her "demons!" She just had to ride it out – whatever it was! She'd always been in complete, control of herself – of her life! She never let her emotions get the better of her!* She sighed with relief. *It felt good to be in control, once again. Besides, there was no way she could shut her mind off. That was impossible! She'd read that it could be achieved but, that was a whole different story. There had to be some other explanation for the insights that she'd gained about her childhood conditioning. She must have read about it somewhere, and then, forgotten all about it. Besides, there was no place like the nothingness! She must have been dreaming....or awake......or WHATEVER!! Damn it! She'd already been down that road!* She sighed, hopelessly.

[If you allow your ego to control you, you'll only end up at another dead-end. Your ego has no commitment to your soul purpose. It's committed to satisfying its own whims, until you awaken to bringing your physical body with alignment with your soul purpose. Your soul doesn't need to be committed - it already is. It has always been; it won't ever stop. And you underestimate the power of your soul to actualize your true purpose. Your mind will accept any answer that your fickle ego dangles in front of it but, you're not beholden to your thoughts – you're bound to your soul purpose. There's no turning back after this kind of transformation. You'll only come up against your soul if you keep resisting – it has the entire Universe behind it. This quest was specifically designed by your soul. It's 'written' in your soul - you couldn't have 'read' about it. Neither can anyone tell you how to go about it – each person's soul path is different]

[Bringing about your quest was no easy feat. Your soul, and Being exercised the power of the Universe to bring about your transformation. Your mind had no role in this. And its role in fulfilling your life purpose

Undefined

is limited. Realizing your purpose isn't a factor of time or experience in your physical world but, of being present as you take each step along your path. Your mind has no concept of the present moment – thanks to your ego. After all, your mind is the only vehicle your ego can use to pursue its never-ending, list of wants. Hence, it's tireless efforts to distract you with an ongoing, barrage of thoughts. Your mind has only ever worked within the confines of your conditioning to perpetuate old patterns of thinking in terms of the 'past,' and 'future.' Neither one exists outside of the present moment. And the only place you can access your Being, and your highest potential is in the now. To be fully present requires you to be one with your Being, and that is totally, foreign to your mind. As is your unlimited potential, and your boundless, capacity for un-conditional love. But, that is all you need to walk your soul path during your lifetime. Your mind will serve you by processing what you 'see' as the observer, when you remain present in your stillness - in a state of no-mind]

But, she was talking to herself!

[You're listening to your Self]

But…… but, she could hear…. voices! She stopped. Not that the "voices" sounded like any human voice that she'd ever heard! It slowly dawned on her that she wasn't hearing, anything. She was "feeling" the words! "Words" that were like tiny, soft "thoughts" coming to her out of nowhere. Subtle, streams of invisible, vibrations - each one with its own tone, and meaning. And she could somehow receive, and interpret their meaning! There were no actual words being spoken!

[That is the power of being present. You're now able to process 'information' from the higher realms through your multi-sensory Being; it acts as a 'transmitter' – receiving vibrations from all around you. Once translated by your heart, those vibrations will become 'thoughts,' and create new patterns of thinking in your brain. That will change how you think, and behave in your physical world. Your Being also transmits your unique code. This process operates between your body, soul and Being, and is beyond your awareness. It's totally, indiscernible. But, it's powerful - it will help you to realize your soul's purpose - the new reality that will equally serve you, and all of humanity. Only by listening to your inner voice will you be able connect to the higher energies that 'speak' to your soul as you walk your path. You've been conditioned over lifetimes to suppress your voice. If it were not for your quest, it would have probably taken as many generations to unlearn everything that's ingrained in your cellular memory, and awaken to your truth. Your quest is the culmination of many soul lessons - over many lifetimes - to bring you to that knowing]

Whether or not, her mind accepted what she heard was immaterial. Each word was being embraced in the silent, stillness within. She sighed, and breathed deeply into the warm cocoon of her open heart space. Once again, amidst all the chaos in her mind she was able to discern a sliver of clarity in the stillness. If her conviction in the unknown was now deeper than any of her previous beliefs in her physical world, then her capability of processing this unfamiliar "information" would also be completely, different. And she needed to trust her soul's knowing to fulfill her purpose – even if her mind had no idea what she was doing. It was no longer necessary to conceptualize every possible scenario to cover when, where or how things would happen. She didn't need to plan the best outcome for her life or accumulate resources to counter every possible mishap. More importantly, she didn't have to worry about whether she would have enough time to fulfill her purpose - her only reason for Being was the realization of her soul purpose. And she already possessed everything that she needed within her Self to co-create her one, true reality in her physical world. Everything else was irrelevant. She smiled. Life really was very simple. Why did she become embroiled in unnecessary complexities before?

[Truth is simple. Illusions of the mind and ego are complex and cause unnecessary suffering, and heartache. Your awareness, and self-love will help you remain in your stillness, and centered in your heart space.

Trust your Self; have faith in the essence of all creation within you]

She didn't know what created her!

[Your mind doesn't know but, your soul does. Your Divine essence will continue to evade all exploration in your physical world, because it doesn't exist outside of you - it lies within. Co-creating your soul's reality isn't about willfully attracting what lies outside of you to manifest a reality. There's nothing outside of you in the entire Universe. You're the Universe. Your true reality already exists. All you need to

Undefined

do is stand in your truth, and remain in alignment with your soul to realize its gifts. There might be many subjective realities in your world but, there is only be one, true reality for you – the one that allows you to access your full potential to bring forth your soul purpose. There is no 'mystery' to life. Everything that you need to know is visible, and readily available to you – when you awaken to your truth. There's no separation between you, and the Divine. All forms of separation are only perceptions of your mind, and reinforced by an ego that's in love with itself. The world as you see it, is its self-portrait]

She'd seldom given any consideration to a Divine force or whether her life had any meaning beyond that imposed by her mind. She'd behaved as though she was some arbitrary product of random selection that could only operate within certain boundaries - boundaries that were already well-established in her physical world. Physically, she might be a product of random selection from the human gene pool – someone capable of taking on any number of roles in her world. Spiritually, however, she was way more than that. She embodied a soul that had a far more significant role to perform during her lifetime – the fulfillment of a very specific purpose. A purpose that would never be known by her mind but, that small detail was unimportant to her soul. And now, she knew which one to follow. As unknown as it was, there was no mistaking the throbbing aliveness in her veins. All she had to do was remain in her awareness – be present with her open heart. And that was no simple task! But, now that she'd uncovered her inner fountain of self-love, she knew that she would have the courage to walk her path. For the realization of her purpose would be contributing to something far greater than she could ever imagine, let alone understand – the elevation of consciousness. And whether that purpose was considered significant by others was immaterial. She would devote what was left of her life to fulfilling it. That would be the final "stake" in the ultimate "ground" – raising consciousness, across all space and time. Albeit one that she would never see the outcome of, during her lifetime. But, that didn't matter. Her soul's knowing would be "visible" across all eternity.

Suddenly, her past ideologies looked utterly frivolous! And completely, out of synch with her soul's truth. So restrictive, compared to the limitless potential within her. Whatever she'd done before might have consumed all her time but, she now knew that she didn't spend her energy wisely.

And with that insight, the meaninglessness of her life became glaringly apparent. She'd tried to force this phenomenon called life, into a box crafted from her age-old conditioning. And for the first time she could see, exactly how small that box was! She'd attempted to reduce the eternal; the magical; the infinite; the undefinable – all of her Being - into something that she could intellectually manage, and control! She'd confined herself to living a small life. She'd thought small. She'd made herself feel small. And in doing so, she'd forced herself to be less than her Being. And no box –none that any mind could conceive – was large enough to contain her Being!

[Your intellect can only help you attain what can be conceived by your mind. And that will always be the smallest portion of your unlimited potential, because your mind can only function in the context of what has been done in the past. And your ego is constrained by its need to be safe. Even if you did go to the moon, your next venture will be to reach whatever lies beyond that. But, if you could achieve every physical objective conjured up by your mind, then what? What will be the next goal that you force upon yourself to escape yourself, and your fears? Where will you go? What role will you take on? No such achievement, destination or role in your physical world will be enough to distract your soul from fulfilling its true purpose. Whatever that purpose is, you can be certain that your soul has designed it to help you overcome your fears, and limitations – to become the highest version of your Self in this lifetime. And that is no small feat. It has taken lifetimes of soul lessons to guide you across the ultimate 'frontier' – the one closest to you; the one within that led you to your stillness. In the process, you've healed your physical body; re-claimed your self-respect, and self-worth. You've learnt to trust the knowing of your soul, and heart to lead you along your soul path. You've found the source of true love – self-love. You've forgiven yourself for the past; for choosing this life, and the family you were born into. You've chosen a path of conscious, soul living over a mindless existence. You've found inner peace. And opened yourself to Being in oneness with the very essence of life. Now you're ready to walk your soul path]

She wasn't a failure?

Undefined

['Failure' is another misnomer in your physical world. You might consider yourself a failure in your mind, because you've judged yourself by the standards in your physical world but, you've not failed by the values held within your soul. You embarked on this quest to seek, and uncover your truth. You went about it instinctively - guided only by soul knowing. Without being aware of it, you went to war with yourself - for the mind-code you lived by previously, wouldn't have allowed you that luxury. You've cut through the various illusions separating you from your Divine Self, and the Universe. In the process, you've encountered your lower self, and your higher Self. And the Being that holds both in love. You've shed the many barriers that separated you from your Self - thereby integrating your physical body with your soul to access to your inherent, unlimited potential, to fulfill your purpose. Although you don't yet know what that entails, it's the equivalent of having access to the Universal Ocean of infinite creation. But, don't attempt to ascribe a value to the worth of your soul in the same way that you valued your physical achievements. Your mind can't comprehend the value of 'priceless' in any realm - let alone, the spiritual one. But, it's priceless, nonetheless. No - you've not failed. Far from it. You've healed and transformed lifetimes of unnecessary pain, and suffering by uncovering your truth. You've uncovered the path to everything – a Universe of endless possibilities - from nothing. You've destroyed the meaningless life that you had, to fulfill your purpose with self-love. You're now free to live the life that your soul desires]

She was now free to live her life? That was hard to believe!

[You've been conditioned to believe that meaning can only be ascribed to your life if it's lived in service of others. That's only partly true. You need to first, and foremost love your Self to own your soul's truth. You can't be of service to others, without first being of service to your Self. And by walking your soul path, you'll also serve others. There's no higher form of service to humanity]

Before she could delve into the ramifications of such a perspective, she was overcome by the sheer joy of feeling free - to fulfill her soul path. It signaled a whole new beginning! It wasn't just a promise of one - she felt it within her soul. And her mind couldn't even conceive her new path – that's how she knew, it was the one meant for her. The only important thing in that moment was to focus on the joy that was flowing from her heart in endless waves. She must have died, and gone to heaven!

[You're in this physical dimension to experience all aspects of your Being, not just the physical aspects associated with a mortal form - like life, and death. As a spiritual Being those two states are but, one and the same. As a Being, you're in life as well as in death, exactly the way that you find yourself now – an infinite beam of love, and light in absolute nothingness. Explore the physicality of your existence but, don't let your experiences define or limit your soul's truth. Until you align your physical self with your soul, everything that you do – everyone that you're with - will only be a reflection of yourself. You'll feel separated from your soul - life will have little or no meaning. And you'll continue going around in circles, trying to find what lies within you]

Her mind felt muggy as she once again, tried to grasp the meaning of her mystical quest. All she wanted to do was surrender to the feeling of oneness within – to connect to the entire Universe. But, somehow she couldn't reach beyond the stillness. She grappled with this invisible "barrier" before she made herself stop, and just be with her stillness. She realized that she was still being surreptitiously manipulated by her ego. And her awareness was an "alarm" bell to any thought that still existed in her mind – it kept her away from the oneness. She realized that she couldn't bear to be separated from the oneness - it was her only connection to anything real! She observed her anxiety increase around her stillness as she pondered her latest dilemma. How could she maintain her connection to the oneness, and still live in her physical world where everything – other than what she could co-create with her soul - would be an illusion!? How could she remain true to the purpose that she had to fulfil without being sucked into the illusion of other subjective realities? Earlier in her quest, she thought that she couldn't go back to her old way of life - not if it meant starting all over again! That contrasted sharply with her truth. She realized that she wouldn't be able to face a life in her physical world - not if it meant compromising the only sense of real value that she'd discovered in the nothingness. Her truth; her Self! And the oneness that connected her to entire Universe! She was certain that there was no longer anything from her past holding her back – physical, mental or emotional. She'd freed herself from those burdens. She now sensed a different kind of limitation; another kind of attachment.

She waited patiently. There was something else that she needed to discover in the silent, stillness. She sat with her eyes closed, and observed her discomfort. She now knew better than to let her frustration rile her. As proven many times before, that would only lead to another dead-end! So she just sat with her question - in the silent, stillness. The answer will reveal itself - she believed that with all her heart. She became aware that the limitation was another fear – the fear of freedom! She'd never known anything like it! And her mind, and ego were reneging furiously! But, she felt it as it silently beckoned her in the stillness. She sensed that whatever she'd called "freedom" in her physical world was in no way close, to what she was about to discover. She realized that it was evident to her now, because she'd released her conditioned baggage. She was open. It slowly dawned on her that this new freedom extended way beyond her physical body - by virtue of her Being. By staying in her stillness, and remaining present in her open heart space, she became conscious of her Being's ability to subtly shift between the different realms. There was her physical body and mind – she could easily relate to its tangibility. And she was aware of her soul's knowing; the special language – the vibrations - that only her heart could translate. But, there was another dimension to the unknown……something else that was connected to her Being.

Her eyes flew open with another revelation. She took a few deep breaths to center herself as she processed her insight. Having freed herself from the confines of her conditioning, and healing her physical body to align with her soul she'd also opened her Self to move between the known; the unknown, and the unknowable – through her Being! There was no need to think about maintaining her connection with the oneness – it would remain intact through her Being. It was the open channel to other realms! There was no separation - between her Self, and anything in the Universe! And even though, there would be challenges in her physical world there was no risk of her being deluded by other subjective realities. She was protected by her awareness, and the stillness that allowed her access to an open channel to other Universal dimensions - courtesy of her Being! She sighed. She'd never felt so liberated! She could surrender to her mind-state (the known), and her soul (the unknown) without any fear.

And she could maintain the connection with the spiritual realms through her higher Self, and still live in her physical world. As the observer, she was granted boundless freedom! Her physical body would no doubt feel her experiences, and her mind would process them but, the channel that existed between her soul, higher Self, and her Being would remain sacred, within her stillness – the zero point that granted her access to the entire Universe!

She didn't have to compromise her soul's desires or her truth in any way. Neither did she need to divorce herself from her emotions – they were an invaluable radar in her physical world. Both states, the physical and the spiritual; the known and the unknown, could coexist within the infinite expansiveness of her Being which was connected to the unknowable. She shifted from the dilemma in her mind, and centered herself in her stillness to revel in this newly discovered sense of liberation. Her physical self also felt inspired, and elevated by all that beckoned from the unknown within, and without. There was no past; no future. Only the full presence of Being. The unknowable space that housed her Being was all that Is. It was nothing by any physical standard and yet, it was everything! It held all of creation. She observed her neutral state – she wasn't in the least bit surprised. There was no form of thought or emotion - she only felt complete, neutrality within her stillness. And her entire life was swirling around her! She felt as though she was in the eye of a storm. *How could she have found peace in all that chaos?*

[Simplicity is the natural order of the Universe, including the 'chaos' that's evident in nature. Everything else is perceived order - the result of your mind attempting to rationalize, and structure what it doesn't understand. Ironically, that results in the man-made chaos that you see around you, because of the projections of your unconscious mind. By overcoming the burdens of your conditioning, and facing your biggest fear of being unlovable you've transcended the stories in your mind, and found your truth - the inner source of your peace. Peace doesn't exist outside of you – it can only be found within you. But, until you root out all the 'stories' that have been clouding your truth you won't be able to feel it. And now that you've healed yourself, the peace within you will form the foundation of your soul's reality]

Undefined

Her head was spinning. *This was all too much! How will she ever know if she was on the "right" path?*

['Right' and 'wrong' belong to your old mind-set. You've already taken the first step onto your soul path. And trusting your inner voice is all that is required to remain on it. If you need verification then turn within, and feel your truth. For as long as you're standing in your truth, you'll always be where you need to be, irrespective of what is happening in your external world]

She glanced around. There was only blackness - nothingness. She groaned. *She wished she could see something. Some sign, at least. What did her soul path look like?*

[It doesn't look like anything – just yet. Whatever form it takes in your physical world is for you to co-create. Take each step from your heart space with love. And only then, will the next step be revealed. Trust your Self. Have faith that everything in the Universe exists to support you living your soul's highest intentions. Nothing needs to be forced; no one needs to get stepped over, hurt or lose their lives, for you to live your best life. You might have intuitive glimpses along your path but, you'll never know the final outcome of your life's journey. Destinations are for your mind, and ego; they can only manifest your intentions within a horizontal level of consciousness. You now fully embody your soul – you abide in the realm of vertical consciousness. If at any time you find yourself thinking that you can pre-determine your soul's destination, know that your ego has taken over. You'll feel your inner harmony disrupted. If you choose to ignore how you feel, you'll only subject yourself to doing an uninspired task. Furthermore, you'll feel disappointed with the results. And you already know what that feels like. But, your time hasn't been wasted. You now know what you don't want for a life. You can now set about co-creating the life that you do want]

[Your quest is over but, your soul's journey has just begun. Walking your soul path in your physical world will continue to expose you to deeper aspects of Self-knowledge. And to other, more subtle ways that you can be distracted by your mind, and ego if you're not centered in your awareness. Life will become somewhat, easier. But, your challenges aren't over yet. In learning the full ambit of your soul's lessons as part of your human experience, you'll be guided through an ongoing evolution of your consciousness. Discernment is key – to uncover even greater, unknown truths to live by. There is so much more to learn about your Divine Self, life, and Being – in this dimension, and many others. The potential you're capable of accessing on your soul path in this physical dimension is but, a small fraction of the total potential that is available to you across all dimensions. But, the 'key' to accessing them remains the same – it lies within you. You're the key to the entire Universe; to all Universes]

In spite of everything that she'd experienced on her quest, she was still having difficulty accepting that the 'key' to her power, lay within her. *Why couldn't she pin-point its exact location? If she could just find it in the vastness within her, she would feel so much better. She didn't want to ever be without it when she started to co-create her new reality in her physical world. She couldn't afford that! She would lose her inner peace! She frowned.* Something just didn't feel right. *How could peace be within her? It was up there – in the heavens. And her body was down here, in the physical world.*

[You're sliding into the realm of your mind, and ego to overcome your discomfort. If you persist on that track, you'll only find your thoughts looping. And you'll end up feeling separated from the oneness. Stay in your stillness; remain in your awareness. There's no 'exact' position for your stillness. It's a feeling - the zero point; the neutral point of balance of all the energies flowing within you. That's being in the 'place' of your limitless power to co-create your soul's desires. There's no 'up' or 'down' – that's just your mind playing games with you. As for time, separation between places is an illusion. In your physical world everything is viewed as separate, because your mind's eye can only perceive limited, low frequencies of light energy in the form of objects. Consequently, your neural pathways have also been limited – your mind won't be able to grasp oneness. To see life – all that Is - you need to see it with your eyes closed - with an open heart. There are no boundaries between the dimensions. It's all oneness; nothingness – around, and within you. It's all of infinity - contained within a single moment. Only your Being is able to interface between multiple dimensions, irrespective of time and space. You're always one

Undefined

with everything, and everyone — whenever you're present with your Being]

She was again, overcome with humility as she reflected on her profound quest in the nothingness. She could now clearly see how limited she'd been in the past. It was very apparent, against the backdrop of being one with the flow of life. There was no distinction between her physical body, and her Being. She felt completely, contained within her physical body and yet, she could detect no boundaries — within or outside of her. She'd never felt so light; so free. She was sitting dead-still and yet, she could sense all of her flowing with an invisible current — a force so powerful that she couldn't imagine the depth or breadth of it. There was no inclination to fight it or even understand where it was taking her. She was comfortable with not knowing. After all. the distinction between knowing, and the known had faded into oblivion. Only the unknown existed. And the unknowable — all that Is. As crazy as that sounded to her mind, it felt right. And real. She was exactly, where she needed to be — with no desires; no plan; no sense of direction; no urge to do anything. No desire to be anywhere or anyone else, other than her Self. It dawned on her that her higher Self had somehow, known that she wasn't on her true path. That's why she'd never found any meaning or felt fulfilled before. And she'd never known the true meaning of freedom; never felt completely one, with life. That truth resonated with her deeply. There wasn't a shred of doubt. She was struck by a revelation. Standing in her truth meant that she would never have to doubt herself - ever again!

"And you……and….and Glow……aren't real?" she whispered sadly. [We're real. We've always been real; always will be. But, we're part of you - not separate from or outside of you. You just needed to be still, and silent long enough to learn to discern your inner voice. Without it, you would never have been able to uncover your truth, and heal yourself. And you won't be able to fulfill your soul purpose - you can't manifest something outside of yourself if it's not your truth. And if you're a seeker of truth, you've no option but, to walk your soul path. Any other road that you force yourself to take will be fraught with unnecessary pain, and suffering. You'll recognize your soul path by the joy that you feel in your heart. Every moment will feel free from the barriers of physical time. And being fully present in each moment, spans all of eternity. Anything that you co-create with your soul in that moment will have the reach of eternity. You now know that you're worthy of your soul. And you deserve a life experience that's more than anything you were conditioned to believe. No false illusion will ever pacify you again. You'll never settle for less than the true worth of your soul]

From having everything in her physical world, to becoming one with nothing; becoming one with her Being, and the Universe. Becoming real - with nothing but, the Divine hand of life guiding her. She felt dazed with wonder. *How was she ever going to remember everything that happened on her quest?* She tried recalling all that she'd learnt – to construct some sort of framework to adopt in her physical life but, her mind failed her. It hit a complete blank. The intricate web of knowledge that she'd gained in the nothingness refused to be unpacked or contained within any kind of familiar structure in her mind. She realized that, as fast as she could conjure up any kind of framework to contain her understanding, it dissolved as quickly into the nothingness from whence it was born, it. She could only begin to fathom the breadth, and depth of her quest by what she felt – a sense of infinite spaciousness filled with love, and joy. It reassured her that she would never lose touch with what she'd found; with who she'd become. She'd had her most real experience of her life, in the nothingness. And it would continue being real as long as it co-created from that empty, infinite space.

[There's no need to remember anything. Nothing is lost – it's all carried within your soul. Listen to your heart – it will guide you. It's the place where your physical body, and soul meet. That's why your heart is the only part of you that will never be controlled by your mind. Every heartbeat, is ordained by the power of the Divine itself]

She felt exhilarated. And completely, vulnerable. It made her succumb again, to her thoughts. She couldn't help thinking that there must be a mistake. She felt far from ready for the huge responsibility of co-creating her life! She'd never taken on anything, on that scale before! Her mind was still flicking through familiar territory – with what made her ego feel safe, and comfortable. And she was aware of it. She tried rationalizing away her awareness. *Yes – that sounded just like her old self! But, in hindsight that way of living was so much easier! It was nothing compared to this.…..this.….. what? This undefinable, un-nerving, uncertainty! This vast, empty, groundless, nothingness!* Despite her thoughts, she couldn't deny that her new way of Being made her feel closer to everything that she'd yearned for, deep within her soul. A connection that called out to her with its silent song; to which she'd responded with every fiber of her Being. She sighed as she felt her mind eventually, give way in acceptance, and surrender. Each day, her adrenaline levels would probably be the equivalent of diving off a cliff - without a parachute! And without the foggiest notion of where she was going to land! She would have to remain in a place of surrender. And trust her inner voice. Her mind – all her physical senses - would be aware of everything that was doing on but, they won't be able to help her navigate her unknown, soul path. Only by keeping her heart open, would she be able to find her way. It would be her soul knowing that would be guiding her. Together with the guidance of other kindred souls that she would encounter along her path. She would continue this way, until the moment of her last, unknown breath.

She looked searchingly into the nothingness. *Could she live her life that way?* She would be continuously, living on the edge! Living life's ultimate adventure – in complete, unison with the unknown. And for as long as she stayed in her truth, she would always be one with the flow of life with every breath that she took; one with the very essence of life. Discovering her truth had been fundamental in helping her understand her Self; to respect this unknown force that flowed through her veins. Since the beginning of her quest, she'd believed that she was being punished. Now she realized that she'd been blessed with a second chance - to heal herself. By destroying her past, and the self that no longer served her. So that she could live the life that she'd always hoped for, in the depths of her soul. She started crying again, humbled by the Divine grace that had accompanied her throughout her quest. She'd never known such patience; such generosity, kindness, and unconditional love in her physical life. When she found herself in the nothingness, she thought that her life was over. That all was lost. But, there she was – still breathing. And feeling more alive than she'd ever felt before. Throughout her life, there was something bigger than herself guiding her to her truth, and the life that she deserved. Somewhere in her heart, and soul she'd remained connected to the same power as this

Divine essence, because both spoke the same language as the Universe. She might be unable to comprehend the language using her mind but, that didn't negate its existence. If someone had forced her to acknowledge the existence of such a Divine force within her, she knew she would have resisted, and engaged in a futile mind-game, debating the pros and cons. She realized that she needed to take on her quest alone – to do this her own way. She might have "failed" to build the life that she believed she wanted but, she now had something far more precious to help her along her soul path – her stillness. And her Self, resurrected from the ashes of her old self. She'd refuted the wisdom behind the timing of her quest but, there was no way she could would have found the courage to do what she'd done without Divine intervention, and guidance. In the process, she'd lost everything that she thought she wanted for her life; and blessed with, exactly what she needed!

She was sobbing, although there was no longer any grief in her heart. She felt totally, at home. At peace. And so very happy over absolutely, nothing - that was now everything. With her newfound sense of Self, she was beginning to grasp the full spectrum of meaning of the emotions on either side of her life's pendulum, and the central fulcrum of Being at which she'd come to rest. She no longer had any idea what her life would be like when she returned to the physical world. There were so many questions that she would never be able to answer. So much that she didn't know. But, all that was irrelevant compared to the trust, and belief in her Self. She'd finally found what she'd been searching for, her entire life – self-love. And that was enough. She was enough. She would be able to co-create a whole new reality; build a whole new life for herself. She had finally, found her place; her home in the world - within her Self. She felt a familiar feeling. She was all tingly, and light. She was again, breaking up into a billion little pieces - into little stars. She was ecstatic. She was going there – no here – all over, again! She was flying. Shining, brilliantly. She was nowhere, and everywhere - all at once! She was nothing, and everything - all at once! All in a single breath. In a single moment. She was where she needed to be. She was peace. Joy. Light. Love. She felt timeless. Free. She felt as one with herself, and everything around her. It was so......so majestically, beautiful. Complete, heaven. She reveled in the feeling. She felt as though she was doing cartwheels in the sky - all ten billion parts of her! She felt as though she was lighting up the entire Universe! She never wanted to let go. She was holding onto it all tightly - in her breath. She felt so vibrantly alive. So in love – with her life. With her Self. As unbelievable as it all seemed, it was more real than anything that she'd ever known.

[It is…..]

So beautiful in all its uncertainty……

[It is…..]

Each moment so eternal…….

[Yes]

But, she had to let it go…….

[Yes]

……and return to her physical world. To complete the rest of her life's journey. Her time in the nothingness might be coming to a close but, she doubted that it would end. It would still be within her when she continued with her soul path in her physical world.

[Yes]

And she could return to the nothingness whenever she needed to?

[Yes]

But, she would never be able to hold onto it? It would never be hers? What if she lost her way somehow?

[It is yours. It always has been; always will be. You wanting to 'hold' onto It, is based on your ego's desire for control. Your Being is It. Your physical body, and soul is from It. However, you'll never own It or be able to control It. It belongs to It-Self. All you can do is feel It enter, and leave your body with every breath that you take. And there is no way that you can lose your Self – not now. Your Self, and the oneness are synonymous with each other. Wherever you go in the Universe, you'll always be with your Self]

She would feel the full essence of the entire Universe in her body but, she'll never be able to hold onto It?

[No. But, you will feel it]

How?

[By feeling the love for your Self. By doing what you love, with love. By remaining open to give, and receive love. Through your feeling of love for everyone, and everything in the world around you. Love is the key – to staying connected to yourself, and being connected to the entire Universe. Always keep your heart open. Let it radiate through every fiber of your Being. Let it be heard with every word that you speak, and visible in everything that you do. See it in everything that you cast your eyes upon. Let it be your guiding light for the remainder of your days on this planet. Together with your truth, you'll always remain in the light. You'll never feel lost or alone, again. Let each heartbeat carry you onwards, and upwards. Hold your truth in love – no matter where it leads you. And as you take each step forward in blind faith, know that love will light your way]

She slowly let out the breath that she was holding onto, so tightly. She didn't even realize that she'd stopped breathing. There was a gush of air through her mouth, and she placed her hands on her heart as she drew in the next life-giving, breath. She didn't know if any of this was true but, that didn't matter. She didn't know where she was going - that didn't matter, either. All she knew was that wherever her path took her, she would take each step with her willing, open heart. She didn't have to worry or doubt herself – ever, again. It was all going to be….. OK. In fact, she believed that everything was going to be more than just….OK. And even if it turned out that she was wrong, that too, would be…..OK. Every moment presented to her by her soul was perfect. And she would experience it, just the way it unfolded.

Her reverie was broken by a strange, scuffling sound. It stopped. She tilted her head, and listened intently. Nothing. Only silence. Then, she heard it again. But, it was too faint for her to say what it was. Whatever it was, it was getting loader, and coming loser. She realized that something was moving very slowly in her direction, in the dark cellar. Then she heard a soft gurgle. Her face lit up with a broad smile. She knew that sound! She would recognize it, anywhere! Her baby! How on earth did she find her way into the cellar!? She heard a little yelp; followed by a whimper. Something – a pebble, perhaps - must have hurt her. But, that didn't stop her for long. The crawling continued – faster, and more determined. She turned to look towards the little doorway in the cellar wall. The darkness made no difference – they "spotted" each other in the same moment! The little toddler, scurried towards her mother on all fours. She opened her arms as her child launched herself into them with a delighted squeal. She just held her baby tightly, and sobbed. Her baby had found her mother's secret, hideaway. No one had ever succeeded in finding it before! She felt the child go still as she sensed her mother's depth of emotion. A tiny hand gently searched her face, in an attempt to place her little fingers in her mother's mouth. She couldn't help it – she burst into laughter. The baby didn't suck her thumb the way her mother had done but, she always made her mother suck her fingers whenever she sensed any sadness. She gently kissed the tiny fingers but, couldn't stop the tears from falling - for the life that was; for all that she'd left behind. And for the life as yet, to be lived. They sat in the dark cellar, hugging each other for a long time; relishing being together, after their brief separation. It was a fun afternoon. She recalled them playing their favorite game of hide-and-seek in the garden. She couldn't remember how she'd ended up in the cellar - she would never have wanted her child to follow her there! She'd never allowed the baby anywhere, near it! And yet, there they were – huddled together in the one place that she never wanted to return to. She felt the baby get slowly heavier in her arms, as she fell into a peaceful sleep. She gazed tenderly upon the outline of the little face for a long time, before making her way out of the cellar. It was time. There was no more fear. Only hope. And love.

She closed her eyes when her knees touched the ground outside. She stood up slowly. Reverently. She knew that she carried the beginning of a whole, new world within her. As did the child in her arms. She knew she could guide her child but, ultimately, she would have to walk her own path. And even if she could no longer be by her side, another mother – a Divine one - would always be watching over her. She smiled, knowingly. Her child was safe. She was safe. She glanced at the cellar door. It had always loomed so large, and ominous in her mind. Now, it looked small. Harmless. Almost too small for her to have entered it, in the first place. She looked up at the rose-kissed, twilight sky. It was no longer out of reach. She knew she would always be able to access it through the open doorway of her heart. She was overcome by gratitude. She'd uncovered her truth, and gained Self-knowledge between those two "doorways." One symbolized the dark, void that she'd been buried in. It no longer existed. And the other – the light of her soul. Again, she became conscious of her breath. Calm, and in perfect harmony with the invisible, flow of life within, and all around her. She looked down at her sleeping child, and felt her heart tremble with love – she never wanted to let her go! She felt the same way about her life. Could she let it all go, when her time came? Would she be able to leave her child? Would she be able to bid farewell to the life that had blessed her with a soul to uncover her truth, and find self-love? She inhaled deeply, as she "heard" her inner voice – straight from her heart - echo boldly across the twilight sky:

Nothing born out of love, will ever be lost. In the meantime, cherish each moment. Your time together will be short as lifetimes go but, time is an illusion. With love in your heart, you'll feel eternity in every breath that you take.

Oh life
You abound with happiness
I have but, to place my lips to your cup
To taste your sweet wine
A cup always full to the brim
Never empty.
I have but, to lift my face
To feel your warmth caress me
Destroying the last shred of emptiness
That crept in, in the dead of night.

All around me
I see your wonderful creation
And hear your beautiful melody
Rising and falling
In harmony with all about you.
Your powerful heartbeat echoes across the sky
I hear it in the growth of the grass
I see it in the blooming of each flower
I feel it with my soul.

Your every breath
Is drawn in
And let out
Silently
And yet, with an inner power and glory.
And another voice within me
Is heard amongst the notes of your silent rhapsody:
"I am one with life"

www.ingramcontent.com/pod-product-compliance
Lightning Source LLC
Chambersburg PA
CBHW021823220426
43663CB00005B/118